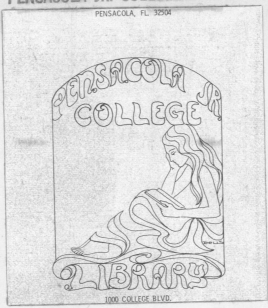

D1399571

A DICTIONARY
OF LIFE IN BIBLE TIMES

W. CORSWANT

A DICTIONARY
OF LIFE
IN BIBLE TIMES

Completed and Illustrated by
ÉDOUARD URECH

Translated from the French by
ARTHUR HEATHCOTE

Foreword by
ANDRÉ PARROT

New York   OXFORD UNIVERSITY PRESS   1960

18,731

FOREWORD

I THINK I met Professor W. Corswant but once, in February 1949, during a lecture tour in French Switzerland. He immediately struck me by the solid and extensive knowledge he had of Oriental antiquity in general and of Biblical archaeology in particular. He was, of course, Professor of the History of Religions and of Biblical Archaeology in the Faculty of Theology at Neuchâtel, and this alertness of mind might appear natural in one who had to teach an exact science. Nevertheless, how many remain on the threshold of a subject, content to have the door ajar! To confine oneself to a study of the texts, without attempting to link them with the realities of the facts or places or people, would be to remain on the threshold of this subject.

Indeed, as our late master Adolphe Lods once wrote, the Bible is "a unique source of spiritual life"; but he at once added that it was also "an historical document". For this reason the Holy Scriptures are not fully understood if they are read without regard to their historical and geographical contexts. Doubtless they contain the "words of eternal life", yet, whether we like it or not, these words were spoken at particular times in particular circumstances, and we cannot be indifferent to that fact. With revelation everything is important. No detail is superfluous. Everything is of value, and its value is only fully appreciated when the setting and circumstances are known with accuracy.

Professor Corswant was one of those men who seek precise and clear knowledge. That is why he was in the forefront of the philological study of the texts, and in the study of places and things. He belonged to the great line of travellers of which Switzerland may be proud, such as Félix Bovet, Lucien Gautier, Edouard Naville, Gustave Jéquier, Max van Berchem, Auguste Gampert, Edouard Montet, to name but a few who are no longer with us. All these understood that it is impossible to speak with authority about the East without having dug in its soil. They all went, some of them several times, to these lands, which do not yield themselves up fully on a first visit, but which always keep in store a harvest of discoveries and many secrets for those who approach them rightly. The scholarly work of all the men we have named is permeated by this direct contact, by a first-hand knowledge which nothing replaces and which ever increases, and by years of labour.

The late Professor left among his papers the almost complete manuscript of a dictionary of life in Bible times. It would have been foolish to have consigned to oblivion so great an achievement. Therefore one of his pupils, M. Edouard Urech, supplied the missing articles and illustrated the book.

There is nothing comparable, or equivalent to it. . . . It covers in detail the whole range of life of Bible times. Where necessary a text—already clear, readable by anyone, and free from over-technical language—is given vivid support by some important or remarkable illustration. Whether in a few lines for the shortest, or in a few columns for the longest, the articles give the information that is requisite and necessary. A wealth of Bible references are clearly set out at the end of each entry for swift and easy consultation.

Conceived and executed in this fashion, the dictionary affords a mine of information of the first order for all who wish to understand Bible ideas more fully or to gain information about aspects of Eastern life which the Bible mentions in passing but does not describe in detail. It is a useful tool for the student. But it is more than that. It is a reliable guide for the reading and fuller understanding of the Book of Books, about which we can never know too much, and which we can only hope to know thoroughly when we understand it in all its aspects.

ANDRÉ PARROT

v

PREFACE

PROFESSOR CORSWANT did not have the pleasure of seeing the completion and publication of his dictionary. He died in 1954, leaving a manuscript of nearly 750 articles. It would have been foolish, as Professor Parrot has said, to have allowed such a work to go unpublished, so M. Edouard Urech, a former pupil of the author's, saw to such revision as was necessary, to the writing of a number of other entries in their entirety, and to the illustrating of the book. It appeared in French in 1956.

It was intended to be of most direct service to all who are engaged in the religious instruction of young people. Technical language is avoided; the articles are concise and often illustrated; references and cross-references are easily followed. Not only is it hoped that it will serve as a valuable reference book for teachers, but pupils from junior grade upwards should have no difficulty in using it.

Every outward and visible aspect of the personal, social, and religious life of the Israelites and early Christians is treated, together with such associated topics as the fauna, flora and minerals of Palestine. Teachers will agree that it is precisely in this field that information is most often needed, and not always easily found. Political history and geography are excluded, along with directly theological or literary questions.

We may quote from the preface which Professor Corswant had written before his death.

"Although we have striven to use simple language, so far as possible avoiding Hebrew or other ancient words, we nevertheless venture to hope that, writing in the light of the results of excavations and of many learned researches—not to mention the two journeys to Palestine which have acquainted us with its life and people—this work of popularization is not unworthy of the serious studies upon which it rests.

"With the idea that the book will be used chiefly for obtaining precise information quickly, we have given it the form of a *dictionary*; the material required can therefore be found at once and without any searching. But in order that it may serve also as a *manual* a systematic classification of the main articles is provided, so that anyone wanting to examine a subject thoroughly is guided to both principal and subsidiary entries where necessary. In this way a wider range of knowledge on a given subject is easily acquired.

"The greatest of care has been given to the Bible references, though of course no attempt has been made to be exhaustive; thus a concordance is by no means superfluous. Moreover, it is important to consult the Bible passages that are given, because they often supplement what is said in the text, and are themselves illuminated by being seen in their context of Bible life and customs."

In preparing the English edition every attempt has been made to preserve the virtues of the original. I am deeply grateful to Mr. P. J. Allcock, B.A., of Leicester, and to my colleague Dr. Joan J. Henry, Ph.D., of Avery Hill College, without whose capable assistance publication would have been much longer delayed and the result much less accurate. However, the responsibility is mine alone for such small alterations as have seemed necessary to the original text and for the checking of all Bible references. The encouragement and patience of Mr. Leonard Cutts of Messrs. Hodder and Stoughton has once again been unfailing.

ARTHUR HEATHCOTE

SIGNS

* and † are used to mark cross references to related articles, which should be looked up under the word so marked.

Biblical references are given for many terms, but it is sometimes necessary to consult alternative versions of the Bible to find the translation that has been used. In some cases the Authorised Version (A.V.), Revised Version (R.V.) or Revised Standard Version (R.S.V.) are specifically mentioned. However, as all word studies are based on the original Greek and Hebrew texts, it occasionally happens that the translation used does not appear in that form in any existing version of the Bible.

par. = parallel passages (usually in the case of Gospel references).

LXX denotes the Septuagint Greek translation of the Old Testament.

In transliterated Hebrew words

' = א; ḥ = ח; ṭ = ט; ʿ = ע; f = ף; ts = צ; š (i.e. sh) = שׁ.

SYSTEMATIC CLASSIFICATION
OF PRINCIPAL ARTICLES

I. SECULAR LIFE

A. DOMESTIC LIFE

1. Family
Family.

2. Marriage
Celibacy, Marriage, Dowry, Levirate marriage*, Adultery, Incest, Divorce.

3. Women
Woman, Widow, Slave.

4. Children
Child, Adoption, Circumcision, Birthright, School, Pastimes.

5. Slaves
Slave, Freedman.

6. Friends and Guests
Friendship, Covenant, Kiss, Hospitality, Politeness, Feast, Chief seat*, Riddle, Elder, Inn.

7. Death and funerals
Funeral, Embalming, Coffin, Will, Tomb, Dolmen, Mourning.

8. Dwellings
Cave, Hut, Tent, House—Corner-stone, Foundation, Lime, Window, Hinge, Key, Lock, Kitchen, Frying-pan, Hearth, Cellar, Rope—Bed, Table, Seat, Lamp, Bushel, Mill, Coverlet, Cushion, Brazier, Cauldron, Pitcher, Bottle, Bucket, Basket—Camp, Gate, City and Village, Cistern, Roads—Lord's Supper.

9. Clothing and care of the body
Dress, Sack(cloth), Shirt, Girdle, Cosmetics, Head-dress, Shoe, Fringe, Hair, Razor, Soap, Beard, Perfume, Aromatics, Tattooing—Bracelet, Ring, Ear-ring, Necklace, Chains, Embroidery, Silk, Cords, Seal, Needle, Clasps, Pearl, Phylactery.

10. Food
Food, Famine—Bread, Flour, Kneading-trough, Mill, Mortar, Dish, Cake—Vegetables—Milk, Butter, Cheese, Cock—Fish—Honey, Spices, Salt—Water, Vine, Vinegar, Strong drink, Abstinence—Knife, Fork, Filter.

B. WORK

1. Hunting, fishing
Hunt, Pit, Fowler—Fishing, Snare—Hook, Fish-hook, Harpoon.

2. Cattle raising
Cattle, Shepherd, Sling—Sheep, Wool, Goat, Bull, Ass (Donkey), Horse, Mule, Camel, Pig—Stable, Crib, Whip.

3. Agriculture
Agriculture—Hedge, Landmark, Dung, Rain, Irrigation—Mattock (Hoe), Spade, Plough, Yoke, Goad, Harrow—Corn, Wheat, Spelt, Millet, Sickle, Glean, Threshing-floor, Threshing-sledge, Flail, Fork, Shovel, Winnow, Sieve, Husk, Straw, Cellar—Tares, Rust, Blight, Grasshopper—Bee.

4. Vineyards, orchards, gardens
Vine, Watch-tower, Press († Olive), Filter, Wine—Olive, Fig tree, Pomegranate—Garden, Vegetables.

Trade and Commerce

5. Trades
Trades—Metals, Smelting, Crucible, Smith (Smithy), Bellows—Precious stones, Seal—Pottery, Clay—Mason, Level, Plumb-line—Carpenter, Pencil, Compasses, Setsquare, Hammer, Nail, Saw—Wood-cutter, Forest, Wood, Axe—Spinning, Weaving, Tow—Dyer, Colours—Fuller, Potash, Nitre—Tanner, Leather—Butcher, Baker—Barber, Perfumer, Razor—Glass—Boat, Raft, Ship's-boat, Ship, Anchor, Rudder, Oar.

6. Commerce
Commerce, Banker, Money-changer, Journey, Balance, Deed of Sale.

Weights and Measures

7. Divisions of time
Day, Night, Hour, Dial, Week, Month, Seasons, Year, Evening.

8. Length, Capacity and Weight

Weights and Measures—Handbreadth, Span, Cubit, Fathom, Furlong, Mile—Line, Measuring-reed, Yoke—Log, Kab, Seah, Ephah, Homer—Hin, Bath—Talent, Mina, Pound.

9. Money

Money—Talent, Mina, Shekel, Didrachma, Drachma, Farthing, Quadrans, Obolus.

C. ARTS AND SCIENCES

Arts

1. Architecture

Architecture, Sanctuary, Palace, Porch (Portico), House, Fortifications, Beam—Cistern, Water, Well, Reservoir, Canal—Tomb.

2. Plastic arts

Sculpture, Pottery, Painting—Colours, Metals, Alabaster, Ivory, Precious stones, Horn, Clay, Cup, Phial, Vessel.

3. Music and dance

Music, Musical Instruments, Flute, Trumpet (horn), Cithara, Harp, Psaltery, Sackbut, Tambourine, Cymbals, Castanet, Sistrum, Triangle, Song, Singers, Dance, Theatre.

Sciences

4. Writing

Writing, Scribe, Inkpot, Pen, Ink, Potsherd, Wax.

5. Astronomy, cosmography, etc.

Astronomy, Astrology, Heavens, Star, Sun, Moon, Eclipse, Rain—Orion, Bear, Pleiades, Zodiac.

6. Medicine

Doctor, Illness, Medicine, Midwife, Apothecary, Eye-salve, Gall, Balms.

D. POLITICAL, CIVIL AND MILITARY AFFAIRS

1. Constitution and Administration

Tribe, Elders, King, Throne, Diadem, Officials, Taxes, Satrap, Sanhedrin, Procurator, Proconsul, Tetrarch, Praetorium, Treasure, Sceptre.

2. Law and Justice

Law—Revenge, Asylum, Crimes and Offences, Punishment, Cross, Crucifixion, Whip—Slave, Woman, Foreigner, Marriage, Levirate marriage*, Divorce, Birthright, Orphan, Inheritance, Will, Property, Deed of Sale, Usury, Pledge, Surety, Debt, Deposit, Find, Poor—Law Courts and Trials, Prison, Witness, Oath.

3. War and Arms

Armour-bearer, Arms, Army, Arrow, Arsenal, Centurion, Chariot, Cherethites and Pelethites, Cohort, Corselet, Cuirass, War, Fortifications, Hireling and Mercenary, Sentry, Runner, Herald, Spy, Horse, Saddle, Catapult, Bow, Devote.

II. RELIGIOUS LIFE

A. HOLY PLACES

1. Ancient Sanctuaries

Altar, Asherah, Sanctuary, Ark, Tabernacle, Sacred Trees*, Pillar, Dolmen, Ephod, Images, Teraphim, Urim and Thummim.

2. Jerusalem Temple

Temple (of Solomon, Zerubbabel, Ezekiel, Herod)—Porch (portico), Cherubim, Candlestick, Chariot, Ash-pan, Snuffers, Censer—Beautiful Gate*, Antonia.

3. Synagogues

Synagogue, Proselyte.

B. HOLY PERSONS

1. Priesthood

Priest—Bishop, Presbyter—Consecration, Anointing, Laying on of Hands *—Ephod, Bell.

2. Holy persons

Levite, Nethinim, Sacred Prostitution*, Nazirate, Rechabites—Deacon, Deaconess.

3. Religious parties

Pharisees, Sadducees, Zealots

C. SACRED SEASONS

1. Weekly and monthly festivals

Sabbath, Sabbath Journey, Preparation, New Moon*—Sunday.

2. Chief annual festivals

Passover—Feast of Weeks * (Pentecost), New Year, Atonement, Tabernacles, Azazel, Fasting.

3. Secondary festivals

Purim, Dedication, Nicanor, Jubilee, Sheep-shearing.

D. SACRED ACTS

1. Sacrifices

Sacrifice, Lamb, Shoulder, Breast, Liver, Fat, Incense, Cake, Firstfruits, Tithe, Taxes, Tongs.

2. Purifications

Uncleanness, Purification, Bath, Red Heifer *— Baptism.

3. Prayer, fasting, almsgiving

Prayer, Blessing, Hallel, Vow, Fasting, Alms, Mite, Corban, Collection, Poor, Phylactery.

4. Magic and superstition

Magic, Divination, Exorcist, Dream, Amulet, Crescents, Incision, Tattooing, Curse.

III. ANIMALS, PLANTS, MINERALS

A. ANIMALS

1. *Domestic*

Ass
Bull
Calf
Camel
Goat
Heifer
Horse
Kid
Lamb
Mule
Pig
Ram
Sheep

2. *Wild*

Antelope
Ape
Bat
Bear
Boar
Cat
Deer
Dog
Elephant
Field-mouse
Fox
Gazelle
Hare
Hart (stag)

Hippopotamus († Behemoth)
Hyena
Hyrax (daman)
Jackal
Leopard
Lion
Mole
Mouse
Rat
Turtle
Wild ass
Wild goat
Wolf

3. *Birds*

Bittern
Buzzard
Cormorant
Diver
Dove
Eagle
Falcon
Gull
Hawk
Heron
Hoopoe
Ibis
Kite
Osprey

Ostrich
Owl (Great, Little)
Partridge
Peacock
Pelican
Quail
Raven
Screech-owl
Sparrows (and other Passeres)
Stork
Swallow
Vulture

4. *Insects, reptiles, etc.*

Ant
Asp
Bee
Chameleon
Fish
Flea
Fly
Frog
Grasshopper
Hornet
Leech
Lizard
Moth
Mosquito
Scorpion

Snail
Snakes († Serpent)
Spider
Viper, horned
Wasp
Worm

5. *Animals mentioned in some versions but which may be errors of translation*

Basilisk
Bearded vulture
Buffalo
Chamois
Crane
Cuckoo
Dolphin
Giraffe
Hedgehog
Louse
Panther
Porcupine
Rabbit
Rhinoceros
Roe-deer
Swan
Weasel
Whale

B. PLANTS

1. *Fruit trees*

Almond
Apple
Caper
Carob
Citron
Fig
Mulberry
Olive

Palm
Pistachio
Pomegranate
Sycomore
Walnut

2. *Other trees*

Acacia
Box

Broom
Cedar
Cinnamon
Cypress
Elm (?)
Henna
Juniper
Laurel
Myrtle

Oak
Pine (?)
Plane
Poplar
Sandalwood
Tamarisk
Terebinth
Thyine
Willow

3. *Trees mentioned in some versions, but which may be errors of translation*

Apricot
Chestnut
Lemon

4. *Other plants*

Aloe
Anemone
Banana
Barley

Bean
Bitter herbs*
Bramble
Calamus
Cassia
Coriander
Crocus
Cucumber
Cummin
Black Cummin*
Dill
Flax
Garlic

Hemlock
Hyssop
Ivy
Leek
Lentil
Lotus
Mandrake
Melon
Mint
Mustard
Nettle
Onion
Orache

Papyrus (Writing §3)
Reed
Rose
Rue
Thistle
Thorn
Vine
Wheat
Wild-gourd
Wormwood

C. MINERALS

Agate
Alabaster
Amethyst
Asphalt
Beryl
Brimstone
Carbuncle

Cornelian († Sardius)
Chalcedony
Chrysolite
Chrysoprase
Clay
Diamond
Emerald

Glass
Jacinth
Jasper
Marble
Metals
Naphtha
Onyx

Opal
Quartz
Ruby
Sapphire
Sardius, Sardonyx
Topaz

PERIODS OF PALESTINIAN HISTORY

Period	Approximate date
Bronze Age I . .	Before 2000 B.C.
II . .	2000–1600
III .	1600–1200
Iron Age I . . .	1200–900
II . .	900–600
Persian and Greek .	600–300
Hellenistic . . .	300–1
Roman	A.D. 1–300

ABBREVIATIONS USED IN BIBLE REFERENCES

Gen.	= Genesis	2 Chr.	= 2 Chronicles	Dan.	= Daniel
Ex.	= Exodus	Ezr.	= Ezra	Hos.	= Hosea
Lev.	= Leviticus	Neh.	= Nehemiah	Joel	= Joel
Num.	= Numbers	Est.	= Esther	Amos	= Amos
Dt.	= Deuteronomy	Job	= Job	Obd.	= Obadiah
Jos.	= Joshua	Ps.	= Psalms	Jonah	= Jonah
Jg.	= Judges	Prov.	= Proverbs	Mic.	= Micah
Ruth	= Ruth	Eccl.	= Ecclesiastes	Nahum	= Nahum
1 Sam.	= 1 Samuel	Cant.	= Song of Songs	Hab.	= Habakkuk
2 Sam.	= 2 Samuel	Is.	= Isaiah	Zeph.	= Zephaniah
1 Kgs.	= 1 Kings	Jer.	= Jeremiah	Hagg.	= Haggai
2 Kgs.	= 2 Kings	Lam.	= Lamentations	Zech.	= Zechariah
1 Chr.	= 1 Chronicles	Ez.	= Ezekiel	Mal.	= Malachi

Wisd.	= Wisdom of Solomon
Ecclus.	= Ecclesiasticus
1 Macc.	= 1 Maccabees
2 Macc.	= 2 Maccabees

Matt.	= Matthew	Phil.	= Philippians	1 Pet.	= 1 Peter
Mk.	= Mark	Col.	= Colossians	2 Pet.	= 2 Peter
Lk.	= Luke	1 Th.	= 1 Thessalonians	1 Jn.	= 1 John
Jn.	= John	2 Th.	= 2 Thessalonians	2 Jn.	= 2 John
Acts	= Acts	1 Ti.	= 1 Timothy	3 Jn.	= 3 John
Rom.	= Romans	2 Ti.	= 2 Timothy	Jude	= Jude
1 Cor.	= 1 Corinthians	Tit.	= Titus	Rev.	= Revelation of John, or
2 Cor.	= 2 Corinthians	Phm.	= Philemon		Apocalypse
Gal.	= Galatians	Heb.	= Hebrews		
Eph.	= Ephesians	Jas.	= James		

INDEX OF CONTENTS

Heavens
Hedge
Hedgehog
Heifer
Heifer (red)
Helmet
Hemlock
Henna
Herald
Herbs, bitter
Heron
High-place † Sanctuary
High Priest † Priest
Hin
Hinge
Hippopotamus † Behemoth
Hireling, Mercenary
Homer
Honey
Hook
Hoopoe
Horn
Hornet
Horse
Hospitality
Hour
House
House of Forest of Lebanon
Hunt
Husk
Hut
Hyacinth † Jacinth
Hydraulic works † Cistern, Reservoir, Water, Well
Hyena
Hyrax (daman)
Hyssop

Ibis
Illness
Images
Imprisonment † Prison, Punishment
Incense
Incest
Incision
Ingathering † Tabernacles
Inheritance
Ink
Inkpot
Inn
INRI
Insects
Interest † Usury
Interpreter
Iron
Irrigation
Ivory
Ivy

Jachin
Jacinth
Jackal
Jasper
Javelin
Jealousy (Law of)
Jerboa † Hyrax
Jewellery † Amulet, Bracelet, Chains, Clasps, Diadem, Earring, Necklace, Ring
Journey
Jubilee (Year of)
Judge † Law-courts
Jujube † Thorn
Juniper
Justice † Law Courts

Kab
Key
Kid
Kidnap
Kidney
King
Kinnôr † Cithara
Kiss
Kitchen
Kite
Kneading-trough
Knife

Labourer † Agriculture, Plough
Ladanum
Ladder
Lamb
Lame
Lamp
Lampwick † Lamp, Flax, Snuffers
Landmark
Lantern
Lapis-lazuli † Sapphire
Lattice † Window, Temple
Laurel
Law
Law-courts, trials
Lead
Leather
Leaven
Leech
Leek
Lemon
Lentil
Leopard
Leprosy
Letter † Writing
Lettuce Bitter herbs*
Level
Leviathan
Levite
Lex talionis † Law §3, Punishment, Revenge

Libation † Sacrifice
Lictor
Lily
Lily-of-the-valley
Lime
Line
Linen
Lion
Litter
Liver
Lizard
Loan † Debt, Usury
Lock
Locust † Grasshopper
Log
Lord's Supper
Lotus
Louse
Love-apple † Mandrake
Lunacy † Epilepsy
Lyre † Cithara

Madness
Magic
Mandrake
Manger † Crib
Manna
Marble
Market-place † Gate
Marriage
Marriage (Levirate)
Marten
Mason
Mattock
Meal † Food, Lord's Supper
Measures † Weights and Measures
Measuring-reed
Meat † Food, Blood
Medicine
Melon
Mercenary † Hireling
Merchant † Commerce
Messenger
Metals
Mezuzah
Midwife
Mildew
Mile
Milk
Mill
Millet
Millo
Mina
Mine
Mint
Mirror
Mite
Mitre † Priest
Mole
Money
Money-changer
Month

Moon
Morning † Day
Mortar
Mosquito
Mosquito-net
Moth
Mother † Child, Family, Woman
Mourning
Mouse
Mulberry
Mule
Murder
Music
Musical instruments
Mustard
Muzzle
Myrrh
Myrtle

Nail
Name † Child
Naphtha
Napkin
Narcissus
Nazirate
Necklace
Needle
Nest
Net † Snare
Nethinim
Nettle
New Year
Nicanor
Night
Nisan
Nitre
Nose-ring † Ear-ring
Number

Oak
Oar
Oath
Oblation † Sacrifice
Obolus
Offences † Crimes and Offences
Offering † Sacrifice
Officials
Oil † Olive
Olive
Omer
Onion
Onyx
Opal
Orache
Oracle † Divination, Magic
Orange
Orchard † Garden
Ordination † Consecration, Laying on of Hands*
Orion

A DICTIONARY
OF LIFE IN BIBLE TIMES

ABIB

The month of the (young) ears of corn; the ancient name of the month in spring (March–April) called Nisan after the Exile. The Hebrew Exodus from Egypt took place in the month Abib.[1]

[1] Ex. 13. 4, etc.

ABSALOM (TOMB OF)

This name is given to a mausoleum cut in the living rock of the Kidron Valley close to Jerusalem, and surmounted by a curious, pointed stone headpiece, which the Arabs called "Pharaoh's Cap". With its semi-columns of Ionic style and its Doric frieze, it

The so-called Tomb of Absalom, near Jerusalem.

plainly dates from the Graeco-Roman period and perhaps from the time of Herod. It cannot, therefore, be identified with the monument—probably a simple pillar—which Absalom erected during his lifetime and which has disappeared.[1]

[1] 2 Sam. 18. 18.

ABSTINENCE

Priests* when on duty,[1] Nazirites († Nazirate) during the time of their vow and Rechabites* throughout their lives abstained from all strong drink, and wine in particular.

[1] Lev. 10. 9.

23

ACACIA

The acacia mentioned in the Bible is not the false acacia (*Robinia*) of our regions, but a tree of the Mediterranean basin; in Palestine it is found only in the southern part of the Jordan Valley. It resembles the mimosa, but its flowers, ball-shaped and separate from one another, are white and its leaves have only a dozen leaflets. Its yellowy-brown wood, hard, extremely slow to rot, and light, was perfectly suitable for building the Ark* of the Covenant and making various articles of furniture.[1] In the Sinai Peninsula only the acacia produces workable timber. The Egyptians used it in boat-building and in making various articles.

Arabian acacia (Mimosa family).

[1] Ex. 25. 5, 10; 26. 15; etc.

ACRE

Our versions translate by this term the Hebrew word for "yoke", which means the area that a yoke of oxen could plough in one day [1] († agriculture). The Roman *jugerum* was 25.18 *ares* (= 3,200 sq. yds.).

[1] 1 Sam. 14. 14; Is. 5. 10.

ADAR

Twelfth month of the post-Exilic Jewish calender (February–March). Mentioned eight times in the Bible.[1]

[1] Ezr. 6. 15; Est. 3. 7, etc.

ADOPTION

The adoption of foreign children into the family does not appear to have been practised among the Israelites. (The princess who adopted Moses [1] was an Egyptian, and Esther was Mordecai's cousin before becoming his daughter.[2]) On the other hand, the childless Israelite wife adopted those which her slave bore to her husband.[3] At times a grandfather raised his grandsons to the status of sons,[4] and a father without male children could marry his daughter to a freed slave and consider the male child of this union as his own son.[5] In Roman law adoption was a sort of purchase before witnesses; doubtless St Paul refers to this when writing to the Galatians.[6]

[1] Ex. 2. 10. [2] Est. 2. 7. [3] Gen. 16. 2; etc. [4] Gen. 48. 5; 50. 23. [5] 1 Chr. 2. 35. [6] Gal. 4. 5.

ADULTERY

From the principles that were at the basis of marriage* in Israel, the two partners did not have the same conjugal responsibilities. The unfaithful wife was always considered an adultress, whereas no law required fidelity of the husband. He committed adultery only by seducing a married or betrothed woman, and then it was a breach of someone else's marriage not his own; it seriously transgressed the husband's property rights, and violated the divine law.[1]

The adultress taken in the very act was punished by death.[2] Under suspicion of adultery she might be subjected to a trial by ordeal or the judgment of God; the "bitter water" which she had to drink brought a curse upon her if she was guilty. The whole ceremony is described at length in Num. 5. 11–31.

A man taken with a married (or betrothed) woman was stoned with her. He only died if he had committed violence in a place where a call for help from the betrothed woman—or doubtless from the married woman also—could not be heard.[3] Seduction of a slave-concubine was not considered as adultery; the guilty parties were "chastised" but not put to death; reparation was due to the slave's owner, whilst a guilt offering was presented in the temple.[4]

[1] Ex. 20. 14, 17. [2] Dt. 22. 22; Lev. 20. 21; Jn. 8. 5. [3] Dt. 22. 22–27. [4] Lev. 19. 20–22.

AGATE

The agate, which is divided into concentric zones and is remarkable for its range of colours, was one of the precious stones which adorned the breastplate of the High Priest*.[1] However, it is not certain that what we call agate is the stone meant by the Hebrew word which is usually so translated.

[1] Ex. 28. 19; 39. 12.

AGORA

The name given to the central square of Athens (cf. the Forum at Rome) where St Paul, during his stay in that city, debated daily with those he met there († gate).[1]

[1] Acts 17. 17.

AGRICULTURE

On their arrival in Palestine, the Israelites, passing from a nomadic or semi-nomadic to a settled way of life, did not have to clear virgin ground; they found land that had been tilled for a long time and fields in full production. However, tillable land constituted only a part of the mountainous regions where they settled.

In October–November the peasant waited impatiently for the first rains on which the success of the crop depended. When the ground was sufficiently moist and thus loosened, it was tilled either by hand (mattock*, spade*) or by the plough*, then levelled [1] by means of a plank or a faggot of thorns which served as a harrow, and finally sown with barley* or wheat*, more rarely with spelt*. The seed was sown broadcast or by seed-pipe, a kind of funnel fixed to the plough; an effort was then made to cover the grain, either by packing the earth, or by taking the plough over the ground a second time, for it was necessary to preserve the seed from possible drought, from ants, and from birds.

Winter, which was the rainy season, fertilized the soil, and the seed quickly developed. In March the rains ceased quite abruptly, but for the crop to be assured, it was necessary that the so-called latter rains should come early in April, at the moment when the ear was forming; the Talmud states that these rains bring more blessings than the ox and the yoke.

The peasant was not spared anxieties: drought was to be feared, as was the parching of the ears by the east or south-east wind,[2] and excess of rain which eroded the fields, hail which dashed the young shoots and locusts*, blight*, and rust*.[3]

Dew, very abundant at times in the mountains, hastened the swelling of the grain, and harvest time—a period of general rejoicing [4]—began with the barley harvest in mid-April on the Mediterranean coast, eight to ten days earlier in the Jordan Valley and as much later in the high plateaux. The wheat came two or three weeks later.

The harvester grasped a handful of corn stalks [5] near the head with his left hand and then cut these with the sickle* about 4 in. below his hand. This procedure effected an immediate separation of the wheat from the weeds († tares), which generally did not grow as tall and which the cattle would graze off when turned into the stubble; further, since the straw was not utilized, it could only be burned, and it blazed less readily in bundles than when standing, so it was usually left uncut and set on fire either immediately after harvest or at the time of tilling. Behind the reaper walked the one who received the bundles, bound them in little sheaves,[6] and packed them in big baskets, which were carried by asses to the threshing-floor, unless a cart was used.[7]

The threshing-floors, common to the whole village, or the private property of some rich peasant, were sited on a natural or artificial terrace, on a hill completely cleared of vegetation and surrounded by low walls. There the sheaves were heaped up and, since it never rained at that time of the year, they were left for some time so that as the grain reached complete ripeness it would be more easily freed from the ear. But each man kept an eye on his own crop, for Bedouin robbers loved to "gather where they had not scattered".[8]

If only a small quantity was to be threshed a stick was used, but on the threshing-floor when the corn had been spread to a considerable depth it was trampled by oxen with iron-shod hooves; urged on by the goad*, they were not muzzled and could eat the corn stalks,[9] a custom oddly referred to by St Paul when speaking of the temporal goods which should be enjoyed by those who sow spiritual benefits.[10] A plank was also used to thresh the grain, a sort of drag or threshing-sledge* fitted with pointed stones or pieces of metal (the *tribulum* adopted by all

ground store, where it was necessary at times to hide provisions.[13] Later, granaries were built, like huge silos, which sometimes had the shape of very high bee-hives; the grain was poured in from the top of a ladder through an opening in the upper part, and it was taken out through a door at ground level († cellar). At Beisan a circular silo with a capacity of about 1,100 bushels has been discovered.

The corn yield varied according to the nature of the soil; it was very low in poorly watered country, but sometimes remarkable in the fertile plains (Jezreel, Gennesaret, etc.). It is known that each grain of corn can produce several stems bearing ears (half a dozen at the most) and that each ear may have up to 80 to 100 grains of very varied size. Thus one grain may yield more than 500. It is obvious that the Parable of the Sower,[14] which is not concerned with

Harvest scenes; Egyptian paintings of the 15th and 13th centuries.

Mediterranean peoples), or a kind of chariot made from a frame, within which were moving rollers fitted with iron blades (*plaustellum*).[11] In time of war these implements were used as instruments of torture beneath which enemies were crushed.[12]

The threshed corn was heaped up to be winnowed, or, more exactly, blown by the wind: they waited for a favourable, but not too strong, wind and with a shovel* or a wooden fork* of two to seven tines, they threw the corn into the air. While the straw and husk were carried away the grain fell back to the ground. This process was repeated several times, and finally the corn was riddled to free it from all foreign matter.

If only small quantities were to be stored, the grain was put into pitchers* or into earthenware containers or even into small pits dug into the ground and lined with sherds or cobble stones. In early times the peasant farming on a larger scale dug out pits in the fields or caves for this purpose—a kind of under-

scientific generalization but with the facts of everyday life, speaks of the yield per ear rather than the yield per grain, in spite of the terms used.

Among the regulations dealing with agricultural work, it should be mentioned that it was forbidden to move boundaries,[15] to mix different kinds of seed,[16] or to yoke together animals of different species (either to spare the weaker animal, or through hatred of all cross-breeding);[17] generosity to the poor was encouraged (i.e., permission to glean in the fields,[18] leaving the sides of the field uncut for their benefit,[19] no turning back for the forgotten sheaf [20]); passers-by were authorized to pluck ears,[21] and a sabbatical year was observed (rest for the land every seventh year).[22]

The unit of surface measure was the yoke († acre), that is, the area that a pair of oxen could plough in a day;[23] the value of ground was calculated according to the grain that was sown in it.[24]

As is well known, the poets of the Bible, the

prophets, Jesus (parables), and St Paul constantly used images borrowed from the life of the fields.[25] Cultivation methods have always been invested with supernatural qualities in the eyes of agricultural peoples; the methods were so wonderful that the people ascribed their origin to the gods. When the Israelites settled in Palestine they at first ascribed those methods to the deities of the country. It was because of this that the prophets accused Israel, the legitimate bride of Yahweh, of adultery, and that they ascribed to their sovereign God the revelation of agricultural science.[26]

(† Fig tree, olive tree, vine, cattle.)

[1] Is. 28. 25. [2] Gen. 41. 6. [3] Amos 4. 9; Hagg. 2. 17. [4] Is. 9. 3; Ps. 4. 7; 126. 6. [5] Ps. 129. 7. [6] Gen. 37. 7; Jg. 15. 5; Job 5. 26, etc. [7] Amos 2. 13. [8] 1 Sam. 23. 1; Matt. 25. 24. [9] Dt. 25. 4. [10] 1 Cor. 9. 4–11. [11] Is. 28. 27. [12] Amos 1. 3. [13] Jer. 41. 8. [14] Matt. 13. 23. [15] Dt. 19. 14. [16] Lev. 19. 19. [17] Dt. 22. 10. [18] Dt. 24. 19; Ruth 2. [19] Lev. 19. 9. [20] Dt. 24. 19. [21] Dt. 23. 25; Matt. 12. 1 par. [22] Ex. 23. 11; Lev. 25. 4. [23] Is. 5. 10. [24] Lev. 27. 16. [25] Matt. 13; 1 Cor. 15. 36 ff.; etc. [26] Is. 28. 26.

ALABASTER

Alabaster, a stone that is normally white but often marked with striated coloured veins, translucent and capable of a very high polish, was especially used in making vases for ointments or perfumes. Excavations in Palestine have occasionally brought to light

Alabaster perfume flasks.

vases or trinkets made from alabaster of Egyptian origin and dating from a very early period. In the Bible alabaster is mentioned only in Mk. 14. 3 par., in connection with a perfume jar, with a slender, fragile neck.

ALMOND TREE

A shrub or tree sometimes growing to a height of 16 ft., the almond grows wild in Palestine but is often cultivated. Its white flowers [1] tinged with pink open before the leaves, as early as the end of January or the beginning of February; hence the name of the almond tree (*šaqed*, which comes from the verb

šaqad = keep watch, be wakeful), for it seems to keep vigil through the winter in order to announce the reappearance of spring, as a sentinel waits in the darkness for the time to proclaim the dawn. This image was used by Jeremiah in his well-known vision.[2] Jacob knew the almond tree, and even in his

Almond blossom (*Prunus cerasus*).

time its fruits were imported into Egypt.[3] Aaron's rod [4] was an almond branch; almond buds and flowers decorated the seven-branched candlestick* in the sanctuary.[5] Orientals have always appreciated almonds, which they eat even before the shell has hardened.

[1] Eccl. 12. 5. [2] Jer. 1. 11. [3] Gen. 43. 11. [4] Num. 17. 8. [5] Ex. 25. 33; etc.

ALMS

Israelite law always recommended benevolence to the poor,[1] and to this end certain ordinances [2] are set forth. Generosity is a virtue which is much liked by Orientals; for the Jews there were many opportunities of showing it: we have only to think of the host of beggars, blind and lame, which figures so large in the Gospel narratives (see also Lk. 14. 21). Almsgiving was the necessary complement of piety.[3] It was characteristic of the righteous man,[4] and the word "righteousness" can signify, in certain cases, simply the practising of good works.[5] It was thought also that almsgiving was meritorious in the eyes of God,[6] especially if it remained secret from other people; "he who gives alms in secret is greater than our master Moses" (Talmud).

Because he preached charity and indifference to

worldly goods, and in view of the social organization of his day, Jesus could only commend true almsgiving;[7] he wants it to be done discreetly [8] and directed by the spirit of sacrifice.[9] He practised it with his disciples.[10] St Paul, too, declares that God loves the man who gives cheerfully,[11] and the first Christians were often distinguished, no doubt, by their good works and their almsgiving.[12] Just as the Jews had drawn up rules for the distribution of money collected in the synagogue, so the Christian community in Jerusalem organized the assistance of widows,[13] and it is well known how carefully St Paul applied himself to collecting for the poor of that city, recommending the Corinthians in particular to set aside each week what they could spare for that work.[14]

[1] Dt. 15. 7–11. [2] Dt. 24. 19–21; Lev. 19. 9, 10. [3] Acts 10. 2; Prov. 17. 5. [4] Ps. 112. 9; 2 Cor. 9. 9, 10. [5] Prov. 10. 2; 11. 4; Dan. 4. 27; Matt. 6. 1. [6] Prov. 19. 17; Lk. 19. 8. [7] Matt. 19. 21; Lk. 11. 41; 12. 33. [8] Matt. 6. 2–4. [9] Lk. 12. 33. [10] Jn. 13. 29. [11] 2 Cor. 9. 7; cf. Heb. 13. 16. [12] Acts 9. 36. [13] Acts 6. 1. [14] Rom. 15. 26–31; 1 Cor. 16. 1; 2 Cor. 8. 9; Gals. 2. 10.

ALOE

This is a valuable and sweet-scented [1] wood which was used as incense or for embalming. The tree from which this wood comes originated in China and Indo-China and must not be confused with the plant which yields medicinal aloe (a purgative). From very early times aloe wood, imported from the Far East, was considered as a luxury commodity. The reference to aloe [2] at a date as early as Balaam arises without doubt from confusion with another tree.

[1] Ps. 45. 8; Prov. 7. 17; Cant. 4. 14; Jn. 19. 39. [2] Num. 24. 6.

ALTAR

The Israelite altar is probably a composite creation derived from the rocky platform provided with cupules (where cultic libations were made in primitive times), from the sacred stones (used for immolations), and from the stone tables (on which burnt offerings of the produce of the fields or of the flesh of victims were sacrificed to the deity).

The Biblical texts often speak of altars and trace them back to the remote past (Noah, Abraham). At the time of the Judges primitive platforms with cupules were still used,[1] but the majority of altars were formed from a simple mound of earth,[2] a block of stone,[3] or from a flat stone supported by a pile of other stones. One ancient prescription demands that altars should have no steps and that the stones used should be unshaped, doubtless because it is not fitting to improve the sacred work of God in nature.[4] These altars could then be very quickly prepared, in

certain cases to be used once only,[5] but most often that altar remained standing in the sacred precinct.

In the course of time the appearance of altars underwent changes; in particular, horns, whose

Altars with horns.

origin is obscure,[6] were fashioned at the four corners; these horns became so important that they had to undergo a special sprinkling with the blood of the sacrifice,[7] and anyone who touched them obtained divine protection († asylum).

Excavations in Palestine have brought to light several platforms with cupules, and a small number of altars, of which two or three have horns. Further, at Megiddo and at Ai the remains of censers have been found, and at Beth-shean some hollow terracotta cylinders decorated with serpents and birds, and some miniature houses, at the windows of which

Censers (?).

can be seen strange figures and symbolic animals; these too may be censers. An "incense altar" discovered at Taanach is perhaps merely a portable brazier like Jehoiakim's.[8]

(For the altar of sacrifice, the table of shew-bread and the altar of incense in the Temple of Jerusalem see temple*, tabernacle*.)

[1] Jg. 6. 19–21; 13. 19; 1 Sam. 6. 14 (?). [2] Ex. 20. 24. [3] 1 Sam. 14. 33. [4] Ex. 20. 25; Dt. 27. 5; Jos. 8. 31. [5] Jg. 21. 4; 1 Sam. 14. 33; 1 Kgs. 18. 32; etc. [6] Amos 3. 14; Ps. 118. 27; Rev. 9. 13. [7] Lev. 4. 30; 16. 18. [8] Jer. 36. 22.

AMETHYST

This is one of the precious stones found in the High Priest's breastplate*, where it occupies the ninth place.[1] It is also mentioned as one of those which adorn the foundations (the twelfth) of the walls of the New Jerusalem.[2] The translation of the Hebrew word used in Exodus is uncertain.

The Eastern amethyst is a fine, very hard stone, usually of a beautiful violet.

[1] Ex. 28. 19. [2] Rev. 21. 20.

AMULET

Considered as charged with magic fluid, and used at all times throughout the world to drive away evil spirits or to ensure certain advantages, amulets are small objects that men, and still more frequently, women wear (for jewels are often no more than amulets), fix at the entrance of their homes, put on the neck of their mounts, or place beside the dead in their graves.

The ordinary people in Israel were far from scorning them, though their religion condemned them in principle. It is true that the word amulet appears only once in the Bible [1] in a list of feminine adornments; but the ear-rings which Jacob buried at Shechem [2] were certainly amulets, and probably, too, those used for the adornment of the Golden Calf,[3] and the crescents hung from the necks of the Midianite camels.[4] Moreover, the considerable number of amulets found in excavations in Palestine is significant; pierced shells, animal teeth, pearls, lunar discs or crescents, perforated stones and small bones, little figurines of deities (Egyptian for the most part), all show how widespread and tenacious was this superstition in Israelite times, as in earlier times, and how great was the extent of foreign influence in this sphere. Often grouped in the form of a collar, amulets sometimes have the shape of animals dedicated to certain divinities, a hippopotamus († behemoth) in lapis-lazuli, or flies* in gold; there are star-shaped pendants, which often have the form of a scarab whose underside bears drawings which doubtless gave magic powers: a god making a vigorous gesture, the victory of the hero over the serpent, a conquered enemy, a nude goddess sometimes reduced to her essential elements. Even in Maccabaean times, some soldiers wore amulets under their tunics.[5] Because of the laws of sympathetic magic the Hittites coloured amulets either red, a reminder of the vital magical liquid—blood—or blue, a propitious colour for protection against the "evil eye", from the particularly malefic blue eye, since blue eyes are quite uncommon in the Orient; but since red was the colour preferred by invaders, the Egyptians attributed evil power to it and a beneficent power to blue; thus with their amulets they exported this taste to their neighbours.

The tufts or tassels, with purple-red cords, which the Israelites wore at the four corners of their outer garments,[6] the little boxes containing passages of the Law which they bound on their arms or their foreheads during prayer (phylacteries*) and those which they fastened and still today fasten on their door-

Amulets in the form of scarabs and pendants, found in Palestine.

posts (*mezuzah*), possibly even the little golden bells* which decorated the High Priest's robe, probably derive from amulets and are related to them.

[1] Is. 3. 20. [2] Gen. 35. 4. [3] Ex. 32. 3. [4] Jg. 8. 21. [5] 2 Macc. 12. 40. [6] Num. 15. 37–41; Matt. 23. 5.

ANCHOR

At the earliest times anchors were simply big stones pierced with holes or fitted with handles through which the anchor rope was passed. The first iron anchors were T-shaped (a), then the arms were bent forward to allow their points to grip more easily (b). Next a cross-bar was added, first in the same plane as the arms (c) then perpendicular to them, which forced the anchor to grip the bottom with one of its lugs (d). Then very big wooden anchors (20 to 25 ft. long) were made, fitted with a lead cross-bar (e);

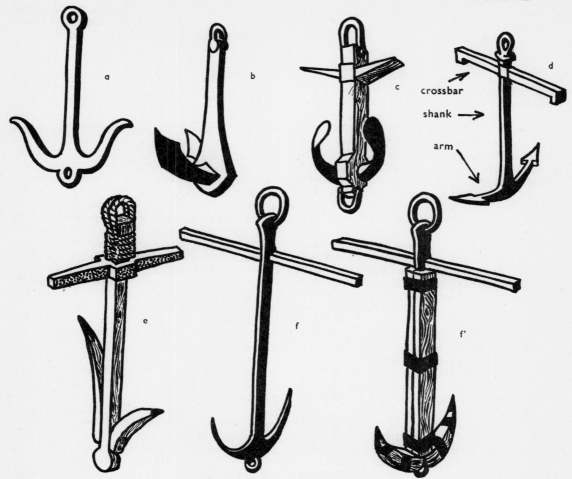

Evolution of the anchor in Bible times.

a certain number of these have been found and their weight varies from 1 to 8 cwt. Finally, long iron anchors were sheathed in wood (f, f[1]). The only passage in the Bible in which anchors proper are mentioned concerns the shipwreck of St Paul, on his voyage to Rome. To prevent the ship from foundering on the reefs, four anchors were thrown from the stern.[1] It is possible that they had earlier thrown over a floating anchor, a heavy piece of wood dragging behind the ship to slow its speed.

The anchor became the symbol of Christian hope because the Epistle to the Hebrews said of hope that it is like an anchor of the soul, sure and steadfast.[2]

[1] Acts 27. 29. [2] Heb. 6. 19.

ANEMONE

It is possible, but not certain, that the lily of the field of whose splendour Jesus spoke [1] was the red

Anemones in a Galilee field.

anemone, which in springtime covers Palestine with the rich red of its flowers († lily).

[1] Matt. 6. 28; Lk. 12. 27.

ANIMALS

According to the creation narratives (Gen. 1 and 2) animals, like men, were formed from the dust of the earth,[1] and the majority of them, apart from birds and the creatures living in the water, were created on the same day as men;[2] men and beasts were to use plants, fruit, and seeds as food;[3] finally, the animal received from God a "soul" housed in the blood.[4] Yet although man is not a separate being in nature, he is called to rule over the other creatures.[5]

Rudimentary classifications of animals are found in Gen. 1 and Lev. 11; thus, Genesis distinguishes creatures living in the air, in water, or on the ground; the ground-dwellers were subdivided into domestic animals, wild animals, and those which crawl on the ground.[6] In addition, the Law draws a distinction between clean and unclean animals [7] († uncleanness). More than once, also, the Law is occupied with animals, either to protect them, or to punish them: thus the ox that kills someone is not only considered as dangerous, but also as guilty, as a criminal; it is stoned and to eat its flesh is forbidden.[8] On the other hand, just as God takes care of animals, man should have some regard for them, and especially for cattle: "A righteous man has regard for the life of his beast: but the wicked have no mercy".[9] The ox and the ass are to have the benefit of Sabbath rest as well as "all beasts";[10] help must be given to the ass which collapses under its load, even if it is "the ass of one who hates you".[11] It is forbidden to yoke ox and ass to the plough together [12] or to muzzle the ox that treads out the grain [13] († agriculture); to cross-breed species [14] or to boil a kid in its mother's milk;[15] and if a nest is found the young may be taken but the mother must be spared.[16] Wild animals are sometimes looked on as a scourge used by God to punish the Israelites,[17] but at the end of time the idyllic age will return when "the wolf shall eat straw like the ox".[18]

It is well known how important was the place occupied by domestic animals in the Israelite cult, which streamed with the blood of sacrifices*. Yet in very marked opposition to the religion of neighbouring peoples, the law and the prophets condemned all worship of animals.[19]

The sympathy felt by the Israelites for the animals which were their daily companions is shown in the way in which children are given the names of domestic animals and birds; perhaps it was desired to endow those bearing such names with the qualities of the chosen animal; it was probably to protect the children against any maleficent evil being that people did not hesitate to give them occasionally the names of savage, wild, or even repulsive animals. (Leah = antelope, Rachel = ewe, Deborah = bee, Jonah = dove, Laish = lion, Simeon = an animal with characteristics of both wolf and hyena, etc.)

[1] Gen. 2. 7, 19. [2] Gen. 1. 24 ff. [3] Gen. 1. 29–30. [4] Lev. 17. 11 ff. [5] Gen. 1. 26; 9. 2. [6] Gen. 1. 25; Acts 11. 6. [7] Dt. 14; Lev. 11; Gen. 7. 8; 8. 20. [8] Ex. 21. 28; Gen. 9. 5. [9] Prov. 12. 10. [10] Ex. 23. 12; Dt. 5. 14. [11] Ex. 23. 5; Dt. 22. 4. [12] Dt. 22. 10. [13] Dt. 25. 4. [14] Lev. 19. 19. [15] Ex. 23. 17, etc. [16] Dt. 22. 6 f. [17] Lev. 26. 22. [18] Is. 11. 6–9. [19] 1 Kgs. 12. 28 ff.

ANOINTING

Oil, and olive oil in particular, was formerly believed to maintain not only the softness of the skin but also the suppleness of the muscles and joints, and to strengthen the body. It was especially used for application after a bath. The use of perfumed oil was favoured; it was a sign of joy and festivity;[1] alternatively, to abstain from anointing was a sign of anxiety or of mourning.[2] Oil was used to soothe wounds [3] and to embalm the dead,[4] or to show respect and esteem for someone.[5] In the last two cases the gesture may already have a religious significance. It is indeed certain that the rite of anointing was a religious symbol, practised by the Israelites, who recognized in it the import of an act of consecration. It was with this in mind that Jacob poured oil on the stone which he had just set up as a stele.[6] It was to appoint them to the kingship on God's behalf that Samuel anointed Saul and David.[7] A picture of this scene in the synagogue at Dura-Europos (which dates from the 3rd century of our era), depicts Samuel holding the horn of oil by the wide end while the oil runs out from the other; it was then in this

Anointing of David by Samuel. Painting in the synagogue at Dura-Europos (3rd century A.D.).

way that the ceremony took place, and excavators have found some of these flasks made from a horn open at the point, and hermetically sealed at the wide end.—Other kings and some prophets were anointed in a similar way,[8] and this was undoubtedly accompanied by a prayer or a formula which gave meaning to the act. Moreover, an analogous ceremony was performed upon kings in Egypt and at Ras Shamra as early as the 15th and 14th centuries.— When anointing was performed by a priest, the oil was considered as the vehicle of supernatural power which was conferred by a deity [9] upon the king, who to some extent became sacred [10] as a result. When, in the course of Israel's social evolution, the priestly office acquired very great importance, the priests too were anointed;[11] cultic objects were so treated in their turn.[12] Then the word "anointed" (in Hebrew = Messiah, in Greek = Christ), which had become a synonym for the king instituted by God's will, took on a wider meaning, sometimes being applied to foreign sovereigns,[13] or to the people of Israel in its entirety,[14] or to a prophet appointed to perform a mission of relief and comfort,[15] and ended by crystallizing the Israelite hope of a deliverer. The disciples of Jesus recognized that he alone deserved this title,[16] and they bore witness to this belief. In the N.T., anointing is primarily a metaphor representing the action of the Holy Spirit.[17]

[1] Ruth 3. 3; Eccl. 9. 8; Amos 6. 6; Lk. 7. 46 . . . [2] 2 Sam. 12. 20–23; 14. 2; Dan. 10. 3; Matt. 6. 17. [3] Is. 1. 6; Mk. 6. 13; Lk. 10. 34. [4] Mk. 16. 1; Lk. 23. 56. [5] Ps. 23. 5. [6] Gen. 28. 18; 35. 14. [7] 1 Sam. 10. 1; 16. 13. [8] 1 Kgs. 19. 15, 16. [9] 1 Sam. 16. 13. [10] 1 Sam. 24. 6; 26. 9; 2 Sam. 1. 14. [11] Ex. 28. 41; 30. 30; 40. 13, 15; Lev. 8. 30. [12] Ex. 30. 26–29; Lev. 8. 10, 11. [13] Is. 45. 1. [14] Ps. 28. 8; Hab. 3. 13. [15] Is. 61. 1. [16] Matt. 16. 16 par. [17] Acts 10. 38; 2 Cor. 1. 21; 1 Jn. 2. 20, 27.

ANT

Several species of ants are found in Palestine. Two of the commonest store certain provisions, either seeds, of which by some means they can stop the germination, or honeydew, which certain of them absorb into their abdomen, which then swells up in an extraordinary way; this honeydew is regurgitated on wet or cold days of the rainy season. These habits, which have been observed by modern entomologists in many countries, had been noticed by the Israelites, and the book of Proverbs [1] praises the wisdom and foresight of the ant in two passages, the only ones where this insect, so remarkable in many respects, is mentioned in the Bible.

[1] Prov. 6. 6–8; 30. 24–25.

ANTELOPE

Dt. 14. 5 lists seven wild animals whose flesh may be eaten. The translation of the names of the last three is dubious; they are probably three sorts of antelopes which are difficult to distinguish from one another: the first, which several versions take for the roe-deer* (A.V., R.V., pygarg) is perhaps the addax antelope, and the second, which the A.V. renders as

31

the wild ox or bull (R.V., antelope) in both Deuteronomy and Isaiah,[1] is probably the leucoryx antelope or the bubal; the third might be the wild

Bubal antelope.

Leucoryx antelope.

Addax antelope.

goat*, but certainly not the giraffe*, as suggested by the Ostervald and Segond versions.

[1] Is. 51. 20.

ANTIMONY

To enhance the brilliance of their eyes, but also and perhaps primarily to protect the eyes from the glare of the sun, Israelite women frequently made up their eyelids and eyebrows with black antimony powder (antimony sulphide), called *pûk* in Hebrew,[1] which was mixed with pure olive oil or clarified fats. One of Job's daughters was called Keren-happuch,[2] meaning antimony-horn or make-up box.

[1] 2 Kgs. 9. 30; Jer. 4. 30; cf. Is. 54. 11 and 1 Chr. 29. 2, where the same word is translated differently in our versions. [2] Job 42. 14.

ANTONIA (Citadel)

This is the fortress mentioned in the account of the arrest of St Paul in Jerusalem (Acts 21–23). Solidly built on a steep rock 80 ft. high, it is situated immediately next to the N-W. corner of Herod's Temple, with which it communicated,[1] and it served the Roman garrison as a barracks. The parapet of this imposing citadel surrounded a large enclosure, in the centre of which stood various buildings, and at each of the four corners was a tower of monumental proportions; the one nearest to the sanctuary and its courts overlooked them from a great height, allowing the soldiers to keep watch on the comings and goings of the Jews.

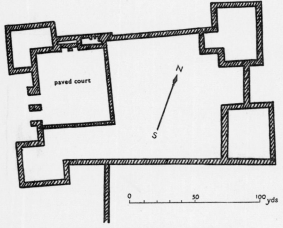

Reconstruction of the plan of the fortress.

As early as the time of Nehemiah [2] there is mention of a fortress attached to the Temple. In the 2nd century B.C., it was rebuilt by the Maccabees, who called it Baris. Herod the Great transformed it, considerably enlarged it, gave it luxurious fittings and furnishings, and called it Antonia in honour of his patron Mark Antony.

[1] Acts 21. 35. [2] Neh. 2. 8.

ANVIL

"He that smootheth with the hammer encouraged him that smiteth the anvil," said Isaiah.[1] It is the only passage in which this tool is mentioned.

[1] Is. 41. 7.

APE

Apes are found neither in Palestine nor in neighbouring lands; those mentioned in the O.T. figure among the curiosities brought from some Asiatic or African land by Solomon's ships.[1] It is impossible to determine the species.

[1] 1 Kgs. 10. 22; 2 Chr. 9. 21.

APOTHECARY

The apothecary is referred to only in Ecclesiasticus in the Apocrypha: "The apothecary . . . makes mixtures . . . through him well-being is spread abroad over the earth." [1] In Hebrew he bears the same name as the perfumer.

[1] Ecclus. 38. 8.

APPLE TREE

Several times [1] the O.T. speaks of a tree and a fruit whose characteristics correspond quite closely to the apple and the apple tree, which is, however, rarely cultivated in modern Palestine. Although the identification is usually accepted, it is not certain, and apricot*, citron*, lemon*, and orange* have in turn been proposed by various exegetes.—The traditional assumption that the forbidden fruit in the Garden of Eden [2] was the apple has no textual support in the Bible.

[1] Prov. 25. 11; Cant. 2. 3, 5; 7. 9; 8. 5; Joel 1. 12. [2] Gen. 2. 17; 3. 3, 6 . . .

APRICOT

This fruit is cultivated today in Palestine. Was it in olden times? There is good reason to think that it was still unknown in Roman times. However, a Hebrew word which modern scholars generally think to be the apple* tree is sometimes translated by "apricot".

ARCHITECTURE

Neither their predecessors in Palestine nor the Israelites themselves produced any original work in architecture. All their buildings, in one way or another, were subject to foreign influence; the situation of the country, and the continual overrunning of which it was the victim, largely explain the absence of an art native to the land and the people.

At an early date the Palestinians were able to build houses* of brick or stone and showed ingenuity in the construction of arching. Excavations have given proof especially of the extensiveness and sound construction of their fortifications*. For their big dwellings and palaces* the Israelites turned to the Phoenicians, who were clever builders and specialists in the shaping of stone. David [1] and Solomon [2] especially had dealings with them, and the close links between the dynasty of Omri and the princes of Sidon [3] are well known.

We have no information about the royal palace which David had built in Jerusalem.[4] On the other hand, I Kgs. 5. 7, 9 speaks in complimentary terms about Solomon's building works. These consisted of a great collection of buildings on the eastern hill of the capital. The Temple*, the glory of Solomon, dominated the buildings, called: (a) the house* of the Forest of Lebanon; (b) the porch* of pillars; (c) the porch of the throne; and (d) the royal palace, with the house of Pharaoh's daughter. If the sanctuary was undoubtedly on the hilltop, it is difficult to say with certainty how the other buildings were grouped; did they succeed one another on the slope in the order given in the Book of Kings? This view has often been held, but, from knowledge gained from excavations in Samaria and elsewhere, archaeologists

As is well known, Herod prided himself on the many buildings which he put up throughout the country, even creating in their entirety new towns, like Caesarea on the coast and the new Jericho. Among these buildings in Jerusalem alone were the Antonia fortress, the magnificent palace where he resided in the shadow of the Hippicus, Phasael and

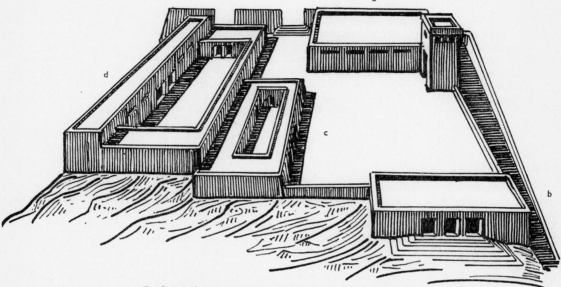

Conjectural reconstruction of Solomon's palace buildings.

today prefer the conjecture that the buildings, adjoining one another, were grouped around one or two towers.—Solomon also busied himself with the fortifications of Jerusalem and of other towns,[5] but his work seems to have been unique; after his reign the kingdom of Judah was weakened by schism and could no longer afford the tastes which cost the son of David such considerable sums. Although the O.T. records, on occasion, programmes of work undertaken by Hezekiah,[6] or Josiah,[7] for example, or Jehoiakim's winter palace,[8] we have to wait for the time of the Herods to see a new flourishing of architecture.

In the northern kingdom the only important buildings are those in Samaria, of which the carefully arranged substructure has been revealed by excavations; the walls show a remarkably advanced technique: living rock outcrops and its sides are shaped to form the framework. Begun by Omri[9] and developed by Ahab[10] and Jeroboam II, the citadel raised its containing walls and the walls of the royal palace at the top of the hill. But Samaria had the finest period of its history in Roman times; it was graced with splendid buildings: Herod the Great erected, among other things, an imposing temple in honour of Augustus.

Mariamne Towers, and especially the Temple which bears his name.

Excavations in Palestine have revealed, in different places, chapels, temples, and imposing structures not mentioned in the Bible; for instance—and without mentioning buildings of the Canaanite period, or fortifications*—there are Solomon's stables* at Megiddo,[11] the "house of the commander" of that city, a sumptuous residence of the Persian period at Duweir (Lachish), and some temples at Bethshean.

(† house, palaces, fortifications, tomb; and articles on hydraulic works, † cistern, etc.)

[1] 2 Sam. 5. 11. [2] 1 Kgs. 5. [3] 1 Kgs. 16. 31. [4] 2 Sam. 5. 11. [5] 1 Kgs. 9. 15 ff. [6] 2 Kgs. 20. 20; 2 Chr. 32. 27 ff. [7] 2 Kgs. 22. 5 ff. [8] Jer. 36. 22. [9] 1 Kgs. 16. 24. [10] 1 Kgs. 16. 32; 22. 39. [11] Cf. 1 Kgs. 10. 26.

AREOPAGUS (= Mars' Hill)

This was a precipitous rock to the west of the Acropolis at Athens where a tribunal with a history dating from the earliest times of Greece used to meet in the open air. This hill, with its staircase of sixteen steps and its rows of seats hewn from the living rock, can still be seen. Deprived of their political power at the time of Pericles, the judges of the Areopagus had retained the guardianship of the laws, of religion, morals, and public education.

After discussions in the Agora* (public square), St Paul must have been taken to the Areopagus, not so much to be judged as to be heard, and it was there, before this famous tribunal, that he must have delivered his speech about the unknown God.[1] Since the Renaissance several writers have argued that the apostle was not taken to the hill, where in his time the judges only sat in exceptional circumstances, but to the Royal Gate (quite close to the Agora), for it was there that the Areopagites held their normal sittings. It is also possible that St Paul did not appear before this tribunal at all, but that he and his hearers merely went up the hill Areopagus in order to be able to hold their discussions more easily, away from the noise of the public square.

[1] Acts 17. 19–33.

ARK

This word comes from the Latin *arca* and means "chest"; sometimes it is used alone and without qualification, but more often the O.T. speaks of the Ark of Yahweh, or the Ark of God, etc., and of the Ark of the Covenant (Law), or the Ark of the Testimony (act of liberation).

Though this sacred object is mentioned in some ancient texts of the Pentateuch,[1] the more recent sources of these first books of the Bible state that the origin of the Ark dates from the events at Sinai; Moses is believed to have built it at Yahweh's command.[2] According to Biblical traditions, it accompanied the Israelites on their wanderings in the desert,[3] went before them when they crossed the Jordan,[4] and played an important part in the taking of Jericho.[5] Once in Canaan, it was placed in the sanctuary at Shiloh;[6] it was removed from there to take part in an ill-fated battle against the Philistines.[7] Captured by them, the Ark was in their possession for seven months, but caused such calamities among them that the conquerors returned it to Israel with strange expiatory gifts.[8] During the whole of the Samuel–Saul period it remained at the house of Abinadab at Kirjath-jearim,[9] but David—after a first attempt marred by an accident[10]—had it removed to Jerusalem in order to increase the prestige of the new capital; there it was placed in a tent put up for the purpose.[11] David used it, at times, to accompany his troops;[12] he went to it to pray to God.[13] Solomon did likewise,[14] but placed the Ark in the Holy of Holies in the Temple,[15] whence it seems never to have emerged, except, perhaps, to appear in certain solemn processions.[16] Then the surprising fact is that after the time of Solomon nothing more is said about it. Was it destroyed at the time of the capture of Jerusalem by Pharaoh Shishak in the

reign of Rehoboam,[17] did it disappear during the other sackings of the Temple, or did it remain there until the fall of the kingdom of Judah? No certainty is possible. At any rate, Ezekiel makes no reference to it in his plan for a new sanctuary,[18] and in the second Temple there is no Ark; because of this there is no reason for surprise at its absence from the bas-relief of the Arch of Titus in Rome, in which the principal sacred objects of the Jews are depicted.

According to Ex. 25. 10–22 and 37. 1–9, the Ark made from acacia wood was not large (4 ft. long, 2 ft. 6 in. wide and 2 ft. 6 in. high, approximately); it was overlaid "within and without" with pure gold and fitted with a lid of pure gold (called the "mercy-seat") on which two golden cherubim* with outspread wings stood facing one another. At each of the four corners was a gold ring; through each pair of these was fitted a bar of acacia* wood, covered with gold, used for carrying the chest.

Tradition also claims that the Ark contained the tables of the Law,[19] but it has been conjectured that this may be a later idea—Heb. 9. 4 lists, in addition to the decalogue, Aaron's rod and a gold jar containing manna—and that originally, according to a widespread belief in Semitic circles, the Ark was a receptacle for some (or one) sacred stones, kinds of fetishes constituting the dwelling-place of the divinity (a reliquary), or even for some divine image (a processional casket) or for two divination stones necessary for consulting Yahweh (a box for oracles). According to another theory, more acceptable, based on more than one text and on some interesting parallels, the Ark was originally a throne, Yahweh's throne, which after a national calamity was later on transformed into a chest containing the sacred texts. However, none of these conjectures is altogether convincing; the question remains open, like that of the exact origin and purpose of this cultic object. It is evident, in any event, that the Ark was the sign and guarantee of Yahweh's presence;[20] it was the national palladium, the banner of Israel.

[1] Num. 10. 33–36; 14. 44. [2] Ex. 25. 10–22; 37. 1–9; Dt. 10. 1–5. [3] Num. 10. 35–36. [4] Jos. 3 and 4. [5] Jos. 6. [6] 1 Sam. 3. 3. [7] 1 Sam. 4. [8] 1 Sam. 5 and 6. [9] 1 Sam. 7. 1. [10] 2 Sam. 6. [11] 2 Sam. 6. 12 ff. [12] 2 Sam. 11. 11. [13] 2 Sam. 7. 18; 12. 20. [14] 1 Kgs. 3. 15. [15] 1 Kgs. 6. 19; 8. 5 ff. [16] Ps. 132. 8; 47. 5 (?). [17] 1 Kgs. 14. 25 ff. [18] Ez. 40–43. [19] 1 Kgs. 8. 9, etc. [20] Num. 10. 34; 1 Sam. 4. 5 ff.; 2 Sam. 6. 5, 14; etc.

ARK (Noah's)

In Hebrew Noah's Ark bears quite a different name (*tebah*) from that given to the Ark* of the Covenant ('*arôn*). *Tebah* is a general term meaning something used as a means of navigation. In the Bible it is used twice:

1. For Noah's Ark. This was an enormous "chest" of gopher wood, coated with bitumen, a kind of floating house, three storeys high; it is difficult to get

34

any clear idea of it, since the text [1] describing it is too obscure. Comparison of the Sumero-Babylonian narrative of the Flood with the Biblical one, which is

Wicker basket.

clearly akin to it, brings no enlightenment. For curiosity and comparison, we append the following table:

	Noah's Ark	Babylonian vessel of the Flood	Liner Lusitania
Length	413 ft.	512 ft.	748 ft.
Breadth	85 ft.	205 ft.	148 ft.
Height	51 ft.	205 ft.	95 ft.

2. For the basket cradle in which Moses was confided to the Nile. From the description given in Exodus [2] it can be identified with the wicker baskets which the river people of the lower Euphrates still make today and which are also found in India, Indo-China, and China. They are made from crushed and plaited stems of papyrus or reeds; the gaps are plugged with straw, and these huge, round or elliptical baskets are daubed inside and out with a coating of asphalt, bitumen, or pitch, more rarely with wood oil. Made in this way, these baskets resist the pressure of water very well.

[1] Gen. 6. 14–16. [2] Ex. 2. 3.

ARMOUR-BEARER

This word has no single Hebrew equivalent, but in the earlier stories of the O.T. young soldiers are often mentioned who carry the weapons or the great shield of a captain or a king. The "servant" of Gideon [1] was doubtless an armour-bearer; Abimelech, Jonathan, and Joab [2] have them; an armour-bearer preceded Goliath, and David is known to have been for a time armour-bearer to the first king of Israel. [3] At the battle of Mount Gilboa the man who accompanied Saul refused, when so requested, to kill his wounded master, and died with him. [4] An armour-bearer supported his master in battle and despatched the enemies he had wounded.

[1] Jg. 7. 10. [2] Jg. 9. 54; 1 Sam. 14. 1, 6, 13; 2 Sam. 18. 15; 23. 37. [3] 1 Sam. 16. 21. [4] 1 Sam. 31. 4–5.

ARMS

The Bible has full documentation on this subject. Soldiers' equipment developed especially from the time of the monarchy, on account of the pressure of

military organization, contact with foreign armies, and progress in the art of war and of siege.—Arms are often used by Biblical authors as figures of speech, as in the famous description of the Christian's armour. [1]

Arms mentioned in the O.T. and N.T. include: (a) defensive arms: helmet—sword—greaves—shoes —shield; (b) offensive arms: sword—bow—sling— spear—javelin—club—axe—chariot of war. (For details, see under these entries.)

[1] Eph. 6. 10 ff.

ARMY

There was no regular army among the Israelites until the time of the kings. Earlier wars were most frequently merely armed raids, razzias, led by a chief with a band of volunteers or servants whose support he had won: Abraham set off with 318 of his most hardened followers to deliver Lot; [1] Gideon chose 300 men to fall upon the Midianites. [2] In serious cases every man capable of bearing arms was called, but sometimes threats were needed to force their decision; [3] in the time of the Judges the tribes never acted as a unit; at the most, in very perilous circumstances, [4] a few of them succeeded in forming a federation. As soon as the campaign was over each man returned home.

It is difficult to know how the army was organized at the time of the Exodus and the conquest of the Promised Land. Later tradition speaks of a militia whose orderliness was in marked contrast with the habits of desert nomads. [5]

It is known, however, that strongholds in Canaan were guarded by troops, frequently mercenaries, who in war were reinforced by all the men of the town. At Ugarit (Ras Shamra) the soldiers in the garrison received a regular wage in silver as well as the other advantages, such as the Code of Hammurabi granted to veterans as early as the 18th century B.C.

One of Saul's first cares after being proclaimed king was to form an army capable of carrying on the struggle against the Philistines. After victories over the Ammonites he kept 3,000 men under arms to meet the first dangers and to form the nucleus of a nation under arms, [6] and he had a bodyguard composed of strong courageous men whom he attached to his personal service. [7] David was the real creator of the Israelite army. Although we lack precise information, it seems clear that at that time the army comprised two elements: on the one hand, proclamation brought together all the fit men from the tribes, mobilized for important campaigns; on the other hand, there was a body of permanent troops, descended from the faithful adventurers who had been David's supporters during his struggles with Saul. [8] This bodyguard, commanded by Benaiah, [9] undoubtedly included some Philistines, past masters in the art of war; it bore the name Cherethites and Pelethites*.[10] The finest warriors ("mighty men") formed an *élite* of thirty men who constituted a kind of General Staff for the king.[11] At the head of these regulars was a general in chief, preferably a relative of the king—Abner was Saul's cousin, Joab his nephew [12]—to whom the king delegated his powers, for he himself did not always take an active part in war.[13] This general had under his command the chiefs of the subdivisions of the army, arranged in groups of 1,000, 500, 100, 50, and 10 men.[14]

In David's time the army consisted entirely of infantry, bearing different weapons († arms); only the chiefs were mounted, on she-asses or mules;[15] it is very curious to discover that David was unable to see the value of the many horses captured from the Syrians, and had them all hamstrung.[16] In contrast, Solomon, who seems to have lavished the greatest care on his army, adopted the methods of his enemies and introduced chariots and cavalry [17] into Israel. Indeed, he had a great number of them and had them stationed in garrison towns and in Jerusalem.[18] To the great annoyance of the prophets, who spoke against the trust given to these weapons by the Israelites to the detriment of confidence in Yahweh,[19] from that time onwards mounted soldiers and chariots constituted an important part of the army.[20] Moreover, the army staff became gradually more influential in the country, and sometimes became involved in political affairs (cf. Jehu's revolution).[21]

In the event of an important war, all men fit to bear arms, aged probably between twenty [22] and fifty years (Josephus), were trained to take part; in early times they were under a moral obligation to do so, whereas it seems that David later instituted special measures for recruitment;[23] in later monarchical times there was a post of secretary in charge of enlistment, who was assistant to the army chief.[24] It seems likely that at this period men were enlisted only in successive contingents [25] and that thus an army of the people tended to replace the mercenary army. Inserted in Deuteronomy there is a curious law, the date of which it is difficult to give precisely, which exempts from war service anyone who has just built a house or planted a vineyard, as well as engaged or newly married men, and even timorous men.[26] Priests and Levites were exempt from all military service.[27]

Mobilization was proclaimed by sounding a trumpet [28] or by the despatch of messengers;[29] signals were also given from the mountains, and the prophets often allude to these measures in their discourses.[30] In early times victualling was not regulated: food [31] for the troops was provided by the district in which they happened to be (see, however, reference to a rudimentary commissariat in Jg. 20. 10); the soldiers also received food from their families.[32] No pay was given to the militia; only the permanent troops received that. On the other hand, every combatant had a share in the spoil,[33] as also did those who had not fought;[34] the chiefs naturally kept certain privileges for themselves.[35]

On many occasions, of course, the O.T., and especially the prophets, speak of the foreign armies with which Israel had dealings: Canaanites riding in their war chariots, strongly armed Philistines, disciplined Egyptians, and finally the Roman cohorts, whose power was to put an end to the political life of the Jews.

[1] Gen. 14. 14. [2] Jg. 8. 4. [3] 1 Sam. 11. 7. [4] Jg. 4 and 5. [5] Num. 1; 2; 20. 14 ff.; 26. [6] 1 Sam. 13. 2. [7] 1 Sam. 14. 52. [8] 1 Sam. 22. 2; 23. 13; etc. [9] 2 Sam. 20. 23. [10] 2 Sam. 15. 18. [11] 2 Sam. 23. 8 ff. [12] 1 Sam. 14. 50 ff.; 1 Chr. 2. 16; 2 Sam. 8. 16; etc. [13] 2 Sam. 10. 7; 11. 1; 1 Kgs. 11. 16. [14] 1 Sam. 8. 12; 17. 18; 18. 13; 2 Sam. 18. 1; cf. Ex. 18. 21. [15] Jg. 5. 10; 10. 4; 2 Sam. 13. 29; 18. 9; etc. [16] 2 Sam. 8. 4. [17] 1 Kgs. 4. 26. [18] 1 Kgs. 9. 19; 10. 26. [19] Is. 2. 7 f.; 31. 1; Hos. 1. 7; Amos 2. 15; etc. [20] 1 Kgs. 16. 9; 22. 8. 21; 13. 7; Is. 2. 7; Mic. 5. 10. [21] 2 Kgs. 9 ff. [22] Num. 1. 3; 26. 2. [23] 2 Sam. 24. [24] 2 Kgs. 25. 19. [25] 1 Chr. 27. 1 ff. [26] Dt. 20. 5–9; 24. 5. [27] Num. 2. 33. [28] Jg. 3. 27; 6. 34; 1 Sam. 13. 3. [29] Jg. 19. 29; 1 Sam. 11. 7. [30] Is. 5. 26; 18. 3; Jer. 4. 5 ff.; Ez. 7. 14; etc. [31] 2 Sam. 17. 27 ff. [32] 1 Sam. 17. 17. [33] Gen. 14. 24; Num. 31. 25 ff.; Dt. 21. 11. [34] Jos. 22. 8; 1 Sam. 30. 24 f. [35] Jg. 8. 24 ff.; 1 Sam. 30. 26 ff.; 2 Sam. 12. 30.

AROMATICS

Various aromatic substances are mentioned in the O.T.; they were used in the preparation of perfumes and in the cult. Apart from incense and coriander*, it is often difficult to determine the exact denotation of some of the Hebrew words; hence our versions are obliged to speak in a loose way of perfume, sweet-smelling perfume, spices, or incense.

Ferula, an umbellifer of the same family from which galbanum was extracted.

We may mention, however, that the galbanum which entered into the composition of the holy incense [1] was a yellowish gum-resin, of penetrating odour, which came from a Persian umbellifer; whilst the onycha (onyx, sweet-smelling nail or shell) referred to in the same passage was not a vegetable

36

product, but came from the horny or calcareous operculum which closed the opening of the shell of certain molluscs. († balm, perfume.)

[1] Ex. 30. 34.

ARROW

For several thousands of years the arrow was the most frequently used weapon; archaeological excavations have unearthed so many of them, from all periods of history, of all shapes and of widely different materials, that the evolution of arrow-heads can be sketched.

So far as Biblical times are concerned, the most ancient arrow heads were made of bronze, although in the earliest times of Israelite history there were, no doubt, heads made from flint flakes and slivers of

(a) Feathering. (b) Incendiary arrow.

bone. The simple shape, like a willow leaf, of the earliest metal arrows was quickly modified when iron came into use; a rib which gave more strength to the edges of the arrow-head was elongated into a tang which fitted into the shaft of reed or light wood; a widened ogival-shaped type was reputed to give particularly serious wounds to horses. When it was noticed that the head did not fit the shaft sufficiently tightly, first a triangular tang was introduced, then a socket which secured the head so firmly that a barb

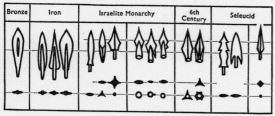

Evolution of arrow points.

could be added with the purpose of aggravating the wound on withdrawal; it seems that this "new" weapon of war was of Assyrian origin. In the 4th century the socket formed part of the head, and finally in Hellenistic times the tang returned as a method of union, for at this period the strength of the breastplate had developed so greatly that the arrow's penetrating power was more important than the extensiveness of the wound it could inflict.

In order that the arrow should retain its initial direction, it was flighted, usually by means of the

two halves of a feather, cut down the middle of the spine (a). Arrows were kept in a quiver carried on the soldier's back or left side, or fixed to the side of a war-chariot († chariot, bow).

Arrows are mentioned in the Bible in the strict and in the figurative sense: Job alludes to poisoned arrows.[1] Elsewhere incendiary arrows are mentioned;[2] one of these incendiary arrows has been found at Shechem: made entirely of metal, the edges of its head are pierced with holes into which was fixed tow soaked in oil which was ignited at the moment it was used (b).

[1] Job 6. 4. [2] Ps. 7. 13; Prov. 26. 18; Is. 50. 11; Eph. 6. 16.

ARSENAL

The development the army underwent in the time of the monarchy necessitated the setting up of arsenals, which are very infrequently mentioned in the O.T.[1] We may recall principally 1 Kgs. 10. 17 and Is. 22. 8, which speak of shields* of gold deposited by Solomon in the house* of the Forest of Lebanon and of the arms in this palace, and 2 Kgs. 20. 13 (= Is. 39. 2), where we simply find a reference to Hezekiah's arsenal, with no further details.

[1] Cant. 4. 4; 2 Chr. 11. 12; Neh. 3. 19.

ART

In comparison with the civilizations of Egypt and Mesopotamia, Israel, in its mountains, gives a rather barbarian impression from the point of view of art. The somewhat harsh nature of the country was hardly favourable to the flowering of the sense of beauty, and the preoccupations of those who were given over to rearing live-stock and to agriculture, when they were not at war, remained primarily utilitarian. Religion, it is true, might have been a source of artistic inspiration, but it is well known how uncompromising Yahwism was in its condemnation of all representation of the things of heaven or earth,[1] since it considered the fine arts as the vehicle of idolatry.

Moreover, in order to flourish art needs patrons, prosperous princes, the power of a great state; but the Israelites enjoyed these circumstances only at the time of Solomon, whose reign was not in the normal Israelite tradition.

Manifestations of a high artistic order cannot then be expected to occur in Israel, and even where production rises above the ordinary, it shows no originality: Palestine, submerged by waves of neighbouring civilizations, constantly borrowed its models from them; it was unable to create an independent art, and its works always show some hybrid quality. Only its literature, nurtured as it was by the religious thought which makes Israel's greatness, shines with true magnificence.

ASHERAH

(For details, † architecture, tomb, hydraulic works [index], painting, sculpture, goldsmith, metals, glass, music, singer, dance.)

¹ Ex. 20. 4; Dt. 5. 8.

ASHERAH

Among the objects to be found in Canaanite sanctuaries was a sacred pole, a branchless tree-trunk; this divine symbol, which was perhaps a substitute for the sacred tree* and which was probably connected with the cult of vegetation, bore the name of "asherah", a term which the majority of Bible versions render in too vague a manner, by the words:

light in Palestinian excavations, and the O.T. does not give a single detail of their form. A small bronze relief found in Elam, which represents an ancient Semitic high-place, sets in line, among other ritual furniture, three tree-trunks without branches; these were undoubtedly asherahs.

¹ 1 Kgs. 14. 15; 2 Kgs. 17. 10; etc. ² 2 Kgs. 23. 6. ³ Jg. 3. 7; 1 Kgs. 15. 13. ⁴ Cf. Jer. 2. 27. ⁵ Dt. 16. 21.

ASHES

In Israel, as among other peoples of antiquity and among some uncivilized peoples today, mourners prostrated themselves in dust or ashes, or sprinkled

A votive tray found at Susa, representing a high-place with asherahs, bowls, offerings, and also, in miniature, a tower ("ziggurat") and a temple. In the middle the king, assisted by a priest, carries out a rite of purification. Bronze, approx. 2 ft. by 1 ft. 4 in. (12th century B.C.).

image, idol, grove. Asherahs (Asheroth) are often mentioned in the O.T., for the Israelites too began to raise them in their high places*;¹ there was even one of them in the Temple at Jerusalem.²

Moreover, of the feminine deities of the Phoenicians mentioned in the O.T.,³ the most important, named Asherah, should not be confused, as too often happens, with Astarte*, the famous goddess of fertility and love. But it is difficult to say what the connection was between the asherahs and the goddess Asherah, and whether the sacred pole took its name from her, for the artificial tree could also represent a male deity.⁴

Deuteronomy⁵ and the prophets categorically condemned the asherahs, which were possibly abolished by the reform of Hezekiah, and certainly by that of Josiah.

These objects were too perishable to have come to

them on their heads and faces. These same actions were carried out, moreover, in any circumstances in which sorrow, humiliation, or penitence were to be expressed. There are many passages in the O.T. alluding to these procedures.¹ In a sense, ashes became the food of the wretched,² so what a wonderful consolation is Isaiah's: "To grant to those who mourn in Zion, to give them a garland instead of ashes." ³ Since outward show naturally threatened demonstrations of this kind, the prophet recalls their vanity, if the heart is not touched, and we know how vigorously Jesus took up this theme and exposed the hypocrisy of outward factitious sorrow.⁴

In the language of metaphor, ashes are the symbol of fragile ephemeral things: "I who am but dust and ashes," says Abraham to his God.⁵ Idols, too, are but ashes,⁶ and the solemn pronouncements of his friends are merely "proverbs of ashes" ⁷ to Job. It

38

is interesting to discover that ashes coming from the burnt offering have a sacred character and must be disposed of in a special place;[8] similarly, the ashes of the red heifer* play an important part.[9] For curiosity's sake, torture by ashes may be mentioned; this was of Persian origin, and is referred to in the second book of Maccabees (Apocrypha); the condemned man was thrown into a tower full of ashes in which he stifled to death.[10]

[1] Jos. 7. 6; 1 Sam. 4. 12; 2 Sam. 1. 2; 13. 19; Job 42. 6; Jer. 6. 26; Matt. 11. 21; Lk. 10. 13; etc. [2] Ps. 102. 9; cf. Lam. 3. 16. [3] Is. 61. 3. [4] Is. 58. 5; Matt. 6. 16–18. [5] Gen. 18. 27; cf. Job 30. 19. [6] Is. 44. 20. [7] Job 13. 12. [8] Lev. 1. 16; 4. 12; 6. 11; etc. [9] Num. 19. [10] 2 Macc. 13. 5–8.

ASH-PAN

It is not always easy to be precise about the utensils used for sacrifices: braziers*, censers*, cauldrons*, etc. But the Book of Exodus mentions vessels to receive the greasy ashes of the altar [1] (coming, not from the burning of wood, but from the offering) and receptacles to take the charred wicks from the sanctuary lamps.[2] The former are made of bronze, the latter of gold. These two kinds of ash-pans have different names in Hebrew.

[1] Ex. 27. 3; 38. 3. [2] Ex. 25. 38; 37. 23; cf. Num. 4. 9.

ASP

English versions of the O.T. often translate by "asp" the Hebrew word *peten*, which appears in six passages [1] in which this creature figures as a particularly venomous snake, much sought after by snake-charmers. The creature in question is probably the

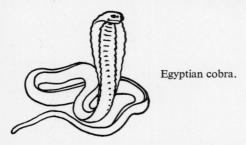

Egyptian cobra.

Egyptian cobra (naja naje), which is now very rare in Palestine (southern). It is known that it has the power to swell its neck, to rear, and sway the forepart of its body before striking and biting; it is the snake "charmed" by flute-players.

[1] Dt. 32. 33; Job 20. 14, 16; Ps. 58. 4; 91. 13; Is. 11. 8.

ASPHALT

In the building of the Tower of Babel [1] asphalt (sometimes translated "bitumen", a more general term) was used as mortar; the historians record that

the walls of Babylon were cemented in this way. Gen. 14. 10 alludes to the asphalt pits in the valley of Siddim, near the Dead Sea, also called (but not in the Bible) Lake Asphaltitis, for pieces of this mineral substance are thrown up from small submarine volcanoes and sometimes float on its surface. Palestinian asphalt is highly reputed. The rush cradle in which Moses was put out on the Nile had been coated with asphalt and pitch.[2]

[1] Gen. 11. 3. [2] Ex. 2. 3.

ASS, DONKEY

Although the wild ass* or onager, now extinct in Palestine, is sometimes referred to in the O.T. in terms stressing its intractable nature and liking for solitude,[1] the domestic ass is mentioned over a hundred times in the Biblical texts. It was indeed highly valued by the Israelites, whom it served in many ways; even today, of all the domestic animals, it is perhaps the most useful to the people of Palestine. Therefore the law is concerned about it and ranks it as highly as the ox.[2]

Big, stronger, more lively and intelligent than ours, the Oriental donkey, grey with reddish markings, has much to recommend it; its steadiness, stamina, and sure-footedness make it an asset which is all the more attractive for being moderately priced and cheap in upkeep. It is used in turn as a beast of burden,[3] as a draught animal for various agricultural tasks,[4] for turning the stone of the large mills,[5] or as a mount; in all periods of history the donkey has been the necessary companion of the Palestinian in all his errands and journeys;[6] it is sure of foot; its easy temper and lively pace make it a pleasant mount, and the rich and great did not scorn it,[7] nor did women of quality;[8] the prophet has no hesitation in hailing the Messiah himself as entering Jerusalem on a donkey and being acclaimed like a king.[9] Females were preferred to males because they were quieter and more manageable;[10] moreover, they gave excellent milk, and their young were a source of wealth. Often today on roads in Palestine one can meet a caravan of heavily laden camels led by a driver riding a female donkey with her colt at heel. White or chestnut-coloured females were especially highly valued and were reserved for the great.[11]

We have only to glance through the lists of animals brought back from the Exile by the Jews [12] to discover how much more widespread was the use of donkeys than that of horses* (6,720 donkeys to 736 horses). The horse was hardly used except in the army* (cavalry and chariots); it was the animal dear to the warrior, while the donkey was just the mount for the Prince of Peace.[13] Herds of donkeys formed a good part of the wealth of big landowners.[14]

The ass's flesh was considered unclean, it was eaten only in times of famine,[15] and the animal, so valuable from many points of view, was never sacrificed.[16]

[1] Gen. 16. 12; Job 39. 5–8; Ps. 104. 11; Is. 32. 14; etc. [2] Ex. 13. 13; 20. 17; 21. 33; 23. 4, etc.; cf. Is. 1. 3; 32. 20; Lk. 13. 15. [3] Gen. 42. 26; 45. 23; 49. 14; 1 Sam. 25. 18; Neh. 13. 15; etc. [4] Is. 30. 24; 32. 20. [5] Matt. 18. 6. [6] Ex. 4. 20; Num. 22. 21; etc. [7] Jg. 10. 4; 12. 14; 2 Sam. 17. 23; 19. 26. [8] Jg. 1. 14; 1 Sam. 25. 23; 2 Kgs. 4. 24. [9] Zech. 9. 9. [10] Gen. 32. 15; 1 Sam. 9. 3; Job. 1. 3, etc. [11] Jg. 5. 10. [12] Ezr. 2. 67; Neh. 7. 69. [13] Mk. 11. 2 ff. par. [14] Gen. 12. 16; 30. 43; Job 1. 3; etc. [15] 2 Kgs. 6. 25. [16] Ex. 13. 13; 34. 20.

ASTARTE

The dispenser of animal and vegetable life, then the goddess of fertility, maternity, love, and also pleasure, Astarte—whose cult at times became quite licentious—was venerated throughout the Semitic East. The Hebrews called her Ashteroth (the Phoenicians, Ashtaret or Ashtart; the Assyro-Babylonians, Ishtar; Astarte, the Greek equivalent, has passed into

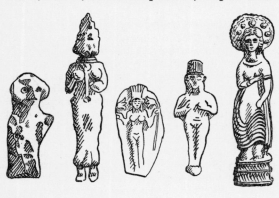

Palestine terra-cotta figurines of Astarte. (*lower illus.*) Bronze Phoenician Astartes of the 14th century.

English). She was held in high honour by the people of Tyre and Sidon, and so to please them Solomon raised a shrine to her "before Jerusalem"; this was later destroyed by Josiah.[1] The Philistines paid homage to her: they hung the weapons of the conquered Saul in the temple of Astarte, probably at Beth-shean or at Ashkelon.[2] Beloved of the Canaanites, among whom she probably replaced Asherah*,

with whom she must not be confused, however, Astarte also had her worshippers in Israel;[3] excavations in Palestine have brought to light a large number of statuettes of this divinity, dating from the Israelite period as well as from earlier times. As Astarte tended to absorb little by little the various female deities of the country, her name became a synonym for goddess: hence the expression "Baalim and Ashtaroth", which is used in the O.T. to denote the ensemble of the Canaanite pantheon.[4] In time, Astarte assumed the character of a celestial deity (daughter of the moon, of the sun, Venus) and we find her again in the O.T. at the end of monarchical times, under the name of "Queen of Heaven"; Jeremiah[5] condemned the preparation of the cakes (stars, crescents, etc.) which were offered to her and eaten in her honour in the cities of Judah, and he inveighed[6] against Jews and their wives, his fellow emigrants to Egypt, who presented incense, cakes, and libations to the Queen of Heaven.

[1] 1 Kgs. 11. 5; 2 Kgs. 23. 13. [2] 1 Sam. 31. 10. [3] 1 Kgs. 11. 33; [4] Jg. 2. 13; 1 Sam. 7. 3, 4; 12. 10. [5] Jer. 7. 18. [6] Jer. 44. 15–26.

ASTROLOGY

Astrology flourished luxuriously in Babylonia,[1] but was not practised in Israel. It is believed that some people at certain times became addicted to this "science", since the cult of the stars was celebrated "in the cities of Judah and the environs of Jerusalem".[2] But astrology is contrary to the religion of Yahweh, who manifests his will by means very different from the intermediary of the stars. None the less, apocalyptic prophets and poets alike have no hesitation in declaring that strange events in the heavens (abnormal colouring of the sun and moon, eclipses, etc.) will precede the great and terrible day of the Lord.[3] Note also the place given to the star of Bethlehem and to the Magi[4] in the Gospel accounts of the birth of Jesus.

[1] Is. 47. 13; Dan. 2. 27; etc. [2] 2 Kgs. 23. 5. [3] Joel 2. 30–31; 3. 14–15; etc. [4] Matt. 2. 1–12.

ASTRONOMY

Since astronomy was the offspring of astrology*, the Israelites paid little attention to it; their knowledge in this field was undoubtedly rudimentary and much inferior to that of the Babylonians († star, sun, moon). The laws of heaven, they felt, surpass human understanding,[1] and rather than plumb the depths of heaven, they bowed before the God whose glory is there displayed.[2] Gen. 1. 14 states, however, that the stars serve as signs to mark the seasons, the days, and the years, but the Israelite calendar is based on simple, straightforward observations and not on astronomical calculations. The dial* of Ahaz,[3] the structure

of which is unknown, was in all likelihood of
Assyrian origin.

¹ Job 38. 33. ² Ps. 19. 1; etc. ³ 2 Kgs. 20. 9–11; Is. 38. 7–8.

ASYLUM

In Israel any homicide, even an unintended one,
set in motion the action of the "avenger of blood"
(*go'el*): the victim's nearest relative was responsible
for putting the killer to death. However, the law
took the unintentional killer under its protection, in
the sense that he could find safety in ancient times
at any shrine and more precisely at any altar*, whose
horns he was quick to grasp.¹ After the cult was
centralized in Jerusalem, six sacred cities (Kadesh in
Naphtali, Shechem, Hebron, etc.), all easily accessible,² were appointed as places of refuge from the
avenger of blood.

A study of the texts—of different periods—relating
to the right of asylum,³ but unfortunately not explicit on certain points, suggests that no murderer
who acted with premeditation (or struck with a
blunt instrument, or even with the hand out of en-
mity) could escape punishment; if necessary he was
dragged from the altar, seized in the city of refuge
and executed by the *go'el*. Only the unintentional
killer was under the protection of the law; in case of
doubt on his behalf, or perhaps even normally, the
refugee was handed over to the elders of the town,
who passed judgment: if adjudged guilty of murder,
he was delivered to the "avenger of blood"; if he
really had killed unintentionally through an accident,
he settled in the city of refuge, which he could not
leave without the danger of falling into the hands of
the *go'el*. No ransom even could set him free. After
the Exile, however, at the death of the High Priest, a
general amnesty was proclaimed for the benefit of
unintentional killers, who could then return home
without fear.

¹ 1 Kgs. 1. 50; 2. 28. ² Dt. 19. 3. ³ Ex. 21. 13 f.; Dt. 4.
41–43; 19. 1–13; Num. 35. 9–34; Jos. 20. 4–9.

ATONEMENT (Day of)

The feast of the Day of Atonement, celebrated on
the 10th day of the 7th month (Tishri), is distinct
from all other Israelite festivals by its serious character, its ritual, and its significance. In time it became if not the one with the greatest attendances, at
least the holiest of the year, until in the end it became
known as "The Day".

1. *Age.* From its earliest days, Israel probably
observed certain expiatory ceremonies; value was
put on them especially after the disasters that led to
the Exile: Zechariah ¹ mentions fasts observed in
the 5th and 7th months, and Ezekiel ² lays down a
brief ritual for the purification of the sanctuary on
the 1st day of the 1st and 7th months. But the Day

of Atonement of the 10th Tishri is mentioned nowhere in pre-Exilic writings; in the form given in
Leviticus,³ this feast does not seem to have been
celebrated even in the time of Ezra, at least not on
the day which has become classical. Indeed, at the
time of the solemn publishing of the Priestly Law by
Ezra, in Jerusalem (444 B.C. at the earliest), there was
no mention of any ceremony whatever on the 10th
Tishri, whereas an important place was given to the
New Year Festival and to the Feast of Tabernacles,
on the 1st and 15th Tishri; ⁴ a fast was even observed
on the 24th of that month, without any reference to
the fast on the Day of Atonement or to its impressive ritual.⁵ Hence it is reasonable to assume that,
at a later date, there became concentrated on the
10th Tishri—the date of the New Year during the
Exile ⁶—a certain number of atonement ceremonies
which had already been in existence in Israel for some
time; and that most of the rites of these ceremonies
were retained, for some of them bear the stamp of
great age.

2. *Ritual.* The ordinances concerning the Day of
Atonement ⁷ are sometimes difficult to interpret because of their composite character, but they demand,
as for any other feast, the complete suspension of
work, under pain of death; but the texts add: "You
shall mortify your souls" (yourselves), in other
words, you shall fast; it is indeed the only general
fast ordained by the Law, and so Josephus, Philo,
and the Acts of the Apostles ⁸ call that day "the day
of the Fast" or simply "the Fast".

Clad in a special robe of white linen, of extreme
simplicity, the High Priest was the principal actor in
the ceremonies which took place in the sanctuary
and for which he prepared himself with a bath of
purification. His first action was to kill, in his own
name, a young bull as an expiatory sacrifice; for the
only time in the year, he went into the Holy of Holies,
which he had already filled with sweet-scented smoke,
for he could not look upon the face of Yahweh, and
he then solemnly sprinkled the blood of the sacrificed
animal. When this rite was completed he left the
sanctuary, killed an expiatory goat in the name of
the people, and once more went into the Holy of
Holies to repeat the sprinkling with the second victim's blood. Then, after mixing the blood of the bull
and the goat, he sprinkled the Holy Place, from
which all the priests had withdrawn, and the altar
"which was before Yahweh" (that is the altar of
sacrifice, not the altar of incense).

The second part of the ceremony opened with an
action of unusual character and strange purpose.
The High Priest placed both hands on the head of a
live goat which had been selected by lot for Azazel*,
"confessed over him all the iniquities of the people
of Israel and all their transgressions, all their sins",
and delivered the animal, thus loaded with the sins
of the people, to a man who was to drive it into a

desolate place. According to a later custom, the animal was led to the desert of Judah, which begins almost at the gates of Jerusalem, and was hurled backwards, from the top of the rocks; signals were sent, and the High Priest, thus informed that the goat had arrived at its destination, was able to continue with the ceremony. A tractate in the Mishnah, dealing with the feast, gives the following formula (perhaps abridged) of the confession: "O God, thy people, the house of Israel, has committed before thee faults, sins and crimes; O God, grant expiation of the faults, sins and crimes which we have committed before thee, according as it is written in the Law of Moses, thy servant."

Finally, the High Priest removed his special robe, bathed, and put on his usual garment again. In his own name and in the name of the community, he sacrificed two rams as burnt offerings. The fat of the bull and the goat killed at the beginning of the ceremony were then burnt on the altar, and the remainder of these two victims burnt outside the sanctuary. It must be noticed that the one who performed this last burning, and also the one who had accompanied the goat for Azazel, were to wash and purify their garments before making fresh contact with the people.

Thus ended the ritual, which lacked neither originality nor grandeur; it took place like a High Mass before the assembly of the Israelites, silent and humbled, who emphasized certain acts by prostrating themselves.

3. *Significance.* The significance of this feast is clear. A double rite of purification is involved—of the Temple and of the people. Defiled by all the ritual faults which had been committed, as well as by sins, involuntary or otherwise, which normal sacrifices had not expiated,[9] the sanctuary was, as it were, reconsecrated at the threshold of the new year; the text says this formally when speaking of the altar: the High Priest shall "cleanse it, and hallow it from the uncleanness of the people of Israel".[10] Moreover, the goat for Azazel bore away all the iniquity of the children of Israel.[11] This procedure, picturesque and popular in its appeal, is an exception among all the bloody rites of Judaism; it is a very curious, and probably very ancient, rite of transmission and elimination, a kind of magic act which has a number of parallels elsewhere; in some respects it recalls the rite in Israel itself of the purification of lepers, in which the priest sacrifices one of two birds given to him, and releases the other alive into the fields, whither it seems to carry away the disease.[12]

In brief, the Day of Atonement was the greatest act of expiation; by making all things clean, it put away all that could separate the people from their God and assured the well-being of the community.

Naturally, formalism took possession of this feast,

but the majority of the Israelites observed it in all sincerity, for it answered to a deep need of pardon and purification; in a striking way, it was a reminder of both the holiness of Yahweh and the defiled state of his children: even the priests publicly admitted their unworthiness, and in this proclamation of unworthiness Israel felt itself to be a people of brothers, a community set apart. It is true that there was a risk of implanting an idea contrary to the one which had inspired the prophets, namely that sin could be atoned for by exterior means, and that it could be shed like a burden; but the Jews were conscious of this danger: "Death and the Day of Atonement [says the Mishnah] effect atonement only on condition that repentance is joined to them. If anyone says, 'I mean to sin, then repent', he will not have the opportunity of being completely penitent. Or if he says: 'I will sin and the Day of Atonement will put all in order again', the Day of Atonement will effect no atonement for him. The Day of Atonement atones for a man's transgressions before God, but it does not atone for transgressions between a man and his neighbour, so long as he is not reconciled to his neighbour."

[1] Zech. 7. 5. [2] Ez. 45. 18–20. [3] Lev. 16. [4] Neh. 8. [5] Neh. 9. [6] Lev. 25. 9; Ez. 40. 1. [7] Lev. 16; 23. 26–32; Num. 29. 7–11. [8] Acts 27. 9. [9] Ez. 45. 20. [10] Lev. 16. 19. [11] Lev. 16. 22. [12] Lev. 14. 4 ff.

AWL

This tool is only mentioned in connection with the ceremony of piercing the ear of a slave who renounces his right to be set free [1] († slave). Awls of bone, bronze, and iron have been found in Palestinian excavations, used chiefly, no doubt, for piercing leather.

[1] Ex. 21. 6; Dt. 15. 17.

AXE

Hebrew has a whole series of words for the different sorts of axes used by the Israelites, but it is difficult to find equivalents in our language: axe, felling-axe, hatchet, pole-axe, adze, etc. Those most frequently mentioned are the wood-cutter's axe or felling-axe; [1] the carpenter's [2] and the idol-maker's [3] axes are mentioned once each; and, perhaps, Ps. 35 and Ps. 74 allude to the battle-axe.[4]

It must be noted that the word normally used for the wood-cutter's felling-axe is found in the Siloam tunnel inscription to denote the miner's pick. Also that David probably did not have the Ammonite captives put under iron axes, nor have them burnt in brick-kilns († brick), as is often suggested by the translation of a curious passage in the Second Book of Samuel;[5] it is much more probable that they were put to forced labour in the making of axes, saws, harrows, and bricks, or even in the mines or quarries.

Different types of axes, especially in bronze—for iron is far less resistant to the ravages of time—have been found in excavations in Palestine, as also have moulds which were used in their manufacture, and small votive axes found in the temples. Primitive ones were of stone (a, b). In Syria semi-circular metal axes, which were fastened to a haft (c), have

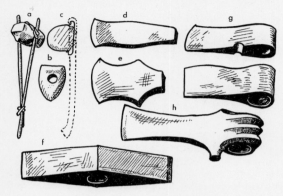

Evolution of the axe in Bible times.

been unearthed, but none have been found in Canaan, where the earliest bronze axes were made of straight pieces which also had to be fastened to a haft (d); as they were not sufficiently firm, points were fashioned between the cutting edge and the heel (e). Finally, a hole was made, centrally placed at first (f), then at the back of the axe head, which was sometimes fitted with a notch (g) and sometimes with a lug (h), both of which allowed firmer fixing.

¹ Dt. 19. 5; 20. 19; Jg. 9. 48; 1 Sam. 13. 20; Ps. 74. 5; Is. 10. 15; Jer. 46. 22; Matt. 3. 10; Lk. 3. 9. ² 1 Kgs. 6. 7. ³ Jer. 10. 3. ⁴ Ps. 35. 3; 74. 6. ⁵ 2 Sam. 12. 31; cf. 1 Chr. 20. 3.

AZAZEL

In the Bible this word, which is of uncertain derivation, is mentioned only in the ritual of the Day of Atonement*. One of the most interesting ceremonies of this religious feast provided for a goat loaded with the sins of Israel ¹ to be sent into the desert. This animal was called the "goat for Azazel". Why? The preposition "for" does not allow us to argue that the word Azazel was applicable to the goat itself and could mean the goat "sent out", or as the Vulgate and certain other versions have it, "the emissary goat". Other exegetes take Azazel as an abstract word and translate "the goat of separation", the goat intended to remove sins, to set them aside. It has also been thought that Azazel might signify the desert country, the wild mountain into which the animal was driven. It seems more reasonable to see

in Azazel the name of a demonic creature (cf. Beelzebul) into whose kingdom the goat is despatched, since the desert is the usual dwelling-place of demons,² and particularly of those pictured as of goat-like form. The goat, loaded with the people's transgressions, was sent to the place where all was uncleanness and sin; the first intention was perhaps to drive out the demon himself, who was incarnate in the goat.—Later Jewish literature places Azazel at the head of the fallen angels (Book of Enoch) or identifies him with Satan (Apocalypse of Abraham).

¹ Lev. 16. 5–10. ² Matt. 12. 43.

BAG

The O.T. recognizes various pouches or bags of leather, cloth, or skin, sometimes fastened by a cord, for containing small or large sums of money ¹ or the weights ² of portable balances*. Sachets or small bags adorned the dressing-table of elegant Jerusalem ladies,³ and sealed money-bags ⁴ provided Bible writers with some good metaphors.⁵ In the N.T. the purse,⁶ properly so-called, must be distinguished from the money-box, divided into compartments, which was entrusted to Judas.⁷

¹ 2 Kgs. 5. 23; Prov. 1. 14; Is. 46. 6. ² Dt. 25. 13; Prov. 16. 11; Mic. 6. 11. ³ Is. 3. 22. ⁴ Gen. 42. 35; Prov. 7. 20. ⁵ 1 Sam. 25. 29; Job 14. 17; Hos. 13. 12; Hagg. 1. 6. ⁶ Lk. 10. 4; 12. 33; 22. 35. ⁷ Jn. 12. 6; 13. 29.

BAKER

Generally in Israel each family made the bread* it needed. This work as a rule fell to the women,¹ and in important households, as in kings' courts,² to maidservants and menservants. Later, in the cities, bread-making became a trade;³ there was a street of bakers in Jerusalem.⁴

¹ Gen. 18. 6; Lev. 26. 26; Matt. 13. 33. ² Gen. 40. 1 . . .: 1 Sam. 8. 13. ³ Hos. 7. 4, 6. ⁴ Jer. 37. 21.

BALANCE

This was used to weigh costly goods, and especially the silver* or metal used in payment. For everyday goods, the measures of capacity were usually adequate. Like some of ours, the balance comprised a beam from which two pans were suspended, just as have been recovered from Megiddo (Palestine) and Carchemish (Assyria). Excavations have provided a great number of weights*. They were originally made of stone. No doubt the steelyard (balance with a single hook) was also known.

The O.T. frequently and significantly insists on the

BALL

need of using "just", i.e. true, balances and weights.[1] The balance is frequently mentioned with a figurative

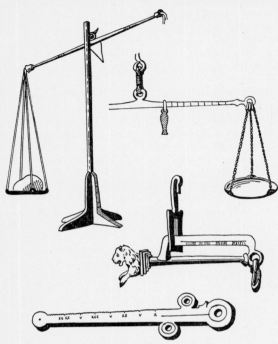

Egyptian, Greek, and Roman balances.

sense in the O.T.,[2] and it is also for the Israelites a symbol of justice.

[1] Lev. 19. 36; Dt. 25. 13–16; Prov. 11. 1; 16. 11; Ez. 45. 10; Hos. 12. 7; Amos 8. 5; Mic. 6. 11. [2] Job 6. 2; 31. 6; Ps. 58. 2; 62. 9; Is. 40. 12, 15; Ez. 5. 1; Dan. 5. 27; etc. Cf. Rev. 6. 5.

BALL

It is referred to as a figure of speech in Is. 22. 18. Ancient peoples played various ball games, which the Israelites would doubtless also know.

BALMS

These are substances of a generally agreeable odour which exude in liquid form from certain plants, then thicken and harden in the air. The Bible mentions myrrh*, bdellium*, and four other substances which cannot be definitely identified: (1) the *naṭaf*,[1] which our versions translate by "stacte", is probably the styrax* obtained by incision in that tree; (2) the *neko't*,[2] translated "spicery" (R.V.), "gum" (R.S.V.), must be gum tragacanth, which comes spontaneously from the stems of certain Astragalus (milk-vetches); (3) the *tsori*,[3] translated "balm", may be the mastic which comes from the mastic tree and which Eastern people often chew; it was said to be

healing and soothing; the Israelites exported it to Tyre,[4] and Jeremiah speaks of it figuratively;[5] (4) the *loṭ*,[6] translated "resin", "myrrh", or "ladanum"

Astragalus and Cistus.

can only be the juice obtained from the leaves and young shoots of the Cistus; it was held in repute for its curative virtues.

[1] Ex. 30. 34. [2] Gen. 37. 25 (1); 43. 11 (3). [3] Gen. 37. 25 (2); 43. 11 (1). [4] Ez. 27. 17. [5] Jer. 8. 22; 46. 11; 51. 8. [6] Gen. 37. 25 (3); 43. 11 (4).

BANANA

This fruit tree flourishes today in the Jordan Valley and on the Mediterranean coast (Jaffa, Acre), but it is not mentioned in the Bible.

BANISHMENT

There is no reference to this punishment before the Exile. The banishment which threatened [1] anyone who did not observe the Law of God and of the king no doubt meant exclusion from the community.[2]

[1] Ezr. 7. 26. [2] Cf. Ezr. 10. 8.

BANKER

In early times the Israelites did not engage in commerce*; so it is not surprising that there were no bankers among them. It was only after the Exile that a small number of them made their living by trade; some of them settled in Damascus, then especially in Egypt, where papyri attesting the existence of Jewish bankers and brokers have been found. This explains why only the N.T. speaks of banks and brokers. However, moneylending was known to the Israelites of Palestine, where Assyrians and Phoenicians had worked in the money-market.—"Why then did you not put my money into a bank?" retorts the master in the Parable of the Pounds [1] to his wicked servant. The same argument is used in the Parable of the

44

Talents: "You ought to have invested my money with the bankers, and at my coming I should have received what was my own with interest."[2] In Greek the word translated "banker" is also used for money-changers*; the latter turned to account the money entrusted to them.—Seventy authors of ancient ecclesiastical literature attest that Jesus pronounced the extra-canonical maxim: "Be good bankers."

[1] Lk. 19. 23. [2] Matt. 25. 27.

BAPTISM

Metaphorical reference to cleansing water is frequent among the prophets;[1] throughout their history the Israelites undoubtedly performed religious ablutions [2] (cf. Mk. 7. 4; Lk. 11. 38; Heb. 9. 10; etc., in which the Greek words for *baptism* and *to be baptized* = "washing" and "to wash"). At approximately the beginning of the Christian era those who changed from paganism to the Jewish religion, adults or children, had to undergo a ceremony which, among other things, included a bath of purification (*tebilah*), a kind of baptism. The Essene sect practised an analogous custom, and it is well known what importance John the Baptist gave to baptism which he performed in the waters of the Jordan,[3] and which Jesus requested for himself.[4]

But the Synoptic gospels (Matthew, Mark, Luke) never show us Jesus or his disciples baptizing those who had been won over by their preaching; only the Gospel according to St John states [5] that Jesus, at the very beginning of his work, baptized people when he had gone with his disciples into Judaea; yet the text makes it clear [6] that it was not the master who officiated, but the disciples. At all events, Jesus, striving always to put the accent on inner purity,[7] seems subsequently to have lost interest in baptism: even in his instructions to the twelve apostles and the seventy disciples, he says nothing about it; the only baptism to which he refers, in a figurative sense, is his approaching death.[8] Hence it is striking to discover that, according to Matt. 28. 19, Jesus gave instructions after his resurrection to baptize in the name of the Father, of the Son, and of the Holy Spirit; it has been suggested that this passage might be a later interpolation or a modification of the original text; in any case, the Acts of the Apostles shows that baptism was given in the early church simply "in the name of Jesus Christ" or "of the Lord Jesus".[9]

From this foundation, and undoubtedly through analogy with what was done for proselytes among the Jews (see above), the early church practised baptism, which became the ceremony, the official act, of entrance into the Christian community. After being baptized himself,[10] St Paul, in his turn, baptized several people: Lydia and her family,[11] the gaoler at Philippi and his whole family,[12] Crispus and Gaius,[13] the family of Stephanas.[14] The baptism of new converts seems a very natural thing to him;[15] yet he expressly states that his mission was not to baptize but to preach the Gospel.[16]

No Biblical description gives exact information of how baptism was originally celebrated. It is very probable that, as in John's baptism, it was performed by immersion;[17] in certain cases, however, and according to circumstances (scarcity of deep water), it is quite possible it was reduced to a simple sprinkling (the word for baptism in N.T. language does not of itself, as we have seen, imply immersion). Whether adults only, or children too, were baptized, it is difficult to say: the texts adduced to support child baptism are not convincing; those advanced to discount it are even less so. Mention should be made of the strange custom by which in Corinth, probably under the influence of the Greek mysteries, certain people had themselves baptized for the dead,[18] probably on behalf of relatives or friends who had been in contact with the Christian community but who had died before being baptized.

Questions concerning the significance of baptism, its meaning to St Paul, or baptism by the Holy Spirit, are the concern of Biblical theology of the N.T. or of dogmatics.

[1] Is. 1. 16, 18; 44. 3; Jer. 2. 22; 4. 14; Ez. 16. 9; 36. 25; 37. 23; Joel 3. 18; Mic. 7. 19; Zech. 13. 1; 14. 8; cf. Ps. 51. 4, 7. [2] Lev. 14. 8; Num. 31. 21–24; 2 Kgs. 5. 10 . . . [3] Matt. 3. 6; Mk. 1. 5. [4] Matt. 3. 13–17; Mk. 1. 9–11; Lk. 3. 21–22. [5] Jn. 3. 22. [6] Jn. 4. 2. [7] Mk. 7. 1–23. [8] Mk. 10. 38; Lk. 12. 50. [9] Acts 2. 38; 8. 16; 10. 48; 19. 5; cf. 1 Cor. 1. 13; etc. [10] Acts 9. 18; 22. 16. [11] Acts 16. 15. [12] Acts 16. 33. [13] 1 Cor. 1. 14. [14] 1 Cor. 1. 16. [15] 1 Cor. 1. 13–17; Eph. 4. 5. [16] 1 Cor. 1. 17. [17] Acts 8. 36–39; cf. Rom. 6. 3. [18] 1 Cor. 15. 29.

BARBER

Ez. 5. 1 alludes to the barber's razor*; it is the only occasion when so much as the name barber appears in the Bible. No doubt Joseph shaved himself before appearing before Pharaoh; the Philistine who shaved Samson's head when he was asleep is simply called a man in the Hebrew text, whilst the LXX and the Vulgate use the name of his profession.[1]

[1] Gen. 41. 14; Jg. 16. 19.

BARLEY

The cultivation of this cereal, very widespread throughout the world, dates, in the eastern Mediterranean, from the very earliest times (Stone Age). The Book of Exodus alludes to fields of barley in Egypt,[1] and it is certain that the plant was known in Palestine long before the Israelites arrived.[2] It is frequently mentioned in the O.T.: Ruth's first gleanings were of barley near Bethlehem;[3] Absalom set fire to a field of barley belonging to Joab,[4] and barley formed part of the supplies which Solomon's district officers sent to the court, as well as part of the payment which Solomon promised to the king of Tyre;[5] etc.[6]

Today, also, barley is sown in many places in Palestine and gives rise to the same type of work as corn*; it is harvested about a month earlier than wheat, at different dates according to altitude, but on the average during April; at the time of the Passover a sheaf was offered in the sanctuary as the firstfruits of the harvest,[7] and it was a golden sheaf, as Josephus and Philo attest. As oats were not grown in Palestine, barley was widely used for feeding horses,[8] mules, etc.; the rabbis even called it "animal food". But bread was also made from barley,[9] coarser than wheat bread, and sold two or three times more cheaply,[10] which was a great boon to poor people [11] or in times of distress. When speaking of the miracle of the loaves, the Fourth Gospel records that they were made of barley;[12] it was barley bread, too, that figured in the narrative in the Book of Kings.[13] Barley's inferiority to wheat explains certain texts in the O.T.[14] and also, perhaps, the presentation of barley-flour as the "jealousy offering" († jealousy).[15]

[1] Ex. 9. 31. [2] Dt. 8. 8. [3] Ruth 1. 22; 2. 17, 23; 3. 2, 15. [4] 2 Sam. 14. 30. [5] 1 Kgs. 4. 28; 2 Chr. 2. 10, 15. [6] 2 Sam. 17. 28; Job 31. 40; Is. 28. 25; Jer. 41. 8; Joel 1. 11. [7] Lev. 23. 10. [8] 1 Kgs. 4. 28. [9] Jg. 7. 13. [10] 2 Kgs. 7. 1, 16, 18; Rev. 6. 6. [11] Ruth 3. 15. [12] Jn. 6. 9, 13. [13] 2 Kgs. 4. 42. [14] Ez. 4. 9; 13. 19; Hos. 3. 2. [15] Num. 5. 15.

BASILISK

A Hebrew word, which is found five times [1] in the O.T., is sometimes translated "basilisk". It is rather the daboia or yellow viper, large in size and particularly dangerous.

[1] Prov. 23. 32; Is. 11. 8; 14. 29; 59. 5; Jer. 8. 17.

BASIN

Several terms used by the O.T. for receptacles of various kinds can be rendered by "basin"; the word is particularly suitable for cultic utensils, doubtless intended for sprinklings.[1] Since they were fashioned in burnished bronze, silver, or gold, they could not have been very large. A basin used for washing the feet is mentioned in Ps. 60. 8 (108. 9), in a derogatory sense, and also in Jn. 13. 5.

[1] Num. 7. 13 . . .; 1 Kgs. 7. 43. 50; 2 Kgs. 12. 13; 2 Chr. 4. 8.

BASKET

The Israelites used different baskets, but it is difficult to form any idea of their size or capacity. Among the most common, we meet in the O.T. the sal [1] which was carried on the head or the shoulder, and in which bread and cakes were presented in the

sanctuary;[2] the dûd, used for transporting fruit [3] and merchandise—the chiefs in Samaria used some of these to send to Jehu the heads of the seventy sons of Ahab whom they had killed,[4] and the Psalmist used this word for the wicker baskets which were carried by the Hebrew labour squads in Egypt;[5] the tene', a provisions basket,[6] probably of considerable size, and the kelûb, an enclosed basket undoubtedly in the form of a cage.[7] (For the tebah, in which the baby Moses was placed, sometimes translated as "basket", see † Ark.)

Two kinds of basket are mentioned in the N.T. Curiously enough, one type was used in the first miracle of the loaves,[8] the other in the second [9] (cf. in particular vv. 9, 10 of Matt. 16 or vv. 19, 20 of Mk. 8). We know that St Paul was lowered from the walls of Damascus in a basket: it bears in the Acts [10] the same name as those mentioned in the second miracle of the loaves, whereas the apostle himself calls it by yet another name in his Second Letter to the Corinthians.[11]

[1] Gen. 40. 16. [2] Ex. 29. 3 . . .; Lev. 8. 2 . . .; Num. 6. 15 . . .; Jg. 6. 19. [3] Jer. 24. 1–2. [4] 2 Kgs. 10. 7. [5] Ps. 81. 6. [6] Dt. 26. 2, 4; 28. 5, 17. [7] Amos 8. 1, 2. [8] Matt. 14. 20 par. [9] Matt. 15. 37 par.; 16. 10 par. [10] Acts 9. 25. [11] 2 Cor. 11. 33.

BAT

These small mammals are very numerous in Palestine, where several species are represented. In the southern part of the Jordan Valley the weather remains so hot that this animal, elsewhere reduced to immobility during the wet season, remains active throughout the year. The O.T. numbers the bat among the unclean animals.[1] Only one other text mentions it: a day will come, says Isaiah, when men will take refuge in the caves, among the rocks before the glory of the divine majesty, and will cast forth their idols of silver and their idols of gold "to the moles and to the bats".[2] A curious thing is that Luther translates the Hebrew word that our versions render by "bat" as "swallow" in Deuteronomy and Leviticus, and as "bat" in Isaiah.

[1] Lev. 11. 19; Dt. 14. 18. [2] Is. 2. 20.

BATH

The heat in Palestine made baths necessary and beneficial. They were taken in rivers, in clear spring water, anywhere where there was enough water.[1] Some rich people had installations built in their homes for this purpose;[2] excavations in Palestine have brought to light a bathroom dating from the time of the 12th Dynasty (2000 B.C.). Though a man washed his whole body before meeting a superior,[3] it was customary to wash the feet frequently, for they were always exposed to the dirt of the roads, since only sandals, and no socks or stockings, were worn; so they were washed before a meal,[4] for example, or before going to bed.[5] The first duty of hospitality was to wash the feet of guests,[6] and a basin of the type used for this purpose [7] has been found. The washing of hands before a meal had become a religious rite.[8] Public baths existed in Palestine from the Hellenistic period, and especially in Roman times; fairly numerous traces of them have been left. At about the beginning of the Christian era the hot springs of Tiberias, of Gadara, or Callirhoe (Moab), and near the Dead Sea were famous for their curative powers (cf. Bethesda [9]).—The Israelites were aware of the properties and uses of saltpetre († nitre), potash*, soap*,[10] and of sponges* too.[11]

For ritual ablutions, see † purification, baptism.

[1] Ex. 2. 5; Lev. 15. 13; 2 Kgs. 5. 10. [2] 2 Sam. 11. 2. [3] Ruth 3. 3. [4] Lk. 7. 44; Jn. 13. 5 . . . [5] Cant. 5. 3. [6] Gen. 18. 4; 19. 2; 24. 32; 1 Sam. 25. 41. [7] Ps. 60. 8; Jn. 13. 5. [8] Matt. 15. 2, 20; Mk. 7. 2, 3; Lk. 11. 38. [9] Jn. 5. 2–4. [10] Job 9. 30; Jer. 2. 22; Mal. 3. 2. [11] Matt. 27. 48.

BATH

A measure of capacity for liquids (water, wine, oil) and probably equivalent to 1·29 cu. ft.:[1] 1 bath = 6 *hins**; 10 baths = 1 *cor**. The bath corresponds to the *ephah** (a measure of capacity for dry substances) and, in general magnitude, to the Greek *metretes*.[2]

(† Weights and measures.)

[1] 1 Kgs. 7. 26, 38; 2 Chr. 2. 10; Is. 5. 10; etc. [2] Jn. 2. 6.

BDELLIUM

This fragrant, yellowish gum-resin († balms) comes from an Indian balsam tree. It is doubtless mentioned in Genesis [1] as found with gold and onyx* in the land of Havila (Arabia?), and in the Book of Numbers [2] it is said to resemble manna*.

[1] Gen. 2. 12. [2] Num. 11. 7.

BEAM

A number of Hebrew words are used for different kinds of beams occasionally mentioned in the O.T.[1] and serving various purposes. In the N.T. Christ speaks metaphorically of a beam in the eye,[2] which comparison is found again in the Mishnah.

[1] 1 Kgs. 6. 15. 16, 36; 7. 2, 12; 2 Kgs. 6. 2; 2 Chr. 3. 7; 34. 11; Cant. 1. 17. [2] Mat. 7. 3; Lk. 6. 41.

BEAN

This vegetable, which was widely cultivated in Palestine, figures in the list of foodstuffs offered to David when he took refuge in Mahanaim.[1] The pod and the seed were both eaten. The seeds, mixed with cereals and lentils, were used, in an emergency, for making flour and bread.[2]

[1] 2 Sam. 17. 28. [2] Ez. 4. 9.

BEAR

David's celebrated statement, "The Lord that delivered me out of the paw of the lion, and out of the paw of the bear, will deliver me out of the hand of this Philistine",[1] the story of the bears of Bethel,[2] as well as certain metaphors of the prophets and Biblical poets,[3] show that the bear was well known in Palestine. Its Hebrew name derives from a root signifying "to walk quietly". This animal was only to be feared when attacked, hungry,[4] or deprived of its young: "It is better to meet a she-bear robbed of her cubs than a fool in his folly." [5] "I will meet them [the Israelites] like a bear robbed of her cubs", are the words put into Yahweh's mouth by the prophet.[6]—The bear figures in the visions of Daniel and in Revelation;[7] Isaiah declares that at the coming of the Messianic peace the heifer and the she-bear will be companions, and that their young will lie down together.[8]

Bears have almost disappeared from Palestine; there were a few until recently in the Hermon massif and in Lebanon; the last few have now taken refuge in Anti-Lebanon.

[1] 1 Sam. 17. 34, 36, 37. [2] 2 Kgs. 2. 24. [3] Is. 59. 11; Lam. 3. 10; Amos 5. 19. [4] Prov. 28. 15. [5] Prov. 17. 12. [6] Hos. 13. 8; cf. 2 Sam. 17. 8. [7] Dan. 7. 5; Rev. 13. 2. [8] Is. 11. 7.

BEAR (GREAT)

According to the majority of commentators, the constellation of the Great Bear is mentioned in two passages of the Book of Job magnifying the power of the creator.[1] But opinions are not unanimous; certain translators prefer the Pleiades, Aldebaran, the Hyades, the Lion, etc. Moreover, it has been thought that the Great Bear is meant in another text of Job's poem [2] in which interpreters now gradually admit that another constellation (Boötes, the Hyades, etc.), or the north wind, is meant.

It is therefore impossible to resolve with certainty these difficult problems of identification.

[1] Job 9. 9; 38. 32. [2] Job 37. 9b.

BEARD

While the Egyptians, in contrast with the "barbarians", wore neither beard nor moustache, the Syrians and the people of Palestine allowed them to grow, as is shown, for example, by funeral decorations in ancient Egypt, or by Assyrian bas-reliefs.

The Israelites lavished great care on their beards, which they considered as a sign of vitality and as essential to manly beauty.[1] However, in common with their Asiatic neighbours, they shaved or covered them as a sign of mourning or grief.[2] On the other hand, to cut off a man's beard or half of his beard was to dishonour him;[3] even today curses such as "May God pluck your beard", "May God burn your beard", "May God let me bury your beard", may still be heard among the Bedouin.

Semitic faces of the 15th and 12th centuries.

To grasp a man's beard in one's right hand, in order to embrace either him or his beard, was a gesture of friendship which has continued in Palestine, and the present author was himself the victim of this gesture in the land of Benjamin.

The prophet Jeremiah inveighs against the people who shaved their temples,[4] and Leviticus forbids the shaving of that part of the beard joining the hair below the temples[5] because this custom had connections with idolatrous and pagan ceremonies. Even today, strict Jews do not cut the locks of hair at the temples and let them hang down in ringlets like those fashionable in the 1830s.

[1] Ps. 133. 2; cf. 2 Sam. 19. 24. [2] Is. 15. 2; Jer. 41. 5; 48. 37; Ez. 24. 17; Mic. 1. 16; 3. 7; etc. [3] 2 Sam. 10. 4; Is. 50. 6. [4] Jer. 9. 26; 25. 23; 49. 32. [5] Lev. 19. 27; 21. 5.

BEARDED VULTURE

Some translators believe that this bird of prey is the second of the birds declared unclean in Dt. 14. 12 and Lev. 11. 13. However, it is not common in Palestine.

(† Osprey.)

BEATING

The Deuteronomic Code alone mentions this punishment, which was probably prescribed for a man who made a false accusation against his wife,[1] but in any case for a quarreller.[2] The number of stripes was proportionate to the fault, but to give a man more than forty stripes was to treat him like a beast; and Israelite law requires human dignity to be respected even in a guilty man. There was nothing rigorous about the figure thus given; it was an

approximation similar to the one that makes an Arab say that he is forty years old as long as he feels in the prime of life. Later, at the time of Pharisaic casuistry, this figure was accepted absolutely and in order not to transgress the law, the Jews ordered forty stripes less one;[3] perhaps the victim received thirteen strokes with a three-lash whip ($3 \times 13 = 39$), and no longer with a rod. The Code of Hammurabi allowed sixty stripes to be given to a man who struck a superior; the Koran orders, in certain cases, eighty or even a hundred stripes.

[1] Dt. 22. 18. [2] Dt. 25. 1–3. [3] 2 Cor. 11. 24.

BED

In the Palestinian house, mats and blankets arranged at ground level along the wall served the native as a bed by night, and a seat by day.[1] But among the Israelites in ancient times, wealthy people used beds standing on legs, and such beds became commoner in Roman times; Jesus himself speaks of the lamp which could be placed under the bushel or under the bed.[2] A whole series of terms, the sense of which it is difficult to grasp precisely, is used in Hebrew to signify this article of furniture; the wealth of vocabulary is rather surprising. It may be possible to distinguish between beds meant for sleep, those used for rest during the day, and those on which people reclined at meal-times, even though

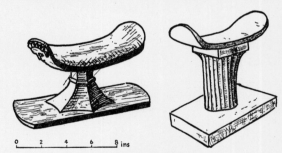

Head-rests of wood and alabaster.

each type was often undoubtedly used for the other purposes.

Beds used for the night's rest might be very fine and high: a low stool was necessary for getting on and off them; among the Egyptians they were sometimes made in the form of a lion (b) or an elongated animal whose paws served as bed legs, and they were decorated with sculpture and inlays. It is thus that we may picture the bed of King Ahaziah: "Thou shalt no more descend from the bed on which thou has gone up, for thou shalt surely die," says Elijah to him, on Yahweh's behalf, during his illness.[3] A bed head-board, often in the form of a crescent, supported the sleeper's head[4] and was wrapped in rich coverings: the adulteress of the Book of Proverbs

48

boasts of having furnished her bed with cushions, spread it with Egyptian materials, and sprinkled it with myrrh, aloes, and cinnamon.[5] In a tomb, a little terra-cotta bed only a foot long has been found; it probably represents one of the type used in the Hellenistic period (c).

But beds could also be much more simple,[6] for example, the one of Egyptian origin found at a site in southern Palestine and dating from the 9th century

Types of beds.

B.C. (a), and those which figure on certain bas-reliefs representing Assyrian tents. They were, moreover, easily transportable articles, as is proved by the picturesque story of David's teraphim,[7] and the account of that monarch's stay at Mahanaim.[8] On several occasions the O.T. speaks of the marriage-bed;[9] of the sick-bed,[10] of the beds on which Jacob, David, and Asa die;[11] beds on which some find sleep with more or less pleasant dreams,[12] but on which

others meditate for long periods and often shed tears.[13] And the Book of Proverbs evokes, not without irony, the idler who turns back and forth on his bed, like a door on its hinges.[14]

Every well-furnished house offered the comfort of divans on which one could rest or sit in the Eastern manner.[15] The great ones of the ancient world also took their meals while reclining on beds, which were often magnificent and highly raised, and in front of which a table was laid: an Assyrian bas-relief depicts King Assurbanipal taking a meal in this way, while the Queen is seated at his feet, on a high arm-chair (d). And the chiefs of Israel behave in no better way, inveighs the prophet.[16] In Roman times couches arranged in a horse-shoe round a common table were used; the guests, half-lying, leaned on the left arm, which left the right one free to pick up the food. This arrangement was well known in Palestine and explains certain details of the account of the woman who was a sinner anointing the feet of Jesus [17] with perfume, or of the last meal that he took with his friends.[18]

[1] Ex. 22. 26; Jg. 4. 18; Is. 28. 20. [2] Mk. 4. 21; Lk. 8. 16. [3] 2 Kgs. 1. 4 (cf. Ps. 132. 3). [4] Gen. 47. 31. [5] Prov. 7. 16–17. [6] 2 Kgs. 4. 10. [7] 1 Sam. 19.15. [8] 2 Sam. 17. 28. [9] Gen. 49. 4; 1 Chr. 5. 1; Cant. 1. 16 (Heb. 13. 4). [10] Ex. 21. 18; 2 Sam. 13. 5; Job 33. 19 (Mk. 7. 30; Acts 9. 33–34). [11] Gen. 49. 33; 1 Kgs. 1. 47; 2 Chr. 16. 14. [12] Job 7. 13, 14; 33. 15; Dan. 2. 28, 29; 4. 5; 7. 1. [13] I Kgs. 21. 4; Ps. 4. 4; 6. 6; 36. 4; 63. 6; Mic. 2. 1. [14] Prov. 26. 14. [15] Amos 3. 12; cf. 1 Sam. 28. 23; 2 Kgs. 11. 2. [16] Amos 6. 4 . . . cf. Est. 1. 6; 7. 8; Ez. 23. 41. [17] Lk. 7. 37 . . . (cf. Jn. 12. 3). [18] Jn. 13. 23 . . .

BEE

Bees are mentioned four times only in the Bible,[1] which, however, makes frequent references to their honey*. The bees of Palestine resemble those of Europe, but they are smaller and more prolific. They live in the wild state all over the country. Since apiculture was known in Asia Minor long before the 14th century B.C., it is natural to think that it was practised from early times in Israel, although we have no direct proof that this is so.

Today bee-keeping is carried on especially in Galilee; for hives the bee-keepers use jars or cylinders of terra-cotta or dried mud, fitted up in primitive fashion and stacked in pyramids; these are covered with earth, a mat or with foliage.

The name Deborah (= bee) was sometimes given to Israelite women.[2]

[1] Dt. 1. 44; Jg. 14. 8; Ps. 118. 12; Is. 7. 18. [2] Gen. 35. 8; Jg. 4 and 5.

BEHEAD

This form of capital punishment is not envisaged in Israelite laws. The decapitations mentioned in the N.T. are penalties inflicted by Herod Antipas [1] (on John the Baptist), by Herod Agrippa I [2] (on the apostle James), and by foreign powers (on the Christian martyrs).[3]—The chief of Pharaoh's bakers did not have his head cut off, as some versions say; Gen. 40. 19 must be translated, "In three days Pharaoh will lift up thy head (above the earth), and shall hang thee upon a tree" (gibbet or impalement).

[1] Matt. 14. 10; Mk. 6. 27. [2] Acts 12. 2. [3] Rev. 20. 4.

BEHEMOTH

Behemoth is the plural of intensity of *behemah* = "beast", unless it is a transcription of the Egyptian *p-ehe-mou* = "water-buffalo". The animal described by the Book of Job [1] as giving a proof of the power of God must have been an enormous creature, and probably it was the hippopotamus. This large amphibian was worshipped by the Egyptians from the most remote antiquity, and it was associated by the Hyksos invaders of Egypt with the cult of Seth; so from the expulsion of these invaders this god, and the animal representing him, were the most hated and the most feared in all the pantheon of Egypt. Amulets* representing a hippopotamus have been found in Palestine. A number of figures of this animal have even been found at Beth-shean, between Mount Gilboa and the Jordan, in temples of the 18th Dynasty.

[1] Job 40. 15–24.

BELL

The High Priest's* surplice had its lower edge decorated with pomegranates alternating with gold bells, the shape and size of which are not given.[1] What was the purpose of this ornament? The text says: The sound of the bells "shall be heard when he [Aaron, that is the High Priest] goes into the holy place before the Lord, and when he comes out, lest he die".[2] These last words are enigmatic; it has been suggested that the bells were to give God a signal of the presence of the officiating priest so that he should not be destroyed, as an intruder, by the divine holiness, or that originally, at least, the bells were meant to drive away the demons who, according to popular belief, prowled near the sanctuary threshold. († Amulet.) Zechariah [3] declares that in God's new kingdom, the words "holy to the Lord" will be engraved even on the bells of the horses. This may not necessarily mean little bells or harness bells, but ornaments, flat metal plates, which could be more easily inscribed, and which clashed together when the horses walked.

[1] Ex. 28. 33 f.; 39. 25 f. [2] Ex. 28. 35. [3] Zech. 14. 20.

BELLOWS

The Egyptians notably, but also the ancient East in general, knew the use of bellows of various forms for stimulating fire, and in particular those for hearths where metals were worked or melted. Isaiah and Jeremiah allude to this equipment.[1]

[1] Is. 54. 16; Jer. 6. 29.

BENJAMIN (GATE)

It seems likely—although this is not the judgment of all commentators—that two gates in Jerusalem bore this name: (1) A gate to the north of the Temple, mentioned in Jer. 20. 2 and called "upper" in relation to the other one, and near which the prophet was imprisoned; Jotham had built it;[1] Ezekiel may also speak of it when he uses the word "upper",[2] and Nehemiah [3] may be referring to it under the name of the Prison Gate (so A.V.).—(2) A gate in the northern wall of the city, mentioned in Jer. 37. 13 and 38. 7; it was through this that the prophet intended going to make for Anathoth, north of Jerusalem. Nehemiah does not mention it, though it has been uncertainly identified with the Old [4] Gate, the Ephraim [5] Gate, or with the Sheep [6] Gate.

The name Benjamin given to these two gates is explained because both lay to the north, in the direction of the land of Benjamin.

[1] 2 Kgs. 15. 35. [2] Ez. 9. 2. [3] Neh. 12. 39. [4] Neh. 3. 6. [5] 2 Kgs. 14. 13; Neh. 12. 39. [6] Neh. 3. 32; 12. 39.

BERYL

Beryl is a precious stone, a variety of emerald, blue, rose, yellow, or colourless, much loved by ancient peoples. It is remarkable for the large size its crystals can reach. For the seer of Revelation beryl was the eighth foundation of the wall of the New Jerusalem.[1]

[1] Rev. 21. 20.

BIRD

The majority of birds mentioned in the Bible appear in the lists of clean or unclean animals;[1] it is particularly difficult to identify the birds of prey; the renderings are very uncertain indeed, as will be seen when the articles on each are read. The general list of birds is to be found in the Systematic Classification of principal articles (p. xi) under the heading Animals.

At all times bird life in Palestine must have been very plentiful; today about 350 species are to be found, among which the birds of prey are remarkable for their variety and quantity. These facts are explained by the geographical situation and formation of Palestine; the country "lies on the bird migration routes between Europe and Africa; it offers a pleasant resting place in winter for birds from the north, in summer for birds from the south. Birds of tropical type live in the hot climate of the Ghôr (Jordan Valley) where certain mountain species go to winter. Each region has its particular residents; one species is so adapted to the desert that it could not live in the mountains; similarly for the maritime plain, the rocky valleys and the orchards—another cause of variety not only within one order, but even within one genus". (G. M. Abel.)

The Biblical texts often allude to the habits of birds, to their flight,[2] to their shelters,[3] their food,[4] their song,[5] and especially their rapacity,[6] which Yahweh often uses to carry out his judgments against the unfaithful members of his people or the enemies of Israel.[7]

While the First Book of Kings states that Solomon spoke with wisdom about animals and birds,[8] the Gospel made famous the words of Jesus on the birds which "sow not, nor reap, nor gather into barns", and which have nests while the "son of man has nowhere to lay his head".[9]

Among the birds only pigeons or turtle doves could be offered in sacrifice;[10] they were sacrificed according to special rules.[11] For the purification of lepers, however, two birds of a species not clearly stated were used.[12]

(† Fowler.)

[1] Dt. 14. 3–20; Lev. 11. 2–23. [2] Prov. 26. 2; Eccl. 10. 20; Is. 16. 2; Hos. 9. 11. [3] Ps. 104. 12; Prov. 27. 8; Is. 31. 5; Ez. 17. 23; 31. 6; Dan. 4. 12, 14; Matt. 8. 20; 13. 32 par. [4] Gen. 40. 17; Matt. 13. 4; Mk. 4. 4; Lk. 8. 5. [5] Ps. 104. 12; Eccl. 12. 4; Cant. 2. 12. [6] Gen. 15. 11; 40. 19; 1 Sam. 17. 44; 2 Sam. 21. 10; Ps. 79. 2; etc. [7] Dt. 28. 26; 1 Kgs. 14. 11; 16. 4; 21. 24, etc.; Is. 18. 6; Jer. 7. 33; 15. 3; 16. 4, etc.; Ez. 29. 5; 32. 4, etc.; Rev. 19. 17–21. [8] 1 Kgs. 4. 33. [9] Matt. 6. 26; 8. 20; Lk. 9. 58; 12. 24. [10] Lev. 1. 14; 15. 14, 29; Num. 6. 10. [11] Lev. 1. 14–17; 5. 8. [12] Lev. 14. 4 . . ., 49 . . .

BIRTHRIGHT

At all times in Israel, the father's first-born son, "his strength and the first fruits of his strength",[1] enjoyed certain privileges. Special deference was due to him as future head of the family, but along with his rights went certain duties also.[2] In the sharing of the patrimony, the law makes it clear that the first-born should receive a double portion which is specifically called the birthright.[3] In early times this right could be lost;[4] Esau traded it,[5] and the father could give it to another of his sons, for example to the son of his favourite wife. Indeed, there is in Hebrew a word meaning "to give the birthright to someone". And so the law to some extent took the eldest son under its protection,[6] by stating that he could not be deprived of his right, even if he were the child of the "hated wife".—This custom was not peculiar to Israel.

[1] Gen. 49. 3. [2] Gen. 24. 50; 37. 22; 43. 33. [3] Dt. 21. 17. [4] 1 Chr. 5. 1; Gen. 49. 3, 4. [5] Gen. 25. 29–34; Heb. 12. 16. [6] Dt. 21. 15–17.

BISHOP

The Greek word *episkopos* which we translate as "bishop" really means "overseer"; he who superintends and keeps watch. It is not limited to the language of the N.T.: without mentioning certain gods who were called *episkopoi* because they watched over their protégés, we know that this name was borne by various magistrates or officers to whom were entrusted the duties of inspectors, administrators, or overseers. Moreover, in the LXX translation several overseers and chiefs mentioned in the O.T.[1] are designated as *episkopoi*.

In the N.T., on the other hand, the word "bishop" is found only five times. The First Epistle of Peter [2] gives this title to the Christ himself when it says: "You were straying like sheep but have now returned to the Shepherd and Guardian [*episkopos*] of your souls." In the other passages, men at the head of the Christian communities are meant. St Paul at Miletus asks the elders of Ephesus to watch over the whole flock of which the Holy Spirit has made them overseers (*episkopoi*),[3] and he addresses the most affectionate of his letters to the Christians as well as to the bishops and deacons at Philippi.[4] The Pastoral Epistles too, in significant lists,[5] enumerate the qualities needed in an *episkopos*, whose office is even praised as being "good".[6]

These few texts may pose more problems than they solve. It may be asked especially whether the *episkopoi*, always distinct from the deacons,[7] have not become confused with the elders* (or presbyters*). In his Miletus speech the apostle to the Gentiles qualifies as *episkopoi* all the elders, without distinction, whom he summoned to him; from the fact that he addresses his letter to the Philippians without mentioning the elders with the bishops and deacons, may we not conclude that the word "elder" (presbyter) and "bishop" are synonymous, a point which seems to emerge from the Epistle to Titus? Exercising supervisory responsibilities, in a general way, the elders were quite naturally called *episkopoi*, especially in pagano-Christian communities, for the word "elder" was of Jewish origin.

But if matters were like this in the beginning, it is possible that in time certain elders became responsible for administrative, disciplinary, or representative duties, which may have carried the title of *episkopoi* for such presbyters, who had now become to some extent purely officials. In any case, 1 Ti. 5. 17 draws a distinction between the elders, by requesting double honour for those of them who had performed their presidential duties well. And this path soon led to the appointment of a chief of the presbyters (the fact that reference is made to the *episkopos* in the singular, in the Pastoral Epistles [8]—and to deacons and elders in the plural—is perhaps significant) and finally to monarchical episcopacy, to the concentration of the community's authority in the hands of a single bishop.

[1] Num. 4. 16; 31. 14; 2 Chr. 34. 12; Neh. 11. 9, 14, 22; Is. 60. 17. [2] 1 Pet. 2. 25. [3] Acts 20. 28. [4] Phil. 1. 1. [5] 1 Ti. 3. 2–7; Tit. 1. 7–9. [6] 1 Ti. 3. 1. [7] Phil. 1. 1; 1 Ti. 3. 1–7 and 8–11. [8] 1 Ti. 3. 1 . . . and 8 . . .; Tit. 1. 5, 7.

BIT

In earliest times and certainly up to the middle of the 2nd millennium horses and donkeys were led by means of a ring passed through their upper lip. The less cruel and more efficacious bit spread rapidly in antiquity, and monuments decorated with figures often depict this metallic part of the harness. Bible

The impression of a Cappadocian cylinder showing a chariot drawn by four quadrupeds (on the left). A bit from Iran (on the right).

texts sometimes make mention of bits (in the true sense) of horses and donkeys,[1] and in one vigorous metaphor the prophet Isaiah pictures Yahweh putting "a bit in the jaws of the peoples", or, again, into the lips of Sennacherib, to make him return to his own country.[2]

[1] Ps. 32. 9; Prov. 26. 3; Jas. 3. 3; Rev. 14. 20. [2] 2 Kgs. 19. 28; Is. 30. 28; 37. 29.

BITTERN

It is very probable that the word *qippod* means the bittern, a wader of the Ardeidae family which includes also the heron and the egret. Some versions translate it by porcupine or hedgehog, though the context makes us think rather of a bird living in the midst of marshes.[1]—When the bittern is angry it distends its plumage and ruffles the feathers of its neck; its call, normally only to be heard at night, resembles a lugubrious bellow. Zephaniah perhaps alludes to this († porcupine).

[1] Is. 14. 23; 34. 11; Zeph. 2. 14.

BLASPHEMY

Any blasphemy, that is any attack on the majesty of God, on the respect due to him, on his authority, on his honour, whether by Jew or foreigner, was punished with death by Israelite law. The prescribed method was by stoning, and those who had heard the guilty man had to place their hand on his head at the moment of execution, in confirmation of their witness.[1]

At about the time of Jesus, the arrogation of God's authority and privileges by a man was also considered a blasphemy, and it was of this crime that Jesus was accused by his enemies.[2] Stephen, the first Christian martyr, was condemned for having uttered subversive and blasphemous words against Moses and against God.[3]

To be witness of an outrage against God was considered as a great misfortune, and so Jews solemnly tore their clothes if they heard anything offensive said against the Lord. The very pronouncing of his ineffable sacred name (Yahweh) was a profanation.

[1] Lev. 24. 15–16; 1 Kgs. 21. 10. [2] Matt. 26. 64–65; Mk. 2. 7; Jn. 10. 33. [3] Acts 6. 11, 13; 7. 56–57.

BLESSING

The Israelites liked to use, in various circumstances, various forms of blessing which were meant to ensure the greatest advantages for those to whom they were addressed. In some degree, these words possessed magic power; they produced their effect of themselves, thanks to the mysterious power inherent in them;[1] often the laying-on of hands* was associated with them. But the primitive idea of this "active blessing" ended by giving place to a more religious and moral conception.

Customary greetings exchanged by people who met one another were blessings: "Peace be unto thee", "The Lord be with you",[2] and on parting people uttered analogous words.[3] The blessings lavished on those setting off on journeys,[4] or the newly married,[5] were of course suited to the occasion; the most solemn and most efficacious were those uttered by the dying.[6] Anyone who had received gifts or had gained privileges gave witness of his gratitude by further vows.[7] The blessing of men of God was especially valued;[8] Jesus too blessed his apostles[9] and the children who were brought to him.[10] The priests called down God's favours on the faithful:[11] the well-known formula from the Book of Numbers[12] has passed into the synagogue and Christian acts of public worship, where it is pronounced at the close. But priests and prophets did not have the monopoly of blessings in the name of the Lord: David blessed the people when the Ark* was removed to Jerusalem[13] and Solomon did the same at the dedication of the Temple.[14]

[1] Gen. 27. 33–40; 48. 13–19; Num. 22. 6. [2] Jg. 19. 20; Ruth 2. 4. [3] Gen. 47. 10; Jos. 22. 6–7; 2 Sam. 13. 25; 19. 39. [4] Gen. 43. 14; etc. [5] Gen. 24. 60; Ruth 4. 11. [6] Gen. 27. 4, 10; 48. 9, 14, 20. [7] Gen. 9. 25 . . .; Ruth 2. 20; 1 Sam. 23. 21;

2 Sam. 2. 5; 1 Kgs. 1. 31. [8] Gen. 14. 19; 49; Ex. 17. 11–13; Num. 23 and 24; Dt. 33; 1 Sam. 1. 17; 9. 13. [9] Lk. 24. 50–51. [10] Matt. 19. 13; Mk. 10. 16; Lk. 18. 15. [11] Lev. 9. 22. [12] Num. 6. 22 . . . [13] 2 Sam. 6. 18. [14] 1 Kgs. 8. 54 . . .

BLIGHT

Hebrew uses a term which means "to become greenish or livid", "to yellow", "to fade", for a disease of corn which is regarded as punishment from Yahweh;[1] it is perhaps the blight which, produced by a small grub, replaces the seeds in the ear by small black galls, very much like the seeds of the corn-cockle, a plant itself most harmful to cereals with which it happens to be mixed. Probably wrongly, a disease afflicting man—gangrene—has also been suggested, at least for Dt. 28. 22.

[1] Dt. 28. 22; 1 Kgs. 8. 37; 2 Chr. 6. 28; Amos 4. 9; Hagg. 2. 17.

BLINDNESS

At all times blind people have been very common in the East, and the place they occupy in the N.T. shows clearly that blindness was the lot of many unfortunate folk in Palestine who benefited from the compassion of Jesus. Although it was sometimes an infirmity of old age[1] or congenital,[2] it was more often the outcome of purulent ophthalmia, caused or aggravated by sun, dust, and dirt.

Leviticus[3] requests that nothing be put in the way of a blind man to make him fall, and Deuteronomy[4] curses anyone who makes a blind man lose his way. Blindness was incompatible with the priestly office.[5] —Texts abound in the O.T. and N.T. which speak of the blind in a figurative sense and of spiritual blindness.

[1] Isaac, Gen. 27. 1; Eli, 1 Sam. 3. 2; Ahijah, 1 Kgs. 14. 4. [2] Jn. 9. 1. [3] Lev. 19. 14. [4] Dt. 27. 18. [5] Lev. 21. 18.

BOAR

This animal—which has in Hebrew the same name as the pig*, and was therefore regarded as impure—is only mentioned once in the O.T.: in a significant comparison the Psalmist[1] alludes to the damage committed by the boar on cultivated land. Still today boars are numerous in Palestine, especially in the thickly wooded and marshy country of the Jordan Valley.

[1] Ps. 80. 13.

BOAT

In Abraham's native city of Ur in lower Mesopotamia, a silver boat, which is probably of the type seen on the Euphrates by the patriarch himself, has been unearthed. In Egypt the Israelites were familiar with various methods of sailing, from the plaited

wicker basket daubed with bitumen († Ark), to the royal barges, and including boats made of papyrus such as can be seen in use today on Lake Chad. In the O.T., however, there is no reference to boats

Scale model of a boat from Ur. Silver. 2800 B.C.

sailing on the lakes or rivers of Palestine. There is mention (and even here the text is very dubious) of only one boat, or more precisely a ferry, which was put at David's disposal to cross the Jordan on his

Papyrus boat as still used on Lake Chad.

return from Transjordania after the failure of Absalom's revolt.[1] On the other hand, the Gospels often speak of the fishermen's boats on the Lake of Gennesaret,[2] which were used by Jesus during his journeyings,[3] or to speak to the crowd assembled on the shore.[4]

[1] 2 Sam. 19. 18. [2] Matt. 4. 21–22; Lk. 5. 7; Jn. 6. 23; 21. 3. [3] Matt. 8. 23; 14. 22; 15. 39; Mk. 4. 36; 5. 18; 6. 32; etc. [4] Matt. 13. 2; Mk. 4. 1; Lk. 5. 3.

BOAZ

This is the name of one of the two pillars which stood at the entrance of the vestibule (porch) of Solomon's Temple*, namely, the one on the left side[1] —not, we may suppose, on the left when entering, but on facing towards the east, as the Semite did to orientate himself, i.e., on the left meant to the north. The other, on the right, i.e., the south, was called Jachin. The meaning of these two proper names is

BOIL

totally obscure. It has in turn been suggested that they were the names of the donor, of revered men, of young sons of Solomon, or perhaps a sort of motto: "*Stet in robore*", etc. Jachin might mean: "He [Yahweh] establishes" and Boaz: "In Him [Yahweh] is strength".

¹ 1 Kgs. 7. 21; cf. 2 Chr. 3. 17.

BOIL

Sometimes in Bible texts reference is made to an inflammation, always denoted by the same Hebrew word which is generally translated by "boil", but which seems to offer varying characteristics. For Exodus ¹ the boils or eruptions of the sixth plague "broke forth with pustules"; Yahweh threatens to strike Israel with the boils of Egypt, which from the knees and thighs infect the whole body; ² Leviticus speaks of a boil in connection with leprosy, ³ and it seems that the malignant boils that torment Job ⁴ from the sole of the feet to the head are tubercular leprosy*; finally, we know that Hezekiah ⁵ was cured of a boil by a poultice of figs, a remedy still today employed by the Arabs for relieving inflammation.

In the N.T. the poor man Lazarus of the parable, lying at the rich man's gate, was covered with boils ⁶ which even the dogs came and licked; and "noisome and grievous" boils attack the worshippers of the Beast in the Apocalypse. ⁷

¹ Ex. 9. 9. ² Dt. 28. 27, 35. ³ Lev. 13. 18 . . . ⁴ Job 2. 7. ⁵ 2 Kgs. 20. 7; Is. 38. 21. ⁶ Lk. 16. 20–21. ⁷ Rev. 16. 2.

BONE

Apart from implements of the Stone Age, there have been found in Palestine excavations various small bone objects, dating from all periods: pins, needles, make-up sticks, mirror handles, etc. There are no Bible references to them, although they are native products.

BOTTLE

In Hebrew, skin bottles, which are of prime importance in domestic and especially nomadic life, have several synonyms according to their shape and purpose. They are still used today in Egypt and the Near East; they are made, as in former times, from the complete skins, softened and tanned, of goats, pigs, etc., and they retain in a strange way the animal's shape. The openings left by the tail and legs are merely carefully sewn up and sometimes sealed with pitch; the neck serves as the outlet; it is closed by tying it tightly.

The Biblical texts frequently refer to bottles for carrying or keeping water,¹ milk ²—which can be

churned in them († butter)—and especially wine.³ The taste taken on by drinks in these skins was far from displeasing to the drinkers. As some Assyrian bas-reliefs show, skins were also inflated to support

A harvester drinking from a bottle. Egyptian painting.

rafts or isolated persons; neither the O.T. nor the N.T. alludes to this procedure. On the other hand, the skin bottle often appears in the figurative language of the Bible.⁴ Elihu, in the poem of Job, says, strikingly, that there is in his heart something like

Raft of inflated skins.

wine which has no way out and which would burst even new bottles.⁵ Jesus's saying about the new wine which bursts old bottles when put into them has become proverbial.⁶

¹ Gen. 21. 14, 15, 19. ² Jg. 4. 19. ³ Jos. 9. 4, 13; 1 Sam. 1. 24; 10. 3; 16. 20; 25. 18; 2 Sam. 16. 1. ⁴ Job 38. 37; Ps. 56. 9; 119. 83. ⁵ Job 32. 19. ⁶ Matt. 9. 17; Mk. 2. 22; Lk. 5. 37–38.

BOW

The bow was a hunting weapon [1] or a weapon of war, very frequently mentioned in Biblical texts. Bent with the hand alone or with the foot (the term

Assyrian and Scythian archers.

then used was "to tread the bow"), it was made of tough elastic wood, sometimes strengthened with binding of tendons; it could be carried in a leather bag. Bows of brass [2] are sometimes mentioned, but this is undoubtedly a poetical expression. The

An archer shooting (Assyrian bas-relief).

bowstring was made of ox or camel gut. The shafts, sometimes metaphorically called "sons of the bow" [3] or "sons of the quiver", [4] were tipped with a head of stone, bronze, or iron according to the period († arrow).

In 2 Sam. 1. 18 (R.V.) David's lament on the death

55

of Saul and his sons is called the "Song of the Bow" because Jonathan's bow is mentioned. The words bow, arrows, quiver, were often used figuratively by the poets and prophets of the O.T. [5]

[1] Gen. 21. 20; 27. 3; etc. [2] 2 Sam. 22. 35; Job 20. 24; Ps. 18. 34. [3] Job 41. 28. [4] Lam. 3. 13. [5] Ps. 37. 14, 15; Ps. 127. 4, 5; Is. 49. 2; Jer. 5. 16; Hos. 1. 5; etc.

BOX TREE

The box was a vigorous shrub with beautiful glossy, green foliage and a very hard wood which the ancients often used. It grew in Lebanon and flourished also in Cyprus. It is probably mentioned in the Books of Isaiah (Lebanon) and Ezekiel [1] (Cyprus), although some authors think that these texts refer rather to a variety of cypress.

[1] Is. 41. 19; 60. 13; Ez. 27. 6.

BRACELET

It was customary for the Israelites to wear bracelets. [1] Fashioned of various materials and in different styles, and worn in various numbers from one upwards, they adorned the wrists or the upper arms. The most valuable were of gold or silver, with varying amounts of decoration, but excavations have

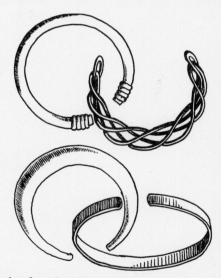

Bracelets from Israelite tombs (Gezer and Beth Pelet).

shown that very simple patterns were usually favoured in Palestine, and especially unclosed bronze rings. Men too wore bracelets, probably and for preference above the elbow, less as adornment, perhaps, than as insignia. [2] The rings which women liked to wear round their ankles were sometimes linked together by small chains which hindered their walking and forced them to take short steps, which were mocked by the prophet Isaiah.[3]

[1] Gen. 24. 22 . . .; Ez. 16. 11; 23. 42. [2] 2 Sam. 1. 10.
[3] Is. 3. 16, 20.

BRAMBLE

The bramble is no doubt included in the O.T. among a number of terms which designate thorny plants († thorn) and which are very difficult to identify; and it is referred to in a Gospel passage [1] where Jesus says: "Do men gather grapes of thorns, or figs of thistles?", and elsewhere: "Of thorns men do not gather figs, nor of a bramble bush gather they grapes." [2]

[1] Matt. 7. 16. [2] Lk. 6. 44.

BRAZIER

In winter, to heat the rooms of wealthy people, containers burning charcoal were used which were undoubtedly analogous to modern braziers.[1] The supposed incense altar*, found at Taanach (Palestine), is possibly only one of these domestic braziers († charcoal).

In various O.T. passages [2] mention is made of a variety of portable cultic utensils of bronze or gold, which are called "braziers" in the majority of our versions; it is difficult to state with certainty their exact shape and use: perhaps they were used for carrying embers from the altar, but they were also used as ash-pans [3] and as incense-burners.[4]

(† Ash-pan, censer.)

[1] Jer. 36. 22. [2] Ex. 27. 3; 38. 3; Num. 4. 14; 1 Kgs. 7. 50; 2 Kgs. 25. 15; Jer. 52. 19. [3] Ex. 25. 38; 37. 23. [4] Lev. 10. 1; 16. 12; Num. 16. 6.

BREAD

Bread was the basic food of the Israelite; the expression "to eat bread" was synonymous with "to have a meal". So it was a highly regarded food. Bread was not given to animals. If a piece of bread was found on the ground it was carefully picked up. When the Arab of today sees us cutting bread with a knife he asks, "Is the bread being killed?" If Is. 58. 7 is well translated it invites us to "*break* bread to the hungry", not to cut it.

It is probable that for a long time people restricted themselves to roasting a few grains (of barley or wheat),[1] and this custom still exists in Palestine. Roasted grains were taken as provisions on journeys.[2]

Normally bread was made from barley; [3] wheat was rare. Flour was obtained by one of three methods:

By pounding the grain in a mortar; [4] this gave a coarse flour which was used for making a kind of gruel, or a kind of cake. By crushing the grain on a flat or concave stone—a method which seems to have been unknown in Babylon, though widely used in Egypt. By using a corn-mill († mill); the women took charge of this work, which was generally done by two of them working together,[5] before sunrise, for each day's bread should be baked early.

The flour* was sometimes sifted, to obtain a higher quality, prime or fine, with which certain pastries were made.

The dough was prepared in a kneading trough, a big wooden container which was not always used exclusively for this purpose; an Egyptian painting († cake) depicts bakers who are kneading dough with their feet!

When the dough was kneaded—half an hour was enough for this task—salt* and leaven* were added; the latter was merely a piece of dough from the previous day kept in reserve for this purpose; but, perhaps because of this, leaven was considered as unclean.[6] Like the Bedouin of today, the Israelites of olden times quite readily used to eat unleavened bread; they made it not only at the Feast of Unleavened Bread, but very often, for example, when they were in a hurry and did not wish to wait for the dough to rise, or especially when they were entertaining a guest—this was the normal practice even when there was a supply of bread in reserve.[7]

Women grinding corn.

Usually bread was baked on a simple round metal plate, about 14 to 20 in. in diameter; the edges were rested on the stones surrounding the fire.[8] Bread made in this way is soft, crustless, and quite flat; this last point has given rise to an Arab proverb which says of a hypocrite: he is like bread baked on a girdle, he has two faces.—Alternatively, a hole in the ground was dug and lined with stones on which the fire was kindled; when the stones were burning hot the embers were swept away and the dough, in flat cakes, was laid on the stones at the risk of having them covered with ash.[9] In an emergency, the bread might even be cooked directly on the embers, when it was necessary to turn the cake in time so that it should not be burnt and uneatable in spite of the appearance of the upper side.[10]

Bread was also baked in the oven. It is uncertain whether the bell-shaped oven, under which the dough was placed and over which the fire was kindled, was used as early as Biblical times. On the other hand, the *tannûr*, mentioned in our texts [11] and depicted by Egyptian painters, was the oven most used, even

Cooking bread in a *tannûr* (*left*),
or on a plate (*right*).

though today its use is almost entirely restricted to the Lebanon. It is a kind of clay stove like a truncated cone with a base diameter of 15 to 24 in. and a height of 2 ft. to 3 ft. 6 in.; normally it consisted of two compartments separated by a horizontal partition containing several wide holes; the fire was made in the lower part and, when the oven was hot, rounds of dough were deftly applied to the inner face of the upper compartment. In this way the bread was very

institution of the Lord's Supper, bread has become the symbol of Christ's presence and activity in the Church, and the expression "to break bread" henceforward means, in the Bible, to take part in the Communion.[13]

[1] Ruth 2. 14; Lev. 23. 14. [2] 1 Sam. 17. 17; 25. 18. [3] Jg. 7. 13; 2 Kgs. 4. 42; Jn. 6. 9. [4] Prov. 27. 22. [5] Matt. 24. 41. [6] 1 Cor. 5. 8. [7] Gen. 19. 3; 1 Sam. 28. 24. [8] Lev. 2. 5; 1 Chr. 9. 31. [9] 1 Kgs. 19. 6. [10] Hos. 7. 8. [11] Ex. 8. 3; Lev. 2. 4; 26. 26; Ps. 21. 9; Hos. 7. 4; Matt. 6. 30; etc. [12] Jn. 6. 35. [13] Acts 2. 42; 1 Cor. 10. 16; etc.

BREAST

With certain sacrifices, the breasts of the animals offered were reserved for the priests,[1] after being subject to a special ritual act.

(† Sacrifice.)

[1] Ex. 29. 26; Lev. 7. 30; 9. 21; 10. 14; etc.

BREECHES

Israelite priests called upon to officiate at the altar, some height from the ground, wore for the sake of decency a pair of short breeches, which had to be made of fine linen like the rest of their attire.[1]

[1] Ex. 28. 42; 39. 28; Lev. 6. 10; 16. 4; Ez. 44. 18.

BRICK

Despite the abundance of stone in Palestine, the use of bricks in house building was general; the extraction of stone necessitated, indeed, metal tools, which for a long time did not exist, and even, at a later date, labour that was more unpleasant and

Egyptian tomb painting showing brick making in the 15th century.

quickly baked. Sometimes this oven was partially buried in the ground, or built into the wall like the one found at Megiddo.

The importance of bread in the general diet of the Israelites makes it understandable why it is used so often in the imagery of the Bible. For example, when a man wished to thank God for the food which he gives to his people it was bread that he brought to the Temple*; also, Jesus reminded people that "man does not live by bread alone", and especially he speaks of himself as the bread of heaven;[12] by the

more costly than that needed to make use of the high-quality clay soils of the country.[1] It is known that in Babylonia and Egypt the nature of the soils had obliged the peoples there to use bricks for the majority of their building works (cf. the decorations of the Beni-Hasan tombs, for example, which depict in lively style the making and utilization of bricks).

Bricks were made by trampling clay or clayey soil in which straw was mixed to bind it and to avoid softening dampness; the Hebrews were employed in this task in Egypt.[2] Originally shaped by hand, bricks were later cast in portable wooden moulds alluded to in the texts.[3] (In these two passages, indeed, brick-moulds are meant—not the brick-kilns of the older translations; David did not condemn the Ammonites to be roasted in kilns, but to work in brick making, a rough toil which was imposed on prisoners and slaves.) Of various sizes, the bricks were then dried in the open or the sun, more rarely in the kiln.[4] Kiln-baked bricks were used in Mesopotamia for the external facing of certain walls, or in the making of pavements; this type of brick was hardly used in Palestine, where stone was profitably used instead. Ordinary bricks were of various dimensions; generally, they measure (12 to 13) in. by ($13\frac{1}{2}$ to 14) in. by (5 to $6\frac{1}{2}$) in. But in the oldest walls, some as long as 21 in. have been found, while the most recent walls have bricks smaller than the average—$3\frac{1}{2}$ to 4 in. thick.—Further, some of the bricks found in excavations have factory marks or even the footprints of dogs, even of a calf in one case, which played about the drying grounds.

The Babylonians and Egyptians knew how to paint and enamel their bricks for the decoration of luxurious buildings.—Isaiah[5] speaks of brick altars which were considered as idolatrous, in contrast with the altars of beaten earth or unshaped stones prescribed by the Law.[6] Note finally that the brick or clay tablet was used as a writing and drawing material.[7]

[1] Is. 9. 10. [2] Ex. 1. 14; 5. 7. [3] 2 Sam. 12. 31; Nah. 3. 14. [4] Gen. 11. 3. [5] Is. 65. 3. [6] Ex. 20. 24 . . . [7] Ez. 4. 1.

BRIMSTONE

Whilst the destruction of Sodom was attributed to a rain of fire and brimstone (sulphur)[1]—a mineral abundant in the Dead Sea region—the Bible writers in their figurative language, the author of Revelation most particularly,[2] speak more than once of brimstone as the agent of divine punishments.[3]

[1] Gen. 19. 24; Dt. 29. 23; Lk. 17. 29. [2] Rev. 9. 17–18; 14. 10; 19. 20; 20. 10; 21. 8. [3] Job 18. 15; Ps. 11. 6; Is. 30. 33; 34. 9; Ez. 38. 22.

BRONZE

The Hebrew term used in the O.T. to speak of copper and, more particularly, the alloy of copper and tin which we call bronze, is usually rendered in our versions by the word brass, the old name for bronze. Indeed, the word bronze (from Brindisi, Brundisium, where it was made) has been in current use for only a few centuries, and the old word brass, considered as a nobler word, has remained in literature; but this terminology is too readily misunderstood, for brass proper is an alloy of copper and zinc which has been known only since the 13th century of our era.

Coming into use later than copper and imported from abroad,[1] bronze appeared in Palestine at the beginning of the 3rd millennium B.C., but it displaced only slowly the crude stone tools with which people remained satisfied. At the same time harder and more fusible than copper, and as readily worked in the foundry as with hammer and chisel, bronze was used for centuries in the manufacture of many things mentioned in the O.T. or unearthed in fair quantities by excavation: chains*,[2] arms*, various utensils of cultic[3] or domestic use, works of art*, bracelets*, needles*, fasteners, clasps*, mirrors*, statues, idols,[4] and later coins.[5] Benefiting from the knowledge of the Phoenicians, who were great importers of bronze and skilled in making all kinds of things in metal, Solomon made great use of it in equipping the Temple*. Bronze held its own for a long time in Palestine, even after the discovery of iron, which did not come into current use in the country until the end of the 2nd millennium B.C.

The copper necessary to the making of bronze came from the Caucasus, the Taurus, and especially from Cyprus; some veins in southern Palestine were also exploited. The tin probably came from Persian and Armenian ores, and, later, from the deposits of the west (Tuscany, the Adriatic, Estramadura, Great Britain, etc.).

The ancients translated as "orichalc" the metal mentioned in Revelation[6] (polished shining brass); this metal has not been successfully identified.

Figurative use of bronze often occurs in the O.T. as a simile for strength, hardness,[7] for bareness of the soil,[8] etc. Jeremiah and Ezekiel[9] compare base worthless men to bronze, because copper was less valuable than gold or silver. (Cf. also 1 Cor. 13. 1, where St Paul refers to the sonorous noise which bronze makes when it is struck.)

[1] Ez. 27. 13. [2] Jg. 16. 21; 1 Sam. 17. 5, 6; 2 Sam. 21. 16; etc. [3] Ex. 25–31. [4] Num. 21. 9; Dan. 2. 32; 5. 4; 10. 6. [5] Mk. 6. 8; 12. 41. [6] Rev. 1. 15; 2. 18. [7] Job 6. 12; 40. 18; Ps. 107. 16; Is. 48. 4; Jer. 1. 18; 15. 12, 20; Mic. 4. 13. [8] Lev. 26. 19; Dt. 28. 23. [9] Jer. 6. 28; Ez. 22. 18.

BROOM

The slight domestic equipment of the Israelites included a broom (besom); we know of it, although it is mentioned only in the vigorous image of the prophet: "I will sweep Babylon with the besom of destruction."[1] In the allegory about relapse Jesus speaks of a house "swept and set in order ",[2] and in the Parable of the Lost Coin about the woman who swept the house in order to recover the lost money.[3]

[1] Is. 14. 23. [2] Matt. 12. 43–45; Lk. 11. 24–26. [3] Lk. 15. 8.

BROOM (SHRUB)

Broom is a shrub, generally stunted but able to attain 12 or 13 ft., which is widely distributed from

Egypt to Phoenicia, in Sinai, and in the Dead Sea basin. It is mentioned only three times in the O.T. Elijah in his flight to the desert slept under a broom tree,[1] the only steppe plant able to offer a little shade. The Psalmist alludes to its use for fuel;[2] its great roots still today provide a charcoal* which gives a particularly fierce heat. Finally, in a terrible metaphor of misery, Job speaks of the roots of broom as the food of unfortunate folk plunged into distress and degradation.[3]

[1] 1 Kgs. 19. 4. [2] Ps. 120. 4. [3] Job 30. 4.

BUCKET

This kind of receptacle was naturally known to the Israelites, as to other ancient peoples. Speaking figuratively, Isaiah says that in the eyes of God the nations are as a drop which falls from a bucket,[1] and they count no more than a grain of dust on a balance. The Samaritan woman remarks to Jesus that he has no bucket to draw water with at Jacob's well.[2] Curiously enough, this utensil is mentioned nowhere else. (The text of Num. 24. 7 is uncertain.)

[1] Is. 40. 15. [2] Jn. 4. 11.

BUFFALO

Is it mentioned in the Bible? Opinions differ, because of the great difficulty of establishing the exact meaning of certain Hebrew names for animals. It seems, however, that what the O.T. says about the re'em[1] could apply to the buffalo. Yet it must be said that although this animal, which originated from India, lives today in some marshy parts of Palestine, it came to the country at too late a time to be re-

Bowl decorated with the head of a wild ox.

ferred to in the O.T., and it would be better to regard the re'em as the wild ox, a savage and ferocious bovine, even more formidable than the buffalo, which the kings of Assyria liked to hunt, as some of their bas-reliefs testify, where it figures under the name rîmu. This interpretation agrees better with what Job 39 says of the re'em and only intensifies the force of the comparisons inspired by this animal.

[1] Num. 23. 22; 24. 8; Dt. 33. 17; Job 39. 9–12; Ps. 22. 21; 29. 6; 92. 10; Is. 34. 7.

BUL

This was the eighth month of the Jewish year.[1] The etymology of the name is uncertain (rain? abundance?). It was the end of October–November, the month of rains. After the Exile it took the name Marḥešvan, which is today abridged as Ḥešvan.

[1] 1 Kgs. 6. 38.

BULL

The richness of Hebrew vocabulary in reference to the bovine race as a whole, and to its different representatives according to age and sex, is proof of the value of these domestic animals to the Israelites. They used them for their different agricultural tasks [1] (ploughing, treading out the corn, carting, etc.); they drank their milk,[2] ate their flesh,[3] and cured their skins. In earliest times the Hebrews, primarily keepers of sheep and goats, had added cattle to their livestock.[4] This probably took place when they came into more constant contact with settled peoples and when they had become semi-nomadic through beginning to cultivate some land.[5]

In Palestine the Israelites kept in their byres [6] the animals necessary for work and milk, as well as those intended for fattening,[7] but the wealthier possessed herds [8] which lived almost wild in certain favourable districts († cattle).—Large numbers of cattle, particularly young bulls, were sacrificed in the cult, to the honour of Yahweh:[9] the priestly texts give detailed information on this subject († sacrifice). Legislation also gave rules about damage caused by these animals,[10] which it did not leave entirely outside its protection.[11] Since the Israelites probably did not practise castration of their animals, it would be better, in our versions, to speak of bulls or bovidae, rather than of oxen, unless this word is used in its widest sense (belonging to the bovine race). It seems that in Palestine cattle rearing was more highly developed than it is today; scarcity of pasture brings difficulties to the improvement of the species.

The role played by the bull as a symbol of life, fertility, and power in the religions of antiquity is well known; Israel too allowed itself, at times, to represent its God in the form of this animal.[12]

(† Cattle, calf, heifer.)

[1] Num. 7. 3; Dt. 22. 10; 25. 4; 1 Sam. 6. 7; 1 Kgs. 19. 19; Hos. 10. 11. [2] Dt. 32. 14; 2 Sam. 17. 29; Is. 7. 21. [3] Gen. 18. 7; Dt. 14. 4; 1 Kgs. 1. 9; Neh. 5. 18; Amos 6. 4; Lk. 15. 23. [4] Gen. 12. 16; 13. 5; 15. 9; 20. 14; 21. 27; 24. 35; 32. 5, 7; cf. Ex. 12. 38. [5] Gen. 26. 12, 14; 34. 10. [6] Jg. 6. 4; 1 Sam. 11. 5; Lk. 13. 15; 14. 19. [7] 1 Sam. 28. 24; 1 Kgs. 4. 23; Prov. 15. 17; Jer. 46. 21; Mal. 4. 2; Matt. 22. 4; Lk. 15. 27. [8] 2 Sam. 12. 2; 1 Chr. 27. 29; 2 Chr. 32. 29; Job 1. 3; 42. 12; Eccl. 2. 7. [9] Gen. 15. 9; 1 Kgs. 8. 63; 2 Chr. 15. 11; 29. 33; 35. 8; Jn. 2. 14. [10] Ex. 21. 28–36. [11] Ex. 23. 12; Dt. 25. 4. [12] Ex. 32; Dt. 9. 16; 1 Kgs. 12. 28; 2 Kgs. 10. 29.

BUSH

The burning bush at Sinai-Horeb, where Moses received his call,[1] was a thorny shrub. Sometimes a kind of acacia, sometimes a species of hawthorn or a variety of bramble (blackberry) has been suggested, but it is impossible to be sure. The Convent of St Catherine in Sinai is said to have been built on the place where this sacred bush grew.

[1] Ex. 3. 2; Dt. 33. 16; Mk. 12. 26; Lk. 20. 37; Acts 7. 30.

BUSHEL

The bushel, equivalent to the Roman *modius*, was a measure of capacity of about 15 pints. The vessel normally used as a dry measure of this capacity could be used as a table or plate by the poor; hence the classic simile in the Gospels of not putting the light under a bushel.[1]

[1] Matt. 5. 15; Mk. 4. 21; Lk. 11. 33.

BUTCHER

The O.T. and N.T. mention no place where meat is sold. The Hebrew word translated "slaughter" means "slaughtering". A number of times the word is used figuratively in impressive comparisons [1] and notably in an allegorical passage which has become classical [2] in its application to the holy victim of Calvary.[3]

In the open country each man killed the animals he needed for food; with important people,[4] or at kings' courts, there were servants charged with this duty, which was included in the functions of a cook; hence the translation of 1 Sam. 9. 23, where "slaughterer" or "butcher" would be more exact.—Later, at least in the towns, slaughtering became a trade; the Talmud speaks of a street of the Butchers in Jerusalem.

[1] Ps. 44. 22 (cf. Rom. 8. 36); Prov. 7. 22; Jer. 11. 19; Zech. 11. 4, 7. [2] Is. 53. 7. [3] Acts 8. 32. [4] Gen. 18. 7.

BUTTER

The word *ḥem'ah*, which we translate as butter, really means: thickened or hard milk; it also means curdled milk (the *leben* of the Arabs), and cream, as well as butter; the meaning is determined by the context. Thus, it is clear that Jael gave cream or curdled milk to Sisera,[1] whereas butter is meant in the curious text of Prov. 30. 33: "For pressing milk produces curds, and pressing the nose produces blood." Indeed, as still is the custom in the Near East, butter was made by shaking, by long churning of sour milk in a leather bottle fastened to a tripod of stakes.[2] Butter takes the place of oil for the Bedouin; because of the climate, butter must be melted and clarified before it is stored in leather bottles or jars, in which it remains in a semi-liquid state; this provides the explanation of eastern hyperboles for

Woman churning butter in a bottle.

abundance of goods, which speak of "torrents of butter" (*leben*) and of bathing one's feet in butter.[3]

[1] Jg. 5. 25. [2] Cf. Gen. 18. 8; 2 Sam. 17. 29; Is. 7. 15. [3] Job 20. 17; 29. 6.

BUZZARD

This bird of prey of the falcon family is perhaps mentioned in the list of unclean birds,[1] but the Hebrew text is uncertain. Its name seems to mean "one who has keen vision".

[1] Dt. 14. 13a (R.V., glede).

CAGE

This object is evoked by Jeremiah [1] in a saying where only a simple osier basket is meant (cf. Amos 8. 2), in which the fowler carries to market the birds he has caught, and by Ezekiel,[2] who speaks of the substantial cage, such as figures on some Assyrian bas-reliefs, in which the lion is shut up by the hunters who have caught him. There are two different Hebrew words for these two kinds of cages.

[1] Jer. 5. 27. [2] Ez. 19. 9.

CAKE

The importance given to the sacrificial presentation of cakes makes it clear that the Israelites did not limit themselves to the making of bread only, but also made all sorts of pastries,[1] which bear various names, but which are difficult to identify. In the sanctuary unleavened cakes mixed with oil and unleavened wafers coated with oil [2] made from the finest flour were given as offerings. Jeremiah inveighs against women of his people who made cakes undoubtedly in the shape of stars, crescents, or moons, which were intended for the cult of the Queen of Heaven [3] (Ishtar—Astarte). Honey wafers are occasionally mentioned in the Book of Exodus.[4] As representation of an Egyptian bakery and confectionery; on the left, at the top, a wicker sieve rests upon a basin; beneath them two servants, leaning on long staffs, knead the cake-mix with their feet. In the centre the baker spreads out the dough and adds the

A royal confectionery. Tomb painting of the 12th century.

for the raisin cakes so often mentioned—David, for instance, distributed them generously to the people when the Ark was removed to Jerusalem [5]—which bear different names in the texts, in every case these were probably quantities of raisins pressed together to form cakes.[6]

On the tomb of Rameses III there is an interesting

seasoning, which two servants bring to him; then he cuts the mixture with geometrical or animal shapes which are placed within arm's reach. Farther on, a pastry cook holds a spiral-shaped cake which he has just baked in the oven under which blazes a wood fire; on the other side of the oven a workman seems to have raised its cover by means of a wooden spatula. Above them the painter has placed some finished pastries, while on the right he depicts a workman busy with something in a pot; he is probably making jam from fruit previously contained in two wicker baskets; in another place a servant is cleaning a bread-oven and various utensils.

[1] Gen. 18. 6; Num. 11. 7–8; 2 Sam. 13. 6–9; 1 Kgs. 14. 3; 17. 13; 19. 6; Hos. 7. 8. [2] Ex. 29. 2, 23; Lev. 2. 4–7. [3] Jer. 7. 18. [4] Ex. 16. 31. [5] 2 Sam. 6. 19. [6] 1 Sam. 25. 18; 30. 12; 1 Chr. 12. 40; 16. 3; Cant. 2. 5; Is. 16. 7; Hos. 3. 1.

CALAMUS

Among the aromatic substances needed to make holy oil, Ex. 30. 23 mentions calamus or sweet-smelling rush.[1] This is Marsh Galingale, a herb which grows in India and Arabia;[2] from its very strongly smelling root an aromatic oil was extracted.

[1] Cant. 4. 14; Is. 43. 24. [2] Jer. 6. 20; Ez. 27. 19.

CALF

It should simply be noted that the calf (young bull) was one of the animals most often presented in sacrifice*. The Israelites deliberately fattened calves in preparation for festive meals († festival),[1] and that,

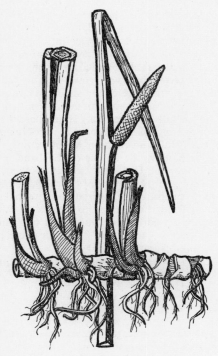

Calamus.

in some cases, the word calf was used in derision for that of bull.[2]

(† Bull, cattle.)

[1] Gen. 18. 7; 1 Sam. 28. 24; 1 Kgs. 1. 9; Jer. 46. 21; Lk. 15. 27. [2] Ex. 32; 1 Kgs. 12. 28; 2 Kgs. 10. 29; Hos. 8. 5–6; 10. 5; 13. 2.

CAMEL

In mountainous Palestine the camel family, of which the dromedary (with one hump) is the most frequently used today, could not be counted among the usual domestic animals. They are naturally adapted to the steppe, the desert, and the long journeys of nomads. So the Biblical texts hardly ever speak of these useful animals except in the narratives of the patriarchs, who possessed many of them,[1] or when telling of the comings and goings of foreign caravans,[2] or of Israel's conflicts with semi-nomadic neighbours (Midianites, Amalekites, etc.).[3]

Camel. Bas-relief from Persepolis.

It should be noted that Joseph's brothers used asses and not camels [4] for their journey into Egypt, and especially that the Israelites had no camels during their desert journey following the Exodus. On the other hand, at the time of the return from the Exile, 435 camels (against 6,720 asses) are recorded.[5]

These ruminants must have been numerous in Transjordania; certain rich landowners had great herds of them (cf. Job 1. 2; 42. 12); and a royal steward had charge of David's herd.[6]

The extraordinary endurance of these animals, and their economy in feeding, is well known. They are used especially as beasts of burden, but also as riding animals [7] and sometimes as draught animals. The camel can carry enormous loads—as much as 10 or 11 cwt.—with which it will cover nearly 30 miles a day. A special saddle permits baskets or merchandise bags to be suspended from it, or a palanquin for carrying women and children to be set on it.[8] Restive, stubborn, often vicious, even very dangerous at certain times, the camel shows no sign of affection for its master, who does not think

the less of it on that account: this "ship of the desert", indeed, not only gives the greatest services as porter or runner, but she-camels can give up to 1½ gallons daily of excellent milk, which the Bedouin make into butter and cheese;[9] the animal's dung is used as fuel; even its urine is useful in washing hair, beard, face, and teeth! Camel meat, forbidden to the Israelites,[10] is eaten by Orientals, though it is much inferior to beef. The hair is used in making material for tents and clothes,[11] and its skin in making harness, bottles, sandals, etc.

O.T. poets rarely allude to the camel; in a strong, stern metaphor, however, Jeremiah compares Jerusalem's passion for idolatry to the wild desire of a young she-camel interlacing her tracks.[12] And in the N.T. two sayings of Jesus have become proverbial: "It is easier for a camel to go through the eye of a needle* than for a rich man to enter the kingdom of God",[13] "You blind guides straining out a gnat and swallowing down a camel".[14]

[1] Gen. 12. 16; 24; 30. 43; 31. 17; 32. 7, 15. [2] Gen. 37. 25; 1 Kgs. 10. 2; 2 Kgs. 8. 9; cf. Is. 30. 6; 60. 6. [3] Jg. 6. 5; 1 Sam. 15. 3; 27. 9; 30. 17; 1 Chr. 5. 21; 2 Chr. 14. 15. [4] Gen. 42. 26; 43. 18; etc. [5] Ezr. 2. 67; Neh. 7. 69; cf. Is. 66. 20. [6] 1 Chr. 5. 21; 12. 40; 27. 30; Job 1. 3; 42. 12. [7] Is. 21. 7; 66. 20. [8] Gen. 31. 34. [9] Gen. 32. 15. [10] Lev. 11. 4. [11] Matt. 3. 4; Mk. 1. 6. [12] Jer. 2. 23–24. [13] Matt. 19. 24; Mk. 10. 25; Lk. 18. 25. [14] Matt. 23. 24.

CAMP

The tents of nomadic tribes are usually scattered irregularly in the area where the people are staying. But if these tribes are in any danger the tents will be grouped in a circle or an open horse-shoe on the hillside. In this way a village of tents [1] is formed, which is sometimes surrounded by a dry-stone wall where protective thorns will grow.—During the rainy season the nomads prefer the sheltered wadis with the river flowing at the bottom; in summer they pitch camp on the hills or on a rocky spur where they can survey the countryside and enjoy the cool breezes.

We have little information about camps set up during wartime by the armies of the Israelites and their enemies; the O.T. only alludes to them.[2] To judge from the Hebrew word, which sometimes means the Israelite camp, we may suppose that it was of circular form; [3] according to Exodus, it was surrounded by an earthwork which had two gates at opposite ends.[4] During the battle the baggage remained in the care of a guard.[5]

[1] Gen. 25. 16; Num. 31. 10; Ps. 69. 26. [2] Jos. 6. 11; 1 Sam. 14. 15; 2 Kgs. 7. 7. [3] 1 Sam. 17. 20; 26. 5, 7. [4] Ex. 32. 26, 27. [5] 1 Sam. 30. 24.

CANAL

Archaeological research has revealed canal systems which were built to bring the necessary water into a town, from a spring or artificial reservoir.

Some of them are open to the sky. But in time of war it was only too easy to divert this water from the besieged town, so tunnels were laboriously dug at some depth in the rocky subsoil. Examples have been found in Gezer, Megiddo, Jericho, and also at Jerusalem. In Jerusalem, indeed, is the best known of these canals; it brings the water from the spring of Gihon to the pool of Siloam. In reality there are two canals there; at the end of one of these an inscription was found in 1880 in ancient Hebrew script († writing), telling how the tunnel was dug; the canal is more than 550 yds. long and was hollowed out at the time of Hezekiah at the end of the 8th century B.C. In wartime the natural access to the spring [1] outside the ramparts was walled up, and the water flowed along the canal beneath the wall, to the pool of Siloam, in the lower part of the town.

[1] 2 Chr. 32. 3.

CANDLESTICK

In the Bible, a stand for one or more lamps is really meant. In every Palestinian house there was at least one "candlestick". When the Shunammite woman prepared a room for the prophet Elisha she put in it a bed, a table, a seat, and a candlestick,[1] and Jesus states that men do not "light a lamp, and put it under the bushel, but on the stand; and it gives light to all in the house".[2] These lampstands are chased in varying degrees; some are very simple, made of clay

Examples of Palestinian lampstands.

or wood, others are of base or precious metals; the candelabrum of King Belshazzar must undoubtedly have been a very choice article of furniture.[3] Excavations in Palestine have brought to light a number of candlesticks, some of which have the lamp itself built in.

According to the First Book of Kings [4] (which, however, does not describe them), ten golden candlesticks stood in the Holy Place of Solomon's Temple*, five on the right, five on the left. These numbers, repeated in Chronicles,[5] are somewhat surprising—in the Tabernacle and the Second Temple there was

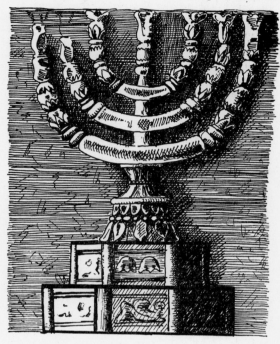

Seven-branched candlestick of the Temple of Jerusalem, as represented on a bas-relief of the triumph Arch of Titus.

only one candlestick, and 2 Chr. 13. 11 states that every evening the gold candlestick (in the singular) with its lamps was lit—but the numbers, from this very fact, seem to be founded on a good tradition, all the more since Jeremiah [6] lists "the candlesticks" among the cultic objects carried away to Babylon when Jerusalem was captured by Nebuchadnezzar (2 Kgs. 25. 15 and 2 Chr. 36. 18, on the other hand, make no reference to them). As for the text of 1 Chr. 28. 15, it speaks not only of golden candlesticks but also of silver ones: in all likelihood it refers to a project which was never completed.

With more certainty we know that a single gold candlestick stood in the Temple rebuilt after the Exile. Carried away and mutilated by Antiochus IV (Epiphanes), then restored and replaced by Judas Maccabaeus,[7] it was retained in the Temple* of Herod. When Jerusalem was taken by the Romans the candlestick was taken to the banks of the Tiber, to figure in the conqueror's triumph, and it was pictured in one of the bas-reliefs on the interior vault of the Arch of Titus, where it can still be seen today. This is probably a rather fanciful reproduction, but it gives on the whole a fair idea of the shape of this sacred object. Moreover, the seven-branched candlestick planned for the Tabernacle, and described at length in Ex. 25. 31–37, was undoubtedly a replica of the one in the Second Temple.—From Rome, after various changes of fortune, the Jewish candlestick was probably taken to Carthage, then to Constantinople, and finally returned to Jerusalem under Justinian (6th century A.D.). It is not known what happened to it after that; perhaps it was destroyed or carried off by Chosroes II, king of Persia, when the Holy City was sacked in A.D. 614.

As the symbol of Jewish faith and hope, the seven-branched candlestick is often represented on the walls of ancient synagogues* or on tombs.

Other golden candlesticks are mentioned in the Bible; in one of his visions [8] Zechariah finds himself before a candlestick—different from the one in the Temple—bearing seven lamps, a metaphor for Yahweh, and framed by two olive trees; the poet of Revelation sees seven golden candlesticks, symbols of the seven churches to which he speaks, and later he too speaks of two olive trees and two candlesticks, allegorical witnesses which stand on the earth [9] before the Lord.

[1] 2 Kgs. 4. 10. [2] Matt. 5. 15; Mk. 4. 21; Lk. 8. 16; 11. 33. [3] Dan. 5. 5. [4] 1 Kgs. 7. 49. [5] 2 Chr. 4. 7, 20. [6] Jer. 52. 19. [7] 1 Macc. 1. 23; 4. 49. [8] Zech. 4. 1–14. [9] Rev. 1. 12, 20; 11. 4.

CAPER

Capers are numerous in Palestine and grow wild. Eccl. 12. 5 is the only Bible passage which mentions

Caper
(*Capparis spinosa*).

capers—though it is not the fruit of this prickly bush, but its flower bud, which was used as a digestive condiment or as a stimulant.

CARBUNCLE

The carbuncle was a stone highly esteemed by ancient peoples. It was bright red, and held against the sun looked like a glowing coal (the name *carbunculus* is a diminutive of *carbo* = charcoal, coal).

In the O.T. the stone referred to may be what is today called the Oriental garnet, or perhaps the Oriental ruby.

The first stone of the second row of the High Priest's breastplate [1] was a carbuncle; along with other precious stones it adorned the robes of the prince of Tyre of which Ezekiel speaks,[2] and it figures among the merchandise sold to Tyre by the Syrians.[3]

[1] Ex. 28. 18; 39. 11. [2] Ez. 28. 13. [3] Ez. 27. 16.

CAROB

In the Parable of the Prodigal Son the pigs ate the carob beans on which the hungry boy himself would gladly have fed.[1] Sometimes the fruit of the carob tree is too vaguely translated as "husks"; it is a very common tree in Palestine and in the Mediterranean

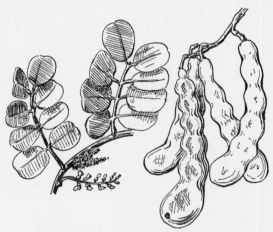

Carob (*Ceratonia siliqua*).

basin, and grows to 40 ft., with a trunk often 6 ft. in girth. Its pods, often leathery and 5 or 6 in. long by over an inch broad, contain a sweetish pulp suitable for animal food, and which is not disdained by some humans, particularly in times of need. They were also used in medical concoctions and in syrup.

[1] Lk. 15. 16.

CARPENTER

In the O.T. carpenters as we understand the word are not meant—there is no such word in Hebrew—but rather workmen, craftsmen "shaping" and working in wood, and practising, often at the same time, the trades of joiner, cabinet-maker, cartwright, turner, and wood-sculptor. Timber-work was hardly ever used except in the construction of important buildings; and it seems that in the time of David and Solomon professional carpenters were foreigners, and especially Phoenicians.[1] Working carpenters are mentioned as employed in the Temple at the time of Joash,[2] but it was probably after the Exile that the Israelites adopted the trade (cf. 2 Kgs. 24. 14, 16; Jer. 24. 1, in which certain versions translate as smith the word usually rendered by carpenter; precisely, it means "shapers" of wood, stone, or metal, craftsmen, workmen who worked in these materials).

Similarly in the N.T., the Greek word translated as carpenter has a more general sense and might mean a house builder; because of this, some exegetes argue

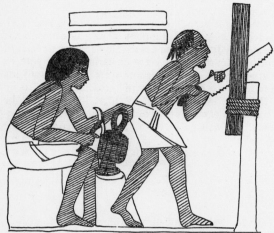

Carpenters. Mural from an Egyptian tomb of the 14th century.

that this was the trade of Joseph [3] and of Jesus [4] before the beginning of his ministry, by pointing out that in Palestine a carpenter's trade is reduced to its simplest expression, that still today many stonemasons originate from Bethlehem and that the references Jesus makes to stone-working [5] are much more numerous than his references to wood-working.[6] We must recognize, however, that the tradition that sees Jesus as a carpenter, a worker in wood, "making yokes and ploughs" as Justin Martyr says, developed at an early age and can be well supported. For the rest, we may note that Jesus himself never spoke of the trade of his youth. († Wood.)

[1] 2 Sam. 5. 11; 1 Kgs. 5. 18; 1 Chr. 14. 1; 22. 15. [2] 2 Kgs. 12. 11. [3] Matt. 13. 55. [4] Mk. 6. 3. [5] Matt. 7. 24; 16. 18; 21. 33; Lk. 14. 28; 20. 17; Jn. 2. 19. [6] Matt. 7. 13; Lk. 23. 31.

CASSIA

This is a kind of inferior aromatic bark provided by a tree closely related to the cinnamon tree. It is more bitter and less aromatic than true cinnamon*. As a perfume [1] it entered into the composition of holy oil,[2] and it was a commodity which Arabia exchanged with Tyre.[3]—Aromatic cassia must not be confused with senna, which came from a leguminous plant and was used as a purgative.

[1] Ps. 45. 8. [2] Ex. 30. 24. [3] Ez. 27. 19.

CASTANET

Some translators think that castanets are mentioned in the last Psalm, where praise for God is called for from all musical instruments.[1] This is not certain, and the etymology of the word can lead to

Egyptian castanets.

different conclusions. However, castanets of metal, bone, and wood have been found in Egypt, and it is not impossible that they were used also in Palestine.

[1] Ps. 150. 5.

CASTRATION

Did the law forbid this operation on animals? The only text which mentions it [1]—even enumerating four methods of mutilation—at least prohibits offering a castrated animal to Yahweh. But Josephus and tradition, which several exegetes follow, think that the text itself prohibits all castration in Israel. It is hard to decide; but in any case it is curious that the law is not more explicit.

[1] Lev. 22. 24.

CAT

The domestic cat, widely distributed and much respected in Egypt, as is known, was very rare in Palestine. In Biblical Hebrew no word exists for cat. Even today, the domestic cat in the East is generally only half tamed. Palestine possesses two or three species of wild cats, which are not mentioned in the Bible. Yet certain commentators think that the Hebrew word, elsewhere translated by the collective "animals (or people, i.e., demons) of the desert",[1] might take—in Is. 34. 14—the more special meaning of "wild cats" because it is coupled in this text with the word for "wild dogs".

[1] Ps. 74. 14; Is. 13. 21; 23. 13; Jer. 50. 39.

CATAPULT

Chronicles records, not without admiration, that Uzziah had machines built in Jerusalem designed to hurl arrows and huge stones from the walls.[1] Although all exegetes are not agreed, this periphrasis might well mean catapults or ballistae. The Assyrians also knew how to make use of these instruments. They are mentioned nowhere else in the Bible.

[1] 2 Chr. 26. 15.

CATTLE

The rearing of cattle in Palestine does not necessarily go together with agriculture*, for, in places where pasture is found, the soil is not suitable for tilling. That is why cattle, sheep, and goats constituted the main source of wealth of the nomadic or semi-nomadic Hebrews and were looked after with great care. Genesis states that Abraham and the patriarchs were very rich in flocks,[1] and the Israelites who settled in the land of Goshen were reported to the Pharaoh as being animal farmers, keepers of sheep and goats.[2]

After Canaan had been settled, the Israelites in Transjordania and the Negev and some other parts of the country continued to devote themselves to their traditional pursuits, while elsewhere agriculture supplanted intensive stock breeding. However, rich arable farmers, and even some townspeople, owned large numbers of livestock which they grazed in suitable districts—the rich pastures of Bashan were especially famous,[3] and several O.T. texts indicate that the kings of Israel and Judah possessed big herds which were supervised by stewards.[4] Even if they are exaggerated, the figures given in the Bible show the scope that stock-rearing could attain: Nabal, at Maon, owned 1,000 goats and 3,000 ewes,[5] and Job in his prosperity had 7,000 ewes, 3,000 camels, 500 pairs of oxen, and 500 she-asses;[6] Mesha, the king of Moab, moreover, paid to the king of Israel a tribute of 100,000 lambs and 100,000 rams.[7] Livestock was so valuable to the Israelite that the Hebrew word for flocks and herds also means wealth; and the proof that God granted his favour to his faithful people was found in the increase of their flocks and herds, when their livestock multiplied.[8] While flocks of sheep, goats, and cattle lived in the open throughout the year, moving from pasture to pasture, draught and sumpter animals, as well as fattening calves,[9] grazed in the fields near the houses [10] or were fed [11] in the byre on chopped straw, barley, bran, or vetches, mixed sometimes with salt or aromatic herbs and put into a manger. The Israelites did not know of oats [12] or the use of hay.

(† Animals, ewe, goat, shepherd, etc.)

[1] Gen. 13. 2; 31. 18; etc. [2] Gen. 46. 32. [3] Ps. 22. 12; Ez. 39. 18; Amos 4. 1. [4] 1 Sam. 21. 7; 2 Sam. 13. 23; 1 Chr. 27. 29 . . .; 2 Chr. 26. 10; 32. 29. [5] 1 Sam. 25. 2. [6] Job 1. 3.

[7] 2 Kgs. 3. 4. [8] Dt. 8. 13; 28. 4; Jer. 31. 27; 33. 12; etc. [9] 1 Sam. 28. 24; Amos 6. 4; Mal. 4. 2; etc. [10] Num. 22. 4. [11] Prov. 14. 4; Is. 1. 3; 11. 7; 30. 24; 65. 25; Lk. 2. 7. [12] Cf. 1 Kgs. 4. 28.

CAULDRON

For cooking food, the Israelites had a whole range of utensils at their disposal; half a dozen Hebrew words are used for them in the O.T., but it is very difficult to identify these objects and to distinguish them from one another; our versions use in turn the words: cauldron, cooking-pot, kettle, pan, pot, basin, bowl, etc. The confusion is all the greater because the same Hebrew word is sometimes rendered in five or six different ways according to the context.—It should be noted that these receptacles of metal or earthenware were of various sizes, with or without lids, and that some were used for storing food, or as bowls. (See in particular the lists in 1 Sam. 2. 14 and 2 Chr. 35. 13.) Some were to be found in the equipment of the Temple and for sacrifices,[1] as well as in the figurative language of the prophets.[2]

[1] Ex. 30. 18; 1 Kgs. 7. 38, 45; 2 Chr. 4. 6; Zech. 14. 20–21; etc. [2] 2 Kgs. 21. 13; Ps. 60. 8; Eccl. 7. 6; Jer. 1. 13; Ez. 11. 3; 24. 3–14; Mic. 3. 3; etc.

CAVE

From Palaeolithic times, the numerous caves in Palestine have been much used as dwellings for succeeding populations, as has been abundantly proved by recent excavations (Carmel, desert of Judah, Nazareth district, etc.). A natural cave was often enlarged with the help of primitive tools and was fitted out more or less comfortably (gutters for drainage of water, cupules for provisions, hearths, stone seats, niches for lamps, mural decorations, etc.). Sometimes several rooms followed one another within the cave, making veritable labyrinths. As temporary dwellings, caves are mentioned in certain O.T. passages.[1]

But, as time went on, caves were hardly used except as stables, storehouses for water or provisions, as tombs (Gen. 23), and retreats in times of war; [2] there, too, according to the prophet,[3] men would hide before the anger of the Lord. Caves served naturally as dens for brigands and thieves, as is borne out by Jeremiah's metaphor quoted by Jesus in his powerful denunciation of the sellers and money-changers in the Temple at Jerusalem.[4]

[1] Gen. 19. 30; Jg. 15. 8; 1 Kgs. 19. 9, 13; etc. [2] Jg. 6. 2; 1 Sam. 13. 6; 22. 1; 1 Kgs. 18. 4; Heb. 11. 38. [3] Is. 2. 19; cf. Rev. 6. 15; [4] Jer. 7. 11; Matt. 21. 13; Mk. 11. 17; Lk. 19. 46.

CEDAR

Remarkable for its impressive appearance, for its long, strong branches, which spread horizontally, for its height (it can grow to more than 100 ft.), and for its longevity, the cedar was the finest of trees in the eyes of the Israelites. It does not grow in Palestine, but the cedars of Lebanon—today reduced to a group of hardly 400—were famous throughout the ancient world.[1] There are many passages in the O.T. which tell of the magnificence and value of this conifer,[2] whose straight-grained aromatic wood was everywhere sought as building timber, as wood for making various articles of furniture, coffins (Egypt), ships, idols, and for panelling rich dwellings.[3] David had obtained this valuable wood from the Phoenicians for fitting out his palace,[4] but it was to Solomon, especially, that Hiram, king of Tyre, delivered large quantities of cedars which were transported to Palestine by sea;[5] the king of Israel used them in the erection of his civil buildings (the house of timber (i.e., the Forest) of Lebanon, throne room, palace, etc.) and in his famous Temple*.[6] The same procedure was used, but undoubtedly on a more modest scale, for the second Temple,[7] and, according to Josephus, King Herod used cedar for the roof of the sanctuary which he restored. We know too that cedar was used in the temple of Diana at Ephesus, and in Caligula's galleys, etc.

This "prince of trees" quite naturally occupies a large place in the figurative language of the Biblical poets and the prophets. It is usually the symbol of grandeur, power, beauty,[8] but also of pride which God will break.[9] As a contrast with the wicked man who passes like grass, the cedar, always green and vigorous, symbolizes the righteous with strong and constant faith.[10] Isaiah speaks of the wonderful times when God will change the desert by planting cedars and other magnificent trees [11] in it, and Ezekiel prophesies that the Messiah will become "a majestic cedar beneath which birds of all kinds will come for shelter".[12]

Israelite law prescribed the use of cedar wood for the purification of lepers and the preparation of the "water which removes defilement", perhaps because of the pleasant smell given off by this wood, and its reputation for incorruptibility.[13]

It is possible that the Hebrew word usually given to the cedar sometimes means trees of related species (pines, for example).

[1] 2 Kgs. 19. 23; Is. 14. 8; 37. 24; Ez. 27. 24; Zeph. 2. 14; etc. [2] Ez. 31. 3–7. [3] Cant. 1. 17; 8, 9; Is. 9. 10; 44. 14; Jer. 22. 14–15. [4] 2 Sam. 5. 11; 7. 2; 1 Chr. 14. 1; 22. 4. [5] 1 Kgs. 5. 6, 9; 9. 11; 2 Chr. 2. 16. [6] 1 Kgs. 6 and 7. [7] Ezr. 3. 7. [8] Jg. 9. 15; 2 Kgs. 14. 9; Cant. 5. 15; Is. 35. 2; Jer. 22. 7; Amos 2. 9; Zech. 11. 1; etc. [9] Ps. 29. 5; Is. 2. 13; Ez. 31. 3; etc. [10] Ps. 92. 12–15. [11] Is. 41. 19. [12] Ez. 17. 22–24. [13] Lev. 14; Num. 19. 6, 9.

CELIBACY

Israelites had a very deep respect for the family*, and considered marriage as a duty and a privilege;

for them celibacy constituted an anomaly, a humiliating state, of which they did not approve. But at about the beginning of the Christian era there appeared in Palestine opponents of marriage: the Essenes considered that it was degrading.

Without placing celibacy higher than marriage, which for him is a divine institution,[1] Jesus recognizes that it may be necessitated in exceptional circumstances, and particularly through fidelity to a vocation which claims entire consecration.[2]

As is known, St Paul had little sympathy with marriage for several reasons, some of an eschatological order; while declaring that the Gospel in no way makes celibacy an obligation, he considers that he who gives his daughter in marriage does well, but he who does not give her in marriage does better.[3] Yet, as time passed, he seemed to look on marriage no longer as the last resource, and he raises it in a well-known simile to a level unknown to Judaism and the pagan world.[4]

Celibacy was not prescribed for the leaders of the early church, and St Peter was himself married.[5]

[1] Matt. 19. 4 . . .; Mk. 10. 6 . . . [2] Matt. 19. 11–12. [3] 1 Cor. 7. [4] Eph. 5. 25–33. [5] Matt. 8. 14; Mk. 1. 30; Lk. 4. 38; 1 Cor. 9. 5.

CELLAR

In important houses in Palestine there were provision-rooms, sheltered from heat and light, excavations where wine, oil, corn, and foodstuffs were stored. Our versions call them cellars or granaries, but the granary as we understand the word did not exist: Israelite houses, ending in terraces, did not

Egyptian granary for corn; tomb painting of 1460 B.C.

have any, and the granary where grain was stored did not differ from the cellar where jars of wine were stored. Cereals were often stored in holes in the ground, in cisterns or silos († agriculture).

Several O.T. texts allude to cellars.[1] In ordinary houses provisions were put away in a corner of the one room or in a secluded room, if the house had several. Sanctuaries owned a large or small number of warehouses where the tithe produce was collected: Nehemiah [2] and Malachi [3] make explicit reference to those of the second Temple.

The story of Joseph has made the Egyptian granaries famous; [4] they are quite frequently represented on Egyptian monuments. The accompanying mural from a tomb of the 15th century B.C. represents a servant carrying a sack of corn, who is about to enter a courtyard surrounded by walls; in the court are three conical granaries, the first of which is hidden by the entrance door; against the other two stand ladders which allow the grain to be poured in from above, while a trap-door is fitted below for extracting the grain when required. The contents of the granaries are represented in the upper half of the painting.

In the N.T. John the Baptist likens the Messiah to a harvester who, with fan in hand, cleans his grain and gathers it into his granary; [5] Jesus himself refers to the granary in the Parable of the Tares, [6] and though the rich fool thinks only of enlarging his storehouses, [7] Jesus observes that ravens, birds of the air, on the other hand, have neither cellar nor granary. [8]

[1] Dt. 28. 8; 1 Chr. 27. 27; 28. 12; 2 Chr. 11. 11; 32. 28; Ps. 144. 13; Prov. 3. 10; cf. Joel 1. 17. [2] Neh. 13. 12, 13. [3] Mal. 3. 10. [4] Gen. 41. 35, 48, 56. [5] Matt. 3. 12; Lk. 3. 17. [6] Matt. 13. 30. [7] Lk. 12. 18. [8] Matt. 6. 26; Lk. 12. 24.

CENSER

Only two O.T. passages [1] mention censers as such, but some fire-pans were used as incense-burners, as other texts show. [2] Since these cultic utensils are nowhere described, their exact form is unknown, but by comparison with those found in Palestinian excavations or used in other religions they can be pictured as either decorated rods ending in a small hand-shaped bowl or as wide shovels with a short handle,

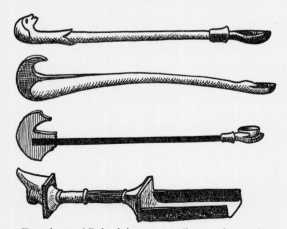

Egyptian and Palestinian censers (incense-burners).

the aromatic substance for burning being placed with the glowing charcoal.

An angel appears in the Apocalypse carrying a golden censer which he throws on the earth, filled with fire from the altar, [3] and there are also golden bowls full of incense, i.e., patens (receptacles with handles) which could be incense-burners. [4]

[1] 2 Chr. 26. 19; Ez. 8. 11. [2] Num. 16. 6; etc.; Lev. 10. 1; 16. 12. [3] Rev. 8. 3, 5. [4] Rev. 5. 8.

CENTURION

This Roman officer was in command of a century, normally a hundred men. Five or six centuries formed a cohort*, and ten cohorts a legion; there were, then, fifty to sixty centuries to a legion. The rank of centurion corresponded, more or less, to that of captain in our modern armies. The centurions mentioned in the N.T. are all sympathetic officers, from the one in Capernaum whose servant is cured by Jesus [1] to the one named Julius to whom St Paul is entrusted during his voyage to Rome, [2] without forgetting the various centurions who took part in the apostle's arrest, [3] and above all the one who was not afraid to pay homage to the crucified Christ at Golgotha, [4] as well as the pious and charitable Cornelius who was baptized by Peter. [5]

There were also commanders of hundreds in the Israelite army; [6] they are especially mentioned in the Books of Chronicles in the reigns of David, Solomon, Joash, and Ahaziah. [7]

[1] Matt. 8. 5–13; Lk. 7. 1–10. [2] Acts 27. [3] Acts 22. 25; 23. 17, 23; 24. 23. [4] Matt. 27. 54; Mk. 15. 39, 44–45; Lk. 23. 47. [5] Acts 10. [6] Num. 31. 14 . . .; 1 Sam. 22. 7; 2 Sam. 18. 1. [7] 1 Chr. 13. 1; 26. 26; 27. 1; 28. 1; 29. 6; 2 Chr. 1. 2; 23. 1, 9 . . .; 25. 5.

CHAINS (FETTERS)

A whole series of texts in the O.T. and the N.T. speak in concrete and figurative terms of these instruments of captivity. Long before iron was used, chains were made of bronze, as one of the Hebrew words for them shows—and the grammatical form of this word (dual) shows that they were double, that is, they were meant to bind both feet and hands, whereas others bound the hands only. [1] In the figurative sense, chains are naturally the symbol of enslavement and captivity. [2] From the Acts of the Apostles, we know that the apostles Peter and Paul suffered this punishment; in prison Peter was flanked by two soldiers to whom he was probably chained, according to Roman custom; [3] Paul, at the time of his arrest, perhaps in the same way, was bound by two chains to which he refers in his speech to Agrippa. Later, in Rome, while enjoying some freedom, he undoubtedly remained bound to his guard. [4]

From the Gospel we know that certain demoniacs were bound; [5] the Epistle to the Hebrews commemorates the martyrs who were subject to fetters (bonds);[6] Jude declares that the bad angels are chained in darkness,[7] and the poet of Revelation sees an angel descend from heaven with a great chain in his hand, seize Satan, the Dragon, and bind him for a thousand years.[8]

[1] Jg. 16. 21; 2 Kgs. 25. 7; 2 Chr. 36. 6; Ps. 105. 18; Jer. 39. 7; 52. 11; etc. [2] 2 Sam. 3. 34; Job 36. 8; Ps. 107. 10; Lam. 3. 7. [3] Acts 12. 6. [4] Acts 21. 33; 22. 30; 26. 29; 28. 20; cf. Eph. 6. 20, etc. [5] Mk. 5. 3–4; Lk. 8. 29. [6] Heb. 11. 36. [7] Jude 6. [8] Rev. 20. 1–3.

CHAINS

Among the trinkets with which Israelite women liked to adorn themselves, chains [1] must be mentioned; they were worn as necklaces*, and bracelets* on the wrist or upper arm (though this custom has been contested, because no chain bracelets have been discovered in excavations and because they are rare in Egypt), as well as with the rings which were worn round the ankles; [2] but the most elegant chains, still common in Palestine today, were fastened at the temples, hanging down both sides of the face, below the chin or down to the chest.[3]

[1] Num. 31. 50. [2] Num. 31. 50; Is. 3. 19–20. [3] Cant. 1. 10–11.

CHALCEDONY

The third of the foundations of the New Jerusalem, according to Revelation,[1] is of chalcedony. This consists of crystallized quartz and silica; several varieties of different colours are recognized. It has been claimed that the Bible writer was thinking of a kind of (green) emerald which came from the copper mines of Chalcedon (an ancient city on the Bosphorus), but this is only hypothetical and cannot be established.

[1] Rev. 21. 19.

CHAMELEON

Lev. 11. 30 mentions five unclean animals which cannot be identified with certainty; the majority of translators regard the fifth one as the chameleon, which is very common in Palestine, while others think the mole is meant, though this is never found there.

CHAMOIS

Some versions, e.g., Luther, Ostervald, translate by chamois [1] the Hebrew name of an animal which is no doubt the ibex (wild goat*). The chamois does not exist, and has never existed, in Palestine.

[1] 1 Sam. 24. 2; Job 39. 1; Ps. 104. 18.

CHANCELLOR

Some translators give this name to two kinds of Israelite officials who might have been archivists,[1] on

the one hand, or scribes or secretaries,[2] on the other. —Luther styles as "chancellor" the magistrate (*grammateus*, secretary, town-clerk) who restored peace at Ephesus at the time of the riot aroused against St Paul.[3]

[1] 2 Sam. 8. 16; 20. 24; 1 Kgs. 4. 3; etc. [2] 2 Sam. 20. 25; 2 Kgs. 18. 18; etc. [3] Acts 19. 35.

CHARCOAL

In the Bible, whenever coals are mentioned, charcoal is meant, since coal was unknown in Palestine in those times. Hebrew has three words, to signify black charcoal, glowing coals, and half-burnt embers. The texts allude, for instance, to the bread being baked, to the cauldron being heated [1] over a glowing fire, to the charcoal used by the blacksmith, and to the broom, the roots of which give a charcoal of high calorific value; [2] this is still sold today by some Arabs. Charcoal was also burnt in the braziers used for heating.[3] The Gospel of John speaks of charcoal fires, one warming those grouped around it, another used for cooking fish.[4]

Many texts mention the glowing or dead embers in a figurative sense, in various metaphors.[5] And the typical expression "to heap burning coals on his head", used in Proverbs and quoted by St Paul,[6] has become proverbial. The Arabs have analogous sayings; for them, for instance, great anxieties are "burning coals of the heart".

In Is. 6. 6 and 1 Kgs. 19. 6, contrary to certain translations, a "glowing stone" is really meant.

[1] Is. 44. 19; Ez. 24. 11. [2] Ps. 120. 4; cf. Prov. 26. 21; Is. 44. 12; 54. 16. [3] Jer. 36. 22. [4] Jn. 18. 18; 21. 9. [5] 2 Sam. 14. 7; Job 41. 21; Ps. 18. 8, 12; 120. 4; 140. 11; Prov. 6. 28; 25. 22; Is. 7. 4; Ez. 1. 13; 10. 2; Amos 4. 11; Zech. 3. 2. [6] Prov. 25. 22; Rom. 12. 20.

CHARIOT

The chariot for war (hunting, racing, or parades) must be distinguished from the cart (for transport or travel).

Since asses and camels were available, carts for carrying merchandise or passengers were rather rare, not only in the mountains of Palestine but also along the banks of the Nile and the Euphrates. The O.T. mentions, among others, the carts sent from Egypt to carry back the wives and children of Jacob's sons and the patriarch himself; [1] those which were used to transport the Ark when it was returned by the Philistines, and later brought to Jerusalem; [2] the litters (or covered carts) offered at the dedication of the Tabernacle; the cart loaded with sheaves (?) used metaphorically by Amos, and those pictured by Isaiah for the return of the dispersed Jews.[3]—In the N.T. the Acts of the Apostles says that an Ethiopian official was returning to his own country from

Jerusalem, seated in his chariot reading the prophet Isaiah.[4]

These vehicles were of wood, since they could be burnt; among the Israelites they were drawn by oxen or by servants,[5] elsewhere by mules or horses. Thanks to Hittite, Egyptian, and Assyrian pictures of these vehicles, we find that they had a flat base, carried on two or four solid or spoked wheels; some had closed-in sides, some had lattice work. Passengers sat on seats or on the bundles of merchandise which were being carried.

Most of the vehicles mentioned in the O.T., however, were chariots for war or parade. The texts refer to those of the Egyptians [6] and of the Pharaoh,[7] to those of the Canaanites,[8] and, later (not to mention other Asiatic neighbours, Philistines, Hittites, Syrians, etc.), to those of the Assyro-Babylonians.[9] Still rare in Israel at the time of David, war chariots

Hand-drawn chariot (Assyrian bas-relief).

became very important from the beginning of Solomon's reign, even though a great part of Palestine was unsuited to their use; although in his father's time, it seems that only the royal princes, Absalom and Adonijah, allowed themselves the luxury of chariots and horses,[10] which were preceded by runners, Solomon provided the army with hundreds of chariots, and thousands of horses* imported from abroad at great cost to pull them; the horses from Cilicia, undoubtedly, and the chariots from Egypt. He stationed them for strategic reasons in a few chosen towns.[11] From that time onwards, though they did not always retain the same importance, military chariots continued to have special attention lavished on them by Israelite kings, particularly those of the Northern Kingdom; from an Assyrian inscription, we know that Ahab placed 2,000 chariots at the disposal of the princes who attacked Shalmaneser in 854 B.C. Generally the prophets were opposed to these armaments, especially at the time when the kings of Judah, with the object of increasing the

restricted number of their chariots, tried to form an alliance with Egypt, which was always well equipped with them: "Woe," says Isaiah, "to those who go down to Egypt for help, who rely on horses, who trust in chariots because they are many . . . and who do not look to the Holy One of Israel." [12]

We know from the pictures on the monuments of

Assyrian parade chariot. 8th century.

antiquity that war chariots and those generally used by the kings of Israel and their principal officers [13] were mounted on wheels with spokes; they were open at the back and more or less open at the sides where the lance and quiver were placed; their lightness allowed great speeds to be reached, though they had bronze or iron armour plating (chariots fitted with

Assyrian war chariot. 7th century.

scythe blades were used only from the time of Cyrus), or were sometimes richly ornamented. The platform on which the occupants stood was often made of a framework surrounding a webbing of cord or straps which deadened the jolts. At the end of the shaft, a sort of yoke lay across the necks of the two horses; they were guided by the driver at whose side stood the fighting man, and perhaps one or two soldiers—shield-bearers—joined the other two. On parade

70

chariots the principal personage was often accompanied by a servant carrying a sunshade or a fan.

In the figurative sense the chariot conveys the idea of power and glory: Yahweh makes the clouds his chariot; even better, his chariots are counted in thousands of thousands.[14]—Elijah carried away in a "chariot of fire" is called—Elisha too—"the chariot of Israel and its horsemen".[15]

There is also the vision of Elisha's servant and Josiah's destruction of the chariots of the sun, which were probably used in idolatrous processions.[16]

[1] Gen. 45. 19; 46. 5. [2] 1 Sam. 6. 7; etc.; 2 Sam. 6. 3. [3] Amos 2. 13; Is. 66. 20. [4] Acts 8. 28. [5] Jos. 11. 6; 2 Sam. 24. 22; Is. 5. 18. [6] Ex. 14. 7, 9; etc.; 2 Kgs. 18. 24; 2 Chr. 12. 3; Jer. 46. 9; etc. [7] Gen. 41. 43; 46. 29; Cant. 1. 9. [8] Jos. 11. 4, 6; 17. 18; Jg. 1. 19; 4. 3; 5. 28; etc. [9] 2 Kgs. 19. 23; Jer. 50. 37; 51. 21; Ez. 23. 24; 26. 7; etc. Cf. Rev. 18. 13. [10] 2 Sam. 15. 1; 1 Kgs. 1. 5. [11] 1 Kgs. 9. 19; 10. 26–29; 2 Chr. 1. 14; 8. 6; 9. 25. [12] Is. 31. 1; Hos. 1. 7; 14. 3; Mic. 5. 10; Zech. 9. 10; cf. Dt. 17. 16; etc. [13] 1 Kgs. 12. 18; 18. 45; 20. 33; 22. 35; 2 Kgs. 8. 21; 9. 20, 21; etc. [14] Ps. 68. 17; 104. 3; Is. 19. 1; 66. 15; cf. 1 Chr. 28. 18. [15] 2 Kgs. 2. 11–12; 13. 14. [16] 2 Kgs. 6. 17; 23. 11.

CHEESE

Cheese was known from very early times, and the Hebrew nomads probably made it, although no text in the Pentateuch alludes to this substance. On the other hand, Jesse, the father of David, sent to the officer under whose orders his sons were serving a present of ten cheeses,[1] perhaps soft cheeses; the exact words are "ten slices [or pieces] of milk". Some "cheeses of cows" were offered to David at Mahanaim for his refreshment at the time of his flight beyond the Jordan.[2] The third and last passage speaks of cheese in a metaphorical sense: [3] "Hast thou not poured me out as milk, and curdled me like cheese?" says Job to God.

The valley running along the western side of the hill of Zion bore the name of the Tyropoeon Valley, i.e., the valley of the cheese makers; but this is probably a deformation of an earlier name.

[1] 1 Sam. 17. 18. [2] 2 Sam. 17. 29. [3] Job 10. 10.

CHERETHITES and PELETHITES

In David's time the royal guard was called the Cherethites and Pelethites.[1] It has been thought that the king made use of the service of Philistine mercenaries: the Cherethites are said to have belonged to a Philistine clan whose name might be connected with that of Crete, according to one hypothesis, whence the Philistines may perhaps have originated.[2] Pelethites could refer to another Philistine clan and might be a corruption of the Hebrew *Pelištim* (Philistines). But it might be more correct to connect Pelethite with Peleth,[3] a clan living in the south of Judah. At Ziklag [4] David made contact with these

people and might have recruited from them soldiers who were particularly seasoned fighters.

[1] 1 Sam. 30. 14; 2 Sam. 8. 18; 15. 18; 20. 7, 23; 1 Kgs. 1. 38, 44. [2] Ez. 25. 16; Zeph. 2. 5. [3] 1 Chr. 2. 33. [4] 1 Sam. 27. 6 . . .; 30. 1 . . ., 26; 2 Sam. 1. 1.

CHERUBIM

These mysterious celestial beings, of which it is difficult to gain a clear idea from Biblical texts, have no connection whatever with the pretty winged heads of children, with fresh pink complexions, made familiar by the works of the great painters. Majestic and strange creatures, the cherubim evoked an idea of strength rather than beauty. Did they have, to the eyes of those who speak of them, human, animal, or half-animal form? The O.T. writers given no precise information and only describe them as having wings. Ezekiel, however, declares that the cherubim adorning the temple of his vision had two faces; "the face of a man turned one way" and "the face of a lion turned the other way"; those which he attempts to describe in the visions in chaps. 1 and 10 are still more complex, having four faces—of a man, a lion, an ox, and an eagle; human hands appear beneath their four wings, they have calves' feet and their whole body is covered with eyes.

The cherubim were probably of Babylonian origin; their Hebrew name *kerûb* is obviously connected with the Accadian *kâribu*. The *kâribu* is a god or intercessory genie belonging to the well-known category of winged bulls and lions, which were set up at the doors of temples or palaces in Mesopotamia; it is distinguished from them in that its functions are not so much those of guardian as of intermediary

Nephthys, a winged Egyptian goddess.

between men and the deity which it adores and prays to perpetually. Clad at first in human form, apparently, it was later provided with wings, varying in number, to become in time a hybrid creature: head and shoulders of a man on the body of a winged quadruped. The Egyptian goddess Nephthys was not unknown in Palestine, and even in Damascus, where her image has been found; she is usually represented in the form of a woman who spreads out protective wings with a broad gesture. The religious role ascribed to her was not dissimilar from that of the Accadian *kâribu*, and this also applies to the two-headed genie whose image has been discovered on a bas-relief at Carchemish. It is certain that these ideas

Double-headed genie discovered at Carchemish.

and imagery exerted, directly or indirectly, an influence on the Biblical *kerûb*, which might have been originally a human being furnished with a pair of wings, but which developed rapidly and was transformed until it assumed the fabulous appearance described by Ezekiel.

Examples of Kâribu, or winged genie.

The lid of the Ark* of the Covenant bore two golden cherubim at its ends,[1] and Solomon had two immense cherubim of wild olive made for the Temple at Jerusalem; they were 16 ft. high, covered with gold, and were meant to protect the Ark.[2] Throughout the sanctuary, the cherubim motif, alternating

with palms and flowers, decorated the walls of the rooms,[3] certain doors,[4] and even the veil of the Holy of Holies.[5] Together with lions, bulls, and palms, cherubim decorated the panels of the wheeled lavers which the priests used in their duties in the Temple.[6] The hangings of the Tabernacle, too, were enhanced with cherubim,[7] and in Ezekiel's Temple there were many more.[8] It is in this prophet's book that cherubim are the object of the most highly developed references. Psalm 18 speaks in a curious way of Yahweh flying on a cherub,[9] which may here personify the storm-cloud, whereas elsewhere vaguer reference is made to Yahweh as seated on the cherubim, or enthroned between them.[10]—Cherubim, placed to the east of the garden of Eden, guarded the way to the tree of life.[11]

The four nameless beasts of Revelation[12] were more probably seraphim*; in the N.T. only one passage in the Epistle to the Hebrews recalls "the glorious cherubim which cover the mercy seat with their shadow".[13]

From these texts it follows that the functions of these marvellous beings were varied, since they are sometimes the bearers of Yahweh and his throne, sometimes guardians of sacred places and objects, sometimes the symbols of uninterrupted prayer.

[1] Ex. 25. 18–22; 37. 7–9; Num. 7. 89. [2] 1 Kgs. 6. 23–28; 8. 7. [3] 1 Kgs. 6. 29. [4] 1 Kgs. 6. 32, 35. [5] 2 Chr. 3. 14. [6] 1 Kgs. 7. 29. [7] Ex. 26. 1, 31; 36. 8, 35. [8] Ez. 41. 18–25. [9] Ps. 18. 10 (2 Sam. 22. 11). [10] Ps. 80. 1; 99. 1; 1 Sam. 4. 4; 2 Sam. 6. 2; etc. [11] Gen. 3. 24. [12] Rev. 4. 8. [13] Heb. 9. 5.

CHEST

Apart from the Ark* of the Covenant, which has in Hebrew the name coffer or chest (*'arôn*), objects of this kind are mentioned only in connection with the mortal remains of Joseph, which were placed in a chest, i.e., in a mummy-chest or coffin,[1] and the collecting box or money-box (*'arôn*) with an opening in the lid, installed near the altar in the time of Jehoash (Joash) for receiving gifts.[2]—The royal treasury (*genez*) mentioned in the Book of Esther[3] was not necessarily a chest. The text of Ez. 27. 24, which the majority of versions take as chests (*genez*) for materials or clothes, is not certain; and we do not know exactly the nature of the receptacle in which the Philistines placed their expiatory gifts that accompanied the Ark of Yahweh on its return to Israel[4]—though it could well be a casket.

[1] Gen. 50. 26. [2] 2 Kgs. 12. 9; 2 Chr. 24. 8. [3] Est. 3. 9; 4. 7. [4] 1 Sam. 6. 8, 11, 15.

CHESTNUT

Some translators (Luther, etc.) think that this tree figures in Genesis and in Ezekiel,[1] but the unanimous opinion of modern versions (and of the Vulgate) is that the plane* tree is meant. The chestnut is not found in the lists of Palestine trees drawn up by experts.

[1] Gen. 30. 37; Ez. 31. 8.

CHILD

For the Israelite, children are a blessing and one kind of wealth: "Like arrows in the hand of a warrior are the sons of one's youth. Happy is the man who has his quiver full of them. He will not be put to shame when he talks with his enemies in the gate." [1] A fine progeny, indeed, not only provided for the father valuable help for his work but also increased his prestige and his authority in the community. Similarly, barrenness in a wife was a great misfortune, which she could remedy by giving her personal servant to her husband as a concubine: the latter's children were considered as the wife's children. [2]

Sons and daughters were the father's absolute property: he could dispose of them at will, [3] he had the right to sell them if need be, [4] and in the earliest times to kill them if they were guilty of a serious fault; [5] later, in similar circumstances, the sanction of the town's elders was necessary, according to rule. [6] The Deuteronomic Law condemns the unruly and rebellious son to death, [7] and like the Code of the Covenant, [8] the Priestly Law states clearly that "everyone who curses his father or mother shall be put to death; he has cursed his father or mother, his blood is upon him" [9] (he alone will be responsible for his own death). But the law and the prophets always condemned child-sacrifice, which was a common practice among Israel's neighbours. [10]

Daughters did not have privileges equal to those of sons, who assured the father's posterity; at marriage, the daughters passed to another family, and so had no share in their father's property († inheritance). The eldest son, on the other hand, the firstfruits of the father's vigour, benefited from a double share († birthright). In cases of twin births, great care was always taken to distinguish the child who had come first into the world. [11] The eldest son belonged to Yahweh, moreover, and five shekels had to be paid to redeem him. [12]

Like present-day Bedouin women, Israelite women gave birth easily [13] (see, however, Gen. 3. 16; 35. 16; Hos. 13. 13); but on occasion they had recourse to midwives, who are mentioned in the Pentateuch. [14] The father did not attend the child's birth; [15] certain Semites hold that it would be shameful for them to be present. For forty days after a boy's birth, and eighty days after a girl's, the Israelite woman was considered as unclean. [16] Here again analogous customs can be found in more than one people. For purification she had to offer a special sacrifice. [17]

A boy's birth was generally greeted with more joy than a girl's, but there was no question in Israel of getting rid of daughters or unwanted children by the barbarous practice of "exposure", to which there is only one Biblical reference—in Ezekiel. [18] On the contrary, the child was surrounded with the greatest care, bathed, rubbed with salt (to be strengthened or perhaps made immune to demonic powers), then wrapped in swaddling clothes. [19] A name was then given by the father, [20] or by the mother. [21] This name —very important, for it was thought to constitute a part of the person—was sometimes a reminder of the circumstances preceding or accompanying the birth, or was a kind of luck-bringer; for reasons easily understood, it often had connections with the name of the deity (theophoric names); but in the course of time certain names continued to be used by tradition and quite independently of their first significance.

Eight days after birth boys were circumcised († circumcision). Normally the mother suckled her child, [22] only in exceptional circumstances was it entrusted to a wet-nurse. [23] Breast-feeding was prolonged for many months, even for two or three years, as is often the custom in the East, even today. A happy feast, accompanied by a sacrifice, often marked the weaning. [24]

The mother attended carefully to the children, who depended on her in their early years. Only God's love surpasses that of a mother: "Can a woman forget her sucking child, that she should not have compassion on the son of her womb? yea, these may forget, yet will not I forget thee." [25] Though the daughter remained with her mother until her marriage, helping in the household tasks or looking after the flock, [26] the boys joined their father, who initiated them into his trade or in the work of the countryside, and they soon became his fellow workers. [27] In wealthy families the children were entrusted to preceptors or tutors. [28]

True Israelites gave great importance to the moral and religious education of their children; it was more important than ordinary instruction. The fathers loved to tell of the great things that Yahweh had done for his people, they made much of explaining the meaning of the different feasts, and sacred customs, [29] they wrote the commandments of the Law on their hearts. [30] "Train up a child in the way he should go: and when he is old, he will not depart from it." [31] It is a fact that Israelite education was rather stern: "He who spares the rod hates his son," [32] says the Book of Proverbs; "If you beat him with a rod he will not die" [33] (or perhaps, more exactly, his faults will not lead him to an early death). "Folly is anchored in the heart of a child, the rod of discipline drives it far from him." [34] († whip.)

Yet paternal and maternal affection was not stinted for the children who were worthy of it. [35] They also knew the joy of relaxation and amusement: the prophet Zechariah pictures the streets of Jerusalem alive with the romps of boys and girls, [36] and Jesus refers to the games of children who imitate

CHISEL

adults and reproduce the noisy exhibitions which accompany weddings and funerals.[37] In excavations, children's toys, and particularly rattles and little animals of clay, have been found.

For instruction, see school*, pastimes*.

Filial devotion was held in high honour among the Israelites [38]—the Talmud is rich in typical anecdotes which illustrate this—and parents considered it as an essential task to procure good marriages for their sons and daughters. The happiness of the children makes that of the parents: "Children's children are the crown of the aged, and fathers are the glory of their children." [39]

It is known how sacred childhood was in the eyes of Jesus, how strongly he rose against those who outraged it, and how warmly he welcomed little children whom he presented as models to those aspiring to the Kingdom of Heaven.[40]

[1] Ps. 127. 4, 5. [2] Gen. 16. 2; 30. 3. [3] Gen. 22; Jg. 11. 34 . . .; 13. 7; 1 Sam. 1. 11. [4] Ex. 21. 7. [5] Gen. 38. 24 (42. 37); Zech. 13. 3 (Prov. 19. 18). [6] Dt. 21. 19. [7] Dt. 21. 18–21. [8] Ex. 21. 15, 17. [9] Lev. 20. 9 [10] Lev. 18. 21; 20. 2–5; Jer. 32. 35; Ez. 16. 20. [11] Gen. 25. 25; 38. 28. [12] Num. 18. 16; Lk. 2. 23, 24. [13] Ex. 1. 19. [14] Gen. 35. 17; 38. 28; Ex. 1. 15. [15] Jer. 20. 15. [16] Lev. 20. 15. [17] Lev. 12. 6–8. [18] Ez. 16. 5. [19] Ez. 16. 4, 5; Job 38. 9. [20] Gen. 4. 26; 5. 3, 29; 21. 3; 41. 51; 2 Sam. 12. 24; etc. [21] Gen. 4. 25; 29. 32; 38. 4; 1 Sam. 1. 20; etc. [22] Gen. 21. 7; 1 Sam. 1. 22. [23] Gen. 24. 59; 2 Kgs. 11. 2. [24] Gen. 21. 8. [25] Is. 49. 15. [26] Gen. 24. 11; 29. 6; Ex. 2. 16; 1 Sam. 9. 11. [27] 1 Sam. 16. 11; Matt. 21. 28 . . .; Lk. 15. 29. [28] 2 Kgs. 10. 1; 1 Chr. 27. 32. [29] Ex. 13. 8; Dt. 4. 10; 11. 19; Jos. 4. 6, 21; Ps. 78. 5, 6. [30] Dt. 6. 7, 20; Prov. 4. 3, 4. [31] Prov. 22. 6. [32] Prov. 13. 24. [33] Prov. 23. 13; 29. 17. [34] Prov. 22. 15; cf. Ecclus. 30. 9–13. [35] Gen. 22. 7; 37. 3, 35; 43. 14; 44. 20 . . .; 1 Sam. 1. 27; 2 Kgs. 4. 17 . . .; Lam. 2. 11, 19; 4. 4; 5. 13; etc. [36] Zech. 8. 5. [37] Matt. 11. 16, 17. [38] Ex. 20. 12; Lev. 19. 3; Prov. 1. 8; 6. 20; 23. 22; 28. 24; Eph. 6. 1–3. [39] Prov. 17. 6. [40] Matt. 11. 25; 18. 2–6; 19. 13–15; Mk. 9. 36–37; 10. 13–16; Lk. 9. 47–48; 10. 21; 18. 15–17.

CHISEL

This tool is mentioned only once in the Bible: the carpenter uses it for carving idols; [1] but the "knife" (or sword; R.V., tool) or iron of Ex. 20. 25 (cf. Dt. 27. 5 and Jos. 8. 31) is also a chisel, since it is used for cutting stone.

[1] Is. 44. 13.

CHISLEV

This was the name [1] given to the ninth month of the Jewish civil year (= November–December). The Feast of the Dedication* is celebrated during it.

[1] Neh. 1. 1; Zech. 7. 1.

CHOENIX

The choenix is a Greek measure of capacity equal to 1·9 pints. It is mentioned in Revelation,[1] but our versions translate this technical word merely by "measure". To say that a choenix of wheat was sold for a denarius ("penny") is to point to a great dearth, because a denarius was a workman's daily pay.[2]

[1] Rev. 6. 6. [2] Matt. 20. 2.

CHRYSOLITE

This is the first precious stone of the fourth row of the High Priest's breastplate (Ex. 28. 20: R.V. beryl; mg. chalcedony). Its Hebrew name appears to indicate its place of origin: it is an abbreviation for "stone of Taršiš" or "Tartessus", a town in the south of Spain. It is a greenish-yellow quartz, also mentioned in other O.T. texts.[1]—The seventh foundation of the New Jerusalem is adorned with chrysolite,[2] which some say is the Oriental topaz of today.

[1] Cant. 5. 14; Ez. 1. 16; 28. 13; Dan. 10. 6. [2] Rev. 21. 20.

CHRYSOPRASE

This precious stone is a variety of chalcedony of a greenish white touched with yellow. The tenth foundation of the New Jerusalem is adorned with it.[1]

[1] Rev. 21. 20.

CINNAMON

The best, genuine cinnamon came from the inner bark of the cinnamon tree, a kind of aromatic laurel which grew in south-east Arabia and in Ceylon. It was used in the preparation of holy oil,[1] and it is

Cinnamon (*Cinnamomum cassia*).

mentioned as a perfume by Proverbs and Revelation.[2] The beloved in the Song of Songs is compared with a cinnamon tree growing in a garden.[3] Today in botany "cinnamon" is used for the group of *Lauraceae* to which belong also camphor and cassia*, etc.

[1] Ex. 30. 23. [2] Prov. 7. 17; Rev. 18. 13. [3] Cant. 4. 14.

CIRCUMCISION

A week after birth all male Israelite children were circumcised,[1] which is a minor surgical operation (removal of the foreskin). Every Israelite had the power to perform this operation, but as a rule it was the head of the family who undertook it; [2] a wife had no authority to perform the task, though in an emergency she could act in the place of her husband.[3] Later, a doctor's help was countenanced; among Jews today, a special official is responsible. Because of its importance, circumcision was permitted on the Sabbath day: [4] "Circumcision sets the Sabbath aside," says a proverb. At this event a name was finally given to the child.[5]

Circumcision is a custom by no means restricted to the Israelites; it exists among several African racial groups, and it is found also in Oceania, South America, and in Asia; there are probably 200 millions of circumcised in the world today. For the Koran, circumcision is such an old and well-established custom that no mention is made of it.

As is shown by examining mummies and certain bas-reliefs in which this operation is depicted, circumcision was known among the Egyptians from the very earliest times. The majority of Israel's neighbours had practised it for varying lengths of time (Midianites, Edomites, Ammonites, Phoenicians, Canaanites); on the other hand, the Babylonians and Assyrians were ignorant of it. But the Philistines were the uncircumcised *par excellence* to the Israelites,[6] for whom the term "uncircumcised" was, moreover, a deadly insult.

The problem of the origins of circumcision is very complex. It is true that it is a very ancient custom, perhaps of African origin. Its antiquity is shown by the use of stone knives for the operation,[7] a custom that persisted for a long time. How was the rite introduced into Israel? It is generally admitted today—though the opinion is not beyond doubt—that the O.T. probably contains three traditional explanations: according to one, circumcision was probably adopted only when the Israelites settled in Canaan (cf. Jos. 5. 2–9, where the original text may have been edited to harmonize it with the other versions); the second source, a very old one, claims that circumcision was a rite borrowed from the Midianites at the time of Moses, since the great prophet was himself uncircumcised; [8] according to a third account, a much later one, but whose author was aware of the pre-Mosaic origin of circumcision, God ordained it to Abraham when the covenant was first made.[9] These variations of the tradition would be quite well explained if circumcision, coming from Africa, had spread via Egypt among the Semites in the Syro-Arabian region as well as among certain Hebraic tribes, finally to become general throughout Israel.

In any event, circumcision did not become firmly established in Israel until after the entry into Canaan. But for a long time it seems to have had a social rather than a religious character: since other nations submitted to it, it could not be the distinguishing sign of Israel; the prophets draw no distinction between the circumcision of their co-religionists and that of other peoples; for them, real circumcision is a wholly moral one—of the heart.[10] The ancient Israelite laws do not speak of the custom, possibly because it was taken for granted, since it was generally observed, and there was therefore no need to legislate on the subject.

Circumcision became a national and religious symbol at the time of the Exile, when the Jews found themselves in daily contact with the uncircumcised peoples of Mesopotamia and Persia. At that time it became, and was to remain increasingly, the sign of belonging to Yahweh, the outward mark, branded in the flesh, of the covenant with God; the more so because, at about the same time, circumcision tended to disappear among the Phoenicians and elsewhere. An uncircumcised Jew was to be cut off from the people,[11] and the slave and foreigner were able to share in the Passover only if they had allowed themselves to be circumcised.[12]

Greek and Roman civilization did not make the Jews give up the custom; it was ineradicable, even though it was a cause of embarrassment to some young men in the gymnasia and public baths.[13] When Antiochus Epiphanes thought he was capable of forbidding the practice, mothers allowed themselves to be put to death rather than give up the circumcision of their sons.[14] Though John the Baptist and Jesus were circumcised according to the Law,[15] it is known that a serious disagreement divided the early Christian: the Christians of Judaea could not conceive of being converted to the gospel without submitting to the Law; all St Paul's tenacity and courage were necessary to prevent circumcision from being made a condition of membership of the Church.[16] Today only the Christians of Abyssinia and the Coptic Church have retained circumcision, without, however, giving it a religious significance.

Although the significance of circumcision among the Jews is very clear in the later period, and it is for them an act of ritual purification as well as the sign of a sacred covenant with God and of membership of the chosen people, it is very difficult to know what was thought about it at other times, what it originally meant. It has been argued (as early as Herod) that it answered needs of a hygienic character, that it was a rite to assure fertility (cf. the "uncircumcised trees" of Lev. 19. 23), or a substitute for child-sacrifice, etc. It is more likely that circumcision was in principle a rite of puberty, a rite of transition: by this act the adolescent passed into the ranks of the adults of the tribe, of the members of the clan, and was then in a position to marry. We cannot list here the arguments showing that circumcision has close connections with sexual life (cf. e.g., Gen. 34. 14–17). By practising the rite on children, it was desired to give them as early as possible the benefit of membership of the tribe. It has even been thought that the text Ex. 4. 24–26 might explain how circumcision came to be performed on children rather than on adults. Then as the rite introduced boys into the social and religious group, a purely religious ceremony for girls was introduced in order to bring them too into the Israelite community. This, like the name given to children, relates circumcision to the Christian baptism of children.

Metaphorically, the O.T. and the N.T. speak, as already mentioned, of the uncircumcision of the heart; [17] or of uncircumcised ears and lips,[18] that is, incapable of attention or without eloquence.

[1] Gen. 17. 12; Lev. 12. 3; Phil. 3. 5. [2] Gen. 17. 23. [3] Ex. 4. 25; 1 Macc. 1. 60. [4] Jn. 7. 23. [5] Lk. 1. 59; 2. 21. [6] Jg. 14. 3; 1 Sam. 18. 25; 31. 4; 2 Sam. 1. 20; etc. [7] Ex. 4. 25; Jos. 5. 2. [8] Ex. 4. 24–26. [9] Gen. 17. 10–14; cf. Jn. 7. 22; Acts 7. 8. [10] Jer. 4. 4; 9. 25–26; cf. Dt. 10. 16; 30. 6. [11] Gen. 17. 14. [12] Ex. 12. 44, 48. [13] Cf. 1 Macc. 1. 15. [14] 1 Macc. 1. 60; 2. 46. [15] Lk. 1. 59; 2. 21. [16] Acts 10. 28; 11. 3; 15. 1–34; Rom. 2. 25–29; 3. 30; 4. 9–12; 1 Cor. 7. 18–19; Gal. 2. 2–6; Phil. 3. 3–5; Col. 3. 11. [17] Lev. 26. 41; Dt. 10. 16; 30. 6; Jer. 4. 4; 9. 25–26; Ez. 44. 7, 9; Rom. 2. 29; Col. 2. 11; etc. [18] Ex. 6. 12, 30; Jer. 6. 10; Acts 7. 51.

CISTERN

Cisterns, for collecting rain-water [1]—in contrast with wells which reach down to a spring or an underground water supply—were originally dug into the rock [2] (limestone), but in time people learned how to make them in any kind of ground, by walling them carefully and by plastering them with a rendering of lime thickened with powdered sherds. They were of various shapes and sometimes of considerable size; many of them resembled enormous pears: the opening remained narrow and the cavity grew wider as the depth increased.

In the towns every important house had its own cistern; [3] the dream of a Palestinian was to drink water from his own cistern; "Make your peace with me," said the king of Assyria to the people of Jerusalem, "and every one of you will eat of his vine and fig tree, and every one of you will drink the water of his own cistern." [4] "Each of you make a cistern in his own house," says the king of Moab to the people of a town mentioned on the Mesha Stone. A number of cisterns have been found in excavations—the earliest dating from 1500 B.C.—and today they are still scattered widely throughout Palestine; the Syrian Orphanage in Jerusalem had forty-four such cisterns for its own use.

Ancient tombs were used as cisterns, which in their turn were used as tombs; sometimes corpses were more or less secretly disposed of in them.[5] When empty, though often muddy and fouled by all kinds

of impurities, they became refuges in times of war [6] or ready-made prisons, as is shown in the stories of Joseph and Jeremiah.[7]

As early as the Covenant Code, regulations were made with regard to negligent owners who might cause accidents through leaving their cisterns uncovered.[8] A fact to notice, explained by the scarcity of water, is that water was not made ritually unclean by the body of an animal falling into the cistern.[9]

Certain important cisterns, such as those at Bethlehem and Ramah,[10] are mentioned in the O.T. Also to be found in Palestine are grottoes or vast excavations which are used as reservoirs and sometimes contain pillars of rock, used at the time of digging for supporting the roof. One of the biggest of these excavations—with a large number of cisterns, some of them very old—is to be found under the esplanade where the Temple of Jerusalem used to stand; fed by canals which bring water from a great distance, it reaches a depth of 42 ft. and is more than 240 yds. in circumference; Tacitus speaks of it, and it was probably made earlier than the time of Herod the Great.

Jeremiah's metaphor about "cracked cisterns that do not hold water" has become proverbial.

[1] Jer. 14. 3. [2] Dt. 6. 11; Neh. 9. 25. [3] 2 Sam. 17. 18; Prov. 5. 15. [4] 2 Kgs. 18. 31; Is. 36. 16. [5] Jer. 41. 7. [6] 1 Sam. 13. 6. [7] Gen. 37. 20; Jer. 38. 6; cf. Zech. 9. 11. [8] Ex. 21. 33; cf. Lk. 14. 5. [9] Lev. 11. 36. [10] 1 Sam. 19. 22; 2 Sam. 3. 26; 2 Sam. 23. 15; cf. 2 Chr. 26. 10.

CITHARA

The Greek LXX version translated the Hebrew word *kinnôr* by *cithara*. It is obvious that we should accept this instead of harp*, as some versions do; better still, all confusion with other instruments is avoided by keeping the Hebrew word, as do some translations.

The *kinnôr* is a stringed instrument of which the O.T. gives no description. From certain Egyptian and Assyrian bas-reliefs, designs on some Greek vases, and certain Etruscan tomb paintings, we are able to see that it was made of a board, more or less rectangular, trapezium, or rhombus shaped; two slender, gracefully shaped wooden arms ran from this board, and their extremities were joined by a cross-strip called the yoke, to which the strings were attached. It is possible that in its primitive form this instrument was made from the skull of a stag or antelope, the horns of which were connected by a yoke.—The strings, made of sheep's gut, were sewn to strips of thick leather which were rolled round the yoke; they passed over a bridge which rested on the board, and at the end of the latter they were fixed to a small board grooved or pierced with fine holes.

More than one Bible text shows that the *kinnôr* could be played while walking.[1] The musician slipped the base of the instrument under his left elbow, which held it in place, while the right hand made the strings vibrate, either directly with the fingers or by means of a plectrum. The strings were exposed; and as there were only six or eight of them the accompaniment of the *kinnôr* could not be very varied. To enrich it the number of strings was increased, even to thirty, but it was difficult to attune

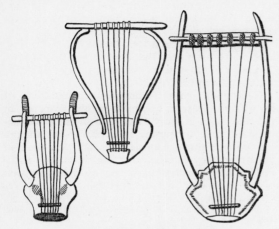

Kinnôrim after Greek and Etruscan paintings.

them. Sometimes two *kinnôrim* were used together, the musician resting the second instrument on his knees.

From the *kinnôr* was derived the lyre, which, judging from illustrations on coins, seems to have been used in the Israelite cult, and also the harp, which in any case was known in Egypt from the 12th century.

Tambourines and *kinnôrim* (Assyrian bas-relief).

Like the *kinnôr*, these two instruments had exposed strings.

This popular instrument,[2] the *cithara*, whose invention was attributed to Jubal, a descendant of Cain,[3] was not used for sad music but, on the contrary, in hours of rejoicing, because it gave a clear sound.[4] It was this instrument which David played before Saul to divert him.[5] It was employed on its own,[6] or along with other musical instruments.[7] It

77

was used for praise of Yahweh, but then it always accompanied the *nebel*, or the *nebel* and cymbals.[8]

The *cithara* is also mentioned in the N.T.;[9] but there again the versions speak of harps. († Music, instruments of.)

[1] Gen. 31. 27; 1 Sam. 10. 5; 2 Sam. 6. 5; Is. 23. 16. [2] Is. 5. 12; 23. 16; etc. [3] Gen. 4. 21. [4] Gen. 31. 27; Job 21. 12; 30. 31; Ps. 137. 2; Is. 24. 8. [5] 1 Sam. 16. 16, 23. [6] 1 Sam. 16. 16; Ps. 43. 4; 49. 4; 147. 7; Is. 16. 11; 23. 16. [7] Gen. 31. 27; 1 Sam. 10. 5; 2 Sam. 6. 5; 2 Chr. 20. 28; Job 21. 12; Ps. 98. 5; Is. 5. 12; Dan. 3. 5. [8] 1 Chr. 15. 16; 25. 1; 2 Chr. 9. 11; 29. 25; Neh. 12. 27; Ps. 33. 2; 57. 8; 71. 22; 108. 2. [9] 1 Cor. 14. 7; Rev. 5. 8; 14. 2; 15. 2.

CITRON

This 15- or 16-ft. tree produces a fruit related to the lemon, but larger and rougher. A century before the Christian era it was very common in Palestine: at the Feast of Tabernacles in Alexander Jannaeus' time the worshippers had their hands full of citrons, and they figured on coins in the Maccabaean age. It is

Citron (*Citrus medica*).

possible, but by no means certain, that the citron was referred to under the term "goodly tree" in Leviticus[1] (concerning the Feast of Tabernacles), just as the Jews of that time, and later times, thought. In any case, that identification would be preferable to one which regards the tree often translated by "apple"* or sometimes by "apricot"* as being a citron tree.

[1] Lev. 23. 40.

CITY and VILLAGE

The word "village" was reserved for a group of houses unprotected by any fortification, whereas the word "city" was used for places surrounded by a wall and dominated by a citadel.[1] In the event of war, the villagers took refuge in the city,[2] but in return the city levied a tax on the villagers. The name "mother"[3] was given to the city, and villages in its district were called its daughters; this metaphor is not conveyed in our versions, which interpret it as "village".[4]

The N.T. also draws a distinction between city and village; but it is no longer a strategic distinction; it is juridical: the city was a locality which had certain rights (especially in matters of justice), recognized by the Roman authorities and not possessed by villages.

CLASPS

Bethphage, Bethany, Bethlehem, and Emmaus [5] were villages, while Nazareth, Capernaum, and Nain were cities.[6]

There is no doubt that certain localities mentioned in the Biblical texts were of Canaanite or even of pre-Canaanite origin; Egyptian documents pre-dating the arrival of the Israelites mention a great number. However, other localities were formed under the monarchy,[7] and we know that certain kings founded cities for political reasons: Omri built Samaria, while Caesarea and Tiberias owed their origin to the Herods.

The name of certain localities alludes to their origin, situation, or reputation: such-and-such a village sited near a spring was called En-gedi (= goat-spring); a village tucked away among the green of fig trees was called Bethphage (= house of figs); near

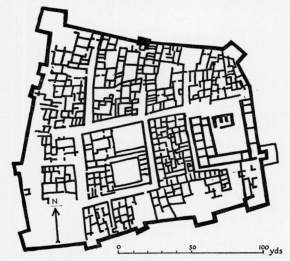

Plan of the city of Marisa in southern Judaea.

the Sea of Galilee there is Bethsaida (= house of fishing); surrounded by corn fields lies Bethlehem (= house of bread), and there is that city famous for its shrine, Bethel (= house of God), and finally Jerusalem itself whose name means "holy city".

Though a village occupied a very limited area, with small houses packed close together, this was even more true of the cities; streets there were narrow and tortuous, often ending in a cul-de-sac; they appear to have been unpaved, and they were extremely filthy: refuse was thrown down by all, and wild dogs acted as scavengers. At times the prophets allude to the mud in the streets.[8] No Public Cleansing Department! Yet at Gezer and Jericho short channels have been found; these were to drain water from the street and were made of bottomless water-pots, fitted inside one another.

There were no public squares († gate); business transactions [9] and official proclamations [10] took place before the city gate or gates, outside the boundaries; law suits were settled there too.[11] Certain gates took their names from these circumstances; in Jerusalem the Fish Gate [12] and the Sheep Gate [13] were so named because the fish and sheep markets were held there.

Formerly, as today (think of the *souks*, i.e. markets), tradesmen of the same kind lived in the same street. We know that in Jerusalem there was a street of bakers.[14]

At night the city gates were locked,[15] and sentries* kept watch all night. But the Psalmist knows that "unless the Lord watches over the city, the watchman stays awake in vain".[16]

Civilization, with its attendant temptations of luxury and pleasure, was more highly developed in the cities than in the villages, and the prophets denounced their corrupting influence.[17] But though the prophets threatened the cities, and Jerusalem in particular, they dreamed that she would be sanctified,[18] a hope which was taken up again in the vision of the "Holy City" in Revelation.[19]

[1] Lev. 25. 29. [2] Jer. 4. 5. [3] 2 Sam. 20. 19. [4] Num. 21. 25, 32; Jos. 15. 45; Jg. 11. 26. [5] Mk. 11. 2; Jn. 7. 42; etc. [6] Matt. 2. 23; 4. 13; etc. [7] 1 Kgs. 12. 25; 15. 17. [8] Is. 5. 25; 10. 6: Mic. 7. 10. [9] 2 Kgs. 7. 1; 2 Chr. 32. 6. [10] Jer. 17. 19; Dt. 21. 19. [11] Amos 5. 12, 15. [12] Neh. 3. 3; Zeph. 1. 10. [13] Neh. 3. 1, 32; 12. 39; Jn. 5. 2. [14] Jer. 37. 21. [15] Jos. 2. 5. [16] Ps. 127. 1. [17] Ez. 9. 9; 24. 6; etc. [18] Is. 1. 26; Ez. 24. 35; etc. [19] Rev. 21. 2 ff.

CLASPS

Gold or bronze clasps are mentioned in texts concerning the Tabernacle*; they were used to join the

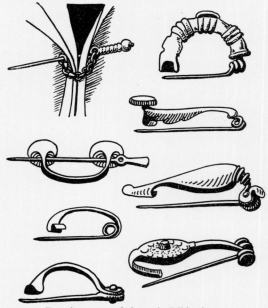

Development of clasps in Bible times.

curtains of this sanctuary.[1] Brooches also figure among the gold objects of Ex. 35. 22. Many fibulae and safety-pins of different styles have been found in Palestine and the Ras Shamra excavations. The earliest Palestinian fibulae go back to the 12th century B.C.; the largest number are post-Exilic.

[1] Ex. 26. 6, 11, etc.

CLAY

Clay, which is one of the earliest materials that man has worked, was used in Israel for making houses*, bricks*, moulds, and pottery*.[1] Consequently it is often mentioned in the O.T. The poem of Job states that man has been moulded like clay, and it compares the human body to a house of clay.[2]

Clay is found in several parts of Palestine, but particularly in the Jordan Valley.

[1] Job 4. 19; Ex. 1. 14; 1 Kgs. 7. 46; Is. 29. 16; Nahum 3. 14; Dan. 2. 33. [2] Job 10. 9; 4. 19, cf. 2 Cor. 5. 1; 4. 7.

CLUB

The LXX Greek translation, followed by some modern versions, has quite reasonably rendered by "club" a word used in Prov. 25. 18, which means, more exactly, the hammer* (of war). The club as such is probably mentioned only in the poem of Job: "The club seems to him [the crocodile] as straw, he laughs at the whizz of the javelin." [1]

[1] Job 41. 29.

COCK

Cocks and hens, which must have been acclimatized in Palestine by the end of the 2nd millennium, are not mentioned in the O.T.; even the laws about clean and unclean animals are silent on the subject. (It is true that some ancient translations have discovered the cock in Job 38. 36, Prov. 30. 31,

Cock engraved upon the seal of Jaazaniah (*Ya' azanyahû*). 6th century B.C.

and Is. 22. 17, but in the first two passages it is doubtful, and in the third unlikely, that this gallinacean appears. The translation "white of egg" in Job 6. 6 is also quite uncertain.) On the other hand, the cock is mentioned several times in the account of Peter's denial;[1] and Jesus takes a beautiful analogy from the hen's solicitude for her chicks.[2] It seems,

moreover, that by the time of Christ eggs had become a familiar food in Palestine.[3] Yet this was not the prime purpose for breeding fowls; it was really to provide cocks for awakening men early in the morning. For this reason the third watch of the night, from midnight to three a.m., was called "cockcrow".[4] Because of this function the cock became the symbol of watchfulness, and as such it was put on many church steeples. Probably for the same reason a leading Israelite, in the 6th century, had a cock engraved on his personal seal, underneath his name and title: Jaazaniah, servant of the king.[5] Certain catacomb paintings make it a resurrection symbol, by looking upon the night in which the cock announces the dawn as parallel to the times of religious obscurity in which the Christian faith proclaims the life of the world beyond.

We have no evidence that cock fights, already so dear to Greeks of the 5th century B.C., were known in Palestine.

[1] Matt. 26. 34, 74–75; Mk. 14. 30, 68, 72; Lk. 22. 34, 60–61; Jn. 13. 38; 18. 27. [2] Matt. 23. 37; Lk. 13. 34. [3] Lk. 11. 12. [4] Mk. 13. 35. [5] 2 Kgs. 25. 23.

COFFIN

Coffins were unknown in Israel; neither the O.T. nor the N.T. speaks of them. The corpse, wrapped in a shroud, was carried in a litter, a kind of stretcher or open bier,[1] and laid straight into the ground or rock, preferably in the family vault. Joseph alone, after his death in Egypt, was placed in a chest or coffin.[2] There is no question, for example, of a coffin

Sarcophagi found in Palestine.

at the time of the death of Lazarus or Jesus.—Excavations have shown that the remains of little children were often placed in pots, and in Palestine recently some specimens of a kind of clay sarcophagus have been found; the bodies were introduced through an opening, which was then closed with a lid nearly oval in shape; this was decorated with a mask conventionally outlining the features of the deceased, while the arms and hands were shown only in a rudimentary and grotesque manner, below the cheeks and chin. These "anthropoid sarcophagi", intended undoubtedly for non-Israelites, date from the end of the Bronze Age (12–13th centuries B.C.).

¹ 2 Sam. 3. 31; Lk. 7. 14. ² Gen. 50. 26.

COHORT

At the time of the Empire the cohort was a subdivision of the Roman legion; the legion contained ten cohorts. But the name cohort was also given to bodies of auxiliary infantry who were more lightly armed than the legionaries, and who served in the less-important provinces, like Judaea. These cohorts were commanded by tribunes or prefects, and were composed of five hundred to six hundred men divided into five or six centuries († centurion); others had a thousand men and ten centuries. Both types were formed either entirely of infantry or of infantry and cavalry.

There are several references in the N.T. to the Roman cohort which formed the garrison at Jerusalem, and which was stationed in the fortress of Antonia; it played a certain part in the arrest and trial of Jesus,¹ and later at the time of St Paul's arrest.² The centurion Cornelius belonged to a cohort named the "Italian", formed from Italian volunteers serving in Caesarea; ³ and on his way to Rome, St Paul was entrusted to a centurion of the Augustan cohort ⁴ (named after the first Roman Emperor, a title of Imperial dignity), which was also garrisoned at Caesarea for a time.

¹ Matt. 27. 27; Mk. 15. 16; Jn. 18. 3, 12. ² Acts 21. 31, etc.; 23. 17, etc. ³ Acts 10. 1. ⁴ Acts 27. 1.

COLLECTION

In conformity with the practice of Jewish "collectors of alms", St Paul organized collections for the poor Christians of Jerusalem.¹

¹ Acts 24. 17; Rom. 15. 26; 1 Cor. 16. 1 . . .; 2 Cor. 8 and 9; Gal. 2. 10.

COLOURS

I. *Colours mentioned in Biblical texts*

A. **Natural colours**

1. *White*. The following were or could be white: byssus, linen, certain materials and clothes ¹—hair (old age) ²—goats (Gen. 30. 35)—teeth (Gen. 49. 12) —wool (Ez. 27. 18)—milk ³—leprosy ⁴—the moon (Hebrew = the white one)—manna (Ex. 16. 31)— marble (1 Chr. 29. 2; Est. 1. 6)—walls (Matt. 23. 27; Acts 23. 3)—snow ⁵—bread (Gen. 40. 16)—the skin, the complexion (Cant. 5. 10; Is. 29. 22; Lam. 4. 7)— the sun, light.⁶

White is the symbol of innocence ⁷—of joy ⁸—of nobility and elegance ⁹—of purity: similarly the clothing of angels, saints, and the glorified Christ ¹⁰ is white.—The following are white in Revelation—a cloud (14. 14)—the throne of God (20. 11)—and certain horses.¹¹ The redeemed soul becomes as white as snow.¹²

¹ Est. 1. 6; 8. 15; Eccl. 9. 8; etc. ² Ps. 71. 18; Hos. 7. 9; Matt. 5. 36; etc. ³ Gen. 49. 12; Lam. 4. 7. ⁴ Ex. 4. 6; Lev. 13. 3; Num. 12. 10. ⁵ Ex. 4. 6; Num. 12. 10; Ps. 51. 7; 68. 14; Is. 1. 18. ⁶ Is. 24. 23; Matt. 17. 2. ⁷ Is. 1. 18. ⁸ Eccl. 9. 8. ⁹ Est. 8. 15. ¹⁰ Matt. 17. 2; Mk. 9. 3; 16. 5; Lk. 9. 29; Jn. 20. 12; Dan. 7. 9; Rev. 3. 4; etc. ¹¹ Rev. 6. 2; 19. 14; cf. Zech. 1. 8; 6. 3. ¹² Ps. 51. 7; Is. 1. 18.

2. *Yellow*. This colour is rare in the O.T. The dove's feathers may have golden yellow (or tawny yellow) ¹ glints.—Mildew is called "corn jaundice".² Jeremiah speaks of faces changing colour and becoming pale yellow (or greenish, livid).³—The colour of the stains of "leprosy" in cloth, leather, and walls are yellowish (or greenish),⁴ and the colour of the horse representing the plague is yellowish too (or pale, livid).⁵

¹ Ps. 68. 13. ² Dt. 28. 22; 1 Kgs. 8. 37; Amos 4. 9; Hagg. 2. 17. ³ Jer. 30. 6. ⁴ Lev. 13. 49; 14. 37. ⁵ Rev. 6. 8.

3. *Black*. The following are or can be black: lambs (Gen. 30. 32, etc.)—hair ¹—the raven (Cant. 5. 11)—the cloudy sky (1 Kgs. 18. 45)—marble (Est. 1. 6)—night ²—the skin, the complexion (Job 30. 28, 30; Cant. 1. 5; Lam. 4. 8)—tents (Cant. 1. 5)—the torrent (blackened by melting ice).³

Black is the symbol of vexation, mourning,⁴ and the colour of certain apocalyptic horses.⁵

¹ Lev. 13. 31; Cant. 5. 11; Matt. 5. 36. ² Jer. 4. 28; Lam. 4. 8; Joel 2. 10; 3. 15; Mic. 3. 6. ³ Job 6. 16. ⁴ Jer. 8. 21; 14. 2; etc. ⁵ Zech. 6. 2, 6; Rev. 6. 5.

4. *Red*, etc. It is the colour of blood ¹—coral ²— wine ³—and in certain circumstances of the eyes (Gen. 49. 12)—of the complexion ⁴—of the sky (Matt. 16. 2)—and the moon (Is. 24. 23).—The marks which appear on the skin of lepers are reddish ⁵—the pottage for which Esau sold his birthright was reddish brown ⁶—as also was the hair (or complexion) of Esau and David ⁷ (not fair in any event)—and certain apocalyptic horses ⁸ (or chestnut, bay, redbrown), as also was the heifer of Num. 19. 2 ff.— while the great dragon of Rev. 12. 3 was fiery-red.

¹ 2 Kgs. 3. 22; Is. 63. 2, 3. ² Lam. 4. 7. ³ Prov. 23. 31; Is. 63. 2. ⁴ Cant. 5. 10; Lam. 4. 7; Joel 2. 6 and Nahum 2. 10 (exact trans.). ⁵ Lev. 13. 19; cf. 14. 37. ⁶ Gen. 25. 30. ⁷ Gen. 25. 25; 1 Sam. 16. 12; 17. 42. ⁸ Zech. 1. 8; 6. 2, 3; Rev. 6. 4.

5. *Green*. Green was the colour of grass, turf ¹— gardens (vegetable) and of orchards (Dt. 11. 10; 1 Kgs. 21. 2; Cant. 6. 11)—of leaves—of fresh wood, of unripe fruit.²

In figurative use, green expresses vigour and prosperity.³

For greenish, see above: yellow.

¹ Gen. 1. 30; 9. 3; Ex. 10. 15; 2 Kgs. 19. 26; Ps. 37. 2; Cant. 1. 16; Mk. 6. 39; Rev. 8. 7. ² Dt. 12. 2; 2 Kgs. 16. 4;

Job 39. 8; Is. 57. 5; Jer. 2. 20; 17. 8; Ez. 6. 13. ³ Job 15. 32;
Ps. 92. 14; Jer. 11. 16; 17. 8; Dan. 4. 4 ff.; Hos. 14. 8.

B. Artificial colours

1. *Blue*. The Hebrew word for this colour, which
Josephus compares to that of the sky, and the LXX
Greek version to jacinth (blue tending to violet), is
too frequently translated by purple, or even by violet.
It was extracted from a gland of a Mediterranean
shellfish (*Helix ianthina*) and was used to dye
priestly,¹ royal,² or costly ³ garments, cloth, hangings,⁴ braid.⁵

¹ Ex. 28. 31. ² Est. 8. 15. ³ Ez. 23. 6; 27. 7. ⁴ Ex. 25. 4;
26. 1 . . .; 27. 16; Num. 4. 6 . . .; Est. 1. 6; cf. Jer. 10 9.
⁵ Ex. 28. 37; Num. 15. 38.

2. *Crimson*. It is the colour obtained by crushing a
tiny cochineal insect (the *Kermococcus vermilio*) or its
dried eggs; this Hemiptera is parasitic on the oak, on
which it develops very rapidly at the expense of the

Kermococcus vermilio, the
cochineal insect of certain
oaks which was still being
used about 1850 for colouring wool and silk crimson.

sap of the tree. The Phoenicians were past masters in
the art of using this colouring matter. In Hebrew the
name of this colour (*tôlaʻ*) comes from a noun
(*tôleʻah*) meaning worm, as the Latin word *vermiculus*
(little worm), from which we have vermilion, means
cochineal. The Bible often speaks of hangings,¹ of
luxurious rich clothes for priests or warriors,² of
ribbons and braids³ as being crimson. Crimson plays
a certain part in purification.⁴ Isaiah's comforting
promise is well known: "Though your sins be as
crimson, they shall be white as snow." ⁵ Revelation
clothes in crimson the woman drunk with the blood
of martyrs; she personifies Babylon the Great, and is
pictured as sitting on a crimson-coloured beast.⁶ Our
versions often replace "crimson" by "scarlet", but
scarlet involves a rather complicated preparation
from cochineal.

¹ Ex. 25. 4; 26. 1 . . .; 27. 16; 35. 6; 36. 8; 38. 18; Num.
4. 8; 2 Chr. 2. 7, 14; 3. 14. ² Ex. 28. 5 . . .; 39. 1 . . .; 2 Sam.
1. 24; Prov. 31. 21; Jer. 4. 30; Lam. 4. 5; Nahum 2. 3; Matt.
27. 28; Rev. 18. 12, 16. ³ Gen. 38. 28, 30; Jos. 2. 18, 21;
cf. 4. 3. ⁴ Lev. 14. 4 . . .; Num. 19. 6; Heb. 9. 19. ⁵ Is. 1. 18.
⁶ Rev. 17. 3–6.

3. *Purple*. This colour, a deep red tinged with
violet, is secreted by a special gland of a marine

81

mollusc with a handsome shell, *Murex trunculus*,
which used to be caught off the coast of Africa, Asia
Minor,¹ and Phoenicia. The Tyrians excelled in its
use as a dye; it was of great value and was the characteristic colour of royalty, power, and fortune. The

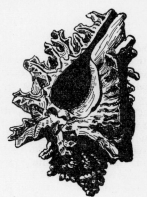

Murex trunculus.

rich man in the parable ² was clothed in it and in fine
linen, and the Biblical texts make it clear that hangings and materials of this colour ³ were very costly,
and that clothes dyed with it were for princes and
those of high degree.⁴

¹ Acts 16. 14. ² Lk. 16. 19. ³ Ex 26. 1, 31, 36; Est. 1. 6;
Cant. 3. 10; Ez. 27. 7. ⁴ Jg. 8. 26; Est. 8. 15; Prov. 31. 22;
Cant. 7. 5; Dan. 5. 7, 16, 29; Jn. 19. 2; Rev. 17. 4; 18. 12;
cf. Jer. 10. 9.

4. *Vermilion*. For certain fresco paintings and for
the colouring of mosaics, the Israelites used minium,
a colouring matter of mineral origin (lead oxide) and
of a fine vivid red (Jer. 22. 14; Ez. 23. 14).

II. *Remarks*

Although the Israelites do not seem to have known
a great number of colours, the relative richness of
their colour vocabulary must nevertheless be recognized: the same colour is often referred to in different
terms which mark certain shades, or which vary
according to the objects described, for their notion of
colour remained concrete, that is, it was linked to the
object coloured in that particular way.—Our versions
sometimes lack precision in rendering Hebrew words
of colour.—The symbolism of colours has often given
rise to interpretations which are very debatable and
fanciful.—The "coat of many colours" given by
Jacob to Joseph ¹ was more probably a fine ankle-
length tunic with sleeves. († Dyer.)

¹ Gen. 37. 3.

COMMERCE

It is rather intriguing to discover that the Israelites,
such clever business-men today, people whom we
readily hold to have a genius for commerce, for long
had no taste for this activity. Anti-Semites confuse

F

acquired and innate characteristics, when they claim that Jews are racially unsuited to agricultural work and have a natural bent for commerce, and especially for the money market. This supposed specialization is explained much more through history than through blood; the prosperity of many Zionist colonies in modern Palestine shows, moreover, how little some theories are based on observation.

When the nomadic or semi-nomadic Israelites settled in Canaan they took up agriculture and continued to tend their livestock; they had neither the need nor the inclination to engage in commerce, and they left that activity to the Canaanites, who had practised it for a long time, because their land lay at the cross-roads of the great trade routes, with the result that the word "Canaanite" was for long to remain as a synonym for the merchant or businessman.[1] Even the Deuteronomic Law has no cognizance of commercial law. Furthermore, the relative isolation of the Israelites in their mountainous territory, their lack of raw materials, the absence of all important industry, their religious separatism, too, and the prohibition of usury, were all obstacles to commercial enterprise. At about the beginning of the Christian era Josephus could still write: "We take no pleasure in trade, we do not like to mingle with foreign nations like business men"; and for certain rabbis of the same period, to stand aloof from business was one of the forty-eight qualities of the pious man.

Yet, from the time of the monarchy, it seems that the Israelites had begun to undertake some commercial exchanges, importing wood, metals, cloth, luxury goods,[2] and exporting cereals, oil and wine, aromatic herbs, honey, and fruit.[3] It is known that David's and Solomon's relations with the Phoenicians were so close that Israel took part temporarily in certain maritime expeditions.[4] With a mind open to progress, and determined to break with routine tradition, Solomon particularly was to draw much profit from the transit of goods over his kingdom, by levying a duty on all caravans [5] going from Egypt or Arabia to Damascus and elsewhere, and vice versa; he even organized trade in horses* and chariots*. These first royal and governmental enterprises instigated others of a private nature, with the result that certain Israelites, especially in the northern kingdom, began to imitate their commercially-minded neighbours; Amos and Hosea draw the unflattering picture of the Israelite merchant who was not above using false balances, and who undertook greedy speculations.[6] But international trade naturally remained in the hands of the Phoenicians and Arabs, and the commercial operations of the Israelites continued on a very modest scale.

It was after the Exile that the Jews engaged more and more in trade; their stay in Mesopotamia, the world centre of commerce, had accustomed them to a life other than that of the fields. Some of them settled down to business and did not return to their own land: many Jewish names appear in the records of a business house at Nippur in the 5th century. Soon—especially from the Hellenistic period—the Jewish business-man appears almost everywhere in the ancient world; the writer of Psalm 107 can even outline the list of dangers run at sea by his people's commercial travellers,[7] and certain chiefs of the nation (Simon Maccabaeus, Herod the Great) were to take a very lively interest in the development of trading. The Jewish community in Alexandria, especially, was to initiate great commercial activity, keeping a tight hold on the grain trade, on which Rome's food supply depended. Jews, dispersed throughout the world after the destruction of Jerusalem, were to follow the example of those of the great city of the Delta, and were soon to become past masters in banking operations and commercial transactions.

After the Exile, too, local commerce became more active: previously it had been to a very large extent the domain of itinerant merchants (in Hebrew, merchant = one who comes and goes), or had been carried on mainly near the sanctuaries at the time of the feasts which were celebrated there and which sometimes had the atmosphere of fairs; now, markets were held regularly at the city gates; such markets were supplied by produce of the countryside, and we know that extensive trade was carried on in the very precincts of the Temple at Jerusalem, for supplying to the faithful the victims necessary for sacrifice.[8]— Shops, too, were not unknown; as early as the Books of Kings [9] we hear of the existence in Samaria of Syrian bazaars (*souks*) and Israelite shops in Damascus; Jeremiah [10] speaks of a street of bakers*, and the Talmud of a street of butchers* in Jerusalem, and Nehemiah recounts that some Tyrians who had settled in the capital sold fish and all kinds of goods.[11] Later, it was the Greeks who often controlled local business, always providing a wider choice of imported articles under Greek and Latin names.

Apart from Ezekiel's lively description of commerce in Tyre,[12] it should be remembered the O.T. frequently alludes to the commercial behaviour of the Jews, often shady, and to the usual bargaining.[13] Ecclesiasticus has this characteristic aphorism: "As a peg is driven in between two stones, so sin enters between sale and purchase." [14] Measures dealing with the conduct of markets were eventually taken by the authorities.—More than one metaphor or piece of information concerning commerce can be found in the N.T.; [15] Jesus was well aware that he was not dealing with farmers only; this significant saying of his, which does not appear in the Gospels, has come down to us: "Be good bankers*." († Weights, money.)

[1] Job 41. 6; Prov. 31. 24; Is. 23. 8; Hos. 12. 7; Zeph. 1. 11; Zech. 14. 21. [2] 1 Kgs. 5. 10; 10. 22; Prov. 7. 16. [3] 2 Sam.

5. 11; 1 Kgs. 5. 11; 2 Chr. 2. 10; etc.; cf. Gen. 37. 25; 43. 11; Hos. 12. 1. ⁴ 1 Kgs. 10. 11, 22; Ez. 27. 12. ⁵ 1 Kgs. 10. 15. ⁶ Hos. 12. 7; Amos 8. 5; cf. Ez. 27. 17; Is. 2. 7, 16. ⁷ Ps. 107. 23 ff.; cf. Prov. 7. 19. ⁸ Matt. 21. 12 ff. par. ⁹ 1 Kgs. 20. 34. ¹⁰ Jer. 37. 21. ¹¹ Neh. 13. 16; cf. 3. 31, 32; Zeph. 1, 11. ¹² Ez. 27. 1–36. ¹³ Gen. 23. 3–20; Lev. 19. 11, 35; 2 Sam. 24. 21–24; Prov. 11. 1; 16. 11; 20. 10, 14; Mic. 6. 10; etc. ¹⁴ Ecclus. 27. 2. ¹⁵ Matt. 13. 44–46; 25. 14 ff.; Lk. 7. 41 ff.; 14. 18; 19. 12 ff.; Acts 16. 14; Jas. 4. 13; etc.

COMPASSES

This is only once mentioned in the O.T.,[1] among the instruments used by the carpenter and, curiously enough, by the maker of idols.

[1] Is. 44. 13.

CONSECRATION

The consecration of the *priest* (in Hebrew, to consecrate = to set apart) gave rise to a solemn complex ceremony which has lengthy treatment in the Priestly Code in Exodus chap. 29 and Leviticus chap. 8.

To free themselves from all defilement and to be in a fit state to present themselves before God, candidates began by taking a bath of purification. Next they dressed in their priestly robes, and then received, at least according to certain texts, an anointing of carefully prepared holy oil. Three sacrifices of great importance followed: a young bull was first offered as an expiation for sin; the consecrated placed their hands on the victim, whose blood was sprinkled on the horns of, and at the foot of, the altar; only the fatty parts of the beast were burnt on the altar; the rest must be burnt outside the sanctuary. As a sweet-smelling sacrifice, a ram was then selected for a burnt offering; this sacrifice, in which the whole victim was burnt on the altar, was particularly important. The third sacrifice was the consecration-sacrifice proper; a second ram, on which the candidates also laid their hands, was sacrificed; the officiating priest took the animal's blood and with it touched the lobe of the right ear, the right thumb and the right big toe of the candidates—a triple symbolic gesture meaning that the priest must at all times listen to the voice of Yahweh, do holy deeds, and walk always in the ways of his God. Blood, a sign of the covenant with Yahweh, or possibly as a symbol of strength and of life, put the priest in close touch with the deity. The rest of the victim's blood was poured over the altar, then this blood, thus consecrated and mingled with the oil of unction, was sprinkled on the candidates and on their clothes in order to sanctify them; then the fat and the right thigh of the second ram, together with a loaf of unleavened bread, a cake made with oil, and a wafer rubbed with oil, were placed in their hands; this offering was made to undergo the rite of waving, and was then taken from the consecrated to be burnt on the altar. The ram's breast was the per-

quisite of the officiant, and the unburnt flesh was prepared and eaten by the priests.

The question of anointing with oil is controversial: according to some texts, this was an integral part of the consecration of every priest; according to others it was reserved for the High Priest alone. It is possible that unction, first applied to the king and then to the High Priest, finally extended to all the priests; or that, originally applicable to all priests, it was finally reserved for the consecration of their chief only.—There has been much discussion, too, about the meaning of the gesture which brings the third sacrifice to an end: why put the victim's fat on the hands of the newly consecrated priests? Why thus fill their hands? Was it an allusion to the priest's right to use part of the sacrificial offerings as food? Or was it rather a symbolic way of stressing the vocation of the priest, who had been called to consecrate to God the gifts he received from the people?

The consecration of the *Levites* [1] was less ceremonious; for them, it was a purification rather than a consecration. After being sprinkled with special water, they shaved their whole body, and washed their clothes; then they sacrificed a bull as a burnt offering and a second as an atonement sacrifice. Finally, they were subjected to the rite of waving, since their very person was considered as an offering to God by the Israelites.

[1] Num. 8. 5 ff.

COOK

The only male cook mentioned in the O.T. is Samuel's [1]—he received the command to serve Saul with a choice portion—but the Hebrew word really means "slaughterer", "butcher"*, the man who kills the animal. Doubtless they existed at kings' courts,[2] as female cooks certainly did, for when the Israelites were impatient to be given a king Samuel told them: "He will take your daughters to be cooks." [3]

Egyptian monuments sometimes depict kitchen scenes, in particular the royal kitchens of Rameses III.

[1] 1 Sam. 9. 23. [2] Cf. 1 Kgs. 4. 22, 23. [3] 1 Sam. 8. 13.

COPPER

In Hebrew, copper bears the same name as bronze* (alloy of copper and tin), and it is the second of these which is meant in the O.T. except in a few passages; thus the mines mentioned in Dt. 8. 9 or Job 28. 2 can only be copper mines, since bronze does not occur in nature (cf. Ez. 22. 18).

Excavations in Palestine have yielded some ancient remains of copper tools which contain little or no tin, but in Canaan we cannot distinguish a Copper Age as a precursor of the Bronze Age. The use of alloys, discovered by accident, undoubtedly spread quickly, since the mingling of copper with other minerals gave a harder, more durable metal which the language did not distinguish from pure copper.

Palestine probably obtained its first copper from Asia (Caucasus, the Caspian, Khorasan, etc.), but during the 2nd millennium B.C. the island of Cyprus, which gave its name to copper as is known, became the main producer of the metal. The mines in the Sinai Peninsula, contrary to what has sometimes been believed, yielded only small amounts of copper. In time, the people of Palestine began to exploit more accessible deposits, notably in the Arabah, to the south of the Dead Sea, where traces of mining installations (huts and furnaces) dating from the 13th century B.C. have been found.

COR

The cor (kor; † homer) is the largest measure of capacity for grain and dry substances,[1] and perhaps for liquids also.[2] From the statements of ancient writers it would be equivalent to about 11 bushels (10·0 to 11·1 bushels). Many commentaries take it as 10·0 bushels.

Solomon delivered 20,000 cors of wheat every year to Hiram, king of Tyre,[3] and he himself required daily 30 cors of fine flour and 60 cors of ordinary flour.[4]

(† Weights and Measures.)

[1] 1 Kgs. 4. 22; 5. 11; 2 Chr. 2. 10; 27. 5; Ezr. 7. 22; Lk. 16. 7. [2] Ez. 45. 14. [3] 1 Kgs. 5. 11. [4] 1 Kgs. 4. 22.

CORAL

The red coral which is found, among others, on the rocky bed of the Mediterranean and Red Sea littoral, is mentioned in comparisons in several O.T. passages;[1] for example, Prov. 3. 15 says that wisdom "is more precious than coral" (A.V., R.V., rubies). The Hebrew word used in the texts (peninim) is no doubt wrongly translated when it is taken as "pearls". Another word (ra'môt), which is met with in Job 28. 18 (first noun) and in Ez. 27. 16, perhaps means "black coral", a modification by sulphurous gases of red coral which has dropped into the ooze.

The Egyptians made ornaments of coral which are to be found in their tombs.

[1] Job 28. 18; Prov. 3. 15; 8. 11; 20. 15; 31. 10; Lam. 4. 7.

CORBAN

This is the name given, in a general way, to all offerings made at the sanctuary. Mk. 7. 11 (cf. Matt. 15. 5 ff.) reminds us that it was possible, by a vow, to declare "corban" (i.e., an offering sacred and devoted to God) any object or possession, which was thereby not allowed to be used in the normal way or given to anyone else. Consequently, it was

possible to refuse even to one's parents what they needed. But Jesus opposed such sophistry.

CORDS

Cords, as accessories to clothing or furniture, were not unknown to the Israelites. For example, Bible texts mention the gold and azure-blue cords which held the High Priest's breastplate and the gold-interwoven cords of his tiara,[1] the girdle-cord at which the Oriental hangs the sword he loves to carry on his person,[2] and the cords of white and purple linen which held up the tapestries in the palace of Ahasuerus.[3]—Twine was also used, for holding the cover of a jar, and for measuring the circumference of a column or basin,[4] etc.

[1] Ex. 28. 14, 28, 37; 39. 17, 21; Num. 15. 38. [2] Gen. 38. 18, 25. [3] Est. 1. 6. [4] Num. 19. 15; 1 Kgs. 7. 15, 23; Jg. 16. 9; Eccl. 4. 12.

CORIANDER

In two O.T. passages[1] manna is compared to coriander seed, an umbellifer well known to the Israelites because it grows spontaneously throughout the Mediterranean region. When fresh, coriander

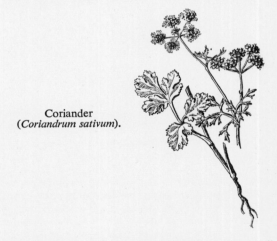

Coriander
(Coriandrum sativum).

gives off an unpleasant fetid odour, but its small, globular fruits, a quarter of an inch in diameter, have an agreeable aromatic scent when dry. They are used in perfume, in medicine, and as spice.

[1] Ex. 16. 31; Num. 11. 7.

CORMORANT

In the list of impure birds,[1] some versions translate by "cormorant"—a large web-footed bird which lives on fish—the name of the third bird in Lev. 11. 18 (the second in Dt. 14. 17) which others render by "vulture" (gypaetus), preferring to find "cormorant" in the second bird of Lev. 11. 17 (the third of Dt. 14. 17).

[1] Lev. 11. 13–19; Dt. 14. 11–18.

CORN

This word is very often used in the Bible in a general sense, without further specification, to cover cereals. Of two more technical expressions, one refers to corn still on the stalk,[1] the other to winnowed corn as it is put into the granary.[2] Usually translations do not reflect these interesting slight variations in meaning.

The two chief kinds of corn grown in Palestine are wheat* and spelt* († agriculture).

[1] Ex. 22. 6; Dt. 16. 9; Jg. 15. 5; 2 Kgs. 19. 26; Is. 17. 5; 37. 27; etc. [2] Gen. 41. 35; 42. 25; Prov. 11. 26; Jer. 23. 28; Joel 2. 24; Amos 5. 11; 8. 5; etc.

CORNER-STONE

In building important Palestinian houses much attention was paid to the foundations and, surprisingly enough, to the corner-stones, which were carefully chosen, cut, and laid.[1] It is probable that a special ceremony often stressed this phase of the construction[2] and that some sort of talisman was inscribed on the corner-stone.[3] This stone served the prophets Isaiah[4] and Zechariah, as well as Jesus[5] and St Paul,[6] for a figure of speech; but the most striking metaphorical use is that of the Psalmist[7] in a verse borrowed by the N.T.[8] and applied to Christ: "The stone rejected by the builders has become the corner-stone."

[1] Jer. 51. 26. [2] Job 38. 5–6. [3] 2 Ti. 2. 19; Rev. 21. 14. [4] Is. 28. 16; 1 Pet. 2. 6; Zech. 10. 4. [5] Matt. 16. 18. [6] Eph. 2. 20. [7] Ps. 118. 22. [8] Matt. 21. 42 par.; Acts 4. 11 f.; 1 Pet. 2. 7.

CORSELET

The corselet (R.V., coat of mail), which is not to be confused with the scaled breastplate (R.V. also coat of mail, or breastplate), is only referred to in passing in Ex. 28. 32 (cf. 39. 23), if the word used here is correctly translated: the robe of the ephod "shall have a hole for the head in the midst thereof: it shall have a binding of woven work round about the hole of it, as it were the hole of a corselet, that the robe be not rent". This allusion to a soldier's equipment is significant—it was perhaps no more than a substantial leathern doublet—and leads us to think that it was more extensively used than we might think from the silence of the texts.

COSMETICS

Among the objects placed in women's tombs, a considerable number of toilet accessories have been

found; these indicate that many kinds of cosmetics were in use in Palestine. There are small earthenware or alabaster jars, tubular bronze (a) or glass (b) containers; there are also innumerable little make-up

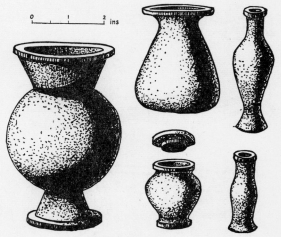

Small alabaster ointment pots.

instruments (c), polishers, scrapers, palettes, and spatulas made of bone or metal; finally, there are cosmetic scoops artistically made in wood or ivory. Some of these were of local manufacture, but the

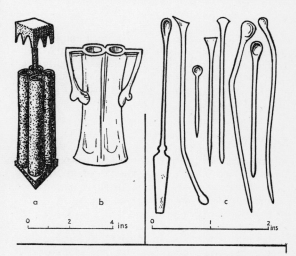

Tubular flasks and small make-up instruments.

majority came from abroad, and especially from Egypt.

The women sometimes made up their own cosmetics, but usually they bought them. In Nehemiah's time there was in Jerusalem a corporation of perfumers*,[1] who possessed a technique which was

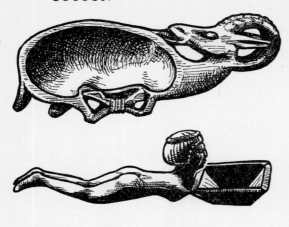

Cosmetic scoops of wood and ivory.

already ancient,[2] or imported their goods from abroad.

[1] Neh. 3. 8. [2] Ex. 30. 25.

COTTON

Cotton does not seem to have been cultivated in Palestine before the time of the Arabs. It is mentioned only in the Book of Esther,[1] as a luxury product: magnificent tapestries of cotton, doubtless from India, adorned the hall where Ahasuerus gave his feast. († Flax.)

[1] Est. 1. 6.

COVENANT

Any covenant contracted between two persons or clans, or with God, was accompanied in Israel by symbolic actions which emphasized its importance and guaranteed its validity.

A simple oath, with or without handshakes, uttered before God was sufficient in certain cases,[1] sometimes it was accompanied by an exchange of clothes [2] or a gift,[3] or a kiss; [4] but most often the pact was sealed with a meal,[5] which was usually preceded by a sacrifice*.[6] To share the same food created in effect a fraternal union; the primitive idea was that two allies were more completely associated if a single item of food contributed mysteriously to their nourishment. It is likely that the Hebrew word meaning covenant (*berit*) comes from the word "to eat together".—It was necessary, too, that the food

should be salted; people said "to eat salt" with someone, to make "a covenant of salt",[7] which by allusion to "the salt of God's covenant" [8] gave the pact an inviolable character. Even today the Arabs offer bread and salt to anyone whom they seek to treat as an ally, and say "there is salt between us". For stronger reasons, any offering to God was to be accompanied with salt*, "the salt of the covenant with your God", says Lev. 2. 13.—Among the majority of peoples and notably among the Semites, blood also plays an important part in the ritual of covenants: if two partners drink one another's blood, after each has cut the other, or dip their hands in the blood of the same victim, then they are brothers from that day forward. In Israel, the sacrificial blood shared between the people, who were sprinkled with it, and God, for whom it was poured on the altar, established the closest communion between the faithful and the deity.[9] Another ceremonial ordained that the sacrificial victim should be divided in two; the parties of the contract then passed between the two halves of the animal, thus showing their willingness to be united as the two parts of the victim had originally been, or to be treated like the beast if they broke their undertaking.[10]

Sometimes a stone was set up or a monument erected as a witness to the agreement.

[1] 2 Kgs. 11. 4; Ez. 17. 18; Prov. 17. 18; 22. 26. [2] 1 Sam. 18. 3. [3] Gen. 21. 27, 30. [4] 2 Sam. 14. 33. [5] Gen. 26. 30; Jos. 9. 14. [6] Gen. 31. 54; Ex. 18. 12; Ps. 50. 5. [7] 2 Chr. 13. 5. [8] Lev. 2. 13; Num. 18. 19. [9] Ex. 24. 2–6. [10] Gen. 15. 10; Jer. 34. 18 ff.

COVERLET

Hebrew possesses several words for coverlets, which were used for different purposes, but principally [1] for covering beds*. The beauty, good quality, and lightness of some of them was much appreciated.[2] But many a poor person had no other covering than his cloak,[3] so the law did not allow it to be taken on pledge beyond the daytime.[4] Though the word is uncertain, it was probably a wetted coverlet that Hazael spread over the face of Benhadad, king of Syria, to suffocate him.[5] The coverlet inspired some vigorous figures of speech for the prophet Isaiah; he said, for example, that in the abode of the dead decay served as a bed and worms as a coverlet for the king of Babylon [6] (cf. also Is. 25. 7; 28. 20; and cf. Dt. 22. 30; 27. 20).

[1] Jg. 4. 18. [2] Prov. 7. 16; 31. 22. [3] Job. 24. 7; 31. 19. [4] Ex. 22. 26–27. [5] 2 Kgs. 8. 15. [6] Is. 14. 11.

CRANE

This tall, migratory wader comes to live in Palestine and in southern countries during the winter, then flies northwards in the spring. It is possible that Isaiah and Jeremiah both mention the crane along with the swallow, the one alluding to the bird's song [1] and the other to its migrations; [2] but, with justification, some commentators think that the Hebrew word translated " crane " is an adjective qualifying the word "swallow", in cases where the swallow is referred to and not the horse, these two (swift) creatures bearing the same name in Hebrew.

[1] Is. 38. 14. [2] Jer. 8. 7.

CRESCENTS

Men and women liked to wear round their neck crescents which were charms rather than jewellery.[1] They were also hung from the neck of camels.[2]

Pendants in the form of crescents.

Palestine excavations have yielded some of them, in silver or gold, mould-cast or repoussé work, and dating principally from the Late Bronze Age (1600–1200).

[1] Is. 3. 18. [2] Jg. 8. 21.

CRIB

In Greek, as in Hebrew, this word not only covers the manger in which domestic animals find their food, but by extension also the stall or stable itself. In the O.T. the latter sense is evident in some passages,[1] while we may hesitate over others; our translations usually favour "crib",[2] for example: "The ox knoweth his owner, and the ass his master's crib." [3]

In the narrative of the birth of Jesus, according to St Luke's Gospel the word "crib" is called for.[4] On the other hand, both senses are possible in Jesus' statement about the sabbath: "You hypocrites, does not each one of you on the sabbath loose his ox or his ass from the 'stall', and lead him away to watering?" [5]

[1] 1 Kgs. 4. 26; 2 Chr. 9. 25; 32. 28. [2] Job 39. 12; Prov. 14. 4. [3] Is. 1. 3. [4] Lk. 2. 7, 12, 16. [5] Lk. 13. 15.

CRIMES and OFFENCES

(see Law* §3 for generalities.)

The Bible texts are unfortunately very brief on the subject of crimes and offences condemned by Israelite penal law. However, we can divide them into five classes.

1. *Outrages against religion.* The severity of the prescriptions in this connection is not surprising, for the people of Israel are the people of Yahweh, the one, holy God.

(*a*) The Covenant* Code punished all *idolatry* and *magic* with death.[1] The Deuteronomic Law was naturally very severe; it wanted death even for anyone who advocated the worship of other gods: "Thine hand shall be first upon him to put him to death . . . and thou shalt stone him with stones, that he die." [2] Priestly legislation is no less categorical: anyone invoking spirits or devoting himself to divination shall be stoned; [3] the cult of Molech (Moloch) with its child sacrifices is particularly blameworthy.[4]

(*b*) There were extreme penalties also for those who violated *cultic* regulations. According to the Priestly Code, the Israelite who does not observe the Sabbath shall be put to death.[5] He who abstains from the Passover celebrations [6] (except for reasons specified), or from humbling himself on the Day of Atonement,[7] or from practising circumcision [8] "shall be cut off from his people". (This expression is ambiguous and doubtless does not always mean put to death, but proscribed—excluded from the promises associated with the keeping of God's covenant.) It is the same for anyone found in a state of uncleanness, who eats the flesh of a peace offering made to Yahweh.[9] The death penalty is also prescribed for a presumptuous person who may refuse to listen to the priest or judge.[10]

(*c*) Any who *blaspheme* († blasphemy) the name of Yahweh, or act in a way that usurps divine authority, merit also the supreme penalty.[11]

[1] Ex. 22. 18, 20, cf. 20. 4. [2] Dt. 13. 9, 10; 13. 6–18; Dt. 4. 15–19, 23; 17. 2 . . . [3] Lev. 20. 6, 27. [4] Lev. 20. 1–5. [5] Ex. 31. 14; 35. 2; Num. 15. 32 . . . [6] Num. 9. 13. [7] Lev. 23. 29. [8] Gen. 17. 14. [9] Lev. 7. 20. [10] Dt. 17. 12. [11] Lev. 24. 15, 16; 1 Kgs. 21. 10; Dt. 18. 20; Matt. 26. 65.

2. *Blows and wounds.* Here all the stages of legislation invoke the *lex talionis*: fracture for fracture, eye for eye, tooth for tooth, wound for wound.[1] But it is probable that with the Israelites, as elsewhere, an incident could be settled by an indemnity, if the injured party consented to it or when the deed had been without premeditation. In any case, the talion was applied only if the blows and wounds left a permanent injury; in the case of temporary incapacity to work, the guilty party was responsible for the medical expenses and paid compensation for loss of time.[2]

It must be noted that the talion came into operation only between free men: "If a man strike the eye of his slave or his handmaid, and destroy it, he shall set them free as compensation for the loss of their eye; and if he smite out . . . a tooth . . . he shall set them free in compensation for the tooth." [3]

There is also an interesting arrangement concerning a pregnant woman: if, in the course of a brawl between men, she happens to be struck and has a miscarriage though suffers no other hurt, the guilty party has to pay the compensation, claimed by the husband, for the loss of the child which might have been his possession.[4] In one very special case, provision is made for the cutting off of a hand.[5]

[1] Ex. 21. 24; Dt. 19. 21; Lev. 24. 20. [2] Ex. 21. 18, 19. [3] Ex. 21. 26, 27. [4] Ex. 21. 22. [5] Dt. 25. 11, 12.

3. *Outrages against life*. Here, above all, blood calls for blood: "Whoso sheddeth man's blood, by man shall his blood be shed." [1] In ancient times—and still today among the Bedouins in Palestine—all murder must be avenged by a member of the victim's family: the vendetta is a sacred right and obligation. But the legislation, which is obliged to recognize it, attempts, though not always with success, to limit its effects. According to Deuteronomic Law, vengeance must be limited to the guilty person alone and not touch the members of his family,[2] and the Covenant Code establishes the essential distinction between assassination (voluntary and premeditated) and accidental manslaughter. A murderer is naturally punished by death († murder), while he who commits unintentional homicide has available the right of asylum*.[3] But the latter no more than the former could escape the consequences of his action by payment of an indemnity.[4]

The right of lawful defence scarcely existed;[5] however, the Covenant Code declares that "if a thief is found breaking in and is struck [in the night] so that he dies, this is not murder; but if the sun has risen, it is murder".[6]

When the perpetrator of murder is unknown, the elders of the town nearest to the corpse must make a special atonement sacrifice.[7]

The law of blood also plays a part in some cases in which we think "civil responsibilities" are involved, as an accident arising from the absence of a parapet round the flat roof of a house,[8] or the death of man, woman, or child from the blow of a horn given by an ox known to be vicious. In the latter case the owner of the animal may in exceptional cases avoid losing his life by the payment of the ransom imposed upon him.[9] (If the ox had not gored before, his owner was absolved, but the animal was stoned and its flesh not eaten.[10])

Here again, the murder of a slave did not have the same consequences as the murder of a free man: the guilty party was punished only if the death were immediate and, in that case, the penalty (which is not specified) was not capital punishment.[11] Moreover, if the victim of a vicious ox (see above) is a slave, the animal is stoned, but its owner only has to pay an indemnity to the slave's owner.[12] But kidnapping a free man to make a slave of him was equated to murder and punished by death.[13]

[1] Gen. 9. 6. [2] Dt. 24. 16. [3] Ex. 21. 12, 13; Dt. 19. 1–13; Num. 35. 16 . . . [4] Num. 35. 31, 32. [5] 2 Sam. 2. 22; 14. 6 . . . [6] Ex. 22. 3a. [7] Dt. 21. 1 . . . [8] Dt. 22. 8. [9] Ex. 21. 29, 30, 31. [10] Ex. 21. 28; cf. Gen. 9. 5. [11] Ex. 21. 20, 21. [12] Ex. 21. 32. [13] Ex. 21. 16; Dt. 24. 7.

4. *Crimes against the family and morality*. Israelite laws are particularly severe against anything that attacks the integrity of the family, the basis of social organization.

A whole series of *consanguineous marriages* and sexual relations is forbidden by the Priestly Code and regarded as incestuous,[1] even though some of them were licit in early Israel: marriage with a brother's widow was then actually obligatory when the brother had died childless [2] (Levirate marriage*), while the new law forbade it. It is the same for marriage with two sisters,[3] marriage with a step-sister,[4] marriage with an aunt,[5] etc. The law does not mention incest of father with daughter: though not exceptional, it must yet always have been condemned (cf., however, Gen. 19. 30 . . .).

Seduction of a young unbetrothed woman was not thought criminal, but the seducer could be constrained to marry his victim or accomplice, and in any case must pay her father a sum equal to her dowry.[6] According to Deuteronomic Law, marriage was obligatory; the sum due was fixed at fifty silver shekels, and the seducer had no right ever to divorce this wife.[7]

Rape of a betrothed woman, and doubtless also of a married woman, was punished by death. Yet if the assault took place in a town where the woman could have cried for help, she also was regarded as guilty, and both of them were stoned "until they died"; if the incident happened in solitude, the man alone was punished.[8]

A proved case of *adultery** involved the death of both the guilty parties.[9]

Though frequent in Israel, *prostitution** was sharply denounced,[10] but only that of the daughter of a priest was punishable: she was condemned to be burnt [11] († fire). The married woman who hid her misconduct was punished by death.[12] Deuteronomy particularly condemns sacred prostitution,[13] which was practised in Canaanite temples and elsewhere.

All *unnatural relationships* (paederasty, sodomy, etc.) were punished by death.[14] The punishment of being "cut off from among the people" is prescribed also for a man who has intercourse with a woman during her period.[15]

Finally, we may notice this significant fact, that a child who curses his parents, strikes them, or rebels against them is liable to the most extreme penalty.[16]

[1] Lev. 18. 6–18; 20. 11 . . .; Dt. 27. 20–23. [2] Dt. 25. 5 . . . and Lev. 18. 16. [3] Lev. 18. 18 and Gen. 29. 27, 28. [4] Lev. 18. 9 and Gen. 20. 12 or 2 Sam. 13. 13. [5] Lev. 18. 12 and Ex. 6. 20 or Num. 26. 59. [6] Ex. 22. 16, 17. [7] Dt. 22. 28, 29. [8] Dt. 22. 23–27. [9] Dt. 22. 22; Lev. 18. 20; 20. 10. [10] Dt. 23. 17; Lev. 19. 29. [11] Lev. 21. 9. [12] Dt. 22. 21. [13] Dt. 23. 18. [14] Ex. 22. 19; Lev. 18. 22, 23; 20. 13, 15, 16. [15] Lev. 20. 18; cf. 15. 24. [16] Ex. 21. 15, 17; Lev. 20. 9; Dt. 21. 18–21; 27. 16; Matt. 15. 4

5. *Attacks on property*. In this realm Israelite legislation is far from being as severe as the Baby-

Ionian, Assyrian, or particularly the Hittite Codes. It demands simply the restitution of the stolen goods, with, it is true, compensation, a kind of amends, amounting to double if it were a case of silver [1] stolen and—a fact worth noticing—four- or even five-fold if it were animals [2] (while in Mesopotamia and elsewhere compensation reached ten, thirty, or even sixty times the value of the goods stolen, with the death penalty, even, in some cases). If the thief was unable to restore what he had stolen he himself was sold to cover the reparation. [3]

A whole series of articles in the Covenant Code give regulations for damage done to property by negligence, accidentally, or wilfully: an uncovered cistern, [4] damage by a vicious ox, [5] havoc to field or vineyard, [6] poor oversight of a beast, [7] fire, [8] borrowing of a beast, [9] deposits*, [10] etc. Removal of boundary marks († landmarks) and the use of false weights* are formally condemned. [11] Appropriation of entrusted goods or of a lost object was regarded as theft. [12]

[1] Ex. 22. 7. [2] Ex. 22. 1–4. [3] Ex. 22. 3. [4] Ex. 21. 33. [5] Ex. 21. 29, 35, 36. [6] Ex. 22. 5. [7] Ex. 22. 10, 13. [8] Ex. 22. 6. [9] Ex. 22. 14. [10] Ex. 22. 7. [11] Dt. 19. 14; 25. 13–16; Lev. 19. 35. [12] Lev. 6. 1–7; Num. 5. 5–10.

CROCODILE

It is curious that the crocodile, which is rarely spoken of in the O.T., is never given there its proper name; it is designated by terms usually given to mythological animals—dragon, sea monster, Leviathan*—for it is evident that it is the crocodile, the sacred animal and emblem of Egypt, to which Ezekiel alludes, [1] while the long description of Leviathan in the poem of Job [2] is, at least to a great extent, of the crocodile.

This animal had long been reported from the marshes of Palestine, drained today, which used to lie at the mouth of the Nahr es-Zerka, north of Caesarea, called by the ancients the "river of crocodiles", and near to the town of Crocodilon. The last specimen of these crocodiles, of modest dimension, is said to have been killed in 1877.

[1] Ez. 29. 3 and perhaps 32. 2. [2] Job 41.

Crocus sativus (Saffron).

CROCUS

The crocus grows wild in all countries of the

89

Levant. From its stigmas there is extracted either a powerful dyestuff (saffron), a perfume, a condiment, or a stimulant and antispasmodic. Saffron is mentioned only once in the Bible, among the sweet-smelling plants praised in the Song of Songs. [1]

[1] Cant. 4. 14.

CROSS

In Greek the word for cross at first meant simply a stake, pale, or gibbet. This instrument of torture (in Latin *crux simplex*) was generally pointed (*crux acuta*), and the condemned man was suspended from it or nailed to it through the hands, or, among some peoples, even impaled upon it, until he died. The O.T. mentions this pole by the name of "wood" or "tree" (our versions usually give "tree", sometimes "gallows"), and records various condemnations to death by this means. [1]

To the upright timber, the Greeks and Romans added a cross beam, which they fixed either to the top of the upright (*crux commissa*, or *patibulata*, in the shape of a T) or into a housing a little below the top (*crux immissa* or *capitulata*, the Latin cross †). As it was enough if the victim's feet could not touch the ground, the length of the uprights was not great; these uprights usually remained standing at the place of execution; but the condemned man was usually forced to carry the horizontal beam, the *patibulum*, a heavy beam which the executioner finally put into place. A wooden pin or block (*sedile* = seat, or *cornu* = horn) was nearly always set in the middle of the gibbet to give support, between the legs, to the victim's body; this piece of wood has never been shown in pictures of the crucifixion of Jesus: on the other hand, a block beneath his feet, the use of which is very dubious, has often been shown.

The Gospels say nothing of the exact form of the cross of Golgotha, but the earliest fathers mention the projection on which the victim was placed and speak of a cross with four ends (*immissa*); in support of this form, the fact that a notice was displayed above Christ's head [2] could be quoted; this notice could have been placed on the *patibulum*, however, since the victim's arms could not remain horizontal. According to the custom the victim of Calvary and Simon of Cyrene probably did not carry the whole cross, which would have been too heavy for one man, but the *patibulum* (also called "cross"), the weight of which was enough to test a man who had been scourged, especially if it were placed across his neck and if his arms were bound to it as a text of Plautus states. The cross of Jesus must have been relatively high, to judge by the merciful gesture of the man who, in order to reach the dying victim's lips, put the sponge on the end of a reed [3]—which, however, was probably not very long. († Crucifixion.)

[1] Gen. 40. 19; 41. 13; Num. 25. 4; Dt. 21. 22; Jos. 8. 29; 10. 26; 2 Sam. 21. 6, 9; Est. 5. 14; 8. 7; 9. 25. [2] Matt. 27. 37; Lk. 23. 38; Jn. 19. 19. [3] Matt. 27. 48; Mk. 15. 36; Jn. 19. 29.

CROWN

The Biblical texts often speak of royal and priestly crowns [1] (cf. also the crown of thorns* worn by Christ [2]), and of those worn by bridegrooms, guests, or athletes,[3] or of those which adorned the victims or officiants in pagan sacrifices.[4]

The crown referred to in 2 Sam. 12. 30, which weighed a talent of gold (more than 110 lb.), was not the crown of the king of the Ammonites, as is generally translated, but that of their idol (Milkom), according to a better rendering of the text; nor did David put it on his head, but he took the precious stone which was set in it for his personal adornment.

It would be impossible to list here the very many passages in which the crown is used in a metaphorical sense, but we know that it is in turn the symbol of royalty, power,[5] prosperity,[6] virtue,[7] victory,[8] glory,[9] etc.

(† Diadem, priest.)

[1] 2 Sam. 1. 10; 2 Kgs. 11. 12; Est. 2. 17; 6. 8; 8. 15; etc.; Ps. 21. 3; Zech. 6. 11, 14. [2] Matt. 27. 29; Mk. 15. 17; Jn. 19. 2, 5. [3] Cant. 3. 11; Is. 61. 10; Ez. 23. 42; 1 Cor. 9. 25; 2 Ti. 2. 5. [4] Acts 14. 13. [5] Jer. 13. 18; Ez. 21. 26; Rev. 9. 7; 14. 14; etc. [6] Ps. 65. 11; 103. 4; Phil. 4. 1; etc. [7] Prov. 1. 9; 14. 18; Rev. 3. 11; etc. [8] 2 Ti. 4. 8; Jas. 1. 12; Rev. 2. 10; 6. 2; etc. [9] Is. 62. 3; Heb. 2. 7; 1 Pet. 5. 4; etc.

CRUCIBLE

The prophets and poets of the Bible very often appeal to the crucible to express the idea of purification, and this figure of speech has become classical.

The Israelites were fully aware of the process of the cupellation of metals, which goes back to remote antiquity. In a vessel of refractory clay the precious metal was subjected to a hot fire and was melted along with certain substances (such as lead) which freed it from all its dross.[1]

In the metaphorical sense it is usually God who tries or purifies, as gold or silver is refined.[2] But the crucible is also the symbol for temptation, for the suffering which puts faith to the test.[3] Moreover, everything that has passed through the crucible is pure and tested, and the same is true of the word of God.[4]

[1] Jer. 6. 27–30; Ez. 22. 20–22; Mal. 3. 2. [2] Ps. 26. 2; 66. 10; Prov. 17. 3; Is. 1. 25; Jer. 9. 7; Dan. 11. 35; Zech. 13. 9; etc. [3] 1 Pet. 1. 7. [4] Ps. 18. 30; Prov. 30. 5; Rev. 3. 18.

CRUCIFIXION

This horrible torture, Oriental in origin († cross) but not practised by the Israelites, was adopted by the Romans as a punishment for slaves, brigands, rebels, etc.; it was considered a dishonourable death, and so was not applicable to Roman citizens, unless they had committed treason. In certain circumstances the authorities put to death whole groups of offenders by this means: Josephus records that, at the siege of Jerusalem by Titus, "space was lacking for crosses, and crosses for the condemned".

Escorted by soldiers, after an obligatory scourging, the wretch who was to die on the cross carried the transverse beam to the place of execution; the reason for his conviction was proclaimed along the road or published on a placard hung round his neck or carried before him; this placard was then fixed to the cross, for the punishment was to be an example. That is also why the crosses, though set up outside the walls,[1] were not placed in isolated places, but near much-frequented localities and roads.

It is difficult to say precisely how the executioners went about their business, for they probably had a good deal of liberty. Stripped naked except sometimes for a loin cloth, the condemned man was either crucified on the ground, horizontally, on the cross-beam, which was then put into place with its human burden, or he was hoisted on to the cross already prepared, and crucified vertically. He was not necessarily nailed to the wood through the hands, but often securely bound with ropes; the feet were either left free or were nailed or bound (a single nail would sometimes suffice, one foot being placed on top of the other).

The wretch remained suspended in this way for hours or even days on end, exposed without food or drink to the heat of the sun or the inclemency of the weather or even to attacks by wild animals or birds of prey. "Crucifixion is indeed one of the most abominable torments that the very inventive genius of torture has imagined. Perhaps it even holds the first place, *crudelissimum teterrimumque supplicium*, the cruellest and most hideous of torments,' says Cicero.

"Nothing so terrifying as the sight of that body alive, breathing, seeing, hearing, still feeling yet reduced to the condition of corpse by forced immobility and absolute powerlessness. It cannot even be said that the victim writhed in his pain, it was impossible for him to writhe. Stripped of all his clothing, unable to beat off the flies which swarmed over his skin lacerated by the preliminary scourging, no longer capable of retaining the most repulsive excreta, a butt to insults . . . the cross exhibited the wretched human being reduced to the last extremity of impotence, suffering, and degradation. Torture, public exhibition, degradation, certain death, but a death distilled out drop by drop—crucifixion embodied all that could be desired. It was the ideal torment." (Alb. Réville.)

Death supervened in various ways, brought on as

much by respiratory as by circulatory disturbance. Sometimes the mercy stroke was given to the dying by the breaking of the legs. The executioners had the right to the clothes of the condemned whose bodies were finally flung to the beasts; however, a decree by Augustus allowed families to receive the bodies after death, except in cases of conviction by the military authority.—Death by crucifixion was abolished by Constantine.

The Gospel narratives recording the death of Christ [2] are remarkably restrained, and their account agrees on the whole with the information about the torment of the cross given by profane authors. We know that Jesus refused the intoxicating drink which the women of Jerusalem, faithful to the prescriptions of Prov. 31. 6–7, gave to the condemned before the execution; and that the "vinegar", that is, water with vinegar added, with which he was glad to moisten his lips,[3] was probably the drink of the soldiers (there was a widespread belief in the East that a man in torment died as soon as he had a drink), and that the sufferings of the Golgotha martyr lasted a relatively short time, if, as Mark says, Christ was crucified at nine o'clock in the morning [4] and died at three o'clock in the afternoon.[5] It is even possible that the crucifixion took place after nine a.m.—we know that there is disagreement on this point between the evidence of the Synoptic Gospels and the Gospel according to St John.[6]

[1] Cf. Heb. 13. 13. [2] Matt. 27. 33–56; Mk. 15. 22–41; Lk. 23. 33–49; Jn. 19. 17–37. [3] Matt. 27. 48; Mk. 15. 36; Jn. 19. 29. [4] Mk. 15. 25. [5] Mk. 15. 34. [6] Jn. 19. 14.

CUBIT

The cubit was the unit of linear measure; it was equal to the distance between the elbow and the end of the middle finger, and was therefore not invariable. Calculations and considerations too difficult to reproduce here lead to the following conclusions: (1) like the Egyptians and Babylonians, the Israelites distinguished between an ordinary or small cubit and a great (royal or sacred) cubit; (2) the great cubit in Israel was one-sixth larger than the small cubit; [1] (3) the ordinary cubit was about 18 in. and the great cubit about 21 in. (the same for Egypt; for Babylonia, 19·8 and 22 in.); (4) when exact conversion to our units is not required an idea of the dimensions given in a Biblical text can be arrived at by taking a cubit as half a yard; (5) since the cubit comprised 2 spans of 3 handbreadths each, and each handbreadth was subdivided into 4 fingerbreadths, the cubit equalled 24 fingerbreadths; 6 cubits equalled 1 measuring-reed*.

In the O.T. the cubit is very often referred to, particularly in connection with the construction of the Tabernacle, the Temple of Solomon, and Ezekiel's Temple and their furnishings. The cubit is men-

tioned only in the N.T. in Jesus' famous saying: "Which of you, by being anxious, can add one cubit to his stature [or 'to his span of life']"; [2] and in two places where it merely gives a measurement.[3]

[1] 2 Chr. 3. 3; Ez. 40. 5; 43. 13. [2] Matt. 6. 27; Lk. 12. 25. [3] Jn. 21. 8; Rev. 21. 17.

CUCKOO

Although the cuckoo is known in Palestine, it does not seem to be mentioned in the Bible. However, in the lists of unclean creatures, the cuckoo has sometimes been identified with the third bird referred to in Lev. 11. 16 and Dt. 14. 15, though the majority of translators prefer "gull"*, which abounds at the waters' edge; the cuckoo is more rare and hard to capture.

CUCUMBER

Cucumbers are grown in great quantities by the inhabitants of Palestine today. They are less indigestible than the European cucumber, and are much relished, whether raw or cooked, as an inexpensive foodstuff. The Israelites regularly ate them in Egypt. They much regretted the loss of them in the desert,[1] but perhaps came across them again in Canaan or introduced them into that country.

To protect cucumber fields, solitary huts were erected on poles—and to these the prophet compares the city of Jerusalem [2]—or scarecrows were used to ward off marauding animals, the jackal* in particular.

[1] Num. 11. 5. [2] Is. 1. 8.

CUIRASS

Information given by the O.T. about this piece of armour is slight. It seems that, in the beginning, the cuirass in Israel was worn only by kings and chiefs—allusion is made to those of Saul and Ahab (R.V., coat of mail, harness) [1]—and that it was not used in arming soldiers [2] until quite late. Yet we know from the list of booty taken at Megiddo by Thutmose III (1479 B.C.) and from a decorated vase, found in the ruins of that city, that the Canaanites wore cuirasses, which were probably leather jerkins strengthened with metal strips and bosses.

1 Sam. 17. 5 states that Goliath was clad in a heavy cuirass made of brass plates, undoubtedly similar to those used by the Egyptians from the 19th Dynasty onwards: leather jackets, with collar and short sleeves, to which were fastened overlapping metal plates riveted together, or more simply stitched with leather directly to the coat along the upper or lateral edges. The Assyrians also used tunics covered with metal plates which have been depicted on certain bas-reliefs and alluded to by Jeremiah; [3] they protected

certain warriors completely from head to foot; later they reached to the knees, or even to the waist only. Remains of them have been found in the ruins of the country, and excavations in Palestine have yielded some specimens of bronze or iron plates.

Metal plates which, sewn on a leather coat, form a cuirass.

Metaphorically, righteousness,[4] or faith and love [5] are considered as a cuirass (breastplate) for the real soldier of God.

The locusts of Revelation have "breastplates like iron breastplates",[6] and the 200 million horsemen who appear at the sound of the sixth trumpet wear cuirasses (breastplates) of the colour of fire and sapphire and sulphur.[7]

[1] 1 Sam. 17. 38; 1 Kgs. 22. 34. [2] 2 Chr. 26. 14; Neh. 4. 16. [3] Jer. 46. 4; 51. 3. [4] Is. 59. 17; Eph. 6. 14. [5] 1 Th. 5. 8. [6] Rev. 9. 9. [7] Rev. 9. 17.

CUMMIN

Cummin, with its Semitic name, was an umbellifer very well known to the ancient world and widely cultivated in Palestine. Its stimulating and diuretic seeds were used both in medicine and as a condiment. Isaiah mentions it in a kind of parable with the reminder that it was threshed with a stick or rod,[1] as still happens in Palestine. Jesus says that the Scribes and Pharisees scrupulously tithed cummin and other fragrant herbs, but neglected what was vital in the law.[2]

[1] Is. 28. 25, 27. [2] Matt. 23. 23.

CUMMIN (Black)

It is no doubt black cummin (Nigella), not corn-cockle, vetch, or dill*, as some translators have thought, that the prophet Isaiah mentions,[1] along with cummin*, saying that they are both threshed with a stick or rod, just as is still done today in Palestine.—Cultivated Nigella (popularly, black cummin, allspice, etc.) is an herbaceous plant whose

Nigella or black cummin.

black, aromatic seeds resemble those of cummin and are similarly used for condiment. Eastern people sprinkle them on certain kinds of bread and cakes.

[1] Is. 28. 25, 27.

CUP

The Israelites used cups of diverse forms, materials, and sizes, designated by a number of terms whose exact sense cannot always easily be determined: cups for secular use intended to take wine, milk, or water [1] or for religious use designed for ritual libations,[2] simple clay cups, or cups worked in alabaster, silver, or gold.[3] Many are the utensils of this kind found in Palestinian excavations.

Iranian and Palestinian cups.

Joseph's cup mentioned in Genesis [4] was a divinatory cup: the movements of oil poured on water or the effects produced by sparkling objects thrown in were observed and interpreted.—Jeremiah [5] alludes to the "cup of consolation" offered to mourners after a funeral. We know the importance which the cup took that Jesus passed round at the Last Supper with his disciples.[6]

Biblical texts often speak of cups in a metaphorical sense,[7] particularly of cups full of divine wrath.

Libation flagon of Prince Gudea; 22nd century.

Jesus reproached the hypocritical Pharisees with cleaning only the outside of the cup and the dish.[8] His passion presented itself to him under the figure of a cup that he asked God to remove from his lips.[9]

[1] Jg. 5. 25; 6. 38; 2 Sam. 12. 3; 17. 28; Prov. 23. 31; Jer. 35. 5; Amos 6. 6; cf. Gen. 40. 11. [2] Ex. 25. 29; 27. 3; 37. 16; 38. 3; Num. 4. 14; 7. 13; 1 Kgs. 7. 26, 50; 2 Kgs. 12. 13; Jer. 52. 19; Rev. 5. 8. [3] 1 Kgs. 7. 26; 10. 21; Jer. 51. 7; Rev. 17. 4; etc. [4] Gen. 44. 2, 5. [5] Jer. 16. 7. [6] Matt. 26. 27; Mk. 14. 23; Lk. 22. 17; 1 Cor. 10. 16; 11. 25, 28. [7] Ps. 23. 5; 75. 8; 116. 13; Jer. 16. 7; Rev. 17. 4; 18. 6; etc.; Is. 51. 17; Jer. 25. 15; Rev. 14. 10; 15. 7; 16. 1; 21. 9. [8] Matt. 23. 25; Mk. 7. 4; Lk. 11. 39. [9] Matt. 26. 39; Mk. 14. 36; Lk. 22. 42; cf. Matt. 20. 22; Mk. 10. 38; Jn. 18. 11.

CUP-BEARER

Cup-bearers, important men, officers of high rank, sometimes eunuchs, were responsible for serving drinks at the courts of kings of antiquity. They are occasionally depicted on Egyptian and Assyrian monuments. They were men of high trust, watching over their master for fear of his being poisoned, and because of this they sometimes had to taste the wine before serving it.

According to tradition,[1] the chief cup-bearer to the Pharaoh played an important part in Joseph's destiny. The Books of Kings and Chronicles record that Solomon had several cup-bearers in his service.[2] Among the important functionaries sent by Sennacherib to Hezekiah[3] was the Rabshakeh, whose name means the great cup-bearer. Most versions make it a proper name. We know that Nehemiah was cup-bearer to Artaxerxes I.[4]

[1] Gen. 40 and 41. [2] 1 Kgs. 10. 5; 2 Chr. 9. 4. [3] 2 Kgs. 18. 17. [4] Neh. 1. 11.

CURSE

Like all Orientals, the Israelites were quick to utter imprecations, curses which they hurled in the teeth of their enemies or which they pronounced to protect themselves against the consequences of a crime,[1] or to underline some of their oaths;[2] most often they were not empty words thrown away on the air, but utterances, formulae, in the efficacy of which there was absolute belief; sometimes, the magic power of the words was strengthened by certain rites.[3]

Once uttered, the curse could not be recalled; sooner or later it would inevitably be fulfilled,[4] unless it was neutralized by a blessing[5] or turned aside: "Upon me be thy curse, my son," said Rebekah to Jacob.[6] In time the idea grew, however, that Yahweh could change a curse to a blessing,[7] and that an undeserved curse was doomed to failure.[8]

As in Greece, Italy, and elsewhere, in excavations in Palestine of strata dating from Hellenistic times, tablets with imprecatory formulae, and lead figurines bound hand and foot, have come to light; these bonds signify in a magical way the bonds of prison, illness, or death for the persons intended or represented. It is well known that the Book of Psalms itself contains terrible words of vengeance against personal enemies, and against the enemies of Israel.[9]

However, no curse should be directed against a leader of the people,[10] nor—a point to be noted—against a man afflicted with deafness;[11] and it was forbidden, under penalty of death, to curse one's father or mother,[12] and of course Yahweh himself.[13]

[1] 2 Sam. 3. 9, 28 f. [2] 1 Sam. 14. 24; 25. 22; 2 Kgs. 6. 31. [3] Gen. 15. 7 . . .; Num. 5. 11 . . .; Jer. 34. 18. [4] Jos. 6. 26; 1 Kgs. 16. 34; Ps. 109. 17; Zech. 5. 3; cf. Num. 23 and 24. [5] Jg. 17. 1 . . .; cf. Ex. 12. 32. [6] Gen. 27. 13. [7] Dt. 23. 5; Neh. 13. 2. [8] Prov. 26. 2. [9] Ps. 35. 4 . . .; 58. 7–10; 109. 2–20; 137. 8; 139. 19–22. [10] Ex. 22. 28. [11] Lev. 19. 14. [12] Ex. 21. 17; Lev. 20. 9; Matt. 15. 4; Mk. 7. 10. [13] Lev. 24. 11, 15; 1 Kgs. 21. 10.

CUSHION

The cushion, or more exactly "pillow", mentioned in one of the narratives of the stilling of the storm,[1] and on which Jesus slept, was placed in the stern of the boat and was probably intended for those who took a turn of sleep during nights of fishing at sea.

[1] Mk. 4. 38.

CYMBALS

Among the musical instruments used by the Israelites for ceremonies and festivals the O.T. mentions quite often,[1] from the time of David onwards, the cymbals, well known to the ancient world. They were either two bronze plates, raised in the centre like modern cymbals, and beaten horizontally while held in the middle by means of a buckle or cord, or else they were hemispherical or conical cymbals also of bronze, but smaller, fitted with a handle and beaten vertically.—The name cymbal was also given to an instrument in the shape of two wooden skittles,

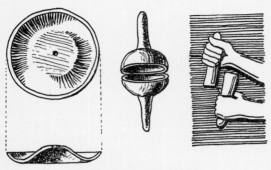

Various forms of cymbals.

elongated and probably grooved. Examples of these instruments, which were beaten or scraped together, are on bas-reliefs. St Paul speaks metaphorically of the "tinkling cymbal" at the beginning of his hymn to love.[2]

[1] 2 Sam. 6. 5; 1 Chr. 15. 19; 16. 5; 2 Chr. 5. 12; Ezr. 3. 10; Neh. 12. 27; Ps. 150. 5; etc. [2] 1 Cor. 13. 1.

CYPRESS

Wild cypress, of which the one growing in our cemeteries is only a cultivated variety, was much in demand because of its hard, aromatic wood, admitting of fine polish and almost rot-proof. Pliny records that the doors of the temple of Diana at Ephesus, made of cypress wood, were as good as new after 400 years.

The O.T. stresses the beauty and grandeur [1] of this evergreen [2] tree and often associates its name—significantly enough—with the cedar, the king of plants.[3] Cypress wood, originating in the Lebanon, which Hiram king of Tyre delivered to Solomon,[4] was used for making the floor of the sanctuary and the leaves of the door.[5] Ezekiel refers to the use of this wood for boat-building.[6] (The text of 2 Sam. 6. 5, which mentions musical instruments of cypress wood, and Nahum 2. 3, which mentions spears of cypress that were brandished, have been corrupted and need to be corrected in an entirely different sense.)

Sometimes the Hebrew word for cypress has been wrongly translated by pine or even fir, but it is possible that under this word were included certain species of trees of similar appearance († juniper).

[1] Is. 55. 13; 60. 13; Ez. 31. 8; Ps. 104. 17; Cant. 1. 17. [2] Hos. 14. 8. [3] 2 Kgs. 19. 23; 2 Chr. 2. 8; Is. 14. 8; 37. 24; Zech. 11. 1. [4] 1 Kgs. 5. 8, 10; 9. 11. [5] 1 Kgs. 6. 15–35. [6] Ez. 27. 5.

DANCE

As with all peoples of antiquity, dance occupied an important place in the life of the Israelites. The Hebrew language possesses as many as eight verbs to describe the action signifying to jump, to dance.

Like those of Oriental peoples today, the dances consisted of round dances, rhythmical actions, jumps, complete turns, movements of a generally lively, joyous pace, regulated by the sound of tambourines and accompanied by songs and music. For the most part the girls danced together; [1] the women also gave themselves up to this pleasure; [2] the men more rarely; and sometimes to show its joy the whole population joined in the festival. It was rare for a male or female dancer to perform alone; but the Philistines sent for Samson to amuse them with dances and feats of strength.[3] The effect produced by Salome's dance upon Herod and his guests is well known.[4]

Quite naturally, dance stresses the happy hours and events of life: [5] people danced at the wine harvests,[6] on the day following a victory,[7] at weddings, on the occasion of solemn feasts.[8] The parable relates that when the prodigal son returned to his father's home and the fatted calf was killed for him, the celebration was accompanied by music and dances.[9]

But eastern antiquity did not practise secular dances only. Among the peoples neighbouring on Israel, dance was an integral part of religious ceremonies: the priests of Baal used to dance round his altars,[10] limping—i.e., on each beat they came down with all their weight on one leg; there existed even among the Phoenicians a "Baal of dance". It was not excluded from the cult of Yahweh; [11] when David brought the Ark* back to Jerusalem he "danced with all his might before Yahweh".[12] Certain ceremonies took place in the Temple of Jerusalem to the sound of timbrels,[13] and religious songs could be accompanied by dances. We know that at the Feast of Tabernacles a torch dance was performed in one of the Temple courts by priests and eminent laymen. Certain passages of the O.T. imply that dances of a fanatical, ecstatic nature were not unknown in Israel.[14] They doubtless resembled those of the dancing dervishes of the East.

More than one text refers to the Israelites' liking of dance; [15] the Song of Songs describes the dance of the Shulammite woman,[16] which recalls the dance of the dagger, performed during Syrian or Bedouin wedding festivities; and Jesus referred to children imitating the dances of their elders in the market-place [17] and to the sound of the flute.

[1] Jg. 11. 34; 21. 21; Jer. 31. 4, 13. [2] Ex. 15. 20; 1 Sam. 18. 6. [3] Jg. 16. 25, 27. [4] Matt. 14. 6; Mk. 6. 22. [5] Is. 5. 12; Jer. 31. 4, 13; Lam. 5. 15. [6] Jg. 9. 27; Is. 16. 10. [7] 1 Sam. 18. 6; 21. 11; 29. 5; 30. 16. [8] Jg. 16. 25; Matt. 14. 6; Mk.

94

6. 22. [9] Lk. 15. 25. [10] 1 Kgs. 18. 21, 26. [11] Ex. 32. 6, 19; 2 Sam. 6. 5; Ps. 149. 3; 150. 4. [12] 2 Sam. 6. 14. [13] Ps. 68. 25. [14] 1 Sam. 10. 5, 10; 2 Sam. 6. 16; 1 Chr. 15. 29. [15] Job 21. 11–12; Eccl. 3. 4. [16] Cant. 6. 13 ff. [17] Matt. 11. 17; Lk. 7. 32.

[1] Ex. 12. 18; Lev. 23. 32; Neh. 13. 19; Ps. 55. 17. [2] Gen. 1. 5; 19. 2; Dan. 8. 14. [3] Gen. 15. 12, 17; 19. 23; 32. 31; Mk. 16. 2. [4] Gen. 19. 15; 32. 24. [5] Gen. 18. 1; 1 Sam. 11. 11; Prov. 4. 18. [6] Jg. 19. 8. [7] Gen. 3. 8; Cant. 2. 17. [8] Gen. 24. 11. [9] 1 Kgs. 18. 29–36; Ezr. 9. 4. [10] Matt. 27. 62; Mk. 15. 42; Lk. 23. 54; Jn. 19. 31, 42.

DARIC

The daric was a gold coin, created by Darius I, weighing about ¼ oz. (0·27 oz.) and worth about 24s. It carried a portrait of the king in the form of an archer. In the time of Persian domination it was current in Palestine. It is mentioned in Ezr. 8. 27 (a gift of twenty gold bowls for the Temple, worth 1,000 darics) and in 1 Chr. 29. 7 (in the time of David, which is clearly an anachronism); some commentators have found it in Ezr. 2. 69 (offerings of 61,000 darics for the rebuilding of the Temple, also an anachronism because it belongs to a period before Darius' time) and in Neh. 7. 70–72 (payment of various offerings to the Temple treasury); but in the two last texts it is probably a matter of gold "drachmas" of the same value, rather than of darics.

Daric.

DAY

Although certain peoples of antiquity made the civil day begin either in the morning, at midday, or at midnight, others (Athenians, Germani, nomads, etc.), and the Israelites in particular, counted their day from one sunset to the other: for them the end of the day coincided with the end of work or with the arrival at the halting-place, and nightfall marked the beginning of a new day.[1] This practice was perpetuated throughout the ages among the Jews, and still today the celebration of the Sabbath and religious festivals begins at nightfall.

But it is clear that the Israelites also understood by "day" the time during which the earth was lit up: the natural day, that of ordinary life, in contrast to night.[2] In ancient times that day was not divided up in a precise way. To indicate the different moments of the day, they were satisfied with general terms: evening, morning, midday, or with more significant expressions: at the rising or going down of the sun,[3] at the arising of the dawn,[4] in the heat of the day or at the height of the day,[5] at the decline of day;[6] they also said "in the cool of the day"[7] (more exactly, at the wind of the day), the time when women go out to draw water,[8] the time of the offering of the evening sacrifice.[9]—The division into hours* was not, apparently, introduced into Israel until after the Exile.

With the exception of the Sabbath, the days of the week bore no special name and were simply numbered, like those of the month. The day (or the evening) preceding the Sabbath was, however, called "the preparation".[10]

DEACON

This word which in Greek signifies "servant" is very often used in the N.T. in its wider meaning: St Paul in particular considers himself as the servant (minister) of God for the Gospel of Christ[1] and as the servant of men.[2]—But in two or three passages the word "deacon" undoubtedly designates an ecclesiastical function. It is thus that the Epistle to the Philippians[3] is addressed "to all the saints in Christ Jesus who are at Philippi, with the bishops and deacons", and that the First Epistle to Timothy[4] enumerates the qualities demanded in the latter. However, we know nothing precise about their office. There is every reason to believe, however, that, as servants of the community and not as "bishops", the deacons were appointed especially to the care of external things, that their activity was exercised essentially in the realm of liberality and mercy and that they looked after the disinherited, the poor and the sick. They had to be without reproach, full of seriousness and loyalty, sober, unselfish, "keeping the mystery of the faith in a pure conscience", husbands of one wife only and directing their children and household well. These demands are significant and show the importance and the serious nature of their task, which was to make them fellow workers of bishops.

The tradition of the Church has always seen in the account of Acts 6[5] the institution of the diaconate. The resemblance between the deacons and the seven elect of Jerusalem is understandable; the latter, men of good renown, full of wisdom and filled with the Holy Spirit, are chosen by the faithful and, having received the laying on of hands from the apostles, are thus solemnly appointed to the service of tables and to the daily distribution of help to the poor; but it must be clearly observed that they are by no means called "deacons" either in this chapter or—in contrast to what certain translations state—in the rest of the Acts of the Apostles;[6] moreover, their activity did not remain limited to tasks of a material nature: Stephen and Philip, in particular, were fervent evangelists.[7]

The diaconate sprang spontaneously into being in various places; its ecclesiastical character gained precision with time, and the deacons found their place in the hierarchy, where they constitute the last of the major orders.

[1] 1 Cor. 3. 5; 2 Cor. 6. 3 . . .; etc. [2] Rom. 15. 25; 2 Cor. 11. 8; etc. [3] Phil. 1. 1. [4] 1 Ti. 3. 8–13. [5] Acts 6. 1–6. [6] Acts 21. 8. [7] Acts 6. 8 . . .; 8. 4 . . .; 8. 26 . . .

DEACONESS

The N.T. gives very little information about the institution of deaconesses. It was only developed later in the Church of the first centuries.—St Paul limited himself to recommending to the recipients of his Epistle to the Romans,[1] Phoebe, deaconess (servant) of the church of Cenchreae (port of Corinth), but it is probable that it was not yet a question of an office, or a function: Phoebe will have freely served the church and the apostle by her kindness, generosity, and devotion. In 1 Ti. 3. 11, in the middle of a passage devoted to deacons*, it is written that (the) "women must be grave, not slanderers, temperate, faithful in all things". It is evident that the author of this text does not mean women in general but a special category, without its being possible to assert whether it is a question of "deaconesses" having an activity analogous to that of the deacons, or wives and female helpers of the deacons, which seems very likely.—In another passage of the same Epistle,[2] there is the question of the registration of widows of over sixty years of age who enjoyed a good reputation. Would they alone have the right to receive help from the church? It has been thought that they constituted a sort of college or order called to render important services to the community, but it does not appear that they were "deaconesses" so-called, holding an office which related them to the clergy.

[1] Rom. 16. 1. [2] 1 Ti. 5. 9, 10.

DEAFNESS

In their metaphorical language the prophets allude to this infirmity,[1] and they also announce a time when the deaf will hear.[2]—The Gospel mentions the recovery of a deaf man and of a deaf-mute.[3] An interesting point of Israelite legislation is that, just as it is forbidden to put an obstacle in the way of a blind man, so a deaf person is not to be cursed [4] (although he does not hear).

[1] Ps. 38. 14; 58. 4; Is. 42. 18; 43. 8. [2] Is. 29. 18; 35. 5; cf. Matt. 11. 5; Lk. 7. 22. [3] Mk. 7. 32 . . .; 9. 24. [4] Lev. 19. 14.

DEBT

Although Israelite law allowed a debtor to make himself a slave in order to be able to pay his debts,[1] and it even demanded that the thief who was unable to repay should be sold because of his theft,[2] it does not appear to authorize the creditor himself to lay hands on the debtor.[3] On the other hand, it seems to allow the practice whereby a father could sell his children to pay his debt.[4] The Second Book of Kings tells of a widow who appealed to Elisha to be saved from selling her two children,[5] and the Book of Nehemiah of parents reduced to selling their sons and daughters to be able to fulfil their obligations.[6] Amos condemns the creditors who sold their Israelite brethren for a pair of shoes.[7] In the N.T. the unmerciful servant of the parable must be sold, together with his wife and children, at the order of the man to whom he owes a large sum of money.[8] The same account tells us, moreover, that imprisonment for debt was not unknown at the time of Christ: the man who has just benefited from the kindness of his master attacks his own debtor and has him mercilessly imprisoned for insolvency.[9]

The relations between creditors and debtors were often very strained in Israel; Jeremiah refers to the hate they bore each other.[10] Many a man in debt preferred to escape all subjection by seeking the open country: the first band of people David gathered about him was largely made up of adventurers of this sort.[11]—It must be recognized, however, that legislation was always sought to protect the debtor and to stem the excesses of creditors († pledge, usury). It prescribed in particular a certain number of very interesting measures in favour of those who had to resort to slavery († slave, Sabbath).

Jesus did not remain insensitive to the people's preoccupation in this respect: apart from the parable mentioned previously, he told the one about the unfaithful steward [12] and the one about the two unequal debtors; [13] and the fifth request of the Lord's Prayer itself, in its exact form, is thus worded: "Forgive us our debts as we forgive our debtors." [14] Moreover, these fine words of St Paul are well known: "Owe no man anything, but to love one another." [15]

[1] Lev. 25. 39, 47. [2] Ex. 22. 3. [3] Cf. Dt. 24. 7. [4] Ex. 21. 7. [5] 2 Kgs. 4. 1–7. [6] Neh. 5. 5; cf. Is. 50. 1; Gen. 47. 18, 21. [7] Amos 2. 6. [8] Matt. 18. 25. [9] Matt. 18. 30. [10] Jer. 15. 10; cf. Job. 22. 6; Ps. 109. 11. [11] 1 Sam. 22. 2. [12] Lk. 16. 5 . . . [13] Lk. 7. 41 . . . [14] Matt. 6. 12; Lk. 11. 4. [15] Rom. 13. 8.

DEDICATION (FEAST OF)

It is stated in Jn. 10. 22 that the Feast of Dedication was celebrated in winter. This refers to neither the dedication of Solomon's Temple nor the dedication of the Temple of Zerubbabel. On the 25th Chislev (about 20th December) of 168 B.C., to the great shame of the Jews, Antiochus IV Epiphanes had begun to offer pagan sacrifices on a little altar set up on the altar of burnt offerings in the Temple of Jerusalem. Three years after, Judas Maccabaeus, having taken the city, purified the sanctuary and dedicated it anew; in the same month and on the same day it had been profaned, the altar was consecrated again, to the singing of psalms, the sound of harps, lyres, and cymbals.[1] It was the 25th Chislev 165; and it was decided to repeat the feast from year to year "with gladness and joy".[2] The illumination of houses and synagogues characterized the celebration of this anniversary; in time it represented the light of the Law which triumphed over the darkness of heathenism, thanks to Judas Maccabaeus. This feast was related to the prophecy of Haggai,[3] who announced a blessing after the 24th day of the 7th month. In this prophecy western Christians were to see the announcement of the birth of Jesus Christ, who is himself the greatest blessing which God has granted to the world.

The Feast of Dedication, which recalled that of Tabernacles*,[4] lasted eight days. During this time, without ceasing to work, people made good cheer and went to special religious services, carrying palms and branches.

This feast subsists in the present-day calender of the Jews under the name of "Ḥanukkah" (dedication).

[1] 1 Macc. 4. 54. [2] 1 Macc. 4. 59. [3] Hagg. 2. 18–19.
[4] 2 Macc. 1. 9; 10. 6.

DEED OF SALE

On the occasion of the sale or purchase of land, witnesses were required to attest the transaction or its terms. In the time of Abraham [1] nothing in our texts suggests a custom of written stipulations at such a contract. However, sale contracts of the 14th century B.C. have been found in Palestine, written on tablets, sealed and signed by a large number of witnesses. When Jeremiah bought some land [2] he seems to have drawn up a contract of sale on papyrus and in duplicate; the original was deposited in a jar with a sealed cover, as an archive record, while the copy was given to the purchaser. Similar ones, dating from the 2nd century A.D., have been found in the Dead Sea caves.

[1] Gen. 23. 10–16. [2] Jer. 32. 10–15.

DEER

The catalogue of clean animals in Dt. 14. 5 (third name), and the list of creatures consumed by Solomon's entourage,[1] refer to an animal which must be the deer, even though it does not seem to have been very common in Palestine, from which it has disappeared today.—Formerly the buffalo, the bubal (antelope) or a variety of roe-deer have been suggested.
(† Hart.)

[1] 1 Kgs. 4. 23.

DENARIUS

As a Roman monetary unit, the silver denarius was current in Palestine from the middle of the 1st century B.C. It was worth a little under ninepence, but its purchasing power then was naturally greater than this would be today: it represented the normal daily wage of a workman [1] (Parable of the Workers in the Vineyard), or an average daily expenditure

(Parable of the Good Samaritan).[2] Jesus asked for a denarius in replying to the captious question of his adversaries; [3] for it was the coin used for paying taxes and it bore the following inscription in Latin round the laurel-wreathed head of Tiberius: "Tiberius, Caesar Augustus, son of the divine Augustus", and on the reverse side, along with a

A denarius of Tiberius, which may be the type referred to in Matt. 22. 19.

symbolic figure, the words: "Chief Pontiff" (High Priest).

The denarius is also mentioned in the Parable of the Unmerciful Servant,[4] in the accounts of the multiplication of the loaves,[5] the anointing at Bethany [6] and the woman who was a sinner,[7] as well as in the Book of Revelation (6. 6).

[1] Matt. 20. 2. [2] Lk. 10. 35. [3] Matt. 22. 19; Mk. 12. 15; Lk. 20. 24. [4] Matt. 18. 28. [5] Mk. 6. 37; Jn. 6. 7. [6] Mk. 14. 5; Jn. 12. 5. [7] Lk. 7. 41.

DEPOSIT

The legislative regulations of the Covenant Code deal with deposits entrusted to other people.[1] In the case of an animal handed over to the care of a keeper, the latter is responsible for it, and, even in the case of theft by a third party, he must compensate the owner; [2] however, if the animal dies or is the victim of an accident (or, perhaps, has been stolen in special circumstances, but the text on this score is not very certain) and if the keeper can swear in the name of Yahweh that he is in no way responsible, the matter is shelved.[3] Similarly, he does not have to repay the owner if the animal has been torn up by a wild animal and if he has been able to present the remains as proof.[4] Certain masters, it is true, cared little for this rule.[5]

If a deposit consisting of money or movable objects is stolen, the thief is condemned to repay twofold.[6] If the thief is not found, the trustee appears before the judges so that it can be found out, by making him take the oath or by a judgment of God (the text does not specify), whether he has "put his hand unto his neighbour's goods".[7] In a similar circumstance the Babylonian Code of Hammurabi, which is more severe, compels the trustee to give compensation, to be repaid, if possible, by the thief.

The Priestly Code, on the other hand, declares that the man who cheats his neighbour in the case of

G

a deposit by appropriating it to himself must return what he has kept, with one-fifth interest, and offer a sacrifice of atonement.[8]

[1] Ex. 22. 7–13. [2] Ex. 22. 12. [3] Ex. 22. 10, 11. [4] Ex. 22. 13; 1 Sam. 17. 34, 35; Amos 3. 12. [5] Gen. 31. 39. [6] Ex. 22. 7. [7] Ex. 22. 8. [8] Lev. 6. 2–5.

DEVOTE

In conformity with a practice found among other peoples and still among some non-civilized peoples today, the Israelites might consecrate to their God beings or objects, which as a result of that became taboo, untouchable. A "ban" or anathema was pronounced on them—they were holy, even dangerous, and so that no one should take possession of them they were usually devoted to total destruction. In Hebrew the word translated by "devoted thing, ban" comes from a root meaning "to cut off, to make unapproachable"; it occurs again in the term "harem", the strictly private apartments of Mohammedan wives.

In ancient times, people had recourse to this practice in case of war in order to stress, for example, its holy [1] nature, or in order to obtain from God particularly efficacious help necessitated by a difficult campaign: "And Israel vowed a vow unto Yahweh, and said, If thou wilt indeed deliver this people into my hand, then I will devote [i.e., utterly destroy] their cities." [2] The Moabites, as we know from the stele of their King Mesha (the Moabite Stone, 9th century B.C.), acted similarly in certain circumstances in order to please their national god. The "ban" forced people to renounce all material gain in victory; [3] everything was remitted to the deity—the enemy was utterly massacred, as also the cattle; houses were destroyed, and plunder burned; [4] at most, some objects were deposited in the sanctuaries. [5] In Israel, woe betide him who had purloined the smallest part of what had been consecrated to Yahweh: the anathema fell upon the guilty one and upon the entire people. The story of Achan, [6] who after the fall of Jericho had reserved for himself gold and silver as well as a costly mantle, is significant in this respect. It has even been wondered whether, originally, the "ban" was not a magical rite, a sort of "strengthened curse", releasing at the same moment a power deadly to the enemies, yet also fatal to any who had violated its rules.

But—and here again it can be seen how closely related are the notions of the holy and the unclean—there also fell under the blow of total destruction not only what was in some way or other offered to Yahweh as a sacrifice of gratitude, but everything which could cast a slur on his holiness and everything contrary to his worship. [7] The "ban" became a punishment on what was tainted with idolatry, with "heathenism". Deuteronomy (and the texts related to it) insists much upon that notion: it consigns to anathema the town which has begun to serve other gods than Yahweh; [8] it even claims that at the time of the conquest of Palestine by the Israelites, all the natives had to be massacred to prevent any infiltration of the abominable practices observed by the Canaanites. [9]

It appears, however, that the "ban", whether consecration or punishment, was a rather exceptional measure. Moreover, more than one text of the O.T. shows that it was not always applied in all its severity; that upon occasion women and children [10] could be spared, or at any rate girls; [11] and that sometimes even the cattle and the booty of the captured town [12] could be kept. As a custom of war, the anathema appears to have disappeared gradually from Israel, but it is nevertheless found in two forms right up to later times: on the one hand, the punishment-ban is transformed into banishment from the community [13] and, at the beginning of the Christian era, into excommunication; on the other hand, the Israelite will always be able personally to consecrate to the Lord what he wants, in a solemn, untransferable way, so that what is thus consecrated is no longer destroyed but remitted to God (that is, to the priests) without the possibility of being redeemed. [14]

(† Corban.)

[1] 1 Sam. 15. 1–3. [2] Num. 21. 2–3; Dt. 7. 2. [3] 1 Sam. 15. [4] Jos. 6. 21, 24. [5] Jos. 6. 19, 24. [6] Jos. 7; cf. 1 Kgs. 20. 42. [7] Ex. 22. 20. [8] Dt. 13. 12–18. [9] Dt. 7. 25–26; 20. 18; cf. Jos. 11. 10–23. [10] Dt. 20. 14. [11] Num. 31. 18; Jg. 21. 12. [12] Dt. 2. 35; 3. 7; 20. 14; Jos. 8. 27. [13] Ezr. 10. 8. [14] Lev. 27. 28; Num. 18. 14; Ez. 44. 29.

DEW

The climate of Palestine is such that in the dry season absolutely no rain falls. Sometimes it ceases completely by March, at a time when the crops are already well developed. Often afterwards, however, the rains called "latter rains" provide advantageous moisture. But after these there is only dew to give the necessary humidity, and when the April rains fail the dew is not merely advantageous but indispensable. It can, indeed, be very abundant in the mountains when the warm air rising from the plains condenses in the coolness of the night. The range of night and day temperatures is very large; in Jerusalem it averages $10 \cdot 8°$ C.

This is why dew is considered a blessing. Isaac bestows it upon Jacob when he blesses him; [1] and the mystery of its origin means that it is regarded as a gift of God. [2] While sometimes it is a symbol for what rapidly passes away, [3] it is, because of its beneficent action, a figure for kindly human speech, [4] and in particular for a king's favour; [5] for the prophet it is as a parable of God's love. [6]

[1] Gen. 27. 28. [2] Job 38. 28; Dt. 33. 13. [3] Hos. 6. 4; Mic. 5. 7. [4] Dt. 32. 2. [5] Prov. 19. 12. [6] Hos. 14. 5.

DIADEM

Diadem has sometimes been used to translate different Hebrew words which signify more exactly: crown*, tiara († priest), turban († head-dress). It appears that the word diadem should be reserved for the noun *nezer*, which implies an idea of consecration, of putting aside. It is the royal insignia *par excellence*, and undoubtedly had the shape of a band round the forehead. Saul wore a diadem which an Amalekite, who boasted of having killed the first king of Israel, brought triumphantly to David;[1] after Joash was proclaimed king, Jehoiada placed a diadem on the head of the young sovereign.[2] It was a diadem, too, which the High Priest wore, made of a leaf of pure gold on which were engraved the words "Holy to the Lord", and it was fixed to a ribbon so that it could be attached to the front of the priest's head-dress.[3]

The Book of Revelation tells, also, of diadems placed on the seven heads of the great red dragon[4] and on the ten horns of the beast rising out of the sea;[5] and the Messiah, the faithful and true, sits on a white horse and wears on his head many diadems[6] (in this way sovereignty over many realms was denoted).

Certain female ornaments undoubtedly recalled royal diadems, but they are not mentioned in the Bible, for in Is. 3. 20 and elsewhere the references are rather to head-bands. A certain number of head-bands or diadems, dating from different epochs and made of beaten and chased gold, have been found in Palestinian excavations.

[1] 2 Sam. 1. 10. [2] 2 Kgs. 11. 12. [3] Ex. 28. 36; 29. 6; 39. 30; Lev. 8. 9. [4] Rev. 12. 3. [5] Rev. 13. 1. [6] Rev. 19. 12.

DIAL

In the Book of Isaiah[1] there is reference to the "steps of Ahaz" upon which the prophet made King Hezekiah see a miraculous backward movement of the shadow of the sun. The two texts are not very explicit. It has been thought to be a kind of sun-dial akin to those used by the people of Mesopotamia and the Egyptians, which Ahaz, the father of Hezekiah, may have brought from Assyria or Damascus;[2] or, more particularly, an obelisk whose shadow moved either over the steps leading up to it or over a graduated circumference. However, the Greek translator of Is. 38. 8 read it as "the steps of the house of thy father", so it might mean, more simply, a return of the shadow on the stairway of the royal palace.

[1] Is. 38. 8 (2 Kgs. 20. 9–11). [2] 2 Kgs. 16. 10 . . .

DIAMOND

The diamond was probably unknown to the Israelites. For this reason, and others besides, the two

99

Hebrew words which have often been translated by "diamond"[1] more probably denote adamantine spar or some other precious stone.

[1] Ex. 28. 18; Ez. 28. 13; Jer. 17. 1; Ez. 3. 9; Zech. 7. 12.

DIDRACHMA

The didrachma is mentioned only once in the N.T.[1] It was a Greek silver coin, worth two drachmas*, that is, almost 1s. 6d., and equivalent to a

A didrachma of Tyre, struck in A.D. 14 and found at Jerusalem.

Jewish half-shekel. It was the sum due yearly from every Jew as a contribution towards the cultus and upkeep of the Temple.[2]

(† Tetradrachma, money, money-changer.)

[1] Matt. 17. 24. [2] Ex. 30. 11 . . .

DILL

Dill, to which Jesus referred[1] in connection with the tithing to which it was subject,[2] is an umbellifer with yellow flowers, a relative of fennel, and abundant in Mediterranean lands, where it grows wild. It is often cultivated for its fragrant seeds, which resemble those of the lentil. They are used in Palestine for condiment and medicine. Dill is not to be confused with black cummin*.

[1] Matt. 23. 23. [2] Dt. 14. 22; Lev. 27. 30.

Dill.

DISH

Dishes of all kinds and from various periods have been unearthed in Palestine excavations. In certain passages the Bible alludes to these utensils which were in common use by the Israelites; thus, the Book of Proverbs[1] says that the sluggard plunges his hand into the dish without having even the energy to lift it to his mouth; Judas put his hand to the dish with Jesus,[2] and Jesus reproached the Pharisees with being content to wash "the outside of the cup and of the dish".[3]—The ministrations in the sanctuary involved the use of dishes made of precious metals.[4]

[1] Prov. 19. 24; 26. 15. [2] Matt. 26. 23; Mk. 14. 20. [3] Matt. 23. 25; Lk. 11. 39 (cf. Matt. 14. 8, 11). [4] Ex. 25. 29; 37. 16; Num. 7. 13, 84.

DIVER

The second unclean bird listed in Lev. 11. 17 (the third in Dt. 14. 17) is probably the diver, which winters even as far south as the Mediterranean. Its Hebrew name, coming from a root which means "to cast down", could also, however, refer to the cormorant* or to any other diving bird.

DIVINATION

The art of interpreting omens, of discovering the future and hidden things of which man could have no direct knowledge, was extremely widespread among the peoples neighbouring on Israel. The O.T. refers to numerous methods of divination practised by the Egyptians, Babylonians, Canaanites, and Syrians. Keeping to Biblical texts there are in particular: *hepatoscopy*, that is, examination of the liver of sacrificial victims; the condition of this organ permitted all sorts of infinitely precious oracles to be derived from it;[1] *cylicomancy*, or consultation by means of a cup, from patterns produced by fragments of precious and brilliant substances thrown into a goblet full of water[2] (cf. *lecanomancy*, an old practice consisting of interpreting the position and shape taken by one or more drops of oil poured on to the water in a metal bowl); *belomancy*, or divination by arrows[3] bearing a name or signs: the first drawn from the quiver indicating, for example, the town to be attacked first; *rhabdomancy*, interpretation of the position taken by rods or sticks which had been dropped.[4] Although observation of the flight of birds, common to the Greeks and Romans, does not appear to have been practised by the peoples of the East, there is perhaps an allusion in the O.T. to the observation of the course of the clouds or serpents[5] (*ophiomancy*). It was also thought that God made his will known by means of dreams, and *oniromancy*, or the interpretation of dreams, which people sometimes tried to cultivate, played an important part in the whole of the ancient world.[6] To obtain the revelation of the future, they went as far as to evoke the dead, the spirits of the dead, and this *necromancy*[7] was often faked with ventriloquism by the soothsayers. As for *astrology**, the important place it occupied from earliest times is well known—particularly among Mesopotamian peoples: for them it was the best means of discovering the mysteries of life and the future.[8] Also mentioned are the practice of *incantations* and of *sacred delirium*, provoked by heady vapours or the use of spirits and narcotics,[9] etc. In the N.T., also, the apostles encounter magicians and exorcists who practise divination: Simon the magician, Bar-Jesus of Paphos, the damsel possessed with a spirit of divination at Philippi, etc.[10]

We can understand that the Israelites found difficulty in freeing themselves from their general environment, for they were tempted to imitate what was going on around them;[11] soothsayers even had a free hand in the reign of certain kings: we have only to think of the witchcrafts of Jezebel,[12] of the statements made in texts such as 2 Kgs. 17. 17, Is. 3. 3 or Jer. 27. 9, of Manasseh and his omens, his necromancers and his wizards,[13] of the evil customs which Josiah's reform abolished,[14] and of the vehement declarations of the prophets.[15] The Law, on its side, forbade the practices of divination,[16] sometimes on pain of death.—But Yahweh had from time immemorial been consulted by drawing lots[17] or by means (teraphim*, ephod*, urim and thummim*, magic*) in some way akin to those used elsewhere;[18] Matthias was chosen an apostle in the place of Judas by the drawing of lots, preceded by a prayer inviting God himself to show the one he had chosen.[19] And it is known that very often Yahweh showed his will by signs[20] and dreams.[21]

[1] Ez. 21. 21. [2] Gen. 44. 5, 15. [3] Ez. 21. 21. [4] Hos. 4. 12. [5] Lev. 19. 26; 2 Kgs. 21. 6. [6] Gen. 40 and 41; Jer. 23. 27; 29. 8. [7] Dt. 18. 11; 1 Sam. 28; 2 Kgs. 21. 6; Is. 8. 19; 29. 4. [8] Dan. 2. 27; 4. 7; 5. 7, 11; etc. [9] Is. 47. 12; Jer. 27. 9; Nahum 3. 4. [10] Acts 8. 9; 13. 6–8; 16. 16; 19. 13 (cf. Rev. 19. 20). [11] 1 Sam. 28; Hos. 4. 12. [12] 2 Kgs. 9. 22. [13] 2 Kgs. 21. 6. [14] 2 Kgs. 23. 24. [15] 1 Sam. 15. 23; Is. 8. 19; Jer. 14. 14; 29. 8; Ez. 13. 6, 23; 22. 28; Mic. 3. 7; Zech. 10. 2. [16] Lev. 19. 26, 31; 20. 6, 27; Dt. 18. 10–12. [17] Jg. 1. 1; 20. 18; 1 Sam. 9. 9; 23. 2; 2 Sam. 2. 1; 21. 1; 1 Kgs. 22. 5. [18] Jos. 7. 14; 1 Sam. 10. 20 . . . ; 14. 36 . . . ; Prov. 16. 33. [19] Acts 1. 26. [20] Jg. 6. 36 . . . ; 2 Sam. 5. 24; Is. 7. 11. [21] Gen. 20. 3; 31. 11, 24; 37. 19; Num. 12. 6; 1 Sam. 28. 6; 1 Kgs. 3. 5; Job 33. 14–18; Dan. 2. 26; etc.; Matt. 1. 20; 2. 12, 13.

DIVORCE

As the woman* in Israel was to some degree the property of her husband († marriage, family), he can repudiate her if she happens to displease him because he has found "some indecency in her";[1] but the wife has no means of separation from her husband other than by trying to make herself hated and be dismissed. No court of law pronounced divorce, but it is probable that, from an early period, the husband had to announce his decision publicly by pronouncing a formula whose echo is perhaps found in Hos. 2. 2: "She is not my wife, neither am I her husband." Later, in the days of the prophets, he was obliged to give her a "bill of divorcement" showing the repudiation and the freedom of the wife.[2] The Talmud has kept a copy of one, and the essential passage is: "Acting in full freedom of mind and without suffering any pressure, I have repudiated, dismissed and expelled you N., daughter of N., . . . of the town of N. and who have been up to now my wife. I now dismiss you, N., daughter of N. In this way you are free and you can, of your full right, marry anyone you wish and let no one prevent you. You are thus free for any man; this is your bill of divorcement, the act of repudiation, the bill of expulsion, according to the Law of Moses and Israel. [There follow the names of the witnesses.]"

The divorced woman, doubtless, usually returned to her father's house; [3] she could marry again, as we have just seen, but her fate was hardly enviable, for the most part.[4] A priest was not allowed to marry a repudiated woman.[5]

Were divorces frequent in ancient times? It is difficult to say. The public declaration, the bill of divorcement, prevented any decision from being made too rapidly, under the influence of anger; the husband risked incurring the hostility of the family of the dismissed wife and lost the money he had paid to his future father-in-law, at the time of the betrothal († marriage). The Deuteronomic Law, in order to combat the levity with which certain husbands might repudiate their wives, forbade them to take them back later if, after remarriage, they had become widows or had been dismissed by their second husbands.[6] (A curious thing is that the Koran possesses on this score a clearly contrary disposition: the husband can take back his repudiated wife only if she has remarried, II, 230.)

Deuteronomy, moreover, refuses the right of divorce to the man who has been forced to marry a girl whom he had humbled [7] and to the husband who wrongly accuses his wife of misconduct before marriage.[8]

The prophets of Israel doubtless always reproved divorce; in any case Malachi condemns the frequency of divorce after the return from captivity, and denounces the conduct of husbands who abandoned the wife of their youth: "I hate putting away, saith Yahweh, the God of Israel." [9] (This translation, however, is contested by some exegetes.)

At the beginning of the Christian era two tendencies were manifested among the Jewish doctors who interpreted differently the motive of repudiation, which is certainly vague, as formulated by Dt. 24. 1 ("some indecency" in the wife, or that "she find no favour in his eyes"). Some, with Hillel—and their point of view prevailed—authorized divorce for the least serious reasons: a blunder, a badly prepared dish, a word spoken to the first-comer, a too powerful voice letting the neighbours hear everything, etc.; Rabbi Akiba would even grant divorce to a husband who found a woman more beautiful than his wife. Others, with Shammai, quite on the contrary, tended to make divorce more difficult: "Even the altar weeps," they said, "over the man who puts away his wife." "A man has not the right to put away his

wife, except it be that he has discovered that she is unfaithful to him." [10]

Finally, the fact is recognized that women also have the right to divorce, in certain cases. Children remained in the care of their mothers (the boys up to six years of age, the girls always), but the father was obliged to maintain them.

It is known that Jesus, when questioned about divorce, clearly declared himself in favour of the indissolubility of marriage, without any reservation according to the Gospels of St Mark and St Luke,[11] with one exception (misconduct of the wife) according to the Gospel of St Matthew.[12] St Paul, dealing in his First Epistle to the Corinthians with marriages in which one of the partners has become a Christian, admits, in order to avoid endless conflicts, that the non-Christian partner may depart, if he (or she) wishes; on the other hand, the Christian partner may not do so of himself (or herself).[13]

[1] Dt. 24. 1. [2] Dt. 24. 1; Is. 50. 1; Jer. 3. 8; Matt. 5. 31. [3] Lev. 22. 13. [4] Is. 54. 6. [5] Lev. 21. 14. [6] Dt. 24. 1–4; Jer. 3. 1. [7] Dt. 22. 29. [8] Dt. 22. 19. [9] Mal. 2. 13–16. [10] Cf. Matt. 19. 9. [11] Mk. 10. 2–12; Lk. 16. 18; cf. 1 Cor. 7. 10, 11. [12] Matt. 5. 32; 19. 2–9. [13] 1 Cor. 7. 12–16.

DOCTOR

Although the curing of disease and especially of internal disease was in ancient times the business of the priest and the magician, there were, at an early date in Egypt and Babylon, men who had some medical and even surgical knowledge; the Babylonian Code of Hammurabi contains some interesting provisions concerning their responsibilities and their rights, and it is known that sometimes a well-known doctor was called in from a great distance.

In Israel there were undoubtedly, in every period, people who were capable of treating sores, setting fractures, and caring for the wounded. The O.T. makes few references to them, yet, at a date as early as the Book of the Covenant, if a man injured another during a quarrel he was obliged to care for him [1] until the latter's recovery; and it seems clear that when King Jehoram was wounded in battle against the Syrians he withdrew to Jezreel [2] in order to be under the care of a "doctor". The prophets too make more than one reference to the medical art.[3] In certain quarters, however, it was thought to be of greater value to trust in Yahweh, the real healer,[4] than to consult doctors.[5] The one did not preclude the other, said Ecclesiasticus (Apocrypha) at the beginning of the 2nd century B.C.: "Honour the doctor according to thy need of him with the honours due to him, for the Lord created him . . . the Lord causes the earth to produce its medicines and the wise man does not scorn them . . . If thou art sick . . . pray to the Lord . . . purify thy heart . . . , offer incense . . . then consult the doctor . . . and let him not forsake thee, for thou hast need of him." [6]

Further, among the office-bearers in the Temple at Jerusalem there was a doctor responsible for the care of the priests, who were likely to suffer especially from enteritis because of the fact that they went barefoot in the sanctuary and had to wash in cold water: he was called "doctor of the viscera".—Elsewhere, the Deuteronomic Code and the Priestly Code made the priests themselves responsible for the diagnosis of certain contagious diseases, especially of leprosy.[7]

From Roman times, doctors were quite numerous in Palestine. The Gospels speak of them sometimes,[8] and the saying of Jesus is well known: "They that are whole have no need of a physician, but they that are sick." [9]—The Epistle to the Colossians conveys the greetings of "Luke, the beloved physician" [10] (a companion of Paul, to whom the composition of the Third Gospel is attributed).

(† Medicine, magic, exorcism.)

[1] Ex. 21. 19. [2] 2 Kgs. 8. 29; 9. 15. [3] Is. 1. 6; 3. 7; Jer. 8. 22; 33. 6; Ez. 30. 21. [4] Ex. 15. 26. [5] 2 Chr. 16. 12. [6] Ecclus. 38. 1 ff. [7] Lev. 13; Dt. 24. 8. [8] Mk. 5. 26; Lk. 4. 23; 8. 43. [9] Matt. 9. 12; Mk. 2. 17; Lk. 5. 31. [10] Col. 4. 14.

DOG

In Bible times the dog was known to all Eastern peoples, who used it as a companion or as a guardian of houses or flocks. In some countries bands of them used to be seen at night coming to clear the streets of the filth that had been thrown there. The Assyrians even covered the dogs they used in warfare with a cuirass. Rome in its decline presented fights between dogs and elephants in the arena. Nevertheless, the dog was always despised everywhere.

Dogs have a relatively important place in the Bible, where they are mentioned some forty times. With more or less of a jackal strain, and the tail of a wolf-dog, they lived in a half wild state in Palestine, wandering everywhere, half-starved, vicious, and voracious.[1] In former times they acted as scavengers, devouring even the filth thrown on the streets; [2] and when the dogs came to lick the sores of poor Lazarus,[3] far from being an act of compassion they simply added to the distress of the unfortunate man, as Jesus depicted him. The corpses of slaughtered foes abandoned to them provided them with a choice banquet, and there was no more wretched end than to be delivered to the dogs.[4] Though dangerous in some circumstances,[5] in general dogs were rather cowardly, and the threat of a stick was enough to induce respect.[6] They were seldom afflicted with rabies.

The Israelites did not pet them; they did not even think of giving them bread, although little dogs would come to devour the crumbs from a meal.[7] Sometimes a dog was used to defend rather than to guard flocks.[8] But far from being appreciated as in Egypt or Babylonia, where they took part in hunting, the dog was thought to be an unclean and contemptible creature.[9] Furthermore, to call anyone a "dog" or the "son of a dog" or "a dead dog" was a grave insult.[10] Yet, in exaggeration and out of humility, sometimes one called oneself by this animal's name.[11] In a famous metaphor Jesus forbade the giving of "that which is holy to the dogs".[12] In addition, "dog", as a figure for shamelessness and obscenity, was the name given to profligates and the prostitutes at foreign temples, whose offerings were forbidden by the Law to be received in Yahweh's sanctuary.[13]

[1] Ex. 11. 7. [2] Ex. 22. 31; Ps. 22. 16, 20; 59. 6, 14–15; Is. 56. 11. [3] Lk. 16. 21. [4] 1 Kgs. 14. 11; 16. 4; 21. 19, 23. [5] Prov. 26. 17; Jer. 15. 3. [6] 1 Sam. 17. 43. [7] Matt. 15. 26–27; Mk. 7. 27–28. [8] Job 30. 1; Is. 56. 10. [9] 1 Sam. 17. 43; 2 Sam. 3. 8; Eccl. 9. 4. [10] 2 Sam. 16. 9. [11] 1 Sam. 24. 14; 2 Sam. 9. 8; 2 Kgs. 8. 13. [12] Matt. 7. 6; cf. Phil. 3. 2; Rev. 22. 15. [13] Dt. 23. 18.

DOLMEN

In Palestine, above all in Transjordania, in Galilee, and in southern Judaea, one quite often comes across monuments made, in their simplest form, of a large horizontal flag-stone placed on other unhewn stones. These rough constructions, analogous to those found in different parts of the world and called dolmens (from the Gaelic: *tol* = table, and *men* = stone), are rarely isolated and nearly always found in groups; it is possible that in Palestine, as elsewhere, they were originally hidden under a heap of stones or earth in the shape of a sepulchral mound, letting only the upper platform appear.

Moabite dolmens.

It is generally admitted that dolmens were sepulchres, but the possibility is not excluded that they acted as primitive altars and offering-tables for the dead. It is difficult to say to which race the men who erected those in Palestine belonged; the Palestinian dolmens are supposed to date from the end of the Neolithic and the beginning of the Bronze Age.

DOLPHIN

Several passages in the Books of Exodus [1] and Numbers [2] mention skins used to cover the Taber-

102

nacle or to wrap certain objects in this sanctuary; there is some doubt as to which animal the skins were taken from, and badger, marten, seal, ram, or dolphin have in turn been suggested. Since the

Dolphin.

dolphin was not easy to capture, it is more likely to have been the dugong (or sea-cow), a mammal akin to the Cetaceae and belonging to the same order as the Manatees, common in the Red Sea and gentle in its habits. Still today the Bedouins use its skin to

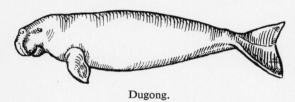

Dugong.

make shoes, which explains the text of Ez. 16. 10. It has also been suggested that, following the Egyptian, it ought to be translated simply by "leather skin". Ancient versions, followed by Ostervald and others, think wrongly that a tint is meant and not an animal, and read "hyacinth-coloured skins".

[1] Ex. 25. 5; 26. 14; 35. 7, 23; 36. 19; 39. 34. [2] Num. 4. 6, 8, 10–12, 14.

DOOR-KEEPER

While town and palace gates were supervised by sentries, watchmen, or porters,[1] the Temple gates at Jerusalem, as well as those of other sanctuaries, required the services of numerous door-keepers; in the time of the kings they were evidently under the control of three priests called "keepers of the threshold", who ranked immediately below the "priest of the second order".[2] From the Books of Ezra and Nehemiah we learn that at the time of the return from Exile the Temple door-keepers formed a group quite distinct from the singers and the Levites,[3] to which later they were assimilated.[4] Belonging to three great families, the door-keepers took turns by lot at the posts that had been assigned to them;[5] however, the problems raised by their history are too complex to be discussed here.

Door-keepers, whose duties were like those of their modern counterparts, kept watch at the entrances of great houses.[6] St John's Gospel speaks of the door-keeper of a sheepfold.[7]

103

[1] 2 Sam. 18. 26; 2 Kgs. 7. 10, 11; Neh. 13. 19; Est. 2. 21; Jer. 37. 13. [2] 2 Kgs. 12. 9; 22. 4; 23. 4; 25. 18; Jer. 35. 4; 52. 24. [3] Ezr. 2. 42, 70; 7. 7, etc.; Neh. 7. 45; 10. 28, etc. [4] 1 Chr. 23. 5, etc.; 2 Chr. 34. 13; 35. 15, etc. [5] 1 Chr. 26. 1–19; etc. [6] Mk. 13. 34; Jn. 18. 16, 17. [7] Jn. 10. 3.

DOVE (Poetic Name of Pigeon)

Four species of doves (pigeons) are met with in Palestine: the *ring dove* (or wood pigeon), which lives by preference in the forests, notably those of Gilead and of Carmel; the *stock dove*, smaller and less common, to be seen in northern Transjordania and round about Jericho; the *rock dove* (or rock pigeon) that breeds in the gorges of the Jordan Valley and on rocks; and the *turtle dove*, of which several varieties exist, including the laughing doves that nest in large numbers on the plain of Jericho.

From remote antiquity pigeons have been tamed in the East, and dove-cotes, sometimes of surprising size, have been found in Palestinian excavations; Isaiah alludes to the chambers of the dove-cote.[1] Although the Bible says nothing about it, the pigeon (which does not figure in the lists of unclean birds [2]) must have been a valuable source of food, as it still is today throughout Palestine. Furthermore, it was the only bird acceptable as a sacrifice—it was offered, in particular, for sacrifices of purification; [3] and folk of modest means were allowed to substitute two turtle doves or two young pigeons for a more expensive victim in the case of certain sacrifices—one of the birds was consumed as a burnt offering, the other went to the priests (the sin offering); [4] many people profited from this concession, which benefited also the parents of Jesus,[5] so that quantities of these creatures were sold in the outer court of Herod's Temple.[6]

It might be said that the dove is the chief bird of the Bible, so many are the allusions to it in the sacred text; one after another, the O.T. mentions the swiftness of its flight [7]—"Who will give me wings like a dove?" says the Psalmist [8]—the migrations of the turtle dove,[9] the flight of doves in flocks,[10] the beauty of their plumage,[11] their plaintive cooing [12]—Hezekiah in his illness moaned like a dove [13]—and their nests on the side of precipices,[14] etc. The dove is the bird of choice in the Song of Songs: [15] the beloved one there is several times called by the name of this sweet and gentle bird [16]—which has become a favourite first name still with Jews today (Jonas)—and the eyes of the beloved are compared with the dove's.[17] In a famous saying, Jesus stressed the innocence of the bird: "Be wise as serpents and guileless as doves." [18]

Some religions have attributed an important role to the dove, often considered a sacred bird. In Christianity it is the messenger of peace, bearing the olive branch that rejoiced Noah in the Flood story; [19] in particular, it is the emblem of the Holy Spirit, who descended in this form on the day of Jesus' baptism, according to the four Gospels.[20] Christian artists have enjoyed developing the symbolism of the dove.

[1] Is. 60. 8. [2] Lev. 11. 13 ff.; Dt. 14. 11 ff. [3] Lev. 12. 6; 15. 14, 29; Num. 6. 10. [4] Lev. 5. 7; 12. 8; 14. 21–23. [5] Lk. 2. 24. [6] Matt. 21. 12; Mk. 11. 15; Jn. 2. 14. [7] Is. 60. 8; Hos. 11. 11. [8] Ps. 54. 6. [9] Jer. 8. 7. [10] Is. 60. 8; Hos. 11. 11. [11] Ps. 68. 13. [12] Is. 59. 11; Ez. 7. 16; Nah. 2. 7. [13] Is. 38. 14. [14] Jer. 48. 28. [15] Cant. 2. 12. [16] Cant. 2. 14; 5. 2; 6. 9. [17] Cant. 1. 15; 4. 1; cf. 5. 12. [18] Matt. 10. 16. [19] Gen. 8. 11. [20] Matt. 3. 16; Mk. 1. 10; Lk. 3. 22; Jn. 1. 32.

DOWRY

In view of the matrimonial system of the Israelites and the fact that the wife becomes to some extent the property of the husband, it is the fiancé who gives a certain sum of money to the father or nearest relative of the fiancée, as well as presents he makes to the girl herself († marriage). Thus she does not need to be provided with a dowry as such. But she does not enter the home empty-handed. She brings with her her own possessions, clothes, jewels and, if of a certain rank, her maidservants,[1] who will remain her personal property; her family also give her certain presents; there is mention, in the Book of Joshua,[2] of the gift of land to a young wife, and the king of Egypt, father-in-law of Solomon, confirmed the marriage of the princess his daughter by a royal gift, the transfer of the town of Gezer,[3] of capital importance to the Israelites, as it covered their frontier on the Philistine side.

Moreover, it seems that a part of the sum handed over by the fiancé served to buy the trousseau of the girl or to make a marriage settlement; as is still the case today, certain arrangements were made which hallowed the alliance of the two families; the Babylonian Code of Hammurabi has some interesting regulations on this subject. At any rate, the author of the account of the marriage of Jacob seems to blame Laban for having kept for himself alone what he had received from his son-in-law.[4]

There is no question of dowry until a very late date: the Talmud requires the father to give his daughter a dowry, but the fiancé's payment remains and always exceeds the future wife's share.

[1] Gen. 24. 59; 29. 24, 29. [2] Jos. 15. 16 . . .; Jg. 1. 12 . . . [3] 1 Kgs. 9. 16. [4] Gen. 31. 15.

DRACHMA

Among all Hellenistic people this coin was the monetary unit in silver. The Attic drachma spread far and wide in the ancient world after Alexander the Great; on the obverse side it bore the head of the goddess Athena, and on the reverse side an owl with its feet resting on a vase, flanked with an inscription and surrounded with a crown of olives. The weight and composition of the drachma varied at different periods; it can be said to have been worth a little under ninepence, that is, much the same as a

Drachmas of Larissa and Athens.

denarius*. The only N.T. reference to this Greek coin is in the Parable of the Lost Drachma.[1]

[1] Lk. 15. 8–9.

DREAM

Like all the peoples of antiquity, the Israelites believed in the value of dreams for knowledge of the future, as omens or admonitions.[1] They even considered them to be one of the ways by which Yahweh had made known his will; [2] this explains how Joseph or Daniel interpreted the dreams of Pharaoh or Nebuchadnezzar.[3] Nevertheless, certain O.T. texts throw a measure of discredit upon dreams by affirming that prophetic inspiration is superior to them and by warnings against the dreams of impostors.[4]

(† Divination.)

[1] Gen. 37. 6, 9; Jg. 7. 13; Matt. 27. 19. [2] Gen. 20. 3; 28. 12; 31. 11, 24; 40. 8; Num. 12. 6; 1 Sam. 3. 3 . . .; 28. 6; 1 Kgs. 3. 5; Job 33. 15; Joel 2. 28; Matt. 1. 20; 2. 13, 19; cf. Acts 23. 11; 27. 23. [3] Gen. 40. 5 . . .; 41. 25 . . .; Dan. 2. 28. [4] Jer. 23. 25–32; 27. 9; 29. 8; Zech. 10. 2; cf. Dt. 13. 1 . . .; Eccl. 5. 3, 7; Ecclus. 34. 1 . . .

DRESS

It is difficult to identify exactly the various articles of clothing worn by the Israelites in Biblical times, first because archaeological excavations cannot bring to light articles of clothing made of perishable materials, but only sculptures, engravings, or paintings, which always have to be interpreted. Also, Biblical texts, which give many names of clothes, obviously do not describe them for us; and the Bible extends over such a long period and introduces us to so many peoples that very different names may designate costumes very similar if not identical.

104

Finally, there is a lack of points of comparison between the clothing habits of other times and our own, which creates a difficulty of translation, as is clearly seen in a comparison of our versions, which use very different words to translate the same term in the original language. However, by comparing all the information available with the present-day clothes of Bedouin and fellaheen, it is possible to gain an idea of the clothes worn by the Israelites of other times.

In the most ancient documents dress is reduced to its simplest expression: a belt is worn round the loins with a loin-cloth in front.

The *Egyptians* used a band of linen of about 6 ft. by 1 ft. It was worn round the waist, and tied in front, where the ends were left hanging (a). But early on they used a longer scarf of linen, of which one end was slipped into a belt; the material was passed between the legs, then spread out and wound

everyone kept as an undergarment; when it is said that Jesus took off his clothes to wash the feet of the disciples,[1] it means that he kept only the costume of the slave and that he already let us foresee in this way the symbolic significance of his action.

However, generally speaking, the Israelites wore a *tunic*, which seems to be the typical dress of the Syrians and the people of Asia Minor. Assyrian bas-reliefs and Egyptian paintings show inhabitants of these regions wearing a long tunic extending sometimes as far as the ankles, sometimes to the knees, but gathered in at the waist by a belt.

The fashion of this dress spread very widely at the end of the 2nd millennium: well-to-do people first adopted it, because of its practical advantages, and soon everyone used it, in Assyria as well as in Egypt.

This tunic was made at first of an animal's skin

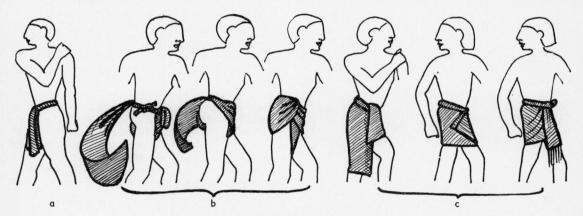

Primitive Egyptian dress.

round the body, forming fan-like folds in the front (b). This was the costume of servants and slaves. But the foremen, and especially people of means, used a shorter and wider piece of material, sometimes fringed, which could be draped in different ways, although a belt was always necessary to keep it in place (c).

It is roughly this same garment that we find in *Babylonia*; but it was made of sheep or goat skin held round the loins by a belt.

The Semites of Syria wore a similar little skirt, but it was more elegant and often decorated with a coloured pattern.

In the mountains, where the *Israelites* had just settled, they were not content with such a simple garment. But a survival of this primitive costume can be recognized in the under-skirt, coarsely woven of camel or goat hair, which the Israelites, both male and female, wore by way of mourning and which is called sackcloth*; and slaves doubtless continued to wear nothing but this little skirt, which generally

(d), then of a square piece of material of which the middle of the upper edge was placed beneath the left armpit while the upper corners were knotted on the right shoulder (e). The opening of the tunic was at the side of the body; it was moved to the front as soon as openings for the arms were made. The length of this garment, made of wool or linen according to countries and climates, varied with the trade of the wearer; often provided with sleeves, it was normally worn with a girdle*.

The "coat of many colours"[2] of Joseph was in fact this tunic, but it had the shape adopted at the time by non-working people. It was either very long or ornamented by a lengthy scarf wound right round the body from top to bottom. The tunic was often composed of several pieces of material sewn together; it was exceptional for it to be made of a single piece of material like Jesus' tunic.[3] It was kept on for work,[4] but taken off at night.[5]

The *coat* was worn over this tunic. Originally the Israelites doubtless draped themselves in a piece of

105

material (it was formerly an animal's skin) thrown over the shoulders or even over the head, as certain Bedouin still do today. But the latter often wear the "abayeh", which is a wide band of coarse material, usually brown with black stripes; it may be a little more than 10 ft. by about 4½ ft., with two holes for armholes, and it rarely has sleeves. The coat of former times seems usually to have had that shape.

The coat was an indispensable garment, although doubtless taken off for work; but it was considered indecent to go about without a coat, and still today any man of self-respect does not appear without a coat. The law, moreover, forbade the keeping of a coat as a pledge after dark.[6]

This garment hardly took into account the Arab proverb which said: Eat for your own pleasure, but dress for the pleasure of others. In fact, it was hardly beautiful, but it had practical advantages: it was a good protection against the cold and the rain, and it acted as a blanket and even as a bed. The

Tunics of animal skin (13th century), linen (15th century), and a tunic with a sash of skin (9th century).

Hebrews, when leaving Egypt, wrapped up in their coats their kneading-troughs and what they contained.[7] Merchants used it as a cloth on which to exhibit their wares for sale. After the war against the Midianites, Gideon spread out his coat before the Israelites, who, one after the other, cast into it a golden buckle taken among their booty.[8] The sword of Goliath, deposited in the temple of Nob, was wrapped in a coat.[9] The coats of Jesus' disciples acted as saddles and carpets on Palm Sunday.[10]

The tunic and the coat were the chief garments of the Israelites, as Jesus implied in his exhortation to kindness: "From him that taketh away thy cloke withhold not thy coat also."[11] But the Biblical texts speak of other clothes and particularly of an outer garment which had the same shape as the tunic but was fuller and made of a finer and pleasanter material. It was worn by princes or important people.[12] Jonathan gave his to David as proof of his friendship.[13]

The Bible also refers to the under-garments of well-to-do people; in particular, they wore a sort of shirt, already familiar to the Canaanites: to reward those who could guess his riddle, Samson offered

thirty shirts,[14] and the wise woman of the Book of Proverbs made that type of garment to sell.[15]

The great, the princes, the townsfolk often wore luxurious clothes. The queen of Sheba was dazzled by the luxury of Solomon and especially "by the apparel of those who served him"; this was probably their livery.[16] Later a special functionary was entrusted with the care of the royal wardrobe.[17] Luxurious garments,[18] clothes of purple [19] imported from Phoenicia, and perhaps even of silk,[20] were known.

Tunic with girdle and coat.

Women's clothes were similar to men's, but were generally fuller and longer, and nearly always had sleeves. Women liked wearing shawls, scarves, and veils, although in olden times they did not cover their faces,[21] except when they were introduced to their fiancés.[22]

Women had at their disposal a great variety of festival clothes, shawls, mantillas, diaphanous robes and robes of fine linen, turbans, and belts; but whereas Saul clothed the daughters of Israel in scarlet,[23] the prophet Isaiah saw only a mark of impiety in the pretension which the beauties of Jerusalem displayed.[24]

[1] Jn. 13. 4. [2] Gen. 37. 3; 2 Sam. 13. 18. [3] Jn. 19. 23. [4] Matt. 24. 18. [5] Cant. 5. 3. [6] Ex. 22. 26; Dt. 24. 12. [7] Ex. 12. 34. [8] Jg. 8. 25. [9] 1 Sam. 21. 9. [10] Matt. 21. 7, 8. [11] Lk. 6. 29. [12] 1 Sam. 2. 19; Ezr. 9. 3, 5; etc. [13] 1 Sam. 18. 4. [14] Jg. 14. 12. [15] Prov. 31. 24. [16] 1 Kgs. 10. 5. [17] 2 Kgs. 22. 14. [18] Jos. 7. 21; Jonah 3. 6. [19] Lam. 4. 5. [20] Ez. 16. 10. [21] Gen. 24. 16. [22] Gen. 24. 65. [23] 2 Sam. 1. 24. [24] Is. 3. 16–24.

DRUNKENNESS

It is surprising what a large number of Bible passages, from Genesis to Revelation, speak in a real or metaphorical sense of drunkenness, and call attention to its ravages. It would be impossible to list them all here, but it is clear that the taking of alcoholic beverages to excess was not rare among the Israelites,[1] that they were drunk in quantity at festivals,[2] and that even meals partaken at the time of sacrifices* might give rise to repellent scenes.[3]

Moreover, the prophets, the Gospels, and St Paul issue warnings against drunkenness.[4] On the other hand, certain groups of Israelites practised abstinence*, and we know that priests could not take wine or intoxicating drink before entering the sanctuary.[5]

(† Wine, Food [drink].)

[1] Is. 5. 11, 22; 56. 12. [2] Gen. 43. 34; Jn. 2. 10; 1 Cor. 11. 22. [3] 1 Sam. 1. 13, 14; Is. 22. 13; 28. 7, 8; Hos. 4. 11. [4] Prov. 23. 20–21; Mic. 2. 11; Hab. 2. 15; Matt. 24. 49; 1 Cor. 6. 10; Gal. 5. 21. [5] Lev. 10. 9.

DUNG

The Israelites knew how to fertilize the soil by spreading dung over the surface of the fields or digging it in at the root of fruit trees. Jesus himself alludes to this second practice in the Parable of the Unfruitful Fig Tree,[1] and in another place he says that tasteless salt is not even any good as manure.[2] Dung was sometimes also used as fuel.[3] A dung pit is referred to in the Book of Isaiah,[4] and one of the city gates of Jerusalem bore the name of Dung Gate or Rubbish Gate.[5]

But this terminology is used especially in the O.T. in a figurative way, principally in prophetic warnings: if Yahweh "lifteth up the needy from the dunghill",[6] he will sweep infidels away like rubbish and their mortal remains shall be like dung scattered over the ground, which they will manure.[7]

Job sat among "ashes" rather than "dung".[8]

[1] Lk. 13. 8. [2] Lk. 14. 35. [3] Ez. 4. 12, 15. [4] Is. 25. 10. [5] Neh. 2. 13. [6] 1 Sam. 2. 8; Ps. 113. 7. [7] 1 Kgs. 14. 10; 2 Kgs. 9. 37; Ps. 83. 10; Jer. 8. 2; 9. 22; 16. 4; 25. 33; Zeph. 1. 17; cf. Lam. 4. 5; Dan. 2. 5; 3. 29; Mal. 2. 3. [8] Job 2. 8.

DYER

We have very little information about Palestinian dyeing in antiquity. No doubt rudimentary processes were resorted to for tinting native woollen goods, while for *de luxe* dyeing application may have been made to foreigners, particularly to Phoenicians. —Some archaeologists believe, and not without reason, that traces of dyers' workshops exist in some Palestinian ruins, though others think these are olive-mills or bath installations.

In any case, certain Egyptian and other records prove that coloured stuffs were in current use from early antiquity in Palestine, and although the Bible texts never mention dyers, they do often speak of clothing, hangings, and veils that were coloured [1]— colours which must have been greatly loved by the Israelites, as they were throughout the East.

(† Colours.)

[1] Ex. 25–39; Jg. 5. 30; 8. 26; Est. 8. 15; Ez. 23. 6; Matt. 27. 28; Mk. 15. 17; Lk. 16. 19; Jn. 19. 2.

DYSENTERY

This was perhaps the cruel, incurable "disease of the bowels" from which Jehoram, son of Jehoshaphat, King of Judah (9th century)[1] suffered and died.

—The Acts of the Apostles records that in the island of Malta St Paul healed the father of the governor of the island who was struck by dysentery.[2] This infectious malady, one that takes the heaviest of tolls in hot countries, is very widespread in the Mediterranean world.

[1] 2 Chr. 21. 15, 18–19. [2] Acts 28. 8.

EAGLE

Eagles are quite often mentioned in the Bible. Since their Hebrew name also covers certain vultures*—with which, however, they must not be confused—translations sometimes vary. But it seems clear that vultures rather than eagles are meant in Job 39. 27 and Micah 1. 16 (and also Matt. 24. 28 par.).—There are several species of eagles in Palestine, of which the commonest are the tawny eagle and the imperial eagle. The law forbade the eating of their flesh,[1] but the O.T. alludes to this bird in magnificent similes inspired essentially by the rapidity and agility of its flight and the care it takes of its brood.[2] Cyrus is compared with the eagle,[3] it appears again in the visions of Ezekiel [4] and of Revelation,[5] and with it is always associated a suggestion of nobility and grandeur.—Josephus relates that Herod the Great put a great golden eagle on the façade of the gate of the Jerusalem Temple, an image for the power of God, but under cover of a riot Jewish rigorists tore it down.—The eagle became associated with St John the Evangelist.

[1] Dt. 14. 12; Lev. 11. 13. [2] Dt. 28. 49; 32. 11; 2 Sam. 1. 23; Job 9. 26; Ps. 103. 5; Prov. 23. 5; etc. [3] Is. 46. 11. [4] Ez. 1. 10. [5] Rev. 4. 7.

EAR-RING (NOSE-RING)

Among the number of jewels with which the Israelite women adorned themselves, and the men also, and which often acted as charms († amulet), must be included ear-rings, round or dangling, and usually made of gold.[1] (Note the simile of Prov. 25.12: "As an ear-ring of gold, and an ornament of fine gold, so is a wise reprover to an obedient

Various ear-rings.

ear.")—But nose-rings, also, were popular with the Palestinians of former times, as they are with the Bedouin of today; in fact, women often wore a big open ring: fixed in the right wing of the nose or in the cartilage separating the nostrils, it descended to beneath the mouth and was sometimes even decorated with pendants which caressed the chin; it is claimed that the Arabs like to kiss their wives through this ring, which is mentioned in certain texts.[2] It is likely that among the Ishmaelites men wore them also.[3] "As a jewel of gold in a swine's snout, so is a

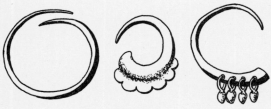

Nose-rings.

fair woman which is without discretion", declares the Book of Proverbs.[4]—Excavations in Palestine have brought to light numerous specimens of rings, ear-rings, and nose-rings of different types, which sometimes show elegance and originality.

A ring was put in the nose or in the jaws of captured animals, and some impressive images of the prophets imply that certain princes, once defeated, were treated in a similar way, in order to be dragged to the triumphal procession of their conqueror.[5] This is confirmed by Assyrian and Persian bas-reliefs.

Finally, there is mention in the O.T. of various animals of gold, silver, or bronze which form many accessories of the tabernacle, the Ark, and priestly garments.[6]

[1] Gen. 35. 4; Ex. 32. 2; Num. 31. 50; Jg. 8. 26; Is. 3. 19; Ez. 16. 12; etc. [2] Gen. 24. 22, 47; Is. 3. 21; Ez. 16. 12; Hos. 2. 13; etc. [3] Jg. 8. 24. [4] Prov. 11. 22. [5] 2 Kgs. 19. 28; Is. 37. 29; Ez. 19. 4, 9; 29. 4; 38. 4; etc. [6] Ex. 25. 12, 14; 26. 24; 27. 4; 28. 23; etc.

EARTH

The Israelites' knowledge of the earth was comparable with that of all their neighbours. Their vagueness is not surprising, for it sprang as much from the fact that their knowledge was usually expressed by way of pictures as from the Biblical writers' instinctive dislike of thinking theoretically and in the abstract; this knowledge interested them only in terms of practical considerations.

For them the earth appeared to be a sort of disc,[1] stretched out above the waters.[2] But there were pillars which held it in position and which at the same time supported the sky;[3] these pillars could

well be the mountains which formed the boundary of the horizon and whose base went down to enormous depths,[4] which ensured their stability and made them the symbol of what was permanent.[5] (It is against this background that we have to view the Bible sayings in which faith removes mountains.[6]) The earth was assuredly solid,[7] and yet one glance from God was sufficient to make it begin to tremble.[8] The Book of Amos tells of an earthquake which occurred in the reign of Uzziah, King of Judah, in the middle of the 8th century B.C., the memory of which remained a long time engraved in people's minds.[9] In 31 B.C. another earthquake is said to have caused thousands of casualties. Such upheavals as these gave people the impression they were shaken about as though in a boat on the water, and that the earth itself also swam on the surface of a primitive ocean (which was called in Hebrew by a name almost identical with the Babylonian term); besides, the existence of springs and even the presence of water at the bottom of a well confirmed this impression. In the time of Noah the waters from below threatened to fill the whole space which separated the earth from the sky, while "the windows of heaven" let in the waters from above.[10]—These various cosmological conceptions explain that the expression "heaven and earth" signifies the whole universe.

The word earth also designates arable land which produces vegetation and feeds man († agriculture), the earth of which pots are made († pottery), and all the inhabitants of the earth;[11] and it became the symbol of visible things in contrast to the invisible.[12]

[1] Ps. 136. 6. [2] Ps. 24. 2. [3] 1 Sam. 2. 8; Job 9. 6; 38. 4–7; Ps. 75. 3. [4] 2 Sam. 22. 16. [5] Ps. 90. 2; 104. 8; Is. 54. 10. [6] Matt. 17. 20; 1 Cor. 13. 2. [7] Ps. 93. 1; 104. 5. [8] Ps. 104. 32. [9] Amos 1. 1; Zech. 14. 5. [10] Gen. 7. 11. [11] Gen. 11. 1; Hab. 2. 20; Lk. 18. 8; 1 Cor. 10. 26; etc. [12] Jn. 3. 31; 1 Cor. 15. 47; Phil. 3. 19; Col. 3. 2.

EBONY

Ebony wood that the ancients imported from India and tropical Africa is mentioned only once in the Bible: according to Ezekiel [1] it was one of the articles of commerce that Tyre imported. Black, and of incomparable density and fineness, this hard wood was used in cabinet-making and for inlay-work, and it served also in the fabrication of idols and images.

[1] Ez. 27. 15.

ECLIPSE

Eclipses as such are not mentioned in the Bible, but like more than one nation, the Israelites doubtless attributed to Leviathan* the power to swallow up the sun or moon,[1] Yahweh triumphing over the monster and giving them back their light.

[1] Job 3. 8–9; 26. 13; Rev. 12. 3–4.

ELDER

Because of the importance of the family in Israel, its head exercised over it complete authority right up to old age. Laws and customs demanded respect for the elder; [1] any departure from this principle was considered scandalous.[2] White hairs were a crown of glory; [3] the experience and wisdom of the elders a blessing; [4] but it is true that they could sometimes be deficient.[5]

Ecclesiastes contains a curious symbolical description of old age,[6] and Ecclesiasticus in the Apocrypha more than one recommendation concerning the respect due to elderly people.[7] The author of the Pastoral Epistles demands that they be treated with gentleness, even if they deserve reproach,[8] but he expects from them dignified conduct.[9]

[1] Lev. 19. 32; Prov. 23. 22. [2] Dt. 28. 50; 2 Kgs. 2. 23; Is. 47. 6. [3] Prov. 16. 31; 20. 29; Job 15. 10. [4] 1 Sam. 2. 31; 1 Kgs. 12. 8; Job 12. 12 (?); Ps. 92. 14; 119. 100; Rev. 4. 4, etc.; Ecclus. 25. 4–6. [5] Job 12. 20; 32. 9. [6] Eccl. 12. 2–7. [7] Ecclus. 3. 12; 8. 6; 32. 9. [8] 1 Ti. 5. 1–2. [9] Tit. 2. 2–5.

ELDERS

In ancient times the Israelites were organized according to the tribal method, in which the chief of the tribe referred always for all important decisions to a sort of general staff or council made up of all the heads of clans or families. In the O.T. these eminent people are called the "elders of Israel" and are the men of confidence of Moses or Joshua.[1]

After their settlement in Canaan the tribal tie disappeared gradually in favour of the communal tie, and the elders of different localities took the place of the elders of earlier times; soon an urban aristocracy was constituted, which took in hand not only the interests of the cities but also those of the villages within their area.[2] Even under the monarchy, the highest authority took little interest in local affairs and the "elders of the town", whose number depended on its importance, kept municipal government and the administration of justice, even at Jerusalem.[3] The elders of several towns occasionally[4] met together and, in important circumstances, the king called together all the elders of the country.[5] It is interesting to note this persistence under the monarchy of an organization of a rather democratic nature.

During the Exile, the part played by the elders was of prime importance: the leadership of the different communities was entrusted to the heads of families.[6] At the return from Exile each locality of Judaea again possessed its own authorities; [7] those of the

capital naturally assumed particular importance, and the body of "Elders of Judah" at Jerusalem finally gave rise to the Sanhedrin*, of which the High Priest was the head.

The early Christian church was modelled on the political organization of the Jews; at the head of the Christian communities, and even at Jerusalem, alongside the apostles, there were elders (†presbyter) who shared the leadership of the flock, the religious services, and teaching.[8]

[1] Ex. 3. 16; 12. 21; 19. 7; 24. 14; Jos. 9. 15; etc. [2] Dt. 19. 12; Jg. 8. 14; 1 Sam. 11. 3; 16. 4, etc. [3] 1 Kgs. 20. 7. 21. 8; 2 Kgs. 10. 1; Is. 9. 15; etc. [4] Dt. 21. 2. [5] 1 Kgs. 8. 1; 2 Kgs. 23. 1. [6] Jer. 29. 1; Ez. 8. 1; 20. 1. [7] Ezr. 6. 7; 10. 8, 14; Lk. 7. 3. [8] Acts 14. 23; 15. 2; 20. 17; 1 Ti. 5. 17; Tit. 1. 5; etc.

ELEPHANT

Although ivory* is mentioned in the O.T., there is no reference to the elephant. On the other hand, the Books of Maccabees in the Apocrypha frequently refer to the presence of this creature in Syrian armies.

ELM

It is perhaps the elm of which the Book of Isaiah speaks in two places,[1] according to which this tree, along with the cypress* and the box tree*, will provide shade in the desert and beauty to the rebuilt Jerusalem. But other translations have been proposed: poplar, pine, ash, plane, and it is impossible to decide with certainty.

[1] Is. 41. 19; 60. 13.

'ELUL

'Elûl was the sixth month of the Jewish civil year (August–September). The meaning of the name is not known. It is cited only once in the O.T.: Neh. 6. 15 states that the walls of Jerusalem were completed on the 25th day of Elul by the Jews returned from Exile.

(† Month.)

EMBALMING

The Egyptians, as we know, tried, out of religious motives, to preserve the bodies of their dead for the longest possible time; for this they used the very complicated processes of embalming. According to Genesis,[1] the burial of Jacob and Joseph followed this custom. The Israelites themselves paid attentive care to corpses, but without practising embalming as such.

(† Funeral.)

[1] Gen. 50. 1–3, 26.

EMBROIDERY

It is certain that the Israelites practised the art of embroidery, which doubtless came from Babylonia, the country of fine materials and luxurious costumes [1] (cf. the clothes of the kings of Assyria and of

Embroidered cover according to an 8th-century Assyrian bas-relief.

8th-century Assyrian flagstone imitating an embroidered cover.

Babylonia as seen on monuments). The Egyptians and the Phoenicians knew it too.[2]—The Song of Deborah ends with the unfolding of embroidered materials [3] which Psalm 45 [4] and numerous passages of Ezekiel also recall.[5]

But the O.T., especially in connection with the description of priestly vestments and materials in the Tabernacle,[6] uses various technical terms which are very difficult to understand and which our versions translate differently. Perhaps it is necessary to distinguish three sorts of needlework: embroidery work, brocaded work (brocades), in which the artist inserted coloured threads in the length of the material, and quilted work, which joined together double material by stitches following diamond shapes or squares.

[1] Ez. 27. 24. [2] Ez. 26. 16; 27. 7. [3] Jg. 5. 30. [4] Ps. 45. 14.
[5] Ez. 16. 10, 13, 18; etc. [6] Ex. 27; 28; 35–36; 38–39.

EMERALD

The oriental emerald is a variety of corundum, the hardest mineral next to diamond, and is a splendid green in colour. Its Hebrew name comes from a root which means "to flash forth lightning". No doubt the Israelites got it from Egypt. It figures on the breastplate of the High Priest [1] (third stone of the first row), and it enhanced the clothing of the prince of Tyre of which the prophet Ezekiel speaks.[2] In Revelation the fourth foundation of the heavenly Jerusalem is adorned with emerald [3] and the throne of God is surrounded with a rainbow "like an emerald to look upon " [4] (in this case a greenish rock-crystal has been suggested, which gives prismatic colours by refraction; ancient people gave the name emerald loosely to stones, jaspers, etc., of a beautiful grass-green).

[1] Ex. 28. 17; 39. 10. [2] Ez. 28. 13. [3] Rev. 21. 19. [4] Rev. 4. 3.

EPHAH

A common measure of capacity for dry goods, the ephah [1] was the tenth part of a homer*; it was sub-divided into three seahs or ten omers.* If we follow the equivalences given by ancient writers it would represent a volume of approximately one bushel.

[1] Lev. 19. 36; Dt. 25. 14; Jg. 6. 19; Ruth 2. 17; Is. 5. 10; Amos 8. 5; Mic. 6. 10; Zech. 5. 7.

EPHOD

This word, the etymology of which is uncertain, signifies: the ancient dress of priests; an essential part of the clothing of the High Priest; and an object pertaining to worship which is not easily identifiable.

1. The ephod, which in ancient times acted as a ritual garment for all priests,[1] may have been, as is generally thought to be the case, a sort of short skirt, or loin-cloth, of linen perhaps, like the one worn by Egyptian priests; it is supposed to have en-

veloped the body from the hips to the knees, but it may have resembled still more closely the ephod of the High Priest (see below) by partly covering the upper half of the body also. The account of the journey of the Ark to Jerusalem proves that the costume was very short: considering himself as a priest, David put on the ephod of linen and "danced before the Lord with all his might". This sight aroused the scorn of Michal, his wife, who could not admit that the king of Israel should have "uncovered himself", as the text says, "in the eyes of the handmaids of his servants, as one of the vain fellows shamelessly uncovereth himself".[2]—When still only a child, Samuel was girded with a linen ephod [3] at the sanctuary of Shiloh.

2. The description of the High Priest's ephod in Exodus [4] chaps. 28 and 39—of fairly late editing—does not enable us to formulate a clear idea of it and permits various interpretations. By recourse to the data of Egyptian and other monuments, we can, by analogy, think of this garment in the shape of a sort of belted corselet, lengthened by an apron-skirt, and held up by two straps bearing on each shoulder an onyx stone. The material of this ephod was magnificent: made of "blue, and purple, and scarlet, crimson, and fine twisted linen", it was embroidered with threads of pure gold; on the onyx stones set in golden bezels were engraved the names of the tribes of Israel, six on the left-hand stone, six on the right, to remind Yahweh of them. The ephod was completed by an oracle-pocket which the High Priest wore on his breast († priest).

3. In several instances there is mention in the O.T. of an ephod which is neither the one worn by the High Priest as described in Exodus nor the ephod of linen worn by Samuel and David. According to certain texts, it even seems that it is a sacred image, a sort of statue. The Book of Judges, in fact, tells that with rings of gold weighing 1,700 shekels (55 to 66 lb.), Gideon made an ephod which he put in his city of Ophrah, "and all Israel went thither a whoring after it there: and it became a snare unto Gideon, and to his house". [5] Micah, also, made an ephod for his house of God, a teraphim, (and perhaps also) an image, and an idol of molten metal. [6] In the sanctuary of Nob the sword of Goliath was kept, wrapped in a cloth, behind the ephod. [7] Hosea declares in a significant survey that, for many years, the children of Israel will remain without sacrifice and without images, without ephod, and without teraphim. [8] It can be seen that these texts do not all definitely imply an image; mention of an ephod beside images and teraphim does not necessarily mean they are identical: something must distinguish these objects pertaining to worship from one another; and why should Goliath's sword have been hung up behind an image? Moreover, other texts, mentioning the

same ephod, seem less favourable still to this hypothesis. David, pursued by Saul, wants to know what the future holds for him: "Bring the ephod," he told Abiathar—the priest who had fled to the future king of Israel "with an ephod in his hand". [9] The same demand and the same consultation were made on the eve of the battle against the Amalekites. [10] But an image is not brought, people go to it; moreover, this alleged fetish, this divine emblem, would hardly have been transported by hand if the sword of Goliath could have been suspended behind it, to say nothing of the weight of Gideon's image. It can be seen from the last texts quoted, and also from others, [11] that the ephod was an object concerned above all with the proclamation of oracles. Sacrifices and religious services were never performed in front of it; it was consulted.

But what was the shape of this divinatory ephod? Considering its name, it seems quite natural to think of a sort of apron, or surplice, with a pocket containing the instruments, the sacred lot, which will proclaim the oracle (in certain cases, the pocket alone, perhaps, was taken with its equipment). This ceremonial garment was related to the linen ephod, and also gave rise to the ephod of the High Priest with its breastplate (and the Urim and Thummim). The priest (or perhaps the consultant, too, sometimes) put it on at the time of calling upon the Lord. Easily transportable, it was usually hung in an *ad hoc*, respected, place where, at Nob, the cloth surrounding Goliath's sword was also found.

Moreover, we may suppose that originally, and wherever there was a representation of the deity, the ephod was worn by the image itself. It either wore it permanently or yielded it to the priest for the consultation. In any case, it has been shown that in Syria, Phoenicia, Asia Minor, Greece, and elsewhere certain images destined to proclaim oracles were covered with a more or less precious surplice (*ependutes*). It is possible that Gideon, and perhaps Micah, may have made a similar image and that, as the name of the part was attributed to the whole, people may have called an image wearing a divinatory surplice by the term "ephod"; in Israel the idol disappears, and the ephod properly so-called alone remains.

The latter was, therefore, still supposed to be a sacred surplice, an oracle case, a ceremonial garment, worn by the deity or by his representative. This solution of the difficult problem of the ephod is only conjecture. It has, however, the advantage of not giving incongruous meanings to the word, while it gives a plausible explanation of all the texts which mention it.

[1] 1 Sam. 22. 18. [2] 2 Sam. 6. 14–16, 20. [3] 1 Sam. 2. 18. [4] Ex. 28. 6–12; 39. 2–7. [5] Jg. 8. 24–27. [6] Jg. 17. 5; 18. 14, 17, 18. [7] 1 Sam. 21. 9. [8] Hos. 3. 4. [9] 1 Sam. 23. 6. [10] 1 Sam. 30. 6–8. [11] 1 Sam. 2. 28; 14. 3, 18, 36; 28. 6; 2 Sam. 2. 1.

EPILEPSY

Among the numbers of sick folk brought to Jesus for healing were found lunatics,[1] i.e., epileptics: it was thought, fancifully enough, that the phases of the moon had a baneful influence upon them, and that they were possessed by unclean spirits or demons. The symptoms of the affliction from which the boy suffered who was restored by Jesus and of which the Synoptic Gospels speak,[2] certainly appear to have been those of epilepsy. But this is unlikely to have been Saul's trouble, which was attributed to an evil spirit sent by Yahweh himself.[3]

(† Illness.)

[1] Matt. 4. 24; 17. 15 (Ps. 121. 6). [2] Matt. 17. 14–21; Mk. 9. 14–29; Lk. 9. 37–43. [3] 1 Sam. 16. 14–15.

ETHNARCH

This Greek title (= ruler of people), the precise meaning of which is uncertain, denotes the representative of a superior power or a kind of governor. Aretas IV, king of the Nabataeans (Arabia), and doubtless a vassal of Rome, had evidently entrusted the administration of the city of Damascus to the ethnarch referred to by St Paul in 2 Cor. 11. 32. We know that Simon Maccabaeus and Archelaus also bore this title.

EUNUCH

Eunuchs, appointed to guard harems, were found in all the palaces in the states neighbouring on Israel, and the Biblical texts mention occasionally Egyptian, Assyro-Babylonian, Persian, or Ethiopian eunuchs.[1]

Among the Israelites, the mutilation of man was forbidden; Deuteronomy declares eunuchs to be unworthy of participating in the congregation of the Lord.[2] But the kings of Israel and Judah none the less imitated the despots of surrounding countries. Foreseen by Samuel,[3] eunuchs appear at the court of David,[4] and their presence is indicated at the court of a whole series of monarchs, from Ahab to the Exile.[5]

However, it is noteworthy that the word eunuch, chief of the eunuchs, signified a high position which was not necessarily linked with the original meaning of the term, but which became synonymous with chamberlain, cup-bearer, etc. (e.g., Potiphar, who was married).[6] In certain texts we do not know whether the references are to eunuchs as such, or to officers of more or less high rank. Several of them combined the two offices.

The word "rabsaris" (chief of the eunuchs), used in the account of the Assyrian invasion in the reign of Sennacherib,[7] is not a proper name, as most of our versions have it, but the title of an officer of the king.

[1] Gen. 40. 2; Dan. 1. 3, 7; Est. 1. 10, 15; 2. 3, 14, etc.; Acts 8. 27. [2] Dt. 23. 1. [3] 1 Sam. 8. 15. [4] 1 Chr. 28. 1. [5] 1 Kgs. 22. 9; 2 Kgs. 8. 6; 9. 32; 23. 11; Jer. 29. 2; etc. [6] Gen. 39. 1, 7. [7] 2 Kgs. 18. 17.

EVENING

It is known that the Israelites reckoned the day* from one evening to the next. The evening naturally represented an important part in Palestinian daily life, and the Bible often speaks of it. Here it is sufficient to mention the killing of the paschal lamb [1] and the second daily [2] sacrifice*, which was made in the Temple "between the two evenings". This expression may mean (as the Samaritans and the Caraites take it) between sunset and the end of twilight (in the dusk of evening), or (as the Pharisees and the Talmud hold) between the sinking of the sun, about the 15th hour, and sunset itself.

[1] Ex. 12. 6; Lev. 23. 5. [2] Ex. 29. 39; cf. 16. 12; 30. 8.

EXORCIST

Like many other peoples, the Jews thought that illnesses of the mind, and other affections also, were due to the presence and action of evil spirits in the body of those who were their victims. Only the expulsion of these demons assured a cure, and it was to this task that the exorcists devoted themselves, by using incantations, exorcisms, adjurations, sacred formulae, or methods depending on magic*.

Exorcism was honoured by the Pharisees. Many Scribes and doctors of law were skilled in it, and exorcists went from place to place to practise their art.[1] They had to follow certain rules in exercising their functions. Thus, the rabbis forbade them to whisper words which embodied religious formulae; these might be taken to be verses from the Bible, which could be regarded as a recourse to magic and an insult to God.

The Gospels clearly let it be understood that Jesus also cast out demons;[2] he did so with authority, in the name and by the power of God, without asking, as he did for other cures he performed, for the collaboration of the patient. The Jews accused him of acting through Beelzebub, the prince of the demons: we know how pertinently he replied to them.[3] Seven cures of people possessed with demons are related to us with a varying amount of detail: the demoniac at Capernaum,[4] a man blind and dumb,[5] the Gerasene demoniac,[6] a dumb man,[7] the daughter of the Syrophoenician woman,[8] the epileptic child,[9] and a woman with a spirit of infirmity, on the Sabbath day.[10]

Jesus conferred upon his disciples this same power "to heal all manner of disease and all manner of sickness".[11] They had certain successes during their master's lifetime,[12] as well as after Pentecost,[13] but they failed sometimes and they learned that certain demons could be cast out only by fasting and prayer.[14] An account in the Acts of the Apostles [15] shows also that exorcism "in the name of Jesus" was not, in itself, necessarily efficacious.

[1] Matt. 12. 27; Mk. 9. 38; Lk. 9. 49; 11. 19; Acts 19. 13. [2] Mk. 1. 34; 3. 11; Lk. 6. 18. [3] Matt. 12. 22 . . .; Mk. 3. 22 . . .; Lk. 11. 14 . . . [4] Mk. 1. 21 . . .; Lk. 4. 33 . . . [5] Matt. 12. 22; Lk. 11. 14. [6] Matt. 8. 28 . . .; 15. 22 . . .; Mk. 5. 1 . . .; Lk. 8. 26 . . . [7] Matt. 9. 32–33. [8] Mk. 7. 25 . . . [9] Matt. 17. 14 . . .; Mk. 9. 14 . . .; Lk. 9. 38. [10] Lk. 13. 11. [11] Matt. 10. 1; Mk. 3. 15. [12] Mk. 6. 13; Lk. 10. 17. [13] Acts 5. 16; 8. 7; 19. 12. [14] Matt. 17. 21; Mk. 9. 29. [15] Acts 19. 13–16.

EYE-SALVE

Though the Israelites were doubtless familiar with eye-salves intended to beautify the eyes [1] († antimony) and comparable with those used by the Egyptians, only the Apocalypse [2] refers, in a metaphorical sense, to medicinal eye-salve, used to improve the eyesight. Because of the verb used this passage probably means, not a dry or liquid eye-salve, but a cream into which were incorporated various beneficial substances.

[1] Cf. 2 Kgs. 9. 30; Jer. 4. 30; Ez. 23. 40. [2] Rev. 3. 18.

FALCON

Several species of falcons live in Palestine, and it would be curious if these birds were not mentioned in the O.T. Perhaps they are included among those that are called *nets* in Hebrew, birds of prey whose flesh could not be eaten.[1] Some translators think that the word *'ayyah* means "falcon"; it occurs as the second name in the two passages Lev. 11. 14 and Dt. 14. 13 and is also found in the Book of Job.[2] Opinions vary; the A.V. takes *'ayyah* as kite (Lev., Dt.) and also as vulture (Job).

[1] Lev. 11. 16; Dt. 14. 15; Job 39. 26 (29). [2] Job 28. 7.

FAMILY

More than elsewhere, perhaps, the family in Israel is the cornerstone of society. In ancient times in particular, the individual hardly counted, the family was everything, and the tribe was only the family on a larger scale. The power of a clan depended on the number of families in it, and the importance of a family on the number of its members. The family and the clan could, if need be, separate itself from the tribe, but it was very difficult for the individual to free himself from the family.

United by ties of the strictest solidarity, the members of the family formed a single body, a single soul; the same blood flowed in their veins; in the case of violent death, it was not the blood of one only which was shed, but that of all his relatives—"our" blood.

According to the stock phrase, each was the "bone and flesh" of his kinsmen. Laban says to his nephew: "Thou art my bone and my flesh"; [1] "Remember also that I am your bone and your flesh," Abimelech reminds the people at Shechem.[2]—A man who belonged to a respected family whose prestige reflected upon him, was fortunate; unfortunate were those whose father was condemned; the whole family, in ancient times, atoned for the faults of its head; we have only to think of the punishment of Achan, stoned with all his family.[3]

In Hebrew the family is commonly called the "house of the father"; the latter is its absolute master: he even possessed for a time the right of life and death over his children; [4] he retained the right to sell them as slaves*.[5] Lot even disposed of the body of his daughters to others,[6] and the Deuteronomic Law had to forbid the father the attribution of birthright to the child he chose.[7] This paternal power derived also from the almost religious functions which the father fulfilled in the midst of the family, of which he was to a certain extent the priest.[8] The family was not only a political unit, it was also a religious association; it celebrated, for example, its special festivals, in which all its members must meet together: one day, Jonathan excused the absence of David from Saul's table by declaring that he was taking part in a family sacrifice.[9] Always—and it is still so today—the Feast of the Passover was a family festival [10] in which was affirmed the religious nature of paternal authority. At the beginning of the Christian era whole families accepted Christianity with the father.[11]

It has been suggested, however, that among the Semites in primitive times the mother might have been the important person of the family: she would have had the ownership of all things, the husband would have entered the family of his wife and lineage would have been established through her. It may be possible to trace survivals of this polyandric and matriarchal regime in the O.T.: the name given to the child by the mother,[12] adoption by the wife of the servant-girl's children,[13] bargainings of Eliezer with the mother and brother of Rebekah, the father remaining in the background, and the declaration of Gen. 2. 24: "Therefore shall a man leave his father and his mother, and shall cleave unto his wife", etc. But it is not certain that these details presuppose an earlier regime of this kind.

However, in historical times, at any rate, there is no trace of a matriarchal regime; the man is indeed the head of the family, the woman leaves her family to join her husband's, and the children are the inheritors of the father.

Whereas with the Babylonians monogamy was the rule, the Israelites practised polygamy, which was so favourable to the development of the family clan and which was not limited by any special enactment. But every man was not able to give himself the luxury of a harem, which remained the prerogative of great men and kings.[14] An ordinary man was usually satisfied with one or two wives.[15] If the wife was barren the Israelite was, so to speak, obliged to marry a second wife or to take a concubine to have descendants. Polygamy favoured the enlargement of the family and, as the Eastern woman ages very quickly, the husband was very tempted to replace the first wife by a younger one. But jealousy very often crept into the home with her, even though the first wife might remain the "wife of youth".[16] The following are significant facts: the second wife was called "the enemy" (enemy of the first), and people distinguished the two wives by calling one "the beloved" and the other "the hated". Deuteronomic Law took the latter under its protection,[17] and it is doubtless in order to spare them painful discord that Leviticus forbade marriage with two sisters.[18]

Even when reduced to bigamy the matrimonial regime of the Israelites engendered much moral misery; and so, while recognizing this fact, legislation tried to attenuate the inconveniences; the spiritual leaders of Israel were obviously in favour of monogamy, which became more widespread with time, especially after the return from Exile. We know with what elevation Jesus spoke of marriage; without formally declaring himself to be against polygamy, he seems to have condemned it implicitly. In the first Christian communities it is specifically stated that the bishop must be the husband of a single wife, and the deacons also,[19] but most commentators are of the opinion that the texts in question point to the prohibition of second marriages, of re-marriage, monogamy having become the rule for the disciples of Jesus.

The Talmud, followed by Mahomet (Koran 4. 3), limits the number of wives to four, for ordinary people at any rate, but if it allows polygamy it does not recommend it.

(† Marriage, woman, child, slave, divorce, crimes and offences.)

[1] Gen. 29. 14. [2] Jg. 9. 2; cf. Gen. 37. 27; 2 Sam. 5. 1; 19. 12, 13. [3] Jos. 7. 24, 25. [4] Gen. 38. 24; 42. 37; Zech. 13. 3. [5] Ex. 21. 7; Neh. 5. 5. [6] Gen. 19. 8; cf. Jg. 19. 24. [7] Gen. 48. 17; 49. 4; 1 Kgs. 1. 13; Dt. 21. 15 . . . [8] Job 1. 5. [9] 1 Sam. 20. 29. [10] Ex. 12. 3; 13. 8. [11] Jn. 4. 53; Acts 16. 34; 18. 8. [12] Gen. 4. 25; 29. 32; 38. 4; 1 Sam. 1. 20; etc. [13] Gen. 16. 2; 30. 3. [14] Jg. 8. 30; 2 Sam. 3. 2 . . .; 5. 13; 1 Kgs. 11. 1. [15] 1 Sam. 1. 2. [16] Is. 54. 6. [17] Dt. 21. 15–17. [18] Lev. 18. 18; cf. Gen. 29. 26, 27. [19] 1 Ti. 3. 2; Tit. 1. 6.

FAMINE

Since Palestine was subject to drought, famines there were not rare events. When the autumn or spring rains were insufficient this scourge threatened the country. Famine could be provoked also by invasions of grasshoppers*, by hailstorms, by war, etc.

The Bible often alludes to this calamity,[1] which might last for several years, and cause some clans or families to go into exile.[2] Those who could get corn from Egypt were fortunate,[3] though even there this affliction was not unknown when the Nile floods failed—we know the measures Joseph took to alleviate the effects of a famine which is said to have lasted for seven years.[4]

The Israelites, and the prophets in particular, looked upon this misfortune as a judgment, a punishment from God.[5]

[1] 2 Sam. 21. 1; 1 Kgs. 8. 37; 17. 1; 18. 2; 2 Kgs. 4. 38; 6. 25; 25. 3; Is. 51. 19; Mk. 13. 8; Lk. 4. 25; 15. 14; Acts 7. 11; 11. 28; Jas. 5. 17. [2] Gen. 12. 10; 26. 1; 47. 4; Ruth 1. 1; 2 Kgs. 8. 1. [3] Gen. 42. [4] Gen. 41. [5] Lev. 26. 19; Dt. 11. 17; Jer. 14. 12; 15. 2; etc.; Ez. 5. 12; etc.; Amos 4. 6 . . .; 8. 11; Rev. 18. 8.

FARTHING

This (the *assarion*) was the unit of the system adopted by the Romans for bronze coins († money). It was $\frac{1}{16}$ drachma*, and was itself subdivided into 4

An *assarion* of Tiberius.

quadrans* or 8 lepta († mite). It was the price of two sparrows.[1] The translation by "farthing" is somewhat misleading.

[1] Matt. 10. 29; Lk. 12. 6.

FASTING

Very common in the whole of the East, the custom of abstaining from food for a varied length of time had been known to the Israelites doubtless since the beginning of their history. Quite naturally, fasting accompanied the external manifestations of mourning[1] or of the grief resulting from a catastrophe.[2] Thus the people of Jabesh fasted for seven days after the death of Saul[3] and the Israelites wept and fasted at Bethel after the defeats they had undergone.[4] But even at that time fasting was probably often practised with the intention of softening the deity, of moving him to pity so that he would refrain from striking and avert the imminent catastrophe. "While the child was yet alive," cried David, "I fasted and wept: for I said, Who can tell whether the Lord will not be gracious to me, that the child may live?"[5]—"Because he [Ahab] humbleth himself before me, I will not bring the evil in his days." [6] But elsewhere God declared: "When they fast, I will not hear their cry." [7] Thus although fasting could be an individual matter,[8] it could also be general: ordered by authority [9] to implore the help of the Lord in favour of his people, it was accompanied by a solemn assembly, sacrifices, confession of sins, and mourning rites.[10]

Perhaps it was sometimes thought in Israel that fasting ensured in itself capacities of a supernatural character: one day Saul had the following curse pronounced to his troops: "Cursed be the man that eateth any food until evening, that I may be avenged on mine enemies." [11] At any rate, abstinence encouraged ecstasy, the receipt of divine orders and communion with God: the fasts of Moses, Daniel, and of Jesus himself are significant in this respect.[12]

With time, the fast became more and more a regular practice with the Jews, an act of penitence and soon a work of merit. The Law ordained it formally only for the Day of Atonement,[13] but from the time of the Exile the anniversaries of national disasters were emphasized by fasting,[14] as the Jewish calender still recalls today (siege of Jerusalem, burning of the city and Temple, etc., see table of festivals*). There is also reference to a fast recalling events which had taken place in the time of Esther.[15]

In the time of Jesus these commemorative fasts multiplied to such an extent that they were celebrated every month; moreover, the Sanhedrin could order national fasts, in the event of drought, for example, and the authorities of the synagogues also prescribed local fasts according to circumstances. To these, of course, were added individual fasts left to private initiative; [16] they were practised especially on Mondays and Thursdays, because Moses, according to tradition, had gone up Mt Sinai on the fifth day of the week and had come down again on the second. The devout even made it a duty to fast regularly on those two days throughout the year: "I fast twice a week," [17] says the Pharisee in the parable. We know that the disciples of John the Baptist imposed similar fasts upon themselves.[18]—The ordinary fast on one day lasted twenty-four hours, but certain rabbis claimed that one could eat during the night, which was certainly the case when the fast lasted more than one day. Abstention from food was combined with various austerities more or less rigorous according to the degree of penitence (it was forbidden to anoint oneself and to wash; wearing of sackcloth and ashes, etc.).

In spite of the high conceptions of the prophets and their admirable words on the subject of fasting,[19] the Jews often held to their regrettable formalism, against which Jesus also protested with well-known vigour, without belittling the value of the true fast.[20] And so the primitive church practised fasting, accompanied by prayers, notably in certain solemn circumstances.[21] St Paul, without recommending it anywhere, keeps an open mind with regard to it, pronouncing words which are of the kind spoken by Christ and the prophets: the kingdom of God is not meat and drink, but righteousness, and peace, and joy in the Holy Spirit.[22]

[1] 2 Sam. 1. 12; 3. 35; Ezr. 10. 6; Ps. 35. 13 . . .; Matt. 9. 14–15; Mk. 2. 18–19. [2] 1 Kgs. 21. 9, 12; Neh. 1. 4; Joel 1. 14. [3] 1 Sam. 31. 13. [4] Jg. 20. 26. [5] 2 Sam. 12. 22. [6] 1 Kgs. 21. 27–29. [7] Jer. 14. 12. [8] Num. 30. 13; Ps. 60. 10; 109. 24. [9] 2 Chr. 20. 2–4; Ezr. 8. 21; Est. 4. 16. [10] 1 Sam. 7. 6; Neh. 9. 1; Jer. 36. 6, 9; Joel 2. 12, 15; Jonah 3. 5–8. [11] 1 Sam. 14. 24; cf. Acts 23. 21. [12] Ex. 34. 28; Dt. 9. 9; Dan. 10. 3, 12; Matt. 4. 2; Lk. 4. 2. [13] Lev. 16. 29; 23. 27; Acts 27. 9. [14] Zech. 7. 5; 8. 19. [15] Est. 9. 31. [16] Lk. 2. 37. [17] Lk. 18. 12. [18] Matt. 9. 14; Mk. 2. 18; Lk. 5. 33. [19] Is. 58. 3 . . .; Zech. 7. 5 . . . [20] Matt. 4. 2; 6. 16; 9. 15; 17. 21; Mk. 2. 20; 9. 29; Lk. 5. 35. [21] Acts 13. 2; 14. 23. [22] Rom. 14. 17; Col. 2. 16; cf. 1 Ti. 4. 1–5.

FAT

Fat is a symbol of fertility, abundance, wealth, of what is best and most succulent; [1] in Hebrew one even says "the fat of the kidneys of wheat " [2] where we might speak of the marrow or fine flour of wheat.

Moreover, in the case of sacrifices the fat was regarded as a choice part, at any rate that which surrounded certain organs [3] (entrails, liver, kidneys, tail of the sheep), and it was surrendered to Yahweh, for whom it was entirely burnt upon the altar.[4]

Because of this, the Priestly Code forbade Israelites to eat beef, mutton, or goat fat,[5] but that probably meant only the fat parts burnt on the altar and not the fat joined to the meat. On the other hand, all the fat of animals which were clean but not acceptable for sacrifices (hart, gazelle, etc.) might be eaten. In certain periods of Israelite history it was the same with all animals killed solely for food. († Sacrifice.) In any case, the prohibition of fat did not have as absolute a character as that of blood.

[1] Gen. 45. 18; Is. 25. 6; etc. [2] Dt. 32. 14. [3] Ex. 29. 13; Lev. 3. 3–5, 9–10, 14–16; 4. 8–10, 31. [4] Lev. 1. 8, 12; 1 Sam. 2. 15; 1 Kgs. 8. 64; Is. 1. 11; etc. [5] Lev. 7. 22–25.

FATHOM

A Roman measure of depth, the fathom [1] was about 6 ft., i.e., the span of the outstretched arms.

[1] Acts 27. 28.

FEAST

On the occasion of their national, rural, or family celebrations [1] the Israelites liked to feast. Circumcision, weaning,[2] betrothals, weddings,[3] return of a relative,[4] funerals, were all celebrated by meals in which the abundance of food usually prevailed over the quality and variety of dishes. Genesis mentions a meal organized for the birthday of the Pharaoh,[5] and the N.T. mentions a feast celebrated on Herod's birthday.[6] Alliances and oaths were sealed by a meal eaten together;[7] in ancient times it also accompanied most sacrifices.[8] The laws of hospitality decreed that every visitor should be honoured by satisfying his appetite.[9]

At the great feasts the guests were invited by slaves or servant-girls sent by the host.[10] In order to participate, a festive garment had to be worn.[11] Greeted by a kiss of welcome,[12] the guest whose feet had been washed at the entrance to the house [13] had his head anointed with scented oil,[14] and sometimes received flowers [15] too, and, once the ritual ablutions had been performed, they sat down to table. For a long time the Israelites ate sitting on seats or on the ground;[16] later, they half lay on cushioned divans.[17] Places of honour were reserved for the guests they wanted to honour,[18] and to these were allotted the best and most abundant portions of the meal.[19] At court and among well-to-do people the feast was accompanied by music, songs, and dances;[20] elsewhere people contented themselves with the charms of conversation animated by stories or riddles.[21] A house-steward often directed the serving,[22] particularly that of the drinks, which occupied an important place in the meals—in Hebrew and in Greek the word "feast" is derived from the verb "to drink"—and gave rise to excesses often condemned by the prophets and, later, by the apostles.[23]

The Book of Esther mentions a large number of sumptuous meals at the court of Xerxes.[24] The feast of Belshazzar described by the Book of Daniel [25] is famous.—Jesus often participated in more modest feasts,[26] and he evokes, in certain of his parables, the festival reunions and the feasts which were the joy of his contemporaries.[27]—All along, the Israelites considered that nothing could better strengthen the ties of solidarity than a meal eaten together.[28] Jesus, also, used this figure to depict the happiness of brotherly communion in the kingdom of God,[29] and we know the importance he attached to the Last Supper which he ate with his disciples, and the part played by love-feasts (*agapé*) in the life of the early church.[30]

[1] Jg. 9. 27; 1 Sam. 25. 2 ff.; 2 Sam. 13. 23; Job 1. 4. [2] Gen. 21. 8. [3] Gen. 24. 54; 29. 22; Jg. 14. 10; Matt. 22. 2; Jn. 2. 1 ff. [4] Lk. 15. 23. [5] Gen. 40. 20. [6] Matt. 14. 6; Mk. 6. 21. [7] Gen. 26. 30; 31. 46, 54; Ex. 24. 11; Lk. 5. 29. [8] 1 Sam. 1. 9; 2. 15; 9. 13. [9] Gen. 18. 6 ff.; 19. 3; 2 Sam. 3. 20; 2 Kgs. 6. 23. [10] Prov. 9. 3; Matt. 22. 3; Lk. 14. 17. [11] Matt. 22. 11. [12] Lk. 7. 45. [13] Lk. 7. 44; Jn. 13. 5 ff. [14] Ps. 23. 5; 45. 7; 104. 15; Eccl. 9. 8; Ez. 23. 41; Amos 6. 6; Lk. 7. 46; Jn. 12. 3. [15] Is. 28. 1. [16] Gen. 27. 19; 37. 25; Jg. 19. 6; 1 Sam. 20. 18, 25; 1 Kgs. 13. 20. [17] Ez. 23. 41; Amos 6. 4; Mk. 14. 15; Jn. 13. 23. [18] 1 Sam. 9. 22; Matt. 20. 21 par.; 23. 6 par.; Lk. 14. 7 ff. [19] Gen. 43. 34; 1 Sam. 1. 5; 9. 23. [20] Jg. 16. 25; 2 Sam. 19. 35; Job 21. 12; Is. 5. 12; Matt. 14. 6; Mk. 6. 22; Lk. 15. 25. [21] Jg. 14. 12. [22] Jn. 2. 8. [23] Ps. 69. 12; Eccl. 10. 16; Is. 5. 11; 28. 1; Hos. 4. 18; Rom. 13. 13; 1 Cor. 11. 17 ff.; Gal. 5. 21; Jude 12. [24] Est. 1; 2. 18; 5; 6. 14; 7. 1; etc. [25] Dan. 5. [26] Matt. 9. 10 par.; Mk. 14. 3 ff. par.; Lk. 7. 36 ff.; 11. 37; 14. 1 ff.; Jn. 2. 2; 12. 2. [27] Matt. 22. 1 ff.; Lk. 14. 15 ff.; 15. 23 ff.; 16. 19. [28] Gen. 26. 30; Ex. 24. 11; etc. [29] Matt. 26. 29; Lk. 13. 29. [30] Acts 2. 46; 1 Cor. 11. 17 ff.; Jude 12.

FESTIVALS

Apart from their family or clan festivals and those occasioned by exceptional events (victories, enthronements, inaugurations, etc.[1]), the Israelites celebrated, from earliest times, different weekly festivals († Sabbath), monthly festivals († moon) and annual festivals († sheep-shearing, Passover, Weeks, Tabernacles, etc.) which stood out pleasantly in their lives, bringing diversions necessary to the people as a whole, as well as to individuals.

Most of these solemn ceremonies had undergone a change. Certain of them went back to the nomadic period and were originally shepherds' festivals; others were clearly agricultural: borrowed apparently from the Canaanites, they celebrated the great moments of peasant life. But all had a decidedly religious character and, what is significant, were related, at a given moment—the annual festivals, at any rate—to certain events in Israelite history; and so they were celebrated not only in honour of the God who blessed the work of the hand and of the soil, but also in honour of Yahweh, who had done great things for his people. In the Priestly Law notably, memory of an agrarian festival was blurred in favour of the historical and religious meaning.

Although in ancient times the festivals were essentially popular and joyous to the point of degenerating into certain excesses,[2] from the Deuteronomic period and, above all, after the Exile, they assumed a more solemn tone: liturgy prevailed over popular rejoicing; less spontaneous, the festival had something more noble about it than it had earlier. Doubtless, the people often held to the easy, pleasant celebration of former times, but ritual sacrifice became more and more the essential act of the festivals, and the Priestly Code carefully laid down the detail of the ceremonies. What is more, the misfortunes of Israel had developed the feelings of guilt and penitence: certain festivals were clearly atoning and purificatory.

The great influence exercised by the festivals from the national and social point of view should be noted. In ancient times they gave the Israelites the opportunity to meet at various sanctuaries in the country, to cultivate the ties which united these sons of the same people, these children of the same God. And so when the prophets wished to speak to the conscience of the Israelites they went and found them at their festivals. Besides, apart from the effect they had on national life, the festivals favoured commercial relations, business: from time immemorial people in Israel carried on transactions analogous to those which, still today, lend the pilgrimages to Mecca their well-known importance. The centralization of the

CALENDAR OF ISRAELITE FESTIVALS

Month		Day	Great feasts	Secondary feasts	Annual fasts
1. Nisan	Mar.–Apr.	14–21	Passover		
2. 'Iyyar	Apr.–May	23		(Capture of citadel of Jerusalem by Simon 142 B.C.)	
3. Sivan	May–June	50th day after 16 Nisan	Weeks (Pentecost)		
4. Tammuz	June–July	9 17			Capture of Jerusalem by the Chaldeans, 586 B.C.—Capture of Jerusalem by Titus (sacrifices suspended), A.D. 70
5. 'Ab	July–Aug.	7 9			Destruction of Temple by the Chaldeans 586 B.C.—Burning of Temple under Titus A.D. 70
6. 'Elûl	Aug.–Sept.	—			
7. Tišri	Sept.–Oct.	1	New Year		Assassination of Gedaliah—586 B.C. (?)
		3			
		10	Day of Atonement		
		15–22	Tabernacles		
		23		Joy of the Law	
8. Marḥešvan	Oct.–Nov.	—			
9. Kislev	Nov.–Dec.	25		Dedication	
10. Ṭebet	Dec.–Jan.	10			Start of the siege of Jerusalem, —587 B.C.
11. Šebaṭ	Jan.–Feb.	—			
12. 'Adar	Feb.–Mar.	13		Nicanor	
		14–15		Purim	

cult at Jerusalem brought the Israelites still more closely together; from all the localities of the country and, later, from all parts of the ancient world, they went up to the Holy City which was packed with people, at the time of the Passover, for example. The caravans met on the way, greeted each other joyfully, and proceeded, singing [3] or accompanied by the pipe, to "the mountain of the Lord, to the Rock of Israel".[4] With their hearts filled with enthusiasm, the pilgrims "walked about Zion, told the towers thereof, marked well her ramparts",[5] and took part in the ceremonies, feeling, in the Temple, in the midst of their country, a single people, the people of Yahweh.

Included here is a calendar of the annual festivals of the Jews, classifying them according to their importance. Some have been celebrated since ancient times, others more or less recently. (For details, cf. articles devoted to the particular festivals.)

[1] Jg. 11. 31; 1 Sam. 18. 6; 2 Sam. 6; 1 Kgs. 8. [2] Dt. 16. 14; Jg. 9. 27; 21. 21; 1 Sam. 1. 13; Is. 28. 7 ff.; Amos 8. 10; etc. [3] Ps. 84; 122. 1–5. [4] Is. 30. 29. [5] Ps. 48. 13.

FEVER

This word is used to translate four different Hebrew terms which cannot be identified with precision, but all of which come from roots implying a notion of heat. As we know, fevers are very common in the East, and the climate of Palestine favours them, at least in certain seasons and in certain districts.

Though the O.T. speaks of fever only in a general way,[1] the N.T. relates Jesus' healing of Peter's mother-in-law, who was suffering from a "violent" (R.V., great) fever,[2] and that of the son of a royal officer at Capernaum who was attacked by a "mortal" fever.[3] St Paul, in his turn, saved the father of the governor of Malta[4] from a fever accompanied by dysentery*.

We know from the Talmud that the remedies generally used by the Jews for fever were bizarre and were dictated by magic and superstition.

[1] Lev. 26. 16; Dt. 28. 22; 32. 24; Hab. 3. 5. [2] Matt. 8. 14; Mk. 1. 30; Lk. 4. 38. [3] Jn. 4. 47, 52. [4] Acts 28. 8.

FIELD-MOUSE

According to some translators (those of the LXX in particular), this little insectivorous mammal may be the first of the animals listed in Lev. 11. 30. Others prefer the hedgehog, ferret, gecko, etc. It is impossible to pronounce with certainty.

FIG TREE

Along with the vine and the olive, the fig tree forms a trio which is characteristic of Palestine. In the fable of Jotham each of these three species is asked in turn to become king of the trees.[1] Together with the vine, the fig tree is mentioned in the promises of prosperity which God makes to his people, and above all in the warnings of the prophets: [2] there will no more be grapes on the vine or figs on the fig tree. This tree, very widespread on the soil of Canaan, is mentioned some fifty times in the Bible.

The fig can grow to 35 or 40 ft. It flourishes even in stony soil, but needs more moisture than the olive, and if it is well tended gives abundant harvests.[3] It was often planted with the vine,[4] and its branches mingled with the latter's foliage to make a high vine-arbour; hence the proverbial expression for the enjoyment of well-being in prosperity and peace: "to be sitting under one's own vine and fig tree".[5]

Under the tree's thick foliage the native enjoyed welcome shade, favourable for meditation.[6] In Genesis the first human beings were clothed with girdles made from the broad palmate leaves.[7]

Fig tree.

But the fig tree was cultivated essentially for its "fruit". Strictly speaking, the fig is not a fruit; it is a pear-shaped receptacle containing the male and female flowers, whose peduncles become fleshy and succulent after fertilization, like the envelope itself. Properly to understand certain Bible passages, it must be understood that the fig tree bears successively three kinds of figs: the *late or autumn figs*,[8] which grow on the current year's wood and furnish the main crop from August right up to the winter; *green or winter figs*,[9] which, not having time to ripen before the leaves fall, spend the inhospitable season on the branches and grow ruddy at the first touch of spring yet are no larger than a cherry; many of them would be blown off by the wind and eaten by the people.[10] The remainder stay on the tree and ripen in summer from June onwards: these are the *first-ripe figs*,[11] much sought after for their freshness and delicious flavour.—Thus, a healthy fig tree bore fruit for about ten months; and Jesus must have expected to find green figs on the tree he cursed, for, as St Mark's Gospel observes, it was not the season for figs (neither first-ripe nor autumnal).[12]—To hasten

the maturing of the figs, some husbandmen today put a drop of oil on the "eye of the fig" while it is still attached to the tree.

Figs are eaten fresh or dried. Cakes or masses were made of them, which were easy to carry and served excellently for food.[13] With reference to their medicinal use as emollient, Isaiah prescribed a poultice of figs to cure the ulcer from which Hezekiah was suffering.[14]

It is not surprising that a fruit so well known entered into numerous similes, metaphors, and proverbs in the Bible;[15] one of the best known is the saying of Jesus: "Are figs gathered from thistles [16] [or from thorn-bushes]?"

[1] Jg. 9. 7 ff. [2] Jer. 5. 17; 8. 13; Hos. 2. 12; Joel 1. 7, 12; 2. 22; Hab. 3. 17. [3] Prov. 27. 18; Lk. 13. 7. [4] Lk. 13. 6. [5] 1 Kgs. 4. 25; Mic. 4. 4; Zech. 3. 10; cf. 2 Kgs. 18. 31; Is. 36. 16. [6] Jn. 1. 48. [7] Gen. 3. 7. [8] Jer. 8. 13; 29. 17. [9] Cant. 2. 13. [10] Matt. 21. 19; Mk. 11. 13; Rev. 6. 13. [11] Is. 28. 4; Jer. 24. 2; Hos. 9. 10; Mic. 7. 1; Nahum 3. 12. [12] Mk. 11. 13. [13] 1 Sam. 25. 18; 30. 12; 1 Chr. 12. 40. [14] 2 Kgs. 20. 7; Is. 38. 21. [15] Jer. 24. 1 ff.; 29. 17; Mic. 7. 1; Nah. 3. 12; Mk. 13. 28; Lk. 13. 6 ff. [16] Matt. 7. 16; Lk. 6. 44; Jas. 3. 12.

FILTER

Filtration is alluded to once in the N.T., when Jesus ridiculed the Pharisees who, under the pretext of observing the Law of Moses,[1] filtered their beverages from fear of swallowing a gnat, while they had no scruples about swallowing a camel.[2] It is a fact that deserves mention, that in hot countries beverages are passed through fine muslin to remove insects or impurities which easily fall into them.

Is. 25. 6, in a prophetic vision, speaks of filtered wines—that is, clarified, purified at the last moment from the dregs at the bottom and consequently of the best quality—which will be served at the sumptuous feast offered by Yahweh to all nations on Mt Zion.

[1] Lev. 11. 20, 23. [2] Matt. 23. 24.

FIND

The three Israelite Codes contain clear regulations relating to animals or objects lost by their owner and found by another. The Covenant Code [1] declares: "If thou meet thine enemy's ox or his ass going astray, thou shalt surely bring it back to him again." Obviously, there was all the more reason to act in that way for an Israelite. The Deuteronomic Code [2] does not mention the enemy and amends the ancient law concerning the obligation to return lost property to its owner: "Thou shalt not see thy brother's ox or his sheep go astray, and hide thyself from them: thou shalt surely bring them again unto thy brother. And if thy brother be not nigh unto thee, or if thou know him not, then thou shalt bring it home to thine own house, and it shall be with thee until thy brother seek after it, and thou shalt restore it to him again. And so shalt thou do with his ass; and so shalt thou do with his raiment, and so shalt thou do with every lost thing of thy brother's, which he hath lost, and thou hast found: thou mayest not hide thyself."—Leviticus [3] adds: ". . . or have found that which was lost, and deal falsely therein, and swear to a lie . . . that he shall restore that which he took by robbery, or the thing which he hath gotten by oppression . . . he shall even restore it in full, and shall add the fifth part more there to: unto him to whom it appertaineth shall he give it, in the day when he makes his guilt offering."

Later, the Jewish doctors interpreted these laws, treating certain particular cases and often attenuating the primitive obligations: "One is not obliged," they said, "to return the found object if it belongs to a Gentile."

[1] Ex. 23. 4. [2] Dt. 22. 1–3. [3] Lev. 6. 3–5.

FINES

Monetary punishments permitted in Israelite law were compensation paid to the injured party rather than fines proper († law §3). This may be judged from the following examples.

If a man left his cistern uncovered and an ox or ass fell into it he had to pay the animal's value to its owner.[1]—A man who quarrelled and did serious injury to his opponent must care for him at his own expense and compensate him for the period of enforced idleness.[2]—Theft of money involved repayment of twice the amount stolen.[3]—Deuteronomy lays down that 100 shekels* of silver should be paid to the father of a woman falsely accused by her husband of not being a virgin at the time of her marriage [4] and 50 shekels to the father of a girl who had been seduced—the culprit also had to marry her.[5]— In certain cases,[6] in addition to the restitution which had to be made, a fifth of the object's value was payable.

At a relatively late date the custom of imposing real fines for certain offences, probably of a cultic nature, seems to have become established; the income went to the priests.[7]

[1] Ex. 21. 33 ff. [2] Ex. 21. 18 f. [3] Ex. 22. 7. [4] Dt. 22. 13 ff. [5] Dt. 22. 28 f. [6] Lev. 6. 2 ff.; Num. 5. 6 ff. [7] 2 Kgs. 12. 16; Prov. 17. 26.

FINGER

This unit of length was equal to the thickness of the middle finger, or, more precisely, to $\frac{1}{24}$ of the cubit or $\frac{1}{4}$ of the handbreadth (i.e., 0·74 or 0·86 in., according to whether it is the small or great cubit*). The bronze columns of Solomon's Temple were four fingers thick [1] (i.e., using the great cubit).

[1] Jer. 52. 21.

FIR

The Vulgate, followed by a number of other versions, often translates by "fir" a Hebrew word meaning cypress*, but under which several other conifers could be included.

FIRE (PUNISHMENT BY)

Adultery, punishable by stoning, was probably punished by burning in primitive times, if the story of Tamar is to be believed; she was ordered to be burned, outside her house and village, for prostituting herself when she was in fact betrothed to Shelah.[1]—Burning was also authorized—not without analogy with the Code of Hammurabi—for the daughters of priests who became dissolute [2] and in a particular case of incest.[3]

There is some doubt as to whether the guilty were burned alive, in Israel, or whether the punishment was inflicted on the dead body, as a way of aggravating the death sentence, like the exposing of bodies in other cases. The question might be settled by the account of Achan, who was condemned to be burned [4] because he had defied the ban, and who seems to have been stoned before being burned, but the text is unfortunately obscure.[5]

The expression "to make his sons and daughters pass through the fire" probably does not refer to a rite of purification, but to the practice of child sacrifice, common in Canaan and sometimes imitated in Israel,[6] although it was forbidden by the law [7] and condemned by the prophets.[8] The victims' throats were cut prior to the burning.

[1] Gen. 38. 24. [2] Lev. 21. 9. [3] Lev. 20. 14. [4] Jos. 7. 15. [5] Jos. 7. 25. [6] 2 Kgs. 16. 3; 17. 17; 21. 6; 23. 10; Mic. 6. 7; cf. Gen. 22; Jg. 11. 31. [7] Lev. 18. 21; Dt. 18. 10. [8] Jer. 7. 31; 19. 5; 32. 35; Ez. 16. 21; 20. 26; 23. 37.

FIRST-BORN

The first-born of animals (clean and unclean) and of men in Israel were the object of regulations closely akin to those relating to firstfruits*, and whether it was a question of men or animals, every first-born, provided it was a male, belonged by right to Yahweh.[1]

The first-born of clean *animals*, no doubt brought in primitive times eight days after their birth [2] to the nearest sanctuary, were subsequently, in conformity with Deuteronomic Law, sacrificed in the Temple at Jerusalem on the occasion of an annual pilgrimage; [3] their flesh, with the exception of what was offered on the altar and on behalf of the priests, acted as a sacred family meal following the sacrifice*.[4] Later, all the flesh returned exclusively to the priests [5] after the sprinkling of blood and the offering of fat. The tainted animal could not be presented at the altar, and the Israelite ate it at home.[6] The first-born of clean animals could not be redeemed.[7] The first-born of unclean animals could be redeemed by a head of smaller livestock, otherwise their neck was broken,[8] at least in ancient times, for there could be no question of offering them for sacrifice; later they were redeemed for money, on evaluation, with an increase of one-fifth, or else they were sold[9] (doubtless by the priests to the benefit of the sanctuary).

Was the sacrifice of the first-born of *men* practised in the earliest days of Israelite history? Certain exegetes think so, by stressing the fact that the Canaanites observed this custom,[10] that Abraham considered himself obliged to sacrifice his son,[11] that sacrifices of children were celebrated in Israel in the time of the kings[12] and on various occasions, and that the Covenant Code even declares clearly: "The first-born of thy sons shalt thou give unto me. Likewise shalt thou do with thine oxen, and with thy sheep."[13] However, it is necessary to note that the children sacrificed by the Canaanites were not necessarily first-born, that the account of the sacrifice of Isaac implies the condemnation of this custom, that the sacrifices of children offered in Israel are without any close relationship to the law pertaining to firstfruits, that the effective killing of all eldest sons would be a demand irreconcilable with the general spirit of Yahweh worship and that in Ex. 22. 29 it seems to be more a theoretical regulation. At any rate, the obligation to redeem the first-born of men was imposed upon the Israelites at an early date: "All the first-born of thy sons thou shalt redeem," says one text,[14] and subsequent legislation specifies that this redemption is made as soon as the child has reached the age of one month and at a cost of 5 shekels* of silver[15] (about 12s. 6d., to be paid to the priests).— In time, the right of Yahweh to the first-born was connected, on the one hand, with the history of the Exodus and of the tenth plague[16] and, on the other, with the consecration of Levites*.[17]

(† Birthright.)

[1] Ex. 13. 2, 12; 34. 19; Num. 18. 15, etc.; cf. Gen. 4. 4.
[2] Ex. 22. 30. [3] Dt. 15. 19. [4] Dt. 15. 20. [5] Num. 18. 17, 18.
[6] Dt. 15. 21, 22. [7] Num. 18. 17. [8] Ex. 13. 13; 34. 20. [9] Lev. 27. 27; Num. 18. 15. [10] Lev. 18. 21; Dt. 12. 31. [11] Gen. 22. [12] 1 Kgs. 16. 34; 2 Kgs. 16. 3; 17. 17, etc.; Jer. 7. 31; 19. 5; 32. 35; Ez. 23. 37; Mic. 6. 7. [13] Ex. 22. 29, 30; cf. Ez. 20. 26. [14] Ex. 34. 20; cf. Ex. 13. 13; Lk. 2. 22 ... [15] Num. 18. 15, 16. [16] Ex. 13. 15; Num. 3. 13. [17] Num. 3. 12, 41; 8. 16 ...

FIRSTFRUITS

In order to express their gratitude to Yahweh and to be able to enjoy in all tranquillity the products of the soil and the flocks, the Israelites, like most peoples of antiquity, offered firstfruits to their God, that is, "the best of the first fruits of thy land", as well as their first-born and those of domestic animals († first-born).

The regulations concerning the firstfruits are not always very clear and raise more than one problem. Briefly, although ancient legislation gives only a general indication,[1] Deuteronomy specifies that the firstfruits—the quantity to be provided, moreover, is not fixed—are due on corn, wine, oil, and the fleece of sheep;[2] they are given to the priests and form part of their endowment.[3] The firstfruits of the earth, in particular, were presented by every Israelite at the sanctuary, in a basket offered with a word of dedication and a prayer;[4] before taking possession of its contents, the priest doubtless burned a small portion of it on the altar.[5] There followed a meal in which the Israelite rejoiced in every good thing that Yahweh had given him, along with his family, the Levite, and the foreigner residing among them.[6]

In the later legislation there appear other offerings of firstfruits which may, moreover, go back to an earlier date: a presentation for the community as a whole, in the course of the Feast of the Passover, of a sheaf composed of the first ripe ears of the year[7] (barley) and, on the day of Pentecost, of two loaves baked with leaven (firstfruits of wheat?[8]); the gift to the priests of all the fruits of the recently planted trees which had reached their fourth year—the possessors could enjoy them only after the fifth year and did not touch them during the first three;[9] finally, the offering by each Israelite of the firstfruits of dough (or of milling), in the shape of a cake[10]; it is not specified in the text whether the first dough of the year is meant, or, as tradition would have it, all preparation of dough.

Two tractates of the Mishnah later laid down all the details concerning the firstfruits, whose presentation at Jerusalem would give rise to beautiful and imposing celebrations. Added to that of the tithes*, the considerable product of the firstfruits was kept in certain special places in the sanctuary for the needs of the members of the priesthood and their families.[11]

[1] Ex. 23. 19; 34. 26. [2] Dt. 18. 4. [3] Dt. 18. 4 (cf. Num. 18. 11–13; Ez. 44. 30). [4] Dt. 26. 1–11. [5] Cf. Lev. 2. 14–16. [6] Dt. 26. 11. [7] Lev. 23. 9–14. [8] Lev. 23. 15–21. [9] Lev. 19. 23–25. [10] Num. 15. 17–21; Neh. 10. 37; Ez. 44. 30. [11] Neh. 10. 35–39.

FISH

There are several references to fish in the Bible, but neither the O.T. nor the N.T. gives the name of any of them. Fish, as the work of the Creator and subjected to man's domination,[1] are not the object of any classification, except that which, ritually, distinguishes[2] between clean fish provided with fins and scales, and unclean fish which lack them (catfish, skate, lampreys, eels, etc.). And so the Israelites could eat fish properly so-called.[3] They had eaten some in Egypt,[4] where fish is one of the chief food resources, and in Palestine they had not only sea fish but also those which abounded in the lakes of Galilee or which lived in the Jordan and its tributaries; however, only the N.T. mentions fishing* in fresh water.

At Jerusalem there was a "Fish Gate",[5] in front of which the fish market was apparently held, stocked by the fisheries of Phoenicia [6] and of Lake Tiberias; but in view of the distance and climate, they doubtless sold there only salted fish or fish dried in the sun. In Galilee fish, together with bread, was the customary food of the population: "What man is there of you," said Jesus, "who, if his son . . . shall ask for a fish, will give him a serpent?" [7] The two multiplications of loaves are accompanied by those of fish; [8] the disciples present grilled fish to their Master after the resurrection.[9]

The sea-water fish of the shores of Palestine are those found in the Mediterranean. Among the fish which prosper in the Lake of Gennesaret and whose flesh is often delicate, are breams, which have the peculiarity of keeping their young in their mouths,[10] and *Clarias macracanthus* (3 ft. long), which emit a sort of mew when they are caught.—It is a well-known fact that the Dead Sea contains no fish and that those which the Jordan carries to it die immediately.

More than one ancient people practised the idolatry of fish.[11] The first Christians symbolically represented Christ in the form of a fish, the five letters of this word in Greek providing the initial letters of the five words, "Jesus Christ, God's Son, Saviour".

[1] Gen. 1. 21, 26, 28; 9. 2; Job 12. 8; Ps. 8. 8; Ez. 38. 20. [2] Lev. 11. 9 . . . [3] Num. 11. 22. [4] Num. 11. 5. [5] 2 Chr. 33. 14; Neh. 3. 3; 12. 39; Zeph. 1. 10. [6] Neh. 13. 16. [7] Matt. 7. 10; Lk. 11. 11. [8] Matt. 14. 19, par.; 15. 36, par. [9] Lk. 24. 42; Jn. 21. 9 . . . [10] Cf. Matt. 17. 27. [11] Cf. Dt. 4. 18.

FISH-HOOK

Hook and line fishing was known in Egypt and in Israel, as the five O.T. and N.T. verses alluding to it in a real or metaphorical sense testify.[1] The hooks in question in these texts were doubtless of metal, but as the word used by the prophet Amos also means "thorns", it is possible that certain thorns were used for taking fish.

Scenes of hook and line fishing are depicted on some Egyptian and Assyrian monuments. A very beautiful copper hook, which dates from the Middle Bronze Age, was found near Gaza.

[1] Job 41. 1; Is. 19. 8; Amos 4. 2; Hab. 1. 15; Matt. 17. 27.

FISHING

On the Mediterranean coasts, in the waters of the Jordan and of the Lake of Gennesaret, fishing was practised, in Palestine as elsewhere, doubtless from remotest antiquity, as the fish-hooks, needles for mending nets, and net-weights which are often found in excavations prove. The Biblical texts mention various nets († snare) and fish-hooks*, speak a number of times of fishermen,[1] and borrow more than one comparison from their work.[2]

Fishing with nets was particularly successful, in the time of Christ, on the banks of the Sea of Tiberias, and fishing has a place in a number of familiar Gospel scenes.[3] The names Bethsaida (house of fishing) and Magdala-of-fish (i.e., Tower of fish; in Greek: Tarichaeae = "fish salting") in Galilee, as well as the existence of a Fish Gate [4] and a fish market [5] in Jerusalem, are significant.

(† Snare §3, fish, fish-hook, harpoon.)

[1] Is. 19. 8; Ez. 47. 10; Matt. 4. 18; 17. 27; Mk. 1. 16 . . .; Lk. 5. 2. [2] Job 41. 1; Jer. 16. 16; Amos 4. 2; Hab. 1. 14–15; Matt. 13. 47. [3] Lk. 5. 4 . . .; Jn. 21. 4 . . .; [4] Zeph. 1. 10. [5] Neh. 13. 16.

FLAIL

Although the threshing of corn usually took place on the threshing-floor* by various methods of crushing († agriculture), for small quantities of grain or for small seeds (cummin, etc.), the Israelites used a stick or staff which did office as a flail.[1] But the technical term "flail" did not exist in Hebrew. On the other hand, staff, rod, and whip are sometimes used in the O.T. in the figurative sense of flail or scourge, or of punishment.[2]

[1] Is. 28. 27; (Jg. 6. 11; Ruth 2. 17). [2] Job 5. 21; 9. 23; Ps. 91. 10; Is. 10. 5.

FLAX

Flax was known as a textile plant from earliest antiquity. It was cultivated in Palestine before the Israelites arrived in that country: the harlot at Jericho hid Joshua's two spies under the stalks of flax [1] spread out on the roof to dry. Mention of the gathering of flax on the ancient Hebrew tablet from Gezer (S-E of Jaffa), which dates from the 10th century B.C., is also significant. Without referring to other texts,[2] it can be said that the land of Egypt [3]—especially the Delta—was the great flax producer. Tomb paintings in the Nile Valley often represent the different tasks which must be carried

Cultivated flax.

out in preparing the plant for spinning and weaving. Flax is not cut but pulled up from the fields (a), and left there to dry. To separate it from the dried foliage and the seeds encased in their round husks, the flax is passed in successive handfuls between the teeth of an iron comb called a hackle (b). These stalks, tied in bundles, are then left for a fortnight in stagnant water. It is this steeping which frees the plant from the remainder of its sap and which makes the cortex

clothes [18] and for the curtains of the Tabernacle.[19] Pharaoh emphasized Joseph's promotion by having him clothed in garments of šeš; [20] Ezekiel pictures Jerusalem as a magnificently clad woman distinguished by her dress of šeš,[21] and the good wife of the Book of Proverbs possesses clothes of šeš and of purple.[22] Some writers have thought that this word

a   b

Harvesting flax. Egyptian tomb painting.

friable. The stalks are re-dried, even scorched by various processes, and are beaten with a notched mallet. This is the 'stripping' which separates out the fibres from the woody parts of the plant. The bast is then cleaned more thoroughly and can eventually be spun and woven.

Flax was used for making measuring-lines [4] and ropes,[5] wicks for lamps (and where our versions speak of the quenched or smoking wick the Hebrew text has "flax" [6]) but primarily for fabric, which is often referred to in the O.T. and under four different names.

Often, in the first place, the name of the plant passed to the fabric: [7] a girdle, breeches, or cap of linen. Priests ministering in the Temple had to be dressed in linen,[8] and all Israelites were forbidden to wear a garment made of both wool and linen together.[9]—Then what is the exact meaning of the words bad and šeš? The former is probably a general term for all linen cloth used for clothing. In Exodus and Leviticus [10] the priests' clothes in particular are called garments of bad; Samuel wears an ephod of bad,[11] as does David when he dances before the Ark; [12] while certain holy personages in the visions of Ezekiel and Daniel are clothed in bad.[13]—If the word bad is a generic term, šeš was doubtless used for a special kind of linen, particularly fine or white, a valuable luxury material, used not only for clothes but also for hangings, canopies,[14] etc. Linen is certainly meant, because the same garment is sometimes said to be of bad,[15] sometimes of šeš.[16] Ezekiel states that šeš comes from Egypt,[17] the place of origin of the word itself. It is not surprising that this precious material was used for the High Priest's

might refer to cotton*, but this view has been criticized, and it seems that the expression "fine linen" usually employed by our versions is the best.

In the case of the word butz it must be noted that it occurs in the most recent texts of the O.T.,[23] in connection with ceremonial vestments, rich stuffs, tapestries, cords, as well as in the N.T. under the name bussos, Latin: byssus, which has passed into various translations. Mordecai wore a robe of byssus and purple; [24] the wicked rich man of the parable was dressed in purple and byssus; [25] and the bride of the Lamb and the armies of heaven in the Apocalypse [26] wore the same pure, shining material. It has been said that, in distinction from Egyptian linen, this word may designate Syrian linen,[27] but it is more likely to be simply the Aramaic name for šeš, and therefore to mean fine linen.

[1] Jos. 2. 6. [2] Hos. 2. 9; Prov. 31. 13; 1 Chr. 4. 21. [3] Ex. 9. 31; Is. 19. 9. [4] Ez. 40. 3. [5] Jg. 15. 14. [6] Is. 42. 3 (Matt. 12. 20); 43. 17. [7] Lev. 13. 47, 48, etc.; Jer. 13. 1. [8] Ez. 44. 17, 18 (cf. Rev. 15. 6). [9] Lev. 19. 19; Dt. 22. 11. [10] Ex. 28. 42; Lev. 6. 10; 16. 4, 23, 32. [11] 1 Sam. 2. 18 (cf. 22. 18). [12] 2 Sam. 6. 14. [13] Ez. 9. 2, 3, 11; 10. 2, 6, 7; Dan. 10. 5; 12. 6, 7. [14] Ex. 26; Ez. 27. 7. [15] Lev. 16. 4. [16] Ex. 28. 39. [17] Ez. 27. 7. [18] Ex. 28. 6, etc.; 39. 2, 5, etc. [19] Ex. 26. 1, 36; 27. 9, 16, 18; 35. 25. [20] Gen. 41. 42. [21] Ez. 16. 10, 13. [22] Prov. 31. 22. [23] 1 Chr. 4. 21; 15. 27; 2 Chr. 2. 14; 3. 14; 5. 12; Est. 1. 6. [24] Est. 8. 15. [25] Lk. 16. 19. [26] Rev. 19. 8, 14; cf. 18. 12. [27] Ez. 27. 16.

FLEA

The flea—plague of the unhygienic East—is mentioned only twice in the O.T.; [1] in both cases by David as a simile. But the second text should no doubt be emended to read: "The king of Israel . . .

seeks me [seeks my life] like the vulture pursues a partridge . . ."

[1] 1 Sam. 24. 14; 26. 20

FLOUR

For bread-making the Israelites used flour of wheat*, of barley*, and in exceptional cases of spelt* (if this is not sorghum) or of millet*. Peasants and the poor regularly ate barley bread.[1] Two qualities of wheat flour were distinguished: ordinary flour and the flour often called in Hebrew [2] the *fat* (or even the fat of the kidneys), i.e., the best, *of the wheat*; it was used to make cakes or festival loaves [3] and was consumed in quantity at Solomon's court.[4]

In early days ordinary flour could be used for sacred offerings,[5] but the Priestly Law prescribed fine flour only; a single exception was made for the sacrifice of jealousy, no doubt a very ancient practice, which provided for barley flour.[6] The loaves of shew-bread were made of fine flour.[7] It was offered in the natural state, moistened with oil, and with incense; or in the form of cakes mixed with, or moistened by, oil.[8] Flour could itself be a sacrificial gift, part of it was generally burnt on the altar, the other part going to the priest.[9] But most usually the offering of fine flour accompanied meat offerings, and was proportional to the importance of the beast which was burnt.[10] Without oil and without incense, it could replace, in the case of the poor, the offerings required as the sacrifice for sin.[11]

[1] Jg. 7. 13; Ruth 3. 15; 2 Sam. 17. 28; 2 Kgs. 4. 42; 7. 1; 2 Chr. 2. 10; Jn. 6. 13. [2] Dt. 32. 14; Ps. 81. 17; 147. 14. [3] Gen. 18. 6; 2 Kgs. 7. 1; Ez. 16. 13; Rev. 18. 13. [4] 1 Kgs. 4. 22. [5] Jg. 6. 19; 1 Sam. 1. 24. [6] Num. 5. 15. [7] Lev. 24. 5. [8] Lev. 2. 1–10. [9] Lev. 6. 15, 16. [10] Ex. 29. 2, 40; Lev. 7. 11–14; 14. 10; 23. 13; Num. 15. 3 ff.; 15. 24; 28. 5, 29. [11] Lev. 5. 11.

FLOWER

In the spring Palestine is magnificently adorned with flowers of all kinds. So the Bible readily speaks of flowers, in a collective sense, or of a particular flower, both with a literal [1] and a figurative meaning; in a figurative sense, as a symbol of the brevity of life, glory, or beauty.[2] Only a few species are named, in particular the lily* (or anemone*?), the daffodil* (according to some translators, this is more likely to be the meadow-saffron or the milk-vetch), almond* blossom, vine* blossom, the mandrake* flower, and the pretty panicles of henna* with a sweet smell.

Furthermore, some cultic objects were decorated with floral patterns,[3] and the Jerusalem Temple was rich in architectural ornaments in the form of open flowers or festoons of flowers.[4]

[1] Num. 17. 8; Cant. 2. 12; Nahum 1. 4. [2] Job 14. 2; 15. 33; Ps. 90. 5, 6; 103. 15; Is. 5. 24; 18. 5; 28. 1; 40. 6–8; Jas. 1. 10, 11; 1 Pet. 1. 24. [3] Ex. 25. 31; 37. 17 . . . [4] 1 Kgs. 6. 18, 29, 32, 35.

FLUTE

It is very difficult to determine precisely what kinds of flutes are meant by the different names given them in the O.T. It seems clear that the Israelites knew most of the kinds in use among their neighbours as ancient bas-reliefs depict them: the straight pipe or shawm, with or without a reed, and with one or two parallel tubes (one for the melody,

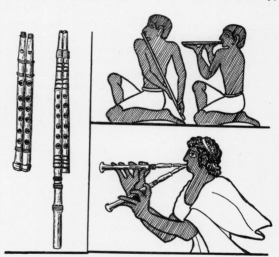

Varieties of flutes and ways of playing them.

the other for the accompaniment); the transverse flute, sometimes very long; the short hautbois and flute (of high pitch); Pan's pipes, with tubes of varying lengths one against the other, which were moved along the lower lip; and a flute mounted on skin bellows, like modern bagpipes.[1]

These instruments were made of reeds, wood, bone, or bronze; they no doubt lacked keys, and their holes probably allowed only a limited range of notes. So far excavations in Palestine have provided only one flute of bone, with a mouthpiece like a

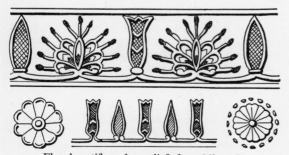

Floral motifs on bas-reliefs from Nineveh.

FLUTE

child's trumpet, and a reproduction in bronze of a woman playing a double-flute.

Bible texts imply that the flute might be played on its own [2] or to accompany other instruments.[3] It enlivened the gaiety of weddings, feasts, and merry-makings; lack of it was a mark of utter grief.[4] Nevertheless, it accompanied funerals: [5] according to the rabbis, "the funeral procession of the poorest Israelite must include at least one who laments and two flute-players".

The titles of the different categories of musicians accompanying Temple ceremonies [6] does not include flautists, though not because they were excluded from the cult; [7] only the very sonorous flutes were needed, and in limited numbers, in an orchestral group.

[1] Dan. 3. 5, 10, 15. [2] Jg. 5. 16; 1 Kgs. 1. 40; Is. 30. 29. [3] 1 Sam. 10. 5; cf. Is. 5. 12. [4] Job 21. 12; 30. 31; Matt. 11. 17; Lk. 7. 32; Rev. 18. 22. [5] Jer. 48. 36; Matt. 9. 23. [6] 1 Chr. 25. [7] Ps. 150. 4.

FLY

The flies which swarm in eastern countries are not lacking in Palestine, where they are very annoying in many places; they propagate the germs of various illnesses by their unpleasant habits of regurgitation and because they drag their long hairy legs in the rotting substances which they seek for food. They lay their eggs in the wounds of living creatures, where their larvae cause all sorts of irritations. They seem to appreciate the particular taste of tears, and so they frequently alight on the corners of the eye-lids, where they very often aggravate ophthalmia.

The O.T. mentions flies only rarely: "Dead flies," says Ecclesiastes,[1] "cause the ointment of the per-fumer to send forth a stinking savour" and, in his colourful style, Isaiah [2] declares that "Yahweh shall hiss for the fly that is in the uttermost part of the rivers of Egypt", that is to say, he will call the troops of that country. A third text [3] relates that Ahaziah, king of Israel, having fallen victim to a serious accident, sent messengers to Ekron to consult Baal-zebub; this name probably signifies the "lord fly" or the "master of the flies". The ancients had noticed a certain relationship between the swarming of flies and the development of certain epidemics; they may have deduced that the flies were demonic creatures, since illnesses* were caused by demons. As a result, the "master" of the flies, their king so to speak, had to be invoked if they were to be pre-served from epidemics, and also, by extension, to be cured of all sorts of illnesses. Golden flies were used as amulets*.

The fourth plague of Egypt [4] apparently consisted of an invasion of flies; the word used by the Book of Exodus and in the Psalms is a collective noun mean-ing "mixture", "cloud", "swarm", without further definition. This expression can be understood when it is known that in theory the descendants of a fly, in five months of favourable climatic conditions, in-crease to the fabulous total of 4,000 billions. How-ever, certain translations mention rather a "mixture of insects", "vermin", "various types of flies", etc., whereas others, following the LXX, refer to horse-flies or even to poisonous flies.

As a matter of interest, one of the permanent miracles that could be noticed in the Temple, accord-ing to the Mishnah, was that there were never any flies in the slaughter-houses of the sanctuary!

[1] Eccl. 10. 1. [2] Is. 7. 18. [3] 2 Kgs. 1. 2, 3. [4] Ex. 8. 21, 24, 29; Ps. 78. 45; 105. 31.

FOOD

Generally speaking, Easterners eat very moder-ately, and the Israelites likewise were fed mainly from the products of the soil.

*Bread** was usually made from barley* flour, less often from wheat* flour. It was not merely supple-mentary to a meal, but an essential part of it. (In Hebrew and Greek [1] to eat bread = to take a meal.) During harvest, in war, or on a journey, they were content simply with roasted corn-grains.[2] But ordinary flour* was used for a kind of porridge, and fine flour for cake* and pastry-making.[3]

Fruit was another important part of diet. Raisins († vine), figs (fig tree*), and dates († palm) were eaten fresh; but when dried and pressed they formed "cakes" useful for carrying.[4] Still today in Damascus apricots are compressed into thin strips that are rolled up like leather. The Israelites also ate pome-granates*, almonds (almond tree*), pistachio* nuts, walnuts, perhaps apples* or apricots*, sycomore* fruits, and, at least after the Exile, lemons*, mul-berries*, and melons*. Apparently the orange and banana were introduced into Palestine only after the Mohammedan conquest. Olives* were used principally for the oil they gave, but it was also known how to prepare them to make them edible.

For the *vegetables* of Palestine the Bible mentions cucumbers*, lentils*, and beans*, from which a sub-stitute flour could be produced in times of want; onions*, leeks*, and garlic*, always beloved of the Jews, and cultivated in Palestine along with bitter herbs* and endives.

Where cattle were raised, *milk** was naturally an accepted foodstuff, and we know that the Israelites were acquainted with its derivatives: cream, butter*, and cheeses* of various kinds.

Meat, on the contrary, cooked and preferably roasted,[5] was a luxury food. Although the court consumed large quantities,[6] ordinary folk killed an animal only at feast times or in honour of a guest,[7] and it was most often a goat* or sheep* (ram*), a kid* or a lamb*; beef († bull) and veal (the fatted calf) was particularly appreciated.—Doves*, pigeons, and sparrows* did not cost much.[8] As for poultry († cock), it is questionable whether it was introduced into Palestine before the Exile, as eggs for food are only mentioned in the N.T.[9] Possibly geese were fattened on King Solomon's farms.[10] So far as game were concerned, the Law allowed among others the hart*, gazelle*, deer*, and roe-deer*,[11] and the Bible speaks of the quail* and the partridge*.

Where *fish* abounded they were food for the poor.[12] Perhaps the fish mentioned in connection with the miracle of the loaves were dried fish.[13]

Like Palestinians today, the Israelites knew how to turn *grasshoppers** to good account, either cooking them in water with salt, or frying them in oil, after removing the head, feet, wings, and entrails, or drying and crushing them to make a kind of cake, whose bitterness was corrected by honey*.

Where there were bees or fruits, *honey* was esteemed, and it took the place of sugar in the preparation of some pastries.[14] Numerous *condiments* are mentioned incidentally in Bible texts: mint*, rue*, dill*, cummin*, mustard*, coriander*, capers*, saffron († crocus), cinnamon*; salt* was naturally in general and constant use.—The Easterner loves fat dishes; it was a delicacy for the Israelite to dip his bread in oil or spread oil on bread.[15] Even in the house of the poorest widow the cruse of oil must not fail.[16]

Along with milk, water* and wine († vine) comprised the essential *beverages*; the wine was drunk new or fermented, sometimes mixed with spices,[17] and workmen slaked their thirst with diluted vinegar (= Roman posca).[18] Wine from fruits, from dates in particular, was familiar, as well as pomegranate must,[19] and doubtless also a form of beer made from barley or millet.

(† Feast, fishing, hunt, strong drink, uncleanness.)

[1] Gen. 37. 25; Mk. 3. 20; etc. [2] Lev. 23. 14; Ruth 2. 14; 1 Sam. 17. 17; 25. 18; etc. [3] Gen. 18. 6; Ex. 29. 2, etc. [4] 1 Sam. 25. 18; 30. 12; 2 Sam. 16. 1; etc. [5] 1 Sam. 2. 15. [6] 1 Kgs. 4. 22 ff. [7] Gen. 18. 7; Jg. 6. 19; 13. 15; 2 Sam. 12. 4; Lk. 15. 23; etc. [8] Matt. 10. 29. [9] Lk. 11. 12. [10] 1 Kgs. 4. 23. [11] Dt. 14. 5. [12] Matt. 7. 10; 14. 17; etc. [13] Mk. 6. 38 par. [14] Ex. 16. 31; etc. [15] Ez. 16. 13; etc. [16] 1 Kgs. 17. 12. [17] Ps. 75. 8; Mk. 15. 23; etc. [18] Ruth 2. 14; Mk. 15. 36 par. [19] Cant. 8. 2.

FOOTSTOOL

The ancients knew of stools for the feet, as certain bas-reliefs depicting them prove. The O.T. mentions only the golden footstool to Solomon's ivory throne [1] (though the text is not very certain), and the Epistle of James alone makes reference to footstools used in places of worship.[2] But Biblical texts speak more than once in a figurative sense of the footstool of the Lord God (the earth, the Ark, or the Temple).[3]

[1] 2 Chr. 9. 18. [2] Jas. 2. 3. [3] 1 Chr. 28. 2; Ps. 99. 5; 132. 7; Is. 66. 1; Lam. 2. 1; Matt. 5. 35; Acts 7. 49.

FOREIGNER

Whereas in Babylonia the law made no distinction between native and foreigner, it was not so in Israel. Moreover, two classes of foreigners are mentioned in O.T. texts, each being denoted by a different word, a distinction which our versions do not always take into account.

The *nokri* (from a root signifying "to stare at, to look at with astonishment") is a foreigner in the wide sense of the term, a foreigner who has only chance temporary relationships with the inhabitants of the country, for he only passes through as a traveller or a merchant. Although, of course, he has a right to hospitality,[1] the usual laws are not applicable to him; [2] Deuteronomy says, for example, that one can demand from these foreigners the interest which it forbids to be asked of the Israelite,[3] or that one can use compulsion towards them for repayment of debts, even during the year of release.[4] It is all the more interesting to note, therefore, that Solomon asks God to answer the prayer of the foreigner who will come to pray in the Temple at Jerusalem.[5]

The foreigner permanently resident in Israel bore the special name of *ger*. Although the *nokri* doing business in Palestine was generally well-to-do and independent, the *ger* was more often than not an unfortunate refugee exiled [6] by war or some such circumstance; he might also be a member of an Israelite tribe who had had to leave his tribe for one reason or another; [7] or even a Canaanite, a former master of the country. Without bonds of relationship with those around him, and not able to rely on any "avenger of blood", he could find security only by placing himself under the protection of an Israelite family, of which he became to a certain extent the dependant and in whose bosom he occupied a special place, but not always an enviable one. But it must be noted that, from the beginning and with significant insistence, legislation upheld the defence, doubtless often necessary, of the *ger*, in whose favour the prophets, too, make it their duty to intervene.[8]

The Covenant Code, while recalling the fact that the Israelites have been *gerim* in Egypt, forbids the molestation and oppression of these foreigners.[9] In return, they naturally have to respect the customs of the country giving them hospitality, and if they are allowed up to a certain point to pay homage to their particular gods, they must especially observe the Sabbath, whose rest is, moreover, a benefit for them.[10]

In view of the spirit pervading Deuteronomy, the sympathy it shows to the *ger* by ranking him with the widows, the poor, and the orphans, is not surprising. The writer of Deuteronomy also recalls the sufferings of the Hebrews in foreign lands,[11] and asks the Israelites to have pity on the *ger*, to help him, and to make him benefit by various advantages.[12] The blessing of Yahweh is akin to this, "For Yahweh your God . . . doth execute the judgment of the fatherless and widow, and loveth the *ger*, in giving him food and raiment." [13] Every difference of opinion between a native of the country and a foreigner must be presented before the judge: [14] "Cursed be he that wresteth the judgment of the *ger* ".[15]

The Priestly Code outbids these regulations: the *ger* is no longer only the object of kindly recommendations, but he is made an equal with the Israelite: "Ye shall have one manner of law, as well for the *ger*, as for the homeborn: for I am Yahweh your God." [16] The cities of refuge are open to him also.[17] In return, the duties of the *ger* are specified: he may no longer give himself up to the "abominations" condemned by the Israelites; he must fast and repent with them and, like them, eat unleavened bread at the appointed time.[18] And woe to the *ger* if he took in vain the name of Yahweh, for immediate death would ensue.[19] It must be noted, however, that the *ger* was not allowed to participate in the Passover meal, unless he allowed himself to be circumcised and by that very act entered the community.[20] With time, and as the nation tended more and more to change entirely into a religious community, the assimilation of *gerim* soon became indispensable, and it was not long before they were merged with the proselytes*.

Our findings, which are all to the honour of Israel, indicate that Josephus is correct when he writes: "It will also be worth our while to see what equity our legislator would have us exercise in our intercourse with strangers; for it will then appear, that he made the best provision he possibly could, both that he should not dissolve our own constitution, nor shew any envious mind towards those that would cultivate a friendship with us. Accordingly, our legislator admits all those that have a mind to observe our laws, so to do: and this after a friendly manner, as esteeming that a true union, which is constituted not only by identity of race, but similarity of conduct: yet does he not allow those that come to us casually only to be admitted into communion with us" (*Cont. Apion* 2. 27, 28).

On the other hand—and even if we think only of the severity of attitude towards marriage with foreign women, especially after the Exile [21]—we must stress the exclusiveness which the Jews practised more and more with regard to foreigners properly so called, for reasons both religious and national.[22] The contrast is great between the declaration made in the Acts of the Apostles: [23] "It is an unlawful thing for a man that is a Jew to associate with, or come unto one of another nation" and that made by St Paul for whom, under Christian law, ". . . there is no difference between Jew and Greek: all have the same Lord who distributes his treasures unto all that call upon him." [24]

[1] Job 31. 32. [2] Gen. 31. 15; Ruth 2. 10. [3] Dt. 23. 20. [4] Dt. 15. 3. [5] 1 Kgs. 8. 41. [6] 2 Sam. 1. 13. [7] Jg. 17. 8; 2 Sam. 4. 3. [8] Ps. 94. 6; Jer. 7. 6; 22. 3; Ez. 22. 7, 29; Zech. 7. 10; Mal. 3. 5. [9] Ex. 22. 21; 23. 9. [10] Ex. 20. 10; 23. 12. [11] Dt. 16. 12; 24. 18, 22. [12] Dt. 14. 21, 29; 16. 11, 14; 24. 19–21. [13] Dt. 10. 18. [14] Dt. 1. 16. [15] Dt. 24. 17; 27. 19. [16] Ex. 12. 49; Lev. 24. 22. [17] Num. 35. 15. [18] Ex. 12. 19; Lev. 16. 29; 17. 10; 18. 26; 20. 2. [19] Lev. 24. 16. [20] Ex. 12. 48. [21] Ex. 34. 15, 16; Dt. 7. 1 . . .; Ezr. 9. 1 . . .; 10. 2 . . .; Neh. 13. 1–3. [22] Neh. 9. 2; Ez. 44. 6–9, 22. [23] Acts 10. 28. [24] Rom. 10. 12; Gal. 3. 28.

FOREST

Forests are often alluded to in the O.T.: [1] in former times Palestine was more extensively afforested than today. Some of the forests mentioned in the texts have disappeared, and woodland vegetation is now fairly abundant only in Upper Galilee, on Hermon, Carmel, and Tabor, and in some parts of Transjordania. For the rest, there are today, as no doubt formerly,[2] copses, thickets, and plantations rather than forests rich in mighty trees; there is (or was) little concern in Palestine for forest conservation, and goats have often caused great damage by eating the young shoots of trees.

Although the Israelites used local wood for fuel, sacrifices and manufacture of utensils, etc., they had to go outside for the large timber for building.[3]

(† Wood, woodcutter, carpenter.)

[1] Jos. 17. 15; 2 Sam. 18. 6; 2 Kgs. 2. 24; Is. 2. 13; 9. 17; 10. 18, 19, 34; etc. [2] Gen. 22. 13; Jer. 4. 7, 29. [3] 1 Kgs. 5. 6 . . .; 6. 9 . . .

FORK

The O.T. nowhere mentions the fork used in agriculture, and excavations have never unearthed any. But it shows us vividly Eli's wicked sons who appropriated certain sacrificial morsels by sticking

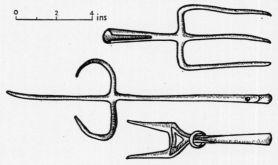

Palestinian forks.

them in "the pan, or kettle, or cauldron, or pot" with a three-pronged fork.[1] Bronze or gold forks also occur in the list of cultic equipment.[2] Similar ones, with two or three prongs, have been recovered from Byblos, Ras Shamra, and Gezer.

[1] 1 Sam. 2. 13–14. [2] Ex. 27. 3; 38. 3; 1 Chr. 28. 17; 2 Chr. 4. 16.

FORTIFICATIONS

From the late Neolithic Age, towns surrounded by walls, still very primitive, arose in Palestine, mainly on a height or a rocky spur. In time, while remaining very modest in area, they multiplied and the technique of fortification made important progress. The excavations in Palestine have provided abundant evidence on this subject, Biblical texts make innumerable allusions to the defence works, to the ramparts, erected in Israel or among the neighbouring peoples.

In view of the impressive Canaanite walls found up to now, one can easily understand the fright experienced by the semi-nomadic Hebrews on their arrival in the Promised Land. "What country are we about to enter!" they said. "The cities are walled, and very great." [1] Once they had become masters of the land, the Israelites soon imitated their predecessors: the O.T. tells of the care which the Kings David, Solomon,[2] Rehoboam,[3] Omri and Ahab,[4] and many others [5] took to fortify their towns and to ensure the defence of the frontiers; several sites of excavation magnificently illustrate the brief indications given on this subject by the texts.—In the days of the Maccabees and of Herod the Great new fortresses arose on new hills and old ones were restored.—Throughout the country from time immemorial numerous small forts were constructed, which were intended to guard and keep watch on passes of importance from the military point of view.

Military architecture concentrated on the two essential parts of fortification: the sloping bank (glacis) and the wall itself.

In order to prevent the enemy from reaching the base of the ramparts, care was taken, from earliest times, to protect the walls by a glacis of beaten earth reinforced by a shield of stones and clay which, often being offset very far forward from the wall, made all sapping extremely difficult.—This glacis, which served only to cover the foot of the rampart, underwent a great development in certain sites in Palestine, and was deployed in a long mound of earth sometimes protected by a dry wall with a relatively moderate slope, but which could attain as much as 65 ft. in height; it exposed the aggressor to an unprotected climb, all the more difficult and perilous, as the mound was often preceded by a ditch of varying width having a counterscarp with a vertical wall.— The huge glacis of Jericho and Shechem, 15 to 20 ft. and 20 to 25 ft. high, seem to have combined the sloping rampart and the shield of stones: with their cyclopian structure of blocks sometimes exceeding 6 ft., they formed a fearful defensive mass.

As for the walls proper, of variable thickness (8 to 20 ft. and over) and made either of stones or of rough bricks resting on a footing of stones, they pre-

sented in the beginning a smooth front and were without flanking parts. Early on, however, they followed the irregularities of the land and adopted a rack lay-out, with alternating salients and re-entrants more or less accentuated; or the line of the crenellated ramparts [6] was interrupted at regular intervals by rectangular towers, the base of which was often fitted with a circular bastion; as they jutted well out, they enabled the defenders to take on the flank and with crossed shooting, those assailants

Reconstruction of a fortified town: Lachish.

who had reached the foot of the wall. Towards the end of the Bronze Age this method became widely used throughout the East in ancient times. It was hardly modified until the time of the Greeks.[7] The towers of the walls of Jerusalem were famous; [8] they bore names preserved by the Book of Nehemiah.[9]

Walls with a double parallel lay-out were frequently constructed, the gap between either being filled with stones or casemated; the rampart on the crest was sometimes defended by a bank,[10] or even

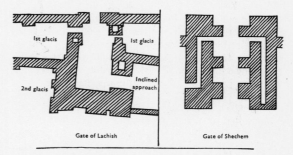

Plans of the gates of Lachish and Shechem.

by several rows of glacis, which took advantage of the natural transverse breaks of the incline, or by some ancient rampart. From the time of Solomon and probably under the influence of Phoenician craftsmen, great progress was achieved in masonry, in the sense that, on the one hand, the walls to be constructed rested upon rock and that, on the other, the wall itself was made of stones carefully hewn, allowing a construction with unmortared joints giving perfect adherence.

The gates were, of course, the vital points of the enclosure; they did not usually build many, and unpretentious towns generally had only one.[11] At Jerusalem they were relatively numerous, and the Biblical texts mention the names of certain of them.[12] Often massive towers ensured the defence of the gate, which was a building in itself. The passage was sometimes zigzagged, but the usual lay-out was pincer-shaped, that is, access was more or less narrowed at two or three points by pairs of buttresses which made between them guard rooms and into which were inserted the leaves of a double or treble gate.[13] The gates proper were composed of two wooden leaves [14] reinforced with pieces of metal.[15] They were closed by iron bolts and bars of wood and metal.[16]

Inside certain fortified enclosures, in the upper part of the town, there often arose a citadel or even an acropolis with its own ramparts; the last attacks were made there when the outer walls had fallen. The traces of several of these fortresses exist still today in Palestine, and the Biblical texts point out some of them.[17]

[1] Num. 13. 28; Dt. 1. 28. [2] Sam. 5. 9; 1 Kgs. 9. 15–17. [3] 1 Kgs. 12. 25; 2 Chr. 11. 5–12. [4] 1 Kgs. 16. 24, 34. [5] 1 Kgs. 15. 17, 21, 22; 2 Chr. 32. 5; 33. 14. [6] Is. 54. 12. [7] 2 Chr. 14. 5–6; 26. 9; Zeph. 1. 16. [8] Ps. 48. 12. [9] Neh. 3; cf. Jer. 31. 38; Lk. 13. 4. [10] 2 Sam. 20. 15; Is. 26. 1; Lam. 2. 8; Nahum 3. 8. [11] Gen. 19. 1; 34. 20; Ruth 4. 1; etc. [12] Neh. 2 and 3; Jer. 19. 2; 31. 38; 38. 7. [13] 1 Sam. 9. 14; 2 Sam. 3. 27; 18. 24. [14] Neh. 7. 3. [15] Ps. 107. 16; Is. 45. 2. [16] Dt. 3. 5; Jg. 16. 3; Neh. 3. 3; Ps. 147. 13. [17] Jg. 9. 51; 2 Chr. 27. 3; Neh. 7. 2; Acts 21. 34, 37; etc.

FOUNDATIONS

Like all the peoples of antiquity and all builders, the Israelites attached great importance to the foundations of their houses and established them with care.[1] And they doubtless offered on that occasion foundation sacrifices analogous to those practised elsewhere. Priestly legislation concerning the Levites* seems to refer to them. Excavations in Palestine have shown that in the Canaanite period—even also in Israelite times—the inhabitants of the country walled-in either a child, a young man, or a girl—sacrificed first, no doubt—in the sub-foundations of the house or under the threshold, probably with the purpose of compensating or appeasing the spirits of the chosen piece of land. The corpses of these victims, accompanied by some utensils, were sometimes placed in huge jars.

Lamp between two bowls—an offering substituted for a foundation sacrifice.

In time these human sacrifices disappeared, but for a long time a lamp, protected by two bowls, was placed as a symbol in the walls of houses. In the time of Ahab, when Hiel rebuilt or fortified Jericho, "he laid the foundation thereof with the loss of Abiram his firstborn, and set up the gates thereof with the loss of his youngest son Segub", as the First Book of Kings [2] says significantly; and this statement is no longer a riddle for us.

Today, new houses in Palestine are often consecrated by means of the blood of a sacrificed animal, and they are protected by various charms: blue balls of glass, buttons, animals' bones, etc.

[1] Cf. Matt. 7. 24 . . .; Lk. 6. 48 . . . [2] 1 Kgs. 16. 34.

FOWLER

Today, as in former times, Eastern people eat small birds, which they catch in snares. Even on the esplanade of the Mosque of Omar in Jerusalem we have seen a fowler use for a decoy the song of a captive bird, while some distance away he deployed a large net-trap. The O.T. alludes to similar equipment.[1] Jeremiah says: [2] "Among my people are found wicked men: they watch, as fowlers lie in wait; they set a trap . . .", and the Psalter glorifies Yahweh, who delivers from the snare of the fowler.[3]

(† Snare.)

[1] Lev. 17. 13; Ps. 124. 7; Prov. 6. 5; Hos. 9. 8; Amos 3. 5. [2] Jer. 5. 26. [3] Ps. 91. 3.

FOX

Two species of foxes live in Palestine, the Egyptian fox in the south and the larger, stronger Syrian fox in the north.—It is possible that the Israelites sometimes used the Hebrew word for fox to designate the jackal* (e.g., Jg. 15. 4 and Ps. 63. 11), but it seems that foxes are meant in the following texts: Neh. 4. 3; Cant. 2. 15; Lam. 5. 18; Ez. 13. 4.—Jesus dubbed Herod Antipas a fox,[1] and in a famous saying alludes to the fox's earth.[2]

[1] Lk. 13. 32. [2] Matt. 8. 20; Lk. 9. 58.

FREEDMAN

Acts 6. 9 mentions a synagogue* called the synagogue of the Libertines (freedmen). This synagogue was a centre in Jerusalem for Jews who had been led away captive to Rome by Pompey in 63 B.C., but had later been liberated; having returned to their homeland, they were able to associate together in worship, along with their descendants.

In 1914 an inscription of the 1st century A.D. was discovered in Jerusalem which mentioned the building of a synagogue, adjacent to an inn and to baths, for Jews come from abroad; it may perhaps be this precise synagogue.

FRIENDSHIP

The Israelites certainly did not lack appreciation for the value and nobility of friendly feelings. As is

128

often the case with primitive peoples even today, in ancient times the bonds which united friends in Israel were sealed by an exchange of gifts and by a religious oath; when Jonathan made a covenant with David [1] it is stated that it was in the name of Yahweh himself.

The word "friend" figures in numerous O.T. texts, showing what place the Jews gave to friendship. The Book of Proverbs in particular,[2] and Ecclesiasticus [3] in the Apocrypha, eulogize it, though admitting, without illusion, the rarity of true friends.

Friends often figure in the Gospels,[4] and Jesus himself expressed touching affection for his immediate associates, for the disciples whom he regarded as his friends, and the three of them whom he regarded as his intimate friends.[5]

[1] 2 Sam. 18. 3; 20. 8. [2] Prov. 17. 17; 18. 24; etc. [3] Ecclus. 6. 5–17. [4] Lk. 5. 34; 11. 5 ff.; 15. 29; Jn. 3. 29; 11. 11; 15. 13, etc. [5] Jn. 15. 14 f.; Matt. 17. 1; Mk. 5. 37; 14. 33; Jn. 19. 26; etc.

FRINGE

The Law called on Israelites to place at the four corners of their outer garment fringes or braid of a sort, or tassels (*tsitsit*), and to fasten to them a purple cord. They were to be a sign; on seeing them, as the text says, they would "remember all the commandments of Yahweh, and do them; and that ye follow not the desires of your own heart and your own eyes, which lead you to be unfaithful".[1]

The wearing of these tassels was an ancient tradition; they may be seen at the bottom of the loincloth worn by Canaanites on some Egyptian monuments. Originally they were in all likelihood a protection against evil spirits, but Jewish practice ended by endowing them with an essentially religious value.

We know from the Gospels that Jesus conformed to the customs of his people and wore a cloak with such fringes: the sick often tried to touch them, convinced that they transmitted from his person sufficient power to cure their disease.[2] In order to make a show of their loyalty to the Law, the Pharisees were addicted to very long fringes.[3]

Even today, some Jews wear *tsitsitot* under their clothes, in the manner of a scapulary, and the shawl which they wear over their shoulders and throw over their heads for prayer is provided with these tassels, which they caress in order to attract blessings from above. Precise rules, dictated by a mystical symbolism, set forth the composition of these cultic ornaments, which became complete emblems of the Law.

[1] Num. 15. 38, 39; Dt. 22. 12. [2] Matt. 9. 20; 14. 36; Mk. 6. 56; Lk. 8. 44. [3] Matt. 23. 5.

FROG

Several species of frogs are common in Palestine, but none are mentioned in the O.T., which refers only to the frogs of Egypt that constituted the second of the plagues related in Exodus.[1] Josephus vividly describes this calamity: "An innumerable multitude of frogs consumed the fruit of the ground; the river was also full of them, insomuch, that those who drew water had it spoiled by the blood of these animals, as they died in, and were destroyed by the water: and the country was full of filthy slime, as they were born, and as they died; they also spoiled their vessels in their houses which they used, and were found among what they ate, and what they drank, and came in great numbers upon their beds" (*Ant. Jud.* II, XIV, 2).

Frogs figure in one vision in Revelation [2] as symbolic of uncleanness.

[1] Ex. 8. 1–15; cf. Ps. 78. 45; 105. 30. [2] Rev. 16. 13.

FRYING-PAN

Contrary to the confusion created by some translations, the Hebrew vocabulary permits a distinction between frying-pans proper,[1] which were concave, and the round convex plates, under which the fire was made which was necessary for cooking the dough,[2] such as the Bedouin still use today.

[1] Lev. 2. 7; 7. 9; 2 Sam. 13. 9. [2] Lev. 2. 5; 6. 21; 7. 9; Ez. 4. 3; 1 Chr. 23. 29.

FULLER

The trade of fuller was not sought after by Israelites, because the scouring of wool, the finishing of new material, the cleaning process of the ancients, and the bleaching of clothes involved operations that were often evil-smelling. Thus fullers generally worked outside populated areas, near a pool or flowing water, which their work required. Three times [1] the O.T. mentions a "fuller's field" situated near Jerusalem, perhaps in the vicinity of En-Rogel, "the fullers' spring" (Job's Well today).

Fullers used large vats where they trod the materials with their feet; they also employed paddles with which they plunged the materials into an alkaline liquid or lye († nitre). The prophet Malachi declares [2] that the day of Yahweh will be "like fullers' alkali [or potash]", and St Mark's Gospel [3] says that on the day of transfiguration Jesus' garments became "exceeding white, so as no fuller on earth could whiten them".

[1] 2 Kgs. 18. 17; Is. 7. 3; 36. 2. [2] Mal. 3. 2. [3] Mk. 9. 3.

FUNERAL

It was a sacred duty for Israelites at all periods to pay the last honours to the dead. No corpse, even that of the man condemned to death,[1] must be left without a sepulchre.[2] It was a dreadful misfortune not to be buried; [3] such a thing was wished only for one's worst enemies,[4] for a lamentable fate was reserved, according to general belief, for those who had not been regularly buried.[5]

Immediately after death, the deceased's eyes [6] were closed with a kiss [7] and his toilet performed. In ancient times the dead man was clothed in his usual attire, for, in the realm of the dead, the king was recognized by his diadem, the warrior by his sword, the prophet by his cloak; [8] but according to the N.T. we know that in Roman times—and the natives of Palestine still today observe the same customs—the corpse, having been washed [9] and scented with aromatic substances,[10] was wrapped in a linen cloth; [11] a napkin was placed on his head [12] and his feet and hands were bound round with little bands.[13] This sort of embalming was very different from that practised by the Egyptians, but certain people devoted considerable sums to the purchase of funeral spices.[14]

Lying on a sort of litter or open bier, the corpse was placed in the middle of the only bedroom of the house or, preferably, in the upper room [15] built on the terrace, where the relatives and acquaintances of the deceased could meet together more easily and honour him by noisily showing grief at having lost him († mourning).

About eight hours after the death—the climate did not allow a longer interval—the corpse was taken to the sepulchre; the bier was usually carried on their shoulders by the friends of the deceased and followed by all those who wanted to surround the dead with their lamentations; [16] professional women mourners and flute-players accompanied the procession, whose size varied according to the deceased's social position. For important personages, large quantities of sweet-smelling substances were often burned near the tomb.[17]

The corpse was laid, with legs stretched out or drawn up to the chin, in the family sepulchre [18] († tomb). It was a misfortune not to be buried with one's forefathers; only the poor, foreigners, and malefactors were placed in common graves.[19] Near the corpse were placed the various objects which abound in ancient tombs.

It is known that the Israelites, like the Arabs of today, did not practise cremation; the cave at Gezer which acted temporarily as a crematorium was used only in the pre-Canaanite period, in Neolithic times, probably.

It must be pointed out that no religious ceremony was celebrated apart from the funeral. The mourners fasted until sunset; when that came, friends or neighbours brought their food, as food in the house of the dead was considered unclean,[20] and urged them to take nourishment.[21] Doubtless the same evening, a meal denoting the end of the funeral rites united the friends of the deceased and the mourners; at a later date goblets of wine were circulated as at the Paschal supper.

[1] Dt. 21. 23. [2] Ez. 39. 14. [3] 1 Kgs. 14. 11, etc.; 2 Kgs. 9. 10; Ps. 79. 3; Jer. 16. 4; Ez. 29. 5; Amos 2. 1. [4] 1 Sam. 17. 44, 46. [5] 2 Sam. 21. 10; Is. 14. 15, 18–20. [6] Gen. 46. 4. [7] Gen. 50. 1. [8] 1 Sam. 28. 14; Ez. 32. 27. [9] Acts 9. 37. [10] Mk. 16. 1; Lk. 24. 1; Jn. 12. 7; 19. 40. [11] Matt. 27. 59; Mk. 15. 46; Lk. 23. 53; Jn. 19. 40. [12] Jn. 11. 44; 20. 7. [13] Jn. 11. 44. [14] Jn. 19. 39. [15] Acts 9. 37. [16] 2 Sam. 3. 31; 2 Kgs. 13. 21; Lk. 7. 12 . . .; Acts 5. 6. [17] 2 Chr. 16. 14; 21. 19; Jer. 34. 5. [18] Jg. 8. 32; 16. 31; Ruth 1. 17; 2 Sam. 2. 32; 1 Kgs. 13. 22. [19] Is. 53. 9; Jer. 26. 23; Matt. 27. 7. [20] Num. 19. 14; Hos. 9. 4. [21] 2 Sam. 3. 35; Jer. 16. 7; Ez. 24. 17.

FURLONG

1. The furlong (*stadion*, equal to 600 feet), which was the measure of road distances most commonly employed by the Greeks, varied, with the value of the foot used, from 600 to 630 ft. approximately. The N.T. mentions it a number of times.[1]

2. The track for foot-races the Greeks used was also called *stadion* (stadium) [2] because its length was precisely that of the measure of the same name. In time these places, which served also for various sports († pastimes) in front of many spectators, were constructed with elaborate care and often took on a monumental aspect.

[1] Lk. 24. 13; Jn. 6. 19; 11. 18; Rev. 14. 20; 21. 16. [2] 1 Cor. 9. 24.

FURNACE

It is difficult to say whether the "burning fiery furnace" into which the three Hebrew youths were thrown of which the story of Daniel speaks [1] was a gigantic bread-oven or a furnace for pottery or metals.

[1] Dan. 3. 6 . . .

GALL

The LXX and the Vulgate, followed by other versions, translate two Hebrew terms by the word "gall", one of which means bile and the gall-bladder, the other a bitter and poisonous plant which is probably the hemlock (others say the poppy). This confusion arose because in antiquity it was thought that the poison of the snake was secreted by the gall-bladder, so that in metaphorical usage poison (hemlock) and bile could be used interchangeably. But today it is necessary to keep the word gall for the second term [1] and to translate the first by poison, hemlock, or poppy, etc.[2]

In the N.T.—apart from Acts 8. 23, which is a saying borrowed from Dt. 29. 18—the word translated "gall" denotes in a general sense, both literally and figuratively,[3] a bitter substance. According to Matt. 27. 34, which refers, no doubt, to Ps. 69. 21, it was mixed with the wine that Jesus refused to drink before his agony, whilst Mk. 15. 23 speaks of myrrh.

[1] Job 13. 26; 16. 13; 20. 14; 20. 25. [2] Dt. 29. 18; 32. 32, 33; Job 20. 16; Ps. 69. 21; Jer. 8. 14; 9. 15; Lam. 3. 5. [3] Acts 8. 23.

GANGRENE

This disease is mentioned only figuratively in the Second Epistle to Timothy,[1] which exhorts readers to avoid the chatter of the godless "whose talk will eat its way like gangrene". Some translators think that gangrene figures among the two or three last curses listed in Dt. 28. 22, but diseases attacking cereals are probably meant.

(† Blight, rust.)

[1] 2 Ti. 2. 17.

GARDEN

Even though gardens made the beauty of the banks and canals of the Nile,[1] though Babylon had hanging gardens and the royal palace of Susa was surrounded by a park,[2] pleasure and amusement gardens were without doubt exceptional in Palestine, where irrigation was often difficult. The Song of Songs describes poetically some very beautiful gardens, flowering and sweet-smelling,[3] but in the O.T. there is hardly mention of any other garden than the "king's garden" at Jerusalem, probably situated at the junction of the valleys of Hinnom and Kidron, where water is less scarce than elsewhere,[4] and of the garden of Uzza near the royal palace where Manasseh and Amon [5] were buried.— According to the Gospel of St John, the sepulchre in which the body of Christ was laid was also in a garden, close to Calvary.[6]—It is difficult to know exactly the nature of the "gardens" in which certain Jews celebrated, even after the Exile still, a mysterious cult which the Book of Isaiah condemns; [7] perhaps they were thickets or sacred woods.

Orchards planted with fruit trees (fig, olive, etc.) were found throughout the land; [8] the "garden" of Gethsemane, whose name signifies "oil-press", was without doubt planted with olive trees.[9]

Herb gardens were also the object of greatest care; the O.T. does not ignore them: [10] King Ahab himself coveted Naboth's vineyard to make a herb garden of it.[11]

In their colourful language the prophets talk of well-watered gardens, of the garden of the Lord or of Eden, or of gardens that have no water.[12] The Book of Numbers itself compares the dwellings of Israel with valleys widely shaded and with gardens on a river's edge . . .[13]

[1] Gen. 13. 10. [2] Est. 1. 5; 7. 7, 8. [3] Cant. 4. 12; 5. 1, 13; 6. 2; 8. 13. [4] 2 Kgs. 25. 4; Jer. 39. 4; 52. 7; Neh. 3. 15; Eccl. 2. 5. [5] 2 Kgs. 21. 18, 26. [6] Jn. 19. 41. [7] Is. 1. 29; 65. 3; 66. 17. [8] Cant. 6. 11; Is. 10. 18; 16. 10; Jer. 29. 5; Amos. 4. 9; 9. 14. [9] Jn. 18. 1, 26; cf. Matt. 26. 36; Mk. 14. 32; Lk. 22. 39.

[10] Dt. 11. 10; Job 8. 16; Is. 61. 11; cf. Lk. 13. 19. [11] 1 Kgs. 21. 2. [12] Is. 1. 30; 51. 3; 58. 11; Jer. 31. 12; Ez. 28. 13; 31. 8; 36. 35; Joel 2. 3; Gen. 2. 15; 3. 23. [13] Num. 24. 6.

GARLIC

The only reference in the Bible to garlic is at the memory of the garlic and onions of Egypt, which the Israelites had left and which haunted them as they crossed the desert.[1] Garlic has always been much appreciated in Eastern countries. It is cultivated in Palestine, and the Talmud attributes to it many, and surprising, virtues. It is known that the Greeks and Romans were fond of laughing at the Jews because they smelt of garlic.

[1] Num. 11. 5.

GATE

In order to be as sheltered as possible from the sun, houses in Eastern cities were cramped closely together and the streets were straight, so that the market-places were found at the entrance of villages or before the gates of towns, and not in their interior. They were used for all the expressions of social life: not only were daily affairs [1] transacted there but justice also was dispensed there; [2] on important occasions the populace gathered there,[3] but they also indulged there in the regular pleasures of talk; [4] deals were transacted there, the unemployed waited for work,[5] the stranger found a host,[6] and the young played,[7] so that market-places were not lacking in animation or picturesqueness.[8]

[1] Gen. 23. 10 ff.; 2 Kgs. 7. 1; Dt. 21. 19; 25. 7; Ruth 4. 1; Ps. 55. 11; Prov. 31. 23; Is. 59. 14; Acts 16. 19. [3] 1 Kgs. 22. 10; 2 Chr. 32. 6; Neh. 8. 1, 3; Is. 15. 3; Amos 5. 15. [4] Matt. 23. 7; Mk. 12. 38; Lk. 20. 46. [5] Matt. 20. 3. [6] Gen. 19. 1; Jg. 19. 15. [7] Zech. 8. 5; Matt. 11. 16; Lk. 7. 32. [8] Prov. 8. 3; Lk. 10. 10; 14. 21.

GATE, BEAUTIFUL

Only the Acts of the Apostles speaks of it.[1] Very likely it was the great gate which gave access from the East to that part of Herod's Temple* which was strictly reserved for Israelite men and women. In that case it would separate the Court of the Gentiles from the Court of the Women, and it was remarkable for its size and splendour. People crowded there on feast days; and unfortunate folk who lived by alms were glad to be installed on the fifteen steps that led up to it.—It is probably a mistake to confuse the Beautiful Gate with the Nicanor* Gate that led from the Court of the Women to the court reserved for male Israelites.

[1] Acts 3. 2.

GAZELLE

The choice flesh of this animal,[1] several varieties of which are still found today in Palestine—the gazelle, *dorcas*, is both the most abundant and the largest of game animals—was regarded as clean and could be eaten, as the Deuteronomic Law definitely states.[2] The majority of O.T. texts speak of the gazelle metaphorically, emphasizing chiefly its agility, timidity, and grace.[3]

Gazelle.

The Hebrew name of the creature, *tsebiyyah* (=gracious one; E.V. Zibiah) was often given to Jewish girls,[4] as was its equivalent, Tabitha in Aramaic, or Dorcas in Greek.[5]

[1] 1 Kgs. 4. 23. [2] Dt. 12. 15, 22; 14. 5. [3] 2 Sam. 2. 18; 1 Chr. 12. 8; Prov. 5. 19; 6. 5; Cant. 2. 9, 17; 4. 5; Is. 13. 14. [4] 2 Kgs. 12. 1; 1 Chr. 8. 9; 2 Chr. 24. 1. [5] Acts 9. 36.

GIRAFFE

Certain versions wrongly translate the Hebrew name of the last of the animals mentioned in Dt. 14. 5 by "giraffe". The exact meaning is not known. It is probably a wild goat (A.V., R.V., chamois*).

GIRDLE

Considering the shape of Israelite dress* (tunic), the girdle was an almost indispensable part of it.[1] Whether it was a cord, band of leather, or a piece of material, it was passed round the loins, and in order to work better or to walk more quickly, the servant, the workman, and the traveller tucked up their tunic into the girdle—a gesture still made today—hence the expression "to gird up one's loins".[2] The girdle was untied in leisure time.[3]

There were a great variety of girdles—from the quite simple girdle of the poor man or of the man in mourning to the magnificently embroidered girdle of the great lady, not forgetting that of the priest, and the belt of the soldier.[4] A beautiful girdle was always a well-appreciated gift,[5] and at the present time, too, the fellah is proud of it. The angel in the Book of Daniel, the Son of Man, and the angels in the Apocalypse wore golden girdles as a mark of their glory.[6] While the warrior put his sword in his girdle, as the Palestinian of our time readily slips a dagger or a pistol into it, the writer hung on it his pen-container († inkpot), and women their sachets.[7] The girdle could act as a wallet[8] and, combined with a fold in the tunic slit upon the breast, it formed a sort of pocket used for various purposes, in which the shepherd could even carry the weary lamb: "Like a shepherd, he shall gather the lambs in his arm, and carry them in [and not 'on'] his bosom."[9]

It must be said that our versions sometimes translate "bosom" and "girdle"[10] by words which vary in suitability.

The girdle is often mentioned in a metaphorical sense.[11] For example, the prophet Isaiah says that when the Messiah comes, "righteousness shall be the girdle of his loins, and faithfulness the girdle of his reins".[12] Taking its inspiration from these images, the First Epistle of Peter exhorts the faithful to be vigilant—"gird up the loins of your mind"[13]—and St Paul recommends the Ephesians to take truth for their girdle.[14]

[1] Ex. 28. 4; Is. 22. 21. [2] Ex. 12. 11; 2 Kgs. 4. 29; 9. 1; Lk. 12. 35, 37; etc. [3] 1 Kgs. 20. 11; Acts 12. 8. [4] Ex. 28. 8, 39; 2 Sam. 20. 8. [5] 2 Kgs. 1. 8; Prov. 31. 24; Is. 3. 20, 24; Matt. 3. 4; Mk. 1. 6; 1 Sam. 18. 4; 2 Sam. 18. 11; Ez. 23. 15. [6] Dan. 10. 5; Rev. 1. 13; 15. 6. [7] Is. 3. 20; Ez. 9. 2. [8] Matt. 10. 9; Mk. 6. 8. [9] Is. 40. 11; Ex. 4. 6; Prov. 21. 14; Lk. 6. 38. [10] 1 Kgs. 20. 11; Ps. 129. 7; Is. 49. 22. [11] 1 Sam. 2. 4; Job 12. 21; Ps. 18. 32; 30. 11; 109. 19. [12] Is. 11. 5. [13] 1 Pet. 1. 13. [14] Eph. 6. 14.

GLASS

In ancient times glass was looked upon as a precious substance; and this is how it appears in the only O.T. passage that mentions it.[1] Until the Persian period it was opaque, but might be coloured; since the art of glass-blowing was unknown—it was introduced in the Roman period—glass could be made only into small vessels: round a mould of clay mounted on metal were placed thin pieces of glass, of similar or different colours, which were then welded together by fusion, worked over, and polished. It was easier, however, to obtain artificial pearls, pieces of jewellery, amulets, etc.; thus quantities of these are found in excavations, particularly in tombs.

Palestinian glassware, from the end of the Bronze Age to the Hellenistic period, was generally imported from Egypt: the glass industry flourished on the banks of the Nile during the 18th, 19th, and 20th Dynasties. While the chance discovery by the Phoenicians of how to make this substance is probably a legend, it is true that fragments of ancient glass have been found at Sarepta and Tyre—however, they may go no farther back than the 5th century B.C., and the workshops of Sidon were famous in the 1st century A.D.—Finds made in particular at Samaria make it possible to establish the variety and to follow the evolution of the glassware used in Palestine, from the 9th century B.C. up to the Roman period.—Eastern peoples did not know how to use glass to make window-panes or mirrors.

In the Apocalypse[2] we hear of a transparent (or glassy) sea like quartz. The cup (of water) spoken of in the Gospels[3] would be an ordinary one of earthenware or metal.[4]

[1] Job 28. 17. [2] Rev. 4. 6; 15. 2. [3] Matt. 10. 42; Mk. 9. 41. [4] Cf. Matt. 23. 25; Mk. 7. 4; Lk. 11. 39.

GLEAN

Israelite law sanctioned the custom—from which Ruth knew how to profit intelligently [1]—of allowing the poor, orphans, and strangers to glean in the fields,[2] and likewise to glean in the vineyards, to gather olives from the trees after they had been beaten and to collect up fruit fallen in the orchards.[3] It is even laid down not to harvest to the extreme limits of a field [4] and to leave for the needy the forgotten sheaf.[5]

[1] Ruth 2. [2] Lev. 19. 9; 23. 22. [3] Lev. 19. 10; Dt. 24. 20–21. [4] Lev. 19. 9; 23. 22. [5] Dt. 24. 19.

GNAT

Naturally there exist in Palestine a large number of small insects of many species that may be called collectively "gnats". In Jesus' famous saying,[1] "Ye blind guides, who strain at the gnat and swallow the camel!", the word "gnat" stands for a Greek word which more usually and more exactly means "mosquito"*.

[1] Matt. 23. 24.

GOAD

This was a long rod carried by the Israelite farmer in his right hand to urge on the beasts that drew the plough*; it ended in an iron tip,[1] and was used as a weapon of war.[2] Twice the word is used figuratively.[3]—Elsewhere, in a proper [4] or in a figurative sense,[5] the word is used for the deadly sting of certain crustacea, and in these places in the English versions is translated "sting".

[1] 1 Sam. 13. 21. [2] Jg. 3. 31. [3] Eccl. 12. 11; Acts 26. 14. [4] Rev. 9. 10. [5] 1 Cor. 15. 55.

GOAT

1. *Male Goat.* The male goat was often presented as a sacrifice by the Israelites (burnt offering and peace offering [1]), but principally it was the victim in the sacrifice* for sin or for atonement.[2]—For the "scapegoat", see Azazel*.

Several O.T. texts refer to the goat-footed demons supposed to haunt desert places as goats or "satyrs"; [3] the name "satyrs" (lit. "hairy ones") was sometimes given to pagan deities in Israel, in order to condemn them.[4]

As the male goat leads the flock,[5] he is used sometimes in the figurative language of the prophets—and in a rather pejorative sense—to mean princes, the powerful, or the rich.[6]

In the well-known Parable of the Last Judgment,[7] when the shepherd divides the sheep (ewes) from the goats, the original text speaks more precisely of kids (v. 33b). Even today in Palestine white ewes and

black she-goats or kids side by side and in large numbers may be met; it is very easy to differentiate between them. Male goats do not go in flocks.

2. *Female Goat.* Together with sheep, female goats are to some extent part of the Palestinian landscape. From Hermon to Hebron, they gambol and graze on the high ground, and often cause serious damage to plantations. At all times flocks of goats, mixed with flocks of ewes, were the wealth of their owners; goats were never absent from any village; the poorest people possessed at least one. Laban and Jacob bred them in hundreds,[8] Nabal had a thousand of them; [9] but the Bible also refers to more modest flocks, such as those to which the Israelites were compared when they faced the numerous Syrian army.[10]

The goat was indeed highly valued, not only for its milk [11] (cheese, butter, etc.) and its meat [12] but also for its skin, from which bottles [13] or clothes [14] were made, and for its hair, from which various materials were manufactured—especially tent-cloth.[15]

Two breeds of goats are widely met in Palestine—the big goat with long hair and sharply curved horns, distinguished by its large pendulous ears,[16] and, in the north, a breed with much shorter ears. Speckled goats [17] are unusual, almost all have black hair, a point which explains the metaphor in the Song of Songs which compares the beloved's hair to a flock of goats moving down the slopes of the mountains of Gilead.[18]

A goat could be offered as a sacrifice, and was in fact frequently so offered.[19] Just as the male goat was especially meant for atonement, the burnt offering of a female was specifically called for, in certain cases, as a sin-offering.[20]

(† Kid, cattle, shepherd.)

[1] Lev. 1. 10; Num. 7. 17, 23; etc. [2] Lev. 4. 23; 9. 3, 15; 16. 7; Num. 28. 15; 29. 38; Ezr. 6. 17; Ez. 43. 22; 45. 23; etc.; cf. Heb. 9. 12. [3] Is. 13. 21; 34. 14. [4] Lev. 17. 7; 2 Chr. 11. 15; cf. Ps. 106. 37. [5] Jer. 50. 8. [6] Ez. 34. 17; 39. 18; Dan. 8. 5; Zech. 10. 3. [7] Matt. 25. 31–46. [8] Gen. 30. 33; 31. 38; 32. 14; etc. [9] 1 Sam. 25. 2. [10] 1 Kgs. 20. 27. [11] Prov. 27. 27. [12] Dt. 14. 4. [13] Gen. 21. 15. [14] Heb. 11. 37. [15] Ex. 35. 6, 23, 26; 36. 14; Num. 31. 20; 1 Sam. 19. 13; Cant. 1. 5. [16] Amos 3. 12. [17] Gen. 30. 32 . . . [18] Cant. 4. 1; 6. 5. [19] Gen. 15. 9; Lev. 3. 12. [20] Lev. 4. 27 . . .; 5. 6; Num. 15. 27.

GOLD

This precious metal, known in the East from earliest times, is named a considerable number of times in the Bible, which describes it as coming mainly from the land of Ophir,[1] the Eldorado of the Israelites (southern Arabia, coast of Somaliland, Madagascar, India, etc.?), and gives it different names according to its condition (solid, pure, fine, etc.).

Abraham, according to tradition, returned from Egypt very rich in cattle, in silver, and in gold; [2]

the stories of the golden calf [3] and of the wedge of gold misappropriated by Achan at Jericho are well known.[4] According to the Chronicles, which speaks hyperbolically, gold was as common as stones in Jerusalem during the time of Solomon,[5] and the First Book of Kings states that the son of David used it liberally for the decoration of his palaces and of the Temple in particular († Tabernacle), for which the altar of incense, the table of shew-bread, the Cherubim, the doors, the candlesticks, and all sorts of utensils for religious services are supposed to have been over-laid with gold or made of gold.[6] The golden shields of Solomon's arsenal were the joy of the Pharaoh Shishak (Sheshonk I) after the pillage of the capital in the time of Rehoboam.[7]— On many occasions the O.T. refers to the gold which the kings of Israel and Judah possessed and which they often had to hand over in order to buy their independence or to offer as tribute.[8]

The second Temple benefited by offerings of gold to which the Books of Ezra and Nehemiah call attention;[9] gold was not spared by Herod the Great, either, in the restoration of the Jerusalem Temple which he undertook.

The vast number of golden objects pointed out by the Biblical texts is also astonishing:[10] jewels of all sorts, plate, clothes woven with gold, idols, etc.; the goldsmiths knew how to work with skill, even in Israel, as is proved by the finds from excavations in Palestine.[11] Objects found at Gaza have suggested that at the end of the Bronze Age there existed there a centre of the gold industry.

In ancient times there was no money minted in gold—the first money used by the Jews dates from the time of Darius (d. 406 B.C.)—but gold, measured by weight, acted as a means of exchange, if not in usual trade, at any rate for big payments.

In the metaphorical language of the Bible, gold naturally plays a large part either as a term of comparison [12]—thus the Law of God, wisdom or even the esteem of men are far superior to it—or else as a symbol of purification:[13] "I will try them as gold is tried", Yahweh announces in the Book of Zechariah,[14] and the Apocalypse, which pictures the Heavenly Jerusalem made of pure gold similar to pure rock-crystal (quartz),[15] says: "I advise you to buy from 'me' gold refined by fire, so that you may become rich." [16]

(† Crucible, money, temple.)

[1] 1 Kgs. 9. 28; 10. 11, 14; 22. 48; Ps. 45. 9; Is. 13. 12; cf. Gen. 2. 11. [2] Gen. 13. 2; 24. 35. [3] Ex. 32. 4 . . . [4] Jos. 7. 21. [5] 2 Chr. 1. 15. [6] 1 Kgs. 6. 20 . . . ; 7. 48 . . . ; 10. 18 . . . [7] 1 Kgs. 10. 16, 17; 14. 26. [8] 1 Kgs. 15. 18, 19; 20. 3, 7; 2 Kgs. 12. 18; 14. 14; 16. 8; 18. 14; 20. 13; 23. 33, 35; 24. 13; 25. 15. [9] Ezr. 1. 4; 2. 69; 7. 15; 8. 26, 27; Neh. 7. 70–72. [10] Jg. 8. 24 . . . ; 1 Sam. 6. 4 . . . ; Ps. 115. 4; Eccl. 12. 6; Is. 2. 7; 40. 19; Ez. 16. 13, 17; Hos. 8. 4; Hab. 2. 19; Matt. 2. 11; Jas. 2. 2; 1 Pet. 3. 3. [11] Jer. 10. 9, 14. [12] Job 28. 15; Ps. 19. 10; 119. 72, 127; Prov. 3. 14; 8. 19; 22. 1; 25. 12. [13] 1 Pet. 1. 7. [14] Zech. 13. 9. [15] Rev. 21. 18. [16] Rev. 3. 18.

GOLDSMITH, SILVERSMITH

These craftsmen are more than once named in the O.T.; apart from the ample evidence of excavations, the abundance of gold and silver objects mentioned by Bible texts, which were certainly not all imported products, implies that the goldsmith's art had skilled exponents in Palestine. In the time of the Judges, a silversmith worked for Micah;[1] the prophets often allude to the idols which goldsmiths made,[2] and Jeremiah declares that goldsmiths are ashamed of the images that come from their hands.[3] The Book of Nehemiah [4] tells of a body of goldsmiths, and we know that the troubles which arose from the proclamation of the Gospel in Ephesus by St Paul were let loose by "a certain man named Demetrius, a silversmith", who made replicas in silver of the temple of Artemis.[5]

(† Smelting, crucible, silver, gold; and articles on jewellery.)

[1] Jg. 17. 4. [2] Is. 40. 19; 41. 7; 46. 6; Jer. 10. 9. [3] Jer. 10. 14. [4] Neh. 3. 8, 31. [5] Acts 19. 24.

GOPHER

The only Bible text which uses this term is the passage in Genesis where God gives Noah the command to construct the Ark*; he tells him to make it of gopher wood.[1] Comparison with similar Assyrian words indicates that it was probably some conifer.

[1] Gen. 6. 14.

GOURD

The Hebrew word for the plant which sprang up over Jonah "that it might be a shadow over his head", but which shrivelled up as rapidly as it had grown, is qiqayôn, which the A.V. translates "gourd".[1] It is difficult to identify, and no Bible plant, perhaps, has aroused such passionate discussion.—Commonly, the castor-bean is proposed, because it can grow to a considerable height and has very large palmately-lobed leaves. But some translators (St Augustine, Luther, etc.) decide for the true gourd, the characteristics of which correspond better to the rapid growth and wilting of Jonah's plant.

Castor-bean.

Ancient versions content themselves with transcribing the Hebrew word. Because of that, curiously enough, the name "kikajons" is frequently given in

French Switzerland to a summer-house, so that the name of the plant made to shelter the prophet has passed to the booth or shelter of branches in the shade of which he sat.

¹ Jonah 4. 5–11.

GOUT

It is possible, but not certain, that the disease of the feet suffered by Asa, king of Judah, in his old age ¹ may have been gout. Apart from that possible allusion, there is no other hint of this infirmity in the Bible.

¹ 1 Kgs. 15. 23.

GRASSHOPPER (LOCUST)

Hebrew has a number of words for grasshoppers and crickets, and perhaps even for these insects at different stages in their development. But the interpretation of the terms presents difficulties which etymology cannot always resolve. This richness of vocabulary, as well as the frequent mention of grasshoppers in the O.T., shows the place they occupied in the preoccupations of the Israelites. Even if some species were harmless, an invasion of locusts—the species which figures most commonly in Bible texts—appeared as a judgment of God.¹ Still today such an event in the East is a catastrophe: when the swarms of these insects, which form clouds able to

A gregarious form of migratory grasshopper.

hide the sun, settle on the ground, all is lost; after half an hour of their passage these innumerable, voracious creatures leave trees completely robbed of foliage and crops entirely destroyed.² Noxious as larvae, grasshoppers were harmful even when dead, because the mass of their bodies gave off pestilential odours.³

The figurative language of the Bible makes several references to grasshoppers;⁴ the comparison of the leaping insect with the horse is easily explicable,⁵ and the prophet Joel's descriptions of the enemies of his nation under the figure of invading grasshoppers are famous.⁶

There was one compensation for the victims of grasshoppers: these insects were edible, and the Israelite law did not prohibit the eating of certain species.⁷ Still today the natives of many regions capture them easily in the morning, when they are

135

numbed by the cold or their wings wet with dew; after removing the head, feet, wings, and entrails, they eat them boiled or roasted, relishing their

A fruit tree which has been ravaged by grasshoppers.

vegetable flavour; others prefer to dry them in the sun, grind them to powder, and makes cakes of them, mitigating their bitterness with honey.

¹ Dt. 28. 38; 1 Kgs. 8. 37; Ps. 78. 46; 105. 34. ² Ex. 10. 15; Is. 33. 4; Joel 1. 4–12; Amos 4. 9. ³ Joel 2. 20. ⁴ Num. 13. 33; Jg. 6. 5; 7. 12; Ps. 109. 23; Is. 40. 22; Jer. 46. 23; Amos 7. 1; Nah. 3. 15. ⁵ Job 39. 20; Jer. 51. 27; Rev. 9. 7. ⁶ Joel 2. 1 . . . ⁷ Lev. 11. 22; Matt. 3. 4; Mk. 1. 6.

GREAVES

The only mention of greaves in the Bible is in reference to Goliath's armour; the text specifies that they were of bronze.¹ None have so far been found in Philistine tombs; if they were normally made of leather, they certainly could not have been preserved.—When Assyrian soldiers wore a long tunic (which became a cuirass* when metal plates were fastened to it), their legs were adequately protected; but when that part of their uniform was shortened they were given higher footwear († shoe); obviously the lower parts wore out more quickly than the uppers, so that this equipment was finally divided into two parts—a sandal and a greave, which was, of

GULL

course, made of leather. Metal greaves have been found at Carchemish, but the discovery was so unusual that they are thought to be an importation from abroad; greaves were part of the equipment of the Greek hoplite.

[1] 1 Sam. 17. 6.

GULL

This creature, whose flesh is tough and indigestible, figures among the unclean birds,[1] but its Hebrew name can doubtless cover other similar small web-footed birds (petrels, terns, etc.), which, like the gull, live on the shores of the Mediterranean and of the Lake of Tiberias. Instead of "gull" some translators prefer "bat"*.

(† Cuckoo.)

[1] Lev. 11. 16 (3); Dt. 14. 15 (3).

HAEMORRHOIDS (EMERODS)

A Hebrew word that figures a number of times in 1 Sam. 5 and 6,[1] for the calamity produced among the Philistines by the presence of the Ark of Yahweh which they had taken from the Israelites, is often translated by haemorrhoids (A.V., emerods). But while recognizing that the author of Ps. 78 [2] and the LXX believed it was this malady, it is possible that it was pustules, or buboes of the plague, to be precise. The consequences of the scourge seem to have been terrible,[3] and it is directly connected with an invasion of rats; [4] it is known that rodents are the usual carriers of the plague.—Reference to buboes, in the series of epidemic afflictions in Dt. 28. 27, also appears more normal than that of haemorrhoids.

[1] 1 Sam. 5. 6; 6. 17; etc. [2] Ps. 78. 66. [3] 1 Sam. 6. 9, 11, 12. [4] 1 Sam. 5. 6 (Gk.); 6. 1 (Gk.); 6. 4; etc.

HAIR

It is difficult to say exactly how the Israelites wore their hair. Egyptian and Assyrian records which could be used in this connection, since certain inhabitants of Palestine are represented on them, perhaps do not deserve all the credence they have sometimes received; and Biblical texts more often than not provide only indirect information. Moreover, the fashion may have varied in the course of centuries, and hair-styles may possibly have depended, also, on social rank.—Whereas the Palestinian peasant of today covers his almost entirely shaved head with his turban, it seems that in general the Israelites let their hair fall in curls on the nape of their neck. An ordinary person did not let it grow long, whereas well-to-do people let their hair cover their shoulders. A fine head of hair emphasized the martial bearing of its owner; he did not hide it

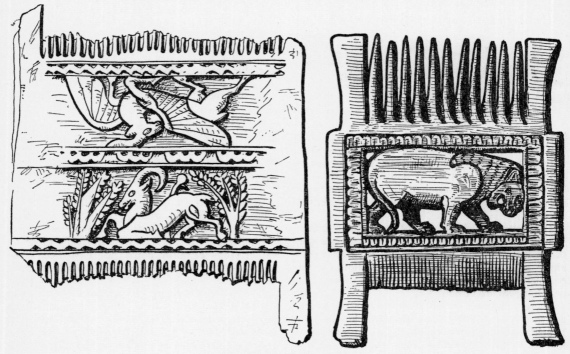

Combs of ivory and wood.

136

under head-gear, but held it back by a narrow band worn round the head. The care which Absalom took of his hair is well known,[1] and the beloved of the Song of Songs praises the locks, "curling and black as a raven", of her loved-one.[2] Samson arranged his hair in locks; [3] Josephus tells that some young men sprinkled their hair with powdered gold to enhance its brilliance. Baldness was a disgrace, as witness the boys of Bethel who scoffed at Elisha's bald head.[4] Priests were ordered to observe a rightful moderation: they must neither shave their heads —as did the priests and high dignitaries of Egypt— nor let their hair grow indefinitely.[5] In the time of St Paul it was not proper for men to wear their hair long.[6] It is well known that the Nazirite († Nazirate) did not touch his until the end of his vow, so that he could offer it in sacrifice.[7]

Women wore their hair long and in plaits, and decorated it in different ways, and even waved it artificially; [8] they doubtless also used combs.[9] It is interesting to note that the Mishnah forbids the plaiting of hair on the Sabbath day. The N.T. recommends Christian women, for whom hair is more a natural veil than an ornament,[10] to give up arranging their hair and to prefer the adornment of the heart to all external adornment.[11]

The Jews anointed their hair with oil and sometimes perfumed it, especially if they were to attend a banquet; [12] it was even regarded as in good taste for the man receiving guests to offer them perfumes.[13] It does not appear that they used either dyes or wigs (which were well known to the Egyptians).

In order to express sorrow, the Israelite left his hair in disorder or tore it violently; as a sign of mourning, he totally or partly shaved his head.[14] There are many texts referring to this practice, which was opposite to that of other peoples, who let their hair grow to show their grief. Among the Arab Bedouin, the women still today cut their hair at the death of a close relation and place it or hang it in long plaits near the tomb.—To untie a woman's hair is to humiliate her [15]—this gesture can also be voluntary [16]—and to shave anyone's hair by force is a grave insult.[17] In certain tribes of Arabia the hair is cut out of vengeance, too: in order not to perpetuate hostility, the assassin is not killed; he is forgiven, but he will not be given his freedom without first having his hair and beard cut, and his head and chin shaved.

In Israel certain purification ceremonies required that the razor be passed over the whole body; it is thus that the Levites had to shave their heads and their whole body for their "consecration".[18]

The hair gives Biblical authors some well-known metaphors: my iniquities "are more than the hairs of my head"; [19] "the very hairs of your head are all numbered"; [20] "there shall not one hair of his head fall to the ground".[21]—In order to show the skill of

the slingers of Benjamin, the Book of Judges claims that they were capable of aiming at a hair without missing it.[22] It is well known that white hair, before which the Israelites bowed with respect,[23] plays a symbolic part in the visions of Daniel and of the Apocalypse.[24]

(† Beard.)

[1] 2 Sam. 14. 26. [2] Can. 5. 11. [3] Jg. 16. 13, 19. [4] 2 Kgs. 2. 23. [5] Lev. 21. 5; Ez. 44. 20. [6] 1 Cor. 11. 14. [7] Num. 6. 18–19. [8] 2 Kgs. 9. 30; Cant. 4. 1; 5. 2; 7. 5; Is. 3. 24; Rev. 9. 8. [9] 2 Sam. 19. 24. [10] 1 Cor. 11. 15. [11] 1 Ti. 2. 9; 1 Pet. 3. 3. [12] Ruth 3. 3; 2 Sam. 14. 2; Ps. 23. 5; Eccl. 9. 8; Is. 3. 24; etc. [13] Matt. 6. 17; 26. 7; Lk. 7. 46. [14] Is. 3. 17, 24; 15. 2; 22. 12; Jer. 7. 29; 48. 37; Ez. 7. 18; 27. 31; Amos 8. 10; Mic. 1. 16. [15] Num. 5. 18. [16] Lk. 7. 38. [17] Is. 7. 20. [18] Num. 8. 7. [19] Ps. 40. 12; cf. 69. 4. [20] Matt. 10. 30; Lk. 12. 7. [21] 1 Sam. 14. 45; 2 Sam. 14. 11; 1 Kgs. 1. 52; Lk. 21. 18; Acts 27. 34. [22] Jg. 20. 16. [23] Lev. 19. 32; Prov. 16. 31; 20. 29. [24] Dan. 7. 9; Rev. 1. 14.

HALLEL (=Praise)

At the great Feasts of Passover, Weeks, and Tabernacles, as well as at the Feast of Dedication, and in other circumstances, the Jews sang the Hallel, or the Egyptian Hallel, which was a little collection of Psalms of praise, so called because it was sung "in the Temple during the sacrifice of the paschal lamb, which called to mind the deliverance from bondage in Egypt". It included Psalms 113 to 118, which were sung also in family gatherings, after the celebration of the Passover, on the first evening of the Feast: Psalms 113 and 114 were chanted at the beginning of the meal before the second cup was circulated; Psalms 115 to 118 after the meal and the handing round of the fourth cup. Jesus and his disciples conformed to this custom, without doubt, to judge by the account of the institution of the Last Supper.[1]

Psalms 146 to 150 also form a Hallel, which has sometimes been called the Great Hallel in contrast with the first, which is considered as the Little Hallel; but these epithets are uncertain and are sometimes interchanged; moreover, the name of Great Hallel is also given to Psalm 136, according to rabbinic tradition.

[1] Matt. 26. 30; Mk. 14. 26.

HAMMER

The Israelites doubtless employed, particularly from Hellenistic times, a whole series of hammers, sledge-hammers, and mallets, analogous to those known from Greek and Roman antiquity. Bible texts allude to tools of this kind, bearing various names which cannot always easily be identified, the less so because Palestine excavations are extremely poor in this field.

Apart from the war-hammer [1] († club) and the tools with which on some occasion the carvings of the sanctuary had been defaced,[2] two names stand out: one which denotes the ordinary hammer used for driving in nails or pegs,[3] for hammering metal,[4] for trimming stones,[5] or for use as a mallet [6]—and the other, the name given to the hammer used for breaking rocks [7] and also for burnishing metal.[8]

[1] Prov. 25. 18. [2] Ps. 74. 6. [3] Jer. 10. 4. [4] Is. 44. 12. [5] 1 Kgs. 6. 7. [6] Jg. 4. 21 (cf. 5. 26). [7] Jer. 23. 29; 50. 23. [8] Is. 41. 7.

HANDBREADTH

A subdivision of the cubit*, the handbreadth (or palm), was equal to the size of the hand or of four fingerbreadths. Three handbreadths made a span, and six handbreadths a cubit. According to the system followed for the latter, the handbreadth corresponded to 3 or 3·4 in.—Sometimes the O.T. mentions it; for example, the Bronze Sea in Solomon's Temple was a handbreadth thick,[1] and the Psalmist writes: "Thou hast fixed [made] my days as handbreadths." [2]

[1] 1 Kgs. 7. 26; 2 Chr. 4. 5. [2] Ps. 39. 5.—Ex. 25. 25; 37. 12; Ez. 40. 5, 43; 43. 13.

HANDS (LAYING ON)

This symbolical act, doubtless often accompanied by freely spoken words or by formulae which it emphasized, is drawn attention to on many occasions in the Bible. The meaning of it is very much discussed; an exact meaning can be arrived at only by taking into account the very different circumstances which demanded this important gesture.

1. *Sacrificial Laying on of Hands.* The ritual of blood sacrifices prescribed for the Israelites demanded that every sacrifice, of cattle or sheep, must be immediately preceded by a laying of *the* hand on the head of the victim. This gesture was made not only at the time of sacrifices* of atonement for sin [1] but also for burnt offerings,[2] for "peace" offerings,[3] and for sacrifices at the consecration of priests.[4] And it was always the one who offered the sacrifice (or the elders in the name of the community [5]) who had to proceed to the laying on of hands, and not the priest—unless of course the latter offered a victim in his own name.[6]

It should be noted that the laying on of the hand was performed also on the head of the Levites when they were dedicated to Yahweh and appointed to his service; [7] and that on the Day of Atonement* the High Priest laid his *two* hands on the head of the goat which he was about to send forth, laden with the iniquities of Israel.[8]

2. *Blessing.* By the laying on of hands Jacob on his deathbed confirmed, in solemn manner, the blessing* which he gave to the two sons of Joseph.[9] It was to bless the little children presented to him

that Jesus laid his hands upon them.[10] It should be noted that he was asked to "touch" them (Mk. 10. 13; Lk. 18. 15) and to pray (Matt. 19. 13), and that the Master also took them in his arms.[11]

Blessing was also given by raising the hands.[12] Elisha placed his on those of King Joash to ensure, magically, a victory to his people.[13]

3. *Healing.* In the N.T. the laying on of the hand or hands often accompanied the cures performed by Jesus,[14] who, however, did not necessarily perform this gesture, even if he was asked to do so; [15] on occasion, he performed others, even more surprising.[16] The disciples practised the laying on of hands also to heal.[17] There is only mention once or twice of prayer accompanying the laying of hands on sick people.[18]

4. *Appointment.* The Book of Numbers [19] reports that Moses received the order to appoint Joshua— "a man in whom the Spirit dwells"—to his office, by laying his hand upon him. Reversing the terms, Deuteronomy [20] declares that Joshua was "full of the Spirit of wisdom, for Moses had laid his hands upon him".

In the Acts of the Apostles the laying on of hands, preceded by a prayer, is performed by the apostles upon the seven men filled with the Spirit and wisdom who are to be appointed to "serve tables",[21] and by the Christians of Antioch, under the influence of the Holy Spirit, upon Barnabas and Saul, entrusted with a missionary journey.[22]—The Pastoral Epistles refer to the gift of grace which was conferred upon Timothy "by prophecy, with the laying on of the hands of the presbytery" [23] and to a laying on of hands which the apostle Paul himself is supposed to have conferred upon his disciple; [24] a third text recommends the same Timothy to "lay hands hastily on no man".[25]

5. *Gift of the Holy Spirit.* Three passages in the N.T. establish a close relationship between the laying on of hands and the gift of the Holy Spirit: Peter and John proceed to this act upon Samaritans who immediately receive the Holy Spirit; [26] Ananias lays hands upon Saul that he might recover his sight and be filled with the Holy Spirit; [27] and the latter descends upon a few disciples at Ephesus after Paul has laid hands upon them.[28]

Other texts [29] show that the gift of the Spirit was not necessarily related to the laying on of hands. On the contrary, baptism plays an important part in the five passages just quoted, whether it precedes or follows the gift of the Spirit.

6. *Miscellaneous.* In order to complete the list of texts which mention the laying on of hands, it should be noted that it is mentioned in a significant list in the Epistle to the Hebrews; [30] that the poem of Job speaks of a judge who might lay his hand upon two litigants; [31] and that when a blasphemer was condemned, all those who had heard him must lay their

138

hands on his head before he was stoned.[32] There is also the fact that Paul twice received the laying on of hands, once at Damascus and once at Antioch.[33]

There is no need to discuss the problems raised by the laying on of hands and which belong to Biblical theology. But it seems evident that this gesture, well known in the history of religions, is initially and essentially a rite of transmission (transmission of blessings, curses, curative virtues, offices, material and spiritual gifts, etc.), the meaning of which has been enriched by connected ideas. In particular, there is some doubt whether the sacrificial laying on of hands had for its aim the transmission of sin to the sacrificed animal or whether it simply marked the yielding of the victim to Yahweh, or whether it was a rite of communion.

[1] Lev. 4. 3, 4, 15, 24, 29, 33. [2] Lev. 1. 4. [3] Lev. 3. 2, 8, 13. [4] Ex. 29. 10, 15, 19; Lev. 8. 14, 18, 22. [5] Lev. 4. 15. [6] Lev. 4. 4; etc. [7] Num. 8. 10, 11. [8] Lev. 16. 21. [9] Gen. 48. 9, 13, 14. [10] Matt. 19. 13; Mk. 10. 16. [11] Mk. 10. 16. [12] Lev. 9. 22; Lk. 24. 50. [13] 2 Kgs. 13. 16. [14] Mk. 6. 5; Lk. 4. 40; 13. 11–13. [15] Matt. 9. 18, 25; Mk. 5. 23, 41. [16] Mk. 7. 32–35; 8. 22–26. [17] Mk. 16. 18; Acts 9. 12, 17; 28. 8. [18] Mk. 7. 34; Acts 28. 8. [19] Num. 27. 18–23. [20] Dt. 34. 9. [21] Acts 6. 6. [22] Acts 13. 3. [23] 1 Ti. 4. 14. [24] 2 Ti. 1. 6. [25] 1 Ti. 5. 22. [26] Acts 8. 17–19. [27] Acts 9. 17. [28] Acts 19. 6. [29] Acts 2. 38; 10. 44–48. [30] Heb. 6. 2. [31] Job 9. 33. [32] Lev. 24. 14. [33] Acts 9. 17; 13. 3.

HANDS (WASHING)

This ritual gesture is ordained by Exodus [1] for the priests, who must wash their hands before fulfilling their office "so that they die not" (because they have presented themselves impure before Yahweh), and, by tradition, for all the Jews, who must wash their hands very carefully before each meal. The Gospels refer to these ablutions, important in the eyes of the Scribes and Pharisees, but which Jesus and his disciples did not trouble to observe; [2] the Talmud gives more than 600 ordinances on this subject. Leviticus demands that every man touched by someone tainted by uncleanness shall wash his hands.[3]

It is well known that this gesture constituted a symbolical profession of innocence; Pontius Pilate has made it famous; [4] but, according to Deuteronomy, at the time of the sacrifice of atonement for a homicide by an unknown man, the elders of the town nearest to the corpse washed their hands over the sacrificed heifer.[5] And the Psalmist exclaims on two occasions: "I wash my hands in innocency." [6]

[1] Ex. 30. 19–21; 40. 30–32. [2] Matt. 15. 1–20; Mk. 7. 2–23; Lk. 11. 38. [3] Lev. 15. 11. [4] Matt. 27. 24. [5] Dt. 21. 6, 7. [6] Ps. 26. 6; 73. 13.

HANGING

The Israelites apparently did not execute by hanging, but sometimes they hanged the bodies of con-

demned prisoners [1] from a tree or gibbet in order to show that they had been executed and, in some cases, mutilated; in early times this was probably done to increase their punishment by depriving them of burial and leaving them as food for beasts of prey. Later the Deuteronomic Law decreed that no criminal should be left hanging from a tree after sunset.[2]

Some exegetes wonder whether the Israelites did not go so far as impaling, since the Hebrew verbs used may include suspension, hanging, and impaling too, or even crucifixion.[3]

The Egyptian baker who, according to Genesis, was a prisoner with Joseph was perhaps beheaded before being hanged,[4] but it seems that at Susa the two eunuchs who conspired against the king, and Haman himself, were hanged (or impaled) alive.[5]

We know that after betraying Jesus, Judas hanged himself.[6]

[1] Dt. 21. 22; 2 Sam. 4. 12; cf. 1 Sam. 31. 10. [2] Dt. 21. 23; Jos. 10. 27; Gal. 3. 13. [3] Num. 25. 4; Jos. 8. 29; 10. 26; 2 Sam. 21. 9. [4] Gen. 40. 19. [5] Est. 2. 23; 7. 10. [6] Matt. 27. 5.

HARE

Hares abound in Palestine; several species are represented, of which the most widespread are, in the north, the Syrian hare, much like our own, and, in southern parts, the hare of Judaea, a smaller-tailed variety than the former. This rodent is listed among the unclean animals in the O.T.,[1] which erroneously takes it for a ruminant, because of the continual movement of its jaws. The Israelites were forbidden to eat its flesh, which nevertheless some people in antiquity very much appreciated. Mohammedans, also, do not eat it.

[1] Lev. 11. 6; Dt. 14. 7.

HARP

The Hebrew word *kinnôr* is usually translated by harp; it would be better to render it by cithara and reserve the term harp for the Hebrew *nebel*, if one does not wish to retain the original Hebrew words, which would be better still. The identity of these instruments is difficult to establish, for, although very often mentioned in the O.T., they are never described there. Some have even maintained that *kinnôr* and *nebel* signified only two sorts of lyres and that the harp was unknown in Palestine; but this opinion can hardly be defended by anyone who knows the relationship of Israel with her neighbours, and the numerous representations of the harp which the Egyptian and Assyro-Babylonian monuments portray.

The essential difference that existed between the *nebel* and the *kinnôr* resides, perhaps, in the presence of a sounding board in the case of the former instrument. But was the *nebel* originally a cymbal made from the shell of a tortoise, covered with the skin of an animal, on which a bridge supported five strings stretched over a lateral trapezium? It is not possible to affirm this (a).—What is certain is that the Egyptians (b, c), Sumerians (d), and Assyrians (e) possessed harps of different size and type, from

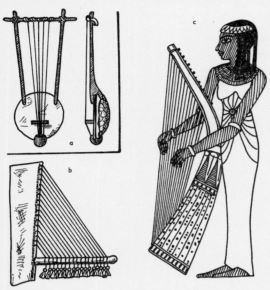

Primitive *nebel* (reconstructed) and Egyptian harps.

instruments still primitive to huge, magnificent harps, decorated with paintings or inlaid work and provided with a varying number of strings; some had to be placed on the ground, others could be used while walking; the strings were sometimes simply attached to the support, with others they were fixed

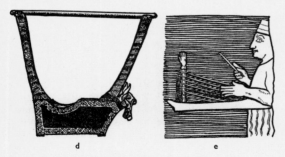

Sumerian and Assyrian harps.

to it by a peg; the sound box of some harps lay at the base of the instrument; at other times it was at the top and the cross-piece at the bottom.

The Israelite *nebel* could be played while walking; rarely mentioned alone in the O.T.,[1] it very often accompanies the *kinnôr*,[2] but both together unite with other musical instruments also;[3] Samuel says

to Saul, "When thou art come thither to the city . . . thou shalt meet a company of prophets coming down from the high place with a harp [*nebel*], and a tambourine, and a flute, and a cithara* [*kinnôr*], before them";[4] and when the Ark was brought to Jerusalem "David and all the house of Israel played before Yahweh on all manner of instruments made of fir wood, even on citharas [*kinnôrôt*], and on harps [*nebalim*] and on tambourines, and on sistra, and on cymbals".[5] Less popular, however, than the *kinnôr*, the *nebel* seems to have been reserved rather for artists and sacred music; there is frequent mention of this instrument in the Psalms, which specify particularly a *nebel* with ten strings.[6]

(† Musical instruments.)

[1] Ps. 144. 9; Amos 5. 23; 6. 5. [2] 1 Kgs. 10. 12; 2 Chr. 9. 11; Ps. 33. 2; 57. 8; 71. 22; 81. 2; 150. 3. [3] 1 Chr. 15. 16; 25. 1; 2 Chr. 20. 28; 29. 25; Neh. 12. 27; Ps. 150. 3; Is. 5. 12. [4] 1 Sam. 10. 5. [5] 2 Sam. 6. 5; 1 Chr. 13. 8. [6] Ps. 33. 2; 92. 3; 144. 9.

HARPOON

In connection with the leviathan-crocodile in the Book of Job[1] a harpoon used in fishing is mentioned, whose Hebrew name comes from a root meaning "to vibrate". It was doubtless a fisherman's straight, metal pike, ending in a barbed point, by which the creature was pierced and hauled closer.

(† Hook.)

[1] Job 40. 26.

HARROW

Biblical Hebrew has no word for this agricultural implement, but the verb used in certain texts,[1] and translated "break the clods" or "harrow", presupposes the use, if not of a harrow similar to ours, at least of a board or a faggot of thorns.

The harrow must not be confused with the threshing-sledge* for crushing grain.

(† Agriculture.)

[1] Job 39. 10; Is. 28. 24; Hos. 10. 11.

HART (STAG)

This animal is no longer found today in Palestine, but it must have been known there in former times, judging from the numerous Bible passages which speak of it. It is true that the question has been raised as to whether these texts signify a species of deer rather than the hart properly so-called; but the discovery of its remains in some caves in Palestine and the representation of this ruminant on certain Assyrian and even Egyptian records would seem to show that in earlier ages it was very widespread in the Near East.

Deuteronomy lists the hart with those animals

whose flesh can be eaten,[1] and Solomon's court was far from despising it; [2] yet this creature was never offered in sacrifice. But it is primarily mentioned in a figurative sense, often in very beautiful metaphors which praise the speed of its flight,[3] the grace of the doe, with which the young wife is compared,[4] and the agility of the young hart, like that of the beloved in the Song of Songs.[5] Psalm 42 has made famous the picture of the thirsty hart bellowing for a water-brook. We may also notice the heading of Ps. 22: "For the Chief Musician; set to 'The hind of the morning' ", which was no doubt a familiar air. Cf. also: Job 39. 1 ff.; Ps. 29. 9; Cant. 2. 7; 3. 5; Jer. 14. 5; Lam. 1. 6.

[1] Dt. 14. 5. [2] 1 Kgs. 4. 23. [3] Gen. 49. 21; 2 Sam. 22. 34; Is. 35. 6; etc. [4] Prov. 5. 19. [5] Cant. 2. 9, 17; 8. 14.

HAWK

This diurnal bird of prey, very common in Palestine, is mentioned only three times in the O.T.: its flesh is forbidden by the law;[1] and the poem of Job alludes to its habit of migration.[2]

Some translators think that in these three texts the references are rather to the kite or falcon.

(† Snare.)

[1] Lev. 11. 16; Dt. 14. 15. [2] Job 39. 26.

HEAD-DRESS

It is difficult to know what was the Israelites' head-dress, and whether they even had one, for the Bible does not make any direct allusion to it, and a few records represent Asiatics, Syrians, and Canaanites with their hair blowing in the wind or else held by a simple band. However, it seems probable that they would have sought early on to protect their heads against the burning rays of the sun. By taking into account certain Egyptian and Assyrian bas-reliefs, in which are represented Bedouins of former times or Israelites, it seems likely that the Israelites wore first a little round bonnet with turned-up edges (a) and which had in the centre a point which fell backwards (b); but doubtless they soon began to wear habitually a head-dress akin to that of present-day Bedouin and of certain Palestinian peasants (c). This comprises a piece of white or many-coloured material folded in a triangle on the head: one of its points falls on the nape of the neck, the two others hang on each side of the face, round which they are often rolled to protect the native from the sun, the cold, or the dust; a coarse double-twisted rope of camel hair or goats' hair—found already on an ancient figurine from Gezer—firmly holds this sort of scarf on the head. The napkin or cloth mentioned in the Gospels [1] is perhaps something analogous to this. At any rate, Jesus did not go bare-headed, any more than his

141

contemporaries did, and one can imagine him with his head covered by a head-dress similar to (c).

In time, in Israel, the well-to-do people began to wear a sort of turban, mentioned sometimes in the O.T.[2] It was a piece of material cunningly twisted round the head; today it is twisted round a white skull-cap or red fez. The priests* and the soldiers (see helmet*) wore a special head-dress.

In time of grief the head was enveloped in a cloak.[3] From a certain period onwards it was so extraordinary to go bare-headed that the law [4]

Semitic head-dresses of the 14th and 8th centuries, and the present day.

forced lepers to walk thus, so that they could easily be distinguished; moreover, the priest uncovered the head of the woman suspected of adultery,[5] when she came before him, at the time of the ceremony envisaged in Num. 5. 11–31.

Contrary to the custom forbidding the Jews to address God without having their heads covered [6]—the Jews today sometimes even put a huge shawl over their usual head-dress—St Paul declares [7] that "every man who prays or prophesies, with his head covered, dishonours his head"; but women, in similar circumstances, must have their heads veiled.

[1] Lk. 19. 20; Jn. 11. 44; 20. 7. [2] Job 29. 14; Is. 3. 23; 62. 3; Zech. 3. 5. [3] 2 Sam. 15. 30; 19. 4; Ez. 12. 6. [4] Lev. 13. 45. [5] Num. 5. 18. [6] 1 Kgs. 19. 13; cf. Is. 6. 2. [7] 1 Cor. 11. 4 ff.

HEARTH

In normal houses* in Palestine the hearth, where certain foods were cooked, was a mere hollow prepared in the earth of the one and only room; the smoke went out by the door or by an opening cut in the wall or through the window.[1] Cooking was also done in the porch of the courtyard of the house.

To get warmth a fire was lit in this courtyard [2] or in the middle of the room itself. A pan like the present Oriental fire-pan or brazier* might be used for this purpose.[3]

[1] Hos. 13. 3. [2] Mk. 14. 54; Jn. 18. 18. [3] Jer. 36. 22.

HEAVENS

The Israelites' conceptions about the universe, clearly related to those of neighbouring nations, often seem very primitive. The sky for them is a solid vault separating the upper world from the lower. God has stretched it over men as a veil or a tent-cloth [1] is spread out, and its extremities rest on the earth, on pillars, or on high mountains placed on the edge of the earth's disc.[2] As for the substance of this firmament [3] (the words which in Hebrew, Greek, and Latin signify the sky come in all three languages from an adjective meaning "solid",

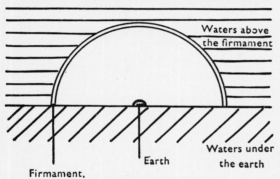

The invisible heaven (heaven of heavens)

Waters above the firmament

Earth

Waters under the earth

Firmament.

The universe according to early ideas.

"firm"), the poem of Job compares it with the metal of which mirrors are made and which can be hammered.[4] Above this solid vault stretches the upper celestial ocean, whose waters constitute the reservoir of rain, snow, hail, and dew; God causes them to fall to the earth through lattice-windows, doors, or channels made in the vault.[5] It is through these that manna also falls, the corn of heaven.[6] In the firmament the Creator has placed the lights which illuminate the earth and whose hosts he causes to march in good order;[7] Ps. 19 states that the sun, in order to run his course, goes forth from a tent erected at the end of the world where heaven and earth meet.[8]

This elementary way of imagining the sky does not prevent the Israelite from exalting its size, its immensity, from being gripped by it, from praising the intelligence and wisdom of him who is the author of it, from feeling the insignificance of man who is incapable of understanding the work of God.[9] In its magnificence, moreover, the sky is nothing compared with God, who is its master and will make it one day return to nothingness to replace it by new heavens.[10]

But, beyond the visible sky, there is the invisible heaven. For the O.T., it is still often related to the starry sky: "It is he that buildeth his chambers in the heaven, and hath founded his vault upon the earth," says Amos; [11] "who layeth the beams of his chambers in the waters," declares Psalm 104.[12] In this palace, in this sanctuary, is his throne,[13] whence he looketh upon all the inhabitants of the earth.[14] This last expression shows that here the metaphorical sense of the words is already being used. Also God is called "He that sitteth in the heavens" [15] and, in the Gospel, "the heavenly father", "the father who is in heaven".[16] However, the Israelites had early on the feeling that God could not be localized anywhere and that "the heaven and the heaven of heavens" cannot contain him.[17] From the notion of a physical heaven they moved more and more to that of an invisible, spiritual world, and when later Jewish literature mentions seven heavens one above the other, or St Paul affirms that he has been caught up to the third heaven (where they placed paradise),[18] we are dealing with images and symbolical language for a heaven of another nature than that which we can see,[19] for the heaven of faith, the abode of the angels, the place of spiritual happenings,[20] the domain of the glorified Christ [21] and of the saints.[22]

[1] Ps. 104. 2; Is. 40. 22; cf. Is. 34. 4; Rev. 6. 14. [2] Job 26. 11. [3] Gen. 1. 6. [4] Job 37. 18; Ez. 1. 22. [5] Gen. 1. 7; 7. 11; 27. 39; Job 38. 22, 25, 37; Ps. 29. 3; 78. 23; 104. 3; 148. 4. [6] Ps. 78. 24. [7] Gen. 1. 16–19; Is. 40. 26. [8] Ps. 19. 4–6. [9] Neh. 9. 6; Job 9. 8; 11. 7; 26. 14; 38. 33; Ps. 36. 5; 96. 5; 103. 11; Prov. 3. 19; Is. 55. 9; etc. [10] Ps. 102. 25, 26; Is. 13. 13; 40. 12; 51. 6; 65. 17; 66. 22; Ez. 32. 7; Hagg. 2. 6; Matt. 5. 18; 2 Pet. 3. 10, 13; Rev. 20. 11; 21. 1. [11] Amos 9. 6; Mic. 1. 2. [12] Ps. 104. 3. [13] Ps. 11. 4; 103. 19; Is. 66. 1; Matt. 5. 34; Rev. 4. 2. [14] Ps. 33. 13, 14; cf. Is. 40. 22. [15] Ps. 2. 4. [16] Matt. 6. 1, 9; 7. 11; 10. 32; etc. [17] 1 Kgs. 8. 27. [18] 2 Cor. 12. 2; cf. Eph. 4. 10. [19] 2 Cor. 4. 18; Heb. 11. 1. [20] Matt. 18. 10; Mk. 12. 25; Heb. 12. 22; Rev. 5. 11; etc. [21] Matt. 3. 17; Jn. 6. 38; etc. [22] Mk. 16. 19; Acts 1. 11; Matt. 13. 43; Lk. 6. 23; Jn. 14. 2.

HEDGE

This kind of fencing, sometimes taking the place of walls, was used in Palestine to protect cultivated land, particularly vineyards,[1] against the depredations of passers-by, thieves, or wild animals. They were usually made of thorny shrubs and, as still today, often bordered the roads.

Hedges are only spoken of in Isaiah's parable and the Gospel parables and, figuratively, in a few infrequent O.T. texts: [2] for example, the prophet Micah said of men that "the best of them is as a brier; the most upright is worse than a thorn hedge".[3]

[1] Is. 5. 5; Matt. 21. 33; Mk. 12. 1. [2] Job 1. 10; Prov. 15. 19; Hos. 2. 6. [3] Mic. 7. 4.

HEDGEHOG

Some translators think, no doubt wrongly, that the hedgehog, admittedly common in Palestine, may be one of the unclean animals mentioned in Lev. 11. 30 which it is impossible to identify with certainty. On the other hand, it is frequently claimed that another Hebrew word used by Isaiah [1] and Zephaniah [2] means hedgehog, though the end of the verse Is. 14. 23 would seem to imply that a creature inhabiting marshes is meant († heron, bittern).

[1] Is. 14. 23; 34. 11. [2] Zeph. 2. 14.

HEIFER

The O.T., which alludes so often to the ox family, sometimes makes special mention of the heifer or young cow as a plough or dairy animal [1] or as a sacrificial victim,[2] notably as atonement for homicide, the perpetrator of which is unknown.[3]

Jeremiah compares Egypt to a fine heifer,[4] and for Hosea, Ephraim is a well-trained heifer which loved to tread the corn.[5]

Several translations use the word heifer in texts where cow would be more correct.

[1] Jg. 14. 18; Is. 7. 21. [2] Gen. 15. 9; 1 Sam. 16. 2. [3] Dt. 21. 3 . . . [4] Jer. 46. 20. [5] Hos. 10. 11.

HEIFER (RED)

In Israel men or objects defiled by the proximity of a human body were purified by the sprinkling of a mixture of "living" water (not from a cistern) and ashes obtained from the burning of a red heifer [1] († uncleanness §3c; purification). This animal, unmarked, without blemish, and untouched by the yoke, was slaughtered in a distant place, in the presence of a priest. The priest dipped his finger in the victim's blood and made seven sprinklings towards the sanctuary; the beast, including its blood, was then entirely consumed by a fire into which the priest threw three purifying substances—cedarwood († cedar), hyssop*, and crimson († colours) (cf. the purification of leprosy*). The ashes of the red heifer were carefully collected and put in a secluded and clean place, where they remained ready to hand for making the "water of impurity" (i.e., water which removes impurity). Those who had performed all these actions were considered as unclean until evening and were obliged to wash their clothes or even to have a bath.

The strange and probably very ancient rite of the red heifer raises more than one question which many hypotheses have sought to resolve. It may merely be noted that the sanctuary was closed to everything which had been in contact with human death; that often in the East, red is a colour which is supposed to possess protecting powers, probably because it is the colour of blood, the principle of life; that the ritual use of purifying water mingled with ashes is found elsewhere among ancient peoples; and that contact with what is clean, or holy, transmits emanations as much to be feared and avoided as contact with unclean things—thus the Jews said that the Holy Scriptures "defiled" the hands and that, after touching them, one should wash.

A whole tractate in the Mishnah is devoted to the rite of the red heifer and sets down the ceremonial in precise detail.

[1] Num. 19. 2–22; 31. 23; Heb. 9. 13.

HELMET

In the few passages of the Bible where helmets are mentioned it is largely a question of those of foreign armies.[1] The Egyptians used them only late in their history, and the Philistines decorated their soldiers with a crown of feathers. On the other hand, from earliest times, the Elamites and Assyro-Babylonians

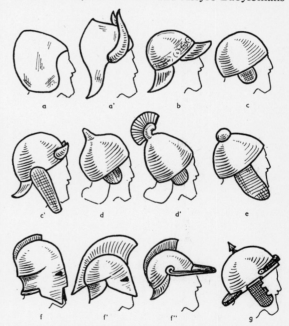

Development of the form of the helmet: a. a´, Babylonian of the 24th century; b, Elamite of the 12th century; c, c´, Babylonian of the 8th century; d, d´, Assyrian of the 7th century; e, Cypriot of the 6th century; f, f´, Greek of the 5th century; f´´, Greek of the 2nd century; g, Roman of the 1st century A.D.

armed their soldiers with a helmet. It is true that in the first place they wore on their heads only a head of a wild ox or bull, either to hide themselves or to frighten the enemy, or else in the hope of thus obtaining the strength of these animals. When this headgear was replaced by leather head-dresses (a, a´) the horns were retained for a long time, and in Babylonia representations of soldiers have been found whose head-dress is decorated with one (a', c') or several pairs of horns. It is the Elamites who seem to have created the metal helmet (b); the Babylonians provided it with ear-flaps (c, c') and the Assyrians with a point in the centre intended to turn aside the blows of adversaries (d). This point became a crest on officers' helmets (d'). An analogous evolution transformed the helmets of other peoples; the Greeks enclosed the whole head in their helmet, then reduced it gradually to a head-dress provided with a vizor, rear-peak, and crest (f, f', f''), prolonged often by a horsetail-shaped plume. The Romans transformed the crest into a buckle useful for hanging up the helmet, or into a point, and made the ear-flaps movable by means of a horizontal hinge (g). Moreover, these two peoples were acquainted with full-dress helmets of remarkable beauty and artistic value. Among the Israelites helmets were at first reserved for leaders,[2] then given to certain troops also.[3] These helmets were probably of leather in the beginning, then they were covered with bronze or iron. Beneath the latter a leather, felt, or woollen bonnet was worn.—In the figurative sense, St Paul, taking up an image used by the prophet Isaiah, speaks of the helmet of salvation and the helmet of the hope of salvation.[4]

[1] 1 Sam. 17. 5; Jer. 46. 4; Ez. 23. 24; 27. 10; 38. 5. [2] 1 Sam. 17. 38. [3] 2 Chr. 26. 14. [4] Is. 59. 17; Eph. 6. 17; 1 Th. 5. 8.

HEMLOCK

In some O.T. passages a plant is mentioned which may be hemlock, and which for two reasons is sometimes associated with the venom of snakes:[1] in the first place, it is fatal like the latter; secondly, its bitter taste suggests gall*, in which ancient science saw the origin of snake venom. The plant is mentioned with wormwood and vinegar,[2] and it gives a bitter drink.[3] But according to Hosea[4] it grows in the furrows of the fields, which hardly accords with hemlock and still less with gall; the expression might be hyperbole for a plant less poisonous than hemlock or even for gall itself; some translators think of the poppy, darnel, or colocynth (wild-gourd). The Vulgate, followed by other versions, does not consider that a plant is meant, but (animal) gall.

[1] Dt. 32. 33; Job 20. 16; Jer. 8. 14. [2] Dt. 29. 18; Ps. 69. 21; Jer. 9. 15; 23. 15. [3] Lam. 3. 19; Amos 6. 12. [4] Hos. 10. 4.

HENNA

"My beloved is unto me as a cluster of henna-flowers in the vineyards of Engedi,"[1] says the Shulammite in the Song of Songs. This is the only text—for Cant. 4. 13 is doubtful—where this shrub, cultivated throughout the East, is mentioned. It must not be confused with privet, as rendered by some versions. Henna grows in the warmer parts of Judaea. Its white scented flowers form panicles which were much sought after by Eastern people for adornment. The dried and crushed leaves provide a powder whose colouring property was used, from ancient times up to the present, to give a reddish or yellowish-orange tint to the inside of the hands, the nails of hands or feet, the hair, the beard, to the mane and tail of horses, or to other things.

[1] Cant. 1. 14.

Henna.

HERALD

This noun is found only once in the O.T., where it is used of Nebuchadnezzar's spokesman;[1] but there are several allusions to his function or to solemn proclamations: a crier went in front of the chariot of Joseph, as prime minister of Egypt;[2] in Nineveh the king issued a public call to penitence[3] and, at Susa, Haman had to proclaim through the city street the glory of Mordecai.[4] On many occasions the prophets are veritable heralds for Yahweh, whose decrees[5] they announce, and the Book of Proverbs tells how Wisdom cries aloud in the streets, lifting up her voice everywhere.[6]—According to the N.T. Jesus presented himself at Nazareth (using a text from Isaiah[7]) as the bearer of good tidings, as the one who announces deliverance and publishes the Lord's year of favour.[8] And the preachers of the gospel are actually termed heralds in the Pastoral Epistles,[9] while elsewhere Noah is looked upon as a herald of righteousness.[10]

[1] Dan. 3. 4. [2] Gen. 41. 43. [3] Jonah 3. 7. [4] Est. 6. 11. [5] Is. 40. 2, 6; 58. 1; Jer. 2. 2; 7. 2; 19. 12; Zech. 1. 14, 17; etc. [6] Prov. 1. 21; 8. 1. [7] Is. 61. 1. [8] Lk. 4. 19. [9] 1 Ti. 2. 7; 2 Ti. 1. 11. [10] 2 Pet. 2. 5.

HERBS, BITTER

Numerous herbaceous plants are mentioned in the Bible: herbs for fodder, aromatic herbs, weeds, flowers*, vegetables*, etc. Necessary information can be found under the particular name.

Here we mention only the "bitter herbs" which had to be eaten with the Passover lamb.[1] The Bible texts do not specify the plants in question, but tradition knows and names them. They varied with time and place, but the principal ones were always no doubt lettuce, endives, and chicory, to which were added cress, parsley, hawkweed, eryngium, etc. There is no mention of these in the Gospel account of the Last Supper. The herbs were to remind those who ate them of the bitterness of the Egyptian bondage.

[1] Ex. 12. 8; Num. 9. 11.

HERON

The majority of modern translations think that the second of the animals mentioned "with its species" in Lev. 11. 19 and Dt. 14. 18 is the heron. Many varieties of this wader live in the marshes of Lake Huleh and on the shores of the Lake of Gennesaret. The LXX and the Vulgate favour the plover. But it is not clear what suggested that translation. Plovers are much less common in Palestine than herons, and herons are quite naturally associated with storks, as at the beginning of the two passages just referred to. The Hebrew word here in question has even been translated parrot, which only shows again how difficult it is to determine with certainty some of the creatures which figure in the Pentateuchal lists.

HIN

A measure of capacity for liquids,[1] one-sixth of a bath*. It was subdivided into $\frac{1}{2}$, $\frac{1}{3}$, $\frac{1}{4}$, $\frac{1}{6}$, and was equal to between 366 and 412 cu. in., following the equivalences given by ancient writers; it is generally evaluated at 410 cu. in.

[1] Ex. 29. 40; Lev. 19. 36; 23. 13; Num. 15. 4; Ez. 4. 11; etc.

HINGE

As excavations in Palestine have shown, even in ancient Israel doors were in use that turned on hinges or pivots of wood or of metal. The lower hinge worked in a socket hollowed in the door-step, which was usually of stone; the upper hinge lodged in a metal cap or in a hole provided in the lintel. The O.T. mentions hinges in a suggestive simile in Proverbs: [1] "As the door turns on its hinges, so does the sluggard on his bed"; and the First Book of Kings asserts that the hinges—or to be more exact, the sockets—of the doors of the Jerusalem Temple were of gold.[2]

[1] Prov. 26. 14. [2] 1 Kgs. 7. 50.

HIRELING, MERCENARY

1. *Workmen.* Independently of slaves* subject to a special régime, the Israelites used, as workmen

145

or hired craftsmen, compatriots or foreigners who, while retaining their liberty, give their work in exchange for a wage; they must not be confused with Israelites, who were forced by necessity to sell themselves and who, according to the Priestly Code, had to be treated "like hirelings" († slave §2).

Although the O.T. mentions chiefly hired workers in the service of certain kings,[1] the Gospel refers to those who worked with Zebedee the fisherman,[2] and to those who work in the harvest fields,[3] and Jesus often introduces them into his parables: servants of the father of the prodigal son, workers hired at different hours, the hireling and the good shepherd,[4] etc.

It is important to stress the understanding shown in the Scriptures for the hard work of the hireling [5] and above all the concern it expresses for his wages; the law ordains that they be not withheld until the morrow, for he is waiting for them.[6] Jesus, for his part, declares that the labourer is worthy of his hire,[7] the prophet Malachi announces the judgment of God against those who withhold the wages of the workman,[8] and the Epistle of James proclaims: "Behold, the hire of the labourers who have mowed your fields, which is of you kept back by fraud, crieth out: and the cries of them that reaped have entered into the ears of the Lord of sabaoth." [9]

2. *Soldiers.* Like their neighbours,[10] the kings of Israel and Judah doubtless took into their pay men of arms who sometimes came from foreign parts, but we have only a little information on this subject. Apart from the adventurers engaged by Abimelech to achieve his undertakings,[11] it appears that Saul and David had a permanent, wage-earning body-guard († army, Cherethites). Chronicles claims that Amaziah, king of Judah, enrolled for a hundred talents of silver a hundred thousand valiant Israelite warriors.[12] It is possible that the hirelings mentioned by the Book of Isaiah are soldiers whose hire contract was for three years.[13]

John the Baptist admonished the soldiers (of Herod? Roman?), who questioned him, to be content with their wages and to be violent to no man.[14]

[1] 1 Kgs. 5. 6, 18; 2 Kgs. 12. 11; 1 Chr. 22. 15; 2 Chr. 2. 10; 24. 12. [2] Mk. 1. 20. [3] Matt. 9. 37. [4] Lk. 15. 17, 19, 22; Matt. 20. 1–16; Jn. 10. 12, 13. [5] Job 7. 1; 14. 6; Is. 16. 14; Matt. 20. 12. [6] Lev. 19. 13; Dt. 24. 14, 15; Job 7. 2. [7] Matt. 10. 10; Lk. 10. 7; cf. 1 Ti. 5. 18. [8] Mal. 3. 5. [9] Jas. 5. 4. [10] 1 Sam. 14. 21; 27. 1 . . .; 2 Sam. 10. 6; 1 Chr. 19. 6; Jer. 46. 21. [11] Jg. 9. 4. [12] 2 Chr. 25. 6. [13] Is. 16. 14; 21. 16. [14] Lk. 3. 14.

HOMER

The word homer (*ḥomer*) [1] etymologically denotes the load that a donkey (*ḥamôr*) can carry. It is the largest measure of capacity (about 10 bushels). It is also called the cor.

(† Cor, Weights and Measures.)

[1] Lev. 27. 16; Num. 11. 32; Ez. 45. 11, 13, 14; Hos. 3. 2.

K

HONEY

Eastern people are very fond of sweet things, therefore honey was always one of the favoured foodstuffs of the Israelites.[1] It was abundant in their land († bee) to such an extent that it was exported,[2] though perhaps the passages which speak of such deliveries to foreign parts refer to the raisin or date honey and not necessarily to the honey of bees. The latter, which in Palestine was very aromatic, was collected from hollows in the rocks (particularly in the desert of Judaea), from holes in trees, etc.[3] The virgin honey that ran from the honeycomb without its being squeezed[4] was particularly appreciated. In times of need or distress honey was a valuable resource.[5] As sugar was unknown, honey was used for cake-making;[6] it was also often taken with milk and with beer,[7] and its medicinal virtues were not unknown.[8]

No offering containing honey could be consumed upon the altar to Yahweh's honour[9]—no doubt it was looked upon as a fermented substance or as liable to fermentation—but nevertheless tithe and firstfruits of it had to be given.[10]

In the figurative language of the Bible honey is a symbol of pleasant things, of the ordinances of God, etc.[11] The Talmud also declares that the sweetness of milk and honey does not equal that of the words of the Law.

(For the expression: a land flowing with milk and honey, see milk*.)

[1] 2 Sam. 17. 29; 1 Kgs. 14. 3; Prov. 24. 13; 25. 16. [2] Gen. 43. 11; Ez. 27. 17. [3] Dt. 32. 13; Jg. 14. 8; 1 Sam. 14. 26, 27; Ps. 81. 16; Matt. 3. 4; Mk. 1. 6. [4] Ps. 19. 10. [5] Jer. 41. 8. [6] Ex. 16. 31; Lev. 2. 11. [7] Is. 7. 15, 22. [8] Prov. 16. 24; 24. 13. [9] Lev. 2. 11. [10] Lev. 2. 12; 2 Chr. 31. 5. [11] Ps. 19. 10; 119. 103; Prov. 5. 3; 24. 13, 14; Cant. 4. 11; Ez. 3. 3; Rev. 10. 9.

HOOK

The O.T. mentions three kinds of hooks: those used for capturing or holding on leash large animals or even prisoners[1] whose lips were pierced (they also used rings, nose-rings [† ear-ring]), those used with tapestry[2] († clasps), and those which were component parts of balances[3] († balance).

[1] Job 41. 2; 2 Chr. 33. 11 (R.V. mg); Amos 4. 2. [2] Ex. 26. 11, 33; 36. 13; etc. [3] Prov. 16. 11; Is. 40. 12.

HOOPOE

This passerine, with its fine, long, curved beak, carries a crest on its head which it can spread out fan-wise. It is found in Palestine from the first week of March to the commencement of winter, when it then migrates to the south. Its nest gives off an unpleasant odour. The hoopoe figures in the lists of unclean birds given in the Pentateuch.[1]

[1] Lev. 11. 19 (3); Dt. 14. 18 (3).

HORN

Here only the use of animal horns as receptacles or as musical instruments need be noted. (For the horns of the altar, see altar*.)

Polished or decorated with patterns, the horns of certain animals were used for keeping precious substances in, such as anointing oil,[1] or powdered antimony*.[2] Excavations in Palestine have yielded a few examples.

Cows' or rams' horns, merely cut at the end to make a mouthpiece, provided primitive trumpets,

An animal's horn used as a trumpet. Bas-relief from Carchemish.

powerful and raucous in tone, which were sounded to give either a short or long note, for announcing an event or a festival, for summoning people or for giving signals, in times of peace or war.[3]

[1] 1 Sam. 16. 1, 13; 1 Kgs. 1. 39. [2] Job 42. 14. [3] Ex. 19. 13; Lev. 25. 9; Jos. 6. 4 . . .; Jg. 3. 27; 6. 34; 7. 8 . . .; 1 Sam. 13. 3; 2 Sam. 20. 22; 1 Kgs. 1. 39, 41; Job 39. 24, 25; Ps. 47. 5; 81. 3; 98. 6; Is. 18. 3; Dan. 3. 5; Amos 3. 6; etc.

HORNET

Hornets, well known in Palestine, are mentioned only in three O.T. passages,[1] in each of which God announces that he will send them or they have been sent as a plague, to drive out the Canaanites and other enemies of Israel. Since the literal fulfilment of this promise is nowhere stated, more than one commentator thinks that these are poetic images, metaphors pointing to supernatural means or to a terror used by Yahweh when coming to the aid of the Israelites.

[1] Ex. 23. 28; Dt. 7. 20; Jos. 24. 12.

HORSE

Coming from Turkestan and the Iranian plateaux, the horse was introduced into Asia Minor in about 2500 B.C. It appeared in Palestine only fairly late: in the course of the 2nd millennium. The movements of population to which was linked the invasion of the Hyksos in Egypt (1720–1550) without doubt favoured its extension; it assumed, at any rate, more and more importance on the banks of the Nile after the beginning of the New Empire and the 18th Dynasty (1550). In the narratives of the earliest patriarchs there is—significantly enough—no mention of horses: Abraham does not possess one and does not receive any at the time of his sojourn in Egypt; [1] they are mentioned only in the time of Joseph, then of the Exodus,[2] but if chariots of war were used in the pursuit of the Israelites, the latter did not take any horses with them and dispensed with them entirely for penetrating into Palestine.

However, the Canaanites possessed military chariots, as is proved, for example, by the list of booty made by Thutmes III at Megiddo (about 1480), by polite forms of expression in some of the Tell el-Amarna letters (about 1350) in which enquiries are made about the state of the recipient's horses, and by the discovery at Ras Shamra of a treatise on hippology dating from the same period, etc. Moreover, the texts of the Bible tell that Joshua, the day following an important victory, cut the hocks of the Canaanite horses,[3] and refer to the war-chariots owned by Sisera,[4] in the battle celebrated in the Song of Deborah. The Israelites had also to brave the attacks of the Philistines' chariots.[5]

As the Israelites lived in mountainous country, hardly favourable to the development of chariots, they did not have recourse to them before the time of the monarchy. Did Saul have horses in his service? No text says so. David also, after his victory over Hadadezer, had the hocks cut of the horses he had seized; he spared a certain number of them, however.[6] From the time of Solomon all these practices changed: the king needed quantities of horses for the chariots with which he had liberally equipped his army. It seems, also, that Solomon traded in these animals. The First Book of Kings [7] claims that he received them from Egypt to sell them to his northern neighbours, but the Hebrew text is defective: it has been suggested that mention of Egypt be replaced by that of the Musri country (Northern Syria), but more recently it has been thought that Solomon had his horses sent from Cilicia to send them to Egypt in exchange for war-chariots which he delivered to the Aramaeans and to Asia Minor. Some large stables* have been discovered which David's son possessed at Megiddo, at the foot of Mount Carmel.

From Solomon's time to the Exile, the Bible texts only rarely mention horses in Israel: they are sometimes referred to in the armies of the northern and southern kingdoms;[8] we learn that the body of Amaziah was brought back to Jerusalem on horses;[9] that the kings of Judah had consecrated horses to the sun [10] and that there was in Jerusalem a "horse

gate"; [11] finally, the prophets make some significant references to them.[12]

But, in their remarks, it is especially the horses of foreign armies which appear (Syrian, Egyptian, Assyrian, Median, etc.), notably in Jeremiah and

Horse in harness, engraved on the golden panel of an Egyptian fan.

Ezekiel. And always the Bible authors insist on the idea that the horse cannot ensure victory: the help of God is worth more than all the cavalries in the world.[13]

It must be noted that, everywhere and for a long

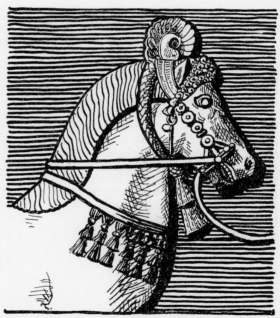

Assyrian harness trappings of the 8th century.

time, horses were used only for drawing chariots; if a few riders were reserved for the transmission of messages, cavalry squadrons were doubtless not organized in the Near East before the 8th century. The O.T. does not tell of any among the Canaanites and the Philistines; it is possible that the Israelites did not use mounted troops before the Exile (cf., however, 2 Kgs. 9. 18; 13. 7 and Amos 2. 15). It was the Assyrians who, from the time of Sargon and Sennacherib, manoeuvred cavalry in great masses; the texts of the Bible henceforth often mention Assyrian and Chaldaean riders, and those of Egypt, too.[14] The Persians proved past masters in this sphere.

On the return from Exile, the Israelites brought back only 736 horses; [15] they did not seem to use this animal very much. The silence maintained by the texts is significant; the horses of foreign peoples [16] are in fact almost the only ones mentioned. Were it not for a reference in the Epistle of James to the horse's bit [17] and the symbolical frescoes of the Apocalypse, it could be said that the N.T. totally ignores this animal; it is very likely that the "beast" [18] of the Good Samaritan, in Jesus' mind, was a donkey rather than a horse.

Egyptian and Assyrian bas-reliefs, and other records, allow us to get an accurate idea of the way in which horses were harnessed; the O.T. mentions bit, bridle, whip, and bells; [19] Isaiah notices that the hooves of the Assyrian horses were as hard as flint [20]—that in former times the horses were no more shod than they are today among the Bedouin; Ezekiel mentions the luxurious materials sometimes put on their saddles.[21]

The Book of Job is enriched by a fine description of the war-horse; [22] the Apocalypse takes up Joel's [23] comparison of the grasshopper and the horse, and the horse appears also in a few brief but sometimes vigorous O.T. similes.[24] Finally, we may notice the horses of fire which carried the prophet Elijah into heaven; [25] those which surrounded Elisha; [26] the important part which these animals, zealous in combat, played in the visions of Zechariah,[27] and especially in those of the Apocalypse [28] —with their gripping pictures of the pale horse mounted by Death, of the innumerable army of horses with lions' heads and serpents' tails, and of the celestial horsemen clothed in fine, pure linen, under the command of one who, on a white horse and wearing a cloak stained with blood, is called the Word of God.

(† Chariot.)

[1] Gen. 12. 16. [2] Gen. 41. 43; 47. 17; Ex. 9. 3; 14. 9; 15. 1. [3] Jos. 11. 4–9. [4] Jg. 4 and 5. [5] 1 Sam. 13. 5. [6] 2 Sam. 8. 4. [7] 1 Kgs. 10. 28. [8] 1 Kgs. 22. 4; 2 Kgs. 3. 7; 13. 7. [9] 2 Kgs. 14. 20. [10] 2 Kgs. 23. 11. [11] Neh. 3. 28; Jer. 31. 40; cf. 2 Kgs. 11. 16. [12] Is. 5. 28; Amos 4. 10; Mic. 5. 10. [13] Dt. 17. 16; Ps. 20. 7, 8; 33. 17; 147. 10; Is. 30. 15–17; 31. 1, 3; Hos. 1. 7; 14. 3; etc. [14] Jer. 6. 23; 8. 16; 46. 4; Ez. 23. 6, 12; 38. 15; Nah. 3. 2; Hab. 1. 8; etc. [15] Ezr. 2. 66; Neh. 7. 68. [16] Hagg. 2. 22; Zech. 14. 15. [17] Jas. 3. 3. [18] Lk. 10. 34. [19] 2 Kgs. 19. 28; Ps. 32. 9; Prov. 26. 3; Zech. 14. 20; Jas. 3. 3; Rev. 14. 20. [20] Is. 5. 28. [21] Ez. 27. 20. [22] Job 39. 19–25. [23] Joel 2. 4; Rev. 9. 7. [24] Is. 63. 13; Jer. 5. 8; 8. 6; Ez. 23. 20; Zech. 10. 3; etc. [25] 2 Kgs. 2. 11. [26] 2 Kgs. 6. 17. [27] Zech. 1. 8; 6. 2–8. [28] Rev. 6. 2–8; 9. 16–19; 19. 11–16.

HOSPITALITY

The peoples of antiquity, and Oriental peoples particularly, regarded hospitality as a duty of honour; it was, moreover, made necessary to a certain extent by the lack of inns and by the difficulties in finding lodging encountered by travellers. Still today, the Bedouin esteems wealth because it enables him to practise generous hospitality, which upholds his prestige and that of his tribe; he would rather be reduced to destitution than fail in the rules of welcome. For the Israelites also, to avoid it would have been to show proof of avarice; to ask shelter of someone,[1] or to respond to his invitation, was to honour him deeply, to refuse it was to do him a grave insult. Fanaticism alone led to scorn of the sacred law of hospitality: every Israelite must experience a feeling of horror on hearing the account of the murder of Sisera who had taken refuge in Jael's tent,[2] and the hate of the Samaritans must have been very strong to make them inhospitable towards other people.[3]

Whether known or unknown, rich or poor, every traveller was, in principle, well received in Israel. His feet were washed, as substantial a meal as possible was prepared for him, kindness was lavished upon him, without even his name being asked first. And the host remained standing at the service of his guests. The account of Genesis 18, showing the alacrity of Abraham towards his unknown visitors, abounds in features that are drawn from life and are very typical. Numerous texts of the Old and New Testaments bear witness to the part played by hospitality in social life.[4] It was naturally not correct to prolong one's stay in another's home (among the nomadic Arabs of today the limit is three days and four hours) unless a share was taken in the cost of food; moreover, he who asked for hospitality often brought his own food and, in exchange for a place at the meal, shared it with those who received him. When he left, the host did not fail to see him off.[5] For the N.T. hospitality is a fruit of love. Jesus recommends it on more than one occasion [6] and specifies also the way in which his disciples must behave when they are receivers of it.[7] Admonitions to practise hospitality leave us to understand that people sometimes tried to ignore this duty: "Devote yourselves to hospitality," says St Paul; [8] the Epistle to the Hebrews [9] adds that by doing so some have entertained angels unawares, and the remark of the First Epistle of Peter [10] is significant: "Use hospitality one to another without grudging".—The Pastoral Epistles declare that none could be a good *episcopos* (overseer, bishop) without being hospitable,[11] and in order to be inscribed on the widows' roll, one must have been known to exercise hospitality.[12]

[1] Lk. 19. 5 ff. [2] Jg. 4. 17 ff.; 5. 24 ff. [3] Lk. 9. 52. [4] Gen.

19. 2; 24. 17, 31, 54; Ex. 2. 19, 20; Jg. 6. 18; 19. 17; 2 Kgs.
4. 8 ff.; Job 31. 31, 32; Lk. 10. 38; Acts 10. 6; 16. 15; 18. 3.
[5] Gen. 18. 16; 31. 27. [6] Matt. 10. 40 ff.; 25. 35 ff. [7] Matt.
10. 11 ff. [8] Rom. 12. 13. [9] Heb. 13. 2. [10] 1 Pet. 4. 9. [11] 1 Ti.
3. 2; Tit. 1. 8. [12] 1 Ti. 5. 10.

HOUR

In the O.T. the word "hour" is found only in the
Book of Daniel,[1] and even then it means a short time
and not a precise division of the day. The Israelites
limited themselves to general terms for the different
periods of the day or night (day*, night*).—The
N.T., on the other hand, proves that at the beginning of the Christian era the division of the day into
twelve hours was common with the Jews; they had
doubtless adopted this system, which is of Babylonian origin, under the influence of Greek or
Roman civilization; the parable of the labourers
hired at different hours [2] is significant in this
respect; the Gospel of St Mark states that Jesus was
crucified in the third hour [3] (nine o'clock) and that
he died in the ninth (three o'clock in the afternoon); [4]
St John's Gospel declares that Christ had sat down
at the sixth hour on the edge of the well in Samaria [5]
and that the nobleman's son was healed in the
seventh hour; [6] Cornelius prayed at the ninth hour,[7]
etc. There is mention in Acts of periods of three
hours or two hours,[8] and Jesus reproaches his
disciples for not having watched one hour with
him.[9]

The length of the hours varied (from 49 to 71
minutes) according to the season and the length of
the day of which they formed the twelfth part, the
first hour beginning at sunrise and the last ending at
sunset.—They probably calculated also according to
the average day, at the time of the equinoxes, from
six o'clock in the morning to six o'clock in the
evening.

A single passage in the N.T. mentions hours of the
night*,[10] generally divided into watches. In a great
number of passages, the word "hour" means only a
period or point of time, and must not be taken in its
exact sense.[11]

[1] Dan. 3. 6; 5. 5. [2] Matt. 20. 1–16. [3] Mk. 15. 25. [4] Mk.
15. 34; Matt. 27. 46. [5] Jn. 4. 6. [6] Jn. 4. 52. [7] Acts 10. 30.
[8] Acts 5. 7; 19. 34. [9] Matt. 26. 40; Mk. 14. 37. [10] Acts 23. 23.
[11] Matt. 8. 13; 9. 22; 10. 19, etc.

HOUSE

The houses of Palestine in archaic times seem to
have had sometimes a circular plan—therefore
these constructions must be thought of as being like
the little domed houses of upper Syria—but they
were much more often almost rectangular. They
were very modest, for their occupants, accustomed
to living in the open air, only expected from them a
protection against heavy rain and, in the dry season,
against sunstroke or the keenness of the night air.

149

However, as soon as a certain well-being was
introduced into the country, and especially as soon
as agglomerations of houses were formed, there
appeared dwellings including several rooms, either
arranged in a suite (I) or distributed round an inner
courtyard (II to IV).

When the techniques of building improved, a
storey over the ground floor was sometimes constructed, and that especially in the towns where the
houses were pressed against one another within the
fortified enclosure. But it seems that this high form
of building was reserved for royal dwellings.

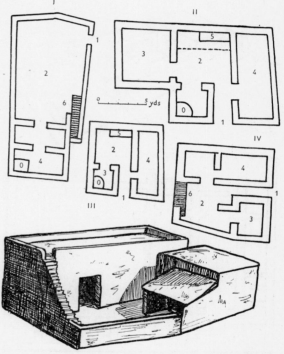

Plan of Jericho houses (9th and 8th centuries), and a
reconstruction following plan IV (1. entrance; 2. courtyard; 3. store-room; 4. living-room; 5. bench; 6. stairway to terrace).

In the Israelite period these various types of buildings are found again, and alongside them soon arise
houses of officials and even palaces* which the kings
have built for themselves with the aid of labourers
from foreign lands.[1]

Of the Persian period there have been found at
Lachish, a humble Judaean township, the ruins of a
beautiful residence of about 120 ft. by 170 ft. An
inner courtyard occupies the centre of the northern
half; it is bordered by little rooms on the east and
north, whereas on the south side there is a loggia
opening on to rooms now completely destroyed.
From the inner courtyard, up a few steps, there is a

vast loggia on the south side, which leads into the entrance-hall of the private apartments; a bathroom, underground pipes, etc., have been discovered.

The Walls. Peasant houses, in former times and still today, had walls of brick*, or even of clay mixed with straw or reeds. These walls were not thick and it was easy to pierce them.[2] Early on, also, the Israelites began to build houses of stone. Our Bible texts mention a certain number of tools used by hewers of stone, but the exact interpretation of this technical nomenclature is difficult. It is known that in the quarries the workmen dug out channels round the blocks they wanted to free, into

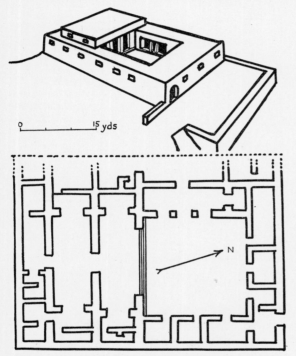

Plan and reconstruction of an important house at Lachish.

which they introduced wooden wedges; when the latter were wetted, they swelled and loosened the stone.

Foundations* were the object of careful attention; they insisted on building on rock.[3] When the walls were made of bricks they were not begun before two or three rows of stones had been arranged on the rock. If, before erecting a stone wall, they did not reach the rock they then built very solid foundations as deep as the height of the wall above the soil. The stone walls were usually very thick.

For mortar they used clay with water added to it, as well as for the rough-casting of walls. They sometimes mixed with it pounded shells or limestone, pulverized potsherds, wood-ash, or even lime

properly so-called. Bitumen, widely used in Mesopotamia as cement,[4] was used very little.

The corner-stone was particularly carefully attended to,[5] and it has even been thought that its laying was accompanied by a ceremony.

The floor of the house was of beaten earth or paved with bricks or stones. Wooden floors are found only in palaces.

The roof, nearly always flat, was of very simple construction, as far as houses of clay and brick were concerned: on a few joists, more or less squared, laid from one wall to the other, were entwined numerous branches, over which was stretched a thick layer of clay mixed with ordinary earth and small stones. In order to fill in all the crevices as much as possible, a roller was passed over it and the grass,[6] which would grow on the roof after the rainy season helped, by reason of its roots, to hold this earthy mass in place. It was, however, a fragile roof, and one can appreciate the need for repairing it after each winter.

An opening in the roof was often made, a sort of fanlight through which the smoke could escape.[7]

As soon as they wanted to enlarge the house, they had to devise a central pillar to prop up the roof. It is astonishing to note that the vault, familiar for a long time in Mesopotamia, was used very little in Palestine in Biblical times; it is found only in burial vaults of small dimensions. This is probably because they did not then know how to cut the arch-stones or even to arrange them so that they would lean firmly one upon the other (*a*, Chaldaean arch), and because they were satisfied with arranging flat stones in overhanging formation (*b*, arch at Megiddo). It is known that Jeremiah was confined in a vaulted dungeon.[8]

It was on the roof that various domestic jobs were performed. Flax was dried there.[9] People walked there in the cool of the evening,[10] and a balustrade had to be built right round this terrace to prevent

(a) Arch with keystone (Chaldaean); (b) cantilever arch (Israelite).

accidents.[11] Guttering went round the edge, and the monotonous, interminable sound of the water which flowed from it in time of rain suggested to the writer of Proverbs some malicious maxims.[12] In time of misfortune or to celebrate a happy event, people went up on to the roof, whence they called to summon their neighbours so that they could take part in these events.[13] But it was there also that serious conversations took place.[14]

Generally everyone could have access to this roof by means of an outside staircase, or in poor houses by means of a wooden ladder. But quite another spirit was introduced into richer houses, which reserved access to the terrace for the family; it could be reached only from inside by a wooden staircase.

Well-to-do families built on the roof a special room called an "upper room", which was often reserved for visitors or for the sick; it was the pleasantest room in the house.[15] It was in such a room as this that Jesus instituted the Last Supper (Lord's* Supper).

The *doorway*, usually fairly low,[16] was often closed only by a curtain; however, early on they were acquainted with the wooden leaf turning on hinges.[17]

Deuteronomy [18] recommended the Israelite to write passages of the Law upon the door-posts. It was there that in former times magic signs were put, which, they believed, sent demons away. Remains of foundation* sacrifices were buried beneath the threshold*, and little idols were hung on the stile of the door.

A lock*, the bolt of which was moved by a key*, sometimes very primitive, may have closed the door.

[1] 1 Kgs. 7. 9. [2] Job 24. 16; Ez. 12. 5; 12. 7; Matt. 6. 19; 24. 43. [3] Matt. 7. 24. [4] Gen. 11. 3; 14. 10. [5] Is. 28. 16; Matt. 21. 42. [6] Ps. 129. 6; Is. 37. 27. [7] Hos. 13. 3. [8] Jer. 37. 16. [9] Jos. 2. 6. [10] 2 Sam. 11. 2. [11] Dt. 22. 8. [12] Prov. 19. 13; 27. 15. [13] Is. 22. 1; Jer. 48. 38. [14] 1 Sam. 9. 25; Jn. 3. 2 (?). [15] 1 Kgs. 17. 19; 2 Kgs. 4. 10. [16] Prov. 17. 19. [17] 1 Kgs. 7. 50; Prov. 26. 14. [18] Dt. 6. 9.

HOUSE OF FOREST OF LEBANON

This edifice, which Solomon constructed in Jerusalem, owes its name to the cedar pillars which were the characteristic feature. It may be that, like the majority of Phoenician and Syrian palaces, it had the form of cloisters surrounding an interior court, above which a series of small rooms had been built. What is certain is that the lower part served as an assembly hall (Josephus the historian attests this), while the first-storey rooms were used as an arsenal.[1]

[1] 1 Kgs. 10. 17; Is. 22. 8.

HUNT

On the face of it, to believe what the O.T. says, it appears that Palestinians did not like and hardly practised hunting. The ideal type of Israelite was Jacob, the quiet man who lived in a tent as he tended his animals, in contrast to Esau, the prowler, the huntsman.—It is said of no king of Israel or Judah that he went to the hunt, though this was a custom very frequent elsewhere among the great, who went in chariots or on horseback, as is proved by certain bas-reliefs from Egypt, Assyria, and Persia, and by a certain golden cup discovered at Ras Shamra (Syria). According to Josephus, Herod the Great was, on the other hand, a fearless huntsman.

On looking closely, however, it can be seen that huntsmen were not lacking among the Israelites and that all of them did not scorn this exercise; the admiration which was apparently felt for the Babylonian Nimrod, "the first mighty man upon earth and a mighty hunter before Yahweh",[1] is significant.

Moreover, hunting was often a necessity, for they had to get rid of the carnivores which threatened the flocks; David, in his youth, bore from the lion's and the bear's mouth the stolen sheep.[2] Besides, game was appreciated: Isaac was very fond of it,[3] and every day some was offered on the royal tables at Jerusalem, in the time of Solomon.[4] The law authorized the eating of hart, gazelle, deer, etc.; but it did not allow the eating of hare or wild boar.[5]

The large number of technical terms referring to hunting, found in the texts, and the abundance of images inspired by it are especially surprising. It appears that the weapons preferably used were the bow and arrow, and the sling, as well as all sorts of snares*, ranging from the net to the pit, including the trap and the lasso, not forgetting the snares of the fowler*, very often mentioned. Hunting dogs are not mentioned, whereas they appear in the records left by neighbouring peoples; and legislative regulations are limited to two recommendations: not to take a female bird sitting on fledglings or eggs [6] (she must be allowed to fly off before the latter are taken!), and to bleed straightway the animal killed in the hunt and to cover up its blood with earth, "for the soul of all flesh is its blood".[7]—Occasionally live animals were caught;[8] we know that the kings of Assyria and Egypt set aside for themselves some game reserves and created something like "zoological gardens".

It would be impossible to review all the metaphors drawn from hunting,[9] huntsmen, their victims, and especially from the traps used. Amongst them are: the snares of death which take by surprise,[10] the cunning of wicked men who "watch as fowlers lie in wait; they set a trap, they catch men",[11] the joy of the "soul escaped as a bird out of the snare of the fowlers: the snare is broken . . .",[12] the snare of the enemy, and especially the proverbs often repeated in the O.T. that: "The wicked man shall fall into the ditch which he has made."[13]—In the N.T. several references of the same nature are found,[14] the most famous aims at those who wanting to become rich "fall into temptation and a snare".[15]

[1] Gen. 10. 8–9. [2] 1 Sam. 17. 34; cf. Amos 3. 12; 2 Sam. 23. 20. [3] Gen. 25. 28; 27. 3, 4. [4] 1 Kgs. 4. 23. [5] Dt. 14. 5, 7. [6] Dt. 22. 6–7. [7] Lev. 17. 14. [8] 2 Sam. 17. 8; cf. Ez. 19. 4. [9] 1 Sam. 26. 20; Ps. 10. 9–10; 11. 1–2; 25. 15; 57. 6; 69. 22;

HUSK

140. 5; Prov. 7. 23; 22. 14; Jer. 16. 16; Mic. 7. 2; etc. [10] Ps. 18. 5. [11] Jer. 5. 26. [12] Ps. 124. 7. [13] Ps. 7. 15; Prov. 26. 27; etc. [14] Lk. 11. 54; 21. 34–35; Rom. 11. 9; 1 Ti. 3. 7; 2 Ti. 2. 26; etc. [15] 1 Ti. 6. 9.

HUSK

Winnowing († agriculture) separates the husk, or capsule investing the grain (glumella), from the grain itself. The husks were often used for stoking the fire, hence the metaphor of John the Baptist.[1] In the O.T. husks—not straw, as some translations have it—carried by the wind symbolize the passing of time,[2] the practice of idolatry,[3] and the scattering of enemies [4] or the wicked.[5]

[1] Matt. 3. 12; Lk. 3. 17. [2] Zeph. 2. 2. [3] Hos. 13. 3. [4] Is. 17. 13; 29. 5; 41. 15 16. [5] Job 21. 18; Ps. 1. 4; 35. 5.

HUT

The hut or booth made only of branches has doubtless been used from early days as a dwelling-place, alongside the cave. Still today among some of the semi-sedentary people of Palestine are found huts of reeds or branches laid over a wooden frame; on the shores of Lake Huleh the stems of papyrus are used, woven in a kind of primitive loom.

As temporary, casual shelter huts have continued to be used by shepherds,[1] or for keeping watch over vineyards and gardens. Isaiah [2] refers to their fragility and Jeremiah [3] to their isolation; for Job they are a figure for the house of the wicked man soon to be destroyed, and for Amos for a crumbling dynasty.[4]

Some versions too frequently use "tent" for the Hebrew word which precisely denotes "hut"; R.V. has in some places "pavilion".[5] The Feast of Tabernacles (=tents) is called in Hebrew the "feast of booths (or huts)" because to celebrate it the Israelites lived, not under tent-covers, but in huts of foliage.

[1] Gen. 33. 17. [2] Is. 1. 8; 24. 20. [3] Jer. 9. 2. [4] Job 27. 18; Amos 9. 11. [5] 1 Kgs. 20. 12, 16; Ps. 31. 20; Is. 4. 6; etc.

HYENA

This carnivore is still very common in Palestine. Perhaps the prophet Jeremiah [1] mentions it, but the text is very uncertain. 1 Sam. 13. 18 speaks of the route from Michmash which overlooked the "valley of hyenas", i.e., probably the Wady abu dabâ', a tributary to Wady el-Kelt, in the land of Benjamin, a ravine where these creatures easily found a lair.

Hyena.

[1] Jer. 12. 9.

HYRAX (DAMAN)

Some infrequent passages in the O.T. speak of an animal whose name has been variously translated porcupine, hedgehog, coney, and jerboa, when it is really the hyrax (daman), a curious little creature of the size of a rabbit often found in Palestine, in the gorges of the Kidron, to the west of the Dead Sea, in the plains of Acre and of Phoenicia, in north Galilee, and in the Lebanon. While the Arabs are very fond of its flesh, the law forbade it to Israelites because it regarded it as a ruminant without a cloven hoof.[1] In reality it is not a ruminant, although it has a two-chambered stomach which relates it to the ruminants, which have four; from its skeleton (number of vertebrae and ribs) and by its feet (five-clawed toes on the anterior limbs and three on the hind limbs) it could belong to the elephant family; but its dentition resembles that of the rhinoceros. So as not to classify it with any one of these three sub-orders of the ungulates a separate order has been created for

Hyrax or daman.

it, that of the Hyracoidea, of which it is the sole species, although it occurs in about a score of forms.

The Psalmist and the Book of Proverbs declare that the hyrax lodges in rocks,[2] which is correct, because it does not dig a burrow but lives in holes in the rock, where it takes refuge at the slightest alarm; from this comes the name it bears in Hebrew, meaning "one who hides". Living in companies and protected by sentinels, the hyraxes are very difficult to capture, in spite of the feebleness which is stressed in Prov. 30. 26. By their manner of life and their thick fur these entirely harmless herbivores closely resemble the marmots.

[1] Lev. 11. 5; Dt. 14. 7. [2] Ps. 104. 18; Prov. 30. 26.

HYSSOP

The plant named *Hyssopus officinalis* (a) is a highly aromatic herb, straight stalked and somewhat woody at the base, a shrubby plant with upright branches, bearing blue or reddish flowers. But as this true hyssop does not frequent Palestine, and even may not have grown there, it is thought that the Hebrews gave this name to other related plants, and in particular to an origanum (b) a near-relative of marjoram, which flourishes in the Mediterranean area.

According to the Bible, hyssop was especially used in a bundle or bunch for the ritual sprinkling of blood or water for purifications,[1] which is why the Psalmist cries: "Purge my sin with hyssop, and I shall be clean".[2]—According to 1 Kgs. 4. 33,

Solomon spoke of trees, "from the cedar that is in Lebanon even unto the hyssop that springeth out of the wall", which has made people think, without any very strong reason, of small plants and mosses and particularly of the caper, which is frequently seen in Palestine in the crannies of walls.—Yet the most puzzling reference to hyssop is found in the Fourth Gospel: at the crucifixion the lips of Jesus were moistened by a sponge fixed "upon hyssop [*hussopo*]"; [3] but the stems of this plant seem too feeble

a   b

Hyssop (*Hyssopus officinalis* L.) and origanum (*Origanum vulgare*).

to support the weight of a sponge filled with vinegar. Perhaps "on a lance [*husso*]" should be read. The Synoptic Gospels speak of a reed.[4] To resolve the difficulty Abbé Migne has suggested the theory that a tuft of hyssop was usually fastened to a reed (which would make it the prototype of the aspergillum or ecclesiastical brush-sprinkler); the soldier may have used this arrangement, since the sponge he had proffered to the Crucified remained fully saturated with liquid.

[1] Ex. 12. 22; Lev. 14. 4, etc.; Num. 19. 6, 18; Heb. 9. 19.
[2] Ps. 51. 9. [3] Jn. 19. 29. [4] Matt. 27. 48; Mk. 15. 36.

IBIS

It is very difficult to identify the unclean bird which is mentioned first in Lev. 11. 18 and third in Dt. 14. 16. It could be the ibis, but heron, swan, flamingo, sultan hen, screech-owl, etc., have also been suggested. The etymology of the Hebrew word

153

gives rise to different conjectures; the context might perhaps suggest an aquatic bird.—It is curious to note that the fifth unclean animal listed in Lev. 11.30 bears the same name, though in this text it is a reference to some kind of lizard or to the chameleon*.—Some versions suppose, probably mistakenly, that the ibis is mentioned third in Lev. 11. 17 (=second in Dt. 14. 16).

Ibis.

(† Owl, swan, screech-owl.)

ILLNESS

Due to a salubrious climate, frugal feeding, and a simple life, the Israelites were a people generally healthy and vigorous, as Tacitus, for one, recognized. But Palestine's position exposed it to the after-effects of the wars of antiquity and to the epidemics encouraged by dust, by heat, which is often very considerable, and by an ignorance of most of the laws of hygiene, the cause of all kinds of disorders; the political and religious fervour of the Jews at certain times in their history no doubt partly explains the rather widespread neurotic complaints among them.

For the Israelites, as for many other people, all illness was divine punishment, caused by some personal or family sin.[1] Yahweh himself struck the guilty one either directly[2] or through the intermediary of an angel[3] or of Satan;[4] he himself sent an evil spirit into the man,[5] or allowed unclean spirits to possess him. In the time of Jesus, certain mental or physical illnesses were usually ascribed to demonic possession.

Although the Bible very often speaks of illnesses in a general sense, it also refers to some in a more precise way; a list in alphabetical order follows, for it would be difficult to classify them scientifically.

Apoplexy, 1 Sam. 4. 18 (Eli); 25. 37–38 (Nabal); 2 Sam. 6. 7 (Uzzah); Acts 5. 5, 10 (Ananias and Sapphira).
Blindness*
Boils*
Bubonic pustules, Ex. 9. 9, 10; Dt. 28. 27.
Burns, Ex. 21. 15; Lev. 13. 24, 28.
Consumption, Lev. 26. 16; Dt. 28. 22; Ps. 106. 15; Is. 10. 16; Ez. 24. 23.
Deafness*
Dropsy, Lk. 14. 2.
Dysentery*
Epilepsy*
Fever*

IMAGES

Fractures, Lev. 21. 19; 24. 20.

Gangrene*

Gout*

Haemorrhage, uterine, Lev. 15. 25; Matt. 9. 20; Mk. 5. 25; Lk. 8. 43.

Haemorrhoids*

Halting † lameness

Hump-back, Lev. 21. 20.

Impotence, 2 Sam. 3. 29; Jn. 5. 3; Acts 3. 2; 14. 8.

Leprosy*

Lunacy † epilepsy

Madness*

Mutilation † eunuch

Palsy (paralysis)*

Peritonitis (?), Acts 12. 23.

Pestilence*

Rash, Lev. 13. 39.

Scab*

Sexual maladies, Lev. 15. 2 . . . ; 22. 4 . . .; Num. 5. 2; 2 Sam. 3. 29.

Stammering, Is. 32. 4; Mk. 7. 32.

Stiffness, Lk. 13. 11.

Sunstroke*

Tumour, Lev. 13. 2, 10, 28; 14. 56.

Withering, 1 Kgs. 13. 4; Matt. 12. 10; Mk. 3. 1; Lk. 6. 6.

Worms (?), Acts 12. 23.

Wounds, Gen. 4. 23; Ex. 21. 25; Dt. 17. 8; 1 Kgs. 22. 35; Is. 1. 6; 30. 26; Hos. 5. 13, etc.

For the treatment of illnesses see doctor*, medicine*.

[1] Job 7. 20; Jn. 5. 14; 9. 2. [2] Ex. 4. 11; 23. 25; Lev. 26. 16; Dt. 7. 15; 28. 22 . . .; 32. 39; 2 Sam. 6. 7; 2 Kgs. 15. 5. [3] 2 Sam. 24. 16. [4] Job 2. 7. [5] 1 Sam. 16. 14.

IMAGES

Like other nomadic peoples or the pre-Islamic Arabs, the Hebrews hardly seem to have used sacred images before their entry into Palestine, if we are prepared to admit that the story of the Golden Calf [1] is the reflection of a later period. But it is certain that, once they had become settled, the Israelites were not long in adopting, very often, the customs relating to worship of the people whom they finally absorbed. Without mentioning other sources, excavations in Palestine have shown decisively the importance among the Canaanites of sacred images used especially in private devotions or by way of charms († amulets), and among the Israelites the part which continued to be played by the familiar statuettes of the goddess of life and fertility, in particular († Astarte). It is to be presumed, and certain indications prove it to be so, that various public sanctuaries were not lacking in images which represented the deity.

Moreover, the O.T. itself makes many references to the cult of images, whether those of false gods or

Phoenician deities. The first on the left is adorned with a collar and girdle of gold.

154

those in close relationship with Yahweh. In the private sanctuary of Micah there was a sacred effigy, a silver image which later became the centre of a high place;[2] Gideon made an ephod* which should probably be considered as an image provided with an oracle-cover or divinatory surplice.[3] David had at home a domestic idol[4] († teraphim). Apart from the bronze serpent to which, probably, for a long time sacrifices were offered in Jerusalem itself,[5] it is known that Jeroboam I placed a golden bull in the two royal sanctuaries of Dan and Bethel.[6] Did these animals symbolize the victorious power of Yahweh, to whom is sometimes given the title of "Bull [or Mighty One] of Jacob" or of "Bull of Israel",[7] or were they merely attributes of the deity or acting as pedestals for Yahweh, who had to remain invisible, or were they indeed representations of the God of Israel? It is not yet possible to reply clearly to these questions and to come to a decision.

The war declared on images also allows us to see how widespread they were. In the beginning, perhaps only metal images[8] were condemned, fostered by the feeling, which was always latent in certain circles, that images were foreign to the original worship of Yahweh, and justified by the growing ascendancy of idolatrous cults. We have only to think, without going back as far as the tolerance of Solomon,[9] of the building by Ahab of a temple of Baal in Samaria,[10] of "the abominable image made in honour of Asherah" by the mother of Asa,[11] of the official patronage granted by Manasseh to the deities of the Assyrian pantheon,[12] of the devotions made to the "Queen of Heaven"[13] on the eve of the Exile, to understand the reaction of prophetic circles.

Hosea was the first to rail upon the "calf of Samaria",[14] and the protests of Isaiah, Jeremiah, and Ezekiel[15] are scathing; their absolute condemnation of all respect for images which represent divine beings is one of the aspects of the struggle waged to establish the cult of a holy God. And so Deuteronomic legislation was categorical: "Take ye therefore good heed unto yourselves . . . lest ye corrupt yourselves, and make you a graven image in the form of any figure . . . for Yahweh thy God is a devouring fire, a jealous God".[16] We know with what vigour Josiah's reform, at the same time (7th century), tried to clean up the country by giving effect to the inspiration of the great adversaries of the "prostitution" of Israel. However, it took the hard times of the deportation and Exile to engrave for ever the horror of idolatry upon the hearts of the Jews; the prophets of those days, and notably Second Isaiah, were able to speak of idols with the scorn of vanquished things which belong only to foreigners.

[1] Ex. 32. [2] Jg. 17. 3; 18. 24, 27. [3] Jg. 8. 27. [4] 1 Sam. 19. 13, 16. [5] 2 Kgs. 18. 4. [6] 1 Kgs. 12. 28; 2 Kgs. 10. 29. [7] Gen.

49. 24; Ps. 132. 2; Is. 1. 24; 49. 26; 60. 16. [8] Ex. 20. 23; 34. 17. [9] 1 Kgs. 11. 5–8, 33. [10] 1 Kgs. 16. 32. [11] 1 Kgs. 15. 13. [12] 2 Kgs. 21. 3, 7, 11; Jer. 19. 13; 32. 29. [13] Jer. 7. 18; 44. 17. [14] Hos. 8. 6; 13. 2. [15] Is. 2. 8, 20; 30. 22; Jer. 2. 28; 10. 1–16; Ez. 14. 1–11; 18. 6; 20. 30–38. [16] Dt. 4. 15–24; 5. 8; cf. Ex. 20. 4; Lev. 19. 4; 26. 1.

INCENSE

Certain Hebrew or Greek words signifying more exactly "perfume" or "sweet-smelling smoke" are often translated by the word "incense". Incense proper, mentioned in several passages of the O.T. and N.T., is a very precious gum-resin obtained by incision of the trunk of the Boswellia tree of the subtropical regions, of southern Arabia in particular (the country of Sheba) whence it was imported into Israel;[1] the Shebans doubtless received some themselves from the land of the Somalis and perhaps even from India. For classical antiquity also the land of Sheba was the land of incense.

The Boswellia, from which incense flows.

It was in honour of gods that this substance was burned, which gave forth a smell of balsam;[2] it was also offered to personalities they wanted to honour.[3]

Among the Israelites, incense had to be used with bloodless sacrifices,[4] except for the simplified sin offering (Lev. 5. 11) and the sacrifice prescribed by the law relating to jealousy*.[5] It also accompanied the shew-bread loaves († bread),[6] being placed, according to tradition, in two gold cups beside or on the loaves; Josephus states clearly that it was burned on the altar of burnt offerings on the morning of each Sabbath day, when the loaves were replaced by others. Moreover, incense was used as an ingredient of certain perfumes* and especially of the sacred perfume burned each day on the altar of incense.[7] In the Messianic Age incense will be brought in abundance into the Temple of Yahweh, so Isaiah and Jeremiah declare.[8]

We know from the Mishnah that one of the collecting-boxes in the Temple at Jerusalem bore as inscription the word "incense". In it was placed the money intended for buying that odoriferous gum, the care of which was committed to the Levites.[9]

Burned on its own or with other aromatic substances, incense is often the symbol of prayer[10] in the Bible; for the prophets its offering is of no value unless it is accompanied by the inclinations of a sincere heart.[11]

[1] 1 Kgs. 10. 2, 10; Is. 60. 6; Jer. 6. 20. [2] 1 Kgs. 11. 8; 2 Chr. 28. 25; Ez. 8. 11. [3] Cant. 3. 6; Matt. 2. 11. [4] Lev. 2. 1, 2, 15, 16; 6. 15. [5] Num. 5. 15. [6] Lev. 24. 7. [7] Ex. 30. 7, 8, 34–38. [8] Is. 60. 6; Jer. 17. 26. [9] 1 Chr. 9. 29; Neh. 13. 5, 9. [10] Ps. 141. 2; Rev. 5. 8; 8. 3. [11] Is. 43. 23; 66. 3; Jer. 6. 20.

INCEST

Israelite legislation forbade a whole series of unions which it considered incestuous; some of them had been legal, however, in ancient Israel.

The following are prohibited:

1. The union of son and mother.[1]—It is strange that the law does not mention the incestuous union of father and daughter, which was doubtless common, but which was none the less reproved and punished, we may suppose.[2]

2. The union of a man with the wife of his father,[3] that is, a wife other than the one who bore him, and of a man with his mother-in-law (mother of his wife).[4]—In ancient times it was permissible to marry them if they were widows.[5]

3. The union of a man with his sister or half-sister.[6]—Abraham married his half-sister Sarah (Gen. 20. 12) and Tamar lets it be understood that she could marry Amnon, her half-brother.[7]

4. The union of a man with his grand-daughter,[8] or with the daughter or the grand-daughter of his wife.[9]

5. The union of the nephew with his paternal or maternal aunt, or his aunt by marriage.[10]—However, the mother of Moses and Aaron was the aunt of their father.[11] No mention is made of union of the uncle with his niece.

6. The union of a man with his daughter-in-law [12] (see, however, Gen. 38).

7. The union of a man with his sister-in-law.[13] This law seems to exclude Levirate marriage*.

8. Marriage with two sisters, when both are still living, is forbidden,[14] whereas it was formerly allowed, as is seen in the case of Jacob marrying Leah and Rachel.[15]

More often than not the death penalty is prescribed for the guilty, man and woman; [16] in one case it is even ordered to cast them into the fire*.[17] "For all these abominations have the men of the land done, which were before you, and the land is defiled; that the land vomit not you out also, when ye defile it, as it vomited out the nations that were before you . . . I am Yahweh your God." [18]

[1] Lev. 18. 7. [2] Cf. Gen. 19. 32 . . . [3] Lev. 18. 8; Dt. 27. 20. Cf. Gen. 35. 22; 2 Sam. 16. 21–22; Ez. 22. 10. [4] Dt. 27. 23; 1 Cor. 5. 1 . . . [5] Ruth 4. 5, 9–10; 1 Kgs. 2. 16 . . . [6] Lev. 18. 9, 11; Dt. 27. 22. [7] 2 Sam. 13. 13; cf. Ez. 22. 11. [8] Lev. 18. 10. [9] Lev. 18. 17. [10] Lev. 18. 12, 13, 14. [11] Ex. 6. 20. [12] Lev. 18. 15. [13] Lev. 18. 16; 20. 21; Mk. 6. 18. [14] Lev. 18. 18. [15] Gen. 29. 27–28. [16] Lev. 20. 11, 12, 17. [17] Lev. 20. 14. [18] Lev. 18. 27–30; Dt. 27. 14 . . .

INCISION

Many religions of former times and of today expect their priests or their zealous devotees to surrender themselves to sanguinary practices in order to appease the deity or make him favourably disposed. The First Book of Kings relates how the prophets of Baal did this on Mt Carmel, striking themselves blows with lances and swords so that the blood gushed out over them.[1]

Again, funeral rites often required the mourners to make incisions on their arms, hands, faces, etc., intended to register their grief, though perhaps also, originally, to offer blood to the dead person in order to establish contact with his soul or to strengthen it. Israel knew such practices,[2] which the law banned—though not always successfully [3]—because they belonged to alien cults.[4]

[1] 1 Kgs. 18. 28. [2] Jer. 16. 6. [3] Jer. 41. 5. [4] Lev. 19. 28; Dt. 14. 1; Jer. 47. 5; 48. 37.

INHERITANCE

We have only a little information about the right of succession among the Israelites, and even this is not completely clear. However, here are the statements it is possible to make:

1. The inheritance was shared among the sons, but in such a way that the father's first-born received a double share. (For details, † Birthright.)

2. If we are to believe the anger of Sarah [1] ("the son of this bondwoman shall not be heir with my son, even with Isaac"), the sons of concubines had a share in the inheritance, but we do not know in what proportion.[2] It is possible that the father made gifts in his lifetime to the sons of his concubines,[3] but more often than not, doubtless, no difference was made between the children of the lawful wife and those of bondwomen. If the children of a concubine were adopted by the childless wife it is obvious that their rights were equal to those of the other sons.

3. Daughters did not inherit, if there were sons. If there were no sons, they had a right to the inheritance, according to the Priestly Code, but on the express condition that they marry into their father's tribe.[4] Job, it is true, gives a share of the inheritance to his daughters, but the case is extraordinary and is explained by the considerable riches of their father.[5]

4. The widow had no right to her husband's inheritance. In ancient times she herself was a part of the deceased's property and passed to the heirs; [6] this custom is found, moreover, among the ancient Arabs before Mahomet, whereas the clauses of the Babylonian Code show proof of a more advanced civilization.

5. If the deceased left no children, his property returned to his nearest relatives, brothers, uncles, etc., and so to the agnates, i.e., to the descendants of

the same male stock, relatives by blood and not by marriage [7] (cf. however, Levirate marriage*).

6. Some texts give us to understand that slaves, in certain circumstances, could inherit from their master.[8]

It should be noted that wills (in favour of friends, etc.) appear only from the Hellenistic period,[9] and that the Parable of the Prodigal Son proves that the youngest son, whose share in the inheritance was half that of the eldest son, could receive it in the lifetime of his father, in order to go and seek his fortune elsewhere.[10]

[1] Gen. 21. 10. [2] Jg. 11. 2. [3] Gen. 25. 6. [4] Gen. 31. 14; Num. 27. 9; 36. 6 ff.; Jos. 17. 3–6. [5] Job 42. 15. [6] 2 Sam. 16. 21; 1 Kgs. 2. 13 ff. [7] Num. 27. 9–11. [8] Gen. 15. 3; 1 Chr. 2. 35; Prov. 17. 2; (30. 23). [9] Gal. 3. 15; Heb. 9. 17. [10] Lk. 15. 12.

INK

The ink used by early people was not a liquid; it was a dry product made from smoke-black mixed with a gum solution, and to write with it water was added. It was easy to efface the marks by merely washing them,[1] but the inscriptions done with ink on ostraca, still perfectly legible today, nevertheless show what a tenacious substance it could prove. From remotest antiquity the Egyptians also used a red ink. made from cinnabar.

Ink is mentioned only once in the O.T.: Baruch, the secretary of Jeremiah, wrote in ink the words that the prophet dictated to him.[2] In the N.T. St Paul asserts that the Corinthians are a letter of Christ, written not with ink but with the Spirit of the living God; [3] and the author of the two Epistles of John tells the recipients of his letters he does not wish to communicate to them by papyrus, pen, and ink all that he desires to say to them, but hopes to come and see them and speak directly to them.[4]

[1] Num. 5. 23. [2] Jer. 36. 18. [3] 2 Cor. 3. 3. [4] 2 Jn. 12; 3 Jn. 13.

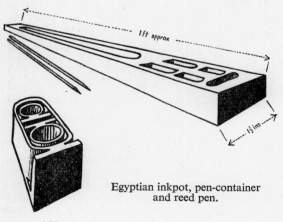

Egyptian inkpot, pen-container and reed pen.

INKPOT

Just as they still do today in the East, scribes or letter-writers used to carry about on their person a pen-container, which comprised an inkpot and the necessary instruments of their profession (reeds, pen-knife, etc.). This little box could be fixed to the girdle, just as the prophet Ezekiel [1] notes in one of his visions—and this, moreover, is the only Bible passage where an inkpot is mentioned.

(† Ink.)

[1] Ez. 9. 2, 3, 11.

INN

In early times, undoubtedly, inns existed neither in the East nor in Palestine. The woman of Jericho who received the Israelite "spies" was a harlot and not an "innkeeper".[1] Along the caravan routes certain primitive resting places [2] (caves, shelters, etc.) were to be found, or khans and caravanserais,[3] spacious courtyards surrounded by walls and huts where, together with shelter from brigands and bad weather, mangers for animals and water could be found. Everywhere else, travellers depended on the hospitality* of the local people.—From Graeco-Roman times onwards inns became common, but they gave little more than a roof; the "inn" of the Good Samaritan [4] was such a place rather than a caravanserai, and the inn at Bethlehem [5] was probably a private house where the occupants extended joint hospitality, if we can believe a custom which still prevails in outlying districts in Palestine.

[1] Jos. 2. 1. [2] Gen. 42. 27; 43. 21; Ex. 4. 24. [3] Jer. 9. 2; 41. 17. [4] Lk. 10. 34. [5] Lk. 2. 7.

INRI

This is an abbreviation of the Latin: *Jesus Nazarenus Rex Judaeorum* (Jesus of Nazareth, the King of the Jews). From relatively recent times (13th century) this superscription has figured above Christ's head in the majority of pictures of the crucifixion. The four Gospels give it (with certain variations) in its full form and not abbreviated; [1] according to Jn. 19. 20, it may have been written in Hebrew (i.e., Aramaic, the language of the Jews), in Latin (the language of the Roman authorities), and in Greek (the universal language of the day).

(† Crucifixion.)

[1] Matt. 27. 37; Mk. 15. 26; Lk. 23. 38; Jn. 19. 19.

INSECTS

The Israelites classified animals* by their habitats; and of those which lived on the earth they recognized three categories—domestic animals, wild animals, and all the tiny animals that moved close to the ground. They included insects in this last group, although not as forming a class apart.[1] However, Deuteronomy, in its list of unclean animals, already distinguished "winged creeping things".[2] Leviticus does the same,[3] but curiously attributes four feet to insects.—Only the following ones are referred to in the Bible: ant*, bee*, flea*, fly*, grasshopper*, hornet*, mite*, mosquito*. To these may be added the spider*—although it is not an insect.

[1] Gen. 1. 24, 25. [2] Dt. 14. 19. [3] Lev. 11. 20.

INTERPRETER

The Bible refers to different types of interpreters: to those who—particularly in Egypt or Mesopotamia—were versed in the art of interpreting dreams*, with Joseph and Daniel[1] outstanding among them, as servants of Yahweh; to those who were go-betweens for people who spoke different languages and who acted occasionally as mediators or ambassadors;[2] and lastly, most important of all, to those in the early church who had the gift of explaining the ecstatic utterance of certain Christians.[3]

Note also that in the time of Christ, when lessons were read in synagogue worship, the sacred Hebrew text of the Law and the Prophets was translated into the Aramaic of popular speech.

[1] Gen. 40. 8; 41; Dan. 2. 4. [2] Gen. 42. 23; 2 Kgs. 18. 26; 2 Chr. 32. 31 (R.V. mg). [3] 1 Cor. 12. 10, 30; 14. 5, 13, 26–28.

IRON

Although iron was used in Asia Minor from the beginning of the 2nd millennium, it supplanted bronze only slowly in Palestine. The first definite references to the new metal in the Bible are found in the Book of Judges, which mentions, among other things, chariots of iron ranged in line by the Canaanite princelings against the Israelites, in whom they inspired great fear.[1] It is an interesting fact that an Egyptian papyrus, of the end of the 12th century B.C., names three towns on the plain of Jezreel as a centre for the production of these chariots. It appears that before being used for the making of weapons, iron was used for ploughing instruments. Goliath's weapons were of bronze; and this precise detail alone is significant—the head of his spear was of iron.[2]

The Phoenicians and the Philistines seem to have had for quite a long time a sort of monopoly over iron.[3] From where was this metal imported? It is not easy to say. At any rate, there were mines between the Taurus and the Anti-Lebanon ranges in Asia Minor, in the island of Cyprus, and in the Lebanon, but also in Transjordania, in Moab, in the Arabah (Edom), and in the Yemen (southern Arabia), to say nothing of southern Spain (Tarshish).[4]

From the time of the Davidic monarchy the use of iron spread among the Israelites; the O.T. mentions on many occasions objects cast or forged in iron: weapons,[5] axes,[6] harrows and saws,[7] chains and fetters,[8] nails,[9] bolts,[10] blades,[11] chisels,[12] engraving tools,[13] idol images,[14] etc.

The Bible texts also refer, in the literal and figurative sense, to the furnaces which heated the ore, and to crucibles.[15] The excavations in Palestine have brought to light numerous specimens of tools and weapons made of iron; there has even been found, at Megiddo, a forge with iron slag.

The name of this metal occurs frequently in Biblical similes in which its hardness, rigidity, and solidity are used symbolically: a sceptre and a yoke of iron, earth and heaven of iron, a pillar of iron, a neck of iron,[16] etc.

(† Smith, lock.)

[1] Jg. 1. 19; 4. 3; 16. 21; cf. Jos. 6. 19–24; 17. 16–18. [2] 1 Sam. 17. 5–7. [3] 1 Sam. 13. 19 ff. [4] Gen. 4. 22 (Dt. 8. 9); Jer. 15. 12; Ez. 27. 12, 19. [5] Num. 35. 16; 1 Sam. 17. 7; 2 Sam. 23. 7; Job 20. 24. [6] Dt. 19. 5; 2 Kgs. 6. 5; Is. 10. 34. [7] 2 Sam. 12. 31; Amos 1. 3. [8] 2 Chr. 33. 11; Ps. 105. 18; 107. 10; 149. 8; Dan. 4. 15. [9] 1 Chr. 22. 3. [10] Ps. 107. 16; Is. 45. 2. [11] Prov. 27. 17. [12] Ex. 20. 25; Dt. 27. 5; Jos. 8. 31. [13] Job 19. 24; Jer. 17. 1. [14] Is. 44. 12; Dan. 5. 4, 23. [15] Gen. 19. 28; Dt. 4. 20; 1 Kgs. 8. 51; Job 28. 2; Is. 48. 10; Jer. 11. 4; Ez. 22. 18, 20. [16] Ps. 2. 9; Rev. 2. 27; etc.; Dt. 28. 48; Jer. 28. 13; Dt. 28. 23; Lev. 26. 19; Is. 48. 4; Jer. 1. 18.

IRRIGATION

Irrigation was not easy in Palestine, for springs were scarce; therefore, well-watered gardens* were appreciated.[1]—A verse in Deuteronomy states that in Egypt the Hebrews used to water cultivated land

Drawing water. Egyptian tomb painting.

with their feet,[2] i.e., either by a foot-operated hydraulic device or as the fellaheen do, opening and blocking in turns the water-channels with earth which they knead with their feet.—Balaam alludes[3] (though the text is very uncertain) to conical-shaped buckets which were used for drawing water and which were hung from a light pole that had a counterbalancing weight; this arrangement—the shaduf—is still used in Egypt, and is also known to the peasants of the Jura uplands.

[1] Is. 58. 11; Jer. 31. 12. [2] Dt. 11. 10. [3] Num. 24. 7.

IVORY

Although in very early days the Egyptians were acquainted with this precious substance and worked it with ability, as did other peoples of antiquity, among the Israelites ivory is spoken of only from the time of Solomon. The ships of the great king fetched it from far away,[1] no doubt from Africa, and the O.T. records that David's son had made for himself "a great throne of ivory overlaid with the finest gold".[2] Biblical texts mention in addition

Plaques of carved ivory, formerly inlaid in furniture.

"houses of ivory" [3] and Ahab's palace of ivory,[4] so-called because the panelling of these luxurious dwellings, and particularly their furniture,[5] were decorated with ivory plaques sculptured in bas-relief. Similar edifices existed in Assyria, Greece, etc. It is an interesting fact that excavations in Palestine have brought to light not only ivory amulets and the fragments of an ivory chest adorned with a design cut with an engraving tool but also—probably from Ahab's own palace—magnificent small ivory plaques, many of which have been inlaid with lapis-lazuli and other coloured substances and plated

159

with gold-leaf (cf. Solomon's throne*). Similar finds have been made at Megiddo at the foot of Mt Carmel, and in Mesopotamia.

The prophet Ezekiel compares the city of Tyre, which did commerce in ivory,[6] to a magnificent ship with benches (or deck) of wood (?) inlaid with ivory,[7] and the Song of Songs alludes to this noble material in some suggestive comparisons.[8] In the Apocalypse ivory occurs among the luxurious merchandise purchased by Babylon the Great, that is by Rome.[9]

[1] 1 Kgs. 10. 22; 2 Chr. 9. 21. [2] 1 Kgs. 10. 18. [3] Amos 3. 15; Ps. 45. 8. [4] 1 Kgs. 22. 39. [5] Amos 6. 4. [6] Ez. 27. 15. [7] Ez. 27. 6. [8] Cant. 5. 14; 7. 4. [9] Rev. 18. 12.

IVY

This plant is mentioned only in the Books of Maccabees in the Apocrypha, since it is not the plant referred to in the Book of Jonah as some translators have thought, notably the Vulgate.

(† Gourd.)

JACHIN

This is the name of one of the two pillars erected at the entrance to Solomon's Temple.

(† Boaz—the name of the other pillar.)

JACINTH

This term covered, and still covers, several varieties of precious stones, to which have been attributed the different colours of the plant of the same name (hyacinth).—The Book of Revelation says that the horsemen (in chap. 9) wore breastplates of fire, jacinth (R.V., hyacinth), and sulphur (R.V., brimstone),[1] and that the eleventh foundation of the Heavenly Jerusalem was adorned with jacinth.[2] The word is not found either in the LXX or Vulgate in the list of the precious stones on the High Priest's breastplate,[3] but the Hebrew name of the seventh stone might perhaps be translated thus.

(† Colours.)

[1] Rev. 9. 17. [2] Rev. 21. 20. [3] Ex. 28. 19; 39. 12.

JACKAL

This carnivore is very common in Palestine and prefers desert places as its habitat. The Biblical texts speak of it almost always in a figurative way, either to say threateningly that Jerusalem, Babylon, Edom, or the cities of Judah would become haunts of jackals [1] or to state, on the other hand, that the jackal's lair would be changed into a place of lush vegetation.[2] In his bitter lament, Job strikingly exclaims that he has become the brother of jackals [3]

JASPER

and the Psalmist mourns because God has cast Israel down among the jackals,[4] while the author of Lamentations contrasts the cruelty "of the daughter of his people" with the jackals, for even they suckle their young.[5]

Jackal.

The Hebrew word meaning fox is undoubtedly sometimes applied to the jackal, e.g., Jg. 15. 4 and Ps. 63. 10, when the jackal is meant rather than the fox, since the latter hunts alone, the former in a pack.

[1] Is. 13. 22; 34. 13; Jer. 9. 11; 10. 22; 49. 33; 50. 39; 51. 37; Mal. 1. 3; cf. Ps. 63. 10. [2] Is. 35. 7; 43. 20. [3] Job 30. 29; cf. Mic. 1. 8. [4] Ps. 44. 19. [5] Lam. 4. 3.

JASPER

The twelfth of the precious stones set in the High Priest's* breastplate was a jasper.[1] Jasper was also part of the king of Tyre's adornment.[2] Revelation states not only that the first of the foundations of the New Jerusalem was decorated with jasper[3] but also that the wall itself was built of the same material;[4] and so when the holy city descends from heaven, it shines like "a very precious stone, a stone of jasper, clear as crystal".[5] In the vision of the throne set up in heaven the seated figure also shines like jasper.[6]

Jasper, siliceous in composition, may be of various colours (red, yellow, green, etc.).

[1] Ex. 28. 20; 39. 13. [2] Ez. 28. 13. [3] Rev. 21. 19. [4] Rev. 21. 18. [5] Rev. 21. 11. [6] Rev. 4. 3.

JAVELIN

It is not always possible to identify exactly all the weapons mentioned in the O.T., and certain renderings remain uncertain, but it is reasonably clear that the Hebrew word *kidôn*, at any rate, means the javelin. This throwing weapon, allied to the lance, differs from it in its small size and its lightness. The Hebrew Bible describes it nowhere,[1] but in Israel, as elsewhere, it was presumably made from a shaft of wood tipped with a metal head († lance). The text which lists the items of Goliath's equipment is alone in saying that the javelin, which the warrior carried over his back, was made of bronze.[2] To make throwing easier, the Greek javelin (sometimes also the Roman one) was fitted with a leather loop.

[1] Jos. 8. 18; Job 39. 23; 41. 29; Jer. 6. 23; 50. 42. [2] 1 Sam. 17. 6, 45.

JEALOUSY (LAW OF)

When an Israelite, seized with "the spirit of jealousy",[1] suspected his wife of adultery, he could subject her to an ordeal, a judgment of God, the witness who knows and sees all. A very old custom, magical in character, was invoked, analogous with those practised among some primitive peoples, and sanctioned by "the law of jealousy".[2]

This took place as follows.[3] The woman was brought to the priest by her husband, who carried, as the prescribed offering in such cases, a substantial quantity of barley flour—not wheat flour, a point which may show the great age of the ritual. Contrary to what took place in other offerings and because of the painful nature of the ceremony, the husband, says the text, "shall pour no oil on it [the offering], and shall put no frankincense on it, for it is an offering of jealousy, an offering of remembrance, bringing iniquity to remembrance".

The priest brought the wife before the altar, unbound her hair—perhaps as a sign of contrition—and placed the offering on her hands. Holding in his hands a clay receptacle containing "the water of bitterness which brings the curse", he made the woman swear an oath while assuring her that if she had not been unfaithful the water would have no harmful effect; if the contrary applied, however, "may this water that brings the curse pass into your bowels and make your body swell, and make your thigh fall away". And the woman answered, "Amen, Amen" (that is, "may it be so").

The priest put these statements in writing and soaked them in the bitter water; he took the flour offering from the woman's hands, presented it to Yahweh according to the ritual, and burned a handful on the altar. Finally, he made the accused drink the preparation—harmless to the innocent, but something to be feared by the guilty, upon whom it acted, apparently, by suggestion.

Overloaded as it is by secondary regulations, this ancient procedure raises many questions. It is sufficient to note that, through fear of divine anger, more than one guilty woman confessed her fault and that if this ceremony was a bugbear for women of easy virtue, it protected some wives from ill-considered accusations.

[1] Num. 5. 14. [2] Num. 5. 29. [3] Num. 5. 11–31.

JOURNEY

Bible texts often speak of journeys and travellers, though the Israelites moved about only under necessity (immigration, flight, trade, pilgrimage) and seldom for pleasure. In fact, journeys were not without difficulties and dangers;[1] hence long trips were made in caravan, under the leadership of a competent guide[2]—the "eye of the caravan" as the

Bedouin still call him. Commonly one went on foot or mounted on a donkey*, and less often by camel* or in a chariot*.

(† Foreigner, hospitality, roads, litter.)

[1] Jg. 9. 25; Ezr. 8. 31; Hos. 6. 9; Lk. 10. 30; 2 Cor. 11. 26.
[2] Gen. 37. 25; Num. 10. 31; Lk. 2. 44.

JUBILEE (YEAR OF)

The Priestly Law [1] ordained that a Year of Jubilee should be celebrated every fifty years. Announced on the 10th day of the 7th month (Tishri, September–October)—the Day of Atonement (ancient New Year)—by a flourish of trumpets or horns (hence probably the name "jubilee", in Hebrew *yôbel*, i.e., ram, then ram's horn, and by extension, a year inaugurated by the sound of the ram's horn), it was marked by the following essential observances (for details, see the text):

1. Sowing and harvesting of corn or grapes was forbidden; only what the earth produced of itself could be eaten.[2]—On this point, the Year of Jubilee was identical with the Sabbatical Year († Sabbath), and it must be noted that since the Year of Jubilee always followed a Sabbatical Year, no sowing or harvesting could take place for two consecutive years.

2. All land was to be returned to its first owner or to his heirs.[3] Ownership of land was therefore not transferable; only the produce could be given up for a certain time: the value of a piece of land was determined by the number of years separating the "sale" from the Jubilee time, for when that came round the owner took back his property, without any liability.

This point, however, did not concern houses situated in walled towns; but in the villages the houses were considered as part of the land itself and were subject to the same conditions. It meant that from a social point of view town property was not so important as rural property.

3. Every *Israelite* slave [4] was to be freed and go back with his wife and children "to his own family, and return to the possession of his fathers". On this point the Jubilee law modified the ancient law by which an Israelite could regain his freedom after six years of labour († slave).

It would appear that the Jubilee Year was unknown before the Exile; texts put forward to prove that it existed in ancient times [5] are relatively unimportant ones, or allude rather to the Sabbatical Year. Moreover, the prophets' complaints against those who sought monopolies may not be a reference to it,[6] and that in itself is a significant fact. On the other hand, according to rabbinical tradition, the Jubilee law was probably not observed after the Exile: no historical text refers to it as an institution, and yet the Book of Nehemiah does mention the Sabbatical Year.[7] Circumstances no doubt precluded the laws envisaged from being put into practice; they must have remained entirely theoretical. It must be appreciated, however, that these laws, which would at times have been difficult to enforce, were inspired by the deep affection which the Israelites felt for the inheritance of their fathers,[8] were the development of ancient laws of redemption,[9] and were founded on fine, generous ideas: an equal distribution of wealth to prevent poverty, a respect for individual freedom and dignity, and belief that Yahweh was the only true owner and master of all things: "The land is mine; for you are strangers and sojourners with me." [10]

[1] Lev. 25. 8 ff.; 27. 16–24. [2] Lev. 25. 11, 12. [3] Lev. 25. 13–17, 23–24; 27. 16–24. [4] Lev. 25. 39–55. [5] Is. 37. 30; 61. 2; Ez. 7. 12 . . .; 46. 17; Lk. 4. 19. [6] Is. 5. 8; Jer. 34. 8 . . .; Ez. 45. 8 . . .; Mic. 2. 2. [7] Neh. 10. 31. [8] 1 Kgs. 21. [9] Ruth 4. 1–8; Jer. 32. 7; 34. 8. [10] Lev. 25. 23.

JUNIPER

This tree is of the same family as the cypress*, and so far resembles it that it is perhaps referred to in some texts by the name cypress. But it is very different from the broom*, with which some translators have occasionally confused it. The plant Jeremiah uses [1] as an image for the abandonment of one whose heart is far from God is very probably the juniper. It may be mentioned again in Jer. 48. 6, but the text is uncertain.

[1] Jer. 17. 6.

KAB

This measure of capacity (*qab*), used both for liquids and as a dry measure, is referred to only in Kings: [1] during a siege of Samaria the famine was such that a quarter of a kab of "dove's dung" was sold for five shekels of silver (about 12*s.*).

[1] 2 Kgs. 6. 25.

KEY

Israelite locks were doubtless similar to those still used today in Syria: the doorpost is fitted with wooden or iron pegs which drop vertically into corresponding holes of a horizontal bolt. To open the door, all that is necessary is to slip into the bolt a key shaped like a wooden ruler and bearing pegs corresponding in number and arrangement to the pegs of the lock and to push them upwards.[1] Since bolts are quite big, keys must be big as well. At Gezer, however, comparatively small metal keys have been found which date from the Hellenistic period.

Since, in big houses, the keys were entrusted to well-tried men, they are the symbol of authority and power [2] in the Bible.—Jesus speaks of the "key of

161

L

knowledge" [3] (knowledge of God and his salvation), monopolized by the doctors of the Law, and the

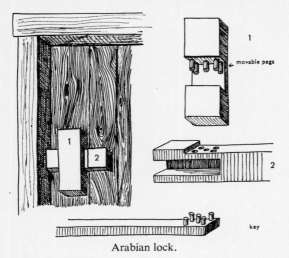

Arabian lock.

Book of Revelation refers to the keys of the resting-place of the dead,[4] which, according to Jewish belief, was provided with doors, and to the key of the bottomless pit or of the shaft of the bottomless pit [5]—a closed passage between the lower world and the earth.

[1] Jg. 3. 25; 1 Chr. 9. 27. [2] Is. 22. 22; Matt. 16. 19; Rev. 3. 7. [3] Lk. 11. 52. [4] Rev. 1. 18. [5] Rev. 9. 1; 20. 1.

KID

The very tender flesh of this animal was a succulent dish that the Israelite readily offered to his guests,[1] as the Bedouin still do today in the desert; furthermore, the kid was killed in preference to the lamb, because the latter was more valuable. Three

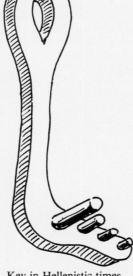

Key in Hellenistic times.

times [2] the O.T. forbids boiling a kid in its mother's milk, and this not only for sentimental reasons but no doubt from fear of drying up the goat's milk. The goat was a welcome gift,[3] and it was also used as a bribe [4] and sometimes the purchase of a field was paid in goats.[5] It was frequently offered in sacrifice,[6] and could even be used as the Passover victim, but the custom of choosing a lamb prevailed.[7]

Isaiah solemnly declares that in the Messianic Age the leopard will lie down near the kid! [8]

[1] Gen. 27. 9; 37. 31; Jg. 6. 19; 13. 15; Lk. 15. 29. [2] Ex. 23. 19; 34. 26; Dt. 14. 21. [3] Jg. 15. 1; 1 Sam. 16. 20. [4] Gen. 38. 17. [5] Prov. 27. 26. [6] Lev. 22. 19; Jg. 6. 19; 13. 19; 1 Sam. 10. 3. [7] Ex. 12. 5; 3 Chr. 35. 7. [8] Is. 11. 6.

KIDNAP

In the Covenant Code [1] and the Deuteronomic Code [2] the kidnapping of an Israelite for a slave, or to sell him, is punishable by death; no other abductions are mentioned in the law.

[1] Ex. 21. 16. [2] Dt. 24. 7.

KIDNEY

When some sacrifices* were offered the kidneys (reins) of the immolated animals might be burnt on the altar of burnt offerings, along with the fat that surrounded them,[1] because they were regarded as one of the most precious parts of the victim, and for that reason reserved for Yahweh.

[1] Ex. 29. 13, 22; Lev. 3. 4, 10, 15; 4. 9, etc.; Is. 34. 6.

KING

1. When the wandering Israelites entered Canaan, they found a social organization in which small states, with a prince or king at their head, were often rivals, but at times tried to federate. This example, as well as a settled life to which they very quickly became accustomed and the fact that the tribes were widely scattered over a mountainous country, were causes which gradually led to a complete transformation of their social system. The first change to come about was the replacement of the tribal division by a town or village grouping. Whereas in early times reference was made to such-and-such a family and to such-and-such a tribe, people came to speak in time of such-and-such a district and the "villages thereof".[1] Then the most important families in these little cities gradually took charge of affairs. Their chiefs called themselves princes or even kings. The name Abimelech, the son of Gideon, means "my father is king".[2]—However, even though the tribal bond among the Israelites was gradually replaced by a communal one, it remained true that people kept their loyalty to the tribe*, that rivalry between the tribes continued, with the result that disorder became more and more prevalent in Israel, where "every man did what was right in his own eyes".[3] To avoid the risk of falling into anarchy and becoming victims of enemies, the country needed a new organization.

2. Without going into the historical circumstances which allowed Saul and David to become kings—a topic which is historical rather than archaeological—

it should be noted that in our Biblical texts there are two opposing versions concerning the institution of the monarchy. The one presents the monarchy as a benefit, a proof of God's love for his people, whereas the other condemns the idea on principle and views it as a national misfortune and a proof of abandonment by God. Even though this second version is later than the other, it is quite probable that from the beginning some Israelites foresaw the dangers of constituting a kingdom, particularly the danger that the king would become to some extent a rival to God, and that politics would act in opposition to religion. However, the great majority of Israelites thought that the king would cement the union of the tribes and uphold the priesthood in their religious task.

3. The royal functions fell into three categories:

(a) The king was a military leader. In the beginning, doubtless, he had to respect the authority of the heads of tribes and towns. But gradually a real army was constituted and the chiefs of earlier times had to give way to officers who had taken to the army as a career, who were chosen from the sovereign's own followers and were entirely dependent on him; Abner was Saul's cousin,[4] and Joab was David's nephew.[5]

(b) Secondly, the king was a judge, the supreme judge of the country. Yet everyone could have access to him in order to claim justice.[6] He strove to be faithful and just.[7] Without doubt, he delegated his authority more and more to officials, and we know that the prophets had to struggle against the corruption of judges.[8]—But it must be noted that executive and juridical powers were not separated, and the king, as judge, was occupied with the administration of his state. At the time of Saul royal officials* were very few, but with the centralization of power they became more numerous, and the heads of tribes, the elders*, and the important families in the towns were in time dispossessed of their rights.

(c) Finally, the king was a priest. He was the head of the priesthood. As such, David wore the ephod*, and Solomon blessed the assembly of the Israelites; on their accession, kings were anointed like priests. Soon they had a sanctuary beside their palaces, where many priests and officiants were on duty.

4. The fact that the king of Israel was king by divine right, that he was in some degree God's representative on earth,[9] rapidly conferred great authority on him. In the prohibition of blasphemy the law sets the king on a level with God: "Thou shalt not revile God, nor curse a ruler of thy people."[10] Even though the king of Israel was never deified, as were many sovereigns in other states, his power was considerable; it was none the less limited, first, by God himself and then by the law, for the law was divine. In Israel people had a lively sense of justice, and there could not be one law for the great and another for ordinary folk; the king himself had to

submit to the law.[11] This does not mean that his kingship was constitutional, nor was it an absolute monarchy. It was in God's name that Nathan rebuked David, that Elijah cursed Ahab and threatened his dynasty, and that Elisha anointed Jehu. It was for this reason that the king of Israel never became an ordinary Oriental potentate.

5. It is impossible to review here the many Biblical texts in which the idea of kingship is used metaphorically. It is sufficient to recall that Jesus was called the King of the Jews,[12] but that his kingdom was "not of this world",[13] and that elsewhere the notion of kingship is a very common metaphor for the authority of God himself, first over the Israelites,[14] then over all believers,[15] and even over the whole world.[16]

[1] Num. 32. 42. [2] Jg. 8. 31; 9. 6; etc. [3] Jg. 17. 6. [4] 1 Sam. 14. 50–51. [5] 1 Chr. 2. 16. [6] 2 Sam. 14; 1 Kgs. 3; 2 Kgs. 15. 5. [7] Prov. 16. 10; Is. 16. 5. [8] Is. 1. 23; 5. 7; Ez. 18. 8; 22. 12; Mic. 3. 11. [9] Ps. 2. 6. [10] Ex. 22. 28. [11] 2 Kgs. 23. 3. [12] Matt. 2. 2; 27. 11, 29, etc. [13] Jn. 18. 36. [14] 1 Sam. 12. 12; Ps. 24. 7, 10; 74. 12; Mal. 1. 14. [15] Eph. 5. 5. [16] 2 Kgs. 19. 19; Ps. 102. 22.

KISS

The Oriental is very demonstrative and readily expresses his feelings with a kiss, so this gesture is often mentioned in Biblical texts.

Kisses were exchanged when a guest arrived at [1] or left [2] his host's house. By a kiss parents showed their affection for their children, and children for parents,[3] brothers for brothers,[4] friends for friends.[5] The kiss sealed the bonds of love,[6] words of reconciliation and peace,[7] or showed the kindly condescension of a superior.[8] To kiss someone's feet was a sign of the deepest respect.[9] The kiss was used hypocritically by more than one traitor.[10] Among the first Christians, it was the sign of brotherly love.[11] The O.T. mocks and condemns the kiss given by idolaters to their gods.[12]

[1] Gen. 29. 11, 13. [2] Gen. 31. 28, 55; Ruth 1. 14; 2 Sam. 19. 39; Lk. 7. 45; Acts 20. 37. [3] Gen. 27. 27; 46. 29; 48. 10; Ex. 18. 7; 1 Kgs. 19. 20; Lk. 15. 20. [4] Gen. 45. 15; Ex. 4. 27. [5] 1 Sam. 20. 41. [6] Prov. 7. 13; Cant. 1. 2; 8. 1. [7] Gen. 33. 4; Ps. 85. 10; Lk. 15. 20. [8] 1 Sam. 10. 1; 2 Sam. 15. 5; 19. 39. [9] Lk. 7. 38, 45. [10] 2 Sam. 15. 5; 20. 9; Prov. 27. 6; Matt. 26. 49. [11] Acts 20. 37; Rom. 16. 16; 1 Cor. 16. 20; 2 Cor. 13. 12; etc. [12] 1 Kgs. 19. 18; Job 31. 27; Hos. 13. 2.

KITCHEN

In the majority of Israelite houses* there was no special part for the kitchen. Meals were prepared in the courtyard or on the ground adjoining the house or in the solitary room which it comprised. The utensils necessary for eating were reduced to their simplest form and a hole in the ground constituted the hearth. In houses of the wealthy and in palaces kitchens properly so-called [1] might be found, as excavations show, though the Biblical texts never mention them; they speak only of the Temple kitchens, where the flesh of the people's sacrifices was boiled.[2]

[1] Cf. 1 Kgs. 4. 22, 23.   [2] Ez. 46. 23, 24.

KITE

The translation in our versions of the Hebrew words for birds of prey, whose flesh was considered unclean, is very variable. Thus, the third name in Dt. 14. 13 (*dayyah*) is translated by vulture (A.V.) or kite (R.V.); the R.S.V., following a number of manuscripts which lack *dayyah* here, takes the second name ('*ayyah*) as kite; the A.V. does the same, but the R.V. has falcon! In Job 28. 7 '*ayyah* is taken by the A.V. as vulture, but by the R.V. and R.S.V. as falcon*. It is impossible to be certain. However, kites of several species exist and are common in Palestine; they have keen vision.[1]

[1] Cf. Job 28. 7.

KNEADING-TROUGH

For kneading their dough the Israelites used vessels of clay, stone, or wood of varying sizes. Strangely enough, apart from the blessings and curses pronounced upon the basket and the kneading-trough,[1] the latter are otherwise mentioned in the Bible only in connection with the Exodus: one text [2] says that the frogs of the second plague even penetrated into the ovens and kneading-troughs of the Egyptians, and the second pictures the Hebrews carrying their dough before it was leavened, "their kneading-troughs being wrapped up in their mantles upon their shoulders"; [3] in this case it is a reference to wooden plates like those used by the Bedouin (who also employ a simple piece of skin).

[1] Dt. 28. 5, 17.   [2] Ex. 8. 3.   [3] Ex. 12. 34.

KNIFE

Excavations in Palestine have shown that stone knives were used for a long period, even until the late Bronze Age. Compared with metal weapons, discoveries of bronze and iron knives in Canaanite soil have been relatively few, but some of them are fitted with interesting handles.

Biblical texts mention the use of stone knives for the operation of circumcision.[1] Huge cutlasses were necessary for cutting up sacrificial animals.[2] Among the equipment in Solomon's Temple are always listed knives, whose purpose it is difficult to give with certainty.[3] In Jeremiah [4] a "penknife" is mentioned: it was used for trimming and splitting the reeds used in writing. As the knives called "table-knives" were not used at meals, the vigorous metaphor in Prov. 23. 2 must refer to a cutting-up knife. As for the idol-maker, he used a chisel rather than a knife.[5]

[1] Ex. 4. 25; Jos. 5. 2 . . .   [2] Gen. 22. 6, 10; Jg. 19. 29; Prov. 30. 14.   [3] 1 Kgs. 7. 50; 2 Kgs. 12. 13; 25. 14 (E.V., snuffers); Ezr. 1. 9   [4] Jer. 36. 23.   [5] Is. 44. 13.

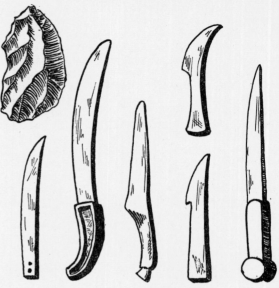

Knives of stone, bronze, and iron.

LADANUM

Genesis mentions that the Ishmaelites coming from Gilead,[1] and later the sons of Jacob,[2] carried ladanum to Egypt, among other products. This fragrant gum-resin, in time past much valued down the Nile Valley for the embalming of bodies, is a natural exudation from the leaves and branches of the rock rose (*Cistus ladaniferus*), a bush with white flowers that grows in the Mediterranean basin, Arabia, Libya, Gilead, and still today in Palestine (Upper Galilee). Some authorities hold that it was a related species; or even that the Hebrew word here used did not denote ladanum but mastic*, the resinous sap of the mastic tree (the lentisk), which was a species of pistachio.

[1] Gen. 37. 25.   [2] Gen. 43. 11.

LADDER

Only the story of Jacob's dream[1] mentions a ladder, which in that context is probably better regarded as an enormous staircase.—Ladders were used in the assault on besieged cities, as some Egyptian and Assyrian monuments prove, as well as the text of 1 Macc. 5. 30.

[1] Gen. 28. 12.

LAMB

While the Psalmist sees the skipping of the lamb as the symbol of joy,[1] the prophets and Jesus associate

164

the lamb with the idea of gentleness, docility, and innocence.[2] But the lamb is mentioned especially in those Biblical texts which speak of sacrifice*. Of all the animals given to the Lord, it was the lamb's blood which flowed most frequently on the altar. No Israelite festival took place without the sacrifice of lambs in greater or lesser numbers (more than a hundred at the Feast of Tabernacles*!); four were sacrificed regularly every Sabbath*, and the daily burnt offering († sacrifice) in the name of the community necessitated the offering, morning and evening, of one of these animals.[3] At the Feast of the Passover* a hecatomb was sacrificed, since each family had to partake of the Passover meal.[4] Moreover, the lamb was one of the victims normally prescribed for certain purification sacrifices (leprosy,[5] childbirth,[6] Nazirate,[7] etc.). All these lambs were to be without blemish and a year old. In the letter of the law a male lamb[8] was involved, unless it was specified otherwise.[9]

From this it can be readily understood that the title of "lamb" given to Jesus in the N.T.,[10] and especially in Revelation (twenty-two passages), is primarily linked with the idea of immolation and the atoning value of sacrifice.

[1] Ps. 114. 4, 6. [2] Is. 53. 7; Jer. 11. 19; Lk. 10. 3. [3] Num. 28 and 29; Ex. 29. 38. [4] Ex. 12. [5] Lev. 14. 10. [6] Lev. 12. 6. [7] Num. 6. 12. [8] Lev. 1. 10; Ex. 12. 5. [9] Lev. 4. 32. [10] Jn. 1. 29, 36; Acts 8. 32; 1 Pet. 1. 19.

LAME

The lame are often alluded to in Biblical texts, either literally[1] or figuratively—sometimes in most beautiful metaphors: "Then shall the lame man leap as an hart," says the Book of Isaiah;[2] Job[3] claims that he was "eyes to the blind and feet to the lame"; and Jesus declares that it is better "to enter into Life lame, than to have two feet and to be cast into the eternal fire".[4] (See also: Jer. 31. 8; Mic. 4. 6; Zeph. 3. 19.)

Lame folk were the object of the compassion of Christ, who healed them.[5]

Just as it was forbidden to offer to Yahweh an animal marked by any blemish,[6] we notice that the lame—and the infirm in general—could not be priests.[7]

[1] 2 Sam. 4. 4; 9. 13. [2] Is. 35. 6. [3] Job 29. 15. [4] Matt. 18. 8. [5] Matt. 11. 5; 15. 30; Lk. 7. 22; 14. 13. [6] Dt. 15. 21. [7] Lev. 21. 17.

LAMP

Excavations in Palestine have brought many ancient lamps to light, and it is not difficult to reconstruct the lamp's evolution. The oldest form was kept for centuries, and is still used in certain parts of Syria: a simple shell or a flat clay cup contained the oil which fed a wick[1] of flax, hemp, or peeled rush;

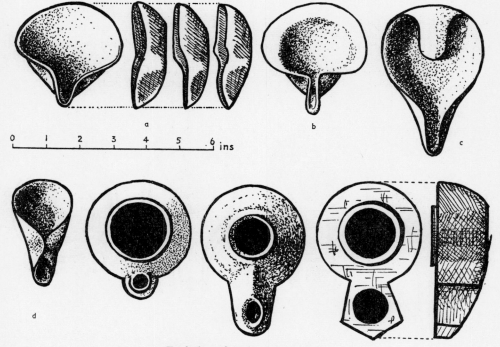

Evolution of the lamp in Palestine.

this wick was kept in place by pinching together the rim of the container (a). In time, a real spout took shape (b, c) and from Hellenistic times onwards the lamp was closed-in except for two holes—one for the wick, the other for refilling with oil (d); hence-

Bronze lamp of the Graeco–Roman period.

forward it was decorated to a greater or lesser degree with various motifs and fitted, at a later stage, with a handle. Metal lamps (e) have also been found. Lamps with several spouts, rare in the Bronze Age, became quite common later on: specimens with two (f) and with seven spouts have been found.

A niche was normally built into the house wall for the domestic lamp,[2] which was also placed on a clay or metal stand,[3] but the lamp could also be a fixture on a tall stand. († Candlestick.)

The lamp was often left burning all day in order to be able to kindle a fire at will; it burned all night too: the lamp of the good wife never goes out at night, states the Book of Proverbs;[4] today also, it is said of the wretch that he "sleeps in darkness". Elsewhere, the light of the wicked grows dim in his tent and his lamp, above him, goes out.[5]

Lamps are also frequently mentioned in the figurative language of the Bible.[6] In particular, the metaphor of a lamp perpetually lit before Yahweh expresses the notion of the continuity and prosperity of a family.[7]

Many lamps along with other articles, doubtless as equipment for the dead, have been found in Palestinian tombs. Symbolically and for magical reasons, a lamp between two bowls sometimes appears in the wall or under the threshold of houses. († Foundations.)

Concerning the confusion which often occurs in translations between lamp and torch, and for the "lamps" of the virgins in the parable, see torch*.

[1] Is. 42. 3; 43. 17. [2] 2 Kgs. 4. 10; Lk. 15. 8; Rev. 18. 23. [3] Matt. 5. 15; Mk. 4. 21; Lk. 11. 33. [4] Prov. 31. 18. [5] Job 18. 5–6; 21. 17; Prov. 13. 9; 20. 20; 24. 20; Jer. 25. 10. [6] Ps. 119. 105; Prov. 6. 23; 20. 27, etc.; Matt. 6. 22; Lk. 12. 35, etc.; Rev. 21. 23; 22. 5. [7] 2 Sam. 21. 17; 1 Kgs. 11. 36; 15. 4; 2 Kgs. 8. 19; Ps. 132. 17.

LANDMARK

Boundary marks showing the limits of fields were well known to the ancients, including the Israelites; we know that the Greeks and Romans placed them under the protection of gods who were honoured by

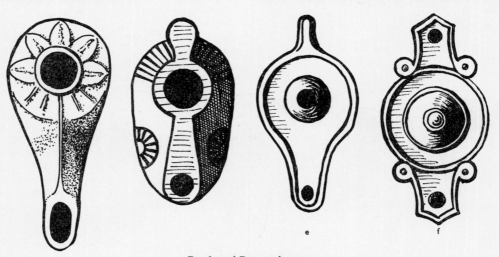

Greek and Roman lamps

a special cult (Hermes, Terminus). In Israel God's curse fell on any who violated property;[1] Yahweh himself watched over the landmarks of the widow and defenceless orphans;[2] displacement or removal of these sacred marks was forbidden[3] and, in a general sense, the paternal inheritance had to be respected in its entirety: "Remove not the ancient landmark, which thy fathers have set," says the Book of Proverbs.[4]

Frontier marks, dating from the Maccabean period, found at Gezer (Palestine) give reason to think that the territory of some districts was carefully delimited, but perhaps these stones (which bear short inscriptions) marked the limit of the zone not to be exceeded on the Sabbath day († Sabbath journey). The frontier between two regions was sometimes marked by a massebah[5] († pillar).

[1] Dt. 27. 17. [2] Prov. 15. 25; 23. 10. [3] Dt. 19. 14; cf. Job 24. 2; Hos. 5. 10. [4] Prov. 22. 28. [5] Gen. 31. 51; Is. 19. 19.

LANTERN

Portable lanterns were well known to the Romans; specimens have been found in Pompeii and in Herculaneum—they are made of bronze, cylindrical

Reconstruction of a lantern from a design painted on a Roman vase.

in shape, and have shutters made of horn. In the Bible lanterns are mentioned only at the time of Christ's passion: the people going to arrest him carried lanterns[1] and torches.

[1] Jn. 18. 3.

LAUREL

It is surprising to discover that neither in the O.T. nor the N.T. is the rose-laurel (Oleander) mentioned, although it is so widespread in Palestine along the water-courses, and its flowers adorn, most notably, the banks of the Lake of Gennesaret.

Some translators have thought that the laurel is mentioned in Ps. 37. 35, but this is most doubtful, and it is better to follow the quite different reading of the LXX. It has recently been suggested that the

tree mentioned at the end of v. 14 of Is. 44 be translated "laurel", but the text is uncertain.

LAW

1. *Common Law.* In the early period no book of written law existed in Israel. However, arbitrariness was by no means the governing principle among the tribes: custom was the rule. (Cf. such expressions as "such a thing is not done in Israel", "it is a folly in Israel".[1]) What custom authorized was just and good, what it condemned was unjust and evil. Not to respect it meant being cast out of the community. Although it was orally transmitted, it was stronger than a written code, and its influence was all the more powerful because it was an expression of the divine will. Any attack on traditional usage was an insult to the deity; conversely, any attack on religion was a violation of the law; the fusion of the two domains was profound: perhaps more than other peoples, the Israelites felt that their God was a just God who loved justice. Thus when custom could not prescribe a line of conduct in new and special circumstances the deity was consulted by the intermediary of the priest; the law was thus enriched by divine oracles which became law. The text of Ex. 18. 16 is assuredly a faithful echo of historical reality: "When they have a dispute, they come to me [Moses]; and I decide between a man and his neighbour, and I make them know the statutes of God, and his oracles [laws]."

So it can be said that, in the beginning, Israelite law was an unwritten law with a religious basis, built up by a body of oral traditions. However, these unwritten rules, while remaining faithful to certain unchanging principles, were naturally subjected to the action of time and circumstances; changes in the political, economic, and social life of the Israelites had to be taken into account, and the influence of certain foreign codes evidently played its part as well. The settling of the Hebrews in Palestine notably, the change over from a nomadic or semi-nomadic life to a sedentary one, and later the institution of the monarchy, could not fail to bring about certain transformations of a juridical nature.

2. *The Israelite Codes.* The time came when the Israelites felt the need of codifying their old customs, as the Mesopotamians and Hittites had done before them. While in the time of the Judges "every man did what was right in his own eyes",[2] as soon as Israel acquired more unity and became organized under the monarchy, the need for setting down the legislation was strongly felt—all the more because it was necessary to take certain new needs into account as well as to give a lead against certain deviations and a reminder of authentic Israelite tradition, the true will of Yahweh.

(*a*) Though there is nothing improbable in the idea that certain rulings of common law were written down at a quite early date, for reference in the sanctuaries, the first real collection of laws probably did not appear until the 10th or 9th century. This *Book of the Covenant*, as it was called, is preserved, in a form which is undoubtedly not the original, in chaps. 20. 22–23. 19 of Exodus. It is, moreover, less a code proper, drawn up according to certain principles, and dealing with all cases (matrimonial law is missing from it), than a collection of ancient decisions, more or less retouched and edited, and a little book intended for the instruction and guidance of the people. Alongside provisions of a juridical order [3] (slaves, protection of life and property) there appear moral injunctions [4] whose social purpose is quite clearly marked, as well as cultic and religious ordinances concerning idolatry, the firstfruits, feasts, etc.

Without speaking of other influences, that of Babylonian law on the Book of the Covenant is certainly striking; though it must not be over-estimated, it is none the less undeniable; yet the differences are great: the whole tenor of Israelite laws shows that they were formulated for a farming people and shepherds, and even sometimes for nomads or semi-nomads; compared with the highly organized state that Babylon had long been, Israelite civilization—with practices such as vendettas and polygamy, or the absence of business-men and state officials—often appears still very primitive. On the other hand, the religious nature of Israel's law is much more marked.

(*b*) A second legal document is to be found in the Pentateuch, where it forms the nucleus of the Book of *Deuteronomy*, chaps. 12–26. This is not a simple collection of rules based on custom, but a real code of law, a charter, directed by a few guiding principles; it was drawn up by priests and disciples of the prophetic and anti-Canaanite movement. This is apparently the law which was given to the people and solemnly promulgated in 622–621; its provisions brought about Josiah's reform.[5] As the object of the love, faithfulness, and favours of Yahweh, Israel has a special relationship with its God; *noblesse oblige*: special responsibilities devolve upon the people, they should be a holy people. Thus, anything not in line with this high ideal is rejected by the new constitution, which revives and transforms ancient customs, and advocates, above all, the centralization of the cult in Jerusalem, the only way of putting an end to dangerous aberrations.

The Deuteronomic Code, moreover, has a close affinity with the Book of the Covenant, the existence of which it presupposes; like that book, it includes juridical provisions and moral pronouncements; it fills the gaps in the earlier collection, it completes and continues it. With a deeply religious inspiration, it gives particular importance to cultic laws, but is also distinct in its pronounced humanitarian and social outlook, without mentioning its style, which gives it a particular character.

(*c*) Finally, a third legal collection occupies an important place in the Pentateuch—the *Priestly Code* (or document). Written as a history of the foundation by God himself of the sacred institutions, it was edited by a whole school of priests with a legal outlook—the school had its centre in Babylon—to guide the life of the Jewish community in Palestine, after the return from Exile. This new charter was indeed solemnly promulgated by Ezra in Jerusalem in the first half of the 5th century B.C. at a date which it is difficult to fix precisely.[6] As its name suggests, it puts in the forefront the rights and duties of the priests, the rules of purity and the rules which should govern the celebration of sacrifices and feasts; it is more the legal code of a Church than of a state.

It must also be carefully noticed that this code not only retained more than one usage inherited from the past but it also brought together, in part or in totality, a variety of bodies of law and, in particular, one special collection, formed at the time of the Exile: the Holiness Code (Leviticus 17–26). These laws were spiritually related to Deuteronomy, and especially to the theoretical laws given by Ezekiel to the community of his dreams, and they form a transition between the Deuteronomic Code and the Priestly Code to which a few more elements were eventually added.

By using the texts of which we have just given the history in broad outline, it is possible to obtain a fair idea of Israelite law, to see the line of its evolution, to discover its nature, and to proceed to a classification of the provisions which it contains. At this point we shall merely glance at the laws which bear on penal and civil offences, although the distinction between them is not always obvious. It goes without saying that, in comparison with our modern bodies of laws, that of Israel often seems very rough and ready.

3. *Penal Law*. Rather severe in nature, penal law was based on a few clear-cut principles, and, at first, on the *lex talionis*. This is expressed at every step of the legislation: "Thou shalt give life for life, eye for eye, tooth for tooth, hand for hand, foot for foot, burn for burn, wound for wound, stripe for stripe."[7] Stern as this law may appear, it sets out to serve the ends of justice and is a step forward from primitive ways in which the idea of revenge was predominant, in which the whole jaw had to be broken for a broken tooth and the man killed in return for a localized injury. Moreover, the *lex talionis*, which was valid only for free men, was not always demanded or applied: if the matter was not serious, it could be settled, indeed, by a financial payment of damages, notably if there had been no premeditation;[8] occa-

sionally a ransom was even authorized to redeem the life of a guilty man.[9] The law made a clear distinction between premeditated murder* and manslaughter—in the latter case, the right of asylum* suspended the effects of the *lex talionis*.—Primitive penal law was to remain for a long time a private law to some extent: the idea of a penalty inflicted in the name of the community was to appear only later.

Another great principle which characterized Israelite law, at least in early times, was the solidarity of the family with the guilty man. The family was responsible for the faults committed by one of its members; if the killer could not be reached, his family was held responsible. This feeling was so deeply ingrained in the ancient Israelites that, according to them, God himself punished the sons for the iniquity of their fathers.[10] The stories of Achan, who was stoned and burned with his sons and daughters, and of Naboth, who was slaughtered with his sons, are typical in this respect.[11] But Deuteronomy fought against this procedure: "The fathers," it decrees, "shall not be put to death for the children, nor shall the children be put to death for the fathers; every man shall be put to death for his own sin." [12] As early as the beginning of the 8th century, Amaziah had refrained from disturbing the sons of his father's murderers.[13] Yet the idea that the entire people may have to answer for the faults of an individual continued in Israel, where a kind of territorial solidarity was shown: the whole district was responsible for a crime committed on its soil by someone unknown.[14] And Deuteronomy itself lays down a collective punishment for the very serious crime of apostasy.[15]

However, the close bond in Israel between law and religion must be stressed. Punishment did not aim at rehabilitating the wrongdoer, who in many cases was executed, nor at compensating the victim, to whom the application of the *lex talionis* brought no material benefit. Primarily, the aim was to awaken the fear of evil, to inculcate revulsion from crime, and to inspire respect for divine law. Evil defiles and is contagious; it must be eliminated: "You shall purge the evil from the midst of you. And the rest of you shall hear, and fear, and shall never again commit any such evil among you." [16] Deuteronomy thus clearly expressed its point of view, and the Priestly Code developed this idea in a masterly phrase: "Be holy, for I am holy." [17] Thus, and with some reservations, motives which led to the fault caused less anxiety than the fault itself; it was the act which counted: Jonathan had to be punished even when he sinned in ignorance; the law had been violated, atonement was called for.[18] And that was why, in certain cases, the animal itself was stoned, as if it were morally guilty, and its flesh was considered as defiled.[19]

169

For crimes* and offences and for punishment*, see the special articles.

[1] Gen. 34. 7; Jos. 7. 15; 2 Sam. 13. 12; etc. [2] Jg. 17. 6. [3] Ex. 21. 1–22. 16. [4] Ex. 20. 22–26; 22. 17; 23. 19. [5] 2 Kgs. 22. 3–23. 27. [6] Neh. 8 and 9. [7] Ex. 21. 23; Dt. 19. 21; Lev. 24. 19, 20. [8] Ex. 21. 18, 19. [9] Ex. 21. 29–30. [10] Ex. 20. 5; 34. 7; Lev. 20. 5; Num. 14. 18. [11] Jos. 7. 24 . . .; 2 Kgs. 9. 26; cf. 2 Sam. 21. [12] Dt. 24. 16. [13] 2 Kgs. 14. 6. [14] Dt. 21. 1–9. [15] Dt. 13. 12–18. [16] Dt. 19. 19, 20; 13. 11. [17] Lev. 19. 2. [18] 1 Sam. 14. 24 . . ., 36–45. [19] Ex. 21. 28.

4. *Civil Law.* Provisions of Israelite codes which can be listed under this heading are relatively scanty; they deal with the law of the individual, matrimonial law, the law of succession and of obligations.

(*a*) There were three types of individual in Israel— free men, slaves, and foreigners. Only the adult free man had full civil status; a son under age, an unmarried daughter of any age, the wife, and slave were all under the authority of the father, husband, or master.—A man came of age probably at the age of twenty, though it is an open question whether, in early times, a son ever reached his majority before his marriage or his father's death.—For the position of the wife († woman), the status of slaves* and foreigners*, see the articles devoted to them. Here it is sufficient to note that a clear distinction must be kept between the Israelite slave and the foreign slave, on the one hand, and on the other between the foreigner who merely passed through the land and the one who settled there.

(*b*) For matrimonial law: see † Marriage, Levirate marriage, and divorce.

(*c*) We have little information about inheritance and the law of succession, which is so important in all civilizations: birthright*, inheritance*.

(*d*) The law of obligations is represented by a few provisions dealing with property*, buying and selling († deed of sale), loans and wages, as well as with debts*. The necessary information will be found under those headings.

5. *Procedure.* See the article on Law Courts* and trials.

* * *

With the Priestly Code, the law received to some extent a definitive form; its 613 commandments constitute a *corpus juris divini* (a code of divine law). But we know that it became the object of almost fanatical study which was the joy and *raison d'être* of the Scribes, and that it was later the subject of abundant explication and commentary by the Mishnah and Gemarah (Talmud).

LAW COURTS AND TRIALS

The administration of justice did not involve in Israel a separate justiciary. Further, "justice is a divine attribute for the Semites". Thus the authority of the judges was a *de facto* authority proportionate to their social prestige, whether religious, political, or even military power was concerned.

1. In early times the head of the family was the only judge. He was the absolute master of his household. He had the power of life and death over his children.[1] As soon as families became grouped into tribes, it was the tribal chief who exercised this power, but his authority was only moral and he had to take account of the opinions of the heads of families; with them he would try to settle any conflict that might arise between two members of the tribe; usually his counsel was followed, but if his advice was not accepted, it was impossible for him to impose his decision; the litigants remained free to take no account of his decision; if he wished to punish even the least important member of his tribe he was liable to his vengeance and that of his family. Certain matters could then be settled only by arms. When the case was particularly complicated, recourse was had to divine judgment through the intermediary of the priest, who would, however, deal only with serious cases, those which human wisdom could not elucidate.

It was thus that, in reality, two kinds of tribunals came to be provided for: the tribunal of one or several heads of households, on the one side, and on the other that of the priest who was later helped by a certain number of assistants.[2]

2. Once settled in Canaan, and after a period of social transformation and adaptation, the elders of the town (who had replaced the tribal elders) acquired such authority that they were able to exercise the power of a judge in a penal case,[3] and were also competent in matters of family law.[4]—The priest continued to be consulted in difficult cases; he was a kind of specialist. Moreover, it was he who received affidavits, oaths pronounced before God.[5]

3. Under the monarchy, the authority of the elders of towns was obviously limited by the king, who became the supreme judicial authority; he could always be appealed to; it was even possible to take the case directly to him. However, the king could appoint an official in his place.[6]

Furthermore, the priest's authority continued; he became either a real judge, while the elders were treated as amateurs, or a higher judge, while the elders acted as justices of the peace. It seems very probable that rivalry existed between them, but it seems that sometimes mixed tribunals [7] were successfully constituted in which laymen and priest-judges acted together. With the adoption of the Deuteronomic Code, however, in 621 B.C. († law), the priests were concentrated in Jerusalem and the elders remained the only judges in their own localities.

4. In the Israel of Ezekiel's prophecies [8] the exercise of judiciary power was reserved for priests alone. But Ezra [9] lets it be understood that the tribunals of elders still continued beside those of the priests.

Finally, in the Greek and Roman period, there existed in the villages what have been called, following Josephus' phrase, "little sanhedrins", composed of laymen, which continued the tradition of the earlier tribunals of elders, but which were subordinate to the great Sanhedrin in Jerusalem.

5. The procedure itself was very simple at all times:

The judges sat at the side of the public square at the gates of the town; however, at Jerusalem Solomon had had a special building erected in which trials took place.—Frequently certain suits were brought before the judges at the time of pilgrimages or religious festivals.—Plaintiff and defendant presented themselves (plaintiff on the right of the defendant [10]) before the judge. There was no official indictment; where there was no complaint, there was no judgment. The accused rarely had a defender.—In early times all was done orally. The plaintiff lodged his complaint and the accused defended himself. He was a fortunate man who could produce proof to support his case. It was to have proof that he was not guilty that the shepherd sought to preserve at least some parts of the animal devoured by a wild beast.[11] If a man could not prove his innocence, he would sometimes swear a solemn oath before God.—The importance given to testimony was great. Two witnesses heard separately were necessary to obtain the judge's conviction,[12] and that was why false witness was considered as a very serious fault.[13] (The Code of Hammurabi condemned the false witness to death.) The witness's responsibility was so deeply involved that, in the event of a death sentence, he cast the first stone at anyone who was going to be stoned.[14] On the subject of witnesses, the Talmud states that neither women nor children were competent.—In doubtful cases, especially in the early period, God was asked to reveal the guilty person and lots were drawn. The test of bitter water was for a long time practised in the case of an adulteress.[15]—On the other hand, torture was not an Israelite method, though we know that it was practised under the Herods.—Execution followed pronouncement of sentence and was carried out in the presence of the judge. Sometimes, it was the avenger of blood († revenge) who was charged with carrying out the verdict.

6. The Israelites had a profound sense of justice. Many recommendations, sometimes very fine ones, were addressed to judges,[16] and the Book of Proverbs has aphorisms about them.[17] If Paul reproaches the Corinthians for taking their differences before pagan judges, it is because true justice can come from God alone. This ancient Israelite conviction also shows through when he speaks of the judgment-seat of God or of Christ.[18]

[1] Gen. 31. 32; 38. 24. [2] Ex. 18. 13–27. [3] Dt. 19. 11–12; 21. 2, 6, 19; 22. 15. [4] Dt. 25. 7–9. [5] Ex. 22. 7–8. [6] 2 Sam.

14. 4 ff.; 15. 2. ⁷ 2 Chr. 19. 11. ⁸ Ez. 44. 24. ⁹ Ezr. 7. 25;
10. 14. ¹⁰ Ps. 109. 6. ¹¹ Ex. 22. 13; Amos 3. 12. ¹² Dt. 17. 6;
19. 15; 1 Kgs. 21. 13. ¹³ Ex. 20. 16; Dt. 19. 16. ¹⁴ Dt. 17. 7;
Acts 7. 58. ¹⁵ Num. 5. 17–28. ¹⁶ Lev. 19. 15, 35; Dt. 16.
18–20; etc. ¹⁷ Prov. 14. 25; 24. 28; 29. 4; 1 Cor. 6. 1–8.
¹⁸ Rom. 14. 10; 2 Cor. 5. 10.

LEAD

Lead was well known to the Israelites,¹ but little
used by them. It is seldom mentioned in Biblical
texts. What was used in Palestine, largely for the
cupellation of metals ² († crucible), came from Syria,
Asia Minor, and the shores of the Black Sea, and,
later on, from Tarshish ³ (in Spain). The poem of
Job seems to allude to lead tablets used for writing,⁴
rather than to characters engraved in exposed rock
into which lead was poured. Zechariah speaks,
curiously enough, of a disc of the metal put on an
ephah ⁵ (a container for measuring corn).

Only a few objects of lead have been found in
Palestine excavations, particularly so for the early
period; among these were lead figures used in
sympathetic magic.

(† Plumb-line.)

¹ Ex. 15. 10; Num. 31. 22; Ez. 22. 18. ² Is. 1. 25; Jer. 6. 29.
³ Ez. 27. 12. ⁴ Job 19. 24. ⁵ Zech. 5. 7–8.

LEATHER

The Israelites at all periods used the skins of their
beasts especially for making bottles*, which nomads
could carry more easily than any pottery; likewise, a
piece of leather spread directly on the ground served
them for a table*. Quantities of leathern objects are
mentioned throughout the Bible: sandals († shoe),
girdles*, tent coverings,¹ cords for slings*, helmets*,
shields*, quivers, bow* cases, and no doubt also
sword sheaths.²

The preparation and handling of leather passed in
the course of time to particular craftsmen.

(† Tanner.)

¹ Ex. 25. 5; 26. 14. ² 1 Sam. 17. 51; 2 Sam. 20. 8; Ps.
37. 14; Jer. 47. 6; Ez. 21. 3, 5, 28; etc.

LEAVEN

In urgent or unforeseen circumstances,¹ and
oftener than is perhaps supposed, the Israelites
would eat unleavened bread, as the Arabs and
certain people of Palestine still do today; they also
knew how to make dough rise ² by adding a substance in a state of fermentation, usually a certain
quantity of old dough from an earlier mixing.

The use of leaven was entirely forbidden during
the Feast of the Passover*, "the days of unleavened
bread" (azumos).³

Since leaven implied an idea of corruption, the
law ⁴ did not allow its use in offerings intended for

the altar,⁵ except for peace offerings († sacrifice) and
for the Feast of Weeks* (Pentecost) ⁶—and then
only in exceptional circumstances. According to
Josephus and the Mishnah, the shewbread († bread)
was also unleavened.

Metaphorically, leaven sometimes represents a
principle of corruption: ⁷ "Beware of the leaven of
the Pharisees", says Jesus,⁸ but generally it is a
symbol of action by an active ferment, for good or
ill, in a given environment.⁹ The Parable of the
Leaven, despite its brevity, is profoundly signi-
ficant.¹⁰

¹ Gen. 19. 3; Jg. 6. 19. ² Hos. 7. 4. ³ Ex. 12. 15, 19, 34;
13. 7; 23. 15; Lev. 23. 6, etc.; Matt. 26. 17; Mk. 14. 12; Lk.
22. 7; Acts 20. 6. ⁴ Cf. Amos 4. 5. ⁵ Ex. 23. 18; 29. 2; 34. 25;
Lev. 2. 11; 7. 12; 8. 2. ⁶ Lev. 7. 13; 23. 17. ⁷ 1 Cor. 5. 8.
⁸ Matt. 16. 6–12; Mk. 8. 15; Lk. 12. 1. ⁹ 1 Cor. 5. 6; Gal.
5. 9. ¹⁰ Matt. 13. 33; Lk. 13. 21.

LEECH

Although leeches were abundant in Palestine, they
are mentioned only in a single text of the Book of
Proverbs ¹ which refers to the creature's insatiable
greed; its Hebrew name comes from the verb "to
adhere"; but some scholars think that in this passage
it may rather be some kind of legendary, blood-
sucking vampire.

¹ Prov. 30. 15.

LEEK

The Hebrew word which almost all ancient and
modern versions translate by "leek" ¹ denoted a
vegetable which was, and is, highly esteemed in
Egypt and in Palestine.

¹ Num. 11. 5.

LEMON

Is this translation apposite? The characteristics
of the tree which in Hebrew bears this name suit the
citron just as much as the lemon tree. The "apples
of gold" spoken of in the Book of Proverbs ¹ might
just be a poetic description of either lemons or
citrons—the orange was not known in olden times
to the Israelites. However, the majority of versions
prefer to think of the apple* or of the apricot tree.

¹ Prov. 25. 11.

LENTIL

The familiar story of the pottage of lentils given
to Esau in exchange for his birthright* ¹ proves that
this vegetable was an Israelite foodstuff. Furthermore, lentils were one of a number of foods offered
to David when he was a refugee in Transjordania ²
at the time of his son Absalom's revolt, and the
Second Book of Samuel speaks of the splendid
exploit of one of David's warriors in defending a

field full of lentils from Philistine attack.³ Mixed with wheat, millet, and spelt, lentils and beans provided a flour which could be used particularly by the poor or in time of want.⁴

¹ Gen. 25. 29–34. ² 2 Sam. 17. 28. ³ 2 Sam. 23. 11, 12. ⁴ Ez. 4. 9.

LEOPARD

This carnivore, which is still to be found today in the Jordan thickets, in the vicinity of the Dead Sea, and even on Carmel, was formerly much less rare in Palestine. In their figurative speech the O.T. prophets allude to its spotted skin,¹ its speed,² its ferocity,³ its lair,⁴ the way it lurks on the watch;⁵ Hosea even compared Yahweh himself to this creature on the watch for prey: "I will be to them [the Israelites] like a lion; like a leopard I will watch out for them on the road." ⁶ One of the four animals Daniel saw in his vision,⁷ and also the Beast the poet of Revelation saw rising from the sea,⁸ were like a leopard.

Some translations speak of panther and not leopard. However, the leopard was only one variety of panther, and the true panther does not occur in Palestine.

¹ Jer. 13. 23. ² Hab. 1. 8. ³ Is. 11. 6. ⁴ Cant. 4. 8. ⁵ Jer. 5. 6. ⁶ Hos. 13. 7. ⁷ Dan. 7. 6. ⁸ Rev. 13. 2.

LEPROSY

This terrible disease, endemic in some countries, Egypt, Arabia, Syria, and Palestine among others, is caused by the introduction of a specific microbe into the system. Today, it is thought to be contagious rather than hereditary and commoner among men than women. Leprosy manifests itself in different ways which are so many variants of the one disease, but its two essential forms, which can follow one another or co-exist in the same individual, are tuberous or tubercular leprosy and anaesthetic leprosy.

The first is characterized by a thickening of the skin, in the form of nodes or tubercles which appear first on the face, where they cause terrible disfigurement, and then spread to the limbs, which they deform, and to the trunk. After a time these swellings soften, suppurate, increase in depth, and slowly eat away the patient's mouth, nose, eyes, fingers, and limbs and damage his whole organism.—In anaesthetic leprosy, which is sometimes arrested for long periods, the sufferer experiences disturbances of touch, sometimes the skin is painful at the slightest touch, sometimes without feeling; it becomes wrinkled, the nerves thicken, the muscles atrophy, the tissues become ulcerated and gangrenous, producing horrible mutilations and the same phenomena of organic destruction as tubercular leprosy; move-

ment becomes impossible, and marasmus and general debility bring on death.

Although science can lessen the effects of the disease, it has not yet succeeded in conquering it. Only severe measures of isolation of sufferers can prevent its spread. Far from being ignorant of leprosy, the Priestly Law established a whole series of rules about it. It sets out at length the signs which allow the priests to diagnose it and distinguish it from other skin conditions; ¹ it orders lepers to wear torn clothes, to go bare-headed, to cover the moustache, to call their defilement to those they meet to give them warning and to live in isolated places; ² but lepers were allowed to live in groups to help one another.³ The priest who succumbed to the disease had to give up eating the sacred food.⁴

The law of purification of the leper presupposed that he could be cured; however, since leprosy was in fact incurable, it is clear that less serious skin troubles ⁵ came under the same heading or that some lepers were allowed to resume normal life during certain periods when the disease was dormant; during these periods, which could sometimes be very long, the danger of contagion was non-existent.⁶— The purification ritual which, without doubt, became more complex as time went on, has a certain interest.⁷ In the time of Herod, it took place in a special court called the Court of the Lepers. The priest took two birds without blemish. He killed one of them over a receptacle full of living (running) water into which the victim's blood flowed; in this he dipped some cedarwood, some crimson, and hyssop, which were probably considered as purifying substances. Then, having plunged the live bird into this mixture, he sprinkled the leper with it seven times, declaring him pure; he then released the live bird, which apparently was thought to carry away the evil power of the disease. The leper then had to wash his clothes, shave himself completely, and have a bath, but he could not return home before repeating these actions seven days later. On the eighth day he finally presented a sacrifice which is described at length in Leviticus and during which, a curious point, the purified leper is the object of a rite similar to that of the consecration* of priests: on the lobe of the right ear, the right thumb, and on the big toe of the right foot of the erstwhile sufferer, the priest placed some blood from one of the sacrificed lambs and repeated the same gesture with oil, which was finally poured on the head of the person, who thenceforth could rejoin the community.

The Priestly Code also laid down a whole series of measures concerning what was termed the leprosy of houses ⁸ and the leprosy of clothes and leather,⁹ that is, about moulds, lichens or saltpetre rot— things which have nothing in common with human leprosy.

The O.T. mentions very few lepers,¹⁰ in particular

Naaman the Syrian general and King Uzziah of Judah.[11] The Gospels stress the kindness which Jesus showed to such unfortunates and tells of the curing of some of them.[12]

[1] Lev. 13. 1–44. [2] Lev. 13. 45, 46; Num. 5. 2–4. [3] 2 Kgs. 7. 3; Lk. 17. 12. [4] Lev. 22. 4. [5] Cf. Lev. 14. 54–57. [6] Cf. Matt. 26. 6; Mk. 14. 3. [7] Lev. 14. 1–32. [8] Lev. 13. 33–53. [9] Lev. 13. 47–59. [10] Num. 12. 10; 2 Sam. 3. 29; 2 Kgs. 7. 3; cf. Ex. 4. 6; Job 2. 7; Lk. 4. 27. [11] 2 Kgs. 5. 1, 27; 15. 5; 2 Chr. 26. 19. [12] Matt. 8. 2–4; Mk. 1. 40–45; Lk. 5. 12–15; Matt. 11. 5; Lk. 7. 22; 17. 11–19; Matt. 10. 8.

LEVEL

The mason's level was well known in antiquity. Only two O.T. texts unquestionably mention it: the one thinks of the level as an instrument symbolic of punishment by Yahweh (the levelling of divine demolitions)—"I will stretch over Jerusalem the line that I have passed over Samaria and the level I have used for the house of Ahab";[1] the other is the magnificent word Isaiah[2] pronounced for his God—"I will take judgment for a line, and justice as a level."

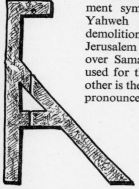

In other passages the reference is perhaps rather to a plumb-line*, which might have been combined with a level; hence the variety of translations.

Mason's level found near Tyre.

[1] 2 Kgs. 21. 13. [2] Is. 28. 17.

LEVIATHAN

In a famous description the Book of Job[1] gives the name leviathan to the crocodile*, whose power and beauty it stresses, showing also the fear it arouses. Anywhere else[2] the references are to a mythical chaos-monster.

[1] Job 41. [2] Job 3. 8; Ps. 74. 14; 104. 26; Is. 27. 1.

LEVITE

1. In the post-Exilic community of Judaea and at the time of Jesus Christ, the Levites, while belonging to the tribe of Levi and enjoying the consideration due to the clergy by the laity, occupied a position very inferior to that of the priests, for whom they were mere servants.[1] They were forbidden to enter the sanctuary proper and to approach the altar under penalty of death.[2] They assisted the priests in preparing the sacrifices (slaughtering and washing the animals, removing the skins, etc.); it was their duty to prepare the shewbread, and to cook the cakes; they looked after the vases and all the sacred utensils, they had the oversight of the shops and the Temple stores; they kept the precincts clean, etc.[3] The writer of Chronicles, who was probably a Levite himself, seeks to show their activities in a good light and declares that certain functions were entrusted to them in civil administration and the exercise of justice[4]—which could be easily explained, since they were nearer to the people than the higher clergy while sharing clerical authority. (It must also be noted that the Chronicler often refers back to the past institutions of his own day and, just as the Priestly source often does, narrates events as they should have taken place according to his conceptions; yet these indications, given quite naturally and in good faith, are not without value, for they reflect the very circumstances of the post-Exilic period.)

The age of entering upon a Levite's duties varies from text to text; fixed at thirty years,[5] it seems to have been reduced to twenty-five[6] and even to twenty,[7] perhaps to overcome an insufficiency in the number of candidates. Levites performed their duties until they were fifty.[8] They were solemnly consecrated († consecration), but they probably wore no special costume.

It is difficult to say precisely how the Levites were organized; but it is known that they belonged to three great families[9] and that in time they were divided into twenty-four classes. The corporation of singers* and door-keepers* finished by uniting with that of the Levites,[10] from whom they were still distinct in the Books of Ezra and Nehemiah.[11] A day even came when the singers considered themselves distinct from the other Levites and claimed the right to wear linen clothes, like the priests.

For their upkeep the Levites enjoyed the greater part of the tithe* which the Israelites subscribed out of the produce of the soil and livestock. They were exempt from taxes.[12]

2. The post-Exilic Priestly Code dates the subordination of Levites to priests from as early as Mosaic times. They were a gift of the people to the priests[13] or, more exactly, the Levites (cf. their consecration) constituted an offering which, by direct orders from Yahweh, the Israelites made instead of their first-born, who belonged by right to God and who, by the letter of the law, should have assumed duties in the sanctuary.[14] The Levites were Yahweh's, and he gave them to the priests as helpers, who were responsible for humble and modest tasks.[15]

This theory is opposed to some ancient texts of the O.T. and, through this, raises a problem which is difficult to solve, and is closely related to that of the origins of the priesthood († priest). It is sufficient to note here that the distinction between Levites and priests did not exist in the early period and seems to have followed the centralization of the cult in Jerusalem—a development which contained the

germ of the distinction. Without doubt, the Deuteronomic Law decreed that country priests who found
themselves without duties, once their sanctuaries had
been suppressed, did not lose their rank, and that
they retained rights similar to those of their colleagues in the capital; [16] but, in reality, it seems
clear that the latter were able to maintain their prerogatives. Though some provincial priests succeeded,
perhaps, in joining the clergy in Jerusalem, the
majority had to be content with minor tasks.[17] In
the main, their position was precarious; the legislator
himself recommends them to the goodwill of the
people.[18] And gradually the word "Levites" which
formerly, and even in the Deuteronomic Code, included all the priests, came to denote officials, certainly members of the tribe of Levi, but of inferior
rank; only members of the Jerusalem clergy were
real priests, the Zadokites, descendants of Zadok the
priest who had been appointed by King David.

In the time of Ezekiel the downfall was completed
and apparently acknowledged: the priest-Levites
who had formerly officiated at the high places could
not claim the title of priests and approach Yahweh
as such; the prophet even views their position as a
divine punishment.[19] The theory of the Priestly
Code is merely another explanation of the inferior
position of the Levites compared with the high
clergy, but it accentuates this distinction by referring
it back, contrary to history, to the distant time of
Moses.

In the Gospels the Levites are mentioned only
once, in company with the priests,[20] but two Levites
of the N.T. are famous: the one, a fictitious character, figures in the Parable of the Good Samaritan,[21]
the other was Barnabas, St Paul's faithful companion.[22]

[1] Num. 3. 6. [2] Num. 18. 3. [3] 1 Chr. 9. 28 . . .; 23. 28 . . .;
26. 20; 2 Chr. 29. 34, 35; 31. 11 . . . [4] 1 Chr. 23. 4; 26. 29;
2 Chr. 19. 11; 34. 13; 35. 3. [5] Num. 4. 3; 1 Chr. 23. 3.
[6] Num. 8. 23 . . . [7] 1 Chr. 23. 24; 2 Chr. 31. 17; Ezr. 3. 8.
[8] Num. 4. 3; 8. 25. [9] 1 Chr. 23. 6 . . . [10] 1 Chr. 23. 5. [11] Ezr.
2. 41 . . .; Neh. 10. 28. [12] Ezr. 7. 24. [13] Num. 3. 1–10. [14] Ex.
13. 13–16; Num. 3. 11 . . .; 8. 16. [15] Num. 18. 6. [16] Dt. 18.
6–8. [17] 2 Kgs. 23. 9; cf. 1 Sam. 2. 35, 36. [18] Dt. 12. 19;
14. 27; 16. 14; etc. [19] Ez. 44. 10–16. [20] Jn. 1. 19. [21] Lk.
10. 32. [22] Acts 4. 36.

LICTOR

The Acts of the Apostles records [1] that at the
Roman colony of Philippi the city authorities sent
their lictors to bring Paul and Silas from prison.—
Lictors were subordinate officials in the service of
Roman magistrates; when they accompanied them
they carried on their left shoulder, as a sign of
authority of their chief, a bundle of rods or sticks
held together by a strap, to which was added a
hatchet, if the magistrate had power of life and death
over the citizens.

[1] Acts 16. 35–38.

LILY

Must the *shôshan*, the favourite flower of the Song
of Songs,[1] and the one of whose sumptuous beauty
Jesus spoke,[2] be identified with the white lily, as is
done by the majority of translators? It is open to
question. This flower is very rare today in Palestine;
was it previously less rare? The Bible references
indicate that the *shôshan* grew in the valleys as well
as in the fields and meadows, in gardens as well as
among thorns; [3] Hosea implies that they were
abundant.[4] Could the lips of the beloved,[5] and the
royal robes of Solomon, which suggest purple-red,
be compared with a lily?

Consequently expositors have suggested, by means
of diverse arguments, an astonishing variety of other
flowers: rose, violet, jasmine, lily-of-the-valley,
amaryllis, gladiolus, iris, narcissus, fritillary, water-
lily, or lotus, and, more recently, a chamomile
(Anthemis), very common in Palestine. But it is perhaps the very beautiful red anemone*, found
throughout the country, which best corresponds to
the conditions stated in the Bible.

It is often thought that the *shôshan* was an ornamentation motif in Solomon's Temple; we read that:
"The chapiters that were upon the top of the pillars
[the two bronze pillars] in the porch were in the form
of a *shôshan*",[6] and later: "The brim [of the Bronze
Sea] was wrought like the brim of a cup, like the
flower of a *shôshan*." [7]

Finally, we must notice that the heading of certain
Psalms [8] may indicate that they were to be sung to a
known tune, of which the first word was *shôshan*.

[1] Cant. 2. 1, etc. [2] Matt. 6. 28–29; Lk. 12. 27–28. [3] Cant.
2. 1, 2, 16; 4. 5; 6. 2, 3. [4] Hos. 14. 5. [5] Cant. 5. 13. [6] 1 Kgs.
7. 19. [7] 1 Kgs. 7. 26. [8] Ps. 45; 60; 69; 80.

LILY-OF-THE-VALLEY

In the Song of Songs [1] some exegetes (Ostervald,
Martin) translate by lily-of-the-valley the Hebrew
name of a flower which is rather the lily* (or anemone), and elsewhere [2] they give it this name!

[1] Cant. 2. 1, 2, 16, etc. [2] 2 Chr. 4. 5; Hos. 14. 5.

LIME

From ancient times Palestinians have known lime,
which they prepared in a glowing fire, for which a
cavity was hollowed out in sloping ground, in such
a way as to leave a vent for draught, as the inhabitants of the country still do today. Isaiah speaks of
blocks of lime that can be powdered.[1] Lime was
essentially used as plaster or whitewash, Eastern
people loving to make the front of their houses
bright. According to Deuteronomy, Moses gave
command to cover with lime the stones set up as a
memorial after the crossing of the Jordan,[2] so that

they should be clearly seen, or to bring into relief the text of the Law that might be written there with a reed or engraved in the stone and then painted black. And in the Book of Daniel [3] it is related that on the lime-whitened wall of Belshazzar's palace a mysterious hand wrote words that terrified the king.

In the last month of the year Jews whitened with lime the rocks where tombs were to be found. so as to put passers-by on the alert, Passover pilgrims in particular, who might be defiled by touching them; hence the powerful comparison which Jesus drew to condemn the hypocrisy of his opponents.[4] St Paul also called the High Priest a "whited wall".[5] As for the prophets, they condemned with no less vigour the guilty people, who would be consumed and burned like lime,[6] and Moab, that had burned to lime the bones of the king of Edom.[7]

[1] Is. 27. 9. [2] Dt. 27. 2, 4. [3] Dan. 5. 5. [4] Matt. 23. 27. [5] Acts 23. 3. [6] Is. 33. 12. [7] Amos 2. 1.

LINE

For certain technical purposes or to evaluate important areas of ground, the Israelites used a measuring cord, a line of variable length.[1] Since the measure was sometimes equated to the thing measured, a "line" became a synonym for a "possession", "part", "lot", or "inheritance". So we translate a Hebrew expression which literally reads: "The lines [for measuring the parts] have fallen to me in pleasant places", by: "An inheritance has fallen to me in pleasant places".[2]

On the other hand, to stretch the line over a place means to make sure that it is horizontal, to level it, for example: "I will stretch over Jerusalem the line of Samaria, and the plummet of the house of Ahab";[3] there shall be stretched over Edom "the line of desolation and the plummet of chaos".[4]

[1] 2 Sam. 8. 2; 1 Kgs. 7. 23; 2 Chr. 4. 2; Is. 44. 13; Jer. 31. 39; Ez. 47. 3; Amos 7. 17; Zech. 1. 16; 2. 1, 2. [2] Ps. 16. 6; cf. Dt. 32. 9; Jos. 17. 5; Ps. 105. 11; Mic. 2. 5, etc. [3] 2 Kgs. 21. 13. [4] Is. 34. 11; cf. Lam. 2. 8.

LINEN

At the time of Jesus, at any rate, when the dead were placed in the tomb they were generally wrapped in a piece of linen which enveloped the whole body,[1] and the Greek name of which, *sindôn*, probably corresponds to the term used by the Hebrews to denote the shirts* of fine material which some of them wore under their clothes; it also denotes the "cloth" left by the young man who fled naked, when Jesus was arrested.[2]—The word linen, or cloth, is used, in the singular, in Peter's vision at Joppa [3] and, in the plural, in John's Gospel as a synonym for shroud;[4] it occurs again with the words *sindôn* and napkin in Egyptian papyri. The napkin* was a kind of scarf [5] of linen which bound only the head of the dead person.[6] There is also a kind of linen towel in the account of the washing of the disciples' feet by Jesus.[7]

[1] Matt. 27. 59; Mk. 15. 46; Lk. 23. 53. [2] Mk. 14. 51, 52. [3] Acts 10. 11. [4] Jn. 19. 40; 20. 5–7. [5] Acts 19. 12; Lk. 19. 20. [6] Jn. 11. 44. [7] Jn. 13. 4.

LION

It may well be said that this "King of Beasts" is also king in the Bible, where it is mentioned almost 130 times. Although the lion has today completely disappeared from Palestine, there were large numbers of them in ancient times;[1] its existence there until medieval times is attested. Amenophis III tells that he liked hunting in Syria and that in ten years he killed 102 lions with his own hand. Other texts and some admirable Egyptian, Assyrian, Hittite, and Persian bas-reliefs tell us of other Eastern kings who liked hunting the lion or who had it captured alive (cf. the den [† pit] of lions in the Book of Daniel [2]); the O.T. refers to no exploit of this kind in Israel.

Lion on Hittite bas-relief of 12th century.

But there are many accounts of fights which had to be undertaken against this beast, which was able to find good lairs in the Jordan thickets, in particular.[3] One day Samson tore a young lion which came roaring against him, as one tears a kid;[4] David bravely defended his young flock against the lion;[5] later, one of his mighty men "went down and slew a lion in a pit on a day of snow",[6] and Amos mentions the shepherd who succeeds in snatching from the lion's jaws two legs or a piece of an ear of the eaten animal, as conclusive evidence.[7]

It is impossible here to draw up a list of Biblical texts which allude to the lion's misdeeds, to his roarings, his appetite, his dens, and ambuscades. Some of them are typical: "A living dog is better than a dead lion," declares Ecclesiastes;[8] the Book

Lion on bas-relief from Nineveh, 7th century.

of Proverbs mocks the sluggard who says: "There is a lion in the road! There is a lion in the streets!" [9] The allegory of the First Epistle of Peter is classic: "Be watchful: your adversary the devil prowls around like a roaring lion, seeking some one to devour." [10] The language of the prophets and poets of the O.T., especially, is rich in metaphors, often striking ones, inspired by the habits and, particularly, by the power of the lion, to which are compared in turn the wicked, foreign nations, warriors, kings, Israel, or God himself: "For I will be like a lion to Ephraim, and a young lion to the house of Judah. I, even I, will rend and go away; I will carry off, and none shall rescue." [11]—The lion also appears, more than once, in the visions of Ezekiel [12] and Daniel,[13] and especially in Revelation,[14] in which, as is well known, the title of "lion of the tribe of Judah" is given to Christ.[15]

The lion was a common motif in ancient, and even in Palestinian, decoration.—Solomon himself had lions carved on the panels of the wheeled baths in the Temple at Jerusalem,[16] and fourteen lions decorated his famous throne of gold and ivory.[17]

[1] 2 Kgs. 17. 25. [2] Dan. 6. 16–24. [3] Jer. 49. 19; 50. 44; Zech. 11. 3. [4] Jg. 14. 5–6. [5] 1 Sam. 17. 34 . . . [6] 2 Sam. 23. 20. [7] Amos 3. 12. [8] Eccl. 9. 4. [9] Prov. 26. 13 (22. 13). [10] 1 Pet. 5. 8. [11] Hos. 5. 14. [12] Ez. 1. 10; 10. 14; 41. 19. [13] Dan. 7. 4. [14] Rev. 4. 7; 9. 17; 13. 2. [15] Rev. 5. 5 (Gen. 49. 9). [16] 1 Kgs. 7. 29, 36. [17] 1 Kgs. 10. 19–20 (2 Chr. 9. 18–19).

LITTER

Several portable couches are mentioned in the O.T. under different names. Apart from the frame for carrying certain utensils for the Tabernacle,[1] we may notice: the wagons acting as litters in Num. 7. 3. and Is. 66. 20; the palanquin mounted on a camel's saddle and provided with curtains, in which women travelled; [2] and the royal litter, sung about in the Song of Songs.[3]

In the N.T. the references are to beds,[4] little beds,[5] portable pallets, and stretchers,[6] on which sick folk hoping to be healed were brought to Jesus or to Peter.

[1] Num. 4. 10, 12. [2] Gen. 31. 34. [3] Can. 3. 7, (9–10 ?). [4] Matt. 9. 2, 6; Lk. 5. 18. [5] Lk. 5. 19, 24. [6] Mk. 2. 4, etc.; Jn. 5. 8, 9; Acts 5. 15.

LIVER

No doubt because it contains much blood, the liver was considered by the Israelites, as well as by other peoples, as being the seat of the principle of life. The word is also used in places where we should speak of the heart or the soul: "My bowels are in a ferment," says the poet of Lamentations,[1] "my liver is poured out upon the earth, because of the destruction of the daughter of my people."

It is known that hepatoscopy (prophecy by observation of the liver) played an important part among the ancient Semites, and particularly among the Babylonians; Ezekiel alludes to it.[2]

The fat (or perhaps the pancreas) clinging to the liver of animals was regarded as sacred and was burnt on the altar and returned to Yahweh when sacrifices were presented.[3]

[1] Lam. 2. 11; cf. Gen. 49. 6; Prov. 7. 23. [2] Ez. 21. 21. [3] Ex. 29. 13, 22; Lev. 3. 4; 4. 9; etc.

LIZARD

It would be surprising if the lizards of all kinds which breed in Palestine were not mentioned in the Bible. The N.T. does not speak of them, but one O.T. text refers to the "various species of lizards". The following verse [2] mentions five small, creeping animals which perhaps are lizards, though it is not possible to identify them with certainty because of gross disagreement between scholars. The first could be the gecko, which makes a distinctive noise but is unpleasant in appearance in spite of its beautiful colours, and the fifth could be the chameleon*.—Rather than a spider*, swallow, or ape, the animal in question in Prov. 30. 28 is also probably a lizard whose species we cannot determine.

Although the Israelites were not allowed to eat these creatures, it seems that Bedouin consumed some varieties, in times of need.

[1] Lev. 11. 29. [2] Lev. 11. 30.

LOCK

The first locks were made to fasten the gates of towns: they consisted simply of heavy beams, rendered in our versions by the terms "bars" or "bolts", the ends of which were dropped into slots cut in the masonry of the gate. Such things are often mentioned in the Bible [1] (a) either in the literal sense, or metaphorically. In the latter case it is a bolt that God strengthens and which speaks of divine protection,[2] or contrarily it is burned or broken and is the foreshadowing of the country's invasion by foreigners.[3]—To strengthen these primitive locks,

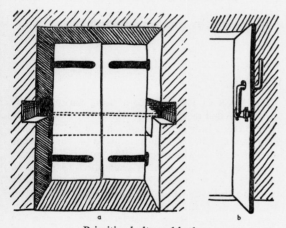

Primitive bolts and locks.

metal ones were made; [4] they were soon reduced in size to be used in locking house-doors and became simple flat bolts. To open the latter from outside, a long iron rod was used; this was bent twice in opposite directions and introduced through a hole in the door itself (b). This key was so big that it was carried over the shoulder.[5]—The bolt was moved to the outside of the door when the idea of shooting it by a secret arrangement of pegs was developed; this led to the lock described in the article on keys*.—It was left to the practical Roman mind, several

centuries later, to move the lock again to the inside of the door, but to operate it by means of a toothed wheel which could be turned equally well from outside or inside.

[1] Dt. 3. 5; 1 Sam. 23. 7; Jer. 49. 31; Ez. 38. 11; etc. [2] Ps. 147. 13. [3] Jer. 51. 30; Amos 1. 5; Nah. 3. 13. [4] Dt. 33. 25; 1 Kgs. 4. 13; Ps. 107. 16; Is. 45. 2. [5] Is. 22. 22.

LOG

As a measure of volume of liquids [1] the log was $\frac{1}{12}$ hin (or $\frac{1}{72}$ ephah), i.e., approximately 1 pint (0·89 to 0·99 pint).

(† Weights and Measures.)

[1] Lev. 14. 10, 12 . . .

LORD'S SUPPER

The many problems set by the last meal taken by Jesus with his followers arise from history, Biblical theology, or dogmatics rather than from archaeology. It is sufficient to say that the room reserved for this "meal in common" was the room of honour, the upper room,[1] which is still found today in the upper part of Eastern houses; it usually opened on to the terrace and was reached by an exterior staircase. The Gospels say that it was large and furnished, which means it contained a "triclinium": a low table, unoccupied on one side to make service easy, while the other sides were lined with couches on which the diners reclined to eat. (For the Passover ritual, see that article.)

Tradition, a very questionable one, identifies this upper room with the place where the disciples met between the resurrection and Pentecost.[2] At an early date a sanctuary marked its presumed site, to the south of the western hill of Jerusalem; the history of this "Church of Zion" is rich in changes of fortune; today it is a mosque, and the Muslims venerate it as the tomb of David.

[1] Mk. 14. 15; Lk. 22. 12. [2] Lk. 24. 33; Acts 1. 13; 2. 2.

LOTUS

The poem of Job [1] speaks of the behemoth* (hippopotamus) as lying under the lotus hidden in the reeds and swamps, and finding shade under the lotus. The Hebrew word used here does not denote the Nymphaea lotus, but probably the Jujube or Ziziphus lotus, which grows in North Africa as thickly branched, thorny bushes, flourishing in the hot and humid marshland.

[1] Job 40. 16, 17.

LOUSE

Some translators think that the insects of the third Egyptian plague [1] were lice; but it is more likely that they were mosquitoes*. The Talmud says that to kill a louse on the Sabbath day is as bad as killing a camel.

¹ Ex. 8. 16; Ps. 105. 31.

MADNESS

Like many other peoples, the Israelites believed that madness was due to the presence in or near the sick person of an alien evil spirit which could even be sent by Yahweh, to whom it was subject.¹ The madman was possessed († exorcist) and therefore untouchable.²

Cases of definite mania are very rare in the Bible: almost the only ones which can be mentioned are Saul's black moods,³ culminating in homicidal crises ⁴ and followed by periods of depression,⁵ the temporary lycanthropy of Nebuchadnezzar,⁶ the wild demoniac madness of the Gadarene.⁷—In addition to David, who feigned madness for a time while among the Philistines,⁸ the term "mad", both in the O.T. and the N.T., was often applied to those who, without being really mad, showed the same manifestations—ecstatic prophets,⁹ or exalted Christians of the early church; ¹⁰ in the eyes of Festus, Paul had lost his reason ¹¹ and Rhoda, the servant, was regarded as mad because she announced the return of Peter, who was in prison; ¹² Jesus himself did not escape this judgment.¹³

On the other hand, there are innumerable Biblical texts (especially in Proverbs and Ecclesiastes) where the word "madness" is used metaphorically to denote an attitude opposed to wisdom (e.g., the foolish virgins of the parable,¹⁴ the madness of idolaters,¹⁵ or that of those who deny or oppose God,¹⁶ etc.).

¹ 1 Sam. 16. 14; 18. 10. ² 1 Sam. 21. 13 . . . ³ 1 Sam. 16. 14; 18. 10. ⁴ 1 Sam. 19. 9, 10; 20. 33; 22. 17. ⁵ 1 Sam. 22. 8; 28. 20. ⁶ Dan. 4. 33. ⁷ Matt. 8. 28–34; Mk. 5. 1–20; Lk. 8. 26–39. ⁸ 1 Sam. 21. 13. ⁹ 2 Kgs. 9. 11; Jer. 29. 26; Hos. 9. 7; 2 Pet. 2. 16. ¹⁰ 1 Cor. 14. 23. ¹¹ Acts 26. 24. ¹² Acts 12. 14, 15. ¹³ Mk. 3. 21. ¹⁴ Matt. 25. 2, 3, 8. ¹⁵ Is. 44. 20; Jer. 10. 8. ¹⁶ Job 2. 10; Ps. 14. 1; 2 Ti. 3. 9; 1 Pet. 2. 15.

MAGIC

Magic, the chimerical science of those who think they can control the lives of men and animals, call up the dead, read the future, work prodigies, etc., was known and practised by all the peoples surrounding the Israelites; but they were at pains to separate themselves from this environment. We know they practised all kinds of divination* and had recourse to magic even in the observance of some religious ceremonies († blessing, riddle, exorcist, Urim and Thummim).

MANDRAKE

The mandrake (love-apple), which is of the same family (Solanaceae) and the same genus (Atropa) as belladonna, is a slightly poisonous, large-leaved, herbaceous plant, whose fleshy and usually forked root suggests the human body with its two legs, and has given rise to all kinds of stories and superstitions. The very strong smell of mandrakes ¹ is

Mandrake.

pleasing to Eastern peoples; they always attributed marvellous, and especially aphrodisiac, properties to the plant.² Its fruit are yellowish berries of the size of a plum.

¹ Cant. 7. 14. ² Gen. 30. 14–16.

MANNA

The Book of Exodus,¹ combining various traditions and using a popular etymology, tells that during their journey through the desert, and for forty years,² the Israelites enjoyed a heaven-sent miraculous food which was called "manna" because, when they first saw it, they exclaimed "*Man hû*", meaning "What is that?" ³ It fell each night with the dew, and when the dew had gone, there lay on the surface of the desert "a small, flake-like (or rounded) thing, small as hoar frost on the ground".⁴ This substance was very like coriander* seed, it was white and tasted like wafers made with honey.⁵ The Book of Numbers makes it clear that manna looked like bdellium*, that it was ground in mills or beaten in mortars ready for cooking or for making into cakes, which tasted like cakes baked in oil.⁶— Every day an omer* (about 7 pints) per head was collected, but early in the day because the sun's rays melted it.⁷ When attempts were made to keep it till the following day, worms spoiled it; ⁸ yet on the eve of the Sabbath, enough was collected for two days— for none fell on the day of rest—and the supply remained unspoilt.⁹ Further, an omer of manna put in an urn was placed "before Yahweh" in order to be kept from generation to generation;[10] the Epistle to the Hebrews further says that the Ark of the Covenant contained a golden vase full of manna.[11]

In addition to the texts in Exodus and Numbers, the O.T. makes a few other references to manna,[12] Psalm 78 [13] calls it "the corn of heaven", the bread of the strong (angels), and Psalm 105 [14] the "bread of heaven". The Book of Revelation [15] promises hidden manna to him who conquers and, in a well-known passage of the Fourth Gospel, Jesus contrasts manna with the true bread which comes down from heaven and gives life to the world.[16]

Still today, the Bedouin of northern Arabia and the Sinai Peninsula gather in small quantities, from certain tamarisks*, little yellowish sweet balls which they call *munn* or *menn* (a lump, ball, grain); this work is done before sunrise, for heat melts the balls and makes them fall in drops. After cleaning this substance, the natives cook it; in this way it can be kept for a long time in leather bottles; they eat it spread on bread like honey, which it resembles in taste.

For a long time, and well into the 20th century, it was thought that manna was an exudation of the tree itself, caused by insect bites. Nowadays, it is established that it is not a vegetable juice, but an animal product (cf. honeydew on certain trees in our country) secreted by a cochineal insect (the *Gossyparia mannifera*) which multiplies very rapidly on the tamarisk concerned, and which feeds on the sap of the tree.

[1] Ex. 16. [2] Ex. 16. 35; Jos. 5. 12. [3] Ex. 16. 15. [4] Ex. 16. 14. [5] Ex. 16. 31. [6] Num. 11. 7, 8. [7] Ex. 16. 18, 21. [8] Ex. 16. 20. [9] Ex. 16. 22–30. [10] Ex. 16. 32–34. [11] Heb. 9. 4. [12] Dt. 8. 3, 16; Neh. 9. 15, 20. [13] Ps. 78. 24, 25. [14] Ps. 105. 40. [15] Rev. 2. 17. [16] Jn. 6. 31 . . .

MARBLE

The marble found in the Lebanon was used only for luxury building in Palestine. Chronicles states that David had prepared for the house of his God all kinds of precious stones and a large quantity of white marble.[1] Among the beauties of the garden of the royal palace at Susa, the Book of Esther mentions columns of white marble and paving stones of malachite, white marble, mother of pearl, and black marble.[2] We also know from Josephus that Herod the Great made extensive use of marble in his sumptuous restoration of the Jerusalem Temple. Revelation, too, mentions marble objects among the number of precious things which merchants imported into Rome.[3]

The Song of Songs boldly compares the legs of the beloved to columns of marble standing on bases of pure gold.[4]

[1] 1 Chr. 29. 2. [2] Est. 1. 6. [3] Rev. 18. 12. [4] Cant. 5. 15.

179

MARRIAGE

Israelite marriage was a business matter and an affair in which the family was more interested than the individual. This can be understood if it is remembered how far among this people the value of the individual was subordinated to the importance of the family*, and that religious and therefore absolute reasons (among others that the father was the family priest) were at the basis of family unity.

1. This foundation of the family explains that, as a rule, it was the father who chose a wife for his son, and that the girl's father decided whether she should leave home or not. At times the girl's brothers might have something to say as representatives of the family. It was not necessary for the girl to be a consenting party. Moreover, the future married couple were not concerned in founding a new family, but rather in augmenting that of the young man's father.[1] All the same, it did happen that the young man made his own choice,[2] but the family viewed such a thing with disapproval. However, account was taken sometimes of the young people's wishes,[3] but it was an exception to the rule.

2. The foundation of the family explains also that the wife was bought in some degree, and by the father of her husband, not by the husband himself. The name *mohar* was given to the payment made to the parents of the bride-to-be. This may sometimes have been in the form of a gift from the young man to his fiancée's nearest relatives; but, even then, it was discussed as part of a contract, in the same way as was done formerly in Babylon, and as occurs today among the fellaheen of Palestine.

The amount of this *mohar* was debated at length in interminable parleys between representatives of the two families. But as soon as the *mohar* was paid over, the girl was legally married; this explains why anyone who seduced a betrothed woman was punished as an adulterer.[4]

How much did the *mohar* amount to? In Deuteronomy it seems that 50 shekels of silver (about £6) was the usual or minimum price.[5] Note, in comparison, that a slave was usually worth half as much. This price is also given in the Babylonian Code. The equivalent could be paid in kind; Jacob paid it off by working for his father-in-law. Some girls were given in exchange for exploits in war; we know that David won Michal for having killed a hundred Philistines.[6]

Over and above the *mohar*, the man owed certain presents which reverted to the fiancée herself. It seems clear that in the long run the *mohar* was used more and more for the bride's trousseau. Sometimes, even, the father gave a special gift to his daughter after the celebration of the marriage.

The payment of the *mohar* implied a kind of proprietary right over the bride by the groom; this explains why he alone had the right to denounce the agreement, that is to decide on divorce*.

3. As a general rule, a wife was chosen from the tribe to which the man belonged. Marriage with a foreign woman was frowned upon, especially as it appeared to carry the temptation to idolatry; at one time it was categorically forbidden.[7] Various consanguineous marriages, and incest, were gradually prohibited also.

4. We have few Biblical details concerning weddings, which must have been the occasion of great rejoicing.[8] Jesus alluded to them more than once, but it is difficult to say exactly how things were conducted. Moreover, usage must have varied from one locality to another.

Here are a few points collected from the customs of present-day Bedouin, compared with what the Bible tells us about weddings in the past:

The autumn was a popular season for marriage; the crops had been gathered in and the nights were of a temperature suitable for merrymaking.

Every wedding was attended by numerous relatives and guests, and the festivity could last a week or even a fortnight.[9]

One of the important moments of the feast was the bride's entry into the husband's house. It was on the eve of the wedding that the bridegroom, accompanied by his friends, went to fetch his bride; he wore his holiday clothes and was crowned with a diadem,[10] which he received perhaps from his mother's hands.[11] The friend of the bridegroom, who acted as master of ceremonies, was an important figure in the procession.[12]

The bride was handed over to those who came to seek her in this way. Her parents pronounced a formula of blessing, which was the only religious act in the marriage.[13]

The bride had her head completely veiled, which explains Laban's success in deceit;[14] she was dressed for the procession,[15] and her friends accompanied her. Amid the music and singing, the shouts and dancing, all these young people went to the bridegroom's house; it has been suggested that the Song of Songs was a collection of nuptial songs sung on such occasions. In any case, the evening was spent in games and singing; the bridegroom took part in it, but the bride stayed in a room which was reserved for her use in the house.

On the following day the young men organized games, competitions of skill in the atmosphere of a popular feast; spectators were numerous, and, towards evening, friends offered their gifts to the bridegroom. A meal was served, but the men and women ate separately. The bride's friends were with her and awaited the bridegroom, who was often delayed at the feasting among his friends. Suddenly the cry arose: "Here is the bridegroom." The girls came forward to meet him and joined the party following him, which moved off towards the house of the newly married couple. According to certain Biblical texts, the wedding meal took place in this house, at this stage.

During these days of feasting, the bridegroom and bride were considered as a king and queen by the local people; a throne was even kept for them at the site of the feasting.

It seems quite clear that there was no religious ceremony proper on the occasion of a wedding.

(† Adultery, divorce, dowry, family, woman, widow.)

[1] Gen. 21. 21; 24. 3, 4; 34. 1–23; 38. 6; Jg. 14. 2. [2] Gen. 26. 35. [3] Gen. 24. 58. [4] Dt. 22. 23, 24. [5] Dt. 22. 28–29. [6] 1 Sam. 18. 25. [7] Dt. 7. 3; Jg. 3. 6; etc. [8] Jer. 16. 9. [9] Gen. 29. 22; Jn. 2. 2. [10] Is. 61. 10. [11] Cant. 3. 11. [12] Jn. 3. 29. [13] Gen. 24. 60; Ruth 4. 11; Tob. 7. 15. [14] Gen. 29. 23–25. [15] Jer. 2. 32.

MARRIAGE (LEVIRATE)

Among the Israelites, as among several peoples today and in ancient times, custom required that if a married man died without a son his eldest brother should marry the widow in order to ensure a posterity for the dead man as well as the preservation of the patrimony: the dead man's name and inheritance reverted to the first son born of this new union.[1] *Levir*, in Latin, means husband's brother, brother-in-law; hence the word "levirate" was given to this ancient institution, which was entirely designed for the dead man's benefit, and which carried more duties than rights in its wake.

There is little agreement on the solutions to the problems raised by levirate marriage. Nor is it always easy to state precisely, to date and harmonize the data supplied in the three texts which speak of it, namely two anecdotic accounts and a legislative passage.[2] It follows from the first two that the two brothers-in-law had to marry the widow in turn and according to age, if death struck them down one after the other, before an heir was born;[3] in default of a brother-in-law, the obligation of the levirate fell on the nearest relative (agnate).[4] However, the widow was not under an obligation, unless morally, to marry the latter,[5] who was also allowed to decline;[6] this at least is implied in the Book of Ruth. These forced marriages, indeed, were not to everybody's taste; they were too onerous, for they could necessitate the purchase of certain lands, since the questions of the dead man's succession and the marriage of the widow were interconnected.

While the Deuteronomic text lays it down that the widow with no son should not marry "outside, with a stranger", but should marry her brother-in-law, it seems to restrict levirate marriage to brothers who "dwell together",[7] that is brothers who worked the same piece of land together or lived in the same district; moreover, it speaks only of the eldest of the brothers-in-law, without mentioning the others or the agnates. But this levir, this brother of the dead man, who in principle had the right to renounce levirate marriage, could decline only at the expense of a demonstration of contempt by the widow. Indeed, if he persisted in his refusal, despite the intervention of the town elders, his sister-in-law took off his sandal in public (to give one's shoe*, that is to renounce a possession; to take off one's shoe, meant to withdraw a right) and spat in his face, saying: "So shall it be done to the man who refuses to build up his [dead] brother's house!" And that man's house was afterwards called in Israel "the house of him that had his sandal pulled off".[8]—This procedure probably aimed at preventing the defection of those who would too easily have evaded the important family duty of levirate marriage.

It follows that from the time when the Priestly Code allowed daughters to inherit,[9] the levirate law applied only if the dead man left neither son nor daughter. Without appearing to consider this case, which must without doubt be set apart, the Levitical law on illicit unions considers the union between brother and sister-in-law as incestuous; it has often been thought, it is true, that this law had sought to abolish levirate marriage, perhaps without succeeding.

In any case, the captious question which the Sadducees put to Jesus about the resurrection [10] proves that, at the beginning of the Christian era, levirate marriage was thought of as Genesis 38 had viewed it, with this one small difference—given that daughters had acquired the right to inherit—that the widow who married her seven brothers-in-law not only had no son, but had no *children*, as the N.T. clearly states.—Further, levirate law is the subject of a long commentary in the Mishnah, which sets down the procedure to the extent of fixing the amount of saliva that a widow who had been refused could eject, at the sandal-removing ceremony!

[1] Dt. 25. 6; Ruth 4. 10. [2] Gen. 38. 6–11; Ruth; Dt. 25. 5–10. [3] Gen. 38. 8; Ruth 1. 11. [4] Gen. 38. 26; Ruth 4. 4. [5] Ruth 3. 10. [6] Ruth 3. 13; 4. 14; cf. 2 Sam. 14. 6–7. [7] Dt. 25. 5. [8] Dt. 25. 7–10. [9] Num. 27. 8; 36. 6 . . . [10] Matt. 22. 23 . . .; Mk. 12. 18 . . .; Lk. 20. 27 . . .

MARTEN

The first of the unclean animals mentioned in Lev. 11. 29 could be the marten, but it is generally regarded as the weasel* and sometimes even the mole*.

MASON

Since ordinary Palestinian houses* were of very simple design, their construction was entrusted to craftsmen who were stone-shapers, masons, and

carpenters* all at once. Specialized workmen were involved only in the building of David's palace and the Temple of Jerusalem or in the repair work which was needed as time passed; masons as such, who bore the name "builders" or "wall-builders", are only rarely mentioned in Biblical texts,[1] but it is clear that the important buildings and works referred to in the O.T. were constructed with their care, and the ruins of fortifications or dwellings in the grand manner of an earlier age bear witness today to the ingenuity of the men who built them. Some of the tools which they used are mentioned in the texts: hammer*, saw*, plumb-line*, level*, measuring-reed*, line* († brick, clay). It is known that David and Solomon—and probably the kings of Samaria as well—had recourse to the services of Tyrian workmen.[2]

[1] 1 Kgs. 5. 18; 2 Kgs. 12. 11; 22. 6; 2 Chr. 34. 11; Ezr. 3. 10. [2] 2 Sam. 5. 11; 1 Kgs. 5. 18; 1 Chr. 14. 1.

MATTOCK

This agricultural implement, more robust than the wooden hoe of the Egyptians, and used for digging and cleaning the ground, is perhaps the one referred to in Is. 7. 25, though some translators favour "spade". But there is wide agreement that the second implement in the list [1] of those which the Israelites went to the Philistines for sharpening was very probably a kind of mattock (or perhaps a hatchet); the same Hebrew word occurs again in the familiar

Various forms of mattocks.

text of Is. 2. 4,[2] where it is generally translated as "ploughshare"; but we could, therefore, more naturally read: "From their swords they shall forge mattocks." Some samples of weeding hoes have been found in Palestine excavations; no doubt some of them were fixed to a curved handle.

[1] 1 Sam. 13. 20. [2] Cf. Joel 3. 10; Mic. 4. 3.

MEASURING-REED

In his vision of the restored Temple, Ezekiel [1] saw a man whose appearance was "like brass", who measured the sanctuary with a cord and a measuring-reed (rush) six cubits long, each cubit a handbreadth more than an ordinary cubit. The ordinary cubit* was probably 18 in., the handbreadth 3 in., so that the cubit here in question was 21 in. and the reed 10½ ft. long.[2]

Similarly, the author of Revelation sees an angel measuring the New Jerusalem, holding in his hand "for a measure a golden reed", which is no doubt the ancient measuring-reed.[3]

[1] Ez. 40. 3, 5 . . . [2] Cf. Ez. 42. 19–20. [3] Rev. 21. 15; cf. 11. 1.

MEDICINE

To obtain the cure of disease, the ancients had recourse to all kinds of magical rites, exorcisms († exorcist), and recipes, but also to natural remedies, prophylactic measures, and medical practices. Circumcision* itself presupposes the observation of agreed methods of care. Certainly the Israelites knew the virtues of certain plants and of some substances of animal or mineral origin. Talmudic literature, the writings of Josephus, and the apocryphal writings of the O.T. provide abundant proof of this. From the canonical writings we may note the use of oil lotions,[1] anointings of balm,[2] fig poultices,[3] eye-salves*. The Good Samaritan of the parable dresses the wounds of the injured man with oil and wine,[4] in accordance with normal usage. Timothy was recommended to drink a little wine, because of his stomach and his frequent indispositions.[5] Ezekiel and the Book of Revelation, in their visions, speak of trees whose foliage can be used as a remedy.[6]—Further, the Book of Proverbs knows that physical health is closely connected with moral health: [7] "A cheerful heart is a good medicine, but a downcast spirit dries up the bones." [8] Finally the importance of hot springs should be noted, the curative value of which was recognized—the pool of Bethesda, baths at El Hamma near Tiberias, at Callirhoe, etc.

(† Bath.)

[1] Is. 1. 6. [2] Jer. 8. 22; 46. 11; 51. 8. [3] 2 Kgs. 20. 7; Is. 38. 21. [4] Lk. 10. 34. [5] 1 Ti. 5. 23. [6] Ez. 47. 12; Rev. 22. 2. [7] Prov. 2. 18; 3. 8; 5. 5; 7. 27; 12. 18. [8] Prov. 17. 22.

MELON

The melon is one of the fruits and vegetables of Egypt which the Israelites sadly missed in the desert.[1] It is the only Bible reference to this member of the gourd family (Curcurbitaceae), so well known in Palestine today and which was also without doubt

cultivated there in former times. The melon particularly familiar in Egypt was the water-melon. It was represented on some bas-reliefs, and its seeds are frequently found in Egyptian tombs.

[1] Num. 11. 5.

MESSENGER

A despatch service with messengers on horseback seems only to have been established in a regular way by the Persians [1] (cf. Herodotus and Xenophon), but couriers were also occasionally employed in Israel as well as in Babylonia.[2] Their swiftness was famous: "My days are swifter than a courier," says Job.[3] But more often kings and private individuals sent their letters with friends or servants,[4] while the authors of the N.T. epistles had no other way of sending them to the churches than by entrusting them to their followers.[5]

[1] Est. 3. 13, 15; 8. 10, 14. [2] 2 Chr. 30. 6, 10; Jer. 51. 31. [3] Job 9. 25. [4] 2 Sam. 11. 14; Neh. 6. 5; Acts 23. 23 . . . [5] Acts 15. 23.

METALS

The various metals mentioned in the Bible are:

antimony	gold	orichalc († bronze)
brass-bronze*	iron	silver
copper	lead	tin

For details see the articles under these names.

For the working of minerals and metals see: mine, crucible, hammer, smith, goldsmith.

MEZUZAH

This Hebrew word (mezûzah) is used in the O.T. for "doorpost", the uprights of the doorway of a house, a holy place which was sometimes marked by blood. Deuteronomy prescribes the writing there of Yahweh's commandments. So the name mezuzah passed to the little box or tube that eventually was hung at the right-hand of the entrance, containing a roll of parchment on which were written, in twenty-two lines, two passages of the Law: Dt. 6. 4–9 and 11. 13–21. The Gospels which speak of phylacteries* and fringes* make no mention of this custom, which is still observed today. Even with modern houses there can be seen a mezuzah fixed to the front door of the Jewish home.

MIDWIFE

Like Eastern women, the Israelites generally dispensed with the services of midwives, for their labour was usually easy. However, Genesis reports that Rachel and Tamar were both assisted by a "midwife",[1] and the Book of Exodus [2] mentions two of them among the Hebrews in Egypt, an absurdly low and significant figure. These are the only texts referring to midwives.

[1] Gen. 35. 17; 38. 27 ... [2] Ex. 1. 15 ...

MILE

The mile (*mille*, 1,000 [double] steps) is a Roman measure of road distances, approximately equal to 8 furlongs, i.e., a little under 1,500 metres (4,920 ft.). Roman routes were marked by milestones or military columns, some of which still survive in Palestine. Jesus said: "Whoever compels you to go one mile, go with him two." [1]

(† Weights and measures.)

[1] Matt. 5. 41.

MILK

Milk has always been an item of prime importance in the diet of nomads, among whom it is often less rare than water; [1] but among the sedentary fellaheen, milk is abundant only in spring, and it is then used mainly in making butter and cheese. The Arabs of today prefer sheep's or goat's milk to cow's milk, which is held to be "hard" for the stomach; in their opinion ewe's milk is superior to goat's; they also drink camel's milk, which is light and mild.

The Biblical texts also mention these different types of milk, [2] while speaking rather of milk in general, without giving details of its origin; [3] the references are perhaps more often to milk in the metaphorical [4] rather than the real sense.

Milk was normally kept in skin bottles, in which it quickly turned sour; it was then used as a refreshing drink. [5] It must be noted that milk was never offered in sacrifice among the Israelites, and that after the time when the camel was considered as an unclean animal, its milk was undoubtedly prohibited as a drink. († Butter, cheese.)

The O.T. very often described Palestine as a land flowing with milk and honey. [6] This expression underlines the country's fertility, but its exact sense has been much discussed; without listing all the hypotheses which have been put forward, it should be noted that some take the words literally—a country in which milk and honey abound—and that others see the words as a picture of the necessary (milk) and the extra (honey), or as a picture of what is best, since the Bedouin like to drink a mixture of milk or of butter and honey. Based on a passage in a myth discovered at Ras Shamra, a more recent suggestion is that we should think of a land in which a good water supply, by developing the grasslands, assures the well-being of livestock (milk, fat) and in a general way makes the vegetation grow (honey); this would not be a nomad's view, but a farmer's.

Concerning the prohibition against cooking a kid in its mother's milk, see † kid.

[1] Jg. 5. 25. [2] Gen. 32. 14–15; Dt. 32. 14; Prov. 27. 27. [3] Gen. 18. 8; 49. 12; Job 10. 10; Is. 7. 22; Joel 3. 18. [4] Cant. 4. 11; 5. 12; Is. 55. 1; 60. 16; 66. 11; Lam. 4. 7; 1 Cor. 3. 2; 9. 7; Heb. 5. 12–13; 1 Pet. 2. 2. [5] Jg. 4. 19. [6] Ex. 3. 8, 17; 13. 5; etc.

MILL

Following a procedure still used today in certain countries to obtain flour, for a long period in Palestine wheat grains were crushed with a roller or muller operated by hand from the front backwards, on a slightly concave slab of hard stone (basalt) (a). In the course of time, the muller was perfected—pierced with a rectangular hopper for admitting the grain; it was also fitted with a horizontal wooden handle, the two ends of which served as hand grips and allowed easier movement in manipulating the stone back and forth. Several statuettes of servants grinding corn have been found in Egyptian tombs.

Woman grinding corn. Egyptian statuette, 10 in. high.

Contrary to what was long thought, the O.T. texts probably allude to these rudimentary mills, [1] sometimes found in excavations, and not to the rotary type, which did not appear until about Hellenistic times. However, ancient rotary mills have been preserved in which the upper wheel is pivoted on the lower; since they were not fitted with any handle, they were turned with both hands, but their small size suggests that they were used for grinding spices or dyes (b).

Rotary flour mills came into use in the later pre-Christian centuries and resembled, with some noticeable variations, the hand-mills which are still in use among the peasants and Arabs of Palestine. In Roman times there was a heavy type in which the lower stone had its cone fitted into the upper stone, which was fitted with a grain funnel varying in width; because of the horizontal bars provided, it could be operated by arm (c) or by an animal (d). It was probably of such a millstone, turned by asses or horses, that Jesus was thinking in his terrible condemnation of those who offend against children.[2]

Although the Romans may have known the principle of the water-mill, they were not able to make use of it for a reason which at first seems surprising: they were unacquainted with wagons of four wheels and a moving front axle. In fact, haulage was very feeble; sacks of grain or flour were carried only on

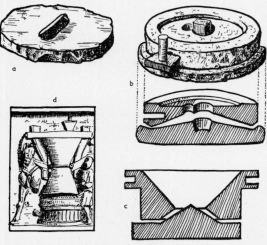

Mills: (*a*) Palaeolithic, made of flint, (*b*) Roman, (*c*) hand turned, (*d*) worked by animals.

the backs of men or animals, which of necessity limited the quantity; a water-mill would not pay under such conditions. Only in the 10th century A.D. does modern harnessing appear, and it is in the Middle Ages that communal mills were built almost everywhere.

Hand-mills of later Bible times comprise two circular stones fitting one inside the other: the upper stone is pierced by a funnel in the middle, is operated by a vertical or oblique handle, and turns on the fixed lower stone which is fitted with a pivot. The flour falls through a slot separating the two stones into a sheet spread on the ground or into a receptacle which forms part of the mill.

The women usually ground enough flour before sunrise to supply the bread for each day. "Two women will be grinding at the mill; one is taken and one is left," says the Gospel.[3] It was tiring work; slaves or prisoners were often set to do the task.[4] Deuteronomy[5] forbids both millstones or even upper millstones to be taken in pledge, for they are indispensable. According to the Book of Judges, Abimelech was killed by a fragment of upper millstone which a woman threw at his head,[6] and the poem of Job compares the hardness of the crocodile's heart to that of the lower millstone.[7] For Revelation

as for Jeremiah, the sound of millstones in the houses is a sign of life and prosperity.[8] (For oil-mills, see † olive.)

[1] Num. 11. 8. [2] Matt. 18. 6; Mk. 9. 42. [3] Matt. 24. 41.
[4] Ex. 11. 5; Jg. 16. 21; Job 31. 10; Is. 47. 2; Lam. 5. 13.
[5] Dt. 24. 6. [6] Jg. 9. 53. [7] Job 41. 24. [8] Jer. 25. 10; Rev. 18. 22.

MILLET

Millet is a species of grass still grown in Palestine for its floury seeds. When necessary it can be used for bread-making instead of barley or wheat. Ezekiel, in the only Biblical text which mentions millet,[1] is commanded to feed himself for more than a year on bread made from wheat, barley, beans, lentils, millet, and spelt (unless the last named is sorghum).

[1] Ez. 4. 9.

MILLO

The Millo was, perhaps, even before David's time, an important bastion [1] in Jerusalem,[2] commanding the hollow which lay between the hill of Zion and the hill where Solomon later raised his palace and Temple. It is possible that David's son, in extending the ramparts of the royal city, filled in this breach [3] to facilitate crossing from the old to the new town [4] and transformed the primitive defence into a kind of esplanade or wide bridge, which was henceforward the Millo. But this explanation, and variations on it, are only hypothetical: it is as difficult to be clear about the history of the Millo as of its structure.

The Second Book of Kings [5] relates that Joash was assassinated as he went down (the Temple hill?) to the Millo and, according to the Chronicler, Hezekiah strengthened this structure.[6]

[1] Cf. Jg. 9. 6, 20. [2] 2 Sam. 5. 9; 1 Chr. 11. 8. [3] 1 Kgs. 9. 15; 11. 27. [4] 1 Kgs. 9. 24. [5] 2 Kgs. 12. 20. [6] 2 Chr. 32. 5.

MINA

The mina, Sumerian in origin, was a weight used to weigh certain kinds of merchandise, and more especially the precious metals which served for money prior to the Exile. As $\frac{1}{60}$ of the talent* it was equal to 50 shekels* in Palestine (1 talent = 60 minas = 3,000 shekels). Whether in gold or silver, the mina represented a considerable sum; if the shekel is estimated at 0·58 oz. the mina equalled 1 lb. 13 oz., i.e., about £112 in gold and about £6 in silver. But these equivalences are very rough approximations and highly contestable († money), and are given only as a general indication; neither must it be forgotten that the purchasing power of silver was much higher in antiquity than in our time.

Minas or their multiples and sub-multiples found in Mesopotamia sometimes have the form of a duck, a crouching lion, or of other animals; they are of varied materials. Minas are seldom mentioned in the O.T.; [1] they are implied in two passages which speak of 50 shekels of gold or of silver. [2] The First Book of Kings relates that Solomon made 300 small gold shields, [3] for each of which were used 3 minas of gold(!), and the Books of Ezra and Nehemiah refer to freewill offerings of 2,000, 2,200, and 5,000 minas of silver. [4]

In the N.T. minas are mentioned only in the Parable of the "Pounds"; [5] here it is a reference to a Greek unit of monetary calculation (*mna*), equivalent to 100 drachmas*, worth about £3 10s.

[1] Ez. 45. 12. [2] Dt. 22. 29; Jos. 7. 21. [3] 1 Kgs. 10. 17. [4] Ezr. 2. 69; Neh. 7. 71–72. [5] Lk. 19. 11–28.

MINE

Palestine properly so-called is not a mining country, and it depended upon other lands for metals. But mines on the periphery of the land were already [1] being exploited, in Lebanon, the land of Moab, and south of the Dead Sea. So the work of the miner was well known to the Israelites; the only important Biblical text which alludes to it forms part of the poem of Job [2] and describes it in a vivid and original manner.

(See articles on various metals.)

[1] Dt. 8. 9. [2] Job 28. 1–11.

MINT

The Gospel reports that Jews in Jesus' time paid tithes even of mint, anise (dill*), and cummin*. [1] Mint is an aromatic herb—the Greek word so translated means "sweet smelling"—very widespread in Palestine, and it was used in perfumes, in food, and especially as a condiment.

[1] Matt. 23. 23; Lk. 11. 42.

MIRROR

The mirror of the ancients consisted of a metal surface (copper, copper and tin, silver), round or slightly elliptical, and polished; it could be held by a handle which was often decorated, sometimes even in the form of a female figure. Some mirrors had a kind of pedestal and could stand on furniture. In the 2nd millennium B.C. mirrors, which were articles of great luxury, were part of the gifts which kings of those days gave to one another: in 1360 the Pharaoh sent thirty-two bronze mirrors to the king of the Hittites, who replied by sending a single one, of silver, in return. A mirror industry seems to have flourished for a long time in Egypt, where many mirrors have been found in old tombs. The majority of those found in excavations in Palestine are of bronze and date from post-Exilic times; those of the Roman period sometimes have no handle.

185

In the O.T. mirrors are mentioned twice only; the Hebrew word comes from the verb "to see"; the Book of Exodus [1] (Priestly document) tells that the bronze laver in the sanctuary was made from the mirrors given by the women, and the poem of Job [2] compares the firmament to a mirror of molten

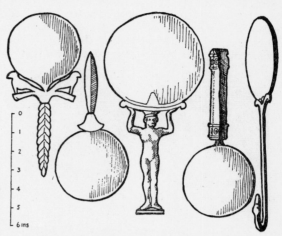

Egyptian, Greek, Syrian and Roman mirrors.

metal.—Several versions mention small mirrors among the toilet accessories listed by the prophet Isaiah; [3] the text is doubtful, perhaps it may rather mean diaphanous materials.

The N.T. also makes only two references to the ancient mirror; [4] the more famous is to be found in the Epistle to the Corinthians: "For now we see in a mirror indistinctly, but then face to face."

[1] Ex. 38. 8. [2] Job 37. 18. [3] Is. 3. 23. [4] 1 Cor. 13. 12; Jas. 1. 23.

MITE

The mite [1] or *lepton* (in bronze) was the smallest coin in circulation in the time of Jesus. 2 lepta = 1 quadrans = ¼ assarion († farthing), and the assarion was worth about ½*d*.

(† Money.)

[1] Mk. 12. 42; Lk. 21. 2.

MOLE

Mole is used sometimes to translate three Hebrew names, of which one [1] may be rather the weasel*, the other [2] the chameleon*, and the third [3] some species of rodent and burrowing animal, in particular, the mole-rat, very common in Judaea, which lives among ruins and stone-heaps or digs long underground run-ways.—The mole properly so-called does not exist in Palestine.

[1] Lev. 11. 29 (1). [2] Lev. 11. 30 (5). [3] Is. 2. 20.

MONEY

1. Before money was minted there already existed a system of exchange which was not merely simple bartering; it was based on an equivalence of value in gold or silver, and in paying for some goods an agreed quantity of precious metal was weighed out. Thus, when Abraham bought the cave of Machpelah he "weighed . . . four hundred shekels of silver, according to what was current among the merchants".[1] The shekel referred to here was a

Tetradrachma of Ptolemy I. The obverse is inscribed ΠΤΟΛΕΜΑΙΟΥ ΒΑΣΙΛΕΩΣ

measure of weight, but it was already also a conventional unit of finance whose status was guaranteed by the usages of the merchants. It was a step towards money minted by the state, guaranteed by it both regarding weight and fine metal content.—This development explains how the same words could have been used for the units of weight and of money, and why the monetary system could have been identical with that for the measures of weight.

Herodian bronze coin, with the words ΕΡΟΔΟΥ ΒΑΣΙΛΕΩΣ

The Bible speaks of talents*, minas*, and shekels* of gold or silver.

There is no information about the grades of the gold or silver used, but we know that gold was worth $13\frac{1}{2}$ to 15 times as much as silver.

2. Coined money appeared in Israel only after the Exile; and even if it sufficed to count it, it might still be weighed.

The most ancient money mentioned in the Bible is the daric*.

Until the 2nd century B.C. the Israelites used the coinage of the foreign countries on which they were

dependent. Hence there have been found in their land coins of the Ptolemies and Seleucids, which were sometimes very beautiful, Phoenician money, and later on Roman. But from the time of the

Denarius of the revolt of Bar-Cochba (A.D. 132–135). Obverse: "Simon"; Reverse: "Of the emancipation of Jerusalem". The bunch of grapes represents Israel.

Maccabaean revolt the first coins of the nation of Israel made their appearance. Unlike these other pieces, the latter did not bear as an image the head of the ruler; but ears of corn, an anchor, olive or palm branches, fruits, the Temple candelabrum, etc., are to be found thereon, usually surrounded by an

Denarius of Bar-Cochba, with the inscriptions: "Simon", "second [year] of the emancipation of Israel", and "Simon [standard-bearer of] Israel", "first year of the emancipation of Israel".

inscription alluding to Israel's deliverance; generally, on the reverse side there is only a second inscription which, like the former, is in old Hebrew characters.

A table of coins mentioned in the N.T. is given below (the equivalences, however, are not rigorously exact).

In bronze:

lepton († mite)
quadrans* = 2 lepta
assarion († farthing) = 8 lepta = 4 quadrans

In silver:

drachma* = 16 assaria
didrachma* = 2 drachmas
shekel* (stater* or tetradrachma) = 4 drachmas

186

In calculations:

talent* = 6,000 denarii
mina* = 100 denarii

3. The evaluation of these coins is very difficult, because neither the grade nor the weight when new are known; moreover, the purchasing power of gold or silver has changed to such an extent over the centuries that even an approximate figure remains conjectural.

However, to give some idea of their value, a rough mean may be taken among the results arrived at *from various methods of estimation*, which gives us the following figures for the value of the coins:

shekel	2s. 6d.
didrachma	1s. 5d.
drachma	8½d.
assarion	½d.
quadrans	⅛d.
lepton	1/16d.

To obtain an approximation to present-day purchasing power, the figures must be multiplied in each case by at least 10.

[1] Gen. 23. 16.

MONEY-CHANGER

Monetary circulation was very complex in Jerusalem (Greek, Roman, and local currencies); and since only Jewish money was accepted for cultic payments, the presence of money-changers near the Temple (they were also bankers*) was a valuable service to the faithful, who, on the eve of the Passover, came to pay the cultic dues; the exchangers also offered service to Jews from all countries who gathered for the great religious festivals. These exchangers, whose love of usury was the cause of noisy argument, had finished by putting up their tables—similar to those still used in Jerusalem and the East—in one of the very courts of the sanctuary, from which Jesus took the initiative of driving them with the authority that is well known! [1]

[1] Matt. 21. 12; Mk. 11. 15; Jn. 2. 15; Lk. 19. 45 does not speak of the money-changers.

MONTH

In the Israelite calendar the twelve months of the year are lunar months, that is they run from one new moon* to the next and last twenty-nine to thirty days; the month started on the evening of the 29th day or the moment when the crescent of the new moon appeared; if it was not observed, the month necessarily had thirty days. At a later period the start of a month was officially announced by means of signals or messengers. Of the two words for "month" in Hebrew, the one implies an idea of

appearance, newness, and the other signifies the moon.

In order to keep lunar and solar years synchronized and to preserve the association between the months and the seasons, it was necessary from time to time to add a supplementary month after the twelfth one.

Before the Exile, the Israelites gave names to the months which were determined by the seasons and which were of Canaanite origin; some of them are found on certain inscriptions; the O.T. mentions only four of them: 'abib [1] (from a root meaning "to sprout") the month of "young ears", the springtime, during which the Exodus had taken place; ziv, [2] month of "the brightness of flowers", the second month of spring; 'etanim [3] (= streams of running water), an autumn month, in which water was to be found only in streams that flowed all the year round; bûl [4] (rain? abundance?), the 8th month.

About the time of the Exile the months are merely numbered, starting from spring (see Ezekiel, for example); later, the Jews adopted the Babylonian calendar, which they have kept up to the present, the names of whose months (all but five) are cited in the O.T.

Post-Exilic Jewish Calendar

1. *nisan*	anc. *'abib*	Mar.–Apr.	Neh. 2. 1; Est. 3. 7.
2. *'iyyar*	anc. *ziv*	Apr.–May	
3. *sivan*	—	May–June	Est. 8. 9.
4. *tammuz*	—	June–July	
5. *'ab*	—	July–Aug.	
6. *'elûl*	—	Aug.–Sept.	Neh. 6. 15.
7. *tišri*	anc. *'etanim*	Sept.–Oct.	
8. *marhešvan*	anc. *bûl*	Oct.–Nov.	
9. *kislev* († chislev)	—	Nov.–Dec.	Neh. 1. 1; Zech. 7. 1.
10. *tebet*	—	Dec.–Jan.	Est. 2. 16.
11. *šebat*	—	Jan.–Feb.	Zach. 1. 7.
12. *'adar*	—	Feb.–Mar.	Ezr. 6. 15; Est. 3. 7; etc.
ve'adar	intercalary month		

[1] Ex. 13. 4; 23. 15; 34. 18; Dt. 16. 1. [2] 1 Kgs. 6. 1, 37. [3] 1 Kgs. 8. 2. [4] 1 Kgs. 6. 38.

MOON

For easily understood reasons the moon has always been an object of veneration, proof of which is amply provided in the history of religions. The Semitic peoples, in particular, had a moon cult which O.T. texts record [1] and which even contaminated the Israelites: the Second Book of Kings states clearly that Josiah drove out the priests who offered incense in the cities of Judah to the moon and the whole host of heaven, [2] and the poem of Job does not conceal the urge to idolatry which the moon exercised as it rose in all its splendour. [3] Thus the O.T. speaks soberly of the moon; it is a work of the Creator, [4] essentially meant to "rule the night", and to "mark the seasons".[5] A certain action on the fertility of the soil was possibly attributed to it;[6] further, moonlight was considered to be dangerous,[7] and certain diseases were attributed to its influence († epilepsy).[8]

While the *full* moon was, it seems, at an early date the occasion for regular rejoicing among the Israelites,[9] while this celebration probably had close connections with the origin of the sabbath*, and while the great Feast of the Passover coincided with the first full moon of spring and the Feast of Tabernacles* with the full moon of the autumnal equinox, it is the importance of the *new* moon that must be underlined here. From the most ancient times the new moon marked among the Hebrews, as among other peoples also, the beginning of a new month; it was greeted with joy [10] and was the occasion of a feast which seems to have been much loved and which is mentioned more than once in the O.T.

In early times, at least, the new moon caused the cessation of work [11] and brought members of a clan together for their traditional sacrifice; [12] the day was used to pay certain visits or to go on certain pilgrimages; [13] the day was propitious for revelations from Yahweh,[14] and we know that at King Saul's court a feast of a sacred character gave particular emphasis to the day,[15] while a special service took place in the sanctuaries.[16] It is a strange thing, and difficult to explain, that the ancient provisions of the Covenant Code and of the Deuteronomic Code make no mention of this feast, though they speak at length of the Sabbath; did the feast contain elements that were incompatible with Yahwism? Whatever the explanation may be, Ezekiel and the Priestly Code refer to the feast: without requiring the suspension of work as on the Sabbath, they give careful directions about the important sacrifices which must be offered on this occasion; [17] these were announced by the sounding of the silver trumpets, the normal thing for solemn occasions.[18] Chronicles always speak of the new moon as a traditional and perpetual institution, inseparable from Sabbaths and feasts,[19] and we know that some Christians observed it under the New Covenant.[20]

(† Month.)

[1] Dt. 4. 19; 17. 3; Is. 47. 13; Jer. 8. 2. [2] 2 Kgs. 23. 5. [3] Job 31. 26–28. [4] Gen. 1. 16; Ps. 8. 3. [5] Ps. 136. 9; Jer. 31. 35; Ps. 104. 19; cf. Jos. 10. 12. [6] Dt. 33. 14. [7] Ps. 121. 6. [8] Matt. 4. 24; 17. 15. [9] Ps. 81. 3; Prov. 7. 20. [10] Num. 10. 10; Hos. 2. 11. [11] Amos 8. 5. [12] 1 Sam. 20. 5, 6, 29. [13] 2 Kgs. 4. 23. [14] Ez. 26. 1; Hagg. 1. 1. [15] 1 Sam. 20. 5, 24, 27. [16] Is. 1. 13; Ez. 46. 1. [17] Ez. 46. 6–7; Num. 28. 11–15. [18] Num. 10 10. [19] 1 Chr. 23. 31; 2 Chr. 8. 13. [20] Gal. 4. 10; Col. 2. 16.

MORTAR

Before they used mills for flour and oil the Israelites, like other peoples (cf. for example Egyptian bas-reliefs), utilized mortars of hard stone (basalt, granite) in which they crushed olives or ground grain which had previously been roasted, using a cylindrical pestle. These mortars survived up to the Christian era for some tasks,[1] and are still today used by the Bedouin. Excavations in Palestine very often bring them to light.

In the Bible mortars are referred to only in connection with the manna which was crushed in them,[2] and in the picturesque statement of the Book of Proverbs: [3] "If you should pound a fool in a mortar with a pestle . . . yet his folly will not be separated from him."—Zephaniah says [4] that a quarter in Jerusalem was called "The Mortar", perhaps because it lay in a hollow.

[1] Cf. Ex. 27. 20; Lev. 2. 14, 16. [2] Num. 11. 8. [3] Prov. 27. 22. [4] Zeph. 1. 11.

MOSQUITO

The Book of Exodus relates that the dust of the earth, struck by Aaron to produce the third plague, changed into small creatures that covered men and animals throughout Egypt.[1] While some translators think of lice which stay on men and animals (v. 18), the majority think that mosquitoes are meant, one of the scourges of Egypt. In any case, Biblical texts only speak of these insects in this passage and in Ps. 105,[2] where the plagues that preceded the Exodus are recalled.

[1] Ex. 8. 16–19. [2] Ps. 105. 31.

MOSQUITO-NET

No mosquito-net is mentioned in the canonical books of the Bible: the object made of goat's hair spoken of in 1 Sam. 19. 13 was not a mosquito-net, as some translators think; it was perhaps a kind of mat, of cloth or plaited hair—the word is unique and the sense uncertain.

It is no more certain that the canopy with which the bed of Holofernes was adorned, according to the Book of Judith in the Apocrypha (13. 9), was a mosquito-net properly so-called.

MOTH

These small lepidoptera, which abound in the East and whose voracious caterpillars do great damage to materials, tapestries, cloth, etc., figure in a number of O.T. comparisons,[1] and also in the N.T. (where "moth" is to be read in preference to "worm").[2]

[1] Job 4. 19; 13. 28; 27. 18; Ps. 39. 11; Is. 50. 9; 51. 8; Hos. 5. 12. [2] Matt. 6. 19–20; Lk. 12. 33; Jas. 5. 2.

MOURNING

Like all Eastern peoples, the Israelites made a great display of their grief; just as they became expansive in the hours of joy, so they gave perceptible form to their troubles. The meaning of some of their actions is not always easy to understand; survivals from a distant past are often involved which were probably linked with the cult of the dead.

Amid weeping and lamentation, the one struck by misfortune, and especially by the death of near relatives, would tear his clothes,[1] as was done among other peoples;[2] even today the wives of some Arabs tear their clothes to the waist. Later, the rabbis laid it down that the tearing should begin at the neck and should not exceed a hand's breadth; it was not to be

Egyptians mourning. Tomb painting of the 13th century.

sewn up again after the death of relatives. Then the mourner put on mourning clothes[3] or, more frequently, bound sackcloth* round his loins, that is he wore a loin-cloth of coarse, dark-coloured material made of goat or camel hair. He went barefoot and bare-headed,[4] completely or partially cut off his hair,[5] shaved his beard or at least covered his chin,[6] and often veiled his face.[7] Neglecting everyday attention to toilet,[8] he would openly sprinkle his head and face with ashes or dust, which he would also throw into the air; sometimes he would even roll on the ground while lamenting.[9] In the well-known expression, "he put on sackcloth and ashes".[10] In some cases, people in mourning even cut themselves till they bled († incision)—a practice finally forbidden by the Law—and beat their breasts or thighs (Is. 32. 12; Jer. 31. 19). Fasting, of course, accompanied any show of sadness.[11]

It is difficult to tell how long mourning lasted;

usually it did not exceed a week, but for a father or mother it probably lasted a month.[12] Jacob was mourned for seventy days,[13] Moses and Aaron for a month,[14] and Saul for seven days.[15] People in mourning were not spared visits from comforters, but these were often silent visits;[16] often today, in the East, friends and acquaintances of the deceased go to the house of death, greet in silence those they are visiting, sit down before them, stay for quite a long time, and retire without speaking a word.

Mourning ended with a ceremony of purification, for everything connected with death and obsequies was considered unclean.[17]

It is known that Jesus was hostile to noisy demonstrations of mourning[18] and that St Paul asked Christians not to behave in affliction like those who are without hope.[19]

[1] Gen. 37. 29; 2 Sam. 1. 11; 13. 31; etc. [2] Est. 4. 1. [3] Gen. 38. 14; 2 Sam. 14. 2; Ps. 35. 13. [4] 2 Sam. 15. 30; Is. 20. 2; Ez. 24. 17; Mic. 1. 8. [5] Job 1. 20; Is. 22. 12; Jer. 16. 6; 48. 37; Amos 8. 10; Mic. 1. 16. [6] Is. 15. 2; Jer. 41. 5; Ez. 24. 17, 22. [7] 2 Sam. 15. 30; 19. 4. [8] Ex. 33. 4; 2 Sam. 14. 2; 19. 24; Dan. 10. 3. [9] 2 Sam. 13. 19; Job 2. 12; Is. 61. 3; Jer. 6. 26; Ez. 27. 30. [10] Est. 4. 1; Dan. 9. 3; Matt. 11. 21; Lk. 10. 13; etc. [11] 1 Sam. 31. 13; 2 Sam. 1. 12; 3. 35; 1 Kgs. 21. 27, etc. [12] Dt. 21. 13. [13] Gen. 50. 3. [14] Num. 20. 29; Dt. 34. 8. [15] 1 Sam. 31. 13. [16] 1 Chr. 7. 22; Job 2. 13; Jer. 16. 5; Jn. 11. 19; Acts 9. 39; Rom. 12. 15. [17] Num. 31. 19. [18] Matt. 6. 16, 18; 9. 23; Mk. 5. 38 . . . [19] 1 Th. 4. 13.

MOUSE

The same Hebrew word covers rats and mice, considered as unclean animals;[1] Isaiah alludes to pagan rites in which, along with pork, rats* (or mice)[2] are eaten. As these creatures were the most dangerous conveyors of the plague, it is interesting to note the simultaneous mention, by the First Book of Samuel, of a grave epidemic striking the Philistines (bubonic plague: † haemorrhoids) and of an invasion of their land by mice; to save themselves they made ex-voto offerings in the form of tumours and mice.[3] Another curious coincidence: according to the Second Book of Kings, Sennacherib's army was decimated one night by a terrible calamity[4] which recalls the pestilence inflicted by Yahweh in David's time;[5] now, Herodotus (II, 141) relates that in his march towards Egypt Sennacherib was held up by an invasion of rodents that made useless in one night the quivers, bows, and shields of his forces.—Many species of mice exist in Palestine and in neighbouring countries.

[1] Lev. 11. 29. [2] Is. 66. 17. [3] 1 Sam. 5. 6; 6. 4 . . . [4] 2 Kgs. 19. 35; Is. 37. 36. [5] 2 Sam. 24. 15–17.

MULBERRY

When one day David consulted Yahweh he was told to go behind the Philistines and "come upon them over against the mulberry trees. When you hear the sound of marching in the tops of the mulberry trees, attack resolutely . . ." [1] The Vulgate speaks of pear trees, and the LXX, thinking of a word derived from the Hebrew verb "to weep", translates: "near to the place where one weeps". This gave rise to versions which combine the two ideas and speak of balsam trees dripping with tears of balm. Because it concerns sounds in the tree tops —or for etymological reasons—the aspen has been conjectured, whose foliage is set quivering by the slightest breeze. Moreover, the Euphrates poplar or aspen is also known as the balsam tree. But the majority of modern exegetes prefer to remain content with the mulberry, although its meaning here is no more certain than in Psalm 84,[2] where the word is used again.

In the N.T. the Third Gospel uses, as well as the sycomore*,[3] another word which resembles it in Greek [4] and which is found in certain ancient authors with the meaning of mulberry; in that case Luke 17. 6 must be translated: "If you have faith as a grain of mustard seed, you would say to this mulberry tree, Be rooted up, and be planted in the sea . . ."

According to tradition, mulberry trees used to be abundant in Palestine, but the Israelites cultivated them only for their fruits. The raising of silkworms, which feed on the leaves of the white mulberry, was introduced into Syrian districts only towards the end of the Roman period, and there it still prospers. Zionist colonies, which began to cultivate the silkworm, have abandoned it; so, without being totally unknown in Palestine, mulberries are cultivated only as ornamental trees.

[1] 2 Sam. 5. 23, 24 (1 Chr. 14. 14, 15). [2] Ps. 84. 6. [3] Lk. 19. 4. [4] Lk. 17. 6.

MULE

From David's time and up to the return from Exile, mules (male and female) are referred to more than once in the O.T.[1] In the early days of the monarchy, particularly, they were held in high regard as military [2] and pack [3] animals: Absalom rode a he-mule in the battle that cost him his life [4] and Solomon a she-mule belonging to his father at the time of his coronation.[5] He-mules were offered to him later as presents.[6] Probably these animals most often came from abroad; [7] there is never any hint of their being bred in Palestine and we know that the Priestly Law forbade the crossing of animals of different species.[8] The he-mule is not mentioned in the N.T.

Contrary to what some translators have thought, there is probably no reference to he-mules in the Book of Esther,[9] nor above all in Genesis; [10] the words for the animals in these texts are quite special and obscure.

[1] 1 Kgs. 18. 5; Ezr. 2. 66; Zech. 14. 15; Ps. 32. 9. [2] 2 Sam. 13. 29. [3] 2 Kgs. 5. 17; Is. 66. 20; 1 Chr. 12. 40. [4] 2 Sam. 18. 9. [5] 1 Kgs. 1. 33 . . . [6] 1 Kgs. 10. 25. [7] Ez. 27. 14. [8] Lev. 19. 19. [9] Est. 8. 10, 14. [10] Gen. 36. 24.

MURDER

In virtue of the *lex talionis* and of the custom of vendetta, the murder of a free man (i.e., with premeditation or by lying in wait) is implacably punished by death according to all the law codes contained in the O.T.[1] It is the avenger of blood († vengeance), the nearest relative of the victim, who executes the sentence, because, according to the law, no murderer can be put to death without prior trial. On the other hand, no ransom could save the guilty party; [2] blood calls out for blood.[3]—The law also reacted against the ancient custom of making a family expiate the fault of one of its members: [4] every one, says Dt. 24. 16, shall be put to death for his own sin († crimes and offences §3).

[1] Ex. 21. 12–14; Num. 35. 20; Dt. 19. 11–13. [2] Num. 35. 31. [3] Gen. 9. 6. [4] Gen. 34. 30; Ex. 20. 5; Jos. 7. 24; 2 Kgs. 9. 26; etc.

MUSIC

While the plastic arts in Israel were reduced to their simplest form, the same cannot be said about music; though it did not reach the level of development which it attained elsewhere and especially among the Greeks, its importance was great among the Israelites, who were sensitive to its beauty and who used it joyously.

Tradition ascribes to Jubal the invention of playing the cithara and the flute,[1] while his brother Jabal was the ancestor of shepherds. Everywhere, and at all times, shepherds have been fond of music; among the Greeks, Pan the god of shepherds was said to have invented the flute, and we know that David was a fine harpist.

No popular or family feast passed without music in Israel, as elsewhere; there was singing and dancing.[2] The court and the great had their singing men and women.[3] During feasts, there was singing to the harp and tambourine; [4] these feasts had their dangers and drew the Israelites into drunkenness and debauchery, so the prophets looked on music as a sign of luxury and dissoluteness.[5]

There was funeral music, too, played at burials and at times of mourning. Perhaps it was originally meant to drive away evil spirits; we know that when David took his harp and played before Saul, the latter was refreshed and "the evil spirit departed from him".[6]

It may be added that music favoured ecstasy; [7] Elisha asked for music one day, and while it was being played "the hand of God was upon Elisha".

Music was also very important in the cult. The

Israelite of olden times knew how to sing to God, how to praise him in dance and in song [8] and through all the sacred instruments. [9]

See musical instruments* for the list of those used by the Israelites; for details about them see the separate articles.

It must, however, be emphasized that the most important form of music was the song*, and that the essential purpose of instrumental music was to underline the thought and to make the sung word more easily understood. It is striking to discover that the use of musical instruments in the cult is especially mentioned in the early texts of the O.T., relatively little in the more recent, and not at all in the N.T. However, this development was probably a corollary of that of the musical instruments themselves, for their potentialities had become more numerous, their sounds fuller and more pleasant, and they had acquired a language of their own, independent of the spoken word; music was self-sufficient and was becoming a means of expression alongside the spoken word and the plastic arts.

[1] Gen. 4. 21. [2] Gen. 31. 27; Jg. 11. 34; 1 Kgs. 1. 39. [3] 2 Sam. 19. 35; Amos 8. 3. [4] Job 21. 12. [5] Is. 5. 12; 23. 16; Amos 6. 5. [6] 1 Sam. 16. 23. [7] 1 Sam. 10. 5. [8] Ex. 15. 20. [9] 2 Sam. 6. 5; Ps. 150.

MUSICAL INSTRUMENTS

Given here is a list of the musical instruments mentioned in the Bible. For details see the individual articles.

1. Wind instruments:
   - bagpipes († pipe)
   - flute*
   - horn*
   - trumpet († horn)
2. Stringed instruments:
   - kinnôr (cithara* lyre)
   - nebel († harp)
   - psaltery*
   - sackbut*
3. Percussion instruments:
   - castanet*
   - cymbal*
   - triangle (?)*
   - sistrum*
   - tambourine*

(† Music.)

MUSTARD

Nothing is said of mustard in the O.T. In the N.T. only Jesus speaks, on two occasions, of this plant, which is very common in Palestine and whose seeds are used to make the condiment of the same name. Both in the parable of the mustard seed [1] and in the forceful saying about faith, that if faith were no greater than a mustard seed it could remove a mountain, [2] the comparison rests on the contrast between the smallness of the seed and the greatness of its possibilities.

While still smaller seeds are known (e.g., of orchids), the mustard at that time represented some-

thing imponderable, something, so to speak, imperceptible. On the other hand, it grew into a veritable shrub in some parts of Palestine, on the branches of which birds could perch, if not make their nests. On the shores of Lake Tiberias black mustard grows woody at the base of the stem and attains a height of 12 or 13 ft.

[1] Matt. 13. 31–33; Mk. 4. 31–32; Lk. 13. 19. [2] Matt. 17. 20; Lk. 17. 6.

MUZZLE

The Deuteronomic Code forbade the muzzling of an ox when treading out the corn. [1] This custom existed in Egypt, as certain monuments decorated with figures show.

[1] Dt. 25. 4; 1 Cor. 9. 9; 1 Ti. 5. 18.

Black mustard (*Brassica nigra*), with seeds.

MYRRH

Myrrh is secreted, spontaneously or after incision, from a thorny shrub, which may become a small tree (*Commiphora Abyssinica*). It does not grow in Palestine, but in southern Arabia and in East Africa, from which it was exported in ancient times to Rome. It is a resinous gum which in the solid, dry state is reddish-yellow or dark brown. Like eastern people in general, the Israelites used it chiefly in the preparation of their perfumes; so it is mentioned a number of times in the O.T., particularly in the Song of Songs. [1]

Myrrh provided a valuable present: the Magi offered it, along with gold and frankincense, before the cradle at Bethlehem, [2] while Nicodemus brought a hundred pounds* weight of myrrh and aloes* to the tomb

Myrrh.

MYRTLE

of Jesus.³ Virgin myrrh—that is, myrrh which flowed spontaneously from the tree—entered, along with other substances, into the composition of the holy oil used for anointing.⁴—It was a Jewish custom to give criminals condemned to death wine mixed with myrrh as an anodyne; Jesus refused it ⁵ († crucifixion).

¹ Est. 2. 12; Ps. 45. 8; Prov. 7. 17; Cant. 1. 13; 3. 6; etc. ² Matt. 2. 11. ³ Jn. 19. 39. ⁴ Ex. 30. 23. ⁵ Mk. 15. 23.

MYRTLE

Myrtle is a sweet-smelling evergreen shrub which grows well on stony ground and is therefore very common in Palestine. At the time of the Feast of Tabernacles after the return from Exile the Jews erected huts made, in part, with branches of olive and myrtle.¹ Along with other trees, it is a plant which symbolizes the Messianic promises.² Zechariah mentions the myrtle in one of his visions,³ but the text is not quite certain. Among the Greeks myrtle was the emblem of glory. Esther owed her Jewish name to it: Hadassah ⁴ (= myrtle).

Myrtle

¹ Neh. 8. 15. ² Is. 41. 19; 55. 13. ³ Zech. 1. 8 . . . ⁴ Est. 2. 7.

NAIL

Nails properly so-called are seldom mentioned in Biblical texts; they must not be confused with pegs, stakes, or hooks, as in some versions. Numerous samples of them, in bronze and iron, have been found in Palestinian excavations. Only five passages in the O.T. speak of them: for the construction of the house of God, David prepared iron in abundance, so 1 Chr. 22. 3 tells us, for clamps and for the nails of the leaves of the doors; 2 Chr. 3. 9 assures us that the nails used in the preparation of the Holy of Holies were of gold; the maker of idols strengthens them by means of nails so that they do not shake, as Isaiah and Jeremiah both declare,¹ and, finally, Ecclesiastes judges that the maxims of wise men, collected together, fix themselves in the mind like well-driven nails.²

In the N.T. Thomas' sceptical words allude to the nails of the cross ³ († crucifixion), and St Paul affirms in a bold metaphor that God has done away with the bill of indictment, which the Law with its many ordinances constituted for men, by nailing it to the cross.⁴

¹ Is. 41. 7; Jer. 10. 4. ² Eccl. 12. 11. ³ Jn. 20. 25. ⁴ Col. 2. 14.

NAPHTHA

This very inflammable bituminous liquid, well known in antiquity, is mentioned only in an addition to chap. 3 of the Book of Daniel in the Apocrypha: the servants of the king of Babylon who, at his command, had thrown the three Hebrew youths into the furnace, stoked it with naphtha, tow, pitch, and brushwood.¹

¹ Dan. 3. 46 (LXX) = Prayer of Azariah v. 23.

NAPKIN

The napkin was a narrow piece of linen,¹ a kind of scarf or handkerchief used for wiping perspiration from the face and also for enveloping the head of corpses.² In the Parable of the Pounds the unprofitable servant kept the mina* that had been entrusted to him in a napkin.³

(† Linen.)

¹ Acts 19. 12. ² Jn. 11. 44; 20. 7. ³ Lk. 19. 20.

NARCISSUS

The identification of this flower, twice mentioned in the O.T.,¹ is probable but not certain. Some translators prefer meadow-saffron, asphodel, rose*, etc.

¹ Cant. 2. 1; Is. 35. 1.

NAZIRATE

As his name indicates (from a Hebrew root signifying: "to separate, consecrate, abstain"), the *nazir* or Nazirite in Israel was a person who separated himself from others by consecrating himself to Yahweh with a special vow.

Originally, the Nazirite vow seems to have bound for life the man or woman who had submitted to it; later it was a temporary vow, of which the Priestly Code carefully regulates the conditions.¹ In effect, the Nazirite must: (1) abstain from wine and all intoxicating drinks, vinegar, and even raisins; (2) not cut his hair during the time of his consecration; (3) not come near a corpse, even that of his father or mother, under pain of making various atoning sacrifices. At the end of his vow the Nazirite had to offer a ewe-lamb as a sacrifice* for sin, a he-lamb as a burnt offering, and a ram as a peace offering, all with the accompaniment of libations and offerings of foodstuffs, then he cut his hair and burnt it in the fire of the peace offering. When the priest had further executed certain ritual acts, the Nazirite was released from his vow. Doubtless, only in part are these prescriptions ancient ones, the Nazirate having become with time an ascetic exercise, a meritorious, ritual activity, to the detriment of its previously pronounced religious character. We have, however, but little information about the Nazirate in the pre-Exilic period: the consecration of Samuel [2] appears to have been of a different nature and the Nazirate of Samson [3] is open to debate, but Amos clearly speaks of Nazirites, whom the people endeavour to deflect from their abstinence.[4] From the time of the Exile, the Nazirate was often practised with the particular aim of gaining certain favours from Yahweh, though doubtless also out of penitence or devotion. Well-to-do Jews facilitated its observance by the poor, by paying the costs of the final sacrifice,[5] in preparation for which Nazirites used a particular little court in the Temple of Herod. Furthermore, casuistry relating to this custom had grown up; a special tractate of the Mishnah is devoted to it, among other things fixing the minimum duration of the Nazirate at thirty days.

Without pausing over the case of John the Baptist, who was probably not a Nazirite, or examining all the hypotheses suggested for explaining the observances which the Nazirate involved and which are met, moreover, outside Israel, it may be said that the abstinence was probably aimed at safeguarding the integrity, the holiness, of the Nazirite: just as wine was forbidden to a priest when officiating, the Nazirite renounced it in order to be more worthy of approaching his God; like the High Priest, he also avoided the defilement of death; finally, the hair, the seat of life or of the divine spirit, the sacred diadem of the Nazirite, could no more be cut than the stones of the altar be defaced by human hands—the hair remained in its natural state until its burning, which ensured its disappearance without fear of profanation.

It is possible that at times the Nazirate marked an attempt to return to the simple life, a protestation against certain abuses, a reaction against certain laxities, but in its essence it seems to have answered a desire for entire consecration to Yahweh; an interesting fact is that it afforded the layman a holiness which was the normal prerogative of the priest. In addition, the asceticism it demanded did not aim, as often elsewhere, at bridling the flesh to make the spirit prevail, but at conserving for the body its complete integrity for the service of Yahweh. Finally, the individualistic nature of the Nazirate must be stressed: those observing the vow formed neither a sect nor an association like the Rechabites*, for example.

[1] Num. 6. 1–21. [2] 1 Sam. 1. 11. [3] Jg. 13. [4] Amos 2. 11–12. [5] Cf. Acts 21. 23, 24.

NECKLACE

Much liked by Eastern people [1] in general, and by the Israelites [2] in particular, necklaces among the latter were very varied, if we judge merely by the different names which they bear in Hebrew. We can get some idea of these ornaments by examining those found in excavations and by comparing them with specimens from Egypt, Assyria, Phoenicia, etc. They were made of very varied materials, ranging from simple shells to the most precious stones and the

Necklaces from Palmyra and Babylonia.

most beautiful pearls; pendants of all sorts and amulets added to their value.

Though the prophets mock at these jewels,[3] the Song of Songs delights in adorning the beloved with them.[4] Among men, particularly among great dignitaries, the necklace was one of the signs of authority.[5] Metaphorically, the necklace was the symbol of wisdom [6] or of beauty,[7] but also of pride.[8]

Amulets fastened to necklaces were sometimes hung round the necks of certain animals—including the camel,[9] strangely enough.

[1] Num. 31. 50. [2] Ex. 35. 22. [3] Hos. 2. 13; cf. Is. 3. 16 ff. [4] Cant. 1. 10; 4. 9; etc. [5] Gen. 41. 42; Dan. 5. 7, 16, 29. [6] Prov. 1. 9; 3. 3; 6. 21. [7] Cant. 7. 1; Ez. 16. 11. [8] Ps. 73. 6. [9] Jg. 8. 26.

NEEDLE

This little instrument is of great antiquity in Palestine, and has been found in excavations; bone needles of the Stone Age were succeeded by ones with bronze eyes made by doubling back the extremity of the shaft, and by iron ones with a perforated eye.

NEST

It is curious that although the verb "to sew" was known in the O.T.,[1] the needle itself is mentioned only in the famous Gospel passage: "It is easier for a camel to go through a needle's eye, than for a rich man to enter into the kingdom of God."[2] Attempts have wrongly been made to extenuate what seems excessive in this paradoxical and entirely eastern figure of speech, by substituting the word "cable" for "camel" (they resemble each other in Greek almost to the letter) or by thinking of the low and narrow postern gate for the use of pedestrians, which flanks some town gates and which may sometimes have been called Eye of the Needle. The vital contrast this saying intended is found, however, in certain expressions in the Talmud, where "camel" is replaced by "elephant".

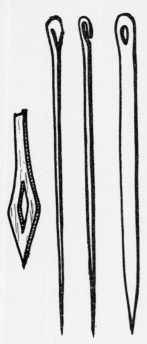

Needles of bone, bronze and iron.

[1] Gen. 3. 7; Job 16. 15. Eccl. 3. 7. [2] Matt. 19. 24.

NEST

Deuteronomic Law forbids anyone finding a nest where a bird is brooding or shielding its young from taking the mother with the fledglings,[1] probably less from pity than with the aim of protecting the species: "Thou shalt let the mother go and only take the young, that it may be well with thee, and that thou mayest prolong thy days."

[1] Dt. 22. 6–7.

NETHINIM

In the post-Exilic literature the servants charged with humble duties in the Jerusalem Temple bore the name Nethinim or Nathinim (= the given).[1] They were reputed to be the descendants of slaves (prisoners of war, etc.) who, in early days, had been given to the priests by kings or special individuals, to do the humbler tasks of the sanctuary.[2] From the time of Solomon, indeed, the priesthood had lay servants and even non-Israelites at its disposal; later on, Ezekiel may have wished them to be

excluded from the Temple as "sons of strangers, uncircumcised in heart and uncircumcised in flesh".[3]

The Nethinim are carefully listed in the Books of Ezra and Nehemiah;[4] some of their families bear names that are clearly of foreign origin. But from the return from Exile, they belonged to the Jewish community,[5] forming a body whose leaders are specially named.[6] They occupied a quarter near the Temple,[7] and an outbuilding of the sanctuary seems to have been reserved for them.[8] The Persian Government exempted them from all taxation,[9] like the priests and like the Levites, whose ranks they no doubt finally entered—for there is no more mention of Nethinim after the early post-Exilic age, and the N.T. never speaks of them.

[1] 1 Chr. 9. 2; Ezr. 7. 7; Neh. 10. 28. [2] Ezr. 2. 55 . . .; 8. 20; (cf. Jos. 9; Num. 31. 47; 1 Kgs. 9. 21). [3] Ez. 44. 5 . . . [4] Ezr. 2. 43 . . .; Neh. 7. 46 . . . [5] Neh. 10. 28 . . . [6] Neh. 11. 21; [7] Neh. 3. 26; 11. 21. [8] Neh. 3. 31. [9] Ezr. 7. 24.

NETTLE

In the three texts where it is found, the Hebrew word often translated "nettle" refers to a plant growing among ruins or on waste land. The field of the idle man is overgrown by it.[1] Isaiah announces that thorns will come up in the palaces of Edom, the "nettle" and the thistle in its fortresses,[2] and Hosea pronounces a similar sentence over Israel.[3]

Yet this translation is doubtful. More than one commentator admits that the nettle is represented rather by another Hebrew word, also found in three passages.[4] And it has been thought that yet a third word must be translated by "nettle" (Is. 55. 13b). It is therefore difficult to reach a decision.

In any case, nettles grow abundantly in Palestine; and their sting is more severe than that of ours.

(† Thorn, thistle.)

[1] Prov. 24. 31a. [2] Is. 34. 13. [3] Hos. 9. 6. [4] Job 30. 7; Prov. 24. 31b; Zeph. 2. 9.

NEW YEAR

The Israelites did not always begin the year at the same time. At first they fixed it in the autumn; then they adopted the Babylonian custom by moving it to the spring, probably for political reasons, but also perhaps in order to separate the old Yahwist Feast of the New Year from the predominantly Canaanite Feast of Tabernacles. After the Exile, the earlier habits gradually returned: at first a religious feast of the New Year was recognized as well as the spring festival, then the religious feast was more and more stressed at the expense of the other; further, the date 10th Tisri seems to have been chosen at first [1] (five days before the Feast of Tabernacles), but was later changed to the 1st of that month. (It may have been a feast lasting ten days, in which the first and last

194

days were made outstanding because of specially important celebrations, but then the first day supplanted all the rest.)

It is thought that at the New Year Festival there was a procession, headed by the Ark, and a ceremony—the principal item—in which God's sovereignty over Israel for the whole of the coming year was recognized; this ceremony was called the "Enthronement of Yahweh". It has even been suggested that Psalm 104 and the first chapter of Genesis may have been liturgical texts in this ceremony. Though this feast seems to have lacked brilliance at the time of the monarchy, it acquired it later: it was announced by the sound of trumpets, and all the people were called upon to take part in the ceremonies.[2] The Day of Atonement* took place ten days after this feast. These two solemn festivals continued in later Judaism and are the greatest Jewish feasts at the present time.

[1] Lev. 25. 9.   [2] Num. 29. 1.

NICANOR

1. *Feast.* On the 13th Adar each year the Feast of Nicanor commemorated the victory of Judas Maccabaeus over the Syrian general Nicanor, who "was the first to fall in the battle" (161 B.C.). The Books of Maccabees do not fail to recount this event, of which Josephus also speaks, but the celebration of this glorious anniversary lapsed in the end.[1]

2. *Gate.* One of the most beautiful gates of Herod's Temple in Jerusalem bore the name Nicanor after its donor, an Alexandrine Jew. It was probably the one leading from the Court of the Women to the Court of the Israelites, but opinions differ about this. (Herod's Temple*.)

[1] 1 Macc. 7. 26–50; 2 Macc. 14. 11–15. 37.

NIGHT

Among the Israelites in ancient times, the night was divided into three watches of four hours each: "I meditate on thee in the watches of the night," [1] says the Psalmist, or: "A thousand years in thy sight are . . . as a watch in the night." [2] The "middle watch" is mentioned in the Book of Judges,[3] the morning watch in Exodus and the First Book of Samuel,[4] the first watch in Lamentations,[5] according to certain translators, but it would be better to render it as "at the beginning of each watch" or "at the entry of the night-watches".

In the N.T. we discover that the Jews had adopted the Roman division into four watches of three hours* each. They are listed in Mk. 13. 35: "evening", "midnight", "cock-crow", and "morning", and more than one text alludes to one or other of them.[6]

[1] Ps. 63. 6.   [2] Ps. 90. 4; cf. Ps. 119. 148.   [3] Jg. 7. 19.   [4] Ex. 14. 24; 1 Sam. 11. 11.   [5] Lam. 2. 19.   [6] Matt. 14. 25; Mk. 6. 48; Lk. 12. 38; cf. 22. 34, 60.

NISAN

The first month (March–April) of the civil year in the post-Exilic Jewish calendar, the month Nisan, used to be called Abib. The word Nisan is used only twice in the O.T.[1] and is not found in the N.T.

[1] Neh. 2. 1; Est. 3. 7.

NITRE

With early peoples it is not a question of nitre (or nitrate) properly so-called, but of natron, a natural carbonate of soda found in Egypt, Syria, and Asia Minor, which possessed purificatory properties; mixed with oil, it formed a kind of primitive soap*. In two vigorous metaphors the O.T. alludes to natron. "Although you wash yourself with natron and are lavish with potash, nevertheless your sin [Israel] will remain as a stain before me [Yahweh]," says the Book of Jeremiah,[1] and Proverbs declares [2] that to sing songs to a person with a heavy heart is pouring vinegar on natron—which would produce strong effervescence; though we perhaps ought to read with the LXX translation: "It is like pouring vinegar on a wound."

It is interesting to note that the words nitre and natron come directly from the Hebrew *neter*, the root of which means "to spring up, to effervesce".

[1] Jer. 2. 22.   [2] Prov. 25. 20.

NUMBER

It is certain that the Israelites were acquainted with numbers from the beginnings of their history and that the decimal system soon took the place of a sexagesimal system, inherited from Babylonia, but some traces of which, however, remained in their weights* and measures. Think of the prayer of intercession of Abraham, who counts down in fives and tens,[1] and remember the importance of the tithe. Moreover, they had names for each unit, for the tens and hundreds, etc., and these, generally speaking, are the terms used by the Bible when writing them out in full.

As for the digits, a system of numbering has been found on the ostraca († potsherd) in Samaria, for the first units in any case; but this system seems not to have been generalized. In later times the Israelites, like many other peoples, used the letters of the alphabet: the units were represented by the first nine letters, the tens by the next nine, the last four letters of the alphabet being used for the first hundreds; above five hundred they used either double letters, the first of which is accompanied by a ·· , or the five letters which have a special form when placed at the end of words. For the first nine thousands they used the first nine letters with a diaeresis above, or simply underlined. Higher numbers were an embarrassment to them, since they often used various periphrases to denote them.[2] With this system, to express the number 15 caused some uneasiness, because, by taking the tenth letter and by putting the fifth immediately after it, the abbreviation of God's proper name was obtained; as people were convinced that words, and especially written words, contained at least a part of the reality they represented, they avoided the risk of finding themselves in the presence of God through writing the number 15 by writing the letters corresponding to 9 + 6.

It must be noted, however, that, for the Israelite, the numbers express approximations of concrete quantities rather than abstract notions.[3] It may be added in this connection that the formula used eight times by Amos, "for three transgressions (of such-and-such a town) and for four, I will not revoke the punishment",[4] signifies that that town has already committed enough crimes, even if one only is cited, for it to suffer the punishment of a sentence of divine justice. Certain numbers (3, 5, 7, 12, 40, . . .) took on a sacred character in Israel, a character which neighbouring peoples ascribed to them in an even greater degree.

In addition, as numbers were represented by letters, efforts were made to establish a relationship between numbers and letters; in particular, the numerical value of the letters of certain names was added up and became a kind of secret pseudonym. The Bible contains an example of this method (isopsephia), with which the Greeks and Romans were well acquainted, but which was Babylonian in origin. Revelation proposes that its readers should "reckon the number of the beast, for it is the number of a man: and his number is 666".[5] This means that the total of the figures corresponding to the letters of the name gives 666. In answer to this invitation, numerical alphabets have been suggested: if A = 86, the number corresponds to Mahomet; the formula A = 55 gives the word "Lutheranos"; this is answered by making A = 73, which gives "lateinos"; with A = 31, we have the Emperor Napoleon, and with A = 100 we find "Hitler". These ingenious procedures forget that the Israelites did not have to make up a numerical alphabet—each letter already had a fixed numerical value; on this basis, the number 666 is obtained by the sum of the usual values of Caesar Nero, and there is every reason for believing that that emperor was meant by the passage in Revelation.

But in the course of the last two centuries before the Christian era the Jews developed these methods considerably by playing with figures and by seeking relationships between the words they represented.

They built up a movement which is called Cabbala, and which is "an extraordinary mixture of sometimes profound speculation with superstitious and extravagant beliefs".

[1] Gen. 18. 22–32. [2] Gen. 13. 16; 15. 5; 1 Kgs. 4. 29; Dan. 7. 10; Rec. 5. 11; 7. 9. [3] Ex. 18. 21; Lev. 26. 8; Dt. 1. 11; 1 Sam. 10. 19; 1 Cor. 4. 15; Rev. 5. 11. [4] Amos 1. 3, 6, 9, 11, etc. [5] Rev. 13. 18.

OAK

Two dozen species of oak grow in Palestine, but the Bible references appear to be essentially to the Valonea oak, a large and beautiful tree whose acorns are very rich in tannin. But Is. 44. 14 particularly mentions the holm oak, a majestic oak which can grow more than 130 ft. high and whose very durable wood is highly valued.

Leaving the oddities of ancient translations on one side, it is a little surprising to read sometimes in our modern versions the word "terebinth" where others translate "oak", and vice versa. From the botanical standpoint the terebinth is quite different from the oak, though also a large tree, and the various Hebrew words used for them both come from related roots which stress priority, height, and sacredness. In consequence, it is easy to confuse these terms, and the Israelites themselves occasionally used them interchangeably.

The oaks of Bashan, in northern Transjordan, were famous for their number and beauty; Ezekiel alluded to the oars made from their wood, used by the Phoenicians;[1] Isaiah and Zechariah make these trees the equals of the cedars of Lebanon;[2] and then, in the figurative language of the prophets, the oak is the symbol of power and might.[3] The abundance of acorns to the north-east of the Jordan explains the breeding of pigs of which the Gospels speak.[4] The hard wood of the holm and the oak were also used, as Isaiah says,[5] for making idols.

In Cisjordan the beautiful oaks grow isolated or in clumps. Because of this they were objects of particular veneration or sometimes of an actual cult, for many people thought that a god lived in them. Hosea reproached the people for burning incense under the oak and terebinth, whose shade was so agreeable.[6] When they settled in Palestine, the Israelites often adopted the sacred places of the earlier inhabitants of the country for the cult of Yahweh. Among these there was, for example, the oak-grove or oak of Mamre, near Hebron, where Abraham built an altar to his God.[7] Still today an "Abraham's Oak" is venerated in this locality. Near Shechem grew the Oak of Moreh, i.e., the oak which teaches, which gives oracles, also celebrated in the Abraham tradition.[8] It was probably under this same tree that Jacob buried the amulets and figurines of foreign gods that his family and relatives possessed;[9] Joshua set up the stele there which was a witness to the covenant made just before his death,[10] and there Abimelech inaugurated his short-lived kingdom.[11] The Book of Judges mentions[12] a "soothsayers' tree", also near Shechem, which perhaps later was identified with the Oak of Moreh. Among other oaks mentioned by the O.T.[13] was the "weeping oak" near Bethel, at the foot of which Deborah, the nurse of Rebekah, was buried.[14]

(† Tamarisk, terebinth, sacred trees*.)

[1] Ez. 27. 6. [2] Is. 2. 13; Zech. 11. 2. [3] Is. 2. 13; 6. 13; Amos 2. 9; Zech. 11. 2. [4] Matt. 8. 30; Mk. 5. 11; Lk. 8. 32. [5] Is. 44. 14. [6] Hos. 4. 13. [7] Gen. 13. 18; 14. 13; 18. 1. [8] Gen. 12. 6; Dt. 11. 30. [9] Gen. 35. 4. [10] Jos. 24. 26. [11] Jg. 9. 6. [12] Jg. 9. 37. [13] Jos. 19. 33; Jg. 4. 11; 1 Sam. 10. 3. [14] Gen. 35. 8.

OAR

Oars, rowing-boats, and rowers are referred to in a few texts of the O.T. and N.T.[1]

(† Ship, rudder.)

[1] Is. 33. 21; Ez. 27. 6, 8, 26, 29; Jonah 1. 13; Mk. 6. 48; Jn. 6. 19.

OATH

The oath was, in general, a form of curse*. He who took an oath prayed that God would destroy him if he did not speak the truth. The words: "as the Lord liveth",[1] implied the conclusion: "so certainly shall I be punished if what I say is false". These were no empty words; it was understood that as soon as the oath was pronounced a formidable potency was let loose whose action could not be arrested.

The Deuteronomic Law recommends swearing by the name of God;[2] and God is called upon as witness.[3] The Priestly Code is indignant at false oaths.[4]

Certain gestures were made on taking an oath: the hand was raised heavenwards,[5] or was merely proffered,[6] etc.[7]

[1] 1 Sam. 19. 6. [2] Dt. 6. 13. [3] Gen. 21. 23; 2 Cor. 1. 23; Gal. 1. 20; Phil. 1. 8. [4] Lev. 19. 12; Mal. 3. 5. [5] Gen. 14. 22; Dt. 32. 40. [6] Ez. 17. 18. [7] Gen. 24. 2; 47. 29.

OBOLUS

The LXX, which some versions follow, translated the word *gerah* (= grain, small Hebrew weight and small coin), used a number of times in the O.T.,[1] by

Massalian obolus, with head of Apollo.

"obolus" (a small Greek coin). Likewise, "obolus" has sometimes been used to render the word *kodrantes* (quadrans: ¼ as [† farthing]) used in the N.T.[2]

(† Money.)

[1] Ex. 30. 13; Lev. 27. 25; Num. 3. 47; Ez. 45. 12. [2] Matt. 5. 26.

OFFICIALS

Although subordinate officials (*šoṭerim*) are found alongside the judges (magistrates)[1] in all Palestine cities from the pre-monarchical period, it was from David's reign that a whole series of more or less elevated civil and military posts were entrusted to outstanding men. They were particularly numerous in the time of King Solomon,[2] but our information about them is too meagre to define accurately their duties or establish their precedence.

The following is a list of the principal dignitaries and officials mentioned in O.T. texts:

1. The *second to the king*[3] and

2. The *friend of the king*.[4] These were doubtless two epithets given to the king's favourites or intimate counsellors, rather than the titles of particular, official functions.

3. The *servant of the king*.[5] What exactly were his duties? It is hard to say. The question is interesting, because a seal has been found at Megiddo, and a seal impression at Tell en-Nasbeh (illustrated under cock*), which give this title to two individuals; and the prophets are sometimes called "servants of Yahweh", not in the sense of slaves, but of some kind of superior official.[6] The "servant of the king" has been regarded as a major-domo or chief of the eunuchs; perhaps we ought rather to think of an adjutant or squire: David, who was the king's armour-bearer,[7] is actually called a "servant of Saul",[8] and Nebuzaradan, "servant of the king of Babylon", is at the same time captain of the guard.[9]

4. *The squire*, the officer "on whose arm the king leaned": in the war-chariot his place was beside the king and the driver, hence the term "third" which was applied to him.[10]

5. *Commander of the bodyguard.*[11]

6. *Commander of the army*, that is, of the contingents demanded by the king from the various tribes, in time of war.[12]

7. *Prefect of the palace* or major-domo, one of the highest of court dignitaries, often referred to, who probably had charge of all domestic affairs.[13]

8. Perhaps the *chancellor*, the *mazkir*, was superior to him, particularly if we regard him as a kind of grand vizier rather than a recorder* or historiographer.[14]

9. The *scribe*[15] was in charge of the royal correspondence with the governors of the country and foreign princes; his importance in antiquity is well known. Two royal scribes[16] are mentioned in

OLIVE

Solomon's time, and no doubt the royal chancellery employed a number of secretaries for copying acts, decrees, letters, and official documents.

10. The *quartermaster* [17] (literally "chief of the resting-place"), charged with preparing accommodation when the sovereign travelled about, unless he was a kind of chamberlain, protector of the royal chamber or tent.

11. The cup-bearer* or *cup-bearers*.[18]

12. The *eunuchs*, guardians of the harem.[19]

13. The governor or *tutor* of the king's sons.[20]

14. The *prefects of the twelve districts* [21] and their head, who was, perhaps, a kind of minister of finance: the division of the kingdom into twelve provinces, superimposed on the traditional tribal system, was aimed essentially at facilitating the collection of taxes and the organizing of forced labour.

15. The *bailiffs* of the royal estates, of which an impressive account has been preserved by the Chronicler.[22]

16. The *overseer of forced labour*.[23]

17. Finally, it should be remembered that the priests* officiating at the royal sanctuary, and their head especially, were all looked upon as servants of the king.[24]

Seal of the "servant of Jeroboam", King of Israel.

All these dignitaries and officials were so many devoted vassals of the crown; moreover, the king often entrusted principal responsibilities to his sons and members of his family. To understand complaints raised against some officials, it seems that among the Israelites this class of society was not exempt from the faults that have characterized the East all too often down the centuries.

Of course, the royal court needed the services of an entire domestic staff of lower grade, of which 1 Sam. 8. 11–13 underlines both the size and variety.

[1] Dt. 1. 15; 16. 18. [2] 1 Kgs. 4. 1 . . . [3] 1 Sam. 23. 17; 2 Chr. 28. 7; Est. 10. 3. [4] 2 Sam. 15. 37; 16. 16; 1 Kgs. 4. 5; 1 Chr. 27. 33. [5] 2 Kgs. 22. 12; cf. 2 Sam. 15. 34. [6] Jer. 7. 25. [7] 1 Sam. 16. 21. [8] 1 Sam. 29. 3. [9] 2 Kgs. 25. 8. [10] 2 Kgs. 7. 2; 9. 25; cf. 5. 18. [11] 1 Sam. 22. 14; 2 Sam. 8. 18; 20. 23. [12] 2 Sam. 8. 16. [13] 1 Kgs. 4. 6; 16. 9; 18. 3; 2 Kgs. 10. 5; 19. 2; Is. 22. 15; 36. 3, 22; etc. [14] 2 Sam. 8. 16; 20. 24; 1 Kgs. 4. 3; etc. [15] 2 Sam. 8. 17; 20. 25. [16] 1 Kgs. 4. 3. [17] Jer. 51. 59. [18] 1 Kgs. 10. 5; 2 Chr. 9. 4. [19] 1 Sam. 8. 15; 1 Kgs.

22. 9; 3 Kgs. 8. 6; 1 Chr. 28. 1. [20] 1 Chr. 27. 32. [21] 1 Kgs. 4. 5, 6 . . . [22] 1 Chr. 27. 25 . . . [23] 2 Sam. 20. 24; 1 Kgs. 4. 6; 11. 28; 12. 18; etc. [24] 2 Sam. 8. 17; 20. 25; 1 Kgs. 2. 27, 35; 4. 4; etc.

OLIVE

1. Together with the vine and the fig tree, the olive is one of the plants characteristic of Palestine,[1] where its ash-grey foliage gives a peculiar charm to the countryside.—For the poor it is a gold mine, because not only can its fruit be eaten (raw or cooked and prepared in various ways), but especially it provides excellent oil widely used in eastern cooking,[2] in which it replaces fat or butter, and which is also used for illumination,[3] for toilet purposes,[4] for

An old olive with hollow trunk.

making ointments or remedies,[5] and for anointings*, royal, sacerdotal, or cultic.—Every food sacrifice had to be accompanied with a libation of oil,[6] which means that it flowed freely in the sanctuary.[7]— Finally, the wood of the olive, yellow veined with brown, very hard, and capable of taking a high polish, was also of value: the cherubim of Solomon's Temple were of wild olive wood, and it was also used for the doorposts of the edifice.[8]

2. Cultivated from ancient time, throughout Palestinian territory,[9] on plain and mountain, the olive does not require particularly careful attention, though some cultivation must be undertaken around

the tree and it must be defended against dangerous parasites. It is easier, the Talmud says, to raise a legion of olive trees in Galilee than to bring up one

Olive branch.

child in the land of Israel. The olive flourishes best on dry, stony, chalky soil, well exposed to the sun, so that Judaea suits it admirably (cf. the Mount of Olives, over against Jerusalem). The olive is grafted

on to a wild plant, and ten years must elapse before the first harvest, thirty before the best; the exploitation of an olive orchard is therefore a long-term affair. It is suited only to a settled population, but is remunerative in the long run, for olive trees attain a great age. A well-developed tree may grow to a height of 40 ft. and give every two years about 20 stone of olives or 6 gallons of oil.—The harvesting of the fruit takes place before it is fully ripe, in September–October; sometimes it is picked, but most often the trees are shaken or beaten. In Israel the olives which remained on the branches were left for the poor.[10]

3. Any extraction of the oil necessitates a preliminary bruising of the fruit. For this they were pounded in a mortar or crushed with a stone roller (a); for large quantities, though only from Hellenistic times onwards, a proper mill was used, with the moving stone turning vertically in a circle over a fixed, hollowed stone (b).

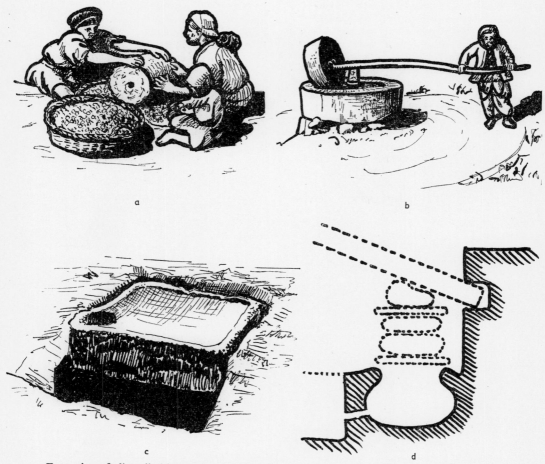

a

b

c

d

Extraction of olive oil: (a) crushing the olives by hand; (b) in a mill; (c) drain; and (d) press.

To get the finest oil all pressure was avoided: the bruised olives were simply put in a basket from which the oil fell drop by drop into a receptacle; or, as is still done in Palestine, the bruised mass was placed in a hollow of rock from which the oil ran slowly through a hole made for the purpose (c); or again, it was sprinkled with hot water, the oil came to the surface and was easily collected. Oil of this first quality fed the lamps of the sanctuary,[11] was used in making cakes for offerings [12] and for holy oil,[13] and it filled the jars which lined the walls of the royal cellars [14]—in the ruins of Samaria there have been found delivery notes for fine oil (strictly, for "washed oil" or "anointing oil") in the palace of Ahab [or Jeroboam II] written on potsherds* or ostraca.

Ordinary oil is obtained by slow and gradual pressure of the bruised olives. No doubt in ancient times the procedure was very primitive, using a heavy stone; true presses, of very varied types, appeared only three or four centuries before the Christian era; owners often set them up in the orchards themselves (cf. Gethsemane = oil press) (d).

Traces of these installations and equipment, from the earliest times down to the beginning of the Christian era, have been found in Palestine (hollowed stones, stones for crushing, mills, millstones, presses), as well as many jars of all shapes in which oil was stored; and even an oil refinery from the period of the Israelite monarchy.

Palestine's abundant [15] oil not only sufficed to meet local needs [16] and was the object of a certain amount of internal commerce,[17] but it was also exported to Egypt and Phoenicia; [18] the First Book of Kings states that Solomon supplied every year to Hiram of Tyre more than 150,000 gallons of superior quality oil.[19]

4. The splendour of the olive is sung by the poets of the O.T.; [20] the tree appears more than once among their metaphors,[21] where it symbolizes above all national or individual well-being.[22] Indeed, the olive is mentioned from the earliest pages of the Bible, since a fresh olive shoot is brought back by the dove to Noah.[23] The oil, too, for the Bible writers, is a figure of prosperity,[24] of joy, friendship, and vigour; [25] but they can also say that the words of a treacherous man are more unctuous, and the palate (the word) of a neighbour's wife smoother, than oil; [26] and to restrain a contentious woman is to take up oil with the hand.[27]

[1] Dt. 6. 11; Amos 4. 9; Hab. 3. 17; Hagg. 2. 19; Jas. 3. 12. [2] Ex. 29. 2; Lev. 2. 4; Num. 11. 8; 1 Kgs. 17. 12, 16; Ez. 16. 13. [3] Ex. 27. 20; Lev. 24. 2; 1 Sam. 3. 3; Matt. 25. 3. [4] Ruth 3. 3; Ps. 104. 15; Eccl. 9. 8; Is. 61. 3; Ez. 16. 9; Amos 6. 6. [5] Is. 1. 6; Mk. 6. 13; Lk. 10. 34; Jas. 5. 14. [6] Lev. 2. [7] Mic. 6. 7. [8] 1 Kgs. 6. 23, 31, 33. [9] Dt. 32. 13; 33. 24; 1 Chr. 27. 28. [10] Dt. 24. 20; Is. 17. 6; 24. 13. [11] Ex. 27. 20; Lev. 24. 2. [12] Ex. 29. 40; Num. 28. 5. [13] Ex. 30. 22 . . . [14] 1 Kgs. 5. 11; 2 Kgs. 20. 13; Amos 6. 6. [15] 1 Chr. 12. 40; Jer. 31. 12; Joel 2. 19, 24. [16] Dt. 8. 8; 2 Chr. 11. 11. [17] 2 Kgs. 4. 7; Neh. 5. 11;

Matt. 25. 9; Lk. 16. 6. [18] Ezr. 3. 7; Ez. 27. 17; Hos. 12. 1. [19] 1 Kgs. 5. 11 (cf. 2 Chr. 2. 10). [20] Hos. 14. 6. [21] Job 15. 33; Is. 17. 6; 24. 13; Zech. 4. 3; cf. Rom. 11. 17; Rev. 11. 4. [22] Ps. 128. 3; Prov. 21. 20; Is. 41. 19; Jer. 11. 16; Hos. 14. 6. [23] Gen. 8. 11. [24] Dt. 33. 24. [25] Ps. 45. 7; 133. 1, 2; 92. 10; Is. 61. 3. [26] Ps. 55. 21; Prov. 5. 3. [27] Prov. 29. 15–16.

OMER

The 'omer [1]—not to be confused with homer*—was a measure of capacity for dry goods. Also called an 'issarôn[2] (i.e., "a tenth"), it was $\frac{1}{10}$ ephah, $6\frac{1}{2}$ to 7 pints (from 6·4 to 7·1 pints according to calculation). Omer means, strictly, a sheaf of corn, and then by extension the amount of grain yielded by a "sheaf"; it is used only in Ex. 16.

[1] Ex. 16. 16, 22, 32, 33, 36. [2] Lev. 14. 10; 23. 13; Num. 15. 4; 28. 5.

ONION

Onions are mentioned only once in the O.T., among vegetables (garlic, leeks) for which the Hebrews sighed in the wilderness.[1] In fact, onions were grown in large quantities on the banks of the Nile; they very often figure on Egyptian monuments. They were eaten either raw or cooked, and were valued for their succulence. Today they are well known in Palestine. Those of the Philistine city of Ascalon have given their name to the shallot (ascalonia).

1 Num. 11. 5

ONYX

1. Probably this precious stone is meant by a Hebrew word which occurs more than once in the O.T. The onyx (Greek for "nail", because its colour is like that of a finger-nail) is a particularly fine variety of agate, marked with parallel and concentric veins of differing colours. (Some scholars, however, think of the cornelian.)

Tradition has it that the onyx was one of the voluntary gifts asked for adorning the ephod and the oracle pouch (breastplate) of the High Priest [1] and among the offerings prepared by David for the Temple at Jerusalem.[2] The second stone of the fourth row of the breastplate was an onyx,[3] as well as the two stones of the shoulder-pieces of the ephod on which the names of the twelve tribes were inscribed.[4]—The onyx has an honoured place in the adornment of the king of Tyre, spoken of by Ezekiel.[5] Genesis claims that this choice stone was found in the land of gold, Havilah [6] (Arabia, India?), and the poem of Job, in a beautiful passage about wisdom, declares that the precious onyx cannot be weighed in the balance against it.[7]

2. The name onyx is also given to the horny shield or operculum of certain molluscs which inhabit particularly the Red Sea. The composition of this oper-

culum is thus akin to that of nail, and hence its popular name of "sweet-smelling onyx". From this operculum, which closes the opening of the shell when the animal retreats inside, there is extracted, still today in the East, a perfume which gives off a penetrating odour when it is burnt. This onyx—sweet-smelling onyx, devil's onyx, sweet-smelling shell—is very probably the "onycha" used in the preparation of the sanctuary perfume.[8]

[1] Ex. 25. 7; 35. 9, 27. [2] 1 Chr. 29. 2. [3] Ex. 28. 20; 39. 13. [4] Ex. 28. 9; 39. 6. [5] Ez. 28. 13. [6] Gen. 2. 12. [7] Job 28. 16. [8] Ex. 30. 34.

OPAL

The opal, whose beauty is produced by iridescent reflections, perhaps figures among the precious stones adorning the oracle-pocket (breastplate) of the High Priest [1] (viz., the first stone in the third row).

[1] Ex. 28. 19; 39. 12.

ORACHE

This plant, with a floral envelope, is of the same family (Chenopodiaceae) as the spinach. It is mentioned only once in the Bible.[1] It is used for food, but its cloying taste quickly nauseates. A species of orache grows as bushes on the shores of the Dead Sea.

[1] Job 30. 4.

ORANGE

Although today it is cultivated abundantly in some parts of Palestine and its fruits are an important article of export, the orange tree is not known in the Bible. Sometimes a tree with sweet-smelling, tasty fruit mentioned in the Song of Songs has been identified with it, but the references are to another plant (apricot or apple but not citron or lemon), because oranges were introduced only much later to the Holy Land, perhaps only about A.D. 1000.

ORION

This constellation—visible in Palestine, as with us, for the greater part of the year—is sometimes mentioned in the O.T.,[1] along with other stars, particularly as one of the Creator's marvellous works.

[1] Job 9. 9; 38. 31; Is. 13. 10 (Hebr.); Amos 5. 8.

ORPHAN

Israelite law always took orphans under its protection; the Covenant Code desired that no harm should be done to widows and orphans,[1] and the Deuteronomic Code, particularly, was very solicitous for those unfortunates who had lost either their

father [2] or their father and mother: not only were their rights to be respected, but they were to share in the great annual feasts and to have a share of the tithe crops.[3]

Probably, orphans often received assistance from relatives, near or distant, or from neighbours and friends,[4] but that their lot was an unenviable one is amply proved by the protestations and threats of the prophets, by the Psalms and the Book of Job: "In you, Jerusalem, the fatherless and the widow are wronged".[5] Justice is not granted to orphans, they are despoiled, and killed; [6] "I will be a witness against those who oppress the widow and the orphan." [7] The curse against the adversary is also significant: "May his children become orphans!"[8] And the comforting assertion, often repeated, that God is the father of the orphans, that with him they will find compassion,[9] leaves it clearly understood that they could not always rely on the compassion of men.

It is nevertheless true that, in keeping with the provisions of the law, the injunctions of the spiritual leaders in Israel are all to the credit of their religion: "Do no wrong or violence to the alien, the fatherless and the widow." [10] "Do not enter the fields of the fatherless." [11] "Be as a father unto the fatherless." [12] In the same spirit, the Epistle of James says: [13] "Religion that is pure and undefiled . . . is this, to visit orphans and widows in their affliction."

[1] Ex. 22. 22. [2] Dt. 16. 11, 14; 24. 17. [3] Dt. 26. 12. [4] Job 29. 12; 31. 17. [5] Ez. 22. 7. [6] Job 24. 3, 9; Ps. 94. 6; Is. 1. 23; 10. 2; Jer. 5. 28. [7] Mal. 3. 5; Dt. 27. 19. [8] Ps. 109. 9. [9] Dt. 10. 18; Ps. 10. 14, 18; 68. 5; 146. 9; Hos. 14. 3; cf. Jn. 14. 18. [10] Jer. 22. 3; Zech. 7. 10. [11] Prov. 23. 10. [12] Ecclus. 4. 10. [13] Jas. 1. 27.

OSPREY

Doubtless the osprey figures in the lists of unclean birds given by Deuteronomy and Leviticus,[1] but translators are not always agreed in their identification; it is the second (or third) of the names listed in either series which may denote the osprey. This bird of prey, with fine wing-spread, armed with a hooked beak and large, powerful talons—from whence comes its Hebrew name—is also called the "fishing eagle". It is hardly found in Palestine outside the Mediterranean coast, the Jordan Valley, and around the Lake of Gennesaret.

[1] Lev. 11. 13–19; Dt. 14. 12–18.

OSTRICH

This creature, which is encountered sometimes still today in the steppes of Syria and Transjordania, was well known to certain Bible writers. The ostrich is, for them, one of the creatures particularly characteristic of wild and desert places.[1] Mic. 1. 8 recalls the plaintive tone of its call (cf. Job 30. 29), and one of the names it bears in Hebrew alludes to its voracity. In a small yet detailed picture, but one reflecting certain popular notions, Job 39.13–18 emphasized the ostrich's speed—"it laughs at the horse and its rider" (v. 18)—but reproves its negligence for its eggs and its harshness towards its young (also Lam. 4. 3); this same passage assumes the bird lacks intelligence; "foolish as an ostrich", say the Arabs also.—The bird figures in the list of unclean creatures in Dt. 14. 15 and Lev. 11. 16.

[1] Is. 13. 21; 34. 13; 43. 20; Jer. 50. 39.

OWL (GREAT)

This nocturnal bird is perhaps the one first named in Lev. 11. 17 and Dt. 14. 16 (cf. Ps. 102. 6), but some translators prefer to see the great owl in the third name of Lev. 11. 17 (= second name in Dt. 14. 16, cf. Is. 34. 11) or even in the first name in Lev. 11. 18 (= third name in Dt. 14. 16). In any case, the great owl certainly seems to figure in these lists of unclean birds. The owl most widely distributed in Palestine is the sparrow-owl, related to the Athenian owl; the Arabs looked upon it as a bird of good omen; it nests in ruins or in the olive woods surrounding villages.

(† Screech-owl.)

OWL (LITTLE)

It is very difficult to identify the birds that were considered unclean, the list of which is twice given in the Pentateuch.[1] It seems that the first and third names that figure in Lev. 11. 17 (= first and second in Dt. 14. 16) denote either the little owl or the great owl, though it is impossible to be definite; some translations accept, no doubt mistakenly, the ibis* for the third name in Lev. 11. 17 (= second in Dt. 14. 16), which is found in Is. 34. 11, where the great owl or little owl is more probably meant than the ibis.—The bird mentioned second in Lev. 11. 16 and Dt. 14. 15 could also be a nocturnal bird of prey, specially an owl, but some versions prefer to speak of the swallow!—Finally, a fourth name, which has reference to the song of the creature that bears it, is commonly translated by "owl": it is found in Is. 13. 21, but according to some writers it could be the jackal.

In any case, several species of owls are known to inhabit Palestine (eagle-owls, horned owls, etc.).

(† Great owl, screech-owl.)

[1] Lev. 11. 13 ff.; Dt. 14. 11 ff.

PAINTING

Painting is hardly mentioned in the O.T. Ezekiel [1] speaks of a kind of bas-relief, the outline of which was marked with a chisel, and whose interior was tinted with the paint-brush to indicate the details of the clothing.—Archaeological exploration, which has found mural paintings in Israel only in a single tomb* at Marissa, has perhaps not yet said its last word on this subject: the paintings in the synagogue at Dura-Europos on the Euphrates which date from the 3rd century A.D. are too fine to have had no predecessors; paintings on pottery*, too, are often very interesting; done predominantly in line decoration, they represent plants, trees, and animals.

[1] Ez. 8. 10; 23. 14.

PALACE

Archaeologists often give the name palace to Palestinian buildings which, in amount of ruins and area occupied, are bigger than ordinary houses. Only large official residences will be discussed here, which, alone, to avoid all misunderstanding, may be conveniently termed palaces. Information about the more sumptuous houses in Palestine can be found in the article on houses.

The O.T. makes only passing reference to palaces

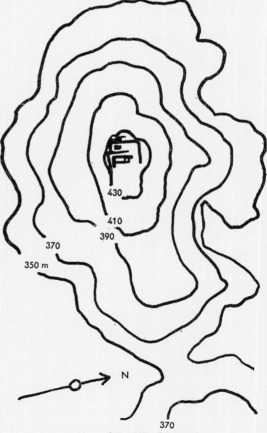

Plan of the hill of Samaria.

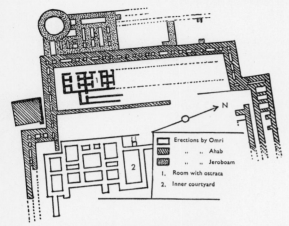

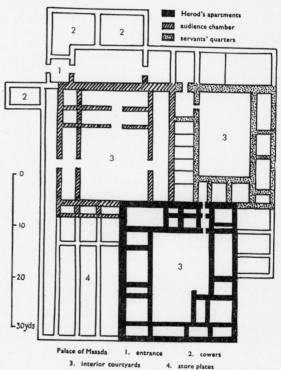

in Egypt, Syria, Babylon, or Persia: they figure on the fringe of some narratives [1] or as the object of prophetic denunciation.[2] But the Bible does little more than mention David's royal palace,[3] or the one built at Tirzah, the ancient capital of the kingdom of Israel,[4] the palace at Samaria,[5] Ahab's palace at Jezreel,[6] Jehoiakim's winter palace,[7] and the palaces at Jerusalem generally,[8] and all the princely dwellings

Plan of the royal palace of Samaria.

in Israel and Judah, which also came under the lash of the prophets' threats.[9]

Only Solomon's palaces receive any description, and we could wish this to be less summary and more precise. From chap. 7 of the First Book of Kings [10] we gather that very close to the Temple, on the eastern hill of Jerusalem, David's son had a whole range of public and private buildings erected, over a period of thirteen years, with the greatest of care and the choicest materials: the house of the Forest of Lebanon, the porch of pillars, the porch of the throne, the palace for his wife, a Pharaoh's daughter, and the royal palace. The text allows us to make only a completely hypothetical plan of these buildings and of their situation in relation to one another († architecture).

A great wall of three courses of freestone, and a course of cedar beams,[11] surrounded the buildings and included the Temple, which dominated them and to which the king could go up from the palace.[12]

Information about the house* of the Forest of Lebanon and the porticoes († porches) can be found under the appropriate headings; as for the sovereign's private apartments, which the author of the text had probably never visited, the Book of Kings restricts itself to saying that they were built in the same style as the other buildings;[13] it is reasonable to think that they were arranged like some Assyrian palaces and that the royal dwellings of Omri and Ahab were similar.

203

The foundations of the last-named buildings were brought to light during important excavations on the hill of Samaria. At its top a rocky terrace had been formed and surrounded by walls. In the southwest corner stood a palace with carefully built walls († architecture), the foundations of which had been sunk to the bedrock; the rooms were built around an interior courtyard. Perhaps begun by Omri, the construction of the Samaria citadel was continued by his son Ahab and was later completed by Jeroboam II; the appearance of the ensemble must have been impressive, and the view of the surrounding countryside from the top of the palace must have been magnificent.

Other palaces more ancient than Solomon's or Omri's had been built in Palestine as early as the Bronze Age; one of them, south-east of Gaza, even had a small bathroom and a sanitary installation. In addition, apart from the commandant's house at

Plan of Herod's palace at Masada.

Megiddo, which is earlier than the Solomon period, the remains of a grandiose palace at Duweir (ancient Lachish) should be mentioned, which dates from the Persian period, and the remains at Masada (west of the Dead Sea) of the palace built by Herod the Great, in which the reception rooms, the private apartments, the interior courts, the ancillary buildings, and store-places occupied a considerable area.

PALM

In his greed for prestige, this monarch built more than one palace besides this—at Caesarea, Jericho, Machaerus, etc. The most famous palace, the magnificence of which has been described by Josephus, the Jewish writer (37–95), stood in Jerusalem itself to the north-west of the western hill.

The Antonia* fortress, also restored by Herod, was citadel and palace combined; and, among other buildings, the Jewish capital could show, between the Temple and Herod's palace, the palace of the Hasmoneans which overlooked the terraces of the sanctuary. The N.T. does not mention it; but in the course of the trial of Jesus there is a reference to the High Priest's palace,[14] which was also probably in the higher part of the city, and indirectly to Herod's palace,[15] perhaps, in which the Roman procurators resided at the time.

(† Praetorium.)

[1] Gen. 12. 15; 45. 1; 2 Kgs. 20. 18; 2 Chr. 36. 7; Neh. 2. 1 . . .; Est. 1. 5, etc.; Is. 39. 7; Dan. 1. 4; 4. 29; 5. 5. [2] Is. 13. 22; 34. 13; Amos 1. 4, 7, 10, 14; 2. 2; Zeph. 2. 13–15. [3] 2 Sam. 11. 2, 9. [4] 1 Kgs. 16. 18. [5] 2 Kgs. 7. 11; 15. 25. [6] 1 Kgs. 21. 1; 2 Kgs. 9. 30. [7] Jer. 36. 22. [8] 2 Chr. 36. 19; Ps. 45. 8, 15; 48. 13; 122. 7. [9] Is. 39. 6; Jer. 9. 21; Hos. 8. 14; Amos 2. 5; 3. 11, 15. [10] 1 Kgs. 7. 1–12. [11] 1 Kgs. 7. 12. [12] 2 Kgs. 11. 19; Jer. 26. 10; 36. 12. [13] 1 Kgs. 7. 8. [14] Matt. 26. 57; Mk. 14. 53; Lk. 22. 54; Jn. 18. 13. [15] Matt. 27. 27; Mk. 15. 16; Lk. 23. 13; Jn. 18. 28, 33.

PALM

The one species of palm which grows in Palestine is the date palm, but it prospers only on the Mediterranean coast, especially south of Gaza, and in the Jordan Valley.[1] No doubt it was more widespread formerly than today, as is suggested by the use made of palms in various circumstances, by the name Tamar (Hebrew for palm) given to certain localities,[2] and by the fact that the palm tree figures on various Jewish and Phoenician coins. The fame of the palm trees of Jericho is attested by several ancient writers, even from the Middle Ages; moreover, the town was called "the city of palm trees" [3] in some texts (like the Tamar of Jg. 1. 16, with which it must not be confused). Josephus believed that these trees, along with many others, made beautiful the plain of Gennesaret. The Book of Judges mentions Deborah's palm tree between Ramah and Bethel.[4]

It must be observed that dates are nowhere mentioned in the O.T. or N.T. (except perhaps indirectly in Cant. 7. 8). While some Easterners go so far as to tell of 360 different uses of the palm, Bible texts speak only of its foliage being used for making booths at the Feast of Tabernacles [5] or waved as a sign of joy and triumph,[6] as well as the palms of gold offered to certain conquerors.[7] Palm branches were waved and spread in front of Jesus when he made his solemn entry into Jerusalem,[8] and the Seer of Revelation sees the elect before the throne of the Lamb

clothed in white robes and holding palms in their hands.[9]

The spiral arrangement of the woody fibres in the trunk of the palm gives it an extraordinary suppleness and a remarkable power of resistance. It raises to 50, 60, or more feet a plume of long leaves whose harmonious curves give the tree an impressive and remarkably beautiful silhouette, still more accentuated at the season of flowering by the appearance of the brilliant golden-yellow male flowers which break forth from the centre of the leafy bouquet. It can be understood how the palm came to be the symbol of

Date palms.

elegance and grace, and that its name was sometimes given to Israelite women;[10] the Song of Songs praises the beloved whose stature is like the palm.[11] The Psalmist declares that the righteous shall flourish like the palm tree [12] (high and straight). The tree inspired certain motifs of the decoration of the Jerusalem Temple [13] (and also certain carvings in synagogues), although we cannot say whether they were simple palm leaves or reproductions of the growing tree or palmettes (i.e., stylized bouquets of palm leaves), after the Assyrian manner.

Because of its peculiar structure, the palm could not be used as wood for building. Even in Egypt, where it is the sole indigenous tree, the trunk has sometimes been used as a support, after slight trimming and squaring, but very rarely as construction beams, and that only at a late period and in small houses.

[1] Cf. Ex. 15. 27; Num. 33. 9; Joel 1. 12. [2] Gen. 14. 7; Jg. 1. 16; 20. 33; 1 Kgs. 9. 18; Ez. 47. 19; 48. 28. [3] Dt. 34. 3; Jg. 3. 13; 2 Chr. 28. 15. [4] Jg. 4. 5. [5] Neh. 8. 15. [6] Lev. 23. 40, 42; 1 Macc. 13. 51. [7] 1 Macc. 13. 37; 2 Macc. 14. 4. [8] Jn. 12. 13. [9] Rev. 7. 9. [10] Gen. 38. 6; 2 Sam. 13. 1; 14. 27. [11] Cant. 7. 8. [12] Ps. 92. 12. [13] 1 Kgs. 6. 29, 32, 35; 7. 36; Ez. 40. 16 . . .; 41. 18–20.

PALSY (PARALYSIS)

Apart from the very special case of Jeroboam,[1] paralysis comes into the N.T. only in connection with the cures wrought by Jesus or his disciples. The malady might affect only one limb (the man with the withered hand [2]), or the paralysis might be more severe, but not complete (the paralytic at Bethesda [3]); the paralytic at Capernaum who was let down from the roof in front of Christ,[4] the Centurion's servant,[5] and Aeneas, of whom the Acts of the Apostles says that he had been in bed eight years,[6] were perhaps more seriously afflicted. Peter healed Aeneas, and in Samaria Philip also restored health to "many that were palsied".[7]

[1] 1 Kgs. 13. 4. [2] Matt. 12. 10; Mk. 3. 1; Lk. 6. 6. [3] Jn. 5. 5, 7. [4] Matt. 9. 2; Mk. 2. 3; Lk. 5. 18. [5] Matt. 8. 6 (Lk. 7. 2). [6] Acts 9. 33. [7] Acts 8. 7.

PARTRIDGE

This gallinacean, whose Hebrew name comes from the root "to cry", abounds in Palestine where a distinction is made between the red (or rock) partridge, with red feet, which breeds particularly in mountainous parts, the yellow (or sable) partridge, much smaller, with orange feet and beak, met with in the desert of Judaea and on the shores of the Dead Sea, and the Francolin, inhabiting the marshy forests of the coastal plain, the Lake of Gennesaret, and the Jordan.

The partridge is mentioned only twice in the Bible: Jeremiah [1] evidently alludes to some popular belief when he compares the man who acquires riches by unjust means to the partridge "sitting on eggs she did not lay"; and in the First Book of Samuel [2] David strikingly says (when the text is emended) that Saul hunts him out "like the vulture pursues a partridge [also translated: wood grouse] in the mountains".

[1] Jer. 17. 11. [2] 1 Sam. 26. 20.

PASSOVER

1. The Feast of the Passover is probably the combination of two feasts which were originally independent of one another:

(a) The Feast of the Passover proper, which was very ancient in Israel; it was a shepherds' feast, and

may have been earlier than Moses. Originally it may have been a feast of the firstfruits of the flock,[1] a feast of thanks to God, from whom came life and the power to procreate. It has been pointed out that it was because the Pharaoh prevented the Israelites from going to offer the first-born of their flocks in the desert that in the last plague the first-born of the Egyptians were struck down, a punishment thus corresponding to the offence—which would show clearly the character of this feast. However, it is probable that this feast of the Passover also sought to assure God's protection of the flocks.

Among the rites of this day was one which was to last through the centuries—the sprinkling of blood: a handful of hyssop* was soaked in the blood of a victim and was then daubed over the lintel and posts of the house-door. (This rite was also practised by many other peoples—Egyptians, Athenians, ancient Germans, etc., and was thought to keep off the demons by putting a part of the sacrifice for them at the entrance of the house.) This suggests the idea that originally the Feast of the Passover was perhaps a ceremony to protect those who were in the house, the members of the family; but when it became a tribal feast, it was more or less combined with the springtime offering of the firstfruits of the flock; it was only later that the link was made between the feast and the Exodus from Egypt.

(b) The Feast of Unleavened Bread, which was an agrarian feast, and therefore pertained to a settled people; it was the feast of the beginnings of harvest. Wafers were made with new corn and were offered to the deities. It did not have a fixed date, since it could not be celebrated until the first grain was ripe for harvest.

When the Israelites settled in Canaan the people naturally adopted the second feast, which they celebrated at the same season and soon at the same time as the ancient feast of the firstfruits of the flock.

2. In the 7th century (at the Deuteronomic period) these two early feasts coalesced, and this Feast of the Passover took place in the month Abib*. As all the religious life of the Israelites was at that time becoming concentrated in Jerusalem, it was there also that people had to go to sacrifice a Passover victim; [2] it is quite clear that the victim could be a big or small animal and not necessarily a lamb.[3] The rite of sprinkling of blood is passed over as if its pagan origin was sensed.

3. At the return from the Exile the rites of the Feast were stated precisely. People must go to Jerusalem, on the 14th Nisan (the new name of the month Abib), and celebrate the Feast for a week. The first day of this week was important, and in the course of it a meal brought between ten and twenty people together, usually from one or two families. Everyone was dressed for a journey, with loins girded, shoes on feet, and staff in hand. The meal consisted of a

roast lamb accompanied by bitter herbs* and unleavened bread. The lintel and the doorposts were marked with the lamb's blood. The command to share in this meal was quite positive, and anyone who absented himself was threatened with death.[4]

4. At the time of Jesus the Feast of the Passover was celebrated in Jerusalem, partly in the Temple and partly "at home", that is in the lodgings that people had found in the capital or in the immediate neighbourhood. The Feast attracted crowds to the Holy City, and many people camped in the orchards and fields in the vicinity.

A tractate of the Mishnah gives precise information about the manner of observing the Feast at this period.

On the afternoon of the 14th Nisan the lambs were sacrificed in the Temple, in the Court of the Priests according to certain rules: blood poured on the altar, skinning of the animal, burning of entrails and fat. It was the first thing that Peter and John did when "they prepared the Passover".[5]

The meal which was then taken "in the houses" was also strictly regulated. When all had washed their hands and sat down, the head of the household took a cup of wine (the first cup), blessed it, and passed it to the others present (at the present day each has his own cup), then each ate a little of the bitter herbs. At this stage the head of the house began the reading of the liturgical texts which recalled the Exodus from Egypt. A second cup was then passed round before the singing of Ps. 113 and 114. Then only came the meal proper, introduced and ended by a prayer from the father. The roast lamb, the bitter herbs, and the unleavened bread were eaten. Then "after supper",[6] a third cup was passed round, called the cup of blessing,[7] and Psalms 115 and 118 were sung: when v. 26 of this last Psalm was being sung, "blessed be he that cometh in the name of the Lord", the fourth cup was brought; it was generally the last. Up to this moment everything was obligatory; everyone had to find the necessary items, and if the poor could not manage to do so, the community had to provide for them.—The evening could end with the singing of Psalms 120 to 137 and the ceremony close with a fifth and last cup.

[1] Ex. 13. 12; 34. 19. [2] Dt. 16. 6. [3] Dt. 16. 2. [4] Num. 9. 13. [5] Lk. 22. 13 par. [6] 1 Cor. 11. 25. [7] 1 Cor. 10. 16.

PASTIMES

Play is not often mentioned in the Bible. At the most Zechariah [1] and Jesus both allude to the children playing in the public squares,[2] and the poem of Job asks whether one can play with Leviathan (the crocodile) as with a bird to amuse little girls.[3]— Some children's toys (animals, clay rattles) have been found in excavations in Palestine, as well as balls, sometimes decorated, dice, pawns, and some sorts of

draughtsmen, all in ivory. At Megiddo several engraved plaques have been unearthed marked with lines and dots arranged in a way that gives every appearance of their being gaming-boards (Fr. *marelle*).

It is certain that the Israelites were fond of dancing († dance) and music, and that, at meals, they liked asking one another riddles*. Some passages of the O.T.[4] give us to understand that certain contests were not unknown to them, that they practised archery,[5] that they liked to handle the sling,[6] organized races, and played ball*,[7] etc.

Small terra-cotta animals; balls, dice, pawns, and a gaming-board in ivory.

The importance of contests between athletes and between animals, chariot races and other competitions in the social life of the Greeks and Romans is well known, and the epistles of the N.T. borrow many metaphors from the different phases of these sporting events.[8]—Further, in the time of the Seleucids a gymnasium was built in Jerusalem itself, where throwing the discus was much in favour,[9] and, later, Herod the Great gave great sums of money for building theatres and stadia († furlong [stadium]) in Palestine and for the sumptuous spectacles that took place in them, to the great displeasure of the Jews, who were opposed to these alien customs.

[1] Zech. 8. 5. [2] Matt. 11. 16 f.; Lk. 7. 32. [3] Job 41. 5. [4] 1 Sam. 17. 10; 2 Sam. 2. 12–16. [5] 1 Sam. 20. 20, 35–39; Job 16. 12; Lam. 3. 12. [6] Jg. 20. 16; 1 Sam. 17. 49; 1 Chr. 12. 2. [7] Eccl. 9. 11; Is. 22. 17; Jer. 12. 5. [8] 1 Cor. 9. 24 . . .; Phil. 3. 12; 1 Ti. 6. 12; 2 Ti. 2. 5; 4. 7; Heb. 12. 1; etc. [9] 1 Macc. 1. 15; 2 Macc. 4. 9–15.

PEACOCK

Five centuries before this bird of Indian origin was introduced into Greece, Solomon had brought it to Jerusalem, where it excited curiosity and emphasized the opulence of the great king. It is true that the meaning of the Hebrew word used in two (parallel) passages, in Kings and Chronicles,[1] is not entirely certain; it figures nowhere else in the O.T., and the N.T. does not speak of the peacock.

[1] 1 Kgs. 10. 22; 2 Chr. 9. 21.

PEARL

Highly valued in antiquity, pearls should have been known in Palestine perhaps from the time of Solomon, but we do not know with certainty what they were called in Hebrew. The Song of Songs [1] speaks of necklaces, into which pearls probably entered, but corals are also suggested. As for the word *peninim* used in the Book of Job [2] and several times in Proverbs,[3] its meaning is disputed: it has been translated, in turn, "precious stones", "rubies" "coral", and "pearls".

In the N.T. there is no doubt that pearls are mentioned in several passages in Revelation,[4] in the First Epistle to Timothy—where women are recommended not to adorn themselves with braided hair, gold, or pearls [5]—and in the Gospel where the Parable of the Pearl [6] is as famous as Jesus' prohibition: "Do not cast your pearls before swine." [7]

[1] Cant. 1. 10. [2] Job 28. 18. [3] Prov. 3. 15; 8. 11; 20. 15; 31. 10. [4] Rev. 17. 4; 18. 12, 16; 21. 21. [5] 1 Ti. 2. 9. [6] Matt. 13. 45. [7] Matt. 7. 6.

PELICAN

The Hebrew name of one of the birds which figures in the lists of unclean birds in Leviticus and Deuteronomy [1] is generally translated by "pelican". Other identifications as wood-owl, bittern, etc., have been proposed for this name, which elsewhere [2] applies to a bird living in the desert and in lonely places; it is impossible to express a confident opinion. In any case, pelicans are well known, particularly in Galilee: they occur in large flocks on the margins of the Lake of Gennesaret, near the Jordan estuary.

[1] Lev. 11. 18; Dt. 14. 17. [2] Ps. 102. 6; Is. 34. 11; Zeph. 2. 14.

PEN

For writing on papyrus († writing §3) or on parchment a calamus was used, that is, a reed stem specially cut for the purpose (*calamus* = reed). To obtain a point which would hold a little ink, a small longitudinal slit was cut at the reed's end, which was then cut obliquely so that the slit was thus obtained at the tip (a). A bronze calamus in the

207

form of a reed has been found, but the tip is much more tapered than any that could be obtained with the plant (b). It was only later, apparently about the 5th century, that goose feathers were used. As a matter of interest, this is how the quills were prepared: the feather was first cut in the same way as

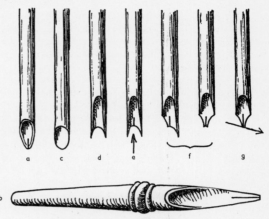

Reed, feather, and metal pens.

the reed (c); then it was turned over to allow a longer cut (d); a short slit allowed the ink to flow (e); then two shoulders had to be cut, one on each side of the slit (f) and closer together or wider apart according to the type of point required; the tip finally received a slightly oblique cut (g).

The O.T. only alludes to this instrument,[1] while John, the writer of the Epistles,[2] gives us to understand that he used them habitually.

[1] Ps. 45. 1; Jer. 8. 8. [2] 3 Jn. 13.

PENCIL

Among the woodworker's tools († carpenter), Isaiah [1] mentions the "pencil". It has been thought that a kind of red pencil was meant, but the article was probably a scriber with a metallic point which allowed lines to be drawn on wood; in any case the root of the Hebrew word used means "to cut into, to engrave".

[1] Is. 44. 13.

PERFUME

The climate, the heat, and their accompanying inconveniences against which people had to contend, explain in a large measure the predilection of Easterners at all times for perfumes and anointing*. Simple or compounded, sometimes mixed into oil which they impregnated, or even into wine, sometimes burnt in special receptacles or acting by evaporation, perfumes in great variety, from antiquity onwards, gave rise to an important trade; [1] the

Egyptians, notably, used great quantities in worship and for the embalming of the dead.[2]—From the time of Solomon, the O.T. texts mention them frequently: the Queen of Sheba came to Jerusalem with camels laden with spices; [3] Solomon received perfumes as annual gifts from his subjects; [4] Hezekiah showed the embassy from Babylon round "all his treasure house, the silver, the gold, the spices, the precious oil . . ." [5] Conforming to the normal procedure, before being presented to the king, Esther perfumed herself for six months with oil of myrrh and for six more months with spices and other ointments.[6] The Song of Songs naturally gives an important place to perfumes,[7] and the harlot used them to gain her ends.[8] Amos reproaches the leaders of Israel for drinking wine from large cups and for perfuming themselves with the most delicate oils, without any thought for the nation's woes.[9] Greek and Roman customs popularized the use of perfumes—the Gospels themselves furnish proof of this.[10] Spices and perfumes played quite an important part in funeral ceremonies and in burials: at his death, Asa [11] was laid on a bier filled with spices, and a "very great" quantity of spices was burnt in his honour; we also know that spices and perfumes had been prepared for the burial of Jesus.[12]

But the cult and liturgy also required the use of choice perfumes; though they were burnt on the idolatrous high places,[13] their smoke also rose in the sacred places of the Israelites and, particularly, in the Temple at Jerusalem, in the adoration of Yahweh.[14] Originally burnt on shovels or in special braziers,[15] the perfumes were offered—from some time before the Exile, if not from Solomon's time [16] († sacrifice, temple)—on a special altar in the sanctuary at Jerusalem, the Altar of Incense which, in Herod's Temple at any rate, stood just in front of the Holy of Holies. Further, although the offering of incense was the indispensable accompaniment of some sacrifices [17] († incense) and some ceremonies [18] († atonement), an offering of incense alone became in the course of time the object of a special regular sacrifice, offered every morning and evening in the Temple; [19] this cultic act is described at length in the Talmudic texts and was considered as one of the most important: the worshippers accompanied it, in all likelihood, with silent prayers which were borne up to God on the smoke of the incense.[20]

Perfume used in the cult was prepared with the greatest of care; [21] it was placed under the supervision of the Levites,[22] and was considered as sacred; any imitation for profane use was strictly forbidden.[23] The oil needed for holy anointing was perfumed as well, and in accordance with a precise and costly recipe.[24]

Independently or not of the liturgical expression: "a sacrifice of a sweet smell", a very common one

in the O.T.,[25] perfume is sometimes used metaphorically by St Paul.[26]

(† Spices, censer, anointing, perfumer.)

List of spices and perfumes mentioned in the Bible:

aloes	cinnamon	myrrh
balm	coriander	onyx
bdellium	galbanum († aromatics)	saffron († crocus)
calamus	incense	spikenard
cassia	ladanum	stacte

(For details see each of these words.)

[1] Gen. 37. 25; Ez. 27. 22; Rev. 18. 13. [2] Gen. 50. 2, 3, 26. [3] 1 Kgs. 10. 2. [4] 1 Kgs. 10. 25. [5] 2 Kgs. 20. 13; Is. 39. 2. [6] Est. 2. 12. [7] Cant. 1. 3; 3. 6; 4. 10; 5. 1, 13; cf. Ps. 45. 8. [8] Prov. 7. 17; Is. 57. 9; Ez. 23. 41. [9] Amos 6. 6. [10] Matt. 26. 6 . . .; Lk. 7. 36 . . .; Mk. 14. 3 . . .; Jn. 12. 1 . . . [11] 2 Chr. 16. 14; cf. Jer. 34. 5. [12] Mk. 16. 1; Lk. 23. 56; 24. 1; Jn. 19. 39–40. [13] Ez. 6. 13. [14] 2 Chr. 2. 4; Jer. 41. 5. [15] Lev. 10. 1; 16. 12–13; Num. 16. 6, 7, 17, 18, 37. [16] Is. 6. 6. [17] Lev. 2. 2, 15; 24. 7. [18] Lev. 16. 12–13; Num. 16. 46–48. [19] Ex. 30. 7–9; Lk. 1. 9. [20] Ps. 141. 2; Rev. 5. 8; 8. 3. [21] Ex. 30. 34–36. [22] 1 Chr. 9. 29. [23] Ex. 30. 36–38. [24] Ex. 30. 23–24; Is. 43. 24; Jer. 6. 20. [25] Ex. 29. 18; Lev. 1. 9; Ezr. 6. 10; Ez. 20. 41, etc.; cf. Gen. 8. 21. [26] 2 Cor. 2. 14–16; Eph. 5. 2; Phil. 4. 18.

PERFUMER

This trade is mentioned in a few O.T. texts. More than once the Book of Exodus speaks of the perfumer's art; [1] Samuel predicts to the Israelites that the king they desire will take their daughters as perfumers, cooks, and bakers; [2] a corporation of perfumers is mentioned in the Book of Nehemiah; [3] the Book of Job may allude to the "perfumer's cauldron",[4] and Ecclesiastes declares that a dead fly taints the perfumer's oil.[5]

According to the Mishnah, the preparation of cultic perfume was in the later period entrusted to a family which had specialized in this art and which had kept to itself certain technical secrets; the way in which the smoke from this family's perfume rose straight up to heaven was especially admired.

[1] Ex. 30. 25, 35; 37. 29. [2] 1 Sam. 8. 13. [3] Neh. 3. 8. [4] Job 41. 20. [5] Eccl. 10. 1.

PESTILENCE (PLAGUE)

The O.T. language has no specific words to denote plague, typhus, cholera, etc. Without distinguishing one from the others, it uses different terms implying the idea of destruction and death when speaking of them. However, bubonic plague is not always and necessarily meant in the many Biblical texts in which the word "plague" appears, but epidemics which brought fear through their virulent character, their rapid spreading, and their ravages. The best known are those which struck the Israelites under David [1] and the Assyrian army in the time of Hezekiah,[2] without forgetting the fifth and sixth plagues which befell the Egyptians.[3] Elsewhere, it is merely a threat when these scourges are mentioned;[4] the trilogy "by sword, by famine and by pestilence" is a set formula in the mouths of Jeremiah and Ezekiel.[5]

[1] 2 Sam. 24. 15. [2] 2 Kgs. 19. 35. [3] Ex. 9. 1 ff.; Amos 4. 10. [4] Ex. 5. 3; Lev. 26. 25; Num. 14. 12; Dt. 28. 21; 32. 24; 1 Kgs. 8. 37, etc.; Lk. 21. 11. [5] Jer. 14. 12; 21. 7; 24. 10, etc.; Ez. 7. 15; 12. 16; cf. 2 Sam. 24. 13.

PHARISEES

The tendencies characteristic of the Pharisees had their origin in the religious transformations which took place in Israel after the return from the Exile and which are usually associated with the names of Ezra and Nehemiah. At that time there was a desire to restore the Law, or more exactly the good, holy, and righteous Israelite doctrine, as it was believed to have been received from God through Moses. This Law assumed the principle of God's sovereignty, and rules were then based on it for everyday living. Obviously those who held these principles could do nothing other than revolt against the attempts of the Seleucids, and particularly Antiochus Epiphanes, to hellenize Palestine by force. They constituted a party of "pious" people (the Hasidim, a word rendered in some versions by Chasidim or Hasidaeans) who were the core of the Maccabaean resistance. But they also became fiercely nationalist in politics, and in religion assiduously attached to the Law[1] and to the rules of the Priestly Code. As they felt themselves the *élite* of the nation,[2] and distinguished themselves from the people by their pietistic tendencies and their strict observance of all the rites and dogmas (including that of resurrection), the people, who never lacked perspicacity, began calling them "the sectarians", that is "the separated ones", which in Hebrew is "Pharisees". They did not object to this title, believing perhaps that it showed respect for their virtues; they intervened in politics as the repositories of religious truth, and took part in governments of the country for nearly a century and a half. As they seemed to know God's Law better than anyone else and strove to carry it out, the people did not stint their admiration—and thus increased the Pharisees' power.

The religious zeal of the Pharisees and Scribes*, who were often associated with them, led them to explain the Law so that it could be applied, to compare and discuss the sometimes very interesting judgments which such-and-such a master had drawn from it. But in order to apply the Law of Moses to a way of life which had been greatly changed by more than a thousand years of history, new arrangements were needed, adaptations, which degenerated into casuistry, and which formed the tradition—a tradition which was accorded as much if not more authority than the Law itself—against which Jesus

spoke.[3] In its development this tradition ended by forming the Talmudic literature.

But though we may ascribe to the Pharisees a place of eminence in history (they saved the Israelite religion from the tide of Hellenism) and recognize their religious zeal (they founded the Jewish mission[4]) and their sense of God's sovereignty, we must deplore their attachment to the letter of the Law rather than to its spirit,[5] an obedience to God that was formal rather than filial. To change the Law into casuistry is to dominate the Law by one's own desires; it is to satisfy oneself while claiming to obey God. This is why the word Pharisee became synonymous with hypocrite. The attachment of these people to the exterior practices of the cult († phylactery), to places of honour,[6] and their habit of being more interested in the form than in the matter,[7] gave the impression that they were always playing a part and were doing it at least to glorify what they knew and believed, if not to glorify themselves.

Everyone knows the reproaches that this pride and hypocrisy evoked upon the Pharisees from Jesus,[8] and we understand why the apostle Paul, after being a very devoted Pharisee,[9] later looked on this connection as a disadvantage.[10]

[1] 1 Macc. 2. 42. [2] 1 Macc. 7. 13. [3] Mk. 7. 8–13. [4] Matt. 23. 15. [5] Lk. 14. 1–6. [6] Matt. 23. 6. [7] Matt. 23. 25. [8] Matt. 23. [9] Acts 23. 6; 26. 5; Phil. 3. 5. [10] Phil. 3. 7.

PHIAL

Twice only in the O.T. is there mentioned a small flask filled with oil for anointing a king.[1] No details are given of the form or material of these phials, parallels to which may doubtless be found in the collections of all kinds of vessels which Palestinian excavations have enabled us to form. On the other hand, it is known that the horns* of some animals were used as receptacles for precious oil or perfume.[2]

[1] 1 Sam. 10. 1; 2 Kgs. 9. 1–3. [2] 1 Sam. 16. 1; 1 Kgs. 1. 39.

PHYLACTERY

Phylacteries (a Greek word derived from the verb "to protect" and meaning "a means of guarding, of protection; a safeguard, an amulet") or *tephillin* (from a Hebrew word meaning "prayer") were small boxes or capsules, made of leather and cubic in shape, and containing four passages from the Law; when they said their daily prayers, the Jews fastened them to their left arm or forehead with long leather thongs. The believer first fastened one on his arm a little above the elbow and facing the heart, by carefully binding the thongs around the forearm, the hand, and the middle finger; then he fastened the second phylactery to the middle of his forehead, where it was held in place by two thongs knotted at

O

the back of the head; the ends of the thongs hung over the shoulders down to the chest. The capsule on the forehead, the more important of the two, contained four compartments; in each one lay a tiny roll of parchment on which was written one of the four prescribed passages of Scripture; the little box on the arm had only one compartment with a single parchment bearing the same four passages, namely: Ex. 13. 1–10 (the Passover law), Ex. 13. 11–16 (consecration of the first-born), Dt. 6. 4–9 (on loving God), and Dt. 11. 13–21 (obedience to the commandments).

The use of phylacteries is based on the injunctions, literally interpreted, which end these four passages: "and these words which I command you this day shall be upon your heart . . . you shall bind them as a sign upon your hand, and they shall be as frontlets between your eyes". But this custom dates only from the last centuries before Christ; there is no reference to it in the O.T. In the N.T. Jesus remarks that, to be noticed by men, the Pharisees broaden their phylacteries [1] (thongs and capsules), though he does not condemn their use.

The orthodox Jew attached great importance to the *tephillin*; everything concerning them was set down in minute detail in the Talmudic writings. Women could use them, though they were not enjoined to do so. They were not worn on the Sabbath or on feast days, since the occasion was sufficient in itself to remind believers of the Law.

It is possible that phylacteries were a sort of substitute for the amulets so dear to Eastern peoples or to the tattoo marks which, in primitive times, were a sign of devotion to the deity.

[1] Matt. 23. 5.

PIG

Perhaps for reasons of hygiene, but especially because the pig played a particular part in certain foreign cults, it was regarded by the Israelites as unclean.[1] When in Maccabaean times the persecutors of the Jews attempted to compel them to eat pork many preferred to die rather than break the Law.[2] Some Jewish doctors even forbade the breeding of pigs; the herds mentioned in Matt. 8. 30, Mk. 5. 11, Lk. 8. 32 and 15. 15 either belonged to non-Jews or to lax Jews, but when Christ made the prodigal son feed swine he did it most certainly to stress the misery into which the unhappy man had fallen. The pig was even taken as a figure for impurity.[3] A saying about the sow is known which had probably become proverbial;[4] and in particular there is the forceful expression of Jesus: "Do not cast your pearls before swine." [5]

Aversion to pigs is found among other people than the Jews; Mohammedans, notably, completely abstain from eating pork. Consequently at the present time the breeding of pigs in Palestine is very limited.

[1] Lev. 11. 7; Dt. 14. 8; Is. 65. 4; 66. 17. [2] 2 Macc. 6. 18 . . .; 7. 1 . . .; cf. 1 Macc. 1. 50. [3] Prov. 11. 22; Is. 66. 3. [4] 2 Pet. 2. 22. [5] Matt. 7. 6.

PILLAR

Semitic peoples often had cultic places near certain stones which, in origin or form, seemed mysterious.

Nowhere in the Bible is any sacred stone expressly recognizable as a meteorite; on the other hand, it speaks of table-rocks and some natural standing-stones. There is the stone of Ophrah,[1] near Shechem, the stone of Gibeon,[2] that of Beth-Shemesh,[3] but especially the rock of Jerusalem, purchased by David as the site of an altar, the same level "threshing-floor" on which Solomon built his Temple.[4]

But it is clear that Israel was especially familiar with mazzebahs, stones artificially erected. (Note in passing that the menhir is a pillar, and doubtless the obelisk as well.) We know that Jacob set up a stone and poured oil upon it.[5] Some of these stones appeared to be essentially commemorative—they were reminders of a covenant between tribes and consequently marked the frontier between them; [6] they could be funeral monuments [7] or memorials of battles.[8] The same word (*matstsebah*, mazzebah) is used to denote the twelve stones taken by Moses to build an altar,[9] and also for those set up by Joshua after crossing the Jordan.[10] Originally these stones were probably the only objects in the Israelite sanctuary. Later the prophets inveighed against them, the more so because later they seem to have been looked on as deities.[11] It is possible that some of the stones may have been kissed by worshippers.[12] Later a certain king was praised because he got rid of the pillars from the high places.[13]

(For their form, see asherah*).

[1] Jg. 6. 11 ff. [2] 2 Sam. 20. 8. [3] 1 Sam. 6. 14. [4] 2 Sam. 24. 21; 1 Chr. 21. 15. [5] Gen. 28. 18. [6] Gen. 31. 45; Is. 19. 19. [7] Gen. 35. 20; 1 Sam. 15. 12; 2 Sam. 18. 18. [8] 1 Sam. 7. 12. [9] Ex. 24. 4. [10] Jos. 4. 1–9. [11] Jer. 2. 27; Hos. 3. 4; 10. 2. [12] 1 Kgs. 19. 18. [13] 2 Kgs. 18. 4.

PINE

The only passage in the Bible where several translations, including the LXX and Vulgate, allow a reference to this tree, is in the Book of Isaiah; [1] but the Hebrew word used is too uncertain for an assured opinion. Some scholars suggest ash, cypress*, or, more acceptably, laurel*.

[1] Is. 44. 14 end.

PINNACLE

"Pinnacle" comes from a Latin word meaning "wing", "battlement". The "pinnacle of the

Temple" which is referred to in the account of the temptation of Jesus [1] apparently means neither the entrance gate of the Temple proper nor the topmost point of the building; it was probably at the south-east corner of the portico which surrounded the Court of the Gentiles; this place, where some people think a tower once stood, overlooked a sheer drop deep into the Kidron Valley.

[1] Matt. 4. 5; Lk. 4. 9.

PIPE

Flutes* bear various names in the O.T. It is likely that one of these, used only four times,[1] meant the pipe, the pastoral or shepherd's pipe, often made from the simple tube of a reed or bark, pierced or not by a number of holes, or made of wood, bone, or ivory.—Some scholars think that it is rather Pan's pipes which are meant, composed of several pipes that the player moves along his lower lip. Tradition holds to the bagpipes, but these appear only belatedly [2] and do not figure on Assyrian or Egyptian monuments.

[1] Gen. 4. 21; Job 21. 12; 30. 31; Ps. 150. 4. [2] Cf. Dan. 3. 5.

PISTACHIO

Pistachio nuts figure among the choice products of the land, sent by Jacob to the governor of Egypt.[1] Although abundant in Syria, the pistachio is rare today in Palestine.

[1] Gen. 43. 11.

PIT

We must distinguish between:

1. The pit, dug by hunters as a trap, which was a large hole covered with branches towards which big game were driven or lured by a bait. In metaphorical language the O.T. often alludes to this snare:[1] "He who digs a pit will fall into it," says the Book of Proverbs,[2] and the Psalm [3] rejoices over the nations which "have sunk in the pit which they made".

2. The pit used as a cistern* and eventually as a rather miry prison.[4] Jesus was probably thinking of a cistern left open by negligence when he spoke of the "pit" into which a child or an ox may fall,[5] while elsewhere, although the word "pit" is used, an ordinary hole in the ground is meant.[6]

3. The pit used as a tomb in which dead bodies were placed.[7] Thus the word pit is very often a synonym of death and corruption:[8] "Thou wilt not abandon my soul to Sheol, or let thy godly one see the pit,"[9] says Ps. 16.

4. The lions' pit immortalized in the story of Daniel [10] is not easy to reconstruct from reading the text. It has been suggested that it was quite spacious

and open to the sky and that a single lateral door gave access to it; but the author seems to think of it as an underground place, a kind of cistern, and as having an opening at the top, which could be closed by a stone.

[1] Ps. 7. 15; 35. 7; 57. 6; Prov. 22. 14; 23. 27; 28. 10; Eccl. 10. 8; Jer. 18. 20; 48. 43; Ez. 19. 4, 8. [2] Prov. 26. 27. [3] Ps. 9. 15. [4] Gen. 37. 20; 2 Kgs. 3. 16; Ps. 40. 2; Jer. 38. 6; Zech. 9. 11. [5] Lk. 14. 5. [6] Matt. 12. 11; 15. 14; Lk. 6. 39. [7] 2 Sam. 18. 17. [8] Ps. 28. 1; 103. 4; 107. 20; Is. 14. 15; 38. 17; Ez. 26. 20. [9] Ps. 16. 10. [10] Dan. 6. 16 ff.

PITCH

This resinous substance was known to the Israelites, but it is only mentioned twice in the Hebrew text of the O.T.;[1] the papyrus basket in which Moses was exposed had been smeared with bitumen and pitch to make it watertight.

[1] Ex. 2. 3; Is. 34. 9.

PITCHER

The Israelites naturally used for different purposes a whole range of earthenware vessels of various sizes and shapes (pottery*). The pitcher proper generally had two handles and was carried on the shoulder or on the head and was mainly used for carrying and keeping water. But as excavation has abundantly shown, and particularly the articles found in tombs, the Palestinians were for centuries familiar with a remarkable variety of smaller pitchers, jugs large and small, etc., varying in style, with flat, rounded, or pointed bottoms, decorated or plain, without handles or with one or two handles, and made from black, grey, red, or ochre clays.

In the East no one went to bed without a little water within arm's reach; the Bedouin of the desert sleeps beside his pitcher of water and his spear, which is stuck in the ground; this explains the episode in 1 Sam. 26. 7–11. Pitchers are also mentioned several times in Biblical texts, whether scenes around wells are being described [1] or Gideon's stratagem to frighten the enemy.[2] A jar and a pitcher were used by the widow of Zarephath to store her flour and oil.[3]

In his allegorical description of old age Ecclesiastes [4] compares the body, struck down by death, to a pitcher broken at the fountain.

[1] Gen. 24. 11 . . .; Jn. 4. 28. [2] Jg. 7. 16, 20. [3] 1 Kgs. 17. 12 . . .; cf. 1 Kgs. 18. 33; 19. 6; Mk. 14. 13. [4] Eccl. 12. 6.

PLANE

This tree, more widespread in Syria than in Palestine, is referred to in only two passages of the O.T.,[1] but the identification of its Hebrew name is fairly certain.

(† Chestnut.)

[1] Gen. 30. 37; Ez. 31. 8.

PLEDGE

As surety of a debt or a loan, the Israelites deposited some object with their creditor,[1] but first the Covenant Code and then the Deuteronomic Code made interesting provisions on behalf of debtors obliged to make such pledges. As a result the creditor had no right to enter the house of his neighbour to take a pledge, he had to wait outside until it was brought to him;[2] both millstones could never be taken in pledge, not even the movable (upper) one: "it would be taking a life in pledge",[3] for the grain for bread-making was ground each day; a widow's garment could not be seized[4] and a cloak taken in pledge had to be returned to its owner before sunset, "for that is his only covering . . . in what else shall he sleep? . . . And if he cries to me, I will hear, for I am compassionate".[5]

But the law was not always respected, and the prophets often had to take up the defence of the wronged, and to curb abuses.[6]

In the time of Nehemiah some Jews complained of being obliged to give in pledge their sons and daughters († slave §2) in order to obtain corn, and to pledge their fields, vineyards, and houses[7]—real mortgages.

[1] Gen. 38. 17–18; Prov. 20. 16; 27. 13. [2] Dt. 24. 10–11. [3] Dt. 24. 6. [4] Dt. 24. 17. [5] Ex. 22. 26–27; Dt. 24. 13. [6] Job 22. 6; 24. 3; Ez. 18. 7, 12, 16; 33. 15. [7] Neh. 5. 2, 3.

PLEIADES

This constellation is very probably invoked three times[1] in the O.T. to the glory of the Creator. Its Hebrew name means: heaping up, a heap.

[1] Job 9. 9; 38. 31; Amos 5. 8.

PLOUGH

The plough used today by many fellaheen in Palestine is very similar to the one formerly used by the Israelites. Simple and slight, it had no wheels and scratched the soil rather than turned it; it was made of pieces of wood roughly squared and assembled—a coulter made from a curved piece of wood, fitted with a handle and tipped, at the lower end, with an iron ploughshare, was the essential part; halfway along its length, the coulter passed through the frame-bar, to which it was fixed by a wooden strut. This assembly was bound to the plough and beam (shaft) to which the yoke was attached, and among the Israelites was drawn by two oxen or two asses (elsewhere by an ox and an ass, horses or camels). With one hand the peasant held the coulter handle, and with the other he urged his animals on with a goad*, which was also useful for breaking up clods of earth. It is well known that the law forbade Jews to yoke to the plough two animals of different species.[1] Egyptian and Babylonian

ploughs pictured on different ancient monuments were of the same type as those used in Palestine, but the coulter had two handles instead of one.

Naturally no ancient ploughs have been found in Palestinian excavations, since they were made of wood; but ploughshares have been found—all made of iron; presumably in the Bronze Age the entire

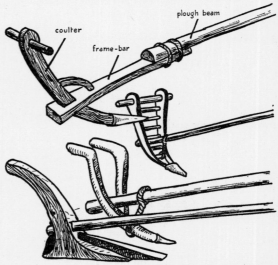

Various forms of ploughs (Egyptian, Assyrian and Palestinian).

coulter was made of wood and merely had its tip hardened in the fire. The Philistines probably played an important part in the introduction to Palestine of iron ploughshares.[2]

It is a curious fact that the word for plough does not appear in the O.T.; it is found only once in the N.T.: "No one who puts his hand to the plough and looks back is fit for the kingdom of God."[3] On the other hand, ploughing and ploughmen († agriculture) are often mentioned in the Bible.

[1] Dt. 22. 10. [2] Cf. 1 Sam. 13. 20. [3] Lk. 9. 62.

PLUMB-LINE

This implement, which goes back to remote antiquity, was doubtless well known to the Israelites, but it is never clearly described in the O.T.

Probably Is. 34. 11, speaking of "stones" of destruction, means the weights of plumb-lines. But could the "stone of tin" of Zech. 4. 10 also be one? Opinions differ. As for the vision of Amos 7. 7–8, some commentators believe that the plummet mentioned in this text should not be equated with the builder's implement, and that it may rather have been a metal weight with which Yahweh would crush his people.

Then in other passages it is less a matter of a

plumb-line as such than of a level* with which, moreover, it might be combined.

POLITENESS

Like all Eastern people, the Israelites made much of form, appearance, external dignity; their courtesy conventions may seem exaggerated at times, but they lack neither charm nor value.—Greetings exchanged by people who met on the road, or especially those exchanged after separations long or short, were accompanied by forms of blessing*,[1] expressive gestures, kisses*, and by lengthy and reciprocal exchanges of news.[2]—The greatest deference was due to superiors: a man must dismount before them,[3] always bow respectfully once, three times, seven times;[4] according to the other's rank, he must prostrate himself before him and kiss his feet,[5] while calling him lord and father, and at the same time he would style himself as a servant, a slave or even as a dog.[6]—Special respect was paid to the aged.[7] Visits required various mutual attentions (washing of feet, anointing*, perfume*, feasting [† feast]); the host hurried to meet his guests [8] and led them in; [9] and, just as they had often offered gifts at their arrival, they did not leave empty-handed.[10]—Even commercial transactions involved ceremonious palaver.[11]

(† Hospitality.)

[1] Gen. 43. 29; Jg. 6. 12; 19. 20; Ruth 2. 4; 1 Sam. 25. 6; 2 Kgs. 10. 15. [2] Gen. 29. 11, 13; Ex. 4. 27; 18. 7; 2 Sam. 20. 9; 2 Kgs. 4. 26 (cf. 2 Kgs. 4. 29; Lk. 10. 4). [3] Gen. 24. 64; 1 Sam. 25. 23. [4] Gen. 18. 2; 19. 1; 33. 3; 1 Sam. 20. 41; 2 Sam. 1. 2. [5] 2 Sam. 9. 6; 2 Kgs. 4. 27; Matt. 28. 9. [6] Gen. 18. 3; 24. 18; 33. 5; 42. 11; 1 Sam. 26. 18; 2 Sam. 24. 21; 2 Kgs. 2. 12; 6. 21; 8. 13; 13. 14. [7] Lev. 19. 32. [8] Gen. 18. 2; 19. 1; 29. 13; Ex. 18. 7. [9] 2 Sam. 19. 31. [10] Gen. 33. 10; 43. 11; 1 Sam. 17. 18. [11] Gen. 23. 3–16.

POMEGRANATE

This little tree, with its fine scarlet-red flowers and succulent fruit, has always been one of the plants characteristic of Palestine: "Yahweh", said Moses to Israel, "is bringing you into a land . . . of wheat and barley, and vines and fig trees and pomegranates",[1] and the spies sent from the desert into the land of Canaan returned not only with a magnificent bunch of grapes, but also with pomegranates and figs.[2] The O.T. mentions pomegranate trees (*rimmôn*) several times; [3] the Song of Songs, notably, sings of the beauty of the gardens where they flourish [4] and compares the beloved's cheek to a partly opened pomegranate [5] (or to half a pomegranate). Today also this fruit, as big as an apple and similar in shape, is much liked in Palestine, and a refreshing drink is made from its juice.[6]

The pomegranate fruit and tree figure as sacred symbols on various Assyrian and Phoenician monuments. In Israel, as elsewhere too, the pomegranate was the emblem of fertility and life because it has so many pips. Was it for this reason or purely for decorative reasons that pomegranates adorned the capitals of the two pillars at the entrance to Solomon's Temple* [7] and that the cloak of the High Priest's ephod* was decorated along its lower hem "with pomegranates of blue and purple and scarlet

Flower and fruit of the pomegranate tree.

stuff and fine twisted linen, alternating with bells of gold"? [8]—The words baluster and balustrade come from the Italian *balustro*, which originally meant the pomegranate flower; the metaphor comes from the bulge of the flower.

[1] Dt. 8. 8. [2] Num. 13. 23. [3] Num. 20. 5; Jg. 20. 45, 47; 21. 13; 1 Sam. 14. 2; Cant. 4. 13; Joel 1. 12; Hagg. 2. 19. [4] Cant. 6. 11; 7. 12. [5] Cant. 4. 3; 6. 7. [6] Cant. 8. 2. [7] 1 Kgs. 7. 18, 20; 2 Kgs. 25. 17; 2 Chr. 3. 16; 4. 13; Jer. 52. 22. [8] Ex. 28. 33; 39. 24–26.

POOR, POVERTY

In principle, as Deuteronomy proclaims,[1] there should have been no poor people in Israel. It is certain that nomadic life, which implies solidarity in abundance and in need, in auspicious and in evil times, was more favourable to social equality than any other way of life; even in the early days of the settlement of Canaan, the system of small properties on the whole excluded individual misery; only the outcast, the exile, or the foreigner* could suffer abandonment and destitution.[2]—But it was not long before pauperism began its ravages: vice, incapacity,[3] disease, and death often made situations precarious or near ruinous. Monopolizers and usurers took advantage of circumstances.[4] From the beginning of the monarchy, and especially with the growth of commerce, the differences between rich and poor became more and more marked. And so the Biblical texts reflect a social unbalance, more or less serious according to the period, which remained through the centuries; everywhere appears the sorry figure in adversity, reduced to beggary and contempt:[5] we have only to think of Nathan's fable, the Parable of Dives and Lazarus, and the stigmatization by the Epistle of James of showing preferences for individuals.[6] Also significant are the continual diatribes by the prophets against the oppressors of the poor,[7] against those who "crush the people and grind the face of the poor",[8] "those whose teeth are swords, and whose jaw-teeth are knives, to devour the poor from off the earth, the needy from among men".[9]

But though these vigorous statements say much about the extortions of some and the sufferings of others, who were even obliged at times to sell themselves as slaves*, they give wonderful proof, too, of the sense of justice possessed by the real Israelites and their suffering at the misfortune of their brethren. —This same care is shown in the many interesting provisions of the law on behalf of the poor: right to glean* corn and grapes,[10] a share in the income from tithes* and at feast meals,[11] a reduction in the expenses caused by sacrifices,[12] the daily payment of wages,[13] the prohibition of lending money for interest († usury),[14] the automatic recovering of liberty for slaves*,[15] the right to redeem an inheritance which had been sold,[16] the benefits assured by the celebration of the Sabbatical Year,[17] the periodic return of the family lands to the one who had been obliged to sell them,[18] etc.

But, assuming that these provisions did not remain as dead-letters, they were naturally insufficient to remedy an evil so deep rooted that Jesus himself—without wishing to make a prediction which was absolute for the future—states that his disciples always "have" the poor with them.[19] We know that almsgiving was one of the signs of Jewish piety, and there are many texts—often fine [20]—which recommend charity and exalt the merits of justice and brotherliness [21] without concealing the fact that there are wicked poor,[22] and that poverty may be a punishment; at the same time, it is recalled that God is the supreme refuge and the liberator of those in distress.[23]

Moreover, in the face of the often corrupting influence of riches, there is a poverty which gives honour to the Israelite who is ready to suffer it worthily, and which is a source of piety and virtue.[24] It was especially to these poor, a veritable *élite* of the nation, morally speaking, that the Gospel was to be preached and by whom it would be accepted.[25]

[1] Dt. 15. 4. [2] Gen. 21. 14 . . . [3] Prov. 24. 30 . . .; Eccl. 10. 18. [4] Mic. 2. 2; Hab. 2. 6. [5] Prov. 10. 15; 14. 20; 18. 23; 19. 7; Eccl. 9. 15. [6] 2 Sam. 12. 1 . . .; Lk. 16. 19 . . .; Jas. 2. 1 . . . [7] Job 20. 19; 24. 4, 9, 14; Is. 10. 2; 32. 7; Jer. 5. 28; Ez. 22. 29; Amos 2. 6–7; 8. 6; Mic. 3. 2. [8] Is. 3. 15. [9] Prov. 30. 14. [10] Lev. 19. 9–10; 23. 22; Dt. 24. 19–21. [11] Dt. 14. 28–29; 16. 11, 14; 26. 12. [12] Lev. 5. 11; 12. 8; 14. 21; 27. 8; [13] Lev. 19. 13; Dt. 24. 14–15. [14] Ex. 22. 25; Dt. 23. 20; 24. 12; Lev. 25. 36. [15] Ex. 21. 1–4. [16] Lev. 25. 23 . . . [17] Ex. 23. 11 . . . [18] Lev. 25. 10. [19] Matt. 26. 11; Mk. 14. 7; Jn. 12. 8. [20] Dt. 15. 7–11. [21] Ex. 23. 6; Job 29. 12; 30. 25; 31. 16, 19; Prov. 14. 21, 31; 19. 17; 22. 9; 28. 8, 27; Is. 58. 7; Lk. 14. 13, 21. [22] Prov. 13. 7. [23] Job 5. 15; Ps. 9. 9; 35. 10; 41. 2; 72. 12, 13; 109. 31; Prov. 22. 22–23. [24] Prov. 19. 1, 22; 28. 6; Lk. 21. 3. [25] Is. 61. 1; Matt. 11. 5; Lk. 4. 18; 7. 22; cf. 2 Cor. 8. 9.

POPLAR

In translating the Hebrew name *libneh*, from a root which means "to be white", scholars hesitate between the storax tree—a shrub which produces a whitish resin (balm*)—and the white poplar, common in Palestine. It is difficult to decide, because the *libneh* is mentioned only twice in the O.T.[1] The translation "storax" has support from the name which the Arabs give to this plant, *loubna*; but the occurrence alongside *libneh* of the almond and the plane,[2] and, more especially, large trees such as the oak and terebinth "whose shade is so agreeable",[3] speaks in favour of the poplar. Some translators think that the Hebrew word normally rendered "mulberry"* may have meant the trembling poplar, i.e. the aspen, or that in place of the willow* we should think of the poplar, or, more particularly, of the Euphrates poplar.

[1] Gen. 30. 37; Hos. 4. 13. [2] Gen. 30. 37. [3] Hos. 4. 13.

214

PORCUPINE

The LXX wrongly translated by porcupine a Hebrew name which means the daman († hyrax).[1] On the other hand, an attempt has been made to identify the animal named in Is. 14. 23, 34. 11 and Zeph. 2. 14 with the porcupine; but the majority of versions prefer the hedgehog*, the heron*, or the bittern*. The flesh of the porcupine—which has nothing in common with pork—is highly esteemed by the Arabs for its delicacy.

[1] Lev. 11. 5; Dt. 14. 7.

PORCH (PORTICO)

While a porch is merely a covered entrance with a roof supported by columns, a portico is an open gallery generally running all round a building, with a roof supported by a colonnade.—The articles on the Temples* of Solomon and Herod provide the necessary information about the porticoes attached to those religious buildings.

The O.T. also speaks of two porticoes (porches) which formed part of the whole ensemble of Solomon's palaces* in Jerusalem: the "portico with columns" and "the portico of the throne" or of judgment. The first, whose purpose is unknown (waiting room?), measured 80 ft. by 50 ft. and was approached through a kind of porch before which was perhaps a flight of steps;[1] in the second, panelled in cedarwood from floor to beams (the ceiling),

the king dispensed justice.[2] The information supplied is so scanty that no choice can be made among the attempts at reconstructing these buildings.

(† Architecture.)

[1] 1 Kgs. 7. 6. [2] 1 Kgs. 7. 7.

POTASH

The Hebrew word translated "potash" (R.V., soap) implies an idea of cleaning, of purity. Doubtless, in ancient Israel, it was a salt used for toilet and for refining,[1] and obtained by burning various halophytic plants that grew on the shores of the Dead Sea and in the salt marshes of the River Jordan.

(† Soap.)

[1] Jer. 2. 22; Mal. 3. 2; cf. Job 9. 30.

POTSHERD

In place of papyrus or other materials († writing), the ancients used potsherds (ostraca, singular: ostracon) for writing brief notes. Excavations in Palestine have yielded a number of these, dating from different periods; the oldest (2nd millennium B.C.) bear only a few archaic characters, the most famous being those found at Samaria and Duweir (Lachish).

The Samaria ostraca, more than sixty in number, were discovered in 1910, in the ancillary buildings of Ahab's palace* and date from the first half of the 9th century. They are well preserved, and the writing is

Development of a design of birds in the decoration of Palestinian pottery (see page 216).

perfectly legible. Rather than labels, as was said, they were probably delivery notes which accompanied jars of wine and fine oil sent from the royal estates to the court.—The eighteen ostraca found at Duweir in 1935 are duty reports, messages sent by subordinates to a military commander, towards the end of the monarchy in Judah (about 580). These two collections of ostraca are very valuable to archaeology, and a study of them allows interesting deductions of a geographical, historical, economic, and even religious, as well as of an epigraphical, nature.

POTTERY

Nomads use receptacles of leather or skin, sometimes of metal; earthenware containers are too fragile and heavy for them. So it was only after their entry into Canaan that the Israelites made any extensive use of clay articles. The Pentateuch refers only rarely to eathenware vessels.[1]

It is known that the potter's is a very ancient trade. As far back as prehistoric times (Neolithic), interesting objects of pottery were in use, and excavation has brought to light sherds from every succeeding period; they differ greatly from one another, however, in the quality of clay used, the method of firing, shape, style, and decoration (painted, chiselled, or engraved). Due to this great variety it is possible to establish, from many comparisons, a system for dating any newly found sherd, and hence the stratum of civilization in which it is found.

Among the Israelites, the trade of potter spread very quickly because vessels of all kinds and sizes were soon needed, not only for holding liquids (water, wines, oil, etc.) but also valuables (jewels,

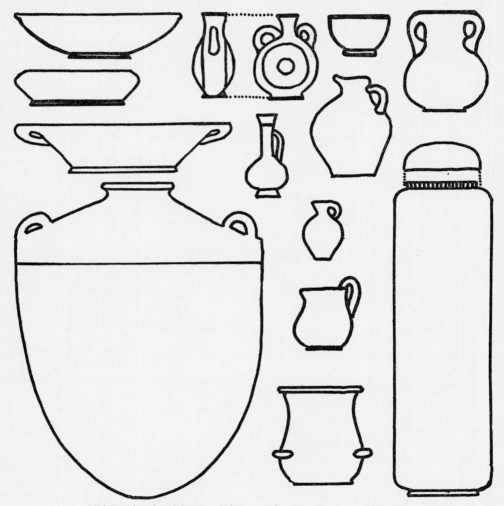

Dishes, bowl, mixing-bowl, jugs and jar from Palestine. Scale $\frac{1}{10}$.

cloth, contracts, etc.), for use as kitchen utensils (dishes and cups, large or small, etc.), primitive piping-systems, and even tombs; the day came when the potter made fire-pans, toys, idols, writing-tablets, etc. Even broken sherds were used: for carrying a light to the hearth, for dipping up a little water,[2] for writing on (ostraca); Job even used them to scratch himself.[3]

The trade was learnt by the Israelites from the Canaanites, who had themselves learnt it from the Egyptians but who had also undergone Greek influence through Cypriot productions. The clay was kneaded with the feet,[4] as is still done today in Tunisia. Originally, the workman modelled the wet clay with his hands only, but later he used a wheel; the Hebrew word for this, and also some texts, suggest that it was made from two wooden discs fixed

Pottery stamps of the royal workshops. Read (*on the left*): "To the king. Socoh", and (*right*): "To the king. Hebron".

at either end of a vertical axis; the bigger disc was operated by the feet.[5] Then the potter had to see to the drying and glazing of his products,[6] and baking them in ovens, a number of which have been found.

The Israelites developed their own style, which they soon marked with brands which show that such articles were made at Hebren, Ziph, Shochoh, or Mensat. There were probably some royal potteries where associations of potters were formed.[7]

Many Biblical metaphors are taken from the potter's trade. The different purposes of vessels made from the same clay struck Solomon as well as the apostle Paul.[8] "What association is there between an earthenware vessel and an iron vessel? One will strike and the other will be broken," said Ecclesiasticus[9] long before La Fontaine. Elsewhere, he adds with a sigh of impotence: "To instruct a fool is like glueing together a broken pot."[10] But it was the fragility of earthenware vessels which was especially noticed and which became the simile for human weakness;[11] while the potter's mastery, as he moulded the clay to his will, was a metaphor for the sovereign power of God who led men even without their knowing.[12]

217

[1] Gen. 24. 14; Lev. 6. 21; 14. 5; Num. 5. 17. [2] Is. 30. 14. [3] Job 2. 8. [4] Is. 41. 25. [5] Ecclus. 38. 29; Jer. 18. 3. [6] Ecclus. 38. 30. [7] 1 Chr. 4. 23. [8] Wisd. 15. 7; Rom. 9. 21. [9] Ecclus. 13. 3. [10] Ecclus. 22. 7. [11] Ps. 2. 9; Is. 30. 14; 41. 25. [12] Is. 29. 16; 64. 8; Jer. 18. 2 ff.; 19. 1 ff.; 19. 10 ff.; Rom. 9. 20–24.

POUND

A Roman weight equal to 11½ oz. Only the Fourth Gospel mentions it: Mary anointed Jesus with a pound of ointment,[1] and Nicodemus brought for the Lord's burial "a mixture of myrrh and aloes, about a hundred pound weight".[2]

[1] Jn. 12. 3. [2] Jn. 19. 39.

PRAETORIUM

In Roman provinces the governor's residence was called the praetorium, but the term was also used for any place where he sat to give justice. In Caesarea[1] the representative of authority lived in a palace called "Herod's praetorium", after its builder. In Jerusalem, according to the Passion narratives, it appears that in front of the building where Pontius Pilate stayed during his visits to the capital there was an open square overlooked by his tribunal, which was set up on a carefully paved (lithostrotos) terrace (gabbatha).[2] But where were this palace and its dependencies (courtyard, barracks, etc.) situated? Opinions have always been divided on this subject, some favouring Herod's old palace* on the western hill in the Upper City, others a palace which formed part of the fortress of Antonia* on the Temple hill, where traces of the lithostrotos are claimed to have been found; still others look elsewhere, particularly near the Xystus* in the declivity of the Tyropoeon.

Varying with interpreters, and depending upon whether St Paul wrote from Rome, as is generally thought, the praetorium mentioned in the Epistle to the Philippians[3] may have been either a building—imperial palace or a barracks—or more probably a body of men—soldiers of the praetorian guard, judiciary officers, etc.

[1] Acts 23. 35. [2] Matt. 27. 27; Mk. 15. 16; Jn. 18. 28, 33; 19. 9, 13. [3] Phil. 1. 13.

PRAYER

In Israel prayer was such a natural thing that it was not commanded. It was generally associated with sacrifice*, and the word normally used for prayer comes from the verb "to sacrifice". So prayer was preferably offered in the sanctuary, where people were especially conscious of being in God's presence, and consequently sure of being heard.[1] But they also prayed away from the holy places;[2] frequently, and especially after the Deuteronomic reform, people would pray facing towards the Temple in Jerusalem.[3]

The attitude of prayer was very free. Sometimes

the one praying simply bowed his head, or he knelt down,[4] and in times of great stress he prostrated himself on the ground.[5] In the N.T. people preferred to pray standing. Often both hands were raised, open, towards heaven.[6] (The custom of putting the hands together probably dates from the 5th century A.D.) Generally, praying was done aloud. Later, phylacteries* were used.

Originally prayer was reserved for special circumstances, but very soon people would pray at any time of the day or night;[7] however, since there were too many who never prayed at all, certain times for prayer were fixed, which varied from one period to another.[8]

In the Bible prayer was addressed to God only, and though it may sometimes have sought to compel him,[9] it remained above magic and conjuration. The worshipper calls on God, who will answer in his own good time, and who may not grant the requests made.[10]

The Bible records some fervent prayers,[11] but selfish ones also,[12] and later Judaism produced some long prayers,[13] the object of which was adulation from men.[14]

The prophets took a stand against a certain formalism in prayer,[15] but others, particularly Jeremiah, show prayer as a real communion of the soul with God.[16]

Finally, it may be said that while the Lord's Prayer seems to be a summary of Jesus' own method of praying, there were already in existence in his day two forms of prayer: one was the "Shema", which was a kind of confession of faith made from the three following passages: Dt. 6. 4–6; 11. 13–21; Num. 15. 37–41; the other was a very interesting prayer called the Eighteen Blessings, which at one time was to be repeated three times daily, and which is still used today in synagogue worship.

[1] Gen. 28. 16–33; 1 Sam. 1. 26; 1 Kgs. 8. 22; Joel 2. 15–17. [2] Gen. 24. 12; Matt. 6. 5; Acts 10. 9. [3] 2 Chr. 6. 24; Dan. 6. 10. [4] Gen. 24. 26; 1 Kgs. 8. 54. [5] Job 1. 20. [6] Ex. 9. 29; 17. 11; 1 Kgs. 8. 22. [7] Ps. 119. 62. [8] Ps. 55. 17; Dan. 6. 10; Acts 10. 9. [9] Gen. 32. 26; Ex. 17. 11; 1 Kgs. 18. 41–45. [10] Ps. 65. 2; 81. 7; 91. 15; 145. 18. [11] 1 Sam. 1. 12 ff.; 1 Kgs. 8. 23 ff.; Ezr. 9. 6; Is. 63. 15 ff.; Dan. 9. 4. [12] Gen. 27. 28; 49. 25. [13] Mk. 12. 40. [14] Matt. 6. 5. [15] Is. 1. 15; 29. 13; Amos 5. 23. [16] Jer. 12. 1 ff.; 15. 15–18; 17. 14; 20. 7–12.

PREFECT

This term is found in some versions of the Bible to denote:

1. Certain royal officials whose task was essentially the collection of tribute or as overseers dividing the work among those who paid taxation in the form of labour service.[1]

2. After the Exile, the Israelites first of all had at their head a Davidic prince, and then a Persian governor who had prefects under his command, who represented his authority in each locality of any importance.

[1] 1 Kgs. 4. 5, 7.

PREPARATION

The Jews called the Friday or the day before the Sabbath [1] the "day of preparation" or "the preparation", and during it they prepared the food and anything else which would have required labour forbidden on the next day.

[1] Matt. 27. 62; Mk. 15. 42; Lk. 23. 54; Jn. 19. 31, 42.

PRESBYTER

From the Greek word *presbuteros* there has come the English word "presbyter" (an elder person), and the commoner word "priest". The N.T. has two additional terms: one for "priest" (*hiereus*) and the other for the overseer of a community (*episkopos*, from which we have "bishop"). *Presbuteros* (which is the comparative of *presbus* = old, aged) has the force of valuable, respectable, venerable.—Information on this subject will be found in the articles: elders, deacon, bishop, priest.

PRIEST

1. *The priesthood in early times*. In ancient times no clergy were necessary among the Israelites; anyone being able to sacrifice was his own priest; [1] it goes without saying, however, that those officiating were preferably men on whom position in the family, the tribe, or country conferred authority.

But wherever there was a shrine, an individual was put in charge at an early date; [2] he would assist those offering sacrifice, would advise them, and ended by arranging and directing the cultic acts; it became more or less necessary to have his services. Moreover, between the worshipper and his God another intermediary also took his place—the seer, who knew by various means how to interpret and transmit the divine will. What more natural than to entrust to him, if possible, the keeping of the holy place. Thus the priest was born, responsible for watching over the altar and speaking in the name of God at the same time. For this double function, there seems to have been a particularly high regard in Israel for those who had perhaps descended from the ancient tribe of Levi and who were the heirs of the traditions of Moses, the tribe's most notable representative; at any rate, those who bore the name "Levites"* had probably specialized in the art of giving oracles and in the duties of the sacrifice.[3]

In the course of time, the priest—and particularly the Levitical priest—became more and more important, especially in places where there were famous shrines (Shiloh, Nob); his duties often became hereditary, the father initiating his sons in his activities;[4] priestly families thus became established.[5] At an early date the priests assumed a special costume—the linen ephod*, the symbol of their dignity.[6] They had a right to certain parts of the sacrifice and received gifts from those who, naturally, did not come empty-handed to the sanctuary; they often acted, too, as counsellors and judges in public or private affairs.

2. *The priesthood in monarchical times.* It is clear that the institution of the monarchy, the building of the Temple in Jerusalem and the division of the kingdom could not fail to produce modifications in the position of the priesthood as well. The priests no longer enjoyed their former independence—the king was their master.[7] Those in the royal sanctuaries (Jerusalem, Dan, Bethel), in particular, were merely public servants,[8] at the orders of the king,[9] appointed and dismissed by the sovereign,[10] who did not necessarily limit his choice only to Levitical priests.[11] On the other hand, the prestige of the priests increased, the glory of the sanctuary reflected on its servants;[12] some of these became great figures in the land. The priest became more and more the indispensable intermediary for the presentation of offerings to Yahweh; it was no longer possible to sacrifice on the royal altars as on the primitive high-places—everything was in the hands of the king and, under him, the priests who were in control; ritual developed and the organization of the cult spread from the principal sanctuaries to the others. The heads of families lost their ancient privileges as sacrificers, and a distinction progressively more marked became established between laymen and the priestly caste. And though the priests hardly ever consulted the oracle in the ancient manner, they nevertheless proclaimed ordinances in the name of Yahweh, of a judicial, moral, or religious nature.[13]

The texts also give evidence of a fairly highly organized clergy; in the Temple at Jerusalem an important personnel was evolved (subordinates of all kinds, men and women musicians, etc.) and a hierarchy began to appear among the priests—besides the High Priest, there is mention of a second,[14] of one in charge of the Temple police,[15] and of three "keepers of the threshold",[16] as well as of priests of the first order or elders.[17]

But, without speaking about the fall of the northern kingdom, it was of course the reform of Josiah which caused the greatest changes in the status of the priests. The centralization of the cult in Jerusalem necessitated that of the clergy; what was to happen to those who held office in provincial sanctuaries? The Deuteronomic Law states that they had rights similar to those of their colleagues in the capital,[18] but in reality the priests of the family of Zadok, in Jerusalem, succeeded in retaining their prerogatives, and their colleagues from elsewhere had to be con-

tent with the duties which the others were willing to leave them;[19] many of them probably preferred to live on their inheritance. A distinction was established between the priests proper, the Zadokites, and their subordinates, for whom the title of Levites was reserved; but the title lost its glorious sense—formerly it had designated the priest *par excellence*; it was to end, as will be seen, as the title of an inferior order of servants.

3. *The priesthood in post-Exilic times and in the Priestly Code.* After the Exile the Israelites who returned to Judah were for a long time politically dependent on foreign kings, but the supreme authority of the Jewish community was in the hands of the Jerusalem clergy and its head. Though the monarchy had disappeared, the High Priest soon seemed like a king. This shows the power acquired by the priesthood, a closed caste; the position of priest was forbidden to anyone not belonging to the clerical aristocracy. The distinction between priests and Levites was now complete for the Priestly Code, the latter not even being priests of the second rank: although they belonged to the holy tribe of Levi, they never had the right and access to the priesthood which was, from the beginning, reserved for Aaron and his descendants (the Zadokites); the Levites were the property of the priests; at the time of Moses they were given to the priests as servants, in the place of the first-born who had to be offered to Yahweh. (For further details, see Levite*.)

The *functions* of the priests were primarily cultic, for they alone had sufficient holiness to present themselves before Yahweh; it was their duty to attend to the care of the sanctuary and the altar, for though they were essentially sacrificers († sacrifice) they also had to renew the shew-bread, see to the candlestick and the Temple utensils, prepare the oils and the sacred perfumes, deal with purifications, blow the trumpets, give Yahweh's blessing to his people, teach them the ritual observances and the rules concerning clean and unclean, supervise and administer the belongings of the sanctuary, police the precincts, and in certain cases administer justice, etc. Several of these tasks were, of course, entrusted to competent specialist priests. The whole body of the priesthood was divided into a number of classes the total of which varied (twenty-four in Chronicles) and which did not all have the same rank. Each class officiated for a week in turn; many priestly families lived in the country and went to Jerusalem only to perform their duties.

The priest "who offered to God" had to have no bodily defect.[20] He was *consecrated* in a complicated ceremony, unknown before the Priestly Code; he had to purify his body, after which, clad in priestly clothes, he offered atonement sacrifices, some of which were repeated on seven consecutive days. Some actions of priests already consecrated, like those of the newly received priest, symbolized their obedience to God.

But the High Priest especially had to be ritually pure and holy, and so he was strictly subject to certain rules—he could not marry a widow, a divorced woman, or a prostitute; he must not eat meat from an animal found dead or torn; he must abstain from all intoxicating drink before performing his duties; he must not cut the corners of his beard, or go near any corpse, etc. The rite of consecration included anointing* with holy oil, the composition of which is specially set down.

From that time onwards the *costume* of the priest was strictly established.[21] Over a pair of shorts, he wore a white tunic and a long belt; this circled his waist two or three times, and its ends hung to his feet. He wore a conical-shaped turban when he was officiating.—The High Priest's costume was more complex. Over the usual priestly garment, he wore a kind of sleeveless surplice, embroidered round the lower edge with violet and red pomegranates alternating with golden bells. Were the latter a survival from pagan times, and were they supposed to keep demons away from the sanctuary? Were they simply to inform God of his servant's presence? There can be no certainty about this. Over this first surplice, he had to wear a second, the ephod*, which had gold shoulder pieces fastened with two onyx stones on which the names of the Israelite tribes were engraved. Finally, on his chest he wore the breastplate, a big square forming a kind of pocket in which were the Urim* and Thummim; on the outside of this pocket shone twelve precious stones, set in threes and bearing the names of the twelve tribes. To complete the costume a special turban, the High Priest's tiara, was adorned with a golden coronet on which these words were engraved: "Holiness unto Yahweh." This costume was well designed to strike the imagination, and its symbolism was not devoid of value. On the Day of Atonement, however, this costume was reduced to a simple garment of white linen.

The *income of the priests* was not inconsiderable. It comprised the firstfruits* of all the animals, fruits and produce of the sacrifices of foodstuffs, sacrifices for atonement and for thanksgiving, all that was put to the ban, etc. All this went to the upkeep of the priests and their families. There are endless directives on how this income should be used.—As for the Levites*, they had the right to the tithes of wheat, maize, and oil, and, like the priests, they were exempt from military service.

[1] Jg. 6. 19; 13. 19; cf. Gen. 12. 7; 13. 18; 22; 28. 18, etc.; 1 Sam. 14. 31 . . . [2] Jg. 17. 5, 13; cf. 1 Sam. 7. 1. [3] Jg. 17. 7; 18. 5, 19. [4] 1 Sam. 1. 3. [5] Jg. 18. 30; 1 Sam. 14. 3; 22. 11. [6] 1 Sam. 2. 18; 22. 18; cf. 2 Sam. 6. 14. [7] 1 Sam. 22. 11–19. [8] 2 Sam. 8. 15 . . .; 1 Kgs. 4. 1 . . . [9] 1 Sam. 2. 35; 2 Kgs. 16. 10; Jer. 21. 1; 37. 3. [10] 2 Sam. 8. 17, 18; 20. 25, 26; 1 Kgs. 2. 26, 27; 4. 4; 2 Kgs. 10. 11; 16. 10, 11; etc. [11] 1 Kgs. 12. 31;

2 Kgs. 17. 32. [12] 1 Sam. 22. 17; Hos. 4. 7. [13] Dt. 33. 10; Mal. 2. 7. [14] 2 Kgs. 22. 4; 23. 4; 25. 18; Jer. 52. 24. [15] Jer. 20. 1; 29. 25. [16] 2 Kgs. 23. 4; 25. 18; Jer. 52. 24. [17] 2 Kgs. 19. 2; Jer. 19. 1. [18] Dt. 18. 6–8. [19] 2 Kgs. 23. 9. [20] Lev. 21. 16 . . . [21] Ex. 28. 4, 40, 43; 29. 8, 9; 39. 27–30; Lev. 8. 13.

PRISON

Although the O.T. occasionally refers to prisons of the Egyptians, Philistines, and Assyrians,[1] it must be recognized that Hebrew law had no punishment which deprived people of their liberty; imprisonment was used only as a preventive measure to be sure of the culprit's whereabouts.[2] Various texts prove, nevertheless, that Israelite kings did not abstain from imprisoning some recalcitrants or from putting them in shackles [3]—Jeremiah himself was more than once thrown into prison.[4]

In post-Exilic times imprisonment became a positive repressive punishment [5] in Palestine too. The N.T. mentions it frequently,[6] and the early Christians and more than one apostle knew its hardships.[7]

(† Stocks.)

[1] Gen. 39. 20; 40. 3; Jg. 16. 21; 2 Kgs. 17. 4; 25. 27; Jer. 52. 11. [2] Lev. 24. 12; Num. 15. 34. [3] 1 Kgs. 22. 27; 2 Chr. 16. 10; 18. 26; cf. Ps. 107. 10 . . . [4] Jer. 20. 2; 32. 2; 33. 1; 37. 15–16, etc. [5] Ezr. 7. 26; Neh. 3. 25. [6] Matt. 5. 25; 14. 3; 18. 30; 25. 36; Mk. 6. 17; Lk. 12. 58; 22. 33; 23. 19. [7] Acts 4. 3; 5. 18; 8. 3; 16. 23 . . ., etc. Heb. 11. 36; Rev. 2. 10.

PROCONSUL

In the Roman Empire senatorial provinces, i.e., those not needing military forces, were controlled by a civil governor. He was sent out by the Senate, bore the title of proconsul, and his mandate lasted (in theory) for one year.[1]

[1] Acts 13. 7; 18. 12; 19. 38.

PROCURATOR

In certain Imperial provinces of secondary importance, such as Judaea (with Samaria), the Roman Emperor himself sent out, for a long or short term, a governor with the title of procurator (= administrator). He was a military commander, with powers of life and death, charged also with the administration of justice and finance. The procurator of Judaea usually lived in Caesarea on the coast and went up to Jerusalem only during the principal feasts. Of the line of fourteen procurators of Palestine only Pontius Pilate, Felix, and Festus are mentioned in the N.T.[1]

[1] Matt. 27. 2 . . .; 28. 14; Mk. 15. 1 . . .; Lk. 3. 1; 23. 1 . . .; Acts 23. 24; 24. 1 . . ., 27; 25. 1 . . .

PROPERTY

Among nomads, property naturally consisted of movable goods, tents, household articles, clothes, jewels, on the one hand, and flocks and herds on the other. Pasture land was considered common property.

But as soon as the Israelites had settled in Canaan, the land was shared out by tribe, clan, and family, and from then on legislation sought to keep real estate in the hands of the same families. Moreover, the Israelite became very quickly attached to the land belonging to his family; the field of his fathers was to some extent sacred.[1]

When, through poverty or the extinction of a family, a sale became necessary, the law made certain particular provisions. First, the nearest relative had a right of pre-emption;[2] on his side the seller could, after a certain time, buy his land back;[3] finally, in the Year of Jubilee*, it returned to its original owner;[4] this did not apply, however, to a house situated in a town.

[1] 1 Kgs. 21. 3. [2] Lev. 25. 25; Jer. 32. 6 ff. [3] Lev. 25. 26–28.
[4] Lev. 25. 13.

PROSELYTE

For a long time the Israelites accepted among them foreigners* who kept their own beliefs. The law protected some of them and authorized them even to enter the Temple at Jerusalem, though only into the outer court, it is true. But when the nation crystallized into a religious community the difference between Jews and pagans became accentuated, and problems of proselytism arose. The missionary idea of this new activity was to be found in the prophetic notion of a single universal God—if there is only one God in heaven and earth he is not the God of one people only to the exclusion of others, and it is necessary to bring foreigners to him and to make them proselytes (literally, those who have been added, newcomers). It must be added that in N.T. times there were many who deplored the pagan inability to raise the moral standards of men and who looked sympathetically on the Jewish religion, which succeeded in maintaining its adherents on a level of healthy life, even though the irony of some Roman historians was always directed against the zeal and skill of the Israelite proselytizers.

The Bible speaks more than once of strangers to the Israelite community who showed their interest in it and gave it their support; they might be more or less Jewish in faith, but they were not full Jews according to the Law. They were called "God-fearers"[1] or "worshippers of God"[2] or "devout proselytes";[3] these terms designate various degrees of half-converts, ranging from those who merely showed a little interest in Judaism to those who came short of being Jews only because they were uncircumcized; but it is not possible to attribute to any one category one or other of these expressions, which seem to designate in general the whole body of those people.

Proselytes could become Israelites in Law, but the Talmud does not allow them to call themselves sons of Abraham, so that they occupied an inferior status in the community. Many proselytes shared in the synagogue worship, but would not agree to become Jews through fear of circumcision, or of changing their religion, or of legal consequences which such changes entailed (the privilege which exempted Jews by birth from worshipping the gods of the Empire did not protect converts, who were accused of atheism). It can be understood how readily Christianity, by freeing proselytes from such fears, would be received by them with joy.

[1] Acts 10. 2. [2] Acts 17. 4; 18. 7. [3] Acts 13. 43.

PROSTITUTION

Hebrew legislation frowned on prostitution,[1] but there was no legal penalty against it (except in a special case).[2] And so although prostitutes were held in contempt, they were common in Israel,[3] and houses of ill-fame were not unknown.[4] Prostitutes were apparently often recruited among foreign women;[5] their trade is naturally condemned in the Biblical texts,[6] at times very realistic, which mention them on many occasions in the literal or metaphorical sense.[7] A priest could not marry a prostitute.[8]

Commonly practised in Canaanite cults and in Semitic ones in general, sacred prostitution* held sway over the Israelites as well, among whom it made sporadic appearances;[9] but all the representatives of Yahwism worked against it,[10] and the Deuteronomic Law proscribed it with vigour.[11]

[1] Lev. 19. 29. [2] Lev. 21. 9. [3] Gen. 38. 15; 1 Kgs. 22. 38; Prov. 6. 26; 7. 10; Is. 23. 16. [4] Jos. 2. 1; 6. 17; 1 Kgs. 3. 16; Jer. 5. 7; Ez. 16. 30, 33. [5] Prov. 2. 16; 6. 24. [6] Prov. 23. 27; Rom. 1. 24; 1 Cor. 6. 9, 18; Gal. 5. 19; Col. 3. 5; etc. [7] Jg. 11. 1; 16. 1; Jer. 2. 20; 3. 2; Ez. 16. 15 . . .; Joel 3. 3; Matt. 21. 31; Lk. 7. 37; 15. 30; 1 Cor. 6. 16; Rev. 14. 8; 17. 1 . . .; 18; etc. [8] Lev. 21. 7, 14. [9] Gen. 38. 21 f.; 1 Kgs. 14. 24; Hos. 4. 14; Amos 2. 7. [10] 1 Kgs. 15. 12; 22. 46; 2 Kgs. 23. 7. [11] Dt. 22. 5; 23. 17, 18; (cf. Rev. 2. 20).

PROSTITUTION (SACRED)

The important Israelite sanctuaries and their clergy used the services of various people who were considered as more or less consecrated to Yahweh, hence the term "hierodule" from the Greek *hieros*, "sacred", and *doulos*, "a slave".

Samuel was dedicated as a child to Yahweh, and, in the sanctuary at Shiloh, he was the servant of the principal priest and keeper of the house of God.[1] The Temple at Jerusalem had foreign slaves who were called "given" (Nethinim*, given by kings or individuals) and who performed the humblest tasks in the sanctuary.[2]

On the model of what happened among the

Semites and especially among the Canaanites, sacred prostitution arose also at the Israelite high-places.[3] The men and women who took part in it, in honour of the deity, were called by a name which underlined their sacred character; but, in contempt, they were also called "dogs".[4] Yahwism always fought against this equivocal custom, despite the religious prestige which surrounded it.[5] Fought by Kings Asa and Jehoshaphat early in the 9th century, then by the prophets Amos and Hosea, sacred prostitution was swept away, almost if not completely, by Josiah's reform.[6]

[1] 1 Sam. 1–3 (cf. Ex. 33. 11). [2] Ezr. 2. 43 ff., 70; 8. 20; Neh. 7. 46 ff., 73; 11. 21. [3] Gen. 38. 21 f.; 1 Kgs. 14. 24. [4] Dt. 23. 18; Rev. 22. 15. [5] Lev. 19. 29; 21. 9; Dt. 23. 17 f. [6] 1 Kgs. 15. 12; 22. 46; 2 Kgs. 23. 7; Hos. 4. 14; Amos 2. 7.

PSALTERY

This stringed instrument is mentioned only in the Book of Daniel.[1] The type of Assyrian origin consisted of a horizontal sounding-board on which a number of strings were stretched, and which was held flat in front of the chest. Others were like a Greek harp, with the sound box at the top.

[1] Dan. 3. 5, 7, 10, 15.

PUNISHMENT

There is a religious concern at the basis of Israelite legislation. Punishment does not aim at the correction and improvement of the guilty, since very often he was put to death; punishment did not seek essentially the compensation of the injured party, for the application of the lex talionis did not necessarily bring anything to him. The main aim was to arouse in everyone respect for God's will as it was expressed in his Law, and as a result to arouse a fear of evil and a loathing of crime.

It was the evil that was punished rather than the wrongdoer; a king's son who broke the law in complete ignorance was to be punished all the same;[1] an animal was punished like a man. That is why there appears more than once the expression "put away the evil from the midst of the people".[2] The holiness of the God of Israel required from his people the same holiness.[3] That is why, when a crime was discovered without any way of knowing its author, it was necessary to offer a sacrifice, the rite of which is reminiscent of an exorcism.[4]

In Israelite law punishment was of three types:

1. *Monetary punishment.* This was especially in compensation for the damage caused. The Covenant Code († law §2) provided that the cattle thief should repay five times what he stole,[5] but generally it was more simply a fixed repayment of double.[6] Fines could be imposed for negligence (e.g., for leaving a cistern uncovered[7]) or for blows or wounds.[8] According to Deuteronomy, 100 shekels were payable for certain calumnies,[9] 50 for seducing a girl.[10] The Priestly Code levied fines on those who lied in order to steal.[11]

2. *Corporal punishment.* Deprivation of freedom was not a punishment prescribed by the Biblical codes. The Priestly Code is alone in recognizing preventive imprisonment.[12] However, it is known that imprisonment was used among the Israelites and that certain prophets (Jeremiah,[13] Micaiah[14]) experienced its bitterness. After the Exile, some wrongdoers were banished.[15]

The *lex talionis*, a rule widely applied by Babylonian and Assyrian law, was also applied by the Israelite codes.[16] Obviously it entailed physical consequences. Yet in Israel the only mutilation expressly prescribed was that of the hand, and that in special circumstances,[17] whereas Babylonian and Assyrian laws savagely require not only that one, but also the cutting off of the tongue, the lips, the eye, sometimes the nose, the breasts, etc.

Beating was also recognized in Deuteronomy,[18] but it was limited to less than forty stripes for fear of degrading the wrongdoer; this punishment did not seem humiliating in itself, but became so when it reduced the victim to a lamentable condition. Later legislation, for fear of going beyond this number (rather than for charity), prescribed "forty stripes less one"; it is possible that they were administered in thirteen strokes of a whip with three lashes ($3 \times 13 = 39$). It must be realized, however, that Assyrian law administered this punishment quite prodigally: for one blow given seven were received, eighteen for calumny, forty-one for some types of prostitution, etc.

3. *Death penalty.* In Israel this was by one means only—stoning. It was to be performed outside the town, before the judge and in the presence of the people.[19] In exceptional cases, however, the Priestly Code admits punishment by fire in two cases for which the Hittite code required the same punishment.[20] It is true that burning after stoning may be involved (in Israel at any rate), as in the case of Achan,[21] a course of action which was a kind of final supreme humiliation. It is also possible that in early times the body was hanged after being stoned to make a show of giving it no burial.[22] Deuteronomy brought some attenuation of this degrading custom by requiring that a body should not be left hanging for more than a day.[23] But the impression remained for a long time that a curse lay on him "who hangs on a tree".[24]

The law did not recognize death by the sword, but it was practised by David; it is true that it was a procedure of summary justice in the two cases in question.[25]—It was in the atmosphere of Roman law that John the Baptist was beheaded and that James died by the sword. Crucifixion*, too, was introduced by the Roman authorities.

[1] 1 Sam. 14. 24–46. [2] Dt. 17. 12; 19. 19; 21. 21. [3] Lev. 18. 24–30. [4] Dt. 21. 1–9. [5] Ex. 22. 1. [6] Ex. 22. 7. [7] Ex. 21. 33, 34. [8] Ex. 21. 19, 22. [9] Dt. 22. 13 ff. [10] Dt. 22. 28, 29. [11] Lev. 6. 2 ff.; Num. 5. 7. [12] Lev. 24. 12; Num. 15. 34. [13] Jer. 37. 16. [14] 2 Chr. 18. 8. [15] Ezr. 7. 26. [16] Ex. 21. 23; Lev. 24. 20; Dt. 19. 21. [17] Dt. 25. 12. [18] Dt. 25. 1–3. [19] Lev. 24. 14; 1 Kgs. 21. 13. [20] Lev. 20. 14; 21. 9. [21] Jos. 7. 15. [22] Jos. 8. 29. [23] Dt. 21. 23. [24] Gal. 3. 13. [25] 2 Sam. 1. 15; 4. 12.

PURIFICATION

Any legal uncleanness had to be removed, in Israel, by washing the body or the clothes,[1] and in certain cases by offering a sacrifice afterwards; thus, after childbirth a woman had to offer, forty to eighty days after the birth of her child, a year-old lamb (or a pigeon, if she were poor) as an atonement sacrifice.[2]—The purification of the leper gave rise to a complicated ceremony († leprosy), and that from uncleanness acquired by touching a corpse or simply by its presence required the use of special water (see red heifer*).

Not only were priests (and Levites) solemnly purified on the day of their consecration*, but they had to cleanse themselves every time they were in a state of impurity;[3] they also regularly washed their feet and hands before going on duty in the sanctuary.[4] No Israelite could go to the Temple without being purified, without having had a wash, or without washing or changing his clothes.[5] It should also be noted that any activity in war*, considered as a holy activity, necessitated the observance of the rites of sanctification [6] and that the Day of Atonement* was the supreme feast of purification for the Temple and the whole nation.

[1] Lev. 11. 24 . . .; 15. 1 . . .; 17. 15. [2] Lev. 12. 6–8; Lk. 2. 24. [3] Lev. 22. 4 . . .; Ezr. 6. 20. [4] Ex. 30. 17–21; 40. 30–32. [5] Gen. 35. 2; Ex. 19. 10, 14; Lev. 16. 26; Jn. 2. 6; Acts 21. 26. [6] Dt. 23. 10–12; 1 Sam. 21. 4–5; 2 Sam. 11. 11; Is. 13. 3.

PURIM

The post-Exilic Feast of Purim was celebrated on the 14th and 15th Adar (or in the 2nd month Adar, when the year* had thirteen months) with great domestic rejoicing, feasting, and exchange of gifts. It is very difficult to know exactly when it first found a place in the Jewish calendar, because its origin is obscure. The Second Book of Maccabees, which is the earliest text to mention it—apart from the Book of Esther—dates from the last century before Christ. It is true that the Book of Esther relates circumstantially the events that gave birth to the Feast of Purim: a minister of Ahasuerus (Xerxes I, 485–465) had resolved to destroy all the Jews found in Persia; the execution was fixed by lot (Pur) for the 13th Adar. But the plan was frustrated, and instead the Jews received permission to massacre their enemies on that day. After the day of carnage the Jews rested

223

and made the 14th Adar a day of feasting and of joy. (Various causes ultimately pushed the Feast forward to the 14th and 15th Adar.[1])—However, it seems that the Book of Esther is only an attempt of little historical value at explaining the Feast, which may in reality have been of foreign origin, Persian or Babylonian, which Jews living in these lands used to celebrate along with the inhabitants, and which ended by finding a place among Jewish customs. The Book of Esther may have been written to justify the adoption of this feast after the event or to substitute a national festival for the foreign one.

At all events, the secular, popular character of Purim must be stressed, which passed also eventually to the synagogue, where the Book of Esther was read amid the applause of the assembly.

[1] Est. 9.

QUADRANS

A small bronze coin current in Palestine in the days of Roman occupation, and mentioned twice in the N.T.[1] As its name indicates, it was equal to a ¼ assarion, and an assarion was worth about a halfpenny. The translation "halfpenny" or "farthing" leads to confusion.

[1] Matt. 5. 26; Mk. 12. 42.

QUAIL

Quails are small migrant gallinaceous birds which leave Europe in autumn, cross the Mediterranean or Palestine and the Sinai Peninsula in innumerable flocks and settle in Africa, which they leave again in spring. Their flight is low and rather heavy; they allow themselves to be carried by the wind, but after a long flight they are sometimes so weary that they fall to the ground and can be caught by hand. Their fat flesh is excellent, although it can cause digestive troubles if eaten in the slightest excess; it is greatly appreciated by the Arabs, who preserve it by drying and salting.—The Israelites leaving Egypt were able to feed on these birds, as the Books of Exodus and Numbers [1] record and as Ps. 105 and 78 [2] recall, in terms which are often corroborated by observations of the birds.

[1] Ex. 16. 13; Num. 11. 31–33. [2] Ps. 78. 25–30; 105. 40.

QUARTZ

Quartz, or rock-crystal, was well known to the ancients. The two words for it in Hebrew originally meant "ice"; and the same is true for its Greek name (krustallos). In one of his visions Ezekiel compares the firmament with the dazzling splendour of quartz,[1] while Job declares that quartz is nothing in comparison with wisdom.[2] The author of the Apocalypse likens, in turn, a sea, a precious stone, and a river to quartz.[3] These are the only places in the Bible where this transparent mineral is mentioned.

[1] Ez. 1. 22. [2] Job 28. 18. [3] Rev. 4. 6; 21. 11; 22. 1.

RABBIT

The Bible never mentions this quadruped, so rarely encountered in Palestine. "Rabbit" has been used in error to translate a Hebrew word which in fact denotes an animal similar to it, though belonging to a different genus, namely the daman or hyrax*.

RACE

Among the sports that the Israelites seem to have known (cf. pastimes*), racing is mentioned only in the statement in Ecclesiastes that "the race is not to the swift".[1] On the other hand, to illustrate his teaching the apostle Paul borrows many a comparison from the sports the Greeks organized, and in particular from the unimpeded race or from the race in armour.[2] The author of the Epistle to the Hebrews also alludes to it in a famous passage.[3]

[1] Eccl. 9. 11 (cf. 2. Sam. 1. 23). [2] 1 Cor. 9. 24; Gal. 2. 2; Eph. 6. 14 . . .; Phil. 2. 16; 3. 12; 2 Ti. 4. 7. [3] Heb. 12. 1.

RAFT

The First Book of Kings and the Second Book of Chronicles say [1] that rafts of floating wood towed by boats were conveyed by sea, in the time of Solomon, from Phoenicia to Jaffa, the nearest port to Jerusalem. The wood was for the royal buildings.

[1] 1 Kgs. 5. 9; 2 Chr. 2. 16.

RAM

The ram was regarded as a favourite animal for sacrifice (cf. Gen. 22. 13). It was given as a burnt offering or as a thank offering († sacrifice)—for example, when priests were consecrated [1] or at the termination of a Nazirite vow.[2] In particular, it was

Bas-relief of the wars of Assurnasirpal. Nimrud; 9th century.

prescribed as a sacrifice for atonement.[3] At the commencement of each month, that is at new moon, a ram was one of the sacrificial victims.[4]

Rams' horns were used for making horns or trumpets.[5]

In the Book of Daniel this powerful, pugnacious animal symbolized the Empire of the Medes and Persians; [6] it is evoked in one or two O.T. comparisons.[7]

Battering-rams, engines of war used in sieges (cf. especially Assyrian bas-reliefs), bear the same name as the animal itself in Hebrew; they are mentioned in the Book of Ezekiel [8] (and in Maccabees).

[1] Lev. 8. 18 . . .; 9. 4 . . . [2] Num. 6. 14. [3] Lev. 5. 15 . . . Cf. Job 42. 8. [4] Num. 28. 11. [5] Lev. 25. 9; Jos. 6. 4. [6] Dan. 8. 3, 4, 20. [7] Ps. 114. 4, 6. [8] Ex. 4. 2; 21. 27; 26. 9.

RAT

One text in the Book of Isaiah [1] speaks of "diggers of holes"; perhaps rats are meant, as many translators think; others prefer moles*. Many species of rats abound in Palestine.

(† Mouse.)

[1] Is. 2. 20.

RAVEN

In Palestine there exist several species of ravens, all of which were regarded as unclean by Israelite law.[1] Six other passages in which this bird is mentioned in the Bible refer to: its black colour, with which the locks of the well-beloved are compared in the Song of Songs,[2] its habitat in the most desolate regions,[3] the habit it is said to have of pecking and eating the eyes of dead, or even of young living, animals,[4] and its voracity, which nevertheless God can satisfy; [5] Jesus himself says: "Consider the ravens, that they sow not, neither reap . . . and God feedeth them." [6] A raven appears in the Flood story of the Bible,[7] but its role is more explicable in the Babylonian narrative of the same cataclysm. Finally, the ravens of the Cherith gorge should be noted, which brought supplies to the prophet Elijah, who had retired to that solitude.[8]

[1] Lev. 11. 15; Dt. 14. 14. [2] Cant. 5. 11. [3] Is. 34. 11. [4] Prov. 30. 17. [5] Job 38. 41; Ps. 147. 9. [6] Lk. 12. 24. [7] Gen. 8. 7. [8] 1 Kgs. 17. 4–6.

RAZOR

The razor, or at least a knife used for shaving, was in common use in Israel from ancient times, to judge from the many texts in which the verb "to shave" occurs. The razor itself is referred to in only four passages, which declare that it must not pass over the head of the Nazirite († Nazirate) or of the boy Samuel,[1] and in one passage ordering, on the contrary, that the Levites use it over their entire bodies on the day of their purification.[2] In three other texts the razor is spoken of metaphorically.[3]

[1] Num. 6. 5; Jg. 13. 5; 16. 17; 1 Sam. 1. 11. [2] Num. 8. 7.
[3] Ps. 52. 2; Is. 7. 20; Ez. 5. 1.

RECHABITES

The status of the Rechabites has much in common with that of Nazirites († Nazirate); but while the latter acted in isolation as individuals, the Rechabites formed an association whose aim was to combat the advance of civilization by preaching and practising a return to the simpler customs of the patriarchs. They held that Israel had travelled a wrong road after the entry into Palestine and that they must return to the nomadic way of life, and reject all the comforts of a sedentary life, which appeared to them as borrowings from foreign civilizations and religions; since the earth could not be cultivated without serving the Baalim who made it fertile, cultivation, especially of the vine, must be abandoned and only the God of the desert must be served.

The Rechabites were descended from Rechab and remained traditionally nomadic; but Jehonadab, the chief of the clan in the 9th century, imposed such rules of life on his descendants as religious obligations. He was a saintly man who exercised a strong influence on the whole country—so much so that it is not surprising that a revolutionary like Jehu[1] sought his collaboration. It is known that, later, Jeremiah had a high regard for them and used their faithfulness to their ancestor as an example to the Israelites. After the Exile they seem to have become an important class of scribes.

It must be noted that the attitude of the Rechabites was not the same as that of the prophets; their principles were mainly negative and disapproving; they show the dangers into which religion runs with the advance of civilization, but they do not overcome those dangers. The prophets worked more deeply by showing that the essence of religion depends less on external circumstances than on the sentiments of the heart.

[1] 2 Kgs. 10. 15, 16; Jer. 35.

RECORDER

Among the royal officials from David's time onwards there is found the *mazkir* (= remembrancer), which most versions take as "recorder". We think of him, in fact, as being charged with recording vital government decisions or, as historiographer, recording events the memory of which merits preservation (cf. the chronicles of the kings of Judah).[1] Yet, given the part played by the *mazkir* in Ezekiel's time, it can be asked whether he was not a much more important person, a court counsellor entrusted with

reminding the king of affairs needing his attention, a chancellor*, a minister analogous to the grand vizier of Oriental kingdoms.[2]

[1] 1 Kgs. 14. 29; 15. 7; etc. [2] 2 Sam. 8. 16; 20. 24; 1 Kgs. 4. 3; 2 Kgs. 18. 18; etc.

REED

A number of species of reeds and rushes grow in almost any part of Palestine, but especially on the banks of the Jordan, of Lake Huleh, and of the Sea of Galilee. These plants are directly referred to[1] more than once in the O.T., and are spoken of figuratively in ways that have in some cases become classic.[2] The reed may grow more than 10 ft. tall (cf. Matt. 27. 48 par.) and was used for measuring († measuring-reed). A pen was a small, cut reed († pen, writing§3). The O.T. also speaks of boats* or skiffs made of reeds.[3]—For the "sweet cane" see calamus*.

[1] Ex. 2. 3; Job 8. 11; 40. 21; Is. 19. 6; 35. 7; etc. [2] 2 Kgs. 18. 21; Is. 9. 14; 36. 6; 42. 3; Ez. 29. 6; Matt. 11. 7; 12. 20; Lk. 7. 24. [3] Job 9. 26; Is. 18. 2; cf. Ex. 2. 3.

RESERVOIR

The supply of water, an important provision in any city, was particularly necessary in Palestine. To own a spring or to acquire a well was a privilege,[1] and, conversely, to fill in a well which someone else had dug was not only an unfriendly act but a veritable declaration of war.[2]

In the towns every important house had its cistern*, but this was not enough to supply all the inhabitants with water, especially in times of drought or war. Public reservoirs big and small were therefore dug.

In Palestine underground chambers in which water was stored—sometimes very large ones—have been found. For this purpose grottoes were sometimes used; they were enlarged, but pillars of rock were left to support the roof. In Jerusalem there are several, and in particular to the south-east of the Temple terrace; there the reservoir called "the king's sea" was situated, which was about 40 ft. deep and 240 yds. in perimeter.

But there were also reservoirs open to the sky, kinds of artificial pools; they were generally cut in the rock, and often partially walled; sometimes, too, a declivity was used, at each end of which a transverse wall was built. These reservoirs were fed by rain or spring water, which was sometimes brought long distances by canal or aqueduct. Such reservoirs were numerous in Palestine; some are anterior to the arrival of the Israelites and date back to a distant past. The O.T. speaks of the pools of Hebron,[3] Samaria,[4] Gibeon,[5] and Heshbon (in Moab).[6] In Jerusalem there were the pools of Mamilla, of the

P

Patriarch, of the Sultan, of Bethesda,[7] and of Siloam,[8] etc.

The most famous reservoirs were perhaps Solomon's, an hour's journey south of Bethlehem. They were three pools partly hollowed out of the rock and partly walled, which were almost 200 yds. long and 50 ft. deep. Innumerable canals collected the water from the neighbourhood. The water was taken by two canal systems to Jerusalem itself. Some archaeologists believe that these installations were undertaken in the time of Herod, but others think that at least a part of the work dates from the time of Solomon himself. It is well known that after the First World War one of the two canals was repaired in order to ensure a supply of water for Jerusalem.

[1] Dt. 6. 11. [2] Gen. 26. 15; 2 Kgs. 3. 19; 2 Chr. 32. 3. [3] 2 Sam. 4. 12. [4] 1 Kgs. 22. 38. [5] 2 Sam. 2. 13. [6] Cant. 7. 4. [7] Jn. 5. 2. [8] Jn. 9. 7

REVENGE

By virtue of the ancient and double principle that blood is thicker than water and that the members of the family and the tribe are interdependent, the Israelites, like many other peoples of former times and of today, were convinced that every murder of a free man, whether voluntary or not, had to be avenged and called for reprisals from the victim's whole family and clan against the criminal and all his kindred.[1] The vendetta was not only a right for them but also a sacred duty; to escape from it cast the gravest slur upon their honour. This system, which acted as an effective incentive to keep a lookout, prevented a certain number of crimes. But with time the barbarity of the custom was bridled by various measures. Without mentioning the distinction soon established between involuntary homicide and murder,[2] the taking of revenge was allowed only to one "avenger of blood", the *go'el* (the vindicator), i.e., to the nearest relative of the deceased;[3] but every murderer was able to take refuge at the altars of the Lord[4] and, later, in a certain number of cities of refuge,[5] where the man not charged with murder could dwell. Moreover, Deuteronomy clearly ordains that revenge can be taken only against the guilty to the exclusion of members of his family.[6]

(† Asylum, crimes and offences §3, murder.)

[1] Gen. 4. 14; Jg. 8. 18–21; 2 Sam. 3. 27; 14. 7; 21. 1 . . .; 2 Kgs. 9. 26; etc. [2] Ex. 21. 12, 13; Num. 35. 16; Dt. 19. 4–6. [3] Num. 35. 19. [4] Ex. 21. 13; 1 Kgs. 1. 50. [5] Num. 35. 22–29; Dt. 4. 41–43; 19. 1–4; Jos. 20. [6] Dt. 24. 16; 2 Kgs. 14. 6.

RHINOCEROS

The Vulgate regards the animal of Job 39. 9 as a rhinoceros, while doubtless it is a wild-ox († buffalo). The creature described in Job 40. 15 is probably the hippopotamus († behemoth) and not the rhinoceros, which was not known in the neighbouring lands of Palestine.

RIDDLE

The Israelites loved to ask and to solve riddles during their feasts; Samson's, for example, is a well-known one.[1] Even kings did not disdain this kind of thing; the queen of Sheba tested the wisdom of Solomon this way.[2] But it was not simply a game; it was no doubt an attempt to assert intellectual superiority, which was equivalent to superiority of power or at least of pretension; anyone who did not discharge the obligations of his defeat provoked almost immediate hostilities, which shows the extent to which these "games" were taken seriously, and retained a background of magic*. Some passages of Prov. 30 have the form of a riddle; thus, in v. 33 the same Hebrew word means "nose" and "wrath". Ezekiel[3] combines riddle and parable in his prophecy in chap. 17. The writing appearing on the wall during Belshazzar's feast[4] was a riddle, and in a way the writer of Revelation was proposing one to his readers when he invited them to "count the number of the beast".[5]

[1] Jg. 14. 10–18. [2] 1 Kgs. 10. 1–3. [3] Ez. 17. 2–10. [4] Dan. 5. [5] Rev. 13. 18.

RING

Rings were known in Palestine from earliest antiquity, as excavations prove. Women wore them not only on their fingers but sometimes on their toes

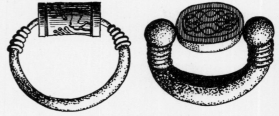

Rings found in Palestinian tombs.

also.[1] Men's rings were often provided with a signet which acted as a seal;[2] they often hung them round their necks, and this custom still prevails today in the East.[3] Kings' and nobles' rings were the sign of their authority.[4]

[1] Ex. 35. 22; Is. 3. 21. [2] Jer. 22. 24; Lk. 15. 22; Jas. 2. 2. [3] Gen. 38. 18; Cant. 8. 6. [4] Gen. 41. 42; Est. 3. 10.

ROADS

As a country of transit between Egypt and the great empires of the north, Palestine was crossed from ancient times by military and commercial highways whose course it is not difficult to trace, but on whose structure we are little informed. Serviceable for armies and war-chariots, they must have been laid down with some care. The Book of Numbers speaks of a "king's way" in the land of Edom and in Transjordan;[1] Josephus claims that Solomon paved the roads leading to Jerusalem with black stones; in his famous inscription the Moabite King Mesha prides himself on having ordered the construction of the road by the Arnon, and Deuteronomy orders that the roads giving access to the cities of refuge be maintained.[2] On the other hand, certain texts of the O.T. imply that the upkeep of ways of communication was so neglected that it was necessary to restore them when the arrival of an important personage was announced.[3] Secondary roads for the use of pedestrians and beasts of burden[4] were mere tracks, with sometimes landmarks and signposts indicating direction;[5] paths naturally linked most places with one another.[6]—Under Persian domination the network of roads was developed significantly, but it was at the time of Roman rule that Palestine was provided with roads worthy of the name. They were paved, maintained, and marked out with milestones showing distances; traces of them are still found today.

[1] Num. 20. 17; 21. 22. [2] Dt. 19. 3. [3] Is. 40. 3; 57. 14; 62. 10; Jer. 31. 9. [4] Jg. 19. 11; 1 Sam. 25. 20; 2 Kgs. 4. 24. [5] Jer. 31. 21. [6] Matt. 13. 4.

ROD

Our translations often render by "rod" two Hebrew words—and a Greek one also—which strictly mean "staff". Thus in the Books of Exodus and Numbers they speak of the rod of Moses and of Aaron;[1] and in many poetic or prophetic texts of the O.T.,[2] and occasionally of the N.T.,[3] of the rod as an instrument or figure of punishment.

[1] Ex. 4. 2, etc.; Num. 17. 2, etc. [2] Job 9. 34, etc.; Ps. 2. 9; 89. 32; Prov. 13. 24, etc.; Is. 9. 4, etc. [3] 1 Cor. 4. 21; Rev. 2. 27; 12. 5; etc.

ROE-DEER

This member of the deer family, no longer met with today in Palestine, is mentioned by some versions in Deuteronomy[1] among the animals whose flesh may be eaten; but more probably a species of antelope* is meant.

[1] Dt. 14. 5 (5).

ROPE

The Hebrew language possesses a whole series of terms to designate ropes, cordage, bonds, tent cords, and bow strings. Different substances were used to make them: flax, palm-tree fibres, camel and goat hair, rush, leather. An Egyptian drawing shows the very simple way in which they were made, by being

227

twisted; plaited ropes were considered as luxury wares.[1]

The passages which mention ropes are very numerous in the O.T. and show the multiplicity of the uses for which they were employed. There is nothing special to notice in connection with them, except that the bonds which tied Samson were particularly well made: they were plaited ropes and cords of catgut.[2] While worn round the neck as a sign of submission,[3] ropes represent figuratively the bonds of sin and iniquity,[4] yet also the bonds of the fatherly tenderness of God.[5] They also represent traps, ambushes, or the anguish of death.[6] In Ecclesiastes[7] human life is compared with a golden lamp hanging on a silver cord. It must be noticed that the expression of the poem of Job which we translate by "the thread of their life" (is broken) signifies literally: "their tent cord . . ."[8]

In the N.T. the same term denotes the ropes with which Jesus made himself a whip when he drove the merchants out of the Temple,[9] and those which served to lower into the sea the skiff of the ship bearing St Paul to Rome.[10] It is known that the sailors sought to strengthen their battered vessel by undergirding it (with cables or strong ropes), but the verb is without a complement in the Greek text.[11]

[1] Ez. 27. 24. [2] Jg. 15. 13, 14; 16. 7, 9, 12. [3] 1 Kgs. 20. 32. [4] Prov. 5. 22; Is. 5. 18. [5] Hos. 11. 4. [6] Job 18. 10; Ps. 116. 3; 140. 5. [7] Eccl. 12. 6. [8] Job 4. 21. [9] Jn. 2. 15. [10] Acts 27. 32. [11] Acts 27. 17.

ROSE

Some versions translate by "rose" the name of a flower mentioned in only two passages in the O.T.,[1] where it is more probably the narcissus*; though other scholars have suggested the crocus, the lily*, the rock-rose, etc. The rose bush seems to have been cultivated in Palestine only for a short time before the Christian era. It is mentioned infrequently in the O.T. apocrypha.—The Acts of the Apostles[2] speaks of a servant-girl called Rose (Rhoda); this was a name widely used in antiquity, as today.

[1] Cant. 2. 1; Is. 35. 1. [2] Acts 12. 13.

RUBY

In two places the O.T. speaks of a precious stone,[1] difficult to identify, which may have been a kind of ruby, the Spinel-ruby; it is deep red, and cuts and engraves well.

[1] Is. 54. 12a; Ez. 27. 16. (R.V.)

RUDDER

Ships in antiquity were furnished with a rudder, which was originally a large oar fixed a little forward from the stern, on the port or starboard side; later, two were used, on either side at the rear of the ship.

RUE

In a storm these rudders were lifted up and fixed at the side of the vessel so that they would not be broken.

The narrative of the shipwreck of St Paul and his companions off the island of Malta implies that this

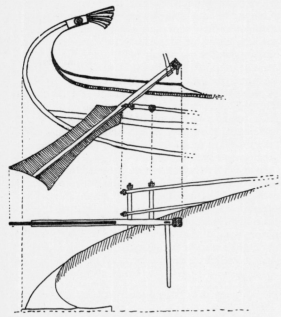

Plan of the rudders of a Roman ship, 1st century A.D.

step had been carried out, and it says that in order ultimately to reach the shore the ropes to the rudders were loosened so that the rudders fell into the sea.[1]

In an original, bold metaphor the Epistle of James compares the tongue with a rudder, which despite its small size directs large ships at the will of the helmsman.[2]

(† Ship.)

[1] Acts 27. 40. [2] Jas. 3. 4.

RUE

This bitter herbaceous plant, used in medicine and also as a condiment, was included among the pot-herbs which were tithed, according to Lk. 11. 42.

Rue.

RUNNER

O.T. texts use the name "runners" for the men who, in Eastern fashion, ran in front of the chariot of a king or royal prince (e.g., fifty runners went before Absalom's chariot),[1] and also for certain soldiers of the royal guard who had, on occasion, to execute their monarch's sentences.[2]

In the N.T. St Paul often alludes to runners eagerly competing in the stadium.[3]

(† Messenger, race.)

[1] 1 Sam. 8. 11; 2 Sam. 15. 1; 1 Kgs. 1. 5. [2] 1 Sam. 22. 17; 1 Kgs. 14. 27; 2 Kgs. 10. 25; 11. 4, 11, etc. [3] Rom. 9. 16; 1 Cor. 9. 24; Gal. 2. 2; 5. 7; Phil. 2. 16; 2 Ti. 4. 7; etc.

RUST

Along with blight*, the O.T. always mentions another disease of cereals, which is perhaps rust.[1] It attacks the plant with reddish or black dust-like spots, caused by a parasitic fungus.

[1] Dt. 28. 22; 1 Kgs. 8. 37; 2 Chr. 6. 28; Amos 4. 9; Hagg. 2. 17.

SABBATH

1. Still at the present time the historical *origin* of the Sabbath is being discussed. It is an institution which appears to stem from Babylonia rather than Egypt, but its source should be sought in the ancient Semitic religion, from which it may have passed in different forms to the Babylonians as well as to the Israelites. It seems originally to have been related to the phases of the moon: first of all, a festival was celebrated on the occasion of the new moon, another at the full moon, then still more were added at the time of the first and last quarters. It is true that, at that time, the interval between these Sabbaths was naturally irregular, since the lunar months do not constantly have twenty-eight days, but twenty-nine and sometimes thirty.

It must have been difficult to obtain a complete cessation of work by wandering shepherds, when they had to let their flocks graze and drink, which was their daily task. However, Yahwism imposed this custom (as early as Moses, perhaps) and gave it a meaning, motives, and a religious origin. It might even be possible that it was in reaction to moon worship that Yahwism established the rule of a Sabbath every seven days.

2. As for the *character* of the Sabbath, it can be noted that in ancient times it was above all a festival, a day of joy,[1] but also a day devoted to Yahweh, which involved the need for rest;[2] it was to make this custom appreciated that its social advantages were pointed out.[3]

But at the time of the Exile, when the pious Israelites who had no Temple could not celebrate their cult nor their festivals, they used to gather together on the Sabbath day; it was this institution alone which constituted the difference between them and their oppressors.[4] To abstain from celebrating the Sabbath soon appeared to them as a very grave fault; much more, obedience to this law assumed a religious value in itself, and ended by becoming a meritorious act; [5] from then on this act had to be codified. The Priestly Code insisted on the Sabbath rest, which it considered a sacred duty: [6] everyone that profanes the Sabbath should be put to death; [7] it was a punishable offence to gather sticks that day or to light a fire.[8] It was on a Sabbath day that in the time of the Maccabees the Syrians attacked some Israelites who, out of faithfulness to their Law, did not bear arms and allowed themselves to be massacred to the last man; the rabbis then decided that in time of war a man could defend himself on the Sabbath day.[9]

In the time of Jesus an entire casuistry regulated the observance of the Sabbath even down to minute details, and the Mishnah devoted to it one of its longest tractates. It was forbidden to carry anything out of one's house, and also to care for the sick or to set a broken leg; it was equally forbidden to write or to undertake a journey, but as it was impossible to forbid people to walk, the number of steps permitted outside one's house was limited to 2,000 cubits, which was "a Sabbath day's journey*". It is true that the Jews used various stratagems to remain within the Law while at the same time violating it, and the rabbis themselves were responsible for attenuating the severity of these observances by allowing derogations and establishing subtle distinctions.

It is understandable that Jesus should have combated such a religion,[10] going as far as to undermine the theological foundation of the Sabbath by pronouncing these revolutionary words: "My father always works." [11] But it must be stated clearly that certain rabbis had already expressed themselves in the same way as Jesus, saying for example: "The Sabbath is laid in your hands, it is at your disposal; it is not you who are in the hands of the Sabbath or who are at its disposal." But the Pharisees could not allow the extension which Jesus afforded to this principle.

3. As a day began at nightfall for the Israelites, it is not surprising that the Sabbath was ushered in by a service on Friday evening in the Temple,[12] with an offering of special sacrifices.[13] Friday was called the "eve of the Sabbath" or the "day of preparation" [14] because people prepared everything so that they did not need to work after nightfall: food for the following day was cooked in advance, the clothes to be worn were made ready, and the lamps were lit for the night.[15]

4. In the application of the rules relating to the Sabbath, certain rabbis had realized that absolute rigidity could not be demanded and that it was necessary to provide for exceptions. In case of accident, they said, it was permissible to help an Israelite by freeing him from the rubble which crushed him, but only if he was in danger of dying. When an animal had fallen into a pit it could be pulled out if there

were risk of its dying, but if not, people had to be satisfied with feeding it there . . . etc. Jesus knew these exceptions,[16] but he gave to their principle the value of a rule, which totally modified its scope.

5. The Romans laughed at the institution of the Sabbath, which they considered as the loss of a seventh of life, but their authorities sometimes took it into account. If we are to believe the Jewish historian Josephus, his co-religionists were supposed to be exempt from military service because they did not bear arms on the Sabbath day. Philo adds that when a distribution of corn was made on a Sabbath day the Jews were authorized to ask for their share the following day.

6. To the institution of the Sabbath is related that of the *Sabbatical Year*. Certain dispositions of the laws prior to the Exile prepared this new law. In fact, it was laid down that certain slaves* should be released after six years' work; every seven years, the land had to be left fallow, and the fruit abandoned on the olive tree and the vine; [17] Deuteronomy declares that this seventh year must be a time of financial release, but it is not possible to specify in what sense, i.e., whether the creditors had to give up their credits entirely, or only the interest on these; [18] if it was the latter case, it may have originated as a consequence of the law requiring that the land should be left fallow; for if the labourer had to abandon the fruits of the earth, how could he pay the interest on his debts?

However, it was only after the adoption of the Priestly Code that the Sabbatical Year was in actual fact celebrated.[19] The earth, throughout the country, must be enabled in the same year to celebrate a Sabbath in honour of the Lord.[20] During these twelve months, nothing must be cultivated, and the law promised magnificent harvests in the sixth year, which would allow people to live the following year.[21] It was in the time of Nehemiah that the Israelites undertook to celebrate the Sabbatical Year,[22] which was undoubtedly respected on more than one occasion.[23] The historians Josephus and Tacitus refer to it: the former, to vouch that the emperor renounced the tax on the Jews one particular Sabbatical Year, and the latter to find in it proof of the Israelites' idleness. But it is not certain that this law was regularly observed; the Talmud bears witness to it indirectly, since it establishes numerous enactments which meet difficulties raised by its application.

7. Finally, *the Year of Jubilee* had to be celebrated every fifty years, i.e., after a week of weeks of years (seven times seven years). On this occasion not only the soil had to be left fallow, as in the Sabbatical Year, but also, and above all, everyone returned to his property and recovered the plots of land which he had had to sell during his life. Finally, an Israelite who had had to sell himself as a slave* had to be freed during the Jubilee Year.[24]

The intentions of this law are very interesting: to proscribe the seizing of rural properties, to apportion public fortune fairly, to respect the dignity of the individual, etc. But the difficulties which this law is supposed to have caused seem considerable, and it appears that it was never applied; this, moreover, is what rabbinical tradition recognizes.

[1] Hos. 2. 11; Is. 58. 13. [2] Ex. 34. 21; Amos 8. 5. [3] Ex. 23. 12. [4] Ez. 20. 12. [5] Is. 56. 6, 7; 58. 13; 66. 23. [6] Ex. 31. 13. [7] Ex. 31. 14; 35. 2. [8] Ex. 16. 22–26; 35. 3; Num. 15. 33–36. [9] 1 Macc. 2. 41. [10] Matt. 12. 5 ff.; Mk. 2. 23 ff.; 3. 1 ff.; Lk. 13. 15 ff.; 14. 5 ff.; Jn. 5. 10 ff.; etc. [11] Jn. 5. 17. [12] Lev. 23. 3. [13] Num. 28. 9, 10. [14] Mk. 15. 42. [15] Lk. 23. 54. [16] Lk. 14. 5; Jn. 5. 10; 9. 14. [17] Ex. 23. 10–11. [18] Dt. 15. 1. [19] Lev. 26. 34, 43. [20] Lev. 25. 1–7. [21] Lev. 25. 20–21. [22] Neh. 10. 31. [23] 1 Macc. 6. 49, 53. [24] Lev. 25. 8–17.

SABBATH JOURNEY

The expression "a Sabbath day's journey" means the length of journey which the Jews were allowed to make on the Sabbath day outside their home. Thus the Mount of Olives was a Sabbath day's journey from Jerusalem.[1] What length was it exactly? While certain rabbis spoke of three different distances according to people and circumstances, the average length of 2,000 cubits (i.e., about $\frac{5}{8}$ mile) was finally adopted. But various means were found, without violating the letter, to evade this injunction —an injunction that itself modified the law,[2] which was hostile to all travelling. If a Jew wanted to travel more than 2,000 cubits on the day of rest it was sufficient for him to leave food at that distance away before the Sabbath began; thus he made for himself a new abode at this spot and, on the Sabbath day, he was able to go not only from his real home to the fictitious one, but also, from the latter, to travel another 2,000 cubits. In the towns the Sabbath day's journey began only at the exit of the locality.

(† Landmark.)

[1] Acts 1. 12. [2] Ex. 16. 29.

SACK, SACKCLOTH

The O.T. has different Hebrew words for sacks for corn, bags for food, the scrip, and the knapsack.[1] In the Gospels Christ forbids his disciples to take wallets (for food?) with them.[2]

But the word "sack"—though we ought perhaps to write "*saq*", following the Hebrew etymology of the word and to avoid any confusion—occurs in many Biblical texts,[3] particularly for loin-cloths of the same coarse material as that from which ordinary sacks were made; men and women [4] put such material round their waists in times of mourning or penitence.

It was usually worn over the tunic, but as a sign of great grief it was worn against the skin as a kind of hair-shirt,[5] with or without other clothing. The sackcloth was kept on by the mourner during the night or was used as a mantle to lie on.[6]—Sometimes

the prophets wore sackcloth, with symbolic significance or as a sign of protest against luxury,[7] for this clothing was very likely a survival of the dress of the ancient nomadic Hebrews.

[1] Gen. 42. 25 . . .; 43. 18 . . .; 44. 1 . . .; Jos. 9. 4; 1 Sam. 17. 40; 2 Kgs. 4. 42. [2] Matt. 10. 10; Mk. 6. 8; Lk. 9. 3; 10. 4; 22. 35–36. [3] Gen. 37. 34; 2 Sam. 3. 31; 1 Kgs. 20. 31; Ps. 35. 13; Is. 15. 3; Jer. 4. 8; Ez. 7. 18; Amos 8. 10; Matt. 11. 21; Lk. 10. 13; etc. [4] Is. 3. 24; Jer. 49. 3; Joel 1. 8. [5] 1 Kgs. 21. 27; 2 Kgs. 6. 30; Job 16. 15. [6] 2 Sam. 12. 16; 21. 10; 1 Kgs. 21. 27; Est. 4. 3; Is. 58. 5; Joel 1. 13. [7] 2 Kgs. 1. 8; Is. 20. 2; Rev. 11. 3.

SACKBUT

The Book of Daniel [1] mentions the sackbut among musical instruments used at the court of the king of Babylon. Oriental in origin, and well known to the Greeks and Romans, it was a stringed instrument in the triangular form of the small portable harp, and was no doubt played by women. It had four or five short strings, giving high-pitched notes, probably set in vibration with a plectrum.

[1] Dan. 3. 5.

SACRIFICE

It is very natural that the occasions, the material, and the ritual of Israelite sacrifice should have been modified in the course of Biblical times.

A. In ancient times

Blood, in which the science of that period saw the principle of life, played the chief part in sacrifices. Still at the time of the Judges people remembered that at all times it was forbidden to sacrifice an animal except in certain places,[1] since its blood had to flow over a special stone, a sort of altar; moreover, they were never allowed to feed on blood.[2] When people wanted to seal a covenant, they began by sprinkling the blood of a victim before the deity, and it was in the presence of the latter that the covenant was effectively sealed. In order that this pledge should be perceptible, certain rites were performed: the sacrificed animal was cut into two pieces, between which the two parties or the deity himself passed;[3] or a meal was eaten together, the essential part of which was the sacrificed animal.[4]

Thus the origin of sacrifice in Israel goes back farther than Moses, and in the days of Jeremiah this was still known, since the prophet was able to declare clearly: "For I spake not unto your fathers, nor commanded them in the day that I brought them out of the land of Egypt, concerning burnt offerings or sacrifices." [5]

B. At the time of the Israelite monarchy

1. *Material.* Whereas before the entry into Canaan, sacrificial rites involved hardly any food offering, after the settlement in Canaan the Israelites

began to offer to God flour (kneaded with oil and perhaps salted), bread (with or without yeast), wine, later water also, but neither milk nor honey. At harvest time roasted ears of corn were offered. It is known, too, that the Canaanites had in certain large sanctuaries a custom which was analogous to that of the loaves of the shew-bread which the Israelites offered in David's time at the sanctuary of Nob.

It seems that everyone offered at will the sacrifices he wished to make; neither quality nor quantity were specified. However, these offerings had less value than the sacrifices of animals, for which there was one prime regulation: only domestic animals could be offered (cattle and sheep), and they must be sound and not too old. Sacrifices were not supposed to be a hardship; they must deserve their name and keep their dignity.

It is known that the Phoenicians and the Moabites practised human sacrifice and that the Israelites, too, were familiar with this in the time of the Judges, but only as an exceptional thing.[6] But it appears that in the last days of the monarchy, when customs, lashed by the ruthlessness of the great dictators of the time, became everywhere more violent, the practice of these sacrifices spread to Israel. The Kings Ahaz and Manasseh offered their own sons as burnt offerings;[7] other Israelites made their sons and daughters pass through the fire.[8] It was in the valley of Hinnom, due south of Jerusalem, that they offered their first-born in sacrifice to God.—It is possible that the account of the sacrifice of Isaac originally had the meaning of an eloquent protest against these abominations, which the prophets always condemned.[9]

2. *Ritual*. The offerings were in the first place presented to God, laid out like the loaves of the shew-bread. Later, they were very commonly burned, but this practice was not so much a way of offering God food, which one tried to share somehow with him, as a good odour of sacrifice.

As these sacrifices could be made almost anywhere, and even without the help of a priest, it was very important to be pure oneself, to be sanctified.[10] People had to have abstained from sexual intercourse,[11] in particular, and to wear clean clothes.[12]

Certain sacrifices were entirely burnt on the altar; these were the burnt offerings. They were not frequent, but reserved for special occasions: the sacrifice of Noah leaving the Ark, of the ram replacing Isaac, of Solomon before his dream, of Elijah on Mount Carmel, etc.—these were burnt offerings. But the richer the kings of Israel became, the more numerous these sacrifices were in the Temple of Jerusalem.

What characterized the other sacrifices was the fact that only one part of the animals was burnt on the altar (the fat parts); a second part was given to the priest, and the rest consumed on the spot in a meal which formed part of the ceremony.[13] The

Bible even means a sacrifice when it mentions eating and drinking before Yahweh.[14] Near the altar there was a room set aside for these meals,[15] which, it must be admitted, easily degenerated into joyful festivals, the excesses of which were condemned by the prophets.[16]

3. *Occasions*. All the circumstances of life could be the occasion of a sacrifice. Most of them, however, were sacrifices of gratitude for harvests granted; and so they were celebrated especially at the time of grain harvests, wine harvests, olive harvests, or sheep shearing. Sacrifice was prepared also on the occasion of a marriage, the making of a covenant, or the reception of a friend.

Certain families made it a rule to offer an animal sacrifice. Before going to war or even when undertaking a fairly important enterprise, sacrifices were similarly made. They were also offered to make supplication to God or with the idea of appeasing him.

C. After the Deuteronomic Reform

As soon as worship was centralized in Jerusalem, modifications were naturally introduced as to the way of regarding and of offering sacrifices.

Regular sacrifices began to be made, daily, weekly, or annually, and this altered their meaning. They became sacrifices of the community, and were no longer private and personal. While the individual was lost in the mass, the priest became the necessary intermediary between the mass and God. The very presence of the Israelite was no longer necessary, and people sacrificed for the sake of sacrificing, and no longer to give thanks or to ask for something.

For its part, the ritual of the sacrifice assumed importance; as sacrifices multiplied in Jerusalem, everything had to be organized exactly. It was then that form triumphed—and to such an extent that it was soon thought that it originated in remotest antiquity and that God himself had revealed it at Sinai; what was still more serious was the fact that people came to think that sacrifice in itself exerted an efficacious influence; thence sprung the idea of the atonement of sins effected by sacrifice. This was a notion which became preponderant in later sacrificial ceremonies.

But this evolution of sacrifice marked a time of spiritual cooling-off in Israel. Sacrifices were no longer offered at home and in all circumstances of life. Family reunions occasioned by these ceremonies were practically suppressed. People were satisfied with meeting everyone at the great festivals only.

D. After the return from Exile

1. It is very understandable that the destruction of the Jerusalem Temple and the suppression of all possibility of offering sacrifices during the fifty years

of Exile were bound to transform sacrificial customs once more, and to a considerable extent.

First of all, a classification was established: on one hand, there were the blood sacrifices, which included thank offerings; the burnt offering, in particular that of a two-year-old lamb, offered morning and evening, and which was also stipulated as the end of a Nazirite vow († Nazirate), and in the case of the woman who had just given birth—but in the last case it could be replaced by the less costly offering of pigeons; [17] and the atonement sacrifice, which was in the nature of a punishment and in which the sprinkling of blood was the essential act, while almost the whole beast was left for the priest.

On the other hand, there were the bloodless sacrifices which occurred only exceptionally on their own. First of all, the offering of the loaves of the shewbread, made now by the Levites* with fine wheaten flour and without yeast, and placed every Sabbath day in two rows on the special table; also the sacrifice of a little flour kneaded with oil offered on behalf of the priest; then there was the sacrifice of the woman suspected of adultery*; and, finally, the sacrifice of incense. But all these sacrifices—and especially the last—very often had to accompany other sacrificial ceremonies.

2. *Ritual.* Meticulously precise details are given concerning the choice of offerings; only pure domestic animals were allowed, so that donkeys, camels, pigs, and dogs were excluded; among birds, only doves and young pigeons were permitted, and then only in exceptional cases. Victims of either sex could not be offered indiscriminately; in each case a stipulation indicated what was required. Naturally the animals always had to be without blemish.

For the food, if it was to be offered with another sacrifice, a *hin* (about 10½ pints) had to be provided and poured in its entirety on the altar. Corn might be offered in roasted or crushed ears, sprinkled with oil and accompanied by a little incense, or as fine wheaten flour, or else as an unleavened cake, kneaded with oil and baked in the oven. The quantities were indicated in detail. Although leaven and honey were forbidden, salt*, the covenant symbol, was always present.

The recipe for incense was scrupulously set out,[18] and had to be followed for religious purposes.

3. *How were sacrifices made?* Having been presented to the priest and submitted to his scrutiny, the victim received the laying-on of hands [19] from the person offering the sacrifice. As this action could have, according to the Bible, various meanings (to bless, to transmit a charge or the responsibility for a fault, to condemn even, etc.), it is not possible to state here its exact significance; it was perhaps quite simply a way of saying: "This animal is mine, I give it to God".—The immolation followed immediately; but it was an act neither symbolic nor important in the sacrifice as a whole. The sprinkling of the blood which followed it was the essential moment of the ceremony: the priest poured the blood round the altar, or, in certain expressly stipulated cases, on the horns of the altar. It was the animal's blood, regarded as being its soul, which was given to Yahweh, and this act had atoning power. The flesh of the victim could be burnt in its entirety on the altar in the case of the burnt offering; in other cases, the fat parts only were burned (the fat covering the bowels, kidneys, the fat lobe of the liver, and in sheep the tail fat), while the rest was given to the priest, unless, in the sacrifice of atonement for the priest, it was burned separately outside the sanctuary.

For a bloodless sacrifice, the offering was often burned altogether on the altar, but sometimes it was given in part or in whole to the priest.

It should be added that often the offering had to be made to God in a waving ceremony, but that this practice, which might be very ancient, seemed to lose some of its value and even to be no longer a religious rite in itself.

4. *What was the meaning of sacrifice for the Israelites?* Without considering here all the solutions which have been offered to this vast problem, it can be said that the fundamental and prime belief of Israelite sacrifice was not so much in a communion or kinship with the deity through the blood, or in the desire to nourish the deity in some way, but rather in the idea of covenant. The worshipper showed this by his desire to be united with God. At bottom, it was always a prayer.—But to this was added an idea of giving, of real offering. It is, however, obvious that in certain circumstances this gift could assume a quality of self-interest or become a homage, an act of thanksgiving, or a supplication.—It is natural that with time, with the progression to sedentary life and after the deprivation of all possibility of making sacrifice for a whole generation, these relatively simple notions should have developed. The ideas of covenant and offering remained preponderant, but soon there mingled with them a quite different element; first of all, the search for a sure and exclusive relationship with God through blood; then sacrifice became an accepted punishment, a sort of penance; and, finally, the notion of atonement effected infallibly by sacrifice. This last way of understanding sacrifice seems to have been developed in the belief that atonement would be more surely effected the greater the sacrifice, and then people sought to pay God a big enough ransom so that he should of necessity forgive them.—The substitution-sacrifice and the atonement-sacrifice raised a whole series of problems, but problems which are the domain of Biblical theology.

[1] 1 Sam. 14. 32–35. [2] Gen. 9. 4. [3] Gen. 15. 17. [4] Gen. 31. 45–54. [5] Jer. 7. 22; Amos 5. 25. [6] Jg. 11. 30–40; 1 Kgs. 16. 34. [7] 2 Kgs. 16. 3; 21. 6. [8] 2 Kgs. 17. 17; 23. 10. [9] Jer.

7. 31; Ez. 20. 26. [10] 1 Sam. 16. 5; 20. 26. [11] 1 Sam. 21. 4.
[12] Gen. 35. 2; Ex. 19. 10. [13] Ex. 24. 11; Jg. 9. 27. [14] Dt.
12. 18; 14. 26; 15. 20; etc. [15] 1 Sam. 9. 22; Jer. 35. 2. [16] 1 Sam.
1. 14. [17] Lev. 12. 8; Lk. 2. 24. [18] Ex. 30. 34–38. [19] Lev. 1. 4.

SADDLE

A saddle, not to be confused with a pack-saddle, was put on the back of a donkey when used for riding; the O.T. mentions it more than once,[1] without description. A camel's saddle is referred to only in the story of Laban pursuing his daughters: Rachel had carried off her father's teraphim* in the kind of basket or cage († litter) with cover and curtains that was fastened on the animal, and in which women travelled,[2] as they still do today.

Certain Assyrian bas-reliefs make it probable that soldiers dispensed with saddles or were content with a simple covering when they rode on horseback.

[1] Num. 22. 21; Jg. 5. 10; 2 Sam. 17. 23; 19. 26; 1 Kgs. 2. 40; 13. 13; etc. [2] Gen. 31. 34.

SADDUCEES

It is not certain that the name Sadducee signifies sons or descendants of Zadok, a High Priest in the time of Solomon; but what is incontestable is the fact that most priests shared the Sadducean tendency much more than the Pharisaic.

The Sadducees appear as conservatives and aristocrats. In religious matters they were conservative in the sense that they confined themselves to the spirit of the Yahwism of former times and rejected resurrection,[1] Messianic beliefs (which is more than hope of a Messiah), and angelology [2] as well as demonology, which they considered to be theological novelties; they regarded themselves as guardians of Israelite religion and wished to know nothing of the tradition constantly mentioned by the Pharisees*. An historian of former times claims that they recognized only the Pentateuch as the written Law. Content with their religious past, they did not regard religious passion or enthusiasm with favour, and slipped, in fact, into a certain rationalism while preserving more religious practices than piety. All this is sufficient to explain that they were opponents of the Pharisees.

Their political activity is less well known than the Pharisees'. They were drawn from the aristocracy, the rich people of Jerusalem, the priests and officials of the Temple, and so they had a situation which carried with it a certain respect, but which made them tend towards political inaction, whereby they avoided all popular agitations, even if it were necessary to submit to the Roman occupation in order to arrive at that position. Already at the time of the invasion of Hellenism (at the beginning of the 2nd century B.C.), they tended to accept certain approximations between Jewish and Greek ideals. And so

the nationalistic Pharisees were not far from considering them as traitors. But behind this attitude of the Sadducees, there was an authentically Israelite notion: the idea of the universalism of the Jewish religion, which lies at the origin of the foundation of Jewish colonies scattered throughout the world and which led to proselytism. However, it has been said: "Triumph of the Sadducean viewpoint might perhaps have saved the Jewish State from destruction at the expense of religion, but the triumph of Pharisaism saved religion at the expense of the State".

[1] Mk. 12. 18 ff.; Acts 23. 6 ff. [2] Acts 23. 8.

SALT

Of particular necessity to a people whose usual diet was vegetables, salt had great importance for the Israelites; they obtained it chiefly from the area south-west of the Dead Sea where veritable quarries of the substance were found.[1] It was used for seasoning food,[2] and for preserving dried fish, olives, and certain vegetables. Often the peasant mixed salt with his beasts' fodder; [3] as the Arabic proverb says: "Sweet provender is camels' bread, salt provender their jam."

But to understand other uses of salt it is important to remember that to eat someone's salt was to eat his bread, and because of that to enter into friendly relations with him: those who eat the same meal, those who eat "bread and salt" together, were united by a special bond; this idea is not peculiar to the Semites. Still today the Arabs say, "There is salt between us" or "I love you as I love salt". So when the Biblical texts speak of a "covenant of salt" they are intending to stress the solemn, solid, irrevocable character of the relationship established.[4] The expression may have come from the obligation to salt all offerings presented in the sanctuary; [5] a custom intended to remind the Israelites of the particular communion uniting them with their God, as Leviticus clearly says; [6] but two other ideas may also be involved— salt must no more be lacking from a meal of the deity than from normal food, and salt possesses a purifying power. Perhaps because of its ability to confer incorruption, salt was mixed with the incense,[7] whose combustion, moreover, it facilitated. Use of salt in the cult meant that reserves of it had to be kept in a special place in the Temple.[8]

It was either to establish a covenant of salt between God and the baby, or simply to strengthen the child, as the Bedouin still believe today, that a child was rubbed with salt at its birth;[9] or the two reasons may perhaps be conjoined here also.—The variously explained phrase in the Book of Ezra: "Now we eat the salt of the palace",[10] perhaps means: "We are in the king's pay", just as the word "salary" originally meant the allowance given to Roman soldiers for the purchase of salt.

As salt makes the soil unproductive, the Semites often sowed it over the sites of cities they had destroyed,[11] to strike them—perhaps magically—with sterility, to mark their downfall.—Salt is also used figuratively in certain N.T. expressions; we need only recall the celebrated words of Jesus: "You are the salt of the earth . . ." [12]

[1] Gen. 19. 26; Ez. 47. 11. [2] Job 6. 6. [3] Is. 30. 24. [4] Lev. 2. 13; Num. 18. 19; 2 Chr. 13. 5. [5] Lev. 2. 13; Ez. 43. 24; cf. Mk. 9. 49. [6] Lev. 2. 13. [7] Ex. 30. 35. [8] Cf. Ezr. 6. 9; 7. 22. [9] Ez. 16. 4. [10] Ezr. 4. 14. [11] Jg. 9. 45; cf. Dt. 29. 23; Job 39. 6; Ps. 107. 34; Jer. 17. 6; Zeph. 2. 9. [12] Matt. 5. 13; Mk. 9. 49, 50; Lk. 14. 34; Col. 4. 6.

SANCTUARY

A. Sanctuaries of primitive Yahwism

1. The Semites in early times surrounded with special reverence springs*, still more trees*, but also mountain-tops and certain stones. However, for the Hebrews at any rate, they were not deities; they were only their dwelling-places.

It is therefore not surprising that Israelite sanctuaries are found near a spring or a large tree. Still today there can sometimes be seen in Palestine certain trees surrounded by a low wall, and on their branches hang pieces of cloth of all colours. These are cultic places where people come to worship or pray to the deity who dwells there. Sometimes it is a thicket and not merely an isolated tree. Sometimes there is only a stone of a more or less striking shape or position, an asherah*, or else a mazzebah, i.e., a stone artificially erected († pillar). Sanctuaries were placed also at the top of certain mountains; for a long time there were some in Moab.[1] Others embodied the tomb of some important personage. In short, it can be said that originally a sanctuary was a particularly impressive place where the divine life seemed to manifest itself, or even where the deity dwelt.

It is hardly possible to give precise details about these primitive sanctuaries. It might be that there was not only a low wall round the holy place, the very soil of which was sacred, but that sometimes an actual sanctuary had been constructed; the most recent excavations seem to point to this and show that some sanctuaries are, at least in part, more ancient than had long been thought.

2. While the Semites generally, and doubtless the Hebrews in particular, knew such sanctuaries, it is certain that *from the time of Moses* the religious life of the Israelites was marked with an original stamp.

Mt Sinai, which other texts call Horeb, was therefore without doubt the sanctuary *par excellence* of Yahweh, God of Israel. It was on Mt Sinai that he revealed himself to Moses for the first time,[2] and it appears, according to the account of Exodus,[3] that the Pharaoh himself knew that it was there that Yahweh dwelt. Finally—and this is important—it was there that God remained after the conquest of the promised land; [4] it was from there that he emerged to come to the help of Israel; [5] it was there Elijah went to find him.[6]

Archaeologically, it is not possible to explain the choice of Sinai as the sanctuary of Yahwism.—The geographical position of this mountain is of secondary importance; various localizations have been suggested: in the south of the peninsula, the Djebel Mousa, or the Serbal, or in Arabia, i.e., outside the peninsula itself, or else in the neighbourhood of Kadesh; the latter hypothesis seems to correspond best with the conditions of the problem, but it is not possible to be certain that it is the correct solution.

3. The Israelites had a portable sanctuary—the Ark*, which accompanied them into the wilderness and which was an object of considerable importance. Here it may simply be noted that, even if this Ark evolved in its meaning and in its form, it always signified the presence of God in the midst of his people; it was a token of the divine protection granted to his people.

4. The most ancient texts which relate the history of Moses' time mention a tent of Yahweh,[7] called also the "tent of meeting" or the "tent of the congregation". It was pitched outside the camp; for divine sacredness forbade profane contacts. It was there that all those went who wanted to consult God through the intermediary of Moses.[8] How was this tent furnished inside? It doubtless had to contain certain precious objects, perhaps an incense altar, probably the equipment needed for giving oracles, and at any rate the Ark of the Covenant; much later on, remembrance of the Ark in the tent prevented David from building a Temple.[9] This tent, which must not simply be equated to the Tabernacle*, was the people's sanctuary at that time, and as such it—and not only its contents—was sacred.

B. Ancient sanctuaries of Israel in Palestine

It is very natural that the establishment of the Israelites in Canaan should have had important consequences in the religious sphere. It was said that the gods of the country assured their protégés of corn, wine, fruits of the earth, and orchards. As they desired this produce, the Israelites were bound to ask for it from those who provided it. Besides, everyone was convinced that each country had its own gods. In the desert the Israelites had known Yahweh; were they not bound to worship the Baalim in Canaan? In actual fact, without denying their God, they began to pay homage also to the gods of the country.[10] However, there were always certain circles and individuals who, in spite of the kinship of these two religions, were able to distinguish between them and remained the defenders of the one they had received in the desert. And so, in spite of the confusion which troubled peoples' minds for a certain time, the primitive Yahwism asserted itself, and in the time of David, but especially under the influence of the great prophets, it was Yahweh himself who became sole master of the country.[11]

This development resulted in the adoption by Yahwism of certain forms of the Canaanite cult and of its religious festivals, but both of them transformed. Archaeological excavations have shown that some sanctuaries had a very long history and that, just as the God of Israel had supplanted the Baalim, so the latter had themselves previously taken the place of certain pre-Canaanite deities.

1. The various sanctuaries of Israel *designate God by different titles*: at Bethel, he is the God of Bethel;[12] at Shechem, God of Israel;[13] at Ophrah, the God of peace;[14] at the well of Beer-lahai-roi, God who sees and is seen;[15] at Beer-sheba, the everlasting God.[16] It appears that in each sanctuary God had a particular title.

2. Some Israelite sanctuaries were *constructed near certain springs* (Beer-sheba, Kadesh, etc.). Others were situated *near trees* or sacred groves; we have only to think of the palm tree beneath which Deborah judged the Israelites [17] and of the famous oak trees of Mamre near Hebron. Finally, there were others which surrounded a sacred stone; the Biblical texts do not clearly refer to any meteorite, but to a few naturally vertical stones and especially some *mazzebot* (stones artificially set up, singular *mazzebah*).

3. *On certain mountains* important sacrifices were made: e.g., the one which sealed the treaty between Laban and Jacob,[18] and Isaac's sacrifice.[19] Other mountains were endowed with sanctuaries: in the north of Palestine, Hermon, at the top of which excavations have revealed ruins of several temples, seems to have been a sacred area; Mt Carmel had an Israelite altar which the worshippers of Baal had overthrown but which Elijah built again;[20] its sacred character survived into Roman times, and Tacitus reports that Vespasian offered a sacrifice there.—Everyone knows that in Samaria are found Mts Ebal and Gerizim, which the O.T. points out as being sacred ground,[21] and which was the place of worship of the Samaritans,[22] who still sacrifice there today at the time of the Feast of the Passover.—On the Mt of Olives there was a sanctuary [23] in the time of David, but Solomon built there a high place for Chemosh, the god of the Moabites.[24]—Finally, we must especially note here Mt Zion, at Jerusalem; this name denoted in the first place the city of David, then the Temple of Jerusalem, then the terrace to the north of this hill, and finally the whole town as a holy city and the holy people who dwelt in it; following the example of certain texts of the N.T.,[25] this name has sometimes been used with reference to the Christian church considered as the true Israel, and even for eternal life under the figure of the Heavenly Jerusalem.

4. *The cult of the high-places* was doubtless derived from that practised on the mountains. Each locality had its high-place; this type of cult, which was very widespread and practised on any height, is characteristic of ancient Israelite religion.[26] The Hebrew name for it has even become a synonym of sanctuary, so much so that, when sanctuaries were constructed in the bottom of a valley,[27] they were nevertheless called high-places!

Originally these high-places were hardly marked; because of their sacred character they were surrounded by low walls, which prevented certain profanations. When it was desired to keep objects of worship in them, small buildings were set up, sorts of chapels which afterwards became temples*.

5. What was the *furniture* in these sanctuaries? In the beginning, people were doubtless satisfied to make libations on the sacred rock or the erected stone, or to hang gifts on the sacred tree or to throw them into the spring.[28] One of these primitive stone altars has been discovered at Gezer, and on it there were eighty-three cavities, ranging from 6 in. to 8 ft. in diameter. Early on, however, the Israelite sanctuary must have included erected stones († pillar) and *asherôt* (singular *asherah**). It is, however, very difficult to determine the exact meaning they might have had in the sanctuary; were they simply commemorative or funeral monuments, or more specifically related to the cult?—Later there was also an altar* in these sanctuaries, which replaced the primitive rock platform, and on which not only incense but also victims were offered and burnt.—By excavating certain places of worship huge cylinders of terra-cotta have been found. These are perhaps incense-burners.—Finally, sacred images* were not lacking in Israel, at first in private life as charms, then introduced into the official cult; all the efforts of the prophets were necessary to banish them from it. —For the ephod*, the teraphim*, and the brazen serpent*, see the individual articles.

[1] Is. 15. 2; 16. 12; Jer. 48. 35. [2] Ex. 3. 1–13. [3] Ex. 5. 1. [4] Ex. 33. 3. [5] Dt. 33. 2; Jg. 5. 4, 5. [6] 1 Kgs. 19. 8. [7] Ex. 33. 7–8. [8] Dt. 31. 14; Num. 11. 16. [9] 2 Sam. 7. 6 ff.; 11. 11. [10] Num. 25. 1–5. [11] 1 Sam. 26. 19; Hos. 9. 3; Jonah 1. 3; etc. [12] Gen. 35. 7. [13] Gen. 33. 20. [14] Jg. 6. 24. [15] Gen. 16. 13. [16] Gen. 21. 33. [17] Jg. 4. 5. [18] Gen. 31. 54. [19] Gen. 22. 4 ff. [20] 1 Kgs. 18. 30. [21] Dt. 11. 29; 27. 4. [22] Jn. 4. 20. [23] 2 Sam. 15. 30–32. [24] 1 Kgs. 11. 7. [25] Heb. 12. 22; Rev. 14. 1. [26] 1 Sam. 10. 5; 1 Kgs. 20. 23; Is. 65. 7; Jer. 2. 20; 3. 23; Ez. 6. 13. [27] Jer. 7. 31. [28] Gen. 28. 18; Jg. 6. 20; 13. 19; 1 Sam. 7. 5 ff.

SANDALWOOD

According to the First Book of Kings,[1] the Phoenician fleet of Hiram brought from Ophir almug (or algum, in Chronicles) trees, from which Solomon made balustrades (?) for the Temple and royal palace, and musical instruments for the singers. The references are to a foreign, rare, and precious wood (cf. 1 Kgs. 10. 12b), and according to most exegetes it was red (or white) sandalwood, coming from India.

A verse in the Second Book of Chronicles [2] speaks of algum trees from Lebanon, which could not supply sandalwood; so the eastern savin or Grecian juniper has been suggested, which affords excellent wood for building. But the word algum in this passage may be an interpolation, for in the parallel passage, 1 Kgs. 5. 8, only cedars and cypresses are mentioned.

[1] 1 Kgs. 10. 11, 12 (= 2 Chr. 9. 10, 11). [2] 2 Chr. 2. 8.

SANHEDRIN

1. The existence of the Sanhedrin at Jerusalem is certain only after the Persian period, at the end of the 3rd century B.C. Its origin is connected with the institution of elders*. It was a sort of aristocratic senate made up of a dozen heads of the principal families in the city. This institution continued into Maccabaean times, as the rulers did not dare to eliminate the Jerusalem aristocracy; it was probably then that the Pharisees were introduced into it. When Pompey suppressed Jewish kingship he maintained the Sanhedrin as a court of justice which pursued its activity in Herod's reign; but after the arrival in Judaea of the Roman procurators (in A.D. 6) the Sanhedrin took the place of Herod and Archelaus, and thus acquired great authority.

2. It was made up of seventy (or seventy-one) members recruited probably by co-option. It included Sadducees, of whom a certain number were called "the souls of the Sanhedrin" and who were doubtless the former High Priests and those who might become High Priests; then there were Pharisees, doctors of the Law who, in the time of Jesus, had a dominant influence; those who belonged to neither of these two factions were called elders. The presidency of the assembly was assured by the High Priest.

3. The Sanhedrin had power only in Judaea, though its moral influence was exerted beyond this territory, even as far as Damascus.[1] It acted as the local superior authority, and took cognizance of all matters. The Romans left it fairly considerable power, limited, however, here and there by certain restrictions: everything that the procurator had not reserved for himself, and everything that a lower tribunal could not decide, was its domain.—Jesus appeared before the Sanhedrin charged with crime against God, Peter and John as pseudo-prophets and seducers of the people, and Stephen as a blasphemer. The Sanhedrin had its police, could arrest, judge, and apply all punishments except the death penalty; if, however, it condemned to death, the procurator

could ratify this sentence or apply Roman law. The murder of Stephen, which seems to be in contradiction to this rule, was rather a case of lynching occasioned by a popular rising. Roman authority had the right to convene the Sanhedrin whenever it wished; for example, to make an inquiry.[2]

4. It might be that, like the small local tribunals mentioned by the historian Josephus, the Sanhedrin itself assembled on Mondays and Thursdays. At any rate, there was no session on feast days or on the Sabbath, and sentence of death could not be passed on the eve of the Sabbath, since such a sentence should be carried out the next day.—At the time of Jesus' trial the Sanhedrin assembled in the palace of the High Priest (at least according to Mark and Matthew); it was an exceptional night session, for the doors of the Temple, where the tribunal usually met, were closed.

It is known through the Mishnah that the members of the Sanhedrin sat in a semicircle (so that they could see each other) and that two secretaries stood in front of them, one writing down the speeches of the prosecution, and the other the speeches for the defence of the accused. In front of them (or perhaps opposite the Sanhedrin) in three rows were the students, the disciples of the scholars who sat on the Sanhedrin.

The procedure was particularly exact when the life of the accused was at stake. First of all his defence had to be examined, and whoever had spoken in his favour was not permitted afterwards to modify his estimation. As for the students, they were allowed to speak only in favour of the accused. A verdict of liberation had to be carried out immediately, and a death sentence had to be carried out the following day. At the time of voting the youngest members voted first, so that their judgment stood no risk of being influenced by the decisions of their elders. Finally, for the liberation of an accused a mere majority was sufficient, but for a condemnation two votes more than half the total number were necessary. If it is remembered that the Sanhedrin consisted of about seventy members, it must be recognized that the difference between these two cases proves that they had especially good intentions; it is true that the attendance of twenty-three members was sufficient for a session to be valid.

[1] Acts 9. 2. [2] Acts 22. 30.

SAPPHIRE

This precious stone is referred to a dozen times in the Bible.[1] It was found on the High Priest's* breastplate,[2] and one of the foundations of the New Jerusalem was adorned with sapphires.[3] No doubt in the Biblical texts it is most often not the true or Oriental sapphire—too hard to engrave—which is meant but lapis-lazuli, an azure [4] or dark-blue mineral, often spangled with brilliant pyrites,[5] which could be cut or engraved without great difficulty.

[1] Job 28. 16; Cant. 5. 14; Lam. 4. 7; Ez. 28. 13. [2] Ex. 28. 18; 39. 11. [3] Is. 54. 11; Rev. 21. 19. [4] Ex. 24. 10; Ez. 1. 26; 10. 1. [5] Cf. Job 28. 6.

SARDIUS, SARDONYX

Sard (R.V., sardius) or cornelian figures as the first stone [1] on the Hight Priest's* breastplate, and it is twice mentioned in the Apocalypse; [2] it is a precious stone, blood-red in colour.—Sardonyx [3] is a variety of onyx* embodying stripes of sard and showing red, white, and black bands.

[1] Ex. 28. 17; 39. 10. [2] Rev. 4. 3; 21. 20 (6th). [3] Rev. 21. 20 (5th).

SATRAP

Darius I, king of Persia (521–486 B.C.), divided his empire into a number of large provinces, subdivided into smaller units. At the head of the former he placed satraps [1] (= protectors of the empire), akin to viceroys and charged with the civil and political administration; they were chosen from the members of noble families, and they gained, in time, considerable power.

[1] Ezr. 8. 36; Est. 3. 12; 8. 9; 9. 3; Dan. 3. 2 . . .; 6. 1 . .

SAW

The use of this implement goes back to prehistoric times. In Palestine itself have been found saws made of flint, very short ones, it is true; they were used right up to the Iron Age. Few examples of metal saws are extant. The infrequent passages of the O.T. that mention them speak of two kinds: those that David condemned the Ammonites to make or use [1] (he put them *to* saws, not *under* saws: see brick*), and also named in connection with the Temple stones which were shaped by saws; [2] and the saw (probably the carpenter's saw) which the prophet Isaiah [3] uses in a metaphor. The Epistle to the Hebrews [4] refers to servants of God who were sawn in two: a Jewish tradition asserts, in fact, that Manasseh inflicted this torture on Isaiah.

[1] 2 Sam. 12. 31 (1 Chr. 20. 3). [2] 1 Kgs. 7. 9. [3] Is. 10. 15. [4] Heb. 11. 37.

SCAB

Skin diseases are very frequent in the East, and the Bible is not unaware of them, but their identification and terminology present difficulties. Leviticus doubtless refers to the scab in some passages [1] and the Book of Job to encrustations of the skin [2] († scurvy, leprosy).

[1] Lev. 13. 2, 6–8; 14. 56; 21. 20; 22. 22. [2] Job 7. 5.

SCEPTRE

Originally simply a staff (crook, staff of command [1]) and then a club or even short sword*, etc., the sceptre has been from ancient times the symbol of authority, the emblem of kingship. Its shape varied considerably with time and place. The Israelites knew its use; we have only to think how many Bible passages speak of it, either literally [2] or, still more, figuratively. [3]

[1] Jg. 5. 14. [2] Num. 21. 18; Est. 4. 11; 8. 4; Ps. 2. 9; Amos 1. 5, 8. [3] Gen. 49. 10; Num. 24. 17; Ps. 45. 6; 60. 7, etc.; Is. 14. 5; Ez. 19. 11; Zech. 10. 11; Heb. 1. 8.

SCHOOL

We are ill-informed on the subject of instruction given to children in ancient times in Israel, but many of them were no doubt taught to read and write. Did the parents assume this task, or did there exist, near the sanctuaries, some kind of schools in which the priests were the teachers? It is difficult to say. At Shechem a tablet of the 15th century has been found containing the grievances of a schoolmaster who did not manage to get his fees paid. This document bears witness to the existence of schools in Canaan before the arrival of the Israelites; but did the latter follow this example? The O.T. is silent on the subject, but more than one text intimates that even if there were illiterates in Palestine,[1] many people could read and write, which is proved also by the use of ostraca* (potsherds used for letters or labels) discovered in excavations. In the Book of Judges [2] it is related that a young man, arrested by chance, it appears, by Gideon, provides him in writing with the names of the heads and elders of the town he lived in; the prophets use tablets intended to be read at a glance, [3] and Isaiah refers to the way a child could count the trees in a devastated forest and write down their number.[4]

After the Exile the synagogue apparently acted as a school, at any rate on the Sabbath day: the hazzan (verger) taught the children to read there. Schools as such for boys, however, were not founded in all the towns of Palestine until the 1st century of the Christian era. The Talmud often mentions them, saying, for example, that "from the age of six the child must be received as a pupil and be fattened with the Law, as a bullock with food", and that "the parents simply give to the child life in this world, whereas the master brings him to the life of the world to come". In these classes instruction remained rudimentary, consisting of exercises in reading, writing, and the memorizing of the principal passages of the Law.

The Scribes* directed higher-grade schools, where they zealously interpreted the Scriptures and tradition. Their courses of casuistry sometimes gave rise to passionate discussions which degenerated into quarrels. The most famous of these masters grouped around them Jews who came from all countries; [5] their teaching was more often than not unpaid, for they practised a trade to earn their living. They attached great importance to memory, to exact repetition of their lessons, comparing their best pupils "to cisterns coated with cement which do not lose one drop of their waters".

[1] Is. 29. 12. [2] Jg. 8. 14. [3] Is. 8. 1; Hab. 2. 2. [4] Is. 10. 19. [5] Acts 22. 3.

SCIENCE

In the Biblical texts there is no science in the modern sense of the word. When mention is made of certain aspects of knowledge, even in abstract matters, it is always practical knowledge which is meant, applied to concrete circumstances (for example: to know God is to serve him [1]). Science, which is supposed to delve into the secret and mysterious relationships of events, is out of man's reach; God alone possesses it. That is what the last speech of Job to his friends expresses throughout.[2] To give an example, we can say that the Bible authors when describing heaven* and earth* use very varied images, behind which lie conceptions that give account of some practical aspect of reality. Thus, God can take snow or hail,[3] storm or wind [4] in specified places and cast them on to the earth when he so desires; the rapid colouring of the sky before sunrise is explained by the image of a young man with wings who traverses the whole of space; [5] the stars* are pictured as people who rejoice in the spectacle of Creation,[6] or perhaps as sailing-ships, of which God must upon occasion tighten the ropes (if it is indeed in this sense that we must understand a passage in Job [7]). Other examples, drawn from the way of considering the human body [8] and the illnesses which can assail it,[9] or from history also,[10] or even the way of calculating by means of figures which frequently retain an approximate value († number), show us that the Israelite of Bible times was not given to theoretical generalizations, and that consequently it is useless to look in the Bible for scientific knowledge in the sense in which we understand it today.

[1] Jer. 4. 22; Gal. 4. 8; 1 Jn. 2. 4. [2] Job 38–42. [3] Job 38. 22. [4] Ps. 135. 7; Jer. 10. 13; 51. 16. [5] Ps. 139. 9. [6] Job 38. 7. [7] Job 38. 31. [8] Job 10. 10. [9] Ex. 11. 4 ff.; Dt. 24. 8; 2 Kgs. 5; Is. 37. 36; etc. [10] Gen. 5. 29; 17. 5; 1 Sam. 1. 20.

SCORPION

Scorpions, as creatures of warm regions, freely breed in the Sinai Peninsula, and some species are frequently encountered in Palestine; their sting is very painful, but seldom fatal. Apart from the dis-

trict south-west of the Dead Sea which bears their name [1] (the Ascent of the Scorpions, 'aqrabbim), scorpions are mentioned only once in the literal [2] and once in the figurative [3] sense in the O.T. In a harsh metaphor the Book of Ecclesiasticus [4] in the Apocrypha declares that an evil wife is like a scorpion. Jesus twice makes reference to these small

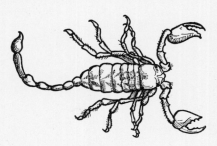

Scorpion.

beasts,[5] and the Apocalypse, inspired perhaps by astrological beliefs, refers to their noxious power.[6] We may recall that certain whips,[7] furnished with points, as well as an engine of war which projected great missiles,[8] bore the name of "scorpion".

[1] Num. 34. 4; Jos. 15. 3; Jg. 1. 36. [2] Dt. 8. 15. [3] Ez. 2. 6. [4] Ecclus. 26. 7. [5] Lk. 10. 19; 11. 12. [6] Rev. 9. 3, 5, 10. [7] 1 Kgs. 12. 11, 14. [8] 1 Macc. 6. 51.

SCOURGING

Among the Jews beating* with a stick, formerly applied to certain offenders,[1] had been replaced, at a period doubtless fairly late but difficult to specify exactly, by scourging with a three-thonged whip* with which thirteen strokes at most were administered. The synagogue authorities had the right to order this cruel punishment, which forced them, moreover, to take certain precautions, notably with regard to those who would not have been able to bear it; it was not, however, debarred from women. Jesus foresaw [2] that his disciples would be whipped in synagogues; Saul of Tarsus admitted that he had had those who believed in Jesus beaten there; [3] he himself, after his conversion, was a victim of this treatment: he wrote to the Corinthians: "Five times from the Jews I received forty stripes less one." [4]

Among the Romans, according to the terms of the Greek N.T. which are sometimes confused in our translations, either rods were used (Acts 16. 22; 2 Cor. 11. 25), or whips* (Matt. 20. 19; Mk. 10. 34; 15. 15; Lk. 18. 33; Acts 22. 25; etc.). Scourging, inapplicable by law to Roman citizens, at any rate after the time of Cato the Elder (about 200 B.C.), was administered to those from whom confessions were sought,[5] or as a punishment [6] or even as a penalty necessarily linked with certain verdicts, including, strangely enough, the death penalty. This terrible torture, sometimes fatal in itself, made the bodies of the unfortunate victims bleed. They underwent the punishment tied to a stake and with their backs turned towards their tormentors. It was added, as we know, to the sufferings of Jesus, who, no doubt, according to the words used in the accounts of the Passion,[7] received the whip*, which was generally reserved for slaves and which was still more cruel than rods.

[1] Dt. 22. 13–19; 25. 1–3. [2] Matt. 10. 17; 23. 34. [3] Acts 22. 19; 26. 11. [4] 2 Cor. 11. 24. [5] Acts 22. 24, 25. [6] Acts 16. 22. [7] Matt. 27. 26; Mk. 15. 15; Jn. 19. 1; cf. Matt. 20. 19; Mk. 10. 34; Lk. 18. 33.

SCREECH-OWL

This nocturnal bird of prey is perhaps mentioned among the unclean birds.[1] Three Hebrew names, very difficult to identify, have been thus translated; in addition to screech-owl scholars have taken them, in turn, not only as great owl and little owl but even as swan and swallow! Ostervald translates with "screech-owl" yet a fourth word, which the great majority of versions render by ostrich.

[1] Lev. 11. 13 . . .; Dt. 14. 12 . . .

SCRIBE

Although Scribes are often associated with Pharisees, nevertheless they did not constitute a party as the Pharisees did, but rather were a class of Israelites.

Before the Exile, the word "scribe" denoted a royal official, a sort of secretary* responsible for the correspondence and perhaps the book-keeping of the king.[1] But in the latter years of the monarchy, in the Exile, and especially after that grievous period of captivity, they had specialized in copying the Law and texts relating to the cult. By working at these sacred writings they learned to know them, and the Scribe's reputation became that of a "scholar", [2] of a specialist in religious matters; up till then they had been priests, but they gradually separated themselves from the priestly class at the time when the latter was drawn into political action. They became the official interpreters of the Law; they were called "doctors of the Law" [3] and "rabbi".[4]

The schools* founded by the Scribes, and by means of which they offered higher studies, had a very particular character. They sometimes assembled numerous pupils in private buildings, or in the constructions included in the porticoes of the Temple*, or even in its courts.[5] The pupils sat on the ground "at the feet" of the master.[6] The teaching was oral and consisted of maxims, questions and answers learned by heart and which, much more than logic, acted afterwards

as a basis for endless discussions, sometimes very lively. In N.T. times some famous schools (directed by Hillel and Shammai) attracted many pupils to Jerusalem; the apostle Paul followed the instruction of Gamaliel.[7]

But the Scribes, entrusted with the task of establishing the "tradition", to which the Pharisees* attached such great importance, also had to administer justice, in the name of that Law of which they knew all the possible applications. But this function of judges was soon handed over to the Sanhedrin*, on which the Scribes were, moreover, represented in large numbers.

Jeremiah reproaches the Scribes with falsifying the meaning of the Law, which is one way of scorning God.[8] In the time of the N.T. they were so happy at being the official interpreters of the Law of God, and so sure of the validity of their knowledge, that a conflict between them and Jesus was inevitable. Jesus' way of teaching, and also the basis of his teaching, were obviously very different from those of the Scribes.[9] Doubtless Jesus recognized their learning; [10] however, he did not refuse to teach them and to reply himself to their questions, even when they contained a trap,[11] in such a way that sometimes he even received approval from them.[12] But he held them responsible for that "tradition" which hinders people from obeying God; [13] he put his disciples on their guard against them [14] and was not afraid to tell them face to face what he thought of them! [15] Moreover, he associated them with the Pharisees in his famous upbraiding of their hypocrisy.[16]

St Luke's Gospel bears witness to the presence in Galilee of a few Scribes,[17] but most of them lived at Jerusalem until the destruction by the Romans both of the Jewish capital and State. After A.D. 70 a large number of Scribes were to be found at Jabneh (Greek Jamnia), a few miles to the south-west of the place where the Jordan flows out of the Lake of Gennesaret; it was there that they founded one of the religious centres whence sprang the monumental work of the Talmud.

[1] 2 Sam. 8. 17; 20. 25; 2 Kgs. 12. 10; 19. 2; 22. 3. [2] Ezr. 7. 11. [3] Lk. 5. 17; Acts 5. 34. [4] Matt. 23. 7. [5] Mk. 12. 35; Lk. 2. 42 ff. [6] Acts 22. 3. [7] Acts 5. 34; 22. 3. [8] Jer. 8. 8, 9. [9] Matt. 7. 29. [10] Matt. 13. 52. [11] Mk. 12. 28; Lk. 10. 25; Jn. 3. 2; [12] Lk. 20. 39. [13] Lk. 11. 52. [14] Mk. 12. 38. [15] Lk. 11. 45 ff. [16] Matt. 23. 13, 15, etc. [17] Lk. 5. 17.

SCULPTURE

For the reasons indicated in the article on art*, the Israelites have always shunned the sphere of the plastic arts. Sculpture is virtually non-existent with them, just as it appears, moreover, to have been mediocre at all times among the Palestinian Semites; in this respect, the almost negative result of excavations is significant: all that deserves to be mentioned here are the ivory* plaquettes discovered at Samaria and Megiddo, together with a basalt bas-relief representing lions and mastiffs confronting each other, and capitals with volutes discovered in the buildings of Megiddo dating from Solomon's time.

For its part, the O.T. simply mentions sculptors of idols,[1] gives some information, often barely explicit, about the artistic works which Solomon had executed at Jerusalem, for the most part by Phoenician workmen (royal throne*, cherubim in wood, decorative

Bas-relief discovered at Beth-shean (14th century B.C.).

panels,[2] etc.), and mentions the sculptures of palm trees and cherubim in the Temple dreamed of by Ezekiel;[3] (cf. also references to the Tabernacle in Ex. 31. 1 ...; 35. 30 ...; etc.). Later, the Jews often became very intransigent with regard to the products of sculpture; their tombs*, for example, are usually very soberly decorated and, in his restoration of the Temple, Herod the Great was obliged to take into account, in part at any rate, the ideas he had received from those under his rule.

[1] Is. 40. 20; 44. 9 ...; 45. 20; Hab. 2. 18. [2] 1 Kgs. 6. 18 ...; 10. 18 ...; 2 Chr. 2. 14; 3. 4; 9. 17. [3] Ez. 40. 16 ...; 41. 17 ...

SCURVY

Without any details being given, scurvy is included among the curses with which God threatens his people;[1] it was one of the illnesses that excluded men from priestly activities[2] and made animals unsuitable for sacrifices.[3] († Scab.)

[1] Dt. 28. 27. [2] Lev. 21. 20. [3] Lev. 22. 22.

SEAH

The *se'ah* is a measure of capacity for dry materials, fine flour,[1] parched grain,[2] etc. It is $\frac{1}{3}$ ephah*, i.e., approximately $\frac{1}{3}$ bushel (2·67 gallons).

(† Weights and measures.)

[1] Gen. 18. 6. [2] 1 Sam. 25. 18.

SEAL

Excavations in Palestine have produced quantities of seals and seal impressions. The earliest date from the end of the 3rd millennium.

They were used as a mark of origin or of ownership, and later as signatures.[1] Jars with contents of value might be sealed; the piece of material, skin, or clay which acted as lid was pasted over with a coating of clay on which the print of the seal was superimposed.[2] And as it was intended to place the goods under a divine guarantee, the imprints, and particularly the seals, took on a religious value; however, among the Israelites, contrary to the custom of surrounding people, seal designs seldom made allusion to religious themes; yet since they were often cut in precious stones, they assumed the value of amulets*. So that the owner might always have the seal at hand, it was made in the form of a ring*. But still more often it was hung from a small chain or simple cord[3] which went round the neck and could easily be hidden under the tunic. In such a case seals sometimes took the form of a scarab or an animal's head,

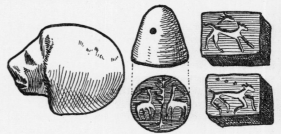

Various forms of seals.

or a cone or cube, though most frequently they were tiny cylinders, $\frac{3}{4}$ to $1\frac{1}{2}$ in. long, engraved on their curved surface; a cord ran through them from end to end, serving to hang them and as an axis of rotation when they were rolled on the wax. There have been recovered from Mesopotamia certain legal decrees of the 2nd millennium, wrapped in clay on which such a cylinder had been carefully rolled until the whole envelope was covered with the design.

Among the most ancient of seals found in Babylonia are some which represent flocks and which were probably intended, by a kind of sympathetic magic, to encourage the reproduction of livestock. Such have also been found in Palestine, dating from a very early period.

From the period preceding the settlement of the

Mesopotamian cylinder seal.

Israelites in Canaan, seals exist decorated simply with geometrical shapes and without picture or writing.

The motifs which occur in imprints from the time of the monarchy sometimes show Egyptian influence —winged-discs, scarabs, sphinx, sometimes along

Various imprints from Palestinian seals.

with certain hieroglyphs; but most often they bear only a word or two in the writing of the time, without any picture.

Seals were engraved in accordance with a professional technique, by specialist craftsmen,[4] who sometimes used diamond points.[5]

In the N.T. it is said that the stone which closed the tomb of Jesus was sealed,[6] and the Apocalypse speaks of a book sealed with seven seals.[7]

Naturally this widespread custom served more

than once in the Bible as a metaphor. God's creation of the world is compared with a man making an imprint in wax with his seal.[8] The seal is like a guarantee of the divine source of prophecy,[9] or of the finality of Jesus Christ [10] or of a vocation.[11] It is also a figure for some kind of conclusive proof: for circumcision, which proves to a Jew that he is in a state of righteousness according to the Law,[12] or for the presence of the Holy Spirit, who assures the Christian of salvation,[13] or for converted Gentiles who attest the validity of the missionary's apostleship.[14]

[1] 1 Kgs. 21. 8. [2] Dt. 32. 34. [3] Gen. 38. 18. [4] Ex. 28. 11, 36; 39. 14. [5] Jer. 17. 1. [6] Matt. 27. 66. [7] Rev. 5. 1. [8] Job 38. 14. [9] Is. 8. 16. [10] Jn. 6. 27. [11] 2 Cor. 1. 22. [12] Rom. 4. 11. [13] Eph. 1. 13; 4. 30; Rev. 7. 2, 4 ff. [14] 1 Cor. 9. 2.

SEASONS

The year in Palestine divides into two seasons,[1] less from variations in temperature than from humidity and dryness: summer, lasting approximately from 15th May to 15th October, during which the sky is almost continuously cloudless, and winter, from 15th October to 15th May, marked by the rains, which increase gradually in volume up to January and then steadily diminish.[2] "To ask for rain after Pentecost would be to require of God a miracle," says the Talmud.—The early rains,[3] so necessary for sowing, must fall before mid-November, at which time the heavy rains [4] of the season begin; and the harvest suffers grave damage if the late rains of March–April fail,[5] even after a very wet winter, for the grain cannot fill out.

[1] Gen. 8. 22; Ps. 74. 17; Is. 18. 6; Zech. 14. 8. [2] Dt. 11. 14; Jas. 5. 7. [3] Ps. 84. 6; Jer. 5. 24; Joel 2. 23; Zech. 10. 1. [4] Ezr. 10. 9, 13. [5] Prov. 16. 15; Jer. 3. 3; 5. 24; Hos. 6. 3; Joel 2. 23; Amos 4. 7; Zech. 10. 1.

SEAT

Usually, the Israelites dispensed with chairs and stools, for they crouched down on the ground or on mats, etc. However, these pieces of furniture were not unknown and were to be found especially in the houses of the well-to-do.[1] Eli fell from his seat on hearing the news of the capture of the Ark of Yahweh [2] and the Shunammite woman took care to put a seat in the room prepared for the prophet.[3] The use of tables* does not necessarily imply the use of chairs, for the guests could sit down on a sort of divan. Ex. 1. 16 doubtless refers to a rudimentary lying-in bed made of two stones, on which, in Egypt, women in labour used to sit.

The N.T. mentions the seats in the synagogues,[4] those of the merchants [5] and Moses' seat (or chair) where the Scribes and Pharisees sat.[6]

Leaving thrones out of consideration here, ordinary seats were made of wooden frames stretched with straw or material—with the result that they have not

SEAT

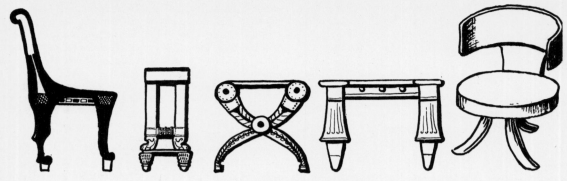

Various seats.

been preserved. However, an idea of their shapes can be formed from ancient paintings which have been brought to light.

[1] 1 Sam. 20. 25; Job 29. 7; Prov. 9. 14. [2] 1 Sam. (1. 9); 4. 18. [3] 2 Kgs. 4. 10. [4] Matt. 23. 6; Mk. 12. 39; Lk. 20. 46. [5] Matt. 21. 12; Mk. 11. 15. [6] Matt. 23. 2.

SEAT (CHIEF)

Among the Israelites, as elsewhere, the seat occupied at table corresponded with the dignity of each guest, and so the chief seats were very much sought after at feasts*.[1] The person whom one particularly wanted to honour sat at the right of the master of the house: Solomon made the queen-mother sit at his right hand,[2] and Salome wanted her sons to sit at the right and left of Jesus.[3] The Messiah sits on the right-hand side of God.[4]

[1] Matt. 23. 6; Mk. 12. 39; Lk. 14. 7; 20. 46. [2] 1 Kgs. 2. 19; Ps. 45. 9; Neh. 2. 6. [3] Matt. 20. 21; Mk. 10. 37. [4] Ps. 110. 1; Matt. 22. 44; Mk. 12. 36; Lk. 20. 42; Matt. 26. 64; Mk. 14. 62; 16. 19; Rom. 8. 34; Col. 3. 1; etc.

SECRETARY

In Palestine, as in other countries, kings and important people employed official scribes, secretaries particularly for writing, for drawing up their letters and corresponding with other lands. From David's time, the O.T. names several of these officials,[1] to whom certain special duties were also entrusted.[2] Again, we know that Baruch was Jeremiah's secretary [3] and that St Paul usually dictated his letters.[4]

(† Officials, recorder, scribe.)

[1] 2 Sam. 8. 17; 20. 25; 1 Kgs. 4. 3; 2 Kgs. 12. 10; 18. 18; 19. 2; 22. 3 . . .; Ezr. 4. 8, 9; Est. 3. 12; 8. 9; Is. 36. 3; Jer. 37. 15. [2] 2 Kgs. 12. 10; 25. 19; 2 Chr. 26. 11. [3] Jer. 36. 18. [4] Rom. 16. 22; 1 Cor. 16. 21; Col. 4. 18; 2 Th. 3. 17; cf. 1 Pet. 5. 12.

SENTRY

The use of sentries for mounting guard was, of course, practised among the Israelites, and in any case they are mentioned more than once in Biblical texts; [1] there were also sentinels who went the round of a town, and watchmen or night-watches posted on towers or walls.[2] But most often sentries figure in the picturesque language of the prophets.[3]

For watchers in vineyards and prison guards see watch-tower*, vine*, prison*.

[1] Jg. 7. 19; 1 Sam. 14. 16; 2 Sam. 13. 34; Matt. 27. 66; 28. 4. [2] 2 Sam. 18. 24; 2 Kgs. 9. 17, 20; Cant. 5. 7. [3] Is. 21. 6–12; 52. 8; 62. 6; Jer. 6. 17; 51. 12; Ez. 3. 17; 33. 1–7; Amos 3. 6.

SERPENT (SNAKE)

Numerous varieties of snakes live in Palestine, but the poisonous ones are relatively rare. Generally, the Bible texts mention serpents without distinguishing between the species [1]—except, however, for the cobra († asp), the horned viper*, and the viper*—and just refer to their crawling,[2] bite,[3] poison,[4] tongue,[5] cunning,[6] and, perhaps, to their hissing.[7]—The beast into which Aaron's rod is changed bears a special name and is more akin to a dragon than to a snake.[8] The "fiery serpents" (*serafim*) of which the Hebrews were victims in the wilderness [9] might be horned vipers; some exegetes liken them to the flying dragons mentioned by Isaiah,[10] fabulous animals haunting the deserts between Palestine and Egypt, according to beliefs still current in the region.

We know the place occupied by the snake in cosmogonies and in ancient cults, and the part given to it in the account of Gen. 3. In the Apocalypse "the great dragon . . . called the Devil and Satan, the deceiver of the whole world" [11] also bears the name serpent, "the ancient Serpent".[12]

[1] Ex. 4. 3; Matt. 7. 10; 23. 33; Mk. 16. 18; Lk. 10. 19; 11. 11; Rev. 9. 19. [2] Dt. 32. 24; Prov. 30. 19; Is. 65. 25; Mic. 7. 17. [3] Prov. 23. 32; Eccl. 10. 8; Amos 5. 19; 9. 3. [4] Dt. 32. 33; Ps. 58. 4. [5] Ps. 140. 3. [6] Gen. 3. 1; Matt. 10. 16. [7] Jer. 46. 22. [8] Ex. 7. 9 . . . [9] Num. 21. 6, 8; Dt. 8. 15. [10] Is. 14. 29; 30. 6; cf. 6. 2. [11] Rev. 12. 9. [12] Rev. 12. 9, 14, 15; 20. 2.

242

SERPENT (BRAZEN)

The Second Book of Kings tells that the pious king Hezekiah ordered a brazen serpent, in honour of which the Israelites burnt offerings,[1] to be broken in pieces; was this type of idol found in the Temple itself [2] or in a sanctuary apart, in Jerusalem or in the neighbourhood? The text does not say. On the other hand, it clearly states that this serpent was called *Nehuštan* (a derivative of the name given in Hebrew to bronze and which also recalls the word "snake", *nahaš*), and it attributes to Moses himself the making of the serpent, in conformity with the account in Num. 21. 6 . . .

The presence of this Nehustan in Israel has given rise to much discussion. Apart from the question of knowing whether Hezekiah would have had the courage to destroy a sacred object going back to Moses himself, it has been wondered whether the brazen serpent was not an image or at any rate a symbol of Yahweh, or else a survival of a primitive cult, and more precisely a divine emblem analogous to the one which the Canaanites (if we are to believe certain indications) surrounded with reverence, in the belief that it protected from illness. At any rate, it is known that in the East, as with the Greeks and Romans, the snake, sometimes entwined around a rod, was the symbol of the gods of healing. Moreover, there have been found in Palestine itself snakes of bronze and terra-cotta and, in certain temple decorations, such an abundance of snakes that it cannot be doubted that there, also, they were associated with the cults of various deities. The touching of holy images is everywhere regarded as having curative value; a mere look can be sufficient for this contact (cf. Num. 21. 8).

[1] 2 Kgs. 18. 4. [2] Cf. 2 Chr. 29. 5 . ..

SETSQUARE

If the LXX and Vulgate versions are to be trusted, this instrument may have been used by the manufacturer of idols spoken of by Isaiah;[1] but the Hebrew word translated in this way comes from a root meaning "to cut, remove, scrape away" and means rather a "chisel". But the setsquare was used in antiquity; it is represented on more than one ancient monument.

[1] Is. 44. 13.

SHEBAT

This was the eleventh month of the Jewish civil year, the latter part of January and the first part of February.[1]

[1] Zech. 1. 7.

SHEEP

Sheep formed one of the main resources of Palestine; they supplied the native not only with milk,[1]

243

meat,[2] and skins but, above all, with their precious fleeces,[3] the shearing of which was the occasion of joyous feasts.[4] The breed still the most widespread is a broad-tailed variety; the head is black, but the body white;[5] the tail, consisting largely of fat, of which the Arabs are as fond as were the Israelites,[6] might weigh twenty pounds—in sacrificing it was particularly stipulated that the tail should be offered whole to Yahweh.[7]

The breeding of sheep was specially practised in Transjordania and in the Negeb (the south of Palestine); sheep and goats often grazed together.[8] The abundance of sheep explains the part they have in the metaphors of the prophets and of Jesus (very many passages) as well as the rôle ovine animals played in sacrificial ritual, notably lambs and rams—though rams also could be presented as thank-offering sacrifices [9] and for sin offerings.[10] It was forbidden to sacrifice a ewe and her lambs at the same time.[11]

(† Lamb, ram, shepherd, cattle.)

[1] Dt. 32. 14; Is. 7. 21. [2] Dt. 14. 4; 1 Sam. 25. 18; Amos 6. 4. [3] Job 31. 20; Prov. 27. 26. [4] Gen. 38. 12 . . .; 1 Sam. 25. 4; 2 Sam. 13. 23. [5] Ps. 147. 16; Cant. 6. 6; Dan. 7. 9. [6] 1 Sam. 9. 24. [7] Ex. 29. 22; Lev. 3. 9; 7. 3; etc. [8] Matt. 25. 32. [9] Lev. 3. 6; 1 Kgs. 8. 5, 63; 2 Chr. 29. 33. [10] Lev. 4. 32; 5. 6; cf. Lev. 14. 10; Num. 6. 14; Jn. 2. 14. [11] Lev. 22. 28.

SHEEP (GATE)

This was a Jerusalem gateway, situated to the north-east of the Temple area and rebuilt after the return from captivity,[1] probably at the spot where there is today St Stephen's Gate, also called the Gate of Our Lady Mary. One early writer thinks that the sheep brought for sacrifice were gathered there and, still in our time, all the sheep needed for the city's food are collected there. Sometimes the Sheep Gate is identified with the Gate of Benjamin*. St John's Gospel states [2] that the Pool of Bethesda was near the *probatike* (probably "gate," understood), i.e., the Gate of Flocks or of Sheep.

[1] Neh. 3. 1, 32; 12. 39. [2] Jn. 5. 2.

SHEEP-SHEARING

This important, lucrative operation took place at the beginning of the summer. It gave rise to a feast [1] that continued in Israel even after the nomadic age; the picturesque story of Abigail [2] is proof of this, as well as the invitation sent on such an occasion by Absalom to all the sons of David.[3] The owner of the flock joined his shearers and provided a feast in which relatives and friends participated.

The Song of Songs [4] compares the white teeth of the beloved to a flock of sheep recently shorn and covered with a new fleece of remarkable whiteness;

and the Servant of Yahweh seems to the prophet like a sheep dumb before its shearers.[5]

[1] Gen. 31. 19; 38. 12.   [2] 1 Sam. 25 (especially vv. 2, 8, 36).
[3] 2 Sam. 13. 23 . . .   [4] Cant. 4. 2.   [5] Is. 53. 7; cf. Acts 8. 32.

SHEKEL

The shekel weight[1] was the unit of weight in Israel; it was subdivided into the half-shekel,[2] quarter-shekel,[3] and one-twentieth-shekel.[4] It is impossible to fix objectively its precise value; it is generally thought to equal 0·58 oz.—The shekel of silver[5] was the money unit; it was $\frac{1}{13}$ of the value of the gold shekel,[6] though here again the equivalences must be

Shekels from a time of Israelite revolt (140 B.C. or A.D. 66). On the first is to be read: "Holy Jerusalem" and "shekel of Israel I (1st year)"; and on the second: "Jerusalem the holy" and "shekel of Israel 2 (2nd year)".

accepted with caution, the more so as we do not know the fineness of grade of ancient gold and silver. Usually the shekel of silver is taken as approximately 2s. 6d.

[1] 2 Sam. 14. 26; 21. 16; Ez. 4. 10.   [2] Gen. 24. 22; Ex. 30. 15; 38. 26.   [3] 1 Sam. 9. 8.   [4] Ex. 30. 13; Ez. 45. 12.   [5] Gen. 23. 15; Ex. 21. 32; Lev. 27. 3 f.; Jos. 7. 21; 2 Kgs. 7. 1.   [6] Gen. 24. 22; Jg. 8. 26; 1 Chr. 21. 25.

SHEPHERD

As the raising of cattle, and particularly of ewes and goats, played a considerable part in Palestine, shepherds were numerous. Generally, flocks were committed to the care of the owners' children[1] or to that of their relations; sometimes the owners themselves assumed this task, but well-to-do people had recourse to the services of hirelings.[2] The shepherd's work was not a sinecure; although it included pleasant hours favourable to conversation, musing,

and flute-playing, it was sometimes painful, the more so as it went on all the year round and in all weathers; the complaints of Jacob to Laban are characteristic in this respect: "The heat consumed me during the day and the cold at night, and sleep fled from my eyes."[3] The flock demanded continual supervision and care: every day, it had to be watered at the well,[4] a frequent cause of rivalry and quarrels;[5] the scattering of the animals had to be prevented; they had to be protected from beasts of prey[6] or thieves,[7] and found if lost; the sick ones had to be cared for, the mother ewes spared of too much walking,[8] the tired lambs carried, and of course the increase of the flock had to be supervised.

In the evening the shepherd gathered his animals either into grottoes or into enclosures surrounded by walls of dry stones,[9] covered in brambles and dominated sometimes by a watch-tower;[10] taking up his position on the threshold of the door,[11] he counted his animals by making them pass beneath his crook,[12] for he was responsible for any which had disappeared, with the exception of those supposed to have been devoured by a wild animal.[13] Shepherds of one area often gathered their flocks together in the same pen for the night and took turns in keeping watch.[14] When morning came, the sheep, attentive to the voice of their master, whom they knew and who called them by name, followed him to the pasture, where they cropped the grass at will.[15]

Besides his crook—which was a long, curved staff allowing him to guide his flock and if need be to seize the recalcitrant ones by the leg—the shepherd possessed, hanging from his wrist by way of a bludgeon, a knotted stick like those still used today in Palestine;[16] but his best weapon was the sling, which he learnt to use with skill.[17] His skin wallet held his meagre provisions.[18] Sometimes, one or two dogs helped him in his work.[19]

The wages of the shepherds were sometimes paid in money,[20] but more often than not in kind, in the form of milk, wool, or sheep.[21]

The O.T. and the N.T. make constant reference to the shepherds' activity: kings and priests must feed the people as faithful guardians of the flock,[22] which God, for his part, embraces with a solicitude like that of a shepherd.[23] The Psalter abounds in images borrowed from pastoral customs;[24] the prophets delved into this same generous fund to translate, in language at the same time poetical and familiar, their appeals or their condemnations;[25] the apostles of Jesus had recourse to the same figures,[26] but the most stirring ones for ever remain those which the Gospel has preserved in their moving simplicity.[27]

[1] 1 Sam. 16.   [2] 1 Sam. 21. 7; Jn. 10. 12.   [3] Gen. 31. 40.   [4] Gen. 24. 20; 29. 3, 8; Ex. 2. 16.   [5] Gen. 21. 25; 26. 20; Ex. 2. 17.   [6] Ex. 22. 3; 1 Sam. 17. 34; Is. 31. 4; Amos 3. 12.   [7] Gen. 31. 39; Job 1. 17.   [8] Gen. 33. 13.   [9] Num. 32. 16.   [10] Gen. 35. 21; Mic. 4. 8.   [11] Jn. 10. 7.   [12] Jer. 33. 13; Ez.

20. 37; cf. Lev. 27. 32. [13] Ex. 22. 10–13; cf. Gen. 31. 38–39; Amos 3. 12. [14] Lk. 2. 8. [15] Mic. 2. 12; Jn. 10. 2–5. [16] 1 Sam. 17. 40, 43; Ps. 23. 4. [17] 1 Sam. 17. 40. [18] *Idem*. [19] Job 30. 1; Is. 56. 10, 11. [20] Zech. 11. 12. [21] Gen. 31. [22] Jer. 3. 15; 23. 4; 25. 34–36; Ez. 34. 2–10; Zech. 10. 2; 11. 5, 7–17; etc. [23] Gen. 48. 15; Is. 49. 9–10; etc. [24] Ps. 23; 49. 14; 78. 71; 79. 13; 95. 7; 119. 176; etc. [25] Is. 40. 11; 53. 6; Jer. 50. 6; Mic. 2. 12; Zech. 13. 7; etc. [26] Acts 20. 28–29; Heb. 13. 20; 1 Pet. 2. 25; 5. 2, 4. [27] Matt. 9. 36; 10. 6; 25. 32; Lk. 15. 3–6; Jn. 10. 2–16; 21. 15–17; etc.

SHIELD

The Hebrew language distinguishes,[1] as do Greek and Latin, between the usual small round shield carried by archers [2] and the shield, twice the size, which protected the whole body and was carried by the shock troops.[3]—Shields were usually wooden— they could be burnt [4]—and covered with thick leather, which was maintained by being rubbed with oil.[5] The covering could also be of bronze.[6] David even captured from the Syrians ceremonial shields of gold, i.e., doubtless, covered in gold,[7] and Solomon had similar ones made, large and small,[8] which

Small and large shields.

delighted Shishak when this Pharaoh pillaged Jerusalem.[9] As he marched, the soldier carried his shield hanging from his shoulder and covered over with a sheath which he removed when he came face to face with the enemy.[10]

In the O.T. the shield is very often a figure for divine protection and salvation; [11] certain texts use, intentionally no doubt, the term which means the *great* shield, which is an interesting shade of meaning with which our versions are generally not concerned.[12] The shield of faith with which the Christian must arm himself is also the great shield.[13]— The princes of the people or the chief men of Israel are sometimes called in the O.T. "the shields of the land".[14]

[1] 1 Kgs. 10. 16; Ps. 35. 2; Ez. 39. 9. [2] 1 Chr. 5. 18. [3] 1 Chr. 12. 8, 34. [4] Ez. 39. 9. [5] 2 Sam. 1. 21; Is. 21. 5. [6] 1 Kgs.

14. 27. [7] 2 Sam. 8. 7. [8] 1 Kgs. 10. 16. [9] 1 Kgs. 14. 26. [10] Is. 22. 6. [11] Gen. 15. 1; Dt. 33. 29; Ps. 3. 3; 18. 2, 30, 35; 84. 11; 144. 2. [12] Ps. 5. 12; 91. 4. [13] Eph. 6. 16. [14] Ps. 47. 9; Hos. 4. 18 (R.V. mg).

SHIP

As the Israelites were not a seafaring people (see however, Gen. 49. 13; Jg. 5. 17), it is surprising to find in the O.T. and N.T. so many references to different types of ships, to their component parts, to their rigging and crews; more than one text reveals an obvious knowledge of the things of the sea.[1] As

Phoenician merchantman.

nearly all the references are to foreign shipping, there is no need to discuss them here; however, Ezekiel's ingenious comparison of Tyre with a first-rank vessel [2] should be noted, and also the fairly frequent mention of "ships of Tarshish",[3] an expression

A light Greek ship.

which people for a long time understood as multidecked Phoenician ships which did the trip between Tyre and Tartessus, near Cadiz in Spain; it is explained that, by analogy, their name was attributed to all ships of heavy tonnage,[4] just as today in French the adjective "transatlantic" qualifies liners traversing seas other than the Atlantic. But this traditional explanation is not very sure. At the present time people prefer, when referring to the etymology of Tarshish (= smeltery), to consider that the vessels of that name transported the products of the foundry at Ezion-geber, which has recently been discovered at the north of the eastern Gulf of the Red Sea.

From this place Solomon initiated ocean voyages with the support of the king of Tyre, notably to the land of Ophir (which has been sought in the south of Arabia, in India, on the Somaliland coast, in Madagascar, etc.), whence they brought back precious metals, ivory, and exotic animals.[5] It does

Roman merchantman.

not appear that this fleet, doubtless considerable, survived Solomon, whose prestige it enhanced. A last resumption of this trading, attempted by Jehoshaphat, came to nothing: the ship, or ships, equipped by the king of Judah,[6] in agreement perhaps with Ahaziah,[7] king of Israel, were wrecked before reaching the high seas.

Without mentioning the short journeys on Lake Tiberias († boat), we may recall, in the N.T., Paul's voyages across the Aegean Sea and, above all, the remarkable account which the Acts of the Apostles gives of St Paul's voyage when he was carried off as a prisoner to Rome.[8] This narrative abounds in details of great accuracy and provides some very useful indications relating to ancient navigation in the Mediterranean, as well as to the manœuvres carried out in the event of storm and shipwreck.

Some interesting Egyptian, Assyrian, Roman, etc., bas-reliefs also enable us to form an accurate idea of ancient ships.

(† Boat, ship's boat, anchor, rudder, rope.)

[1] Ps. 107. 23–30; Prov. 23. 34; 31. 14; Is. 23. 1 . . .; 33. 21 . . .; Dan. 11. 30, 40; Jonah 1; Rev. 18. 17. [2] Ez. 27. 4 . . . [3] Ps. 48. 7; Is. 2. 16; 23. 1; 60. 9; Ez. 27. 25. [4] 1 Kgs. 10. 22; 22. 49. [5] 1 Kgs. 9. 26–28; 10. 22; 2 Chr. 8. 17, 18; 9. 21. [6] 1 Kgs. 22. 49, 50. [7] 2 Chr. 20. 35–37. [8] Acts 27.

SHIP'S BOAT

At the time of the storm which swept away the ship on which St Paul was travelling on his way to Rome, one of the first concerns of the sailors was to hoist on board—not without difficulty—the ship's

Ship's boat attached to the stern of a vessel. Fragment of a Roman mosaic.

boat, or lifeboat, so that it should not be carried off by the wind or knock against the ship.[1] It is the only Biblical text in which this sort of boat is mentioned.

[1] Acts 27. 16–17.

SHIRT

Only well-to-do Israelites seem to have worn, under the customary tunic, an undergarment reaching to the knees—a shirt, in fact. This way of dressing became common in the 1st century A.D., especially in the towns. Some authors think that this shirt is meant by a word which they translate by "shirt" or "fine linen" (R.V., linen garment), which is found in Isaiah's list [1] concerning women's dress, in the account of the prizes Samson promised to anyone who should solve his riddle [2] and in the panegyric on the virtuous wife who makes fine linen and sells it.[3]

(† Dress.)

[1] Is. 3. 23. [2] Jg. 14. 12. [3] Prov. 31. 24.

SHOE

If, in conformity with eastern customs, stockings were not worn by the Israelites, shoes, on the other hand, had been in common use since ancient times, just as they often had been among neighbouring peoples. Numerous Biblical texts [1] prove this to be so; on a certain Egyptian record dating from about 2000 B.C. Asiatic people can be seen with footwear,

the men wearing sandals and the women shoes (a
and b). "I have led you forty years in the wilderness . . . without your sandals wearing out upon
your feet," said Moses.[2]—The usual shoe was, in
fact, the sandal; only the poor were without them:
upon the return of his son, whose destitution was
complete, the first care of the Prodigal's father was to
have shoes put upon him, together with a robe and a

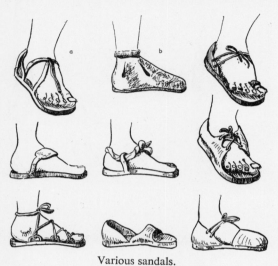

Various sandals.

ring.[3] When Jesus commanded his disciples, who
were sent on a mission, not to "carry" (the Greek
verb means "to carry a burden") purse, nor scrip, nor
sandals,[4] we must apparently understand by that that
they were not to take a change of shoes with them
but to be satisfied with the sandals they had on their
feet (as the Gospel of St Mark states [5]). Still today,
it is rare for a man to go barefoot; a fellah would

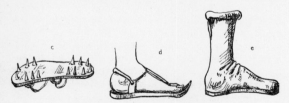

Hobnailed sandals and Oriental shoes.

blush to be met without shoes even if he were carrying them in his hand. Women dispense with them
more readily: at Beisan we saw a native woman on
leaving a place take off the shoes she had carefully
kept on her feet while going through it.

Sandals (the Hebrew word is supposed to come
from a root meaning "to protect, secure") are made
of a wooden, leather, reed, or palm-bark sole, held
on the foot and at the ankle by thongs;[6] a leather
ring is often made for the big toe to pass through.

There is great variety among these shoes: some sandals are even hobnailed (c). The Mishnah forbade
the wearing of such shoes on the Sabbath day. Amos
reproached the Israelites for selling the poor for a
pair of sandals; [7] these, indeed, were of no great
value. Doubtless well-to-do people often used a type
of shoe which figures on an Assyrian obelisk: King
Jehu's envoys who brought the tribute to Shalmaneser III wore on their feet babouches whose
pointed raised tip, like the Hittite shoe, protected the
toes (d). Assyrian soldiers were equipped with rather

Greek shoes.

high bootees (e) [8] which the great ladies of Palestine
hastened to imitate by having the shoes of different
coloured skins made to which Ezekiel refers.[9] In the
Greek period the Greek national shoe (krepis, Lat.
crepida) was introduced all the more easily as it was
a sandal; and when the Romans in their turn established themselves in the country they brought with
them their style of shoes also: the calceus was worn

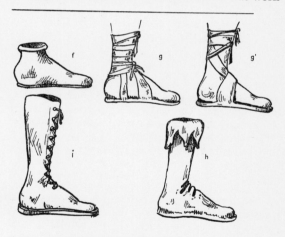

Roman forms of footwear.

by the Roman citizen (f), but if provided with four
thongs it was the mark of the Senator (g and g'); the
embas was a leather half-boot with revers (h), the
origin of which is to be found in the shoe worn by
the Assyrian warrior (e); finally, the endromis was a
half-boot in which the two front parts were pulled
together by a lace passed through eyelet-holes or
looped over buttons (i).

Sandals were not worn indoors, which explains certain scenes in the Gospels; [10] soiled by the dust or the mud of the roads, the feet were washed when the sandals were taken off, and it was the first duty of hospitality to offer all that was necessary for this purpose.[11] As is the practice still today in Mohammedan countries, the Israelite took off his shoes as soon as he trod on holy ground; [12] the priests also went barefoot in the sanctuary,[13] and this obligation was not without risk to their health. Just as captives marched without sandals,[14] so those in mourning or sadness did not wear them either: at the time of Absalom's revolt, David left Jerusalem barefoot.[15]

With the Israelites, probably, as with other peoples, to put one's foot on something or to cast one's sandal on a piece of land meant to take possession of it; [16] moreover, an old custom required that in a case of sale or transfer, the former owner should take off one of his sandals and give it to the new owner; the sandal was thus like a symbol of the right of ownership.[17]

In the N.T. the shoe which is part of the Christian's armour is the symbol of eagerness to proclaim the gospel of peace.[18]

[1] Gen. 14. 23; Ex. 3. 5; 12. 11; Jos. 5. 15; 9. 5; 1 Kgs. 2. 5; Is. 11. 15; etc.; Matt. 3. 11; Acts 12. 8. [2] Dt. 29. 5. [3] Lk. 15. 22. [4] Matt. 10. 10; Lk. 10. 4; 22. 35. [5] Mk. 6. 9. [6] Gen. 14. 23; Is. 5. 27; Lk. 3. 16; Jn. 1. 27; Acts 13. 25. [7] Amos 2. 6 (8. 6). [8] Is. 9. 5 (R.V. mg). [9] Ez. 16. 10; cf. Cant. 7. 1. [10] Lk. 7. 38, 44; Jn. 12. 3. [11] Gen. 18. 4; 19. 2; 24. 32; 43. 24; Jg. 19. 21; 1 Sam. 25. 41; 2 Sam. 11. 8; Lk. 7. 44; Jn. 13. 5; 1 Ti. 5. 10. [12] Ex. 3. 5; Jos. 5. 15; Acts 7. 33. [13] Ex. 30. 19. [14] 2 Chr. 28. 15; Is. 20. 2. [15] 2 Sam. 15. 30; cf. Ez. 24. 17. [16] Ps. 60. 8. [17] Ruth 4. 7; cf. Dt. 25. 9. [18] Eph. 6. 15.

SHOULDER

The LXX and Vulgate, followed by other versions, translate by "shoulder" the choice piece referred to in certain sacrifices [1]—the part put aside by Samuel for Saul; in fact, it was the right thigh of the hind leg of the animal.

[1] Ex. 29. 22; Lev. 7. 33; 8. 25; etc.; 1 Sam. 9. 24.

SHOVEL

This name is sometimes given by our versions to differing utensils for which the Hebrew has special terms: the winnowing shovel,[1] the spade (or mattock),[2] the tent-peg which could be used to dig the soil,[3] and utensils used to remove the ashes of sacrifices.[4]

[1] Is. 30. 24. [2] Is. 7. 25. [3] Dt. 23. 13. [4] Ex. 27. 3; 1 Kgs. 7. 40; 2 Kgs. 25. 14; Jer. 52. 18.

SICKLE

This implement, used in the harvesting of corn and barley, is mentioned only four times in the O.T., and under two different names: [1] it is possible that one means a toothed sickle and the other a sickle with a plain blade. In one of his parables [2] Jesus mentions a sickle, and the Apocalypse several times in a symbolic passage.[3]

Excavations in Palestine have provided us with some examples of slightly curved sickles; the oldest

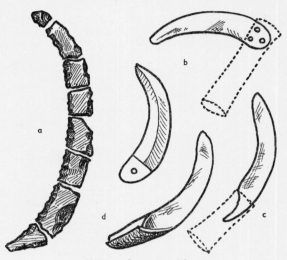

Sickles of stone and iron.

are made of notched flints, joined together and fixed with bitumen into a wooden frame (a); use of these was long continued; the bronze sickles which succeeded them are rare; iron ones were fixed to a handle by rivets (b), by a tang (c), or by a socket (d).

[1] Dt. 16. 9; 23. 25; Jer. 50. 16; Joel 3. 13. [2] Mk. 4. 29. [3] Rev. 14. 14–20.

SIEGE

The siege of fortified towns in ancient times necessitated all sorts of operations and the use of various measures illustrated admirably by certain eastern bas-reliefs and mentioned by numerous Biblical texts. If the Israelites were at first dismayed by the Canaanite fortifications, they too learnt with time how to seize the most solid ramparts, and to defend their own. But the masters in the art of besieging towns (poliorcetia) were above all the Assyrians, Greeks, and Romans.

The besiegers began by investing the town, which they did by cutting possible water channels and by surrounding it if necessary with entrenchments and palisades [1] in the hope of conquering it by famine. If the town resisted, they had to try to approach the walls to undermine them,[2] make breaches in them,[3] or burn down the gates; [4] huge shields or roofs protected the soldiers,[5] and ladders* enabled them to scale the walls.[6] But, in order to achieve their aim, the attackers also used battering-rams* and engines of war,[7] increasingly improved, or else they constructed earth-banks, mounds, and earthworks [8] and, later, movable towers (*heleopoleis*, 1 Macc. 13. 43) fitted with draw-bridges enabling them to attack the defenders on the level or to dominate even the top of the walls.

As for the besieged—who had previously made ready their water [9] and food supplies—they used their bows* and arrows* [10] from the top of their fortifications, threw down upon their assailants lighted torches and various missiles,[11] set up catapults* and engines of war [12] upon their battlements, while endeavouring to overthrow those of the enemy by means of chains fitted with grappling hooks. If possible the breaches in the walls were repaired immediately, if need be by demolishing houses to obtain the necessary stones; [13] the inhabitants of the encircled towns even attempted dangerous sorties [14] to take the adversary by surprise, to overthrow the operations for approaching the town and to relieve it, and in the event of the withdrawal of their soldiers they hoisted them rapidly up the walls to avoid opening the gates.

The O.T. often tells in a lively fashion of the hazards of such sieges,[15] of the cunning and treason which they occasioned,[16] and it stresses the dreadful plight into which the defenders might fall.[17] This type of warfare naturally provided the Bible writers with numerous images and comparisons.

(† Fortifications, war.)

[1] 2 Kgs. 25. 1; Is. 29. 3; Jer. 52. 4; Ez. 4. 2; 17. 17; 26. 8; Lk. 19. 43. [2] 2 Sam. 20. 15 (R.V. mg). [3] 2 Kgs. 25. 4; 1 Macc. 13. 43. [4] Jg. 9. 49, 52; Jer. 51. 58. [5] Ez. 26. 8; Nahum 2. 5. [6] Joel 2. 7. [7] Is. 29. 3; 1 Macc. 6. 31, 51; 11. 20; 2 Macc. 12. 15. [8] Dt. 20. 20; 2 Sam. 20. 15; 2 Kgs. 19. 32; Is. 37. 33; Jer. 6. 6; 32. 24; Eccl. 9. 14; Ez. 4. 2; 17. 17; 26. 8. [9] Nahum 3. 14. [10] 2 Sam. 11. 24. [11] Jg. 9. 53; 2 Sam. 11. 20, 21. [12] 2 Chr. 26. 15. [13] Is. 22. 10. [14] 2 Sam. 11. 17; 1 Kgs. 20. 16; 1 Macc. 6. 31. [15] 1 Kgs. 20. 22; 2 Kgs. 18. 19; Nahum 2. 5 . . . [16] Jos. 8. 10 . . .; Jg. 9. 34 . . .; 2 Sam. 5. 6. [17] Dt. 28. 52 . . .; 2 Kgs. 6. 24 . . .; 7. 1 . . .; 18. 27; Jer. 51. 30.

SIEVE

After being winnowed († agriculture), the grain was then passed through a sieve to remove foreign matter. Sieves, which must be distinguished from riddles for flour, were constructed of leather thongs or cords of gut.

In the Bible sieves occur in comparisons and in three passages only.[1] But Amos complains that the merchants sell "the refuse of the wheat". [2]

[1] Is. 30. 28; Amos 9. 9; Lk. 22. 31. [2] Amos 8. 6.

SILK

Some exegetes and some versions of the Bible suppose that Ezekiel was speaking of silk when he represented Yahweh as carefully clothing Jerusalem with a veil of *meši*, among other beautiful materials; [1]

but the translation of this word is by no means certain. On the other hand, the Book of Revelation names silk in the list of precious materials commonly sold in the markets of Babylon the Great.[2]

[1] Ez. 16. 10, 13. [2] Rev. 18. 12.

SILVER

From ancient times this metal has been known in the land of Palestine, where it was used in making jewellery and by silver-smiths,[1] and as a standard of exchange in trade, in the form of discs, rings, ingots, and small bricks often of known weight [2] or which were weighed when a purchase was made.[3] The earliest silver "money" used in Palestine was the Persian daric; shekels of silver were minted only by the Jews in the Maccabaean period († money).

It follows from numerous O.T. texts that the Israelites could melt and mould silver, and also work it with the hammer. The prophets and poets often allude to these operations.[4] All sorts of things were made of silver: vessels, cups, jewellery, ornaments, musical instruments [5]—though for a long time the Phoenicians kept a monopoly of the industry.

Palestine had no silver mines; the metal was imported from abroad, notably from Ophir and Tarshish († metals).

[1] Gen. 24. 53; Ex. 3. 22; cf. Ex. 25 ff. [2] 1 Sam. 9. 8. [3] Gen. 23. 16; 44. 2; Jos. 7. 21; Jer. 32. 10; etc. [4] Ps. 12. 6; Prov. 25. 4; 26. 23; Is. 1. 25; Ez. 22. 18, 22; Zech. 13. 9; Mal. 3. 2 ff.; etc. [5] Num. 10. 2; 2 Sam. 8. 10; 1 Kgs. 10. 25; 2 Kgs. 12. 13.

SINGER

From ancient times doubtless musicians and minstrels travelled round in Israel, and their songs broke the monotony of the days or brightened festival programmes.[1] The lot of most of them must have been pretty wretched, especially that of the women singers, who often degenerated into courtesans.[2] The position of men and women singers taken into the service of kings was quite different; David maintained at his court men and women singers who entertained him during meals; Amos refers to songs in the palace [3] and we know, thanks to an Assyrian record, that men and women musicians were part of the tribute which Hezekiah had to hand over to Sennacherib (701 B.C.).

The talents of these singers were put to the service of worship, and the sanctuary at Jerusalem had its recognized singers. If we are to believe the Book of Chronicles, liturgical music—which the Law does not mention—had been organized by David on an impressive scale: 4,000 sacred singers are said to have functioned in his time.[4] Even if it is obvious that "imagination reported of the first Temple what was only true of the second", and that the writer of Chronicles often related the events as they should

249

have happened according to his own ideas, nevertheless the origins of cultic music may well date from the time of the earliest kings. Who knows if the instruments Solomon had made "for the singers" [5] were not destined for the official Temple singers, and if the words of Amos: "I will not regard the peace offerings of your fat beasts. Take thou away from me the noise of thy songs; for I will not hear the melody of thy viols", [6] do not attack a well-organized ritual? At any rate, we know that many singers were among the Israelites returning from Exile. [7] Although we must not confuse these singers with those of Ezra 2. 65 and Neh. 7. 67, who are rather wandering musicians accompanying the caravan, we can conclude from them that an institution was already firmly established well before the fall of Jerusalem.

Whatever the case may be, after the return from Exile sacred music was to play an ever greater part and the position of singers to become more important. The king of Persia was full of solicitude for them—they were exempt from all taxes. [8] Divided finally into three guilds, they lived in their own villages in the neighbourhood of Jerusalem, and their twenty-four groups used private rooms when they were in turn on duty in the Temple. [9] The value of their singing was so appreciated that it was considered by the author of Chronicles [10] to be of the nature of prophecy. It is true that he was so well disposed towards the singers that he was perhaps one of them, as has been suggested. At any rate, from being subordinate functionaries in the time of Ezra, [11] they were raised to the rank of Levites, [12] and according to Josephus, were finally allowed, under Agrippa II, to wear linen clothes like the priests. (The writer of Chronicles attributes this costume to them in the time of David. [13])

[1] Ez. 33. 32. [2] Is. 23. 15. [3] 2 Sam. 19. 35; Eccl. 2. 8; Amos 8. 3. [4] 1 Chr. 23. 5. [5] 1 Kgs. 10. 12. [6] Amos 5. 22, 23. [7] Ezr. 2. 41; Neh. 7. 44. [8] Ezr. 6. 8; 7. 24; Neh. 11. 23. [9] 1 Chr. 9. 33; 15. 19; 25; Neh. 12. 29; Ez. 40. 44. [10] 1 Chr. 25. 1. [11] Ezr. 2. 41; Neh. 7. 44; 10. 28. [12] 1 Chr. 16. 5–7; 23. 6. [13] 2 Chr. 5. 12.

SISTRUM

At the time when the Ark was first brought to Jerusalem, so the Second Book of Samuel says, [1] David and all the people danced before Yahweh and sang to the accompaniment of sistra, along with other instruments. This is the only Bible text which

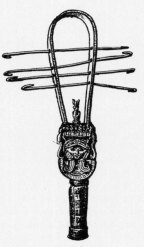

Egyptian sistrum.

mentions this percussion instrument, so much beloved by the Egyptians and often represented on the monuments of their land.

[1] 2 Sam. 6. 5 (R.V. mg).

SIVAN

This third month of the Hebrew year, May–June, is mentioned, in the Book of Esther, [1] on only one occasion.

(† Month.)

[1] Est. 8. 9.

SLAVE

"Fodder, a stick, and burdens, for an ass; bread, and discipline, and work, for a slave. Set thy slave to work, and thou shalt find rest: leave his hands idle, and he will seek liberty. Yoke and thong will bow the neck: and for an evil slave there are racks and tortures. Send him to labour that he be not idle; for idleness teacheth much mischief. Set him to work, as is fit for him; and if he obey not, make his fetters heavy." These terrible words of Ecclesiasticus [1] (in the Apocrypha) might make us believe that slavery, quite a natural and indispensable institution for the Israelites as for the other peoples of the ancient world, was particularly hard in Palestine. In actual fact, it was undoubtedly practised there more liberally, more humanely, than anywhere else. The text just quoted ends, in fact, with these words: "But be not excessive toward any; and without judgement do nothing. If thou hast a slave, let him be as thyself . . . treat him as a brother . . . If thou treat him ill, and he depart and run away, which way wilt thou go to seek him?" [2] These words, it is true, are relatively late, but it is a fact that Israelite legislation has always been kindly with regard to slaves, whose number, moreover, must never have been very great in Palestine. [3] There is reason, however, to distinguish clearly between those of foreign extraction and slaves of Israelite origin.

1. *Foreign slaves.* The slave of foreign extraction, bought for silver (30 shekels [4] on an average in ancient times, i.e., about £4) and either a war captive or son of a slave, [5] was the absolute property of his master, who could re-sell him, give him away, or hand him on as inheritance. In the accounts of the patriarchs the slave is frequently ranked with the cattle; [6] the laws of justice which were valid for the free man are not applicable to him († law). But his owner is not allowed to kill him; [7] if the slave died under the blows he suffered in punishment, or if he died within a day afterwards, his master was blameworthy; however, if death only occurred later, justice did not intervene, as the master was considered to be punished sufficiently by the very loss he suffered. [8] On the other hand, if the slave were maimed as the result of brutal treatment (loss of an eye or even a

tooth), he had a right to immediate liberation.[9] Contrary to what happened in Rome, Deuteronomy does not admit that a fugitive slave should be returned to his master; [10] he profited by a sort of right of asylum, for it was felt that he had not fled without serious cause, but this legal disposition was perhaps only valid for refugees from abroad.[11]

The slave enjoyed the day of rest [12] and, once circumcised,[13] he took part in worship and religious festivals: [14] it is obvious that he was considered a member of the family to the extent that a servant "acquired with money" by the man offering the sacrifice could eat sacred things, which was forbidden even to the daughter of the priest if, by her marriage, she was united to a non-priestly family.[15]

And so intelligent, well-beloved slaves—they are not lacking in the O.T.—were invested with all the confidence of their master,[16] and especially those born in his house; their opinions were asked for and listened to; [17] they could even be entrusted with important offices, and with delicate missions.[18] Enjoying high esteem,[19] some of them finally owned slaves themselves,[20] married their master's daughter,[21] or profited from her legacies.[22] A woman slave could also become the wife of her master's son.[23]

The following insistence on the part of Deuteronomy is significant also: Israel must remember, in her relations with slaves, that she was a captive in Egypt.[24] Job was careful not to scorn their rights, for, he said—and these words are not lacking in depth—"Did not he that made me in the womb make him [the slave]? And did not one fashion us in the womb?" [25] The Book of Proverbs does not wish a slave to be slandered before his master.[26]

2. *Israelite slaves.* One can expect that the position of Israelite slaves was generally better still than that of foreign slaves; the law was closely concerned with their lot. Whereas it was forbidden, on pain of death, to enslave an innocent Israelite against his will,[27] he could be constrained by penury, or in order to pay his debts, to sell his children as slaves or to sell himself [28] († debt); the thief unable to repay had to pay with his person.[29] But an essential arrangement, though not valid for foreigners, enabled the Israelite slave, after six years' service and in the course of the seventh year, to recover his liberty.[30] (With the Babylonians, enslavement for debt was limited to a period of three years.) Slavery, however, was so little considered as a catastrophe that the Covenant Code had already foreseen the case where in order not to abandon his family, out of fear of independence accompanied by want, or for other reasons, the Israelite preferred to remain in his master's house. In such a case the latter solemnly pierced (the lobe of) his (right?) ear, thus stamping him with the indelible seal of slavery for life.[31]

The Deuteronomic Law [32] maintained these arrangements without mentioning, it is true, the obligation on the part of the freed slave to give up the wife given him by the master, and his children.[33] But we cannot necessarily conclude from such an omission that this clause was abrogated. But, with customary generosity, Deuteronomy exhorts the master not to dismiss the freed slave empty-handed, but to make him a few presents in kind,[34] doubtless in order to make easier for him the return to a life of freedom.

Were all these laws always observed? It seems not, if we read the complaints and threats of Jeremiah [35] in this connection.

It is nonetheless true that the Priestly Code itself would no longer hear speak of Israelite "slaves"; they could only be "servants". It was to Yahweh that the Israelite belonged by right. He could not be subjected to any man.[36] "And if your brother who dwells by you becomes poor, and sells himself to you, you shall not make him serve as a slave; he shall be for you as a hired servant, and as a sojourner . . . They shall not be sold as a slave is sold . . . Both your bondmen and female servants, whom you shall have, shall be from the nations that are round about you." [37] On the other hand, these servants were freed only every fifty years, in the Year of Jubilee*.[38] Moreover, the Priestly Code provided that an Israelite who sold himself (to a foreigner living in the land, it was said) had the power to redeem himself—a proof that he was able to amass some wealth—or get himself redeemed by a close relative.[39]

3. *Women.* The position of the female slave (foreign or Israelite) was always a special one because of the fact that she very often became the concubine of the man who had bought her, or of his sons. If so, she was not freed after six years, even if she was an Israelite.[40] But the law took her under its protection. Unfortunately the text [41] is not very clear on this point and gives rise to various interpretations. However, if the Israelite slave ceased to please her lord, the latter had no right to sell her: he had her redeemed by a member of the family to which she belonged.[42] If he took a second concubine he had to assure the first of a suitable income and her keep, otherwise she had the right to be freed.[43]—The Deuteronomic Law extended emancipation to female Israelite slaves after six years' service, if they wanted it,[44] but this doubtless referred only to those who were not concubines.

The foreign slave, too, could not be sold by the man who had had conjugal relations with her. For the Arabs even today, to act otherwise would be to lay oneself open to general scorn, especially if the woman were a mother.[45] It is noteworthy that the slave who belonged personally to the wife [46] could not become, without the latter's consent, the concubine of the husband.[47] Finally, Deuteronomy allowed the captive woman to mourn her father and mother for a month before the marriage was consummated.[48]

SLING

Even if the Israelites, who were victims of certain raids, were sold in the market-places abroad,[49] it does not appear that their people indulged in slave traffic; this was in the hands of the Phoenicians and neighbouring nations.[50]

In the N.T. there is frequent mention of slaves. (It is true that versions often translate by "servant", "handmaid", and the like, Hebrew and Greek words signifying "slave".) Jesus makes them figure in several of his Parables (Tares, Wicked Husbandmen, Unmerciful Servant, Talents, Great Supper, Prodigal Son) or alludes to their position [51] and their tasks, as does St Paul, who likes to call himself the slave of Jesus Christ; [52] we know that the Epistle to Philemon is a note of commendation on behalf of a fugitive slave; and we know the classical exhortations made as much to the masters as to the slaves by the apostle to the Gentiles.[53] The Essenes had given up the practice of slavery; Jesus and the N.T. writers never attacked it directly, but its condemnation was implicit in their liberating message.

Eastern politeness demanded that one should term oneself the "slave" of the superior one was addressing; [54] consequently this word is often used in the Bible texts in its metaphorical sense.

[1] Ecclus. 33. 24–28. [2] Ecclus. 33. 29. [3] Neh. 7. 67. [4] Ex. 21. 32. [5] Gen. 14. 14; 17. 12; Eccl. 2. 7. [6] Gen. 12. 16; 24. 35; 30. 43; Ex. 20. 17. [7] Ex. 21. 20. [8] Ex. 21. 21. [9] Ex. 21. 26, 27. [10] Dt. 23. 15. [11] Gen. 16. 6; 1 Sam. 25. 10; 1 Kgs. 2. 39–40. [12] Ex. 20. 10; 23. 12. [13] Gen. 17. 12, 13, 23, 27. [14] Ex. 12. 44; Dt. 12. 12, 18; 16. 11, 14. [15] Lev. 22. 10–13. [16] Gen. 24. 2; Matt. 24. 45–46. [17] Jg. 19. 11; 1 Sam. 9. 5–10; 25. 14–17. [18] Gen. 24; 2 Sam. 10. 2–4. [19] 1 Sam. 9. 22. [20] Gen. 9. 25 (?); 2 Sam. 9. 10. [21] 1 Chr. 2. 35. [22] Gen. 15. 2; Prov. 17. 2. [23] Ex. 21. 9. [24] Dt. 5. 15; 15. 15; 16. 12; 24. 18, 22. [25] Job 31. 13, 15. [26] Prov. 30. 10. [27] Ex. 21. 16; Dt. 24. 7. [28] Ex. 21. 2; Dt. 15. 12; Lev. 25. 39; 2 Kgs. 4. 1. [29] Ex. 22. 3. [30] Ex. 21. 1–4. [31] Ex. 21. 5, 6. [32] Dt. 15. 12–18. [33] Ex. 21. 4. [34] Dt. 15. 13–15. [35] Jer. 34. 8–22. [36] Lev. 25. 42, 55. [37] Lev. 25. 39 . . . [38] Lev. 25. 40. [39] Lev. 25. 47–55. [40] Ex. 21. 7. [41] Ex. 21. 7–11. [42] Ex. 21. 8. [43] Ex. 21. 10, 11. [44] Dt. 15. 12, 17. [45] Dt. 21. 14. [46] Gen. 16. 6; 24. 61; 25. 12; 29. 24, 29. [47] Gen. 16. 1–2; 30. 3, 9. [48] Dt. 21. 13. [49] Joel 3. 6; Amos 1. 6, 9. [50] Ez. 27. 13. [51] Matt. 10. 24–25; 20. 27; 24. 45–47; Lk. 12. 35–48; 17. 7, 8; Jn. 8. 35. [52] Rom. 1. 1; Phil. 1. 1. [53] Eph. 6. 5 . . .; Col. 3. 22 . . .; Tit. 2. 9, 10 (1 Pet. 2. 18). [54] Gen. 32. 18; 43. 28; Num. 32. 25; Ruth 3. 9; 1 Sam. 25. 41; etc.

SLING

The sling was used by the shepherd to defend his flock, and was also used by the huntsman. We know with what skill David handled it,[1] and the poem of Job declares that slingstones are no more than stubble for leviathan (the crocodile).[2] But the sling was still a military weapon; Egyptians, Assyrians, Greeks, and Romans mobilised troops of slingers, and the O.T. alludes to those of Jehoram and Uzziah.[3] The men of Benjamin were past masters, it appears, in the art of slinging: [4] "Every one could sling a stone at a hair and not miss! " As soldiers they were armed both with bows and slings.[5] Made of a leather thong, or of plaited cords, widened in the centre to take in its "hollow" [6] a round, smooth stone,[7] the sling was given a swift rotary motion, and the missile flew off

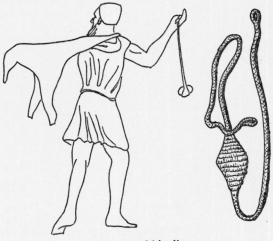

A slinger and his sling.

the moment one of the ends of the thong was suddenly released.

[1] 1 Sam. 17. 40, 49. [2] Job 41. 28. [3] 2 Kgs. 3. 25; 2 Chr. 26. 14. [4] Jg. 20. 16. [5] 1 Chr. 12. 2. [6] 1 Sam. 25. 29. [7] 2 Chr. 26. 14; Zech. 9. 15.

SLUG

Only Ps. 58. 8 alludes to this mollusc: "Let them [the wicked] be like the slug, which melts as it goes along." (That was how the sticky trail left by the creature was explained.) Because the slug unprotected by a shell is rare in Palestine, some translators think the Psalmist was referring to a snail*.

SMELTING

If by a bold anachronism whose religious meaning is obvious the Israelites dated the origins of metallurgy [1] from the first era of the world, it is nonetheless certain that Palestine received early on from abroad the knowledge necessary for the working and, strangely enough, for the smelting of metals. Industrial furnaces, somewhat broken down, have been uncovered at several town sites in Palestine; the O.T. is acquainted with them [2] and often alludes also to objects, notably idols, made of metal cast in moulds prepared for the purpose.[3] The decoration of Solomon's Temple (pillars, bowls, cultic utensils, etc.) necessitated much smelting work directed by a Tyrian master-workman who had settled in the Jordan Valley, where he found water and the clay essential for the creation of casting-moulds.[4]

Certain Bible authors were not ignorant of the methods used to refine and purify precious metals († crucible).

(† Metals, bronze, copper, silver, tin, etc.)

[1] Gen. 4. 22. [2] Gen. 19. 28; Prov. 17. 3; 27. 21; Jer. 6. 29. [3] Ex. 32. 4; Jg. 17. 2–4; Jer. 10. 14; cf. Acts 19. 24. [4] 1 Kgs. 7. 13 . . ., 46.

SMITE

To strike an Easterner on the cheek is to do him a grave wrong; indeed, in later Judaism the culprit was heavily fined. The O.T. only mentions a single affront of this kind.[1] On the other hand, Jesus and Paul were struck several times.[2] A number of Biblical texts speak of smiting in a figurative sense.[3]

[1] 1 Kgs. 22. 24 (2 Chr. 18. 23). [2] Matt. 26. 67; Mk. 14. 65; Jn. 18. 22; 19. 3; Acts 23. 2; 1 Cor. 4. 11. [3] Job 16. 10; Is. 50. 6; Lam. 3. 30; Mic. 5. 1; Matt. 5. 39; Lk. 6. 29; 2 Cor. 12. 7.

SMITH (SMITHY)

There was no special word in Hebrew to signify the smith, and he simply bore the name of workman, artisan, literally "cutter",[1] or more precisely: cutter of bronze or of iron;[2] they also spoke of "one who smites the anvil".[3]

Tradition has it that the smith's trade goes back to the dawn of history, when it is said[4] that "Tubal Cain was an instructor of every artificer in bronze and iron". In reality, work in metal, which is not

Smiths. An Egyptian tomb painting.

native to Palestine, was introduced into that country at about the beginning of the 3rd millennium. The Phoenicians and Philistines seem to a certain extent to have had the monopoly of it for a long time,[5] but the Israelites finally applied themselves to it:[6] there are numerous objects of iron*, among other things, mentioned in the texts—texts which are not unacquainted with the anvil or the smith's hammer,[7] while the bellows spoken of by Jeremiah[8] are those of the smelter.

The smiths readily plied their trade from place to place in order, strangely enough, to repair ploughing

instruments or to make new ones. The traces of an Israelite smithy, complete with plough-shares, have been dug up in Palestine; an Egyptian tomb painting represents in an interesting way two smiths working a smithy bellows, and Ecclesiasticus evokes in a few words the effort and care of these artisans: "So is the smith sitting by the anvil, and considering the unwrought iron: the vapour of the fire will waste his flesh; and in the heat of the furnace will he wrestle with his work: the noise of the hammer will be ever in his ear, and his eyes are upon the pattern of the vessel; he will set his heart upon perfecting his works, and he will be wakeful to adorn them perfectly."[9]

[1] 1 Sam. 13. 19; 2 Kgs. 24. 14; Zech. 1. 20. [2] Is. 44. 12. [3] Is. 41. 7. [4] Gen. 4. 22. [5] 1 Sam. 13. 19. [6] 2 Chr. 24. 12; Is. 44. 12; Zech. 1. 20; cf. 2 Ti. 4. 14. [7] 1 Kgs. 6. 7; Is. 41. 7; cf. Jer. 23. 29. [8] Jer. 6. 29. [9] Ecclus. 38. 28.

SNAIL

These molluscs with coiled shells are represented in Palestine by a large number of species. There is no reference to them in the Bible if the mollusc mentioned in Ps. 58. 8 is taken as a slug*, but this is not certain.

SNARE

In the O.T. and in the N.T. there are a dozen terms used to signify different snares whose exact form cannot always be specified; and so our versions cannot be very strict on this matter and often give the wide sense of traps, snares, toils, and nets to words whose technical meaning we do not know and which are, moreover, used in many cases as synonyms. However, this hunting gear and fishing tackle can quite naturally be grouped in three categories according to its use.

1. *The bird-catcher's snares.* These traps, of various shapes and names, functioned automatically or were operated from a distance. They were generally equipped with a bait, and doubtless resembled those still used today in Palestine. The Bible generally mentions them in a figurative sense: "Surely he shall deliver thee from the snare of the fowler," says, for example, Ps. 91. 3 (cf. also Ps. 124. 7; Prov. 1. 17; 7. 23; Eccl. 9. 12; Jer. 48. 43; Hos. 7. 12; 9. 8; Amos 3. 5; Lk. 21. 35).

2. *Hunting snares.* These were nets stretched over the path of the game or meshed snares intended to bring it down. Several kinds are mentioned in the O.T. by way of similes, as: "Thy sons [Jerusalem!] have fainted . . . as an antelope in a net."[1] "The nations are sunk down in the pit that they made; in the net which they hid is their own foot taken."[2] "I will spread my net upon him [King Zedekiah], and he shall be taken in my snare, and I will bring him to Babylon."[3] (Cf. also: Job 18. 8, 9; 19. 6;

Ps. 31. 4; 57. 6; 69. 22; etc.; Prov. 22. 5; Jer. 18. 22; Ez. 12. 13; 19. 8; etc.)

Some of these snares may be combined with a hole covered over with branches into which the victim falls. The Egyptians and the Assyrians—their bas-reliefs prove this—generally practised hunting or the capture of birds by means of tackle analogous to that quoted by the O.T.

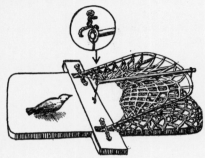

Fowler's net.

3. *Fishing-nets*. Various types are occasionally mentioned, generally metaphorically in the O.T. books, but it is the Gospels in particular which speak of them. Apart from the nets, in the generic sense of the word, which Jesus' disciples mended, washed, or cast at their Master's command,[4] it is necessary to distinguish the "casting net", which was a wide, circular, weighted net of 10 to 15 ft. span, which the fishermen skilfully cast on the water to imprison the fish in its mesh,[5] and the *sagene* (drag-net, seine-net,

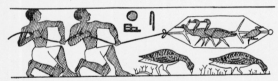

Hunting net.

trail-net), which was a long net that collected everything; the fishermen cast it from the height of the boats or as they entered the water and slowly folded it back upon itself, laden with its often strange contents, either in a closed circle or towards the shore, where the edible fish were sorted out (Parable of the Drag Net [6]). The Egyptians also were acquainted with these two sorts of nets, which are still commonly used in Palestine, where we have witnessed scenes perfectly illustrating the Gospel stories.

[1] Is. 51. 20. [2] Ps. 9. 15. [3] Ez. 17. 20. [4] Matt. 4. 21; Mk. 1. 19; Lk. 5. 2, 4, 6; Jn. 21. 6. [5] Matt. 4. 18; Mk. 1. 16. [6] Matt. 13. 47, 48.

SNUFFERS

This instrument, used to cut or trim the burning wicks of lamps, is included among the gold utensils made by Solomon for use in the Temple.[1] Snuffers were also part of the Tabernacle equipment.[2] In Hebrew the same word also occurs for the tongs with which one of the seraphim took a glowing stone from the altar in Isaiah's vision.[3]

[1] 1 Kgs. 7. 49; [2] 2 Chr. 4. 21. [2] Ex. 25. 38; 37. 23; Num. 4. 9. [3] Is. 6. 6.

SOAP

No doubt, like other people, the Israelites used a coarse and primitive soap, obtained by mixing the ashes of wood or of certain plants with a fatty substance. The poem of Job alludes to it.[1]

(† Nitre, potash.)

[1] Job 9. 30.

SONG

Beloved by Oriental people, in Palestine, also, singing accompanied the labour of the workmen, especially at the time of harvesting the crops and at the wine harvest.[1] It was normal at feasts, and public and private rejoicings: weddings, family festivities, welcome to the conquerors on their return from war, etc. Laban, when reproaching Jacob for his secret departure, said to him: "I might have sent thee away with mirth, and with songs, with tabret, and with harp"; [2] as they met the victorious Saul and David, the women of all the towns of Israel came out, singing and dancing; [3] and songs and dances also enhanced the great feast which the father of the prodigal son gave in his honour.[4] But if God smites his people "they shall no more drink wine with a song"; to cause the noise of singing and the sound of harps to cease was a significant threat in the mouth of the prophets.[5] As certain meals gave rise to abuse, the wise men of Israel scourged the cynicism of wicked men who "sing to the timbrel and harp, and rejoice at the sound of the pipe" and the heedlessness of the chief men that "sing idle songs to the sound of the viol".[6]

Although people sang as they danced,[7] funeral ceremonial also included elegiac songs which are often referred to; Jesus even called to mind the children who in their games imitated adults singing funeral dirges.[8]

Beside the elegies given in the Second Book of Samuel,[9] the song sung after the crossing of the Red Sea and, above all, the magnificent Song of Deborah celebrating the victory over Sisera,[10] a few vestiges of secular songs have remained in the O.T., in particular the Song of the Well, and even a fragment of a Tyrian song.[11] Some of the melodies to which certain Psalms had to be sung were perhaps secular songs (cf. the titles of Ps. 8, 22, 56, 80, 84).

But music* and song served, above all, to express the intensity of religious life. That is why the sacred song was particularly held in honour by the Israelites. When they went up to Jerusalem for their great festivals they struck up spiritual songs; [12] when they went through the doors of the Temple their joy burst forth in hymns to the glory of God.[13] Ps. 68, recalling the triumphal procession in the sanctuary the day after a victory, declares: "The singers went before, the minstrels followed after, in the midst of the damsels playing with timbrels." [14] To express their hopes and their faith, the devout had at their disposal a whole collection of hymns with joyful strains: we have only to think of the "Songs of Zion", whose beauty was appreciated by foreigners and which the deported refused to sing in the land of Exile; [15] or of those Hallel Psalms [16] which ended the meal Jesus took with his disciples before his arrest.[17] Even in the cults celebrated in the sanctuary, the songs of laymen had their place,[18] and the sacrifices of thanksgiving in particular enabled the faithful to express their feelings aloud.[19]

However, liturgical songs properly so-called, especially after the Exile, were sung by singers* and the official musicians of the Temple; the Psalter has preserved several of them, which magnificently enhanced the great festivals of Israel [20] or which accompanied sacrificial offerings; seven Psalms, for example, were assigned to each day of the week to be sung at the morning service.[21] The people themselves took part in these hymns with "Amens" and "Hallelujahs", or by singing refrains or responses.[22] These choruses were accompanied by instrumental music;[23] it appears that people always sang in unison.[24] They readily took part in antiphonal singing, whereby the massed choir replied to a soloist or one group to another group; [25] at the time of the completion of the rebuilding of the walls of Jerusalem Nehemiah even organized two huge choirs in procession.[26]

It is likely that a certain place in the synagogue service was given at an early date to the singing of Psalms. As for the first Christians, it is known that they liked to give full scope to their inner joy by singing: Paul and Silas in prison sang the praises of God, and before the throne, in the Book of Revelation, new songs resound.[27] "Teach [cf. Dt. 31. 19] and admonish one another in psalms and hymns and spiritual songs," writes St Paul to the Colossians, "singing with grace in your hearts to the Lord." [28]

The Eastern song sounds differently from ours; it is a singing speech rather than a melody. The range of notes, with the Hebrews, was doubtless not very extensive, and they did without any harmony. But they probably much enjoyed, as do the Arabs today, half-tones, singing through the nose, trills, and a special vibrato obtained by exerting a slight pressure on the throat (an Assyrian bas-relief represents this gesture). But, above all, it was the rhythm which counted, for the song was accompanied by various movements, marches and counter-marches,

clappings of hands, and dances*.[29] Even sacred song did not scorn these manifestations, and dance played its part in religious processions.[30]

[1] Is. 9. 3; 16. 10; Jer. 48. 33; Hos. 2. 15; etc. [2] Gen. 31. 27. [3] 1 Sam. 18. 6. [4] Lk. 15. 25. [5] Is. 24. 8; Jer. 16. 9; 25. 10; Ez. 26. 13; etc. Cf. Rev. 18. 22–23. [6] Job 21. 12; Amos 6. 5. [7] 1 Sam. 18. 6; 21. 11; Lk. 15. 25; etc. [8] 2 Chr. 35. 25; Jer. 9. 20; Amos 5. 16; etc. Matt 11. 17; Lk. 7. 32. [9] 2 Sam. 1. 18; 3. 33. [10] Ex. 15. 20–21; Jg. 5. [11] Num. 21. 17–18; Is. 23. 15–16. [12] Ps. 120–134. [13] Ps. 100. [14] Ps. 68. 25. [15] Ps. 137. [16] Ps. 113–118. [17] Matt. 26. 30; Mk. 14. 26; cf. Is. 30. 29. [18] Ps. 26. 6, 7; 27. 6. [19] Ps. 22. 22; 66. 16; 116. [20] 2 Chr. 29. 26–30. [21] Ps. 24, 48, 81, 82, 92, 93, 94. [22] 1 Chr. 16. 36; Ps. 99. 3, 5; 106. 48; 136. [23] 1 Chr. 15. 19 . . .; 25. 1; etc. [24] 2 Chr. 5. 13. [25] Neh. 11. 17; 12. 24; Ps. 24. 7–10; Is. 6. 3; Rev. 19. 4–5. [26] Neh. 12. 27 . . . [27] Acts 16. 25; Rev. 5. 9; 14. 3; etc. [28] Col. 3. 16; cf. Eph. 5. 19; Jas. 5. 13. [29] Ex. 15. 20; Jg. 11. 34; 1 Sam. 18. 6; Jer. 31. 4; etc. [30] Jg. 21. 21; 2 Sam. 6. 5; Ps. 149. 3; 150. 4; cf. Ex. 32. 19.

SOUNDING-LINE

Although the idea of sounding, probing, trying is common in the Bible in a figurative sense, the only reference to a sounding-line is in the shipwreck of St Paul.[1]

[1] Acts 27. 28.

SPADE

Some versions translate thus the last tool mentioned in 1 Sam. 13. 20 and that referred to also in Is. 7. 25, but the identification of agricultural implements is questionable. In both cases the R.V. gives "mattock"*.

SPAN

The span is a measure of length equal to half a cubit* or three handbreadths*; it was 8·9 or 10·3 in., according to whether the ordinary or the royal cubit was used. It was the stretch of the open hand from the thumb to the tip of the little finger.—The High Priest's breastplate was a square of side one span.[1] This was also the size of the rim of the sacrificial altar in Ezekiel's Temple.[2] In poetic vein, when Second Isaiah sings the praise of the Creator God he declares that "he measured the heavens with a span".[3]

[1] Ex. 28. 16; 39. 9. [2] Ez. 43. 13. [3] Is. 40. 12.

SPARROWS (AND OTHER PASSERES)

Palestine is rich in passerine birds of all varieties; the majority of those familiar to us are found there (tits, finches, robins, warblers, larks, blackbirds, etc.) with other species in addition. The Hebrew noun which designates the whole group is no doubt applied particularly to the sparrow which abounds there; but, apart from one or two exceptions, no particular species of passerine bird is named in the Bible: thus, even the law relating to the purification of lepers [1] is not precise about what particular small birds have to be brought to the priest. The O.T. texts otherwise make only simple passing allusions to their resting-place,[2] flights,[3] migration,[4] song,[5] and the nets which snare them.[6] In the N.T. Jesus, recalling the low market value of sparrows, nevertheless asserts that not one of them is forgotten before God, and adds: "Fear not therefore: you are of more value than many sparrows." [7]

[1] Lev. 14. 4 . . . [2] Ps. 84. 3; 102. 7; Ez. 17. 23. [3] Ps. 11. 1; Prov. 26. 2. [4] Hos. 11. 11. [5] Ps. 102. 7; Eccl. 12. 4. [6] Prov. 6. 5; 7. 23; Amos 3. 5. [7] Matt. 10. 29, 31; Lk. 12. 6–7.

SPEAR

Our translations use the word spear for two weapons which have different names in Hebrew: one (hanit) was more like a javelin, hardly over 4 ft. long and was probably a kind of pike, hunting-spear, a nomad's ancient weapon, used in hunting as well as in war, perhaps a sign of authority also; the other

(rômaḥ) was probably a spear proper: longer and heavier, and measuring up to 6 ft. long, it was generally used in the hands of troops who also bore a shield.

Both weapons are often mentioned in O.T. texts; the spears of Goliath and Saul, for example, were probably of the first type,[1] the lances of Rehoboam's and Asa's soldiers, of the second.[2] It must be recognized that this distinction, probable as it may be, is nevertheless beset with some difficulties. Thus Goliath's spear had a shaft "like a weaver's beam", that is as thick as the two rollers carrying the warp, in weaving-looms; the length of the weapon must have been in proportion, with the result that this javelin was perhaps as big or even bigger than a spear. In any case, these weapons were all made from a wooden shaft into which the "tang" of the spear head was fitted; usually the head had a socket into which the shaft was driven. The other end was fitted with a ferrule which allowed the spear to be driven into the ground, as Saul did; [3] even today, among the Bedouin, a spear stuck in the ground at a tent door indicates that it belongs to a chief. Many spear heads of various shapes, made of bronze or iron,[4] have been found in excavations in Palestine.

The spear with which a soldier pierced Jesus' side is the only one mentioned in the N.T.[5]—Though the prophet Joel exclaims, "Beat your pruning-hooks into spears!",[6] we know that Isaiah and Micah, reversing the expression, looked forward to the time when the nations would beat their spears into pruning-hooks.[7]

[1] 1 Sam. 17. 7; 18. 11; 19. 10; etc. [2] 2 Chr. 11. 12; 14. 8; cf. Jg. 5. 8; Neh. 4. 13; Jer. 46. 4. [3] 1 Sam. 26. 7. [4] 1 Sam. 17. 7. [5] Jn. 19. 34. [6] Joel 3. 10. [7] Is. 2. 4; Mic. 4. 3.

Development of the metal parts of the spear in Palestine.

SPELT

There is a Hebrew word found only three times in the O.T. which is generally translated by "spelt". We are told in the Book of Exodus [1] that the seventh plague in Egypt of hail destroyed the flax and the barley which were already in the ear, but did not damage the later-maturing wheat and spelt. Isaiah speaks of the good sense of the farmer who sows wheat and barley in his field and spelt at the edges.[2] Spelt can be sown in poor soil. Ezekiel is commanded to mix wheat, barley, beans, lentils, millet, and spelt to make bread.[3]

Some exegetes and botanists, doubting whether spelt was cultivated in Egypt, Palestine, or Babylonia, prefer to think of sorghum (Indian millet); then the Ezekiel passage would be grouping the grains in pairs: wheat and barley, beans and lentils, millet and sorghum. However, it has recently been possible to verify that early Egyptian bread was made of spelt flour.

[1] Ex. 9. 32. [2] Is. 28. 25. [3] Ez 4. 9.

SPICES

The vegetable substances with an aromatic smell or a piquant taste, which the Israelites used to flavour their foodstuffs, all came from plants cultivated in the country. Those mentioned in the O.T. and N.T. are as follows:

dill	mustard
coriander	rue
cummin	saffron († crocus)
mint	

For details see the individual articles.

SPIDER

Although many kinds of spiders exist in Palestine, the Bible speaks only of the spider's web as a figure for vain [1] or delusive [2] achievements. Sometimes the word *semamit* in Prov. 30. 28 has been translated by "spider" (Luther, A.V., etc.), but more likely a lizard is meant.

[1] Is. 59. 5. [2] Job 8. 14.

SPIKENARD

In the O.T. only the Song of Songs speaks, on three (?) occasions,[1] of this perfume with its particularly agreeable odour. The N.T. records [2] that Mary poured it upon Jesus' head (Matt. and Mk.) or on his feet (Jn.), during the meal at the house of Simon the leper. While Matthew speaks of the ointment as very precious, Mark and John actually say that it was spikenard, pistic (genuine?) nard, and all three lay stress on its value: it could have been sold for more than 300 denarii and given to the poor, some of them murmur. It had a subtle odour; the Fourth Gospel remarks that the house was filled with it.—It is possible that the ointment poured upon the feet of Jesus by a sinful woman [3] was also spikenard; in any case, it was contained in a phial of alabaster like that used at the Bethany anointing.

Spikenard is an aromatic oil, made from the roots and radical leaves of a plant which belongs to the Valerianaceae and which grows on the slopes of the Himalayas. Since it was imported from this remote country, it was very expensive. Horace, in one of his poems, promises Virgil a whole cask of good wine for a small phial of spikenard.

[1] Cant. 1. 12; 4. 13, 14. [2] Matt. 26. 6 . . .; Mk. 14. 3 . . .; Jn. 12. 1 . . . [3] Lk. 7. 36 . . .

SPINNING

From pre-historic times spinning has been practised in Palestine, as testified by the stone balancers with which the spindles were weighted and which have been found in excavations. Through the centuries it has remained one of the chief occupations of women at home. The main raw material used was wool,[1] then goat's hair [2] or camel's hair [3] and—at an early date on the banks of the Nile but later elsewhere—flax.[4]

The spinners of antiquity used neither a wheel nor probably even a distaff. They obtained the necessary twisting of the fibres by merely rotating a spindle,[5] stuck into a stone acting as a steadying factor and on whose shaft the thread was wound. Several Egyptian paintings and reliefs represent young Egyptian

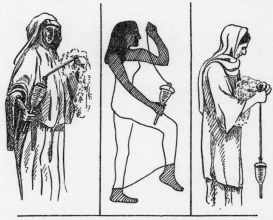

The three main movements of the spinner.

women busy at this work, and their traditional gestures are performed still today by Bedouin women; as they walk along they twist the wool which they carry over their arm or hidden in a fold of their clothing, giving a rapid rotary movement to the spindle by rubbing it against themselves, then letting it hang down so that the twist should be regular.

Christ refers to the work of the spinner in the famous text: "Consider the lilies of the field, how they grow; they toil not, neither do they spin: Yet I say unto you, that even Solomon in all his glory was not arrayed like one of these." [6]

[1] Job 31. 19 ff. [2] Ex. 35. 26; 36. 14. [3] Matt. 3. 4; cf. 2 Kgs. 1. 8. [4] Jos. 2. 6. [5] Prov. 31. 19. [6] Matt. 6. 28; Lk. 12. 27.

SPITTLE

Not only does the Easterner spit on the ground before someone he detests or merely at the mention of his name, but he will go up to him to spit in his face. This was even a recognized action among the Israelites by a widow to the brother-in-law who had refused to marry her [1] (Levirate marriage*), and a father could even express indignation against his daughter in this way when he was displeased.[2] Job complained of being treated thus by those who derided him,[3] while the servant of Yahweh accepted such humiliating chastisement.[4]

SPONGE

We know that Jesus did not escape this kind of insult from the Jews [5] and the Roman soldiers; [6] he had foreseen as much.[7]

[1] Dt. 25. 9. [2] Num. 12. 14. [3] Job 30. 10. [4] Is. 50. 6. [5] Matt. 26. 67; Mk. 14. 65. [6] Matt. 27. 30; Mk. 15. 19. [7] Mk. 10. 34; Lk. 18. 32.

SPONGE

Unknown in the O.T., sponge is mentioned only in the narrative of Christ's passion: the lips of the crucified, tortured by thirst, benefited from the vinegar-water (a drink of Roman soldiers) which one of the helpers at the crucifixion had soaked up in a sponge and then put on the end of a reed.[1] Had it been expressly prepared for the victims, or were the soldiers using it for other purposes? We are not told.

[1] Matt. 27. 48; Mk. 15. 36; Jn. 19. 29 (on a lance?).

SPRING

It can easily be understood that in the East, and in a country as deprived of water as Palestine, water should have been an object of great veneration and of a cult. It is even more precious for the nomad than milk, which he possesses in abundance; moreover, by encouraging vegetation it promotes the existence of shade, which is a blessing in the midst of the sunny, barren steppe. How could one not see something divine in the water which springs forth mysteriously from the earth or which lies at the bottom of a well? And when the spring is intermittent, warm, sulphurous, when it not only quenches the thirst but also works wonders in certain illnesses, how could it fail to be sacred?

It is known that cults have been celebrated in the sanctuary at Dan near the most abundant of the springs of the Jordan. In the time of Jeroboam I a golden bull could be found there.—The kings of Jerusalem were consecrated near a spring: Adonijah at the spring of Rogel, but Solomon at the spring of Gihon, the present Virgin's Fount and the starting-point of the famous Siloam tunnel.—To the northeast of Bethany the spring and sanctuary of Ain Shems is known, now called the Apostles' Fountain. —It was near the spring of Beersheba that Abraham planted a sacred tree; [1] Isaac set up an altar [2] there, and offered a sacrifice.[3]—Finally, Kadesh, whose name comes from the verb meaning "to be holy", was also a spring near which there was a place of worship.

In the figurative sense, "spring" expresses the idea of origin.[4] But there are springs whose water is tainted, and which are a figure for the righteous giving way before the wicked; [5] there are springs which dry up—a symbol of God's punishment; [6] but there are also springs of living water—those which gush forth from faith in Jesus Christ; [7] they are also a symbol of the happiness of the elect in heaven.[8]

(† Sanctuary.)

[1] Gen. 21. 33. [2] Gen. 26. 25. [3] Gen. 46. 1. [4] Job 38. 16; Prov. 4. 34; etc. [5] Prov. 25. 26. [6] Hos. 13. 5. [7] Jn. 7. 38. [8] Rev. 7. 17.

SPY

Espionage, familiar in all countries and all ages, was not unknown to the Israelites. In the Bible texts the references are not always to spies properly so-called,[1] but to "scouts", "informants", men designated to "explore" some particular region.[2]

The narrative of the sending of spies to Jericho leads us to think that the association between espionage and prostitution already existed.

[1] Gen. 42. 9; Jos. 2. 1 . . .; 6. 22; 1 Sam. 26. 4. [2] Num. 13 and 14; 21. 32; Dt. 1. 22 . . .; Jg. 7. 10; 18. 2; 2 Sam. 10. 3.

STABLE (STALL)

In Palestinian houses* in the country there was often a stable or a cattle-stall for the animals being fattened [1] or for the beasts of burden and draught-animals [2] in the lower part of the only room, the other animals living in the pasture the whole year round.—But the O.T. declares that Solomon "had forty thousand stalls for horses* for his chariots*" [3] (cf. 2 Chr. 9. 25—"four thousand"), and that Hezekiah made "stalls for all manner of beasts".[4] It is an interesting fact that the stables which Solomon possessed at Megiddo were discovered in about 1930

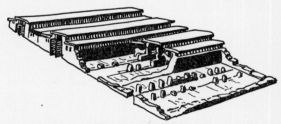

Solomon's stables at Megiddo (reconstruction).

in the ruins of this fortified town at the opening of the pass through the Carmel Range.[5] Each of them comprised a rectangular covered hall; in the centre, formed by the pillars supporting the roof, there was a wide corridor on to which the stalls of the horses faced from both sides. Between the pillars there remain a few stone mangers; and one can even see that certain holes made in the pillars eventually became polished by the rubbing of the bridles passed through them. The stables at Megiddo could perhaps shelter in all nearly 400 horses.

(† Shepherd, crib.)

[1] 1 Sam. 28. 24; Amos 6. 4; Mal. 4. 2; Lk. 15. 30. [2] Hab. 3. 17. [3] 1 Kgs. 4. 26. [4] 2 Chr. 32. 28. [5] 1 Kgs. 4. 12; 9. 15.

STACTE

Styrax officinalis is a shrub which grows everywhere in the Mediterranean region and especially in

A shoot of *Styrax benzoin*.

its eastern parts. Its brown, vanilla-flavoured gum was probably used by the Israelites as one of the constituents of incense.[1]

(† Balm.)

[1] Ex. 30. 34.

STAFF

This was the indispensable item of the traveller's equipment,[1] which he must have to defend himself against enemies[2] or against the savage dogs*[3] sometimes so common in Palestine; he needed it for removing the stones that hindered access to water in cistern or spring,[4] or simply for striking his mount. It served the peasant for beating out a little grain († agriculture), and also anyone who inflicted a beating*. On occasion some Israelites used it for divination.[5] Often it was decorated in such a way that it could be identified among many others.[6] Yet it continued to be a figure for poverty; not to have a staff was misery indeed.[7] This fact, moreover, resolves the famous contradiction which occurs between Matt. 10. 10 and Mk. 6. 8: "A traveller with only a staff", and "A traveller without even a staff" are two expressions meaning, "A very poor traveller"; they only superficially contradict each other, basically they mean exactly the same thing.—Figuratively, the staff represents the punishment (beating) Yahweh will bring upon Israel,[8] and yet again it symbolized God's protection, like a shepherd's* in defence of his flock.[9]

(† Rod.)

[1] Ex. 12. 11; Jg. 6. 21; 1 Sam. 14. 27; 2 Sam. 23. 21; 2 Kgs. 4. 29 ff.; Is. 10. 15. [2] Mic. 5. 1; Matt. 26. 47 par. [3] Lk. 16. 21. [4] Num. 21. 18; Num. 22. 27. [5] Hos. 4. 12. [6] Gen. 38. 18. [7] Gen. 32. 10. [8] Is. 10. 24. [9] Ps. 23. 4.

STANDARD

The Book of Numbers[1] attributes to the Israelites marching in the desert a banner or standard for each tribe, probably, and ensigns for the clans. But it is

impossible to specify the nature or form of these distinctive objects; according to the rabbis, they were differentiated from one another by the colour and the emblems with which they were decorated (lion, bull, eagle, etc.).

In the O.T. the references are more often than not to the *nes*, meant to be seen from a distance to act as a signal of alarm, of mobilization, or for a rallying point.[2] It was usually set up on a bare mountain or a

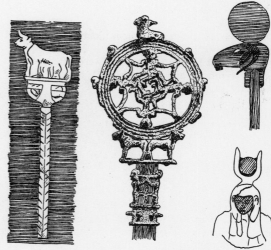

Ensigns from Mari (mother of pearl); Iranian (bronze); Egyptian (wood).

high hill,[3] and was doubtless a mast or pole,[4] to which was probably attached a gaudy piece of cloth. In a few texts the *nes* accompanies the army[5] or even means a ship's flag.[6]

The word is used particularly in the metaphorical sense by the prophets: Yahweh lifts up his standard to bring together the sons and daughters of Israel or on the contrary, to call the nations against them.[7] During the battle against the Amalekites, Moses with his arms uplifted was a living standard for his people;[8] after the victory he erected an altar which he called "Yahweh nissi", "Yahweh is my standard."[9]

[1] Num. 1. 52; 2. 2; 10. 14; cf. Cant. 2. 4. [2] Jer. 51. 27. [3] Is. 13. 2; 18. 3; 30. 17; Jer. 6. 1. [4] Num. 21. 8, 9; 26. 10. [5] Is. 31. 9; Jer. 4. 21. [6] Ez. 27. 7. [7] Is. 5. 26; cf. 11. 10, 12; 49. 22; 62. 10; Jer. 4. 6. [8] Ex. 17. 10 . . . [9] Ex. 17. 15.

STAR

The innumerable multitude of the stars,[1] created by God,[2] who called them all by the names he had given them,[3] and differing in glory and brightness,[4] ruled over the night and gave light to it.[5] They composed part of the great army of the skies which was under the orders of Yahweh its head.[6]

STATER

In order to understand some Bible passages we must remember that in accordance with ancient, popular belief the stars were thought of as living beings: thus, they applauded the magnificence of creation [7] or came to aid heroes in battle.[8] (Observe also the place St Paul gives them in 1 Cor. 15. 40 ff.) Worship of them, so widespread among Israel's neighbours, was introduced into Palestine at certain periods,[9] but was severely condemned by the Law and the prophets.[10]

The Israelites were acquainted with various constellations; some are mentioned in the O.T. († Bear, Orion, Pleiades), though their identification is not certain.

In Biblical language the stars were often used as poetic symbols and metaphors,[11] notably in the Apocalypse.[12]

[1] Gen. 15. 5; 22. 17; 1 Chr. 27. 23; Neh. 9. 23; Heb. 11. 12. [2] Gen. 1. 14, 16; Neh. 9. 6; Ps. 8. 3. [3] Ps. 147. 4; Is. 40. 26. [4] 1 Cor. 15. 41. [5] Ps. 136. 9; Jer. 31. 35. [6] Gen. 2. 1; Dt. 4. 19; Ps. 148. 3; Is. 24. 21. [7] Job 38. 7. [8] Jg. 5. 20. [9] 2 Kgs. 17. 16; 21. 5; 23. 4, 5; Zeph. 1. 5; Acts 7. 42. [10] Dt. 4. 19; 17. 3; Jer. 8. 2; 19. 13. [11] Gen. 37. 9; Dan. 12. 3; 2 Pet. 1. 19; Jude 13. [12] Rev. 1. 16 . . .; 2. 28; 12. 1; 22. 16.

STATER

The stater was a Greek coin, once referred to in the Bible,[1] worth four drachmas or one shekel; it was another name for the tetradrachma.

[1] Matt. 17. 27.

Silver stater from Cilicia.

STEWARD

"Steward" represents a Greek word (*oikonomos*) which means one who manages a household.

On two occasions [1]—and most strikingly in the Parable of the Unfaithful Steward—Jesus alludes to the duties of stewards or bailiffs, to whom was confided the administration of large houses which they tended and whose estates they developed. For his part, St Paul declares that the apostles must be regarded as "stewards" or administrators of the divine mysteries.[2] The Epistle to Titus calls a bishop the "steward of God", [3] and the First Epistle of Peter desires Christians to be good stewards of divine grace.[4]

The treasurer of some Greek towns also bore the title *oikonomos*. A disciple of Paul's called Erastus was *oikonomos* of Corinth.[5]

[1] Lk. 12. 42; 16. 1–13. [2] 1 Cor. 4. 1. [3] Tit. 1. 7. [4] 1 Pet. 4. 10. [5] Rom. 16. 23.

STOCKS

Hebrew vocabulary has three or four words for instruments of punishment used upon prisoners; it is impossible to distinguish one from another, but they probably included stocks and collar, that is, a structure made of two large pieces of wood into which the prisoner's feet were inserted and sometimes perhaps his hands and neck as well. It was thus that Jeremiah was put into the stocks by the overseer in charge of the Temple,[1] and that King Asa threw the prophet Hanani into "the house of the stocks".[2] The Book of Job twice mentions figuratively these instruments of punishment. They appear only in later Bible passages, so that the question can be raised whether they were known in early days in Israel.

In the N.T. the Acts of the Apostles records that at Philippi Paul and Silas were thrown into an inner prison, where the gaoler made fast their feet in the stocks.[3]

[1] Jer. 20. 2–3; cf. 29. 26. [2] 2 Chr. 16. 10; Job 13. 27; 33. 11. [3] Acts 16. 24.

STONES (PRECIOUS)

In every age in great demand by Eastern peoples, precious stones—or "stones of desire" [1] or "stones of grace",[2] as they are also called in Hebrew—entered into the structure of jewellery, crowns, seals, and the ornamentation of royal and priestly robes. The Israelites got them direct from foreign parts (Ophir, Arabia, Egypt, Media, India) or through the intermediary of Phoenicians and Egyptians; [3] no doubt they were usually already cut, but in Palestine, also, workmen were found who were capable of cutting, mounting, and engraving them.[4]

It is not always easy to determine the exact variety of stone meant by the Hebrew terms used in the O.T., and in any case the opinions of scholars sometimes diverge. While precious stones are very often mentioned in Bible texts, both collectively [5] and individually, it is useful to notice in particular the three lists which group, as in three caskets, all the Israelites thought most beautiful in this realm: the twelve stones of the High Priest's breastplate,[6] the gems adorning the king of Tyre [7] according to Ezekiel, and the jewels which the Book of Revelation named as adorning the foundations of the wall of the New Jerusalem.[8]

Palestine excavations have enabled us to recover all kinds of gems, particularly cornelians, amethysts, jaspers, agates, onyx, and quartz.

List of the precious stones mentioned in the Bible

agate	jacinth
amethyst	jasper
beryl	onyx
carbuncle	opal
chalcedony	quartz
chrysolite	ruby
chrysoprase	sapphire
cornelian († sardonyx)	sardonyx
diamond (?)	topaz
emerald	

To this list may be added corals and pearls, as well as alabaster and marble, although their origin is different.

(For details, see the entry for each of the above stones.)

[1] Is. 54. 12. [2] Prov. 17. 8. [3] 1 Kgs. 10. 11; Ez. 27. 16, 22. [4] Ex. 35. 33. [5] 1 Kgs. 10. 2; 2 Chr. 32. 27; Ez. 27. 22; 1 Cor. 3. 12; Rev. 17. 4; 18. 12. [6] Ex. 28. 17–20; 39. 10–13. [7] Ez. 28. 13. [8] Rev. 21. 18–20.

STONING

Many texts in the O.T. and N.T. show that the Israelites at all times were quick to throw stones at those who aroused their anger and that they were quite ready to lynch any such people.[1] The reproaches of Jesus against the Jews who stoned the prophets are famous; [2] it is known that he himself was several times threatened with stoning,[3] that Paul was actually stoned at Lystra, where he barely escaped death,[4] and that Stephen was executed in this way by the people.[5]

Israelite law prescribed stoning as the capital punishment for the following numerous offences:

idolatry, Dt. 13. 10; 17. 5 (13. 5).
blasphemy*, Lev. 24. 14; 1 Kgs. 21. 10; Jn. 10. 33.
child sacrifice, Lev. 20. 2.
divination, Lev. 20. 27.
violation of the Sabbath*, Num. 15. 32–36.
adultery*, Dt. 22. 22, 23; cf. Ez. 16. 40; 23. 47; Jn. 8. 4, 5.
misconduct, Dt. 22. 21.
rebelliousness of children, Dt. 21. 20, 21.
dangerous ox, Ex. 21. 28.

Furthermore, the O.T. records that at Mt Sinai anyone who touched the mountain sanctified by Yahweh's presence was to be stoned [6] and that, after the capture of Jericho, Achan was stoned by order of Joshua for breaking the law about devoted* spoil.[7]

Those condemned to be stoned were taken outside the town; [8] the witnesses, whose responsibility was thus deeply involved, had to cast the first stones [9] and the people, as executors of the verdict, then carried

261

through the sentence.—According to Jewish traditions, the guilty party was almost completely stripped of clothing and, with hands bound, was hurled [10] by the first witness to the bottom of a hollow in the ground; if he did not die as a result of the fall, the second witness threw a heavy stone at his head or chest, and the people then pelted the dying man. The corpse was buried in a special place with the stone which had inflicted the fatal blow; no mourning ceremony was permitted.

[1] Ex. 17. 4; Num. 14. 10; 1 Sam. 30. 6; 2 Sam. 16. 6; 1 Kgs. 12. 18; Lk. 20. 6; Acts 5. 26; 14. 5. [2] Matt. 21. 35; 23. 37; Lk. 13. 34; (2 Chr. 24. 20–22; Heb. 11. 37). [3] Jn. 8. 59; 10. 31, 33; 11. 8. [4] Acts 14. 19; 2 Cor. 11. 25. [5] Acts 7. 58–59. [6] Ex. 19. 12, 13; Heb. 12. 20. [7] Jos. 7. 24, 25. [8] Lev. 24. 14, 23; Num. 15. 36; 1 Kgs. 21. 10, 13; Acts 7. 58. [9] Lev. 24. 14; Dt. 13. 9; 17. 7; Jn. 8. 7. [10] Lk. 4. 29.

STORK

Two species of these waders, which ancient peoples already surrounded with a certain veneration, are found in Palestine: the common white stork is to be seen on the plains bordering the Mediterranean and in the Plain of Jezreel, in spring at the time of its migration northwards; and the wilder black stork, seen in winter in the south of the land. The Hebrew name for the stork (= pious, kind) shows that its gentleness to its young and its dutifulness had been remarked upon.—The Law forbade eating its flesh.[1] The four other passages in the Bible where it is mentioned refer to its maternal wings and their power, to its knowledge of the seasons (for its migrations) and to its habit of nesting, in the East, in high trees.[2]

[1] Lev. 11. 19; Dt. 14. 18. [2] Job 39. 13 [16] (text uncertain); Zech. 5. 9; Jer. 8. 7; Ps. 104. 17.

STRAW

In Israel reapers cut the corn high up on the stalks and left the tall stubble in its place; this was always burnt in the fields to give manure.[1] The chopped straw, which has a different name in Hebrew from stubble, and which must be distinguished also from husks*, meant the bruised stalks which remained after the trampling and winnowing of the corn sheaves († agriculture, threshing-sledge). The distinction is clearly drawn in the account of the making of bricks by the Hebrews in Egypt; [2] "Ye shall no more give the people straw to make brick [said the Pharaoh] ... So the people were scattered abroad throughout all the land of Egypt to gather stubble for straw." [3] It was used, in fact, to make the bricks* firmer before they were dried. Straw was used mainly as stable-litter and as food for animals; [4] Isaiah says that in the Messianic Age the lion will eat straw like the ox.[5]

In the symbolic language of the O.T. straw and stubble, sometimes assimilated one with the other, are often a figure for things of no value, for adversaries, for potentates, for the unfaithful and the wicked, which the wind [6] will carry away or the fire consume.[7] The Gospel saying about the straw (strictly, a fragment of straw) and the beam has become classical.[8]

[1] Ex. 15. 7; Is. 5. 24; 47. 14; Joel 2. 5; etc. [2] Ex. 5. 6–18. [3] Ex. 5. 7, 12. [4] Gen. 24. 25, 32; Jg. 19. 19; 1 Kgs. 4. 28. [5] Is. 11. 7; 65. 25. [6] Job 21. 18; Ps. 83. 13; Is. 40. 24; 41. 2. [7] Ex. 15. 7; Is. 5. 24; 47. 14; Obd. 18; Mal. 4. 1. [8] Matt. 7. 3; Lk. 6. 41–42.

STRONG-DRINK

The beer that ancient people made with barley or other cereals is styled in this way. Some versions use the word to translate a Hebrew term often employed in the O.T. (and in parallel with the word "wine"), which means etymologically "intoxicating drink", and from which it is impossible to tell whether beer, wine made from honey or from fruits, or all of these drinks together are intended.[1]

[1] Lev. 10. 9; Num. 6. 3; Jg. 13. 4; 1 Sam. 1. 15; Prov. 20. 1; 31. 6; Is. 5. 11; 56. 12; etc. Cf. Acts 2. 13.

STYLUS

The style or stylus was the instrument used for writing on lead, and later, on wax tablets († writing §3). It was made of bronze, iron, silver, or bone. One end, which was pointed, dug into the lead or wax; the other, spatula-shaped, was used to wipe out what was written by repeated pressing.

Metal stylus.

It is this latter use to which the prophet's threat may refer, as it is found in some versions: "I will efface Jerusalem as one effaces what is written on tablets; I will make the stylus pass and repass often over it until nothing remains there"; [1] but this translation is doubtful. Nevertheless, the expression "to efface someone's name" [2] very probably connects with this practice.

[1] 2 Kgs. 21. 13. [2] Dt. 9. 14; 25. 6; 29. 20; 2 Kgs. 14. 27; Rev. 3. 5.

SUICIDE

Judging from the O.T., suicide appears to have been rare in Israel; the laws do not speak of it. Only seven cases, really very varied ones, are given in the Biblical texts, namely the deaths of Abimelech,[1] Samson,[2] Saul and his armour-bearer,[3] Ahithophel,[4] Zimri, king of Israel,[5] and Judas Iscariot.[6] The Second Book of Maccabees in the Apocrypha gives an account of the highly dramatic suicide of a Jerusalem elder.[7]

[1] Jg. 9. 54. [2] Jg. 16. 30. [3] 1 Sam. 31. 3–5. [4] 2 Sam. 17. 23. [5] 1 Kgs. 16. 18. [6] Matt. 27. 5; cf. Acts 1. 16 ff. [7] 2 Macc. 14. 37–46.

SUN

Our modern mind is surprised to notice that in the first chapter of Genesis light should be created independently of the sun and before the sun.[1] This is because the Israelite regarded light, and darkness also, as very fine substances, while the sun, moon, and stars were for him no more than light-bearers. Sometimes, however, the sun seems to be considered as though it were a personal being, like a young hero who leaves his chamber every morning and rejoices to run his course.[2] In his daily course he is preceded by the dawn,[3] who seems to have the appearance of a young man with powerful wings.

Before the arrival of the Israelites in Palestine, the Canaanites practised a form of sun worship. It was, indeed, a cult common to all the heathen peoples of this region. It appears, however, that this cult developed in Israel only under the influence of the Assyro-Babylonians. In the time of Manasseh, altars had been constructed in the Temple of Jerusalem to present offerings "to all the host of heaven"; [4] in the sanctuary there were horses and a chariot dedicated to the sun,[5] and later still, a short time before the destruction of the city, Ezekiel perceived with indignation twenty men within the Temple, facing the east, and prostrating themselves before the sun.[6]

In a general way, the Bible considers the sun to be one of the most glorious works of the Creator.[7] But although it recognizes the sun's obedience to the orders of God,[8] and considers its light as a blessing for the earth,[9] its moderation remains striking in comparison with the famous hymns dedicated to the sun by other religions.

The Bible writers compare God himself with the sun.[10] The splendour of this star and its brilliance are symbols of all that is beautiful,[11] and specially of the glory of those who love God,[12] the glory of the righteous,[13] and of Christ at prayer.[14] At the end of time the brilliance of the sun shall be darkened,[15] but in the future city the redeemed will dispense with light from the sun, because the glory of God will shine upon them, and the Lamb will be their lamp.[16]

(† Dial.)

[1] Gen. 1. 4, 16; Ps. 74. 16. [2] Ps. 19. 5. [3] Ps. 139. 9; Job 3. 9. [4] 2 Kgs. 23. 4, 5. [5] 2 Kgs. 23. 11. [6] Ez. 8. 16. [7] Ps. 74. 16; 148. 3. [8] Job 9. 7; Matt. 5. 45. [9] Dt. 33. 14; 2 Sam. 23. 4; Eccl. 11. 7. [10] Ps. 84. 11; 89. 36; 2 Sam. 23. 4. [11] Ps. 50. 2; Cant. 6. 10; Is. 9. 2. [12] Jg. 5. 31. [13] Matt. 13. 43. [14] Matt. 17. 2. [15] Is. 13. 10; 30. 26; Matt. 24. 29; Rev. 6. 12; etc. [16] Is. 60. 19; Rev. 21. 23.

SUNDAY

Was Sunday already observed in N.T. times—a Sunday which in the Christian Church ended by replacing the Sabbath, though without retaining its character? [1]

We know that the first Christians faithfully observed the Law, and consequently respected the Sabbath day. It is very difficult to specify the period when Sunday was substituted for it. Only three passages in the N.T., which unfortunately are very uninformative, probably imply that the Lord's day was singled out from the beginnings of the apostolic church.

The most ancient of these texts, 1 Cor. 16. 2, is a recommendation of St Paul: "Upon *the first day of the week* let each one of you lay by him in store, as he may prosper, that no collections be made when I come." Is that the first mention of Sunday? It is very possible. But as it is only an act performed in the privacy of the home, and not when believers gather together, which is in question here, it has been wondered if the apostle did not simply suggest that the day when the craftsmen and workmen of Corinth received their pay be chosen for putting some money aside.—The second text provides a more conclusive witness. St Paul has been at Troas for a few days; "*the first day of the week*", says Acts 20. 7, "when we were gathered together to break bread, Paul discoursed with them, intending to depart on the morrow; and continued his speech until midnight". It seems that this was not a particular meeting, but that the first day of the week had been set aside and reserved for the breaking of bread at Troas, if not in all the churches. Paul will not set off before the next day in order to be able to spend "Sunday" (but the word, it should be noted, is not yet used) with the Christians of the locality.—Finally, the author of the Apocalypse himself declares clearly that he fell into a trance "on the Lord's day"; [2] that expression could hardly mean, as it has been claimed, Easter day or some such other solemn day; it seems certain that we have here the most ancient distinct mention of Sunday.

The first day of the week had evidently been chosen in memory of the resurrection of Christ [3] and perhaps also of the descent of the Holy Spirit upon the apostles. References to the celebration of the Lord's day become more and more precise in the course of the 2nd century.

[1] Rom. 14. 5; Gal. 4. 9 . . .; Col. 2. 16 . . . [2] Rev. 1. 10. [3] Matt. 28. 1; Mk. 16. 2; Lk. 24. 1; Jn. 20. 1; cf. Jn. 20. 19, 26.

SUNSTROKE

Sunstroke was normally very frequent in Bible lands, because of their climate. No doubt that was the trouble with the Shunammite's son mentioned in the Second Book of Kings, [1] and the prophet Jonah at Nineveh. [2]

In sayings full of significance for Easterners, the Psalmist affirms that the sun "will not smite" the pilgrim to Jerusalem, [3] and the prophet makes the same promise to the people who will return there from captivity. [4] The Apocalypse, also, is confident that in the Heavenly Jerusalem neither the sun nor any burning heat will overwhelm any longer those who come out of the great tribulation. [5]

[1] 2 Kgs. 4. 18 . . . [2] Jonah 4. 8. [3] Ps. 121. 6. [4] Is. 49. 10. [5] Rev. 7. 16.

SURETY

Acting as surety is not mentioned in Israelite law, but it was not unknown there, [1] and more than once the Book of Proverbs warns earnestly against the risks it entails: "The man is without sense . . . who becomes surety for his neighbour." [2]

[1] Cf. Job 17. 3. [2] Prov. 17. 18; 6. 1; 11. 15; 20. 16; 22. 26.

SWADDLING-CLOTHES

Among the Israelites, as with Palestinian people today, babies were enveloped in swaddling-clothes. Ezekiel implies that to be deprived of them was a curse. [1] The poem of Job compares with swaddling-clothes the thick clouds that covered the primeval sea. [2] St Luke's Gospel records that Mary swaddled her son Jesus before laying him in the manger. [3]—These are the only instances of swaddling-clothes in the Bible.

[1] Ez. 16. 4. [2] Job 38. 9. [3] Lk. 2. 7, 12.

SWALLOW

Two Hebrew words, perhaps to be translated by swallow or swift, refer to this bird, which is very common in Palestine, where several species of it have been noted. The O.T. briefly alludes in turn to its nest, [1] its rapid flight, [2] its song, [3] and its migrations. [4]

[1] Ps. 84. 3. [2] Prov. 26. 2. [3] Is. 38. 14. [4] Jer. 8. 7.

SWAN

In the lists of unclean birds (Lev. 11 and Dt. 14), which are so difficult to identify, some versions, and the Vulgate in particular, give the name swan to the first creature listed in Lev. 11. 18 (= third in Dt. 14. 16). But, of northern origin, the swan is very rare in Palestine and Egypt. Some commentators have therefore suggested the ibis or moor-hen, but the bulk of modern versions accept screech-owl* or great owl*.

Development of the dagger in Bible times.

Development of the sword in Bible times.

SWORD

The pre-eminent offensive weapon of the Israelites was the sword, whose Hebrew name seems to have covered the dagger and even the poniard. It is therefore not always easy to specify exactly the type of blade meant in a given text. No description, moreover, is given of a sword in the O.T., where it is often mentioned; there was doubtless a very great variety of these weapons.

In ancient times the sword was made of bronze, then of iron [1] and was no doubt usually straight,[2] very sharp,[3] and two-edged.[4] It served both for cutting and thrusting, that is to say, to pierce through the adversary,[5] or to cut, "to put to the sword", "to smite with the edge of the sword".[6] Sheathed in leather,[7] it was worn at the belt [8] and not on a shoulder-strap. In the N.T., where it is sometimes mentioned,[9] it is spoken of also as an instrument of execution: [10] Roman justice often condemned people to death by the sword.

Excavations in Palestine have brought to light numerous specimens of swords, daggers, and poniards. The most ancient ones go back to Neolithic times. Some are of bronze, others of iron; they are of various dimensions, curves, and outlines. In Israelite times the blade of the poniards was at first separate from the handle of wood, bone, or horn, to which it was fixed by a few rivets (a); then the blade was furnished with a long tongue which passed through the handle and curved up at its base (b); later the blade and the handle were in one piece (c); the hilt was sometimes decorated with horn or ivory (d); of particular interest is the poniard of the year 1000 B.C., the blade of which was of iron, while the handle was of bronze (e).—Among the swords which have been discovered, it is possible to follow the same evolution in the handle; there have also been brought to light a certain number of curved swords (f), a sort of scimitar with a convex edge. These weapons seem to have been only for show, the official symbols of the power of those who carried them.

Frequently compared by the Bible to a fierce devouring [11] animal, the sword often symbolizes, in turn: war [12] or divine punishment,[13] divisions [14] or evil words,[15] suffering,[16] or again the penetrating Word of God.[17]

[1] 1 Sam. 13. 19. [2] 1 Sam. 31. 4, 5. [3] Ps. 7. 12; 64. 3; Ez. 21. 14. [4] Jg. 3. 16; Ps. 149. 6; Prov. 5. 4; Rev. 1. 16. [5] Jg. 3. 21; 2 Sam. 2. 16; 20. 10; Is. 14. 19. [6] Jos. 6. 21; 8. 24; 10. 28; Jg. 21. 10; 1 Sam. 17. 51; 1 Kgs. 3. 24–25; Job 1. 15, 17. [7] 1 Sam. 17. 51; 2 Sam. 20. 8; 1 Chr. 21. 27; Jer. 47. 6; Ez. 21. 9; Jn. 18. 11. [8] 1 Sam. 17. 39; 25. 13; 2 Sam. 20. 8; Neh. 4. 18; Ps. 45. 3. [9] Matt. 26. 47 . . .; Lk. 22. 38, 49, 52. [10] Acts 12. 2. [11] Dt. 32. 42; Is. 1. 20; Jer. 2. 30; 12. 12; 46. 10. [12] Lev. 26. 6, 25; 2 Sam. 11. 25; Jer. 5. 12; 46. 16; Ez. 7. 15. [13] 1 Chr. 21. 12; Ps. 7. 12; Is. 34. 5–6; 66. 16; Rev. 19. 15. [14] Matt. 10. 34. [15] Ps. 55. 21; 57. 4; 59. 7; Prov. 12. 18; 30. 14. [16] Lk. 2. 35. [17] Is. 49. 2; Eph. 6. 17; Heb. 4. 12.

SYCOMORE

This tree, with its thick foliage and its lower branches only a short distance from the ground,[1] generally reaches a considerable height and has a fine expanse. The sycomore-fig (*sukomorea*) belongs to the fig family; its foliage resembles, it is true, that of the mulberry (Greek: *morea*), but its fruits are fig-like (*sukon*). To make the fruits ripen it was necessary to prick or cut them, as did the prophet Amos; [2]

Sycomore.

they were of but mediocre taste but always abundant, so they served for the poor. Sycomores were native to Egypt and always widespread there.[3] In Palestine they flourished at Jericho [4] and on the coastal plain, and were common on the western slopes of the mountains of Judaea.[5] The wood, light and easy to work, but inferior to cedarwood,[6] was used for buildings and, in Egypt, for mummy-cases.

[1] Cf. Lk. 19. 4. [2] Amos 7. 14. [3] Ps. 78. 47. [4] Lk. 19. 4. [5] 1 Kgs. 10. 27; 1 Chr. 27. 28. [6] Is. 9. 10.

SYNAGOGUE

Synagogues, as their name indicates (*sunagoge* = a bringing together, a gathering), are not little temples where God may reside, but houses where people gather together to read the Law and to pray. Hellenistic Jews even more readily called them houses of prayer.

1. Origin. In N.T. times worship in the synagogue was an established institution, a deeply rooted custom. It had been established for generations,[1] and Ps. 74, which appears to date from the Maccabaean period, already seems to mention its existence.[2]— But Josephus and Philo attribute its foundation to Moses himself, while the Targums speak of synagogues of the patriarchs. It must be recognized that these last statements have no historical value.

Archaeologically, the oldest synagogue attested by an inscription is an Egyptian synagogue at Schidia near Alexandria, and dedicated to Ptolemy II (247–221). For such an institution to have been formed abroad, it must have been accredited already in Israel itself. Theologians are very nearly unanimous in thinking that synagogues may have been founded at any rate at the time of Ezra, at the time, that is, when religion was considered essentially as a collection of regulations—and must not this Law be known? must it not be taught? and how could that

Above: painting from the synagogue at Dura-Europos, showing golden candlestick to the left, sacrifice of Abraham to the right.—*Below:* sculptured reliefs from the synagogue at Capernaum (2nd–3rd century A.D.).

be done without gathering the faithful together?—However, the synagogue can be thought to have an earlier origin still. The loss of all Temple worship at the time of the Exile may have caused the religious leaders of Israel to gather together the faithful to mourn for the lost cult, and yet also to turn their thoughts to God and to think again about his will; the same reasoning may be applied to the Deuteronomic reform which, by centralizing worship at Jerusalem, at the same time deprived all the other localities of their worship at the high-places; it is not impossible that there were at that time already a few small religious gatherings which, without observing a synagogue form of worship properly so-called, may have known some prototype of it.

2. *Architecture.* They tried to build a synagogue on high ground "so that no one may live higher", the rabbis said. But in the Diaspora, in which the Jews were not authorized to build a place of worship in the towns, synagogues lay outside the cities, if possible beside rivers,[3] which facilitated the purification rites. According to the synagogues whose ruins have

been studied, it can be said that they conformed usually to local style. There were often three doors arranged on the one frontage, and which led through a pillared vestibule into the sanctuary itself; this was generally rectangular, and on three sides there ran a gallery supported by pillars and reserved for the women. Many ornaments, paintings, sculptures, and above all mosaics have been discovered which decorated these places of worship. It is possible that it was under Christian influence that an apse was built in which the Torah cupboard was placed, flanked by two candlesticks.

3. The essential *furniture* consisted of a cupboard closed by a curtain, which contained the scrolls of the Law carefully wrapped in linen and placed in a case. Next, a platform for the elders was necessary, and a sort of desk at which the man expounding the Scriptures sat. Finally, there were lamps, and

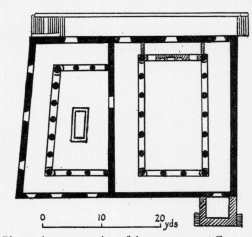

Plan and reconstruction of the synagogue at Capernaum, 2nd–3rd century A.D.

trumpets to announce fast days, and horns* to announce the New Year.

4. *Sabbath-day worship* usually proceeded in the following way: after a long prayer pronounced by one of the assistants while the faithful stood and faced Jerusalem, others of the congregation came

266

and read the passage for the day—for the Bible was divided into sections to be read each Sabbath day; in order that this reading should acquire its full value certain rules had to be respected: seven people at least had to take part in it, and none of them had to recite a single verse by heart. In N.T. times each verse was read in Hebrew and immediately translated into Aramaic.—Next came a freely chosen Bible reading taken from the Prophets; it was followed by an oral commentary or a paraphrased explanation of the text with edifying observations. Any member of the congregation could give this commentary.[4] Lastly, the service ended with a blessing preferably spoken by a priest.

It does not appear that at the time of the N.T. there was any specially appointed official for the reading, the exposition, and the prayer; however, already at that time we know there was a chief of the synagogue (who chose the commentator and the reader),[5] receivers of alms, and a "sexton" who carried the Scriptures,[6] taught the children to read, and carried out punishments.[7]

5. The institution of the synagogue made it possible for the religion of Moses to flourish independently of the Temple and its ceremonies. What is more, it displaced the centre of worship: it was the spoken word and no longer the ceremony which mattered, and due to that fact deeper piety became possible. It must not be forgotten that, after finding an audience in the synagogues, the apostle Paul set up with those who followed him a sort of Christian synagogue,[8] and that in this way the Christian form of worship sprang from that of the synagogue.

[1] Acts 15. 21. [2] Ps. 74. 8. [3] Acts 16. 13. [4] Mk. 1. 21, 39; Lk. 4. 20 ff.; 6. 2; 6. 6; 13. 10; Acts 13. 5; etc. [5] Acts 13. 15. [6] Lk. 4. 20. [7] Matt. 10. 17; 23. 34; Mk. 13. 9; Acts 22. 19. [8] Acts 13. 5, 14; 14. 1; 17. 1, 10, 17; 18. 4; 18. 19; 19. 8.

TABERNACLE

The Tabernacle is described in our texts [1] as a rectangular court bounded by a curtain of fine linen five cubits high, stretched over pillars with bronze sockets and silver hooks. In the centre the altar for burnt offerings was of wood but covered with bronze. The sanctuary itself was made of a palisade of planks of acacia wood covered in gold, as were also the bars which held them together; their bases were of silver. The hangings covering the whole were fastened with golden pins, and protected first by a covering of goat's hair and then by two covers of animals' skins. The two inner parts of the sanctuary had the same proportions as Solomon's Temple, with which it has striking points of resemblance. In the Holy of Holies there was a gold-covered table for the shew-bread; all the dishes, chalices, and cups used in the sanctuary were also of gold, as was the candlestick and the top of the altar

of incense. The Ark itself, with its lid and cherubim, were obviously also covered in this precious metal.

The Tabernacle was interpreted symbolically at an early date. The Epistle to the Hebrews [2] saw religious principles reflected in it. Josephus and Philo saw in it an image of the world, and since then there have been numerous people who have indulged in strange fantasies in respect of it. They have gone as far as to see in the sanctuary the form of the human body: the courts are supposed to be the limbs, the Holy Place the soul, the Holy of Holies the spirit, the palisade the skeleton, etc.—On reading attentively our texts concerning the Tabernacle we are obliged to recognize that the description of this sanctuary must spring from a confusion: its sumptuous appearance is surprising in the midst of a very poor people; the raw materials used, the equipment necessary for transport, and the transport itself can hardly be explained in the desert circumstances known from other descriptions; the Ark could not be at the same time in the tent of meeting († sanctuary) and in the Tabernacle; the period of the Judges and of the kingdom before Solomon knows nothing of the Tabernacle, and at the building of Solomon's Temple there is not the slightest reference to the earlier sanctuary which resembled it so strangely . . . etc. That is why, in the almost unanimous opinion of theologians, it can be said that the Tabernacle did not exist in that form. At the time of the redaction of the Priestly Code, with which our texts on this subject are connected, it was thought that the Israelite cult had always been what it then was, and that the sanctuary in the wilderness could only have been a prefiguration of the Temple of Solomon; thus ancient history was given the pattern of a relatively recent event, so that the Tabernacle in fact appears as a transposition of Solomon's Temple into the early history of Israel.

[1] Ex. 25–27, 30, 36–40. [2] Heb. 9. 1 ff.

TABERNACLES (FEAST OF)

This autumn feast, which the Israelites probably inherited from the Canaanites, was in ancient times the great feast of the year, and so great that it was called simply "the feast". It was a harvest festival,[1] but at the same time it marked the beginning of the year; it is very likely that this second aspect of the feast was of Israelite origin.

From the time of the monarchy, this solemn ceremony no longer bore the name of Feast of Ingathering, but was called the Feast of Tabernacles (i.e., of booths or huts), because usually at the time of gathering olives and grapes it was customary to leave the villages and to live in the orchards or vineyards during the whole harvest-time; that created an atmosphere of camp life, which people liked to feel when they went to spend the seven days of the feast at Jerusalem.[2] One of the important acts of this feast was the one which consisted of offering to God a basket full of all the fruits harvested.[3] This act of gratitude was made more definite and was transformed on the return from Exile, at the time when the Priestly Code—forced to teach the rules of religious life to a people who, lacking a Temple, had lost its tradition for half a century—was codifying the rites of the festivals. At that point they had to remember the time when Israel lived in tents in the wilderness, and especially in the promised land; they thought also of all the other and more recent sufferings of the people, and above all of all the deliverances God had granted them; and so life in tents at the time of the Feast of Tabernacles assumed a new meaning: it aimed at something like a renewal of life in the wilderness.[4] Some lived in tents, others built huts;[5] processions were perhaps made; numerous sacrifices were prescribed.[6]—Thanks to the Talmud, which devotes a whole tractate to this feast, we have precise information about the way in which it was celebrated in the days of the N.T. Every day the priests in procession went round the altar shouting Hosannahs and waving a bunch of three different branches; the congregation sang Ps. 118. At v. 26 ("Blessed be he that cometh in the name of the Lord") they prostrated themselves, waving the branches which they, too, held in their hands. On the seventh day they celebrated the water rite: a priest would go and fetch water from the spring of Siloam, and on his return he was received solemnly, and the water he brought back was poured out before the altar of burnt offerings to the sound of trumpets and to the acclamations of the Levites. Finally, a sort of night feast took place on this occasion in the Court of the Women: by the light of four golden candela-

bra, a few men would dance, holding lighted torches in their hands, while the onlookers sang Ps. 120–134. It has been thought that it may have been on this occasion that Jesus spoke the words: "I am the light of the world."[7]

[1] Ex. 23. 16; 34. 22; Jg. 9. 27; 21. 19; 1 Kgs. 8. 2; etc. [2] Dt. 16. 13. [3] Dt. 26. 2. [4] Lev. 23. 42. [5] Lev. 23. 40; Neh. 8. 15. [6] Num. 29. 12–38. [7] Jn. 8. 12.

TABLE

In the nomadic period the Israelites used, for a table, a mat or a round piece of leather around which they squatted for meals.[1] If we are to believe certain Bedouin customs, this piece of leather could be closed like a purse and hung on the camel's saddle, for it was equipped with loops which could be fastened by means of a little cord. This way of eating continued after settlement in Palestine;[2] at best, an upturned bushel* or a little stool could sometimes act as a table. Only the well-to-do and people of a certain rank used tables of varying heights having three or four curved legs, of which certain bas-reliefs give an idea. Already the Book of Judges implies that a Canaanite princeling used to eat off a piece of furniture of this sort;[3] there is often mention of the tables of Saul, David, and Solomon,[4] although "to eat at the king's table" also meant to be fed at his expense.[5] Out of consideration for Elisha, the Shunammite woman put a table in the room carefully prepared for the prophet.[6] The Gospel speaks twice of the crumbs which fall from a rich man's table;[7] though it seems likely that with time the use of tables became fairly general. Before the Hellenistic period, four guests at most could probably find room round one table, so that several were necessary for big receptions.

The money-changers used for their trade little tables[8] from which they derived their Greek name, just as the word "banker" stems from "bank".

(† Feast, Lord's Supper, Temple.)

[1] Gen. 37. 25; Ex. 32. 6. [2] Ruth 2. 14. [3] Jg. 1. 7. [4] 1 Sam. 20. 24 . . .; 2 Sam. 9. 7; 19. 28; 1 Kgs. 2. 7. [5] 1 Kgs. 4. 27; 18. 19; cf. Neh. 5. 17. [6] 2 Kgs. 4. 10. [7] Matt. 15. 27; Mk. 7. 28; Lk. 16. 21. [8] Matt. 21. 12; Mk. 11. 15; Jn. 2. 15.

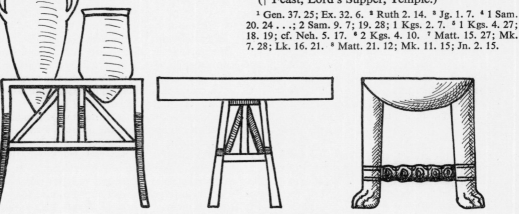

Egyptian and Assyrian tables (8th and 9th centuries).

268

TABLE-CLOTH

Table-cloths were unknown to ancient peoples, so it is better to use "linen cloth" or "great sheet" for the object Peter saw in his vision at Joppa.[1]

† (Linen.)

[1] Acts 10. 11.

TALENT

In Babylonia a talent was known of 130 lb., which was divided into 60 minas* of 60 shekels each. Originally it was a measure of weight, but since it was used to weigh gold and silver, it also represented the value of these precious metals. A talent of silver, and still more a talent of gold, represented a very large sum; it comes into the picture only for the payment of tribute or taxes,[1] or for particularly important goldsmiths' work.[2] In Israel the talent apparently at first comprised 60 minas of 60 shekels each, but it seems to have been devalued to 50 minas of 60 shekels, i.e., 3,000 shekels in all.[3]

In the N.T. the talent, which is mentioned several times, was a Greek unit of money-reckoning equal to 6,000 denarii.

The attempts made to evaluate the weight and the value of the talent have given very varied results, depending on the method used: from 75 to 130 lb.; the talent of silver was worth from £170 to £320, while the talent of gold is estimated at £5,600 to £6,100. In spite of this wide range, the order of magnitude arrived at is sufficiently precise for us clearly to understand the Parable of the Talents,[4] or the Parable of the Unmerciful Servant.[5]

[1] 2 Kgs. 18. 14; 23. 33. [2] Ex. 37. 24; 38. 24; 2 Sam. 12. 30. [3] Ex. 38. 25 ff. [4] Matt. 25. 14–30. [5] Matt. 18. 24.

TAMARISK

Many species of this tree grow in the Mediterranean regions; their tapering, gracefully curved, branches carry very small leaves, and tiny flowers of a more or less vivid pink colour, arranged in spikes. In Egypt, Palestine, and Syria the tamarisk can attain remarkable proportions and become a tree of great height. Three are mentioned in the O.T., which without doubt were regarded as sacred: the one planted by Abraham at Beersheba,[1] that at the high-place in Gibeah,[2] and the tamarisk under which the bones of Saul and his sons were interred.[3] (Chronicles says, a terebinth.[4])

(† Manna.)

[1] Gen. 21. 33. [2] 1 Sam. 22. 6. [3] 1 Sam. 31. 13. [4] 1 Chr. 10. 12.

TAMBOURINE

This percussion instrument (R.V., timbrel), known from remote antiquity and generally handled by women, accompanied the dances and songs at festivals. It is very often mentioned in the O.T., either alone or along with other instruments (harp, flute, etc.).[1] The use of tambourines even in religious ceremonies is attested by various passages in the Psalms.[2]

[1] Gen. 31. 27; Ex. 15. 20; Jg. 11. 34; 1 Sam. 10. 5; 18. 6; Job 21. 12; Is. 5. 12; 24. 8; 30. 32; Jer. 31. 4. [2] Ps. 68. 25; 81. 2; 149. 3; 150. 4.

TANNER

Although leather objects were known to the Israelites, the O.T. speaks neither of tanners nor curriers (workmen who manipulated leather to soften it). On the other hand, the Acts of the Apostles relates that Peter stayed some days at Joppa (Jaffa) with a tanner named Simon.[1] The trade of tanner and currier was scorned by the Jews, not only because it involved evil-smelling tasks but also because dead animals were regarded as unclean; the trade was followed outside a town, sometimes on the seashore, which was where Simon's house was situated.[2]

[1] Acts 9. 43. [2] Acts 10. 6, 32.

TARES

The tares spoken of in the Gospel [1] are a species of the grass family which mix with cereals and whose seeds—or, more accurately, the microscopic fungus they always carry—produce symptoms of poisoning, nausea, and a kind of drunkenness, which has given the plant its French name ("ivraie"; "ivresse" = drunkenness); the mixing of these seeds with those of the corn is distinctly detrimental to the quality of the flour.

The plant in the blade resembles wheat; its roots are hard to extirpate, and get mixed up with those of the nearby grain. But when fully developed the tares, with their lateral spikelets, are clearly distinguished from the cereal, more especially as they are under 3 ft. in height. At harvest-time separation is easy,

Tamarisk.

either by pulling up the tares as soon as they are seen or by reaping the wheat above them and abandoning the tares for the fire. When the seeds are riddled a complete separation is assured, for the seeds of the tares are much smaller than those of the wheat.

Roman legislation anticipated and punished the practice of sowing tares in a field for the purpose of revenge.

[1] Matt. 13. 24–30, 36–43; cf. Job 31. 40.

TATTOOING

Tattooed designs, which even today Orientals so much like, were forbidden to Jews by the Priestly Code.[1]

To advertise that they belonged to a particular master or leader, or to honour their deity, ancient Semites made tattoo marks on the palms of their hands or on their foreheads; some Bible passages allude to this.[2] There are scholars who even think that the prophets of Israel followed for some time an analogous practice [3] by bearing on their forehead the "sign of Yahweh", which could also have been a mark of protection.[4] Again, in the Apocalypse there is reference to the mark of the Beast which is borne on forehead and hand by those who belong to him,[5] while the elect are stamped with the "seal of the living God".[6]

[1] Lev. 19. 28. [2] Ex. 13. 9, 16; Dt. 6. 8; cf. Gal. 6. 17; 1 Ti. 4. 2. [3] 1 Kgs. 20. 38; Is. 44. 5; (49. 16); Zech. 13. 6. [4] Ez. 9. 4; cf. Gen. 4. 15. [5] Rev. 14. 9. [6] Rev. 7. 2–3; cf. 14. 1.

TAXES, DUES, TOLLS

A. Civil taxes

1. Where ancient times are concerned, we have little information about the Israelites' civil dues. Moreover, there is no question of them before the time of the monarchy, and even if Samuel "told the people the manner of the kingdom, and wrote it in a book, and laid it up before Yahweh",[1] Saul, in the first simplicity of the new régime, was apparently satisfied, besides the revenues of his lands and his share in war booty, with the voluntary gifts offered by those who enjoyed his support or wanted to pay him homage.[2] One text, however, implies—though it is perhaps guilty of a slight anachronism—that the first king of Israel could exempt from all burdens those who deserved his favour.[3]

The situation was modified with David, who already cut the figure of an eastern sovereign: his counsellors and his ministers, his officials, those who lived with him, his general staff, his hirelings, to say nothing of his harem, cost him dearly;[4] it is true that the victories of his valiant captain won him the benefits (booty, presents, tribute) necessary to his mode of life;[5] however, it has been thought that the census

he made of the people [6] was not only a prelude to levies of troops but also of taxes. Whatever the case may be, from the time of his successor, at any rate, measures were obviously taken to assure Solomon of the considerable resources he needed: the country was divided up into districts which, in turn and under the direction of twelve officers, provided for the upkeep of the court for one month.[7] Moreover, foreigners and Israelites were compelled to do forced labour [8] without which David's son would not have been able to erect the buildings of which he boasted. The texts also like to point out the presents he received from his guests;[9] but more certain still were the revenues from his properties or from the monopoly he possessed of certain trading [10] or the tolls he exacted from the caravans passing through his country.[11]

Some of the measures taken by Solomon aroused bitter recriminations:[12] they ended, as we know, by starting a schism, although they alone do not account for it; it is significant that at Shechem the official in charge of forced labour or taxes was stoned.[13]—The O.T. is silent on the score of the financial organization of the kingdoms of Judah and Israel; at most we learn that the Omrides had, like Solomon, their kingdom divided into districts,[14] that a considerable tribute was paid them by the king of Moab,[15] that—according to Chronicles—"all Judah brought presents to Jehoshaphat",[16] and the Ammonites to Uzziah,[17] that the latter and Hezekiah possessed numerous flocks, vineyards, fields, and storehouses.[18] —Moreover, the Samaria ostraca (way-bills or accountancy documents, written on potsherds and discovered in 1910) mention consignments of oil and wine doubtless coming from Ahab's domains. As for the official stamps on earthenware jars, found only in Judaea, which bear, along with a place name, a reference "for the king", these might perhaps imply dues furnished for the royal administration, but opinions differ as much on this topic as on that of the date of these brief inscriptions.

Finally, let us recall that in times of crisis in the history of the northern and southern kingdoms it was necessary to make capital levies: Menahem, to pay the tribute to the Assyrians, imposed a contribution of 50 shekels (about £6) upon all well-to-do Israelites,[19] and Jehoiakim, in order to acquit himself where Pharaoh Necho was concerned, demanded of all the inhabitants of Judah a proportionate share of their wealth.[20]

2. After the Exile, Judaea naturally paid tribute to the kings of Persia,[21] Egypt, or Syria, to which she was in turn a vassal. In the reign of Herod the Great the financial responsibilities of the Jews were often very heavy, in spite of the remission he occasionally granted.

In order to understand more than one narrative in the N.T., it is important to know the fiscal arrangement to which Palestine was subjected by Roman authority. Two sorts of taxes were customary: direct tax and indirect tax.[22] The first of these, which was very heavy and was collected by the agents of the Imperial treasury, affected, on the one hand, the owners of land (a property tax) and, on the other, the owners of a certain amount of personal property (a personal tax, on the subject of which the Pharisees questioned Jesus one day, thinking to compromise him [23]).—Indirect tax hit merchandise at the entrance or at the exit of certain tariff districts, and it was collected at various points (bridges, cross-roads, entrance to certain towns,[24] etc.). The collection of these dues, farmed out by the State, under the overall direction of a financial procurator, to societies or private individuals—who naturally sought to derive the largest profits—was made by means of subordinate agents, the publicans or tax-collectors, who in their turn did not usually shrink from extortion or embezzlement.[25] Because of this, they were hated by the tax-payers, but above all they were disliked for being in the service of foreigners, and they were ranked with sinners, that is to say, with those who neglected the practices of the Jewish Law.[26]

B. Religious dues

Independently of the tithes* prescribed by the Law from post-Exilic times, every Israelite, resident or not in Jerusalem, had to pay annually a Temple tax intended to ensure the outlay of money on public worship and the upkeep of the sanctuary. This uniform tax of a half-shekel [27] ($= \frac{1}{3}$ of the shekel used in Babylonia [28]) and later of two drachmas [29] († didrachma) was paid, at any rate in Palestine, in the month Adar*; the money collected in Jewish communities throughout the world was sent to Jerusalem. People readily discharged this contribution, which, in all, represented a considerable sum of money and betokened the solidarity of the Jewish people.

[1] 1 Sam. 10. 25. [2] 1 Sam. 10. 27; 16. 20. [3] 1 Sam. 17. 25. [4] 2 Sam. 8. 16 ff.; 20. 23 ff.; 1 Chr. 18. 14 ff. [5] 2 Sam. 8. 7–12. [6] 2 Sam. 24. [7] 1 Kgs. 4. 7 ff.; 4. 27. [8] 1 Kgs. 5. 13, 14; 9. 15 ff.; 11. 28. [9] 1 Kgs. 10. 10, 25. [10] 1 Kgs. 9. 28; 10. 11, 28 f. [11] 1 Kgs. 10. 15. [12] 1 Kgs. 12. 4. [13] 1 Kgs. 12. 18. [14] 1 Kgs. 20. 14. [15] 2 Kgs. 3. 4. [16] 2 Chr. 17. 5, 11. [17] 2 Chr. 26. 8. [18] 2 Chr. 26. 10; 32. 28 ff. [19] 2 Kgs. 15. 20. [20] 2 Kgs. 23. 35. [21] Ezr. 4. 13; Neh. 5. 4. [22] Rom. 13. 6, 7. [23] Matt. 22. 17; Mk. 12. 14; Lk. 20. 22. [24] Matt. 9. 9. Lk. 19. 2. [25] Lk. 3. 13; 19. 8. [26] Matt. 9. 11; 18. 17; Mk. 2. 15–16; Lk. 5. 30; 15. 1; 18. 10 . . . [27] Ex. 30. 11 . . . [28] Neh. 10. 32–33. [29] Matt. 17. 24.

TEBET

Tebet was the tenth month of the Jewish year: end of December–early January. It is mentioned only once in the O.T.[1]

[1] Est. 2. 16.

TEMPLE

1. Archaeological excavations in Palestine have brought to light the ruins of temples dating from before the arrival of the Israelites, in particular on Gerizim (18th century), at Beth-shan (15th century), and at Lachish (14th century).

One ancient temple mentioned by Bible texts is that at Shiloh. In spite of the opinion of certain archaeologists, it cannot be agreed that this temple was a mere tent; incidentally, in fact, the texts mention doors and rooms, and the place is called a house or a palace—so many terms that it would be hard to explain them with reference to a tent. The Ark was deposited there. It was the central sanctuary at the time of the Judges. People went there on pilgrimage.[1] It was on the occasion of one of those feasts that the Benjamites carried off girls to marry them.[2] The temple was probably destroyed by the Philistines at the time of the ruin of Eli's family. A Christian sanctuary was built there eventually, where at the present time there is a Mohammedan mosque.—There was perhaps a temple at Nob [3] which may have taken the place of the one at Shiloh.—Our texts quote another temple called the house of Micah,[4] another at Ophrah,[5] and yet another at Shechem.[6]

2. *Solomon's Temple*

The centralization of worship at Jerusalem was one of the consequences of the building of Solomon's Temple; it was in no way one of the causes of it. The king thought only of making a private chapel for himself, but one which, according to his tendency towards megalomania, was to outshine the other places of worship. That in no way prevented people from continuing to sacrifice on high-places for yet another three centuries.

Tradition reports that David had already intended to build a Temple in his capital, but that he was dissuaded from it by a conservative party whose spokesman was Nathan and which wanted to retain the simplicity of worship at the high-places.

It is well known that Solomon renewed with the king of Tyre the treaty which David had made with him to obtain the wood necessary for his buildings; [7] he had the stone hewn by a large number of forced labourers; a foundry was even set up on the Jordan plain.

Were the architects of Solomon's Temple inspired by what had been done elsewhere, or did they create an original piece of work? The question has been discussed at length, and comparisons have been sought in Egypt, Babylonia, among the Hittites, and even in Mycenaean civilization. It is understandable that each time new ruins of an ancient temple are discovered, comparisons should be sought with the Bible texts which mention Solomon's Temple, the more so as these texts are not always clear to us.

It can be said, it seems, that the first Temple of Jerusalem was a product of northern rather than Egyptian architecture, but conceived in Oriental fashion. It was on the eastern hill of Jerusalem, the hill of Zion, that the site of the Temple was chosen, immediately

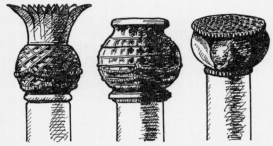

Various reconstructions of the capitals of the bronze pillars of Solomon's Temple.

to the north of Solomon's palaces* between the Kidron valley and the declivity of the Tyropoeon. It is there that the Haram-esh-Sherif is found today and the Mosque of Omar, in the middle of which rises the famous holy rock probably marking the site of the Temple altar of former times.

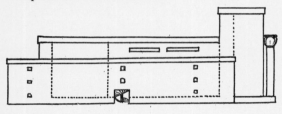

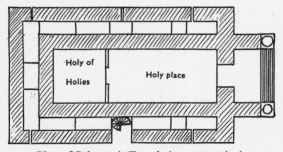

Plan of Solomon's Temple (reconstruction).

General lay-out. The sanctuary itself was of extremely modest dimensions. Inside it measured 60 cubits long, 20 wide, and 30 high (= about 90 ft. long, 30 ft. broad, 45 ft. high). It was preceded by a vestibule of the same width but higher by 10 cubits. Moreover, side buildings, 15 cubits high, leaned against the north, west, and south walls; it was in

the middle of the south front that the entrance to this annexe was situated. The annexe comprised three storeys reached by a winding staircase. Our texts, which describe windows furnished with wooden lattices in the upper and central part of the Temple, do not say whether there were any in the side building. If there were any to give a little light in the rooms of these different storeys they must have been small and few. The roof, built of cedar beams and planks, must have been flat, since later on certain kings of Judah set up altars there where incense and libations were offered to the astral gods.[8]

The Temple was contained in the general enclosure surrounding the palaces of Solomon, but a second wall round it produced an inner court called more exactly the forecourt.[9] This wall was made of three rows of free-stone and one row of cedar beams. It had two doors in it, one on the west side, through which came the faithful on their way from the city, and the other on the south, which was the private entrance of the king.

The Temple door itself was flanked by two hollow columns of bronze. They were about 27 ft. high and about 6 ft. in diameter, and were very likely situated a little farther forward than the door, on the left and right of the ten steps which led to it. They were topped by capitals 8 ft. high, described at length but so obscurely that it is impossible to arrive at a reconstruction which would satisfy most specialists. Their significance is no less disputed.

Having crossed the porch, one penetrated into the Temple by way of a door with two leaves of cedar and cypress, and entered the first chamber 40 cubits long, dimly lit by the light filtering through the window lattices which were placed high up to left and right. This was the Holy Place, the "hekal". The whole of this room was covered with panels of carved wood, in which could be found motifs of cherubim, palms, crowns, flowers, etc. Some enthusiastic texts probably exaggerate when they say that the whole was overlaid with gold; it is, however, possible that certain panels were covered with this precious metal. The rectangular form of the place attracted one's attention to the far end of the room, where there was a light wall, with a door with two olive-wood leaves, and "with five angles", that is to say, the upper line was raised in the centre, thus making the fifth angle. It was through that door that one penetrated into the second chamber, the Holy of Holies, the "debir", absolutely cubic in shape, and without any windows.[10] It was there that the famous rock appeared on which the Ark was placed.

Furniture of the Temple. In the courtyard there was the altar of burnt offerings, made of natural stones overlaid with bronze; it was about 30 ft. long, 30 ft. wide, and 15 ft. high. Access to it was by means of a stairway placed on the west side.—A few paces to the south, there was the Bronze Sea.[11] This was a huge container 7½ ft. high and 15 ft. in diameter, placed on 12 oxen. We do not know anything about it—its shape, how it was filled and emptied, the reason for its position in the Temple courtyard . . . It appears, however, that this water-container had a utilitarian purpose and served for ablutions.—We are told that on both sides of the altar there were wheeled lavers; their rims were 9 to 10 ft. from the ground, and they could perhaps be used from the top of the altar. Containers of this sort have been discovered in Cyprus, Greece, and Babylonia.

In the Holy Place there was the table for the shew-bread. An altar of this type doubtless existed already in the temple at Nob, if we are to believe the story of the loaves which David came to seek there.[12] But the one in Solomon's Temple was covered with

Bronze cultic basin found at Cyprus.

gold leaf. The Book of Chronicles later mentioned ten tables, five on the right and five on the left . . . but that is a confusion with something else.—For a long time it was thought that there was no altar of incense in this first Jerusalem Temple, but at the present time, on the contrary, its presence beside the table for the shew-bread is fairly generally admitted, it being added that it was in the time of Ezekiel that people tried to forget it, because it was considered to be too much like pagan customs.—Finally, ten candlesticks gave useful service in the Holy Place where light hardly penetrated.

In the Holy of Holies there was only the Ark*, protected by two cherubim* with their heads turned towards the entrance and with their wings outspread.

Fate of Solomon's Temple. This Temple, a little heavy in its outer form, but not without artistry and riches inside, could not have failed to impress and cheer the inhabitants of Jerusalem, whose status as capital was enhanced by this sanctuary.—For a long time cults were celebrated there alongside those at the high-places. It was only in Hezekiah's time that a

first attempt at centralization was made, but without much success, it appears. Various circumstances led to the Deuteronomic reform which made Solomon's Temple the Israelites' sole place of worship.

This Temple was repaired through the care of several kings of Judah (Jehoash,[13] Jotham,[14] Ahaz[15]). In time of war it was naturally an object of envy and submitted to pillage by Shishak[16] and by Jehoash[17] of Israel. Some kings of the realm had on several occasions to strip it of its riches (Ahaz,[18] Hezekiah,[19] Asa,[20] Jehoash[21]). Others again set up altars there to foreign gods, urged perhaps by political necessity (Manasseh[22]).

Finally, Nebuchadnezzar pillaged the Temple at the time of the first siege of Jerusalem,[23] and eleven years later (in 586) he destroyed it completely.[24] Everything of bronze was broken and carried away to Babylonia as well as everything of gold or silver.

3. *The Temple of Ezekiel*

One of the visions of Ezekiel[25] describes the plan of reconstruction of the Temple as envisaged by the prophet; it is not only a symbolical picture; recalling the destroyed sanctuary, Ezekiel wished to inspire and announce the restoration of this place of worship.

The plan is distinguished by the perfect symmetry of the Temple and by its isolation. The latter point is explained by the prophet's desire to separate the sacred from the profane. The same reason prompts him to foresee two courts, one for the people and the other for the priests.

A wall of 6 cubits containing three porches, with one on the east and the others on the south and north sides, encloses a square of 500 cubits. Inside the first court, against the wall, store-rooms, halls, and offices would be installed. The second wall separating the two courts has also three doors corresponding to the entrance porches. Exactly in the centre of the whole would stand the altar of burnt offering. As for the sanctuary itself, it would include a porch, a Holy Place, and a Holy of Holies, very similar to those of the former Temple.

4. *The Second Temple*

We are unfortunately very little informed about this Temple, which was not lacking in a certain glory, since it was the centre of the magnificent Israelite resistance to foreign oppression. It is likely that on their return from Exile the Israelites simply set up an altar on the site of Solomon's Temple. Following the prophet Haggai, a whole movement was begun in favour of the restoration of the Temple. Accompanied by the prophet Zechariah, he approached the governor Zerubbabel, who was soon won over to the cause; this explains why sometimes this governor's name is given to the Temple. However, several years' effort was necessary before, in the year 515, the new sanctuary could be opened.

This building must have had about the same dimensions and the same arrangements as the preceding one. According to Hecataeus, the Greek historian of the beginning of the 3rd century B.C., the court is said to have been about 500 ft. by 140 ft.; in it the sacrificial altar made of non-hewn stones [26] stood before the Temple itself. It seems likely that a second court surrounded it, against whose wall were ranged the rooms mentioned by numerous texts of Ezra and Nehemiah. The people, however, had access to both courts, contrary to Ezekiel's plans. But one day when the King and High Priest, Alexander Jannaeus, was officiating at the altar he was pelted with citrons by the people; and so, in order to prevent the recurrence of such incidents, he had a barrier set up round the altar to which henceforth only the priests had access.

The Holy of Holies was empty, and in the Holy Place there was only the golden candlestick and the table for the shew-bread.[27] It was a mere curtain that separated these two parts of the Temple.

This Temple, as we know, was pillaged and dishonoured by Antiochus Epiphanes,[28] but purified afterwards by Judas Maccabaeus, who restored the whole building as well as the altar, endowed the Temple, and fortified it with outer walls and towers.[29]

A century later, Herod transformed it from top to bottom, which explains why this new building bears his name, although it was only a restoration of the second Temple.

5. Herod's Temple

For reasons more political than religious Herod undertook after 20 B.C. to enlarge the Temple at Jerusalem. This sovereign, who saw things on a large scale, considerably extended the Temple area to the extent of giving it, by the construction of high retaining walls on the south side, about the extent of the present Haram-esh-Sherif (about 1,500 ft. by 1,000 ft.). A strong wall decorated with crenellated towers surrounded it completely, except for the north-west corner, where the fortress of Antonia* rose. On the opposite side the top of the corner tower on the south-east was 500 ft. above the Kidron valley, and it was from that point that a sentry announced every morning the first hour of day. It is not impossible that it is that tower which is referred to in the account of Jesus' temptation.[30]

On the side of the city this huge terrace was entered by four gates, upon one of which there abutted a bridge crossing the Tyropoeon. Still today its sub-foundation to the south of the terrace can be seen. Finally, on the north side there was also a fortified gate, and on the long side there was a single door which was little used, for at this point the land sloped away steeply.

Everyone could go into this outer court, called the Court of the Gentiles, which was completely paved with flagstones and mosaics, and surrounded by porticoes on the four sides. The whole thing must have had the appearance of a long basilica. "The columns," says the historian Josephus, "were so large that three people could hardly encompass one." The other porticoes had only two rows of columns and measured 50 ft. in width; the one going the length

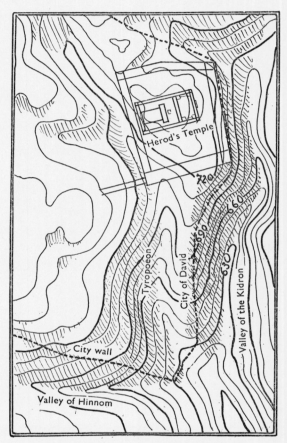

Location of the City of David and of the Temple.
(*Heights shown in metres*)

of the eastern wall was called Solomon's Porch.[31] The ceilings of these porches were made of carved cedar. In these colonnades a few halls and rooms had been built, and it is probably in one of them that the discussion between the twelve-year-old Jesus and the doctors of the Law took place.[32] The rabbis had a habit of walking along these porches, and even of sitting down in them.—As it was necessary to climb up from all sides to reach this huge terrace, some merchants dealing in beasts for sacrifice had obtained permission to establish themselves inside, near the doors, but they sometimes ventured into the porticoes and right into the middle of the place; it is well known with what energy Jesus chased them out of it.[33]

A little to the north of centre of this court a stairway was climbed to reach another terrace on which the sanctuary itself was built. But before arriving at the foot of this stairway, a low stone wall had to be passed through. This was 3 to 5 ft. high, and at its openings an impressive inscription in Greek and Latin forbade all foreigners, on pain of death, to go into the Jewish sanctuary. Two copies of this inscription have been discovered. It ends with the words that any foreigner who "is caught will have himself to blame that his death ensues". The upper

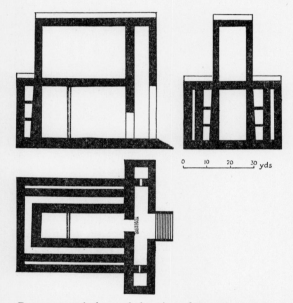

Reconstructed plan and elevation of Herod's Temple.

terrace was some 10 ft. higher than the other, and the stairway which surrounded it on three sides had two flights, one of fourteen and the other of fifteen steps.

The Jewish sanctuary with east-west axis was divided into two parts: on the west side the Temple properly so-called and its courtyard; on the east side the Court of the Women. Nine doors gave access to it; the most remarkable, on the east, was fronted by decorations that encroached upon the stairway, which at that point had only fifteen steps; this is probably what was called the Beautiful Gate.[34]

The *Court of the Women* formed a square with sides of about 210 ft., but each corner was occupied by a little courtyard whose name indicated its purpose: court of the wood, lepers' court, court of the Nazirites, and the court of oil and wine. It was in this area that the chests intended for various offer-

ings were also found; certain of them were called *šôferôt* (from *šôfar* = horn, trumpet*) because they had a hole in the shape of a horn.

From the Court of the Women one passed into the western part of the sanctuary through the Nicanor Gate. This was a door with very heavy leaves and was difficult to move; it had solid bolts, and was shut every evening at eight o'clock. It had perhaps a few steps leading up to it. One then reached a new court, of which a strip of 15 to 20 ft. wide was reserved for men—on the east side only, say some sources; right round the Court of the Priests, say others.

The *Court of the Priests* must have sometimes had a strange appearance: in the centre was the sacrificial altar, a huge mass 50 ft. square and 13 ft. high, with upper corners lengthened into the shape of horns; a fire was lit there, and quite close to it beasts were brought along a gently sloping ramp. Other beasts awaited their turn, attached to four rows of six rings fitted into the ground, to the north of the altar. Farther to the north still, eight posts provided with huge butcher's hooks formed part of the house called "the slaughter-house", to which they were linked by cedar beams. Quite near there, marble benches for the cutting-up of the animals could be seen. Still other tables bore all the instruments used at the altar, to the west of which rose the black mass of a huge bronze, probably rectangular, container. It is difficult to imagine a religious ceremony which included at one and the same time the bellowing of the victims, running blood, the sickening smell of burnt fat, and in which the robed sacrificers officiated with solemnity, in spite of the inevitable disorder of such a scene.

The *Temple properly so-called* was set out in the same way as its predecessors. There was no entrance door, but a porch above which Herod had had a golden eagle placed—which was torn down in an insurrection a few years before the king's death, such a representation being contrary to the Law. The vestibule was only 17 ft. deep. A stairway of twelve steps led to it, except at the end of the vestibule which gave access to the door of the Holy Place. This door had two leaves, each made of two panels which could be folded back. During the daytime this door remained open, but a curtain always closed the opening. Origen and Jerome think that it was this curtain which was rent asunder at the time of Jesus' death.[35] Above the door there was a huge decoration in gold, representing an immense vine-branch. (A Latin historian took advantage of it to deride the Jewish cult, which, he claimed, was addressed to Bacchus!)

From there one penetrated into the "hekal" (60 ft. by 30 ft., by 60 ft. high), doubtless panelled and decorated with various ornaments which were overlaid with gold. It is there that the golden candlestick* was found, the table for the shew-bread and the altar of incense, both the latter overlaid with gold also. Two parallel curtains closed this part of the sanctuary on the west side, but there was no entrance between the curtain and the wall except on the south side for the first curtain and on the north side for the second, so that neither light nor gaze would be able to penetrate into the Holy of Holies. Moreover, in the Holy of Holies there was absolutely nothing. It was on a simple large stone that the High Priest, once a year on the Day of Atonement, would come and set down the censer, after passing the short distance between the curtains. It was from this stone, according to the Koran, that Borak, Mohammad's wonderful horse, leapt forth with the prophet to bring him before the throne of God himself.

As in the previous Temples, a side building surrounded the central body of the construction and contained thirty-eight rooms divided into three storeys. Perhaps there was again an external corridor which linked all these rooms, but it is not certain. Above the Holy Place and the Holy of Holies there was a large building, reached on the south side by way of the side building; the purpose of this structure is unknown. A marble balustrade 3 cubits high went round the Temple roof, which itself, says Josephus, "was as though bristling with very slender gold points to prevent the birds alighting there and dirtying it".

Such as it was, the Temple of Herod filled the Israelites with enthusiastic admiration, of which we have a few echoes in the Gospel.[36] But Jesus says, "There shall not be left one stone upon another, that shall not be thrown down." In fact we know that this Temple was completely destroyed on the 10th August in the year A.D. 70.

6. Jewish temples in Egypt

In spite of the centralization of worship at Jerusalem, advocated by the Deuteronomic and Priestly Laws, temples were raised to Yahweh outside the frontiers of Israel.

In the 6th century B.C. there lived in Elephantine in Egypt a Jewish colony which seems to have been formed from soldiers in garrison in that locality; a batch of papyri and ostraca has been discovered in that region which makes the fact known to us. These documents, written in Aramaic, tell us that there was in Elephantine a temple built of stone, decorated with columns, and covered with a cedar roof; priests who used silver and gold utensils offered up sacrifices and incense; there is even a list of the names of those who gave two shekels of silver for Yahweh. This temple, which Cambyses had protected in his conquest of Egypt (530–522), was destroyed in 410 B.C. by the fanaticism of the Egyptians, who, in some of their cults, regarded as divine the animals which the Jews offered in sacrifice.

In order to rebuild their temple the Jews asked for permission and help from Jerusalem, which seems not to have been forthcoming. Moreover, the colony at Elephantine might well have disappeared in 404 when, after a general insurrection, Egypt was delivered for about sixty years from Persian domination.

We must also mention a Jewish temple which existed at Leontopolis near Cairo, in about 170 B.C. All that is known about it is that it had been built on the model of the second Jerusalem Temple, and that it remained until A.D. 73; it was at that date that the Romans closed it.

[1] 1 Sam. 1. 3, 24. [2] Jg. 21. 19. [3] 1 Sam. 21. 1. [4] Jg. 17. 5. [5] Jg. 8. 27. [6] Jg. 9. 27. [7] 1 Kgs. 5. 2–11. [8] 2 Kgs. 23. 12. [9] 1 Kgs. 6. 36. [10] 1 Kgs. 8. 12. [11] 1 Kgs. 7. 23 ff.; 2 Chr. 4. 2 ff. [12] 1 Sam. 21. 4. [13] 2 Kgs. 12. 5. [14] 2 Kgs. 15. 35. [15] 2 Kgs. 16. 14. [16] 1 Kgs. 14. 25. [17] 2 Kgs. 14. 14. [18] 2 Kgs. 16. 17. [19] 2 Kgs. 18. 16. [20] 1 Kgs. 15. 18. [21] 2 Kgs. 12. 18. [22] 2 Kgs. 21. 3 ff.; 23. 4 ff. [23] 2 Kgs. 24. 13 ff. [24] 2 Kgs. 25. 9. [25] Ez. 40–42. [26] 1 Macc. 4. 44. [27] 1 Macc. 1. 21; 4. 49. [28] 1 Macc. 1. 21, 45, 57; 4. 38; 2 Macc. 6. 2. [29] 1 Macc. 4. 56, 60. [30] Matt. 4. 5; Lk. 4. 9. [31] Jn. 10. 23; Acts 3. 11; 5. 12. [32] Lk. 2. 46. [33] Matt. 21. 12 ff. [34] Acts 3. 2. [35] Matt. 27. 51. [36] Mk. 13. 1–2.

TENT

A tent is the classical dwelling of nomads. Noah already dwelt in a tent,[1] and Israelite tradition, when telling us of the wanderings of the patriarchs, refers frequently to this type of dwelling.[2] Life in tents was so closely linked with the very existence of the Israelites that after their settlement in Canaan their language remained impregnated with it. Instead of "to depart", they said "to pull out" (the tent-pegs, understood). When the Israelites of the north separated from Solomon's son they did not say,

Assyrian military tents.

"Let us return to our houses", but rather, "To your tents, O Israel." [3] The day after the destruction of Jerusalem Jeremiah put into the mouth of those deported the significant words: "My tent is spoiled, and all my cords are broken: my children are gone forth of me and they are not: there is none to stretch forth my tent any more." [4] The "tent (E.V., tabernacle) of God" is his Temple.[5] Jesus himself uses the word tent for the dwelling-place of souls in the world beyond,[6] and the apostles use it for the human body in which the soul resides [7] and even for the future dwelling-place of God.[8]

The Israelites did not completely abandon the use of tents at the time of their settlement in Canaan; shepherds continued to use them;[9] the Rechabites[10] remained faithful to them on principle; and following the example of the Assyrians, the Israelite armies doubtless used small tents, either conical or triangular.[11]

The Bible texts give us no information about the shape of the patriarchs' tents; they cannot have differed much from those of the present-day Bedouin. The poles which support the tent-cloth vary in number according to the importance and wealth of the owner; however, there are at least nine, which are arranged in a rectangular pattern. They reach from 5 to 7 ft. in height, the one in the middle being slightly higher than the others.

Inside, the tent is divided into two parts by a mere curtain, but its seams make a strong partition. Whereas in the daytime an expanse of the tent-cloth when hooked up gives ample access to the first part of the tent for everyone, even for the stranger, the

Bedouin tents.

rest of the dwelling, completely shut, is strictly reserved for women and children.[12] There may be also, marked out by other curtains, several rooms for the servant-girls and slaves. Sometimes a rich tribal chief takes away the whole of this part of his dwelling and has a separate tent set up for the women.[13]

In the first place the tent was covered with animals' skins. Early on, however, they began to spin and weave camel and goat-hair, which gives a brown, almost black material;[14] long bands of it were made, as wide as the looms of the time allowed. Particularly appreciated were the materials made with the wool of Cilician goats, called "cilicium"; they resisted the most drenching rains, but, being a little stiff, they were more difficult to cut and assemble than other cloths, so that this activity soon constituted a distinct trade. It is known that the apostle Paul, who came from Cilicia, was just such a maker, cutter, or sewer of tents.[15]

When the tent is to be put up the cloth is first of all spread out on the ground; one slips underneath it, with the necessary poles, on which it can be raised at certain reinforced support points. Then one has only to attach long ropes to the wooden toggles sewn on the edges of the cloth, and to tie the other

end of them to tent-pegs stuck in the ground; basically, it is a job which does not take much time; yet the taking down of the tent may be accomplished still more quickly.

The furniture in the tent is rudimentary: carpets, cushions, straw mats; an earthenware lamp*; the table* is often only a circle of leather; a few water-bottles*; the flour-mill, a few metal vessels—those made of earthenware are too heavy and too fragile for nomads; two or three baskets; a few wooden spoons; the mallet with which the tent-pegs are driven in; and that is all.

Ordinarily, the tents of one tribe are dispersed throughout an area, but at the danger signal they are gathered together and grouped in horse-shoe formation. That is the *douar*, or village of tents.[16]

[1] Gen. 9. 21. [2] Gen. 4. 20; 9. 27; 13. 3, 5, 12; 18. 9; 24. 67; 25. 27; 26. 25; 31. 33; etc. [3] 1 Kgs. 12. 16; Jg. 7. 8. [4] Jer. 10. 20. [5] Ps. 15. 1; 27. 5. [6] Lk. 16. 9. [7] 2 Cor. 5. 1, 4; 2 Pet. 1. 13. [8] Rev. 21. 3. [9] Is. 38. 12. [10] Jer. 35. 6–10. [11] 2 Kgs. 7. 7. [12] Jg. 15. 1; Cant. 3. 4. [13] Gen. 24. 67; 31. 33. [14] Cant. 1. 5 . . . [15] Acts 18. 3. [16] Ps. 69. 25.

TERAPHIM

On several occasions the O.T. mentions objects of worship bearing the name of "teraphim". (Although in Hebrew it has a plural form, this word can denote a single object.) Rachel stole her father's teraphim,[1] Micah made one;[2] David's teraphim acted as a picturesque hoax;[3] the prophets and Josiah condemned them,[4] and the king of Babylon consulted them.[5]

What were teraphim? It is difficult to know. More often than not we think of domestic idols,[6] household gods, grotesque figures, like the little protective statues of the family hearth brought to light by Palestinian excavations; but there have also been suggested heads or cultic masks, images of ancestors, figurines handed down to an inheritor, the possession of which constituted a claim to the inheritance; furthermore, it is certain that teraphim were connected with soothsaying.[7] Given the variety of the objects which the texts seem to presuppose, some scholars consider that the word teraphim is one of those insulting words like "shame", "abomination", "filth" which the Jews of the later period substituted for abhorred heathen terms, and the word could from then on signify as much an idol as a magic or divinatory object.

[1] Gen. 31. 19, 34, 35. [2] Jg. 17. 5; 18. 14 . . . [3] 1 Sam. 19. 13, 16. [4] 2 Kgs. 23. 24; Hos. 3. 4; Zech. 10. 2; cf. 1 Sam. 15. 23. [5] Ez. 21. 21. [6] Gen. 31. 30. [7] 1 Sam. 15. 23; Ez. 21. 21; Zech. 10. 2.

TEREBINTH

A number of times the O.T. mentions a tree whose Hebrew name implies height, robustness,[1] but it is not possible to be certain of the species. It is generally thought to be the terebinth, one of the Pistachia, a beautiful tree, common in Palestine, able to attain a height of nearly 50 ft. and with outspreading branches. Its deciduous foliage resembles that of the olive, its fruit encloses an edible seed, and its resin is a turpentine.

Apart from the narrative of the death of Absalom, whose hair caught in the branches of a "terebinth",[2] almost all the Bible references allude more or less

Terebinth.

directly to the religious veneration which surrounded these trees, regarded as sacred,[3] and which often served, along with others, as sanctuaries for the Semites.

(† Oak, sacred trees*, tamarisk.)

[1] Is. 6. 13; 61. 3. [2] 2 Sam. 18. 9, 10, 14. [3] Gen. 35. 4; Jg. 6. 11, 19; 1 Sam. 17. 2, 19; 1 Kgs. 13. 14; Is. 1. 29, 30; 57. 5; Ez. 6. 13; Hos. 4. 13.

TETRADRACHMA

A frequently used coin and one often found in archaeological excavations. Its name shows that it

Attic tetradrachma of the 5th century.

was worth four drachmas, which was equivalent to one shekel.

TETRARCH

Etymologically, a ruler governing one-quarter of a region divided into four parts, in the Roman Empire the tetrarch was a princeling inferior to kings and ethnarchs, who yet enjoyed certain royal prerogatives.[1] Herod Antipas, ruler of Galilee and Peraea, Philip his brother, and Lysanias are three tetrarchs named in the N.T.[2]

[1] Matt. 14. 9; Mk. 6. 14, 22, 25, 26; Lk. 3. 19. [2] Matt. 14. 1; Lk. 3. 1; Acts 13. 1.

THEATRE

Unknown among the Israelites, who knew nothing of dramatic art, the theatres of Graeco-Roman antiquity were vast open-air structures, comprising tiered semicircles of stone seats, with stairways and entrances; facing these was the *orchestra* (dancing place), at ground level where the chorus danced and the stage was raised up on a stone platform, open to the audience and enclosed on the other three sides. Public gatherings were also held in these places. The only theatre mentioned in the N.T. is the one at Ephesus, the imposing ruins of which have been recovered, where the riot related in the Acts of the Apostles took place.[1]

[1] Acts 19. 29 . . .

THISTLE

It is impossible to identify the numerous prickly plants of the Bible. Two of them in the O.T. may correspond to two species of thistles; the first is mentioned only twice;[1] the second is mentioned in several texts as being a plant harmful to cereals, a foul growth, springing up in the fields or among ruins, which, with the nettles*, it overruns;[2] though here some translations prefer "thorns" to "thistles".

In the N.T. the Epistle to the Hebrews uses the metaphor of useless soil which produces only thorns and thistles,[3] and in the Sermon on the Mount Jesus asks his listeners whether figs are gathered from thistles.[4] On the shore of Lake Tiberias one type of thistle grows to a height of over 13 ft.

[1] Gen. 3. 18; Hos. 10. 8. [2] 2 Kgs. 14. 9; Job 31. 40; Prov. 26. 9; Cant. 2. 2; Is. 34. 13; Hos. 9. 6. [3] Heb. 6. 8. [4] Matt. 7. 16.

THORN

Considering the very large number of thorny plants which flourish in Palestine, because of the dryness of the climate, it is not surprising to discover that the Bible mentions almost a score of species. Yet they cannot be identified with certainty, and our versions are obliged to translate the different names in a loose way by "thorns" or "thorn bush". Some of the names already have, moreover, a generic force. Only the plant spoken of in Job 40. 21–22 can be specified. It is a kind of spiny lotus, the Jujube tree, in the shadow of which behemoth* (the hippopotamus) loves to lie.

Thorns presented a serious obstacle to agriculture in Palestine.[1] Fire was used to get rid of them; this had the advantage of fertilizing the soil; but the lazy man let them overrun his field.[2] On the other hand, they were excellent for fuel;[3] and they were also used for protective hedges, while camels, donkeys, and goats occasionally ate some species. Gideon used them for the punishment he inflicted on the men of Succoth.[4]

But, above all, the O.T. writers speak of thorns figuratively, as a symbol for evildoers,[5] for the enemies of Israel,[6] for difficulties which are for ever

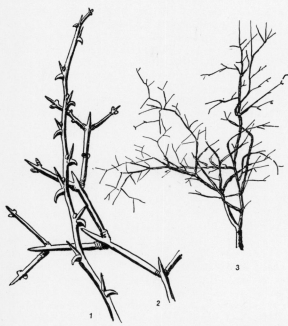

Various thorny plants popularly called thorns of "the crown of Christ".

recurring,[7] for a curse,[8] for the desolation of a country,[9] and, in particular, for calamities with which the writers threaten their people.[10]—The beloved one in the Song of Songs is a lily in the midst of thorns;[11] and the part played by the thorn in the fable of the trees which wanted a king[12] is familiar enough, as are also the thorns in the Parable of the Sower.[13] Jeremiah said, "Do not sow amongst thorns",[14] and he used the expression "to sow wheat, and reap thorns".[15] Jesus, for his part, asked if one could "gather grapes of thorns".[16]

Many suggestions have been made about Christ's crown of thorns,[17] but it is impossible to be sure which plant was used; Thorny Burnet (*Poterium spinosum*: 3) and two prickly shrubs (Paliurus: 1; and the Jujube: 2) are often called "the thorns of Christ". It

279

is sufficient for us to know that brambles and thorns abounded up to the very gates of Jerusalem.

[1] Gen. 3. 18; Matt. 13. 7, 22; Mk. 4. 7, 18; Lk. 8. 7, 14; Heb. 6. 8. [2] Prov. 24. 30 . . . [3] Ex. 22. 6; Ps. 58. 9; Eccl. 7. 6; Is. 32. 13. [4] Jg. 8. 7, 16. [5] 2 Sam. 23. 6; Mic. 7. 4. [6] Num. 33. 55; Jos. 23. 13; Ez. 28. 24. [7] Prov. 15. 19; 22. 5; Hos. 2. 6. [8] Gen. 3. 18. [9] Job 30. 7; Is. 9. 18; 10. 17; 27. 4; 34. 13; 55. 13; Zeph. 2. 9. [10] Is. 5. 6; 7. 23; 32. 13; Hos. 9. 6; 10. 8. [11] Cant. 2. 2. [12] Jg. 9. 14. [13] Mk. 4. 1–9 par. [14] Jer. 4. 3. [15] Jer. 12. 13. [16] Matt. 7. 16; Lk. 6. 44. [17] Matt. 27. 29; Mk. 15. 17; Jn. 19. 2, 5.

THRESHING-FLOOR

This is where the threshing, winnowing, and sifting of corn was carried out († agriculture).

Threshing-floors could be prepared in the fields themselves where the harvesting was done, but generally they were set up near the village at high points,[1] where the breeze needed for winnowing made itself felt. They were usually circular platforms of beaten earth or terraces either of natural rock or artificially paved, surrounded by low walls. The corn might be exposed there for a time—for it did not rain in the harvest season—watched over by its owners, who spent the night near their sheaves.[2] This was the season thieves chose for coming to gather from the threshing-floors what they had not sown.[3] Even today at threshing time everybody goes off to the hills to work, and the villages are temporarily abandoned. Very often in the Bible threshing-floors are referred to in the literal sense; sometimes figuratively.[4]

[1] 2 Sam. 24. 16. [2] Ruth 3. 7. [3] 1 Sam. 23. 1. [4] Jer. 51. 33; Matt. 3. 12.

THRESHING-SLEDGE

To separate the grain from the ear, the Palestinian farmer, among other methods († agriculture), used one or two animals to drag over the corn, which was spread out in a fairly thick layer, either a heavy wooden platform—bent back at the front and fitted with sharp stones or metal points, on which he himself stood to increase its weight—or a sort of carriage provided with a seat for the driver, which rested on rollers fitted with iron strips.[1] Such

Threshing-sledges: board and roller forms.

THRESHOLD

implements are still used in Egypt and in the Mediterranean regions. The prophets make striking figurative references to them,[2] and the poem of Job compared the first kind with the underside of the crocodile as it drags across the mud.[3]

[1] 2 Sam. 24. 22; (1 Chr. 21. 23.) [2] Is. 28. 27; 41. 15; Amos 1. 3. [3] Job 41. 30.

THRESHOLD

The threshold of houses had a sacred character;[1] it was there that demons might enter the home, so it was there that they should be appeased if their evil influences were to be diverted. For this reason there were foundation* sacrifices, the remains of which are often found under thresholds. Some idolaters, moreover, used to leap over the threshold,[2] and the Israelites began to imitate this custom.[3] Sacred images were hung in the doorway; Isaiah condemned these idols[4] (though the text is uncertain), and Josiah, in his drive against idolatry, destroyed in particular the one belonging to the house of the governor of Jerusalem.[5] The sacred character of the threshold carries over to the container called the "mezuzah"* which Jews fix to their doorposts, and which encloses certain Bible passages.

[1] Ex. 21. 6. [2] 1 Sam. 5. 5. [3] Zeph. 1. 9. [4] Is. 57. 8. [5] 2 Kgs. 23. 8.

THRONE

Among the thrones spoken of in the literal sense in the Bible,[1] only Solomon's is actually described, and that but briefly.[2] Doubtless its name of "throne of ivory" arose from an ornamentation similar to the carved ivory* pieces which have been found at Samaria and Megiddo. With its six steps, its armrests, and the figures of lions and bulls, betraying

Throne, carved on an ivory plaque from Megiddo.

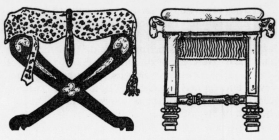

Thrones: Syrian (14th century) and Assyrian (9th century).

foreign artistic influences, this royal seat was probably of imposing appearance and emphasized the prestige of David's son.

[1] Ex. 11. 5; 1 Kgs. 2. 19; 2 Kgs. 25. 28; Jer. 43. 10; 52. 32; Acts 12. 21. [2] 1 Kgs. 10. 18–20; 2 Chr. 9. 17–19; cf. 1 Kgs. 7. 7.

THYINE

This fragrant wood, rich in hue and finely marked, came from a north African conifer, an evergreen 20 to 25 ft. in height. It is mentioned in the Apocalypse among precious products which great merchants sold in Rome;[1] cabinet-makers used it for tables and luxury furniture, highly valued in antiquity.

[1] Rev. 18. 12.

TILE

Roofs in Palestine were flat or cupola-shaped, so tiles were not in use there. Those curiously spoken of by Luke in the healing of the paralytic let down "through the tiles" in front of Jesus,[1] present a minor problem which exegetes have sought to resolve in various ways, some of which are more satisfactory than others. It is possible that as the author of the Third Gospel was writing for an imperial public he was thinking of the roofs of Graeco-Roman houses. The parallel narrative in Mark's Gospel,[2] where tiles are not in question, is in any case perfectly clear.

[1] Lk. 5. 19. [2] Mk. 2. 1 ...

TIME

The Israelite scarcely had as rigorous a notion of time as ours. In order to speak of the length of a generation and to express his age, he doubtless used a number, but that rather expressed a state, e.g., the man of forty may have that age for many years running, for that means he feels in the prime of life. Moreover, the number forty is found more than once in the Bible without necessarily expressing what our modern usage would see in it.[1]

This is why the Israelites have no exact chronology

such as that of the Greeks and Romans, who relied on an important and well-known event (Olympiads, foundation of Rome). They could have taken the Exodus from Egypt, or the giving of the Law, or the building of Solomon's Temple, or the return from Exile; some of them did so regard these events, and in the Books of Maccabees there is the idea of a Seleucid era and of a Maccabaean era, but they were not consistently applied.

In the period of the monarchy years were reckoned from the coming to the throne of an Israelite or foreign king.[2] An important event could also serve as a landmark; thus Amos dates one of his prophecies from "two years before the earthquake".[3]—Apocalyptic writings determine certain periods by means of the Sabbatical or Jubilee Years (7×7 years), and the Book of Daniel speaks of weeks of years.[4]

Let us add that the Talmud reckons events from the creation of the world, but it was only in the Middle Ages (to be exact, since R. Scherira, who died in A.D. 1019) that the chronology recognized today by the Jews was adopted, one which places the beginning of the world in 3761 B.C.

As for the Christian church, so far as we can judge, it first reckoned events by means of cycles of fifteen years, beginning with the victory of Constantine over Maxentius in 312. 1960 is the 13th year of the 109th cycle ($1960 - 312 = 1648$; and $1648 \div 15 = 109$, leaving 13).—Finally, it was Denis the Small who in 531 fixed the date of the birth of Jesus in the year 753 of the foundation of Rome; but it was the Venerable Bede (died 735) who spread the use of this Christian era, and it was Charlemagne who imposed it upon all his States.

For the division of time see †year, hour, day, month, night, seasons, week.

[1] Num. 14. 34; Jg. 3. 11; 4. 3; etc. [2] Neh. 2. 1; Est. 1. 3; Jer. 32. 1; etc. [3] Amos 1. 1. [4] Dan. 9. 24–27.

TIN

Used essentially in the making of bronze*, tin was well known to the Israelites. It is named by Ezekiel among the metals that Tyre sought for from Tarshish (in Spain?);[1] but the Phoenicians imported it also from Cornwall and elsewhere in Great Britain, and they no doubt also drew upon the deposits round the Adriatic. It is possible that before this Palestine imported tin from Persia and Armenia.—During the second half of the 1st millennium B.C., the trade in tin passed into the hands of the Greeks at Marseilles. Tin figures in the list of metals in Num. 31. 22.

[1] Ez. 27. 12; cf. 22. 18, 20.

TITHE

The deduction of the tenth part of the income for use by the civil authority or the religious sanctuaries

was customary among more than one ancient people. The institution also existed in Israel; unfortunately we are not well informed on the subject: texts are few in number and are often inexplicit. Thus, we do not know whether the monarchy did in fact exact the tithe which Samuel, according to 1 Sam. 8. 15–17, had feared for his people; perhaps the word should be understood in the general sense of dues and taxes.

It is probable that the tithe sacred to Yahweh was an early introduction into Israel. Two or three O.T. texts,[1] which may perhaps refer to the early period, speak of it. In any case, Yahweh was considered as the owner of the soil; men could not therefore enjoy the fruits of the earth without reserving a part for him, and the gratitude shown to him could only bring new blessings [2] on the faithful. For the rest, nothing could be less unpleasant than the manner in which matters were conducted as these are reflected in the later Deuteronomic legislation: [3] apart from what was undoubtedly offered to Yahweh in sacrifice and what was given to the priests, the Israelite himself benefited in the end from the majority of the produce set aside for his God. Indeed, he consumed it with joy before Yahweh in the local sanctuary near his home or in one of his choice, in a sacred ritual meal in which he was in some sense the host of Yahweh and which was shared by all his family, his servants, male and female, and any poor whom he wished to invite.

The centralizing of the cult in Jerusalem naturally necessitated new rules and caused changes dealt with in the legislative texts. In Deuteronomy, it seems—for the texts are not always very clear—that the tithe levied solely on the produce of the soil [4] (corn, oil, wine) was to be brought for two consecutive years to the Temple in Jerusalem,[5] at the time of a pilgrimage, perhaps at the Feast of Tabernacles. And sacrificial family meals similar to those formerly held in the local sanctuaries were organized in the central sanctuary; the Levites, whose condition was often very poor, were to be invited guests.[6] If the Israelite lived far from Jerusalem it was permissible for him, in order to simplify his journey, to change the produce reserved for the tithe into money, and to bring the equivalent to the capital.[7] In the third year, on the other hand, the family feast appears to have been omitted; it was replaced by the deposit of the whole tithe—in each man's home district—for the benefit of the Levites, foreigners, orphans, and widows who "shall come, eat and be filled".[8]

The tithe ordered later by the Priestly Code was quite another matter. Instead of being an opportunity for the family to gather before Yahweh or to show charity, it became a levy which the clergy took in its entirety.[9] It was a tax due to the Levites, who in their turn had to pay a tenth of the collected tithe to the priests. At one stage even, the Levites went in person, under the supervision of a priest, to collect what the agricultural population had to pay,[10] and livestock also was now tithed.[11] And when the Israelite wished to redeem a part of what was normally paid in kind, he had to add to it a fifth of its value.[12]

It may have been the extension of the tithe system laid down by the Priestly Law that made its collection difficult after the Exile. Malachi [13] complains of deceit in the payment of tithes, and Nehemiah [14] of negligence which he sought to rectify. Elsewhere, the Gospel and the Talmud show that far from losing any importance with time, tithe was paid by strict Jews even on vegetables and the smallest culinary plants.[15]

[1] Gen. 14. 20; 28. 22; Amos 4. 4; cf. Heb. 7. 1–10. [2] Dt. 26. 15; Mal. 3. 10, 11. [3] Dt. 14. 23, 26. [4] Dt. 14. 22, 23. [5] Dt. 12. 11, 12, 17. [6] Dt. 14. 23, 26, 27. [7] Dt. 14. 24–26. [8] Dt. 14. 28, 29; 26. 12. [9] Num. 18. 21–32; Lev. 27. 30. [10] Neh. 10. 37. [11] Lev. 27. 32, 33. [12] Lev. 27. 31. [13] Mal. 3. 8–12. [14] Neh. 13. 10–13. [15] Matt. 23. 23; Lk. 18. 12.

TOMB

1. In order to acquire some archaeological information about the answers given in former times on the question of life after death, tombs had to be violated; and it is not surprising that the excavations carried out, especially in the first half of our century, should have brought to light a considerable number of them, and particularly in Palestine. Thus, some large cemeteries are known (for example, at Jericho, Marissa, Jerusalem) which are situated outside the towns, as well as private burial places, tombs of sovereigns, kings, princes. But a certain number of isolated tombs have also been found. The O.T. recalls that sometimes some dead were interred in the land attached to their own houses,[1] or beneath a tree (perhaps a sacred tree),[2] or in a field.[3] It appears, however, that the use of family tombs was very widespread, a custom which gives rise to the expression "to be gathered to [i.e., buried with] one's fathers".[4] It is possible to state that sometimes these last-mentioned tombs were abandoned for several generations, but were used again two or three centuries later; people then contented themselves with putting on one side, often in a little box of clay, the bones found there, thus making a sort of ossuary. The Israelites who owned no land where a family tomb could be built were buried "in the graves of the children of the people",[5] that is to say, in a common grave.

2. Tombs of prehistoric times have been studied, the most important of which are the dolmens*, and what have been called the Neolithic crematoria of Gezer and Jerusalem—sorts of caves, the floors of which were covered with incompletely calcined human bones and human ashes. Of the period preceding the entry of the Israelites into Canaan, tombs formed in two parts are known: a ramp or a shaft giving access and a funeral chamber, which was sometimes faced with stone and often closed by a little wall (a).

At the beginning of the Israelite period it appears likely that the people newly arrived were content to imitate the funeral customs of their predecessors. But in the time of the monarchy the side shaft of access was suppressed and replaced by a simple hole bored at one end of the ceiling, and through it people jumped into the tomb (b). Sometimes a second opening closed by a simple slab of stone was made in the middle of the ceiling; but it is not possible to give its purpose.

So that the corpses should not be simply laid on the ground, a stone bed was built in some tombs. This was changed into a bench and later into a deep niche into which a coffin* could be introduced.—Sometimes several tombs, natural or enlarged grottoes, were situated near each other with entrances opening on to a sort of courtyard common to them all, an inner courtyard whose gate was

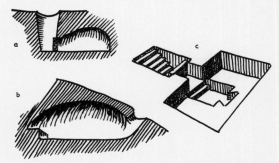

Development of tombs: (*a*) Canaanite; (*b*) early Israelite; (*c*) with benches.

later carefully constructed. More and more, the dead were laid on benches which sometimes lined the walls of the funeral chamber (c); they were usually laid on their left side with their knees raised to their chin.

With time, the Israelite underground tomb became more and more architectural. Inside first, the funeral beds were surmounted by arcades cut into the rock; the body was then laid on the bed on its back, with its head sometimes resting on a head-stone. But these forms of tomb only allowed the burial of two or three people in each chamber. The idea was conceived of hollowing out narrow, deep niches at right-angles to the wall, closed by a square stone slab as soon as a body had been laid there. Sometimes two storeys of niches were hollowed out.—The courtyard, first of all open to the sky, on to which the chambers of the tomb opened, was itself soon cut into the rock against which the entrance door sometimes assumed the appearance of a monumental façade. However, more often than not this entrance door was simply closed by a huge stone frequently in the shape of a mill-stone, which explains the question asked by

Mary Magdalene, Mary the mother of James and Salome, when they drew near Jesus' tomb on Easter morning: "Who shall roll us away the stone?" [6]

In Roman times two very well-known tombs were built at Jerusalem; the Tomb of the Judges, which comprises a vestibule 13 ft. wide surmounted by a carved triangular pediment, and a whole collection of chambers and niches hollowed out of the rock; certain authors claim that judges of the Jewish tribunal were buried there; at any rate, these are not the judges mentioned by the Book of Judges.—Then the Tomb of the Kings; it is of the same type as the preceding one, with a vestibule formerly supported by two columns and whose cornice is fairly well preserved; in a central chamber, four new doors give access to four chambers (with annexes) in the walls of which are hollowed deep niches; this tomb has

Tomb door in the form of a mill-stone.

nothing to do with the kings of Israel; it is very likely the mausoleum of Queen Helena of Adiabene (in Assyria) and of her family; having taken refuge in Jerusalem at the end of the 1st century A.D., she had become a Jewish proselyte.

It is from this same period that the Tombs of Absalom* and of St James date, and also the Pyramid of Zacharias in Jerusalem.

3. There are no paintings decorating the tombs, as there are in Egypt. Of the hundreds of excavated tombs, only one has been found (at Marissa) which bore a painted decoration; it is an exception.

But there is clear development in the objects deposited in the tombs. In Canaanite tombs are found dishes, weapons, objects of adornment laid near the corpses, or placed apart; terra-cotta vessels which contained food; large earthenware jars are accompanied by little pitchers, which seems to indicate that the first were filled; one often gets the impression that certain vessels had been purposely broken as if in that state (dead, as it were) they could the better serve in the beyond.

283

But in Israelite tombs it seems that the realism of some of the Canaanite conceptions was abandoned in favour of development towards more abstract notions. Amulets then appear frequently, as if a magic power could be more useful to a dead man than food. Soon oil lamps became the most characteristic element of funeral furniture.

4. Tombs sometimes acted as places of worship. In order to convince oneself of this fact it is sufficient to remember that an artificially erected stone had been set up near Rachel's tomb.[7] It is not impossible that by not mentioning the sites of Moses' tomb it was desired, among other things, to protest against this type of cult.

[1] 1 Sam. 25. 1; 2 Chr. 33. 20. [2] Gen. 35. 8; 1 Sam. 31. 13. [3] Jos. 24. 32. [4] Gen. 49. 29; Dt. 31. 16; Jg. 2. 10; 1 Kgs. 11. 21; etc. [5] 2 Kgs. 23. 6. [6] Mk. 16. 3. [7] Gen. 35. 20.

TONGS

Among the utensils needed at the altar for burnt offerings was to be found one whose Hebrew name has been translated as tongs, fork, fleshhook.[1]

(† Snuffers.)

[1] Ex. 27. 3; 38. 3; 1 Chr. 28. 17; 2 Chr. 4. 16.

TOPAZ

Topaz is a yellow form of corundum, but, by the name of "oriental topaz" a beautiful yellowish-green stone is generally meant. It was the second stone on the High Priest's* breastplate,[1] the ninth foundation of the walls of the New Jerusalem,[2] and it adorned also the robes of the king of Tyre.[3] The poem of Job declares that the topaz of Ethiopia cannot equal wisdom.[4]

[1] Ex. 28. 17; 39. 10. [2] Rev. 21. 20. [3] Ez. 28. 13. [4] Job 28. 19.

TORCH

Made of several pieces of wood coated with oil or pitch, the torch was known in Palestine from ancient times as a means of lighting or as a taper. The O.T. mentions it several times,[1] but nearly always metaphorically: the eyes of the angel seen by Daniel [2] shone like "burning torches", torches shot forth from the mouth of Leviathan,[3] and the prophet will not be silent until the salvation of Jerusalem is resplendent as a "burning torch".[4] Certain versions sometimes translate wrongly the Hebrew word for lamp* by torch.

In the N.T. the same mistake has sometimes been made, or else a reverse mistake in rendering by "lamp" the Greek word meaning precisely "torch" found in several passages.[5] (It must, however, be recognized that in the papyri this Greek word currently meant the ancient lamp.) Even in the Parable of the

Ten Virgins, torches might be meant—kept alight by means of oil in the East—and not lamps, whose little flame would be difficult to protect in the open-air. However, as it could hardly be admitted that "torches" lit up the room at Troas where Paul prolonged his speech until midnight,[6] it is better to

A "fire vase" figured on an Assyrian bas-relief.

think that in this narrative, and consequently in the Parable of the Ten Virgins also,[7] the references are to the "fire vases" represented on certain ancient bas-reliefs: this type of copper goblet was filled with pitch, oil, and rags for burning. It had a base which, upon occasion, could be fixed to the end of a stick.

[1] Gen. 15. 17; Jg. 7. 16; 15. 4, 5; Ez. 1. 13; Nahum 2. 4. [2] Dan. 10. 6. [3] Job 41. 19. [4] Is. 62. 1. [5] Matt. 25. 1; Jn. 18. 3; Acts 20. 8; Rev. 4. 5; 8. 10. [6] Acts 20. 8. [7] Matt. 25. 1.

TOW

On the basis of two O.T. texts we can affirm that the Israelites were acquainted with tow, a by-product of the combing of flax: the Book of Judges [1] relates that Samson "broke the withes, as a string of tow is broken when it touches the fire", and Isaiah [2] announces to a guilty people that their strength will be like tow and will be consumed by fire.

[1] Jg. 16. 9. [2] Is. 1. 31.

TRADES

1. *General matters.* Among ancient nomads there was no question of trades; each man made the things he needed for his own use—clothes, tents, tools, etc. The Palestinian peasant was almost independent of tradesmen and could even build his own house, except possibly for a little help from his neighbour. However, work in metal and the making of water-pots required special material; it is possible that in Israel, as in Palestine today, blacksmiths travelled at times from village to village to make any necessary repairs and that potters hawked their wares.

Trades only developed in the towns when political circumstances allowed; at the time of the Philistine wars the work of Israelite blacksmiths [1] was stopped, and Solomon called on the help of the Phoenicians in his building projects. It took the ancient Hebrews some time to equal the manual skill of those they had supplanted; excavations in Palestine reveal a halt or even a setback in civilization after the Israelites arrived in the land. Moreover, broadly speaking, industry never flourished there, nor showed originality in its products; often it was subject to foreign influences—and how could it compete with the technical marvels or the art of Egypt, Mesopotamia, or even Phoenicia?

Trades were usually handed down from father to son; guilds were formed [2] and men of one craft worked in the same street or the same part of the town, as they often do today in the East: Jeremiah speaks quite clearly of a street of bakers in Jerusalem,[3] Josephus of a street of smiths, and the Talmud of one of butchers. Certain districts specialized in particular industries: Netaim and Gederah had their potters,[4] as Gaza has today, and Beth-Ashbea its weavers,[5] as Nablus has its soap-making today; excavations have shown, for example, that almost all the houses in ancient Beit Mirsim (Debir) were weaving sheds, and that near Haifa there was a great distributing centre for Aegean pottery in Palestine.

While the Greeks and Romans often despised all manual work, the Jews loved to say that a man who did not teach his son a trade was teaching him to be a vagabond; notable rabbis were butchers, shoe-makers, blacksmiths, etc., and it is well known that St Paul was a weaver of tent-cloth. Only occupations which endangered ritual purity or morality were disliked.

2. *List of principal trades mentioned in the Bible texts.*

(For details, see the articles indicated.)

Wood:	Metals:
Woodcutter*	Smelter († smelting)
Carpenter*	Blacksmith († smith)
Sculptor († sculpture)	Goldsmith, Silversmith*
Stone:	Leather:
Stonecutter	Currier
Mason*	Tanner*
Sculptor († sculpture)	Clothes, etc.:
Clay:	Weaver († weaving)
Potter († pottery)	Dyer*
Brickmaker († brick)	Fuller*
Food:	Perfumer*
Baker*	Barber†
(Butcher)*	
Cook*	

See also: † seal, precious stones.

[1] 1 Sam. 13. 19. [2] Neh. 3. 8, 31. [3] Jer. 37. 21. [4] 1 Chr. 4. 23. [5] 1 Chr. 4. 21; cf. 4. 14.

TREASURE

Independently of their lands, flocks, food stores, etc., the kings of Israel and Judah, like the monarchs of antiquity,[1] and contrary to the thought of Deuteronomy (17. 17), possessed a treasure containing gold, silver, precious stones, and objects of price;[2] Solomon's was particularly remarkable.[3] Deposited in special chambers,[4] these riches were entrusted to the supervision of high officials (treasurers).[5] The Bible texts mention this royal treasure especially in connection with the successive pillages or depletions which it had to sustain many times.[6]

The sanctuaries of Palestine and the Temple of Jerusalem, in particular, also hid in their subsidiary buildings a treasure[7] which was increased by war booty,[8] acts of generosity by kings and well-to-do people, the voluntary offerings of the faithful, and, at a later period, what was forthcoming from the collecting boxes († treasury) and the Temple tax*. Established by David and Solomon,[9] the treasure in the Jerusalem Temple was under the supervision of officials and special guardians.[10] Like the royal treasure, it constituted a sort of state bank from which the city could draw in case of need;[11] of course, the conquerors of Jerusalem did not fail to pillage it.[12]

[1] Ezr. 7. 20; Est. 3. 9; 4. 7; Ez. 28. 4. [2] 2 Kgs. 20. 13. [3] 1 Kgs. 10. 14 . . ., 23; 2 Chr. 9. 13. [4] 2 Kgs. 20. 13; 2 Chr. 32. 27. [5] 1 Chr. 27. 25; cf. Acts 8. 27; Rom. 16. 23. [6] 1 Kgs. 14. 26; 15. 18; 2 Kgs. 14. 14; 16. 8; 18. 15; 2 Chr. 12. 9; 16. 2; etc. [7] Jos. 6. 19, 24; Jg. 9. 4. [8] 2 Sam. 8. 11, 12; 1 Chr. 18. 11. [9] 1 Kgs. 7. 51; 1 Chr. 29. 1, 8; 2 Chr. 5. 1. [10] 1 Chr. 9. 26; 26. 22–28; cf. Jn. 8. 20. [11] 1 Kgs. 15. 18; 2 Kgs. 12. 18; 16. 8; 18. 15; 2 Chr. 16. 2. [12] 1 Kgs. 14. 26; 2 Kgs. 14. 14; 24. 13; 2 Chr. 12. 9; 25. 24.

TREASURY

According to the Mishnah, somewhere in what was called the Court of the Women in Herod's restored Temple in Jerusalem, probably in the place called the treasury,[1] thirteen chests received sanctuary offerings. Doubtless because of their shape they bore in Hebrew the name "trumpets"; notices indicated what each one was for (burnt offerings, wood, incense, freewill offerings, etc.). Here the widow mentioned in the Gospel placed her two mites*. The word used in the Gospels seems to cover both the collecting-boxes and the treasure-room(s) of the Temple.[2]

[1] Jn. 8. 20. [2] Mk. 12. 41 . . .; Lk. 21. 2; cf. 2. Kgs. 12. 9.

TREES, SACRED

All peoples have venerated the mysterious life-force which manifests itself in trees. The Semites most particularly made them the object of a definite cult. Even today the fellaheen and the Bedouin of

Arabia regard the sacred tree as the dwelling-place of a superhuman being, of a saint buried under its roots.

The Canaanites shared similar ideas, and when they reached Palestine the Israelites all too quickly fell back into practices connected with that belief, such as those they had observed in the pre-Mosaic period. The O.T. mentions a series of trees whose sacred character is almost certain: the terebinth or holm oak which was at the sanctuary of Yahweh in Shechem and which was called the oak of Moreh (= giver of oracles),[1] that of Mamre near Hebron,[2] a favourite resort of Abraham, the tamarisk of Beer-sheba,[3] the terebinth at Ophrah, where God appeared to Gideon,[4] the "weeping oak" on the tomb of Deborah, Rebekah's nurse,[5] perhaps identical with the palm tree under which Deborah the prophetess sat,[6] the tamarisk of Jabesh, under which the bones of Saul were interred,[7] and the tamarisk, also of Gibeah, where Israel's first king dispensed justice,[8] etc.

But still more significant are the denunciations of the prophets who rose up with such energy against the cults celebrated "under every green tree" and thus demonstrate their importance: "they [the Israelites] burn incense under oaks and poplars and terebinths";[9] "you shall be ashamed of the terebinths in which you take delight";[10] "are you not children of transgression inflaming yourselves among the terebinths, under every green tree?";[11] "upon every high hill and under every green tree thou didst bow thyself, playing the harlot".[12] (Cf. also 2 Kgs. 16. 4; 17. 10; 2 Chr. 28. 4; Jer. 3. 6, 13; 17. 2; Ez. 6. 13; 20. 28.)

Deuteronomy ordered[13] the abolition of these idolatrous customs, which Josiah's reform sought to end.

[1] Gen. 12. 6; 35. 2–4; Jg. 9. 6. [2] Gen. 13. 18; 14. 13; 18. 1. [3] Gen. 21. 33. [4] Jg. 6. 11. [5] Gen. 35. 8. [6] Jg. 4. 5. [7] 1 Sam. 31. 13. [8] 1 Sam. 22. 6. [9] Hos. 4. 13. [10] Is. 1. 29. [11] Is. 57. 4, 5. [12] Jer. 2. 20. [13] Dt. 12. 2.

TREES, SHRUBS

Trees are often used symbolically by the Bible writers. We only have to think of the trees of the Garden of Eden,[1] of the allegory of the trees seeking a king,[2] of chap. 31 of Ezekiel, with its splendid comparison of Assyria with a cedar, and of the parables of Jesus, at once simple and effective, about good and bad trees.[3] Elsewhere, the righteous man or he who trusts in God is said to be like a green and fruitful tree;[4] or the tree is sometimes a figure for pride, for arrogance,[5] sometimes for longevity;[6] while four times the Book of Proverbs speaks of the "tree" of life, where we should say "source" of life.[7] (Cf. also Is. 7. 2; Ez. 17. 22; Job 14. 7; 19. 10; 24. 20; Jude 12; etc.—† Trees, sacred; forest.)

TRENCH

[1] Gen. 2 and 3, cf. Rev. 2. 7; 22. 2; etc. [2] Jg. 9. 8–15. [3] Matt. 3. 10 par.; 7. 17 par.; 12. 33. [4] Jer. 17. 8; Ps. 1. 3. [5] Is. 2. 13; 10. 33. [6] Is. 65. 22. [7] Prov. 3. 18; 11. 30; 13. 12; 15. 4.

TRENCH

The Hebrew word used for the trench that Elijah dug round his altar [1] means in all other instances a "water-channel", a "conduit".

(† Fortifications.)

[1] 1 Kgs. 18. 32.

TRIANGLE

A percussion instrument, which is referred to once in the O.T.,[1] and the Hebrew name of which comes from the number three, perhaps corresponds to the triangle our musicians use.

[1] 1 Sam. 18. 6.

TRIBE

1. The nomads and semi-nomads have no conception of a State, and the basis of their organization is the tribe. The Israelites are no exception to this rule; they lived in the atmosphere of the tribe, for as long as they were not tied to a country and specific places; and even after the conquest of Canaan, they kept certain elements of the tribal constitution for a long time.

The tribe is an association of clans and families whose members are united by blood and constitute an entity. In theory, all the individuals who are part of it descend from a common ancestor, which is the basis of the brotherly spirit which they owe each other reciprocally. In fact, a tribe is generally formed of a nucleus of individuals really related to each other, around which strangers come and group themselves—for example, slaves bought or set free, fugitives from other tribes, isolated individuals, small families scattered by war or separated from their first tribe after dissensions; thus when the tie of natural kinship is lacking, it is replaced by a mystic tie established by a more or less magic ceremony, whose form is very variable, ranging from the simple meal to the mingling of the contractants' blood. But this ceremony effects between those participating in it a very deep bond, a religious bond. The tribe is in effect a religious community. Each individual must be linked not only to the other members of the tribe but also, and above all, to its god; for each tribe has its god, or its sanctuary, or at any rate its own way of practising its worship, its own rites, and its particular sacrifices. It can happen, however, that several tribes participate in the same cult. Several centuries after the settlement of the Israelites in Canaan certain clans still kept these ancient tribal habits. Thus it is

known that Samuel's father went up each year to Shiloh "with his house" to offer the annual sacrifice.[1] Later David excuses his absence to Saul by evoking a family sacrifice at which he had to be present.[2]

2. The tribe is divided into a certain number of clans which subdivide themselves into families, and these in their turn split up into households.

It appears that it is the clan which constitutes the real social unit, the basis of this organization. It is the clan which suffers the consequences of a crime committed by one of its members; it is the clan which assumes the responsibility of the vendetta when one of its members has been killed.

However, at the head of the tribe there is a leader who is at the same time a judge and a military leader; but even in these functions he must take the advice of the most highly regarded men of the tribe and in particular of the leaders of the various clans. His authority is primarily moral and results, above all, from his personality, his courage, his intelligence, his shrewdness.

It is striking to notice to what extent each individual in the tribe is fundamentally free; no one intervenes in his private life; the family is mistress in its own home. A whole clan may become free if it is powerful enough to detach itself from the tribe. But the attachment of each one for his tribe is very deep; each individual loves his tribe and cannot imagine a situation more dreadful than that of a man expelled from his tribe.

Tribal constitution is thus, in spite of its simplicity, perfectly adapted to the needs of nomads, whom it assures of indispensable protection and freedom.

3. At the time when the Israelites were still living in the nomadic state a tribe might be called by the name of its ancestor, so that in our Bible texts some proper names indicate a collectivity rather than an individual, in spite of appearances; some covenant or even marriage narratives are often interpreted as an echo of the historical associations of certain tribes. A number of passages show us the tribe of the Calebites, formerly more or less independent and of Edomite origin, which associated with the tribe of Judah and ended by being absorbed by it.[3] On the other hand, the tribe of Benjamin detached itself from that of Joseph, and the latter was again divided into two groups: the tribe of Ephraim and the tribe of Manasseh.—Thus the number of tribes of Israel has varied; not one ancient text, moreover, mentions a division of the nomadic Hebrews into twelve simultaneous tribes. It was later that people tried to split them up in that way, although the method of counting the tribes has not been constant. Furthermore, we must add that it is extremely difficult to reconstruct the history of Hebrews in those days.

The dividing up of the tribes in the recently conquered land of Canaan is a matter for history rather than archaeology. Finally, it should be said that even after the suppression of tribal organization, the people remained very attached to the memories it had left behind, and transposed them into the future, so that they appear in the N.T. and in particular in the Apocalypse.[4]

[1] 1 Sam. 1. 21. [2] 1 Sam. 20. 29. [3] Num. 13. 6; 32. 12, 13; Jos. 14. 6, 13; 15. 13. [4] Acts 26. 7; Rev. 7. 4 ff.; 21. 12.

TRIBUNE

A superior officer in the Roman army. In Jerusalem a tribune commanded the cohort quartered in the fortress of Antonia*, at the north-west corner of the Temple area.[1]

[1] Jn. 18. 12; Acts 21. 31–23. 35.

TRUMPET, HORN

The horn or trumpet is very often mentioned in the O.T., which distinguishes the cow's or ram's horn (actually, or of this shape), from the straight trumpet of metal.

The horn, which gave a low-pitched, staccato, or prolonged note, is without doubt more ancient than the metal trumpet. It could be of various dimensions.[1] The Israelites used it mainly to give signals of alarm [2] or of war,[3] but also to enhance certain solemn and joyful [4] activities, and even to praise Yahweh (Ps. 47. 6; 98. 6; 150. 3). The New Year festival was announced by the sound of the trumpet,[5] and this practice has been perpetuated until our times in the synagogues. According to the Mishnah, at a later date the Sabbath day and other feast or fast days also began with similar signals.

Bronze or silver trumpets were made of a straight tube, without valves, terminating in a bell. They gave a clear sound. Their size doubtless varied: those of the Temple of Jerusalem, reproduced on Titus' Arch in Rome, are longer than the usual Egyptian trumpets and than those rather roughly represented on certain Jewish coins. In ancient times they were used for non-religious signals,[6] but it seems likely that the trumpet became with time, among the Jews, an essentially cultic instrument, reserved for the priests; [7] the writings of the post-Exilic period even ascribe to it, in the past, a rôle similar to that at the time of writing: [8] trumpet calls (cf. our bell-ringing) enlivened feasts and the sacrificial ceremonies to which they gave rise; [9] there is even reference to a body of 120 priests bearing these instruments.[10] Through the Mishnah we know that, later still, different signals were given daily in the Temple by the sound of trumpets (sunrise, sacrifices, etc.).

In the N.T. the trumpets of the Apocalypse [11] are famous, and three passages mention the trumpet of God, which will gather together the elect.[12]

[1] Is. 27. 13. [2] Neh. 4. 18; Jer. 4. 5; 6. 1; Hos. 8. 1; Joel 2. 1; Amos 3. 6. [3] Jos. 6. 5; Jg. 3. 27; 6. 34; 7. 18; 1 Sam. 13. 3; 2 Sam. 2. 28; Job 39. 25; Jer. 4. 19; Hos. 5. 8; Amos 2. 2; Zech. 9. 14. [4] 2 Sam. 6. 15; 1 Kgs. 1. 34; 2 Kgs. 9. 13; 1 Chr. 15. 28; 2 Chr. 15. 14. [5] Lev. 23. 24; cf. 25. 9; Num. 29. 1. [6] 2 Kgs. 11. 14; 2 Chr. 23. 13; Hos. 5. 8. [7] Num. 10. 8; 2 Kgs. 12. 13; 1 Chr. 15. 24; 16. 6; 2 Chr. 7. 6; 13. 14; 29. 28; Ezr. 3. 10. [8] 1 Chr. 15. 28; 16. 42; 2 Chr. 29. 28. [9] Num. 10. 10. [10] 2 Chr. 5. 12. [11] Rev. 8. 2–9. 11. [12] Matt. 24. 31; 1 Cor. 15. 52; 1 Th. 4. 16 (cf. Is. 27. 13; Joel 2. 1).

TURTLE

Several species of land turtles and aquatic turtles exist in Palestine, but it is unlikely that they are named in the list in Lev. 11. 29, 30, where the references are rather to various lizards.

UNCLEANNESS

Like so many other peoples, the Hebrews attached great importance to the notions of cleanness and uncleanness. From ancient times, we note in their customs the existence of prohibitions of all sorts, alimentary or others—real taboos, of which it is not our concern here to seek the often distant origin, nor the motives, which are as diverse as they are difficult to explain. At any rate, the Israelites' conceptions on this subject were very different from ours: for them, for example, the freshest and cleanest pork was absolutely impure, whereas bread baked beneath a layer of dung was perfectly pure. The problem is, above all, of a religious and cultic nature. Thus the Deuteronomic Law insisted on the need for ritual purity: Israel must be distinguished from other nations, for it was holy before Yahweh.[1] And the Priestly Code drew the full consequences of this principle by initiating a careful regulation of observances which resulted in the casuistry of the Mishnah. At the beginning of the Christian era the religious life of the Israelite demanded submission to all sorts of recommendations against which Christ reacted on many occasions with the freedom and boldness which are so well known.[2]

Leaving to Biblical theology those questions which are within its scope on this topic, listed below are the chief uncleannesses recognized, at a more or less late date, by the O.T. texts.

1. *Animals*. A whole series of animals which it is forbidden to offer in sacrifice or to consume are considered unclean. As regard quadrupeds and fish, legislation tried to have recourse to certain principles of discrimination: those animals are clean which have the horn of their hoof cleft and which chew the cud (ox, sheep, hart, giraffe, etc.); those which chew the cud, or seem to do so, but have no cleft hoof are unclean (camel, hare, etc.), also those which have a cleft hoof but do not chew the cud (pigs), and again those which walk on the sole of the

foot and not on hooves [3] (dogs, cats).—Of the animals which live in water, only those are clean which have both fins and scales, i.e., fish, with the exclusion of cetacea, mollusca, crustacea, etc.

For birds, there is no general rule: those which are forbidden are mainly, but not solely, birds of prey.— All reptiles and insects, with the exception of certain grasshoppers, are unclean.

The two important lists are found as follows: Dt. 14. 3–20 and Lev. 11. 2–23, 41–47.

2. *Food.* It is forbidden to consume not only meat from unclean animals but also that of any beast mauled by a wild animal or which has died of an illness.[4]—Moreover, the blood of any animal is strictly forbidden,[5] not because it is in itself unclean, but because it is the life-principle of every creature and belongs to Yahweh.[6] (It can be seen here how close are the domains of the clean and the unclean; what is holy can also contaminate, "defile"; so the Jews wash their hands when they have touched the Holy Scriptures.[7])

3. *Death.*

(*a*) The corpse of an *unclean* animal defiles for a whole day people who touch it or carry it.[8] The Priestly Code goes as far as to state exactly—and this is the beginnings of casuistry—that several sorts of "little animals which move on the ground", weasels, mice, etc., make unclean any *object* on which they chance to fall when dead, with the exception of springs, cisterns (which cannot be dispensed with), and seeds [9] (protected by their skin, as long as it is dry).[10]

(*b*) The corpses of *clean* animals which have not been correctly slaughtered for food defile for one day those who touch them or carry them or eat of their meat.[11]

(*c*) The human corpse makes unclean, for seven days, the man who touches it,[12] as well as the tent in which it is laid. The tent, in its turn, makes unclean all those who enter it, and even every vessel not provided with a lid.[13] Whoever, moreover, touches in the fields a man killed by the sword or who has died a natural death, or human bones or a sepulchre, is unclean for seven days.[14] Everything which touches what is unclean becomes unclean, and the person who touches it is unclean until the evening.[15]

4. *Leprosy.* Every man suffering from leprosy* is unclean and must live apart from those not afflicted with his illness; he wears torn clothes, lets his hair fall loosely, and covers his upper lip.[16] The Priestly Code considers that objects of wool, linen, leather, and even houses can be attacked by "leprosy" and, in that case, come under the law of uncleanness.[17]

5. *Women in child-bed.* The woman in child-bed is considered unclean, not because she has given birth to a child, but because she has spilt blood. In the case of a boy she is unclean for seven days, and in the case of a girl for fourteen days; and the law adds that she shall remain at home and touch nothing holy for thirty-three days if she has had a boy, and sixty-six days if she has had a girl, until the days of her purification be accomplished.[18]

6. *Secretions.* Different secretions, normal or pathological, make unclean for one or for several days those who are afflicted with them or even the objects with which they come into contact. Chap. 15 of Leviticus gives the necessary precise information on this subject.

7. *Paganism.* As Palestine is holy land, Yahweh's country, every foreign land is considered unclean [19] and also the bread eaten there.[20] Every uncircumcised male is unclean, as well as everything concerning the worship of foreign gods, magic, certain funeral customs,[21] etc. He who practises them pollutes the territory of Israel in its entirety.[22] From the N.T. we know that the Jews are forbidden to enter the houses of "pagans" or to eat with them, and that the presence of non-Israelites in the Temple pollutes the sanctuary.[23] "Thou wentest in to men uncircumcised, and didst eat with them" [24]—such is the reproach levelled at Peter. And the riot provoked by the Jews who accused Paul of having introduced Greeks into the Temple at Jerusalem was a serious one.[25]

Most of the uncleannesses in the list we have compiled, when they do not disappear of themselves,[26] are removed by the thorough purifications* prescribed by the Law. In certain cases, however, the violation of orders incurs the death of the guilty party [27] on the same score as attacks on sexual prohibitions, which, more than uncleannesses, are acts of unchastity and crimes against morality.[28]

[1] Dt. 7. 6. [2] Matt. 15. 1–20; 23. 23–28; Mk. 7. 1–16; Lk. 11. 37–44; cf. Col. 2. 16; Heb. 13. 9. [3] Lev. 11. 27. [4] Ex. 22. 31; Lev. 17. 15; Dt. 14. 21; Ez. 4. 14. [5] Gen. 9. 4; Lev. 7. 26; 19. 26; (cf. its rôle in sacrifices), Dt. 12. 16; 15. 23; Acts 15. 29. [6] Lev. 17. 10 . . . ; Dt. 12. 23; 1 Sam. 14. 32–34. [7] Cf. Lev. 11. 27–28; Num. 19. 1–10; Is. 65. 5; Ez. 44. 19. [8] Lev. 11. 8, 24, 27–28, 31. [9] Lev. 11. 29–37. [10] Lev. 11. 38. [11] Lev. 11. 39–40. [12] Lev. 21. 1; Num. 9. 6; 19. 11. [13] Num. 19. 11, 14–15. [14] Num. 19. 16; 31. 19. [15] Num. 19. 22; Hagg. 2. 13. [16] Lev. 13. 3, etc.; 45–46. [17] Lev. 13. 47–59; 14. 33 . . . [18] Lev. 12. 1–8; Lk. 2. 22. [19] Amos 7. 17. [20] Ez. 4. 13; Hos. 9. 3. [21] Lev. 19. 26–28; Dt. 14. 1; Jer. 2. 23; Acts 15. 29. [22] Jer. 2. 7; 3. 2, 9; Ez. 36. 18. [23] Jn. 18. 28; Acts 10. 28. [24] Acts 11. 3. [25] Acts 21. 28. [26] Lev. 11. 24, 39. [27] Lev. 17. 10; 20. 6. [28] Lev. 20.

URIM AND THUMMIM

These two mysterious words of unexplained etymology, almost always mentioned together (two passages alone speak only of Urim [1]), designate the sacred lots by means of which the priest [2] consulted Yahweh. Most likely he used them much in the way of "heads or tails", getting either "Urim" or "Thummim" as the answer.[3] But the precise nature of the Urim and Thummim is as unknown as their origin

—the plural form of the words does not necessarily imply a plurality of objects. Many guesses have been made: two small stones, rods, images, etc., of differing form or colour have been suggested, kept in a special pocket of the priestly garment, or some kind of dice, the one bearing the first letter of the Hebrew alphabet and the other the last, with which the words 'ûrim and tummim commence; furthermore, it must be observed that in some cases the oracles gave no reply.[4]

Biblical texts dealing with the early days mention many consultations with Yahweh, probably by this method, although most often it is not stated.[5] But it seems that in time this way of learning the divine will was eclipsed by prophetic revelations and suffered as a result of the condemnation of divination and magic by the Law. Did the Urim and Thummim come back into favour after the Exile,[6] as some have imagined? It is unlikely. Though perhaps these mysterious objects had then a symbolic value—a guarantee, as it were, of priestly rank. The Priestly Code says that the High Priest must carry them in the breastplate († priest) which was an essential part of his dress.[7]

(† Priest, ephod, divination.)

[1] Num. 27. 21; 1 Sam. 28. 6. [2] Dt. 33. 8. [3] 1 Sam. 14. 41 (LXX). [4] 1 Sam. 14. 37; 28. 6. [5] Jos. 7. 14; Jg. 1. 2; 20. 18; 1 Sam. 10. 22; 23. 9; 2 Sam. 2. 1; etc. [6] Ezr. 2. 63 (Neh. 7. 65). [7] Ex. 28. 30; Lev. 8. 8.

USURY

From early days right up even to the post-Exilic period the Israelites did not deal in money; a loan was an act of kindness, a service to be rendered and one which was enjoined: "Thou shalt not . . . shut thine hand from thy poor brother: but thou shalt surely open thine hand unto him, and shalt surely lend him sufficient for his need, whatever it may be." [1] Consequently it was unfitting to demand any sort of interest, at least from an Israelite (interest rates were very high in Egypt and Babylonia); on this the law is definite: "Thou shalt not lend upon usury to thy brother; usury of money, usury of victuals, usury of any thing that is lent upon usury." [2] On the other hand, it was permissible to ask interest from a well-to-do foreigner*, the merchant who had come to do business in the country.[3]

But it seems that the law had often been broken; Ezekiel, in bemoaning the crimes of Jerusalem, cries: "In thee have they taken bribes to shed blood; thou hast taken usury and interest" [4]—and the Hebrew word for "usury" signifies "something bitten off", so it was perhaps interest deducted in advance from the capital loaned.

(† Banker, debt.)

[1] Dt. 15. 7, 8; Prov. 19. 17. [2] Dt. 23. 19; Ex. 22. 25; Lev. 25. 36; Neh. 5. 7; Ps. 15. 5; Prov. 28. 8; Ez. 18. 8, 13, 17. [3] Dt. 23. 20. [4] Ez. 22. 12.

VEGETABLES

Bible texts sometimes mention vegetables in a general way, and reference is made to vegetable gardens* as well as to pot-herbs,[1] which the Pharisees felt themselves obliged to tithe.[2] From fear of defilement by eating food which was impure, Daniel and his companions would eat only vegetables.[3] A piquant text in the Book of Proverbs declares: "Better a dish of vegetables where love is than rich beef with hatred." [4]

Only the following vegetables are mentioned by name: garlic, cucumbers, beans, lentils, melons, onions, and leeks. (For details see the separate articles devoted to them, and also † herbs.)

[1] Matt. 13. 32; Mk. 4. 32. [2] Lk. 11. 42. [3] Dan. 1. 12, 16; cf. Rom. 14. 2. [4] Prov. 15. 17.

VESSEL

As receptacles for liquids and dry materials, the Israelites ordinarily used clay* vessels († pottery, pitcher), but they were also familiar with vessels of wood and stone.[1] Among well-to-do folk, and in palaces and temples, were to be found precious vessels of alabaster*, bronze*, silver*, or gold*; [2] more than one king offered such to the Temple at Jerusalem.[3] Not to mention those that King Jehoash of Israel took,[4] these sacred vessels were carried off by the Chaldeans when the city fell in 586; but Cyrus returned them to the Jews.[5]

In figurative speech, vessels are the subject of many similes in the O.T. and N.T.

(† Cup.)

[1] Ex. 7. 19; Jn. 2. 6. [2] Ex. 25. 38; 27. 3; 37. 16; 38. 3; Num. 7. 84; 2 Sam. 8. 10; 1 Kgs. 10. 21; Matt. 26. 7; Mk. 14. 3. [3] 2 Sam. 8. 11; 1 Kgs. 7. 45; 15. 15. [4] 2 Kgs. 14. 14. [5] 2 Kgs. 25. 14; Ezr. 1. 7 . . .

VINE

Cultivation of the vine was formerly very extensive in Palestine. Moses' spies were dazzled by grapes which were one of the characteristic products of the mountains of Hebron, but Isaiah's invectives against the drunkards of Ephraim [1] and the sales of wine to which the Samaria ostraca bear witness clearly show that this culture was also widespread in the north of the country. The culture of the vine was practised so abundantly by the Israelites that the prophets often represented the nation by the image of a vine; [2] for that reason Jesus used numerous features of the trade in his parables, and even on certain Jewish coins a bunch of grapes became the emblem of the nation.

In his famous song about the vine [3] Isaiah reviews the labour of which the vine is the object. First of all, it is necessary to choose a very exposed hillside, to establish terraces on it, perhaps, an enclosing wall [4] or a hedge; above all, it must be emptied of stones, ploughed or dug over with a mattock*, and finally a particularly good vine plant must be chosen; often a little tower († watch-tower) was built, in which the necessary installations for wine-making and the storage of wine were frequently arranged, and from the terrace of which the vineyard keepers could easily exercise the necessary supervision at harvest-time.

Gathering and crushing of grapes in Egypt (14th century).

The custom was to let the vine grow almost freely; it could be left to creep along the ground, or be supported by props; more frequently still it was planted near fruit trees, in whose branches it entwined naturally, or it was arranged in cradles from one tree to the next.[5] This latter practice explains the proverbial expression which evokes the peace of the agricultural worker: to dwell beneath one's vine and beneath one's fig tree.[6] The tasks of looking after the vine were not excessive; it was enough to pull up the

Grape-treading scenes. Mosaic fragment.

weeds, to maintain the wall or walls[7] and to see, if need be, to the watering of the vine.[8] The time came when it must be pruned; that was because the flowering was over and the sap must make the grapes grow rather than increase still further the length of the shoots.[9] The thorns pulled up and the prunings were usually burned on the spot.[10]

Then came the vine harvest, which was a period of joy.[11] People even left the villages to go and camp in the vineyard.[12] The bunches of grapes were cut by means of a sharp little pruning-hook.[13] The harvest was gathered in with joy; people sang and danced;

and out of the noisy gaiety thus spread over the vine-yards the Bible writers painted sometimes a picture of the most wholesome joy,[14] sometimes a picture of the distress of the last judgment.[15]

Some of the grapes were eaten fresh. Some were dried, too, even a large quantity, so that they became a food very much appreciated in the bad season; [16] special cakes were made of them, which the Bible sometimes mentions.[17] But those were only accessory uses of the grape.

Usually the press was in the vineyard itself. A certain number of them have been discovered. More often than not they are made of a first shallow vat, cut into the rock. This is barely 2 yds. by 3 yds. A few workmen who removed their shoes trampled on the grapes to the rhythm of songs and shouts,[18] while the must flowed away through a little channel into a second vat, usually smaller and deeper. But that was only a means of crushing the grapes; they still

Ancient press.

had to be pressed, which was sometimes done in cloths which were twisted, but usually by placing what remained in the large vat into baskets put under pressure: a long beam had its fulcrum behind these baskets and rested on them, and it was sufficient to attach a stone to the end of the beam for this primitive press to function († olive). The Bible texts do not give us any information about the detailed care given to the wine. It is probable that it was first left undisturbed to clarify and stabilize; then it was filtered and transferred into huge earthenware jars whose apertures were carefully closed and sealed. Wine was also put into skin water-bags, where it sometimes caused accidents, when the wine which was immature fermented undetected.

It can be noted here that it was red wine which was drunk [19] and that people did not know how to preserve non-fermented wine. The Greeks and Romans prepared mixed wines for themselves: "they multiplied the mixtures, sweetenings, dilutions, and made ample use of perfumes to obtain a beverage which had the consistency of syrup and which could not be

Pressing of grapes in Egypt.

drunk unless diluted with water". In the composition of these wines were included honey, aloes, thyme, myrrh berries, resin, flowers, etc. The Israelites, who knew of mixed wines,[20] seem seldom to have practised such complicated mixtures, and usually drank their wine neat.

Wine is mentioned 141 times in the Bible. Certain texts praise wine,[21] and the Book of Proverbs points out that it must not be reserved for the great only, but that some must be granted to the unfortunate also.[22] Wine was not lacking at any banquet,[23] and Jesus himself drank some.[24]—But intemperance, which was very common in antiquity, was also common in Israel, and the texts mentioning it are often very realistic.[25] The Bible reacts energetically and recalls the fact that intemperance is first of all a lack of wisdom,[26] then a source of poverty[27] and debauchery,[28] but above all that it dishonours man[29] and leads him to scorn his God.[30] The N.T., which recommends wine for the sick,[31] is not less energetic in its struggle against drunkenness, which was so frequent in the first centuries of the Christian era.[32]— It should be added on this question that wine was forbidden to the priest performing his duties, who must appear before God in the integrity of his nature.[33] The abstinence of the Nazirite († Nazirate) was of the same order. The Rechabites,[34] also, abstained from drinking wine, much more by way of reaction to the necessarily sedentary life of a vine-grower than to combat drunkenness.

The culture of the vine provides popular language with sayings,[35] and the prophets and Bible writers with very numerous metaphors. The vine is sometimes a symbol of fertility[36] in the Bible, and the punishment of God is often represented in the image of the destruction of a vine,[37] whereas the forgiveness of God is pictured among other ways by the reconstitution of a flourishing vine.[38] But the vine is, above all, a symbol for Israel itself, the people of God.[39] The parables of Jesus move within the same perspective.[40] Finally, we should notice here the striking metaphor of the Fourth Gospel which represents God as the husbandman, Jesus Christ as the true vine, and his disciples as the branches.[41]

[1] Is. 28. 1, 3. [2] Gen. 49. 11–12; Is. 5. 7; etc. [3] Is. 5. 2–7. [4] Prov. 24. 31. [5] Ez. 19. 11; Lk. 13. 6. [6] 1 Kgs. 4. 25; 2 Kgs. 18. 31; Mic. 4. 4; Zech. 3. 10. [7] Prov. 24. 30–31. [8] Is. 27. 3. [9] Jn. 15. 2. [10] Ez. 15. 4–5. [11] Jg. 21. 20, 21. [12] Is. 16. 10. [13] Rev. 14. 18. [14] Is. 16. 10. [15] Jer. 25. 30. [16] 1 Sam. 25. 18; 30. 12; 2 Sam. 6. 19; 16. 1. [17] Jer. 7. 18; Hos. 3. 1. [18] Jer. 25. 30; 48. 33. [19] Gen. 49. 11; Dt. 32. 14; Ecclus. 39. 26; 50. 15. [20] Ps. 75. 8; Prov. 9. 2, 5; Cant. 8. 2; Is. 5. 22. [21] Jg. 9. 13; Ps. 104. 15; Eccl. 10. 19; Zech. 10. 7. [22] Prov. 31. 6. [23] Is. 25. 6. [24] Matt. 11. 19; 26. 29; Jn. 2. 1–11. [25] Is. 5. 22; 28. 7–8; Hos. 7. 5; etc. [26] Prov. 20. 1; 31. 4; Eccl. 2. 3, 11; Ecclus. 31. 25–31. [27] Prov. 21. 17; 23. 21. [28] Prov. 23. 31, 33; Hab. 2. 15; Ecclus. 19. 2. [29] Is. 28. 7; Hos. 4. 11. [30] Is. 5. 11 ff. [31] 1 Ti. 5. 23. [32] Rom. 13. 13; 1 Cor. 6. 10; Eph. 5. 18. [33] Lev. 10. 8–10; Ez. 44. 21. [34] Jer. 35. 6–7. [35] Jg. 8. 2; Jer. 31. 29. [36] Ps. 128. 3; Ez. 19. 10. [37] Is. 7. 23; 32. 10; Jer. 8. 13; Hos. 2. 15. [38] Joel 2. 22; Mal. 3. 11. [39] Is. 3. 14; 5. 6, 7; Jer. 2. 21; 12. 10; Ez. 15. 1–6; Hos. 10. 1; etc. [40] Matt. 20. 1; Mk. 12. 1 ff.; etc. [41] Jn. 15. 1–8.

VINEGAR

This liquid, derived from grape wine,[1] and pure or mixed with spices or fruit juices, was used as a condiment; but diluted with water (or a little oil), it afforded a refreshing beverage (Greek: *oxukreton*) which is still today enjoyed in the East; workmen often soak their bread in it,[2] and under the name of *posca* it was also in use among Roman soldiers. We know how, to appease the thirst of Christ on the cross, one who witnessed his sufferings brought to his lips a sponge soaked with this liquid.[3]—Vinegar was forbidden to anyone under a Nazirite vow.[4]

[1] Cf. Prov. 10. 26; 25. 20. [2] Ruth 2. 14. [3] Matt. 27. 48; Mk. 15. 36; Jn. 19. 29, 30; cf. Lk. 23. 36. [4] Num. 6. 3.

VIPER

Several species of vipers exist in Palestine; one of the most dangerous is the little sand viper that lives in the Jordan Valley. Only three O.T. texts[1] mention these reptiles, whose "tongue" it was said gave a mortal wound.[2]—The First Gospel records that

VIPER

Jesus called the Scribes and Pharisees a "generation of vipers" [3]—an expression John the Baptist had used to stigmatize the Pharisees and Sadducees, or even any who listened to him.[4]—The Greek word customarily translated "viper" covers all venomous snakes; it occurs in the Acts of the Apostles [5]—in which passage some scholars think it means some small constrictor that resembled a viper but did not make a wound.

[1] Is. 30. 6; 59. 5. [2] Job 20. 16. [3] Matt. 12. 34; 23. 33.
[4] Matt. 3. 7; Lk. 3. 7. [5] Acts 28. 3.

VIPER, HORNED

This most dangerous snake is mentioned only once in the O.T.; [1] it still occurs today in Arabia Petraea. It is up to $\frac{1}{2}$ yd. long, and each eye is surmounted by a small pointed horn (hence the name). Frequently it slips into the sand and lurks there for the animals on which it feeds. Its venom can kill a man in half an hour. Endowed with extreme alertness and capable of moving in any direction, it strikes swiftly at anything that approaches, so that the terror horses show when they see one is understandable. The comparison of the tribe of Dan with this redoubtable little beast is most pertinent.

Possibly the "fiery serpents" of which the Israelites became victims in the wilderness [2] were horned vipers.

[1] Gen. 49. 17. [2] Num. 21. 6; Dt. 8. 15.

VIRGINITY

If a husband questioned the virginity of his wife at the time of marriage and spread slanderous rumours abroad about her, the parents of the young woman produced the signs of their daughter's virginity before the local elders*. Refuted in this way, the husband was "chastised" (which probably means struck), and had to pay a fine of 100 shekels to his parents-in-law and he lost the right of divorce. If the proofs were lacking the woman was stoned. At any rate, these are the measures prescribed by the Deuteronomic Law.[1]

[1] Dt. 22. 13–21.

VOW

To dedicate to the deity, by a vow, some present or future possession was a very common custom in antiquity; and in Israel too, as is proved by numerous texts of the O.T.[1] These voluntary offerings were far from being always disinterested, and often constituted a sort of bargain concluded with Yahweh, from whom the faithful expected favours or deliverance; [2] the vitality still today of this popular form of piety is well known. The most frequent vows provided for the presentation of a sacrifice which was doubtless accompanied by songs of praise,[3] but the Israelite could vow to his God—with the chance of redeeming them from him—houses, his own person, or that of his children. The Priestly Law codifies various rules on this subject.[4] It states also that although the vow of a man, a widow, or a repudiated woman is irrevocable, that of a girl or a married woman must be made with the assent of the father or the husband.[5] Moreover, it was better not to pronounce vows rather than to make them lightly; [6] these commitments are perfectly free,[7] but once they are made, it must not be long before they are fulfilled.[8]

The N.T. alludes to a vow made by St Paul himself, but its nature is not known, or its cause; [9] on the other hand, the same apostle took upon himself the cost of a vow which four of his compatriots had imposed on themselves.[10] A whole tractate of the Mishnah is devoted to casuistry concerning vows.

(† Corban, devote, Nazirate.)

[1] 1 Sam. 1. 11, 21; 2 Sam. 15. 7–8; Job 22. 27; Ps. 65. 1; 132. 2; Prov. 7. 14; Is. 19. 21; Jer. 44. 25; Jonah 2. 9; Nahum 1. 15; Mal. 1. 14. [2] Gen. 28. 20–22; Jg. 11. 30; 17. 3–4; Jonah 1. 16. [3] Ps. 66; 116. 18. [4] Lev. 7. 16; 22. 18, 21, 23; 27. 2–29; Num. 15. 3 . . . [5] Num. 30. 3–16. [6] Prov. 20. 25; Eccl. 5. 4, 5. [7] Dt. 12. 6. [8] Dt. 23. 21–23. [9] Acts 18. 18. [10] Acts 21. 23.

VULTURE

This bird of prey, regarded as unclean, is probably mentioned in the lists of Lev. 11. 13 and Dt. 14. 12; but translations vary because the identification of the birds of prey is very uncertain. Perhaps the Great Vulture is meant by the first term used in these texts; but other scholars think that it figures in the third place in these same passages, to say nothing of other theories. In any case, the context shows that vultures rather than eagles are meant in the texts of Job [1] and Micah [2] (and also in Matt. 24. 28). Moreover, four species of vultures live in Palestine.

(† Bearded vulture.)

[1] Job 39. 27 (30). [2] Mic. 1. 16.

WALNUT

Only the Song of Songs [1] mentions the walnut, or, rather, the tree which produces it: "I went down into the garden of walnuts" (R.V., nuts; Moffatt, walnut-bower) says the Shulammite, or perhaps her beloved—"to see the green plants of the valley". Josephus assures us that walnuts were cultivated abundantly in the Plain of Gennesaret. Today these trees are rare in Palestine.

[1] Cant. 6. 11.

WAR

From the time of the Exodus to that of the Exile, the Israelites had numerous wars to wage or suffer.

In the desert they fought against the Amalekites; penetration into Palestine often brought them to grips with the inhabitants of Transjordan and the Canaanites; and there was the long, fierce struggle with the Philistines. Next, numerous conflicts arose with the other neighbours of Israel: Ammonites, Midianites, Moabites, Edomites; and soon, to say nothing of the sacking of Jerusalem by the Pharaoh Shishak,[1] civil wars set the kingdoms of Israel and Judah against each other. Later, they had to face terrible adversaries in the people of Damascus and Syria, and finally to set up vain and desperate resistance to the Assyrians and Babylonians—the fight of dwarfs against a giant.

So several books of the O.T. echo with the sound of the wars in which Yahweh himself participates as "a man of war", "strong and mighty in battle".[2] Israel's enemies are his.[3] From Sinai he rushes to the fight,[4] he strikes his adversaries with terror, he casts both horse and rider into the sea, and makes huge stones fall on the fugitives whom he has put to flight.[5] The ancient Song of Deborah curses "those who have not come to the help of Yahweh" against the mighty,[6] and the Book of Numbers refers to a book, since lost, entitled "The Book of the Wars of Yahweh".[7] David, like Moses and Joshua in former times, "fights Yahweh's battles" by waging the national battles of Israel;[8] up to the time of Solomon, at any rate, the Ark of the Covenant manifests the presence of the God of Israel in the ranks of those who fight with him and for him.[9]

War henceforth is considered to be sacred: every warrior is "consecrated to Yahweh"[10] and must submit himself, before and during the campaign, to the abstinences of sanctification.[11] Certain of these customs are to be found, moreover, among many peoples, and like them, Israel doubtless preceded her wars by religious ceremonies and sacrifices;[12] no expedition was undertaken, at any rate, without Yahweh's being consulted in one way or another.[13]

For a long time the warlike instincts of the sons of Joshua and David asserted themselves; Isaiah still likes to refer to the victories of former times,[14] to the shouts of joy which accompanied the sharing out of booty,[15] and he describes, with barely restrained admiration, the great Assyrian army.[16]—However, it is obvious that the agricultural labour to which the Israelites devoted themselves made them like the benefits of peace and the times when, without fear of annoying surprises, everyone could eat the fruits of his vine and fig tree.[17] The very notion of the national, warlike Yahweh of former times was remarkably modified under the influence of the prophets: "He will be the judge among the nations", a famous text later proclaimed, "and they shall beat their swords into plowshares, and their spears into pruninghooks".[18] This does not mean that the old

feelings were never to be aroused; Jeremiah goes so far as to pronounce this curse which Gregory VII used for his motto: "Cursed be he that doeth the work of the Lord negligently, and cursed be he that keepeth back his sword from blood."[19] Significant, too, is the favour granted to the savageries of the Book of Esther. On the other hand, the rising of the Maccabees and the tragedy which culminated in the taking of Jerusalem by Titus shows the Jews' dynamism and power of resistance until the last period of their ancient Palestinian history.

Hostilities usually began in the spring.[20] They were generally prepared by secret investigation of the enemy[21] († spy), sometimes preceded by a declaration of war, by acts of provocation,[22] but more often than not released unexpectedly. Mobilization was accomplished by means of various signals or the sending of messengers[23] († standard). Single combat, stressed by reciprocal invective, occasionally acted as a prelude to battle.[24] To the sound of trumpets and uttering their war cries,[25] the soldiers rushed into the affray, which consisted mainly of fierce hand-to-hand fighting.[26] Strategy consisted, above all, of cunning, surprises, ambushes, of turning movements,[27] too, for the Israelites often manœuvred by dividing their army into two or three contingents;[28] with time they became capable of withstanding the most fearful adversaries. (For the war of siege see † fortifications, siege.)

Every campaign, every victory especially, was naturally accompanied by acts of cruelty and reprisals: the putting to death of enemy leaders, mutilation of survivors, pillages and devastations, taking of slaves,[29] etc. Like other Asiatic peoples, the Israelites practised, in certain circumstances, for quite a long time the custom of putting to the ban (devote* or make anathema) which made horrible massacres and destruction obligatory.

Songs and dances celebrated the triumphs gained,[30] stones erected perpetuated their memory;[31] as a sign of gratitude people deposited in the sanctuaries weapons or precious objects;[32] those who deserved it were rewarded,[33] but in the sharing out of the booty[34] those were not forgotten who had been on guard, and the memory of those who had fallen as heroes[35] was piously honoured.

Israelite legislation is little concerned with war. Whilst letting certain men eligible for mobilization enjoy exemption from military service,[36] Deuteronomy seems to want timidly to modify the rules about putting to the ban († devote); curiously enough, it does not allow that the enemy's fruit trees be felled: "For is the tree of the field a man, that it should be besieged of thee?"[37] It is likely that, with time, certain barbaric customs were more or less eliminated in Israel; the ban itself finished by disappearing altogether. One interesting text in the

WASP

Book of Kings [38] claims even that the Israelite kings had the reputation of being open to pity. It is well known, on the other hand, that the Assyrians inflicted dreadful tortures upon the enemies which they had defeated.

Finally, it must be noticed that the Priestly Code asks the warriors returning from a campaign to submit themselves to the purifying rites [39] imposed on those who have killed men or touched corpses.

(† Arms, army.)

[1] 1 Kgs 14. 25 . . . [2] Ex. 15. 3; Ps. 24. 8; cf. Dt. 32. 41; 2 Sam. 5. 24; Ps. 18. 14; Is. 31. 4 . . .; etc. [3] Jg. 5. 31; 1 Sam. 30. 26. [4] Jg. 5. 4. [5] Gen. 35. 5; Ex. 15. 1, 21; 23. 27; Jos. 10. 10, 11. [6] Jg. 5. 23. [7] Num. 21. 14. [8] 1 Sam. 18. 17; 25. 28. [9] Num. 10. 35; 1 Sam. 4. 6, 7; 2 Sam. 11. 11. [10] Is. 13. 3. [11] Jg. 20. 26; 1 Sam. 21. 5; 2 Sam. 11. 11. [12] 1 Sam. 7. 9; 13. 9; Ps. 20. [13] Jg. 1. 1; 20. 18, 28; 1 Sam. 14. 37; 23. 2; 28. 6; 1 Kgs. 22. 5; etc. [14] Is. 9. 4. [15] Is. 9. 3. [16] Is. 5. 26 . . . [17] 1 Kgs. 4. 25; 8. 56; 2 Kgs. 18. 31; Mic. 4. 4; Zech. 3. 10. [18] Is. 2. 4; Mic. 4. 3. [19] Jer. 48. 10; cf. Joel 3. 10. [20] 2 Sam. 11. 1. [21] Num. 13. 1 . . .; 21. 32; Dt. 1. 22 . . .; Jos. 2. 1 . . .; 6. 22; Jg. 1. 23; 7. 11; 18. 2; 1 Sam. 26. 4; 2 Sam. 10. 3; 15. 10. [22] Jg. 11. 12; 1 Sam. 11. 1 . . .; 2 Kgs. 14. 8. [23] Jg. 3. 27; 6. 35; 7. 24; 2 Sam. 20. 1; Jer. 42. 14; Hos. 5. 8. [24] 1 Sam. 17. 40 . . .; (2 Sam. 2. 14). [25] Num. 10. 9; 1 Sam. 17. 52; Job 39. 25; Is. 42. 13; Amos 1. 14; 1 Cor. 14. 8. [26] Ez. 21. 9 . . . [27] Jos. 8. 2, 12; Jg. 7. 16 . . .; 20. 36; 1 Sam. 15. 5; 2 Sam. 5. 23; 2 Kgs. 7. 12. [28] Jg. 7. 16; 9. 43; 1 Sam. 11. 11; 2 Sam. 10. 9–11; 18. 2. [29] Dt. 20. 11 . . .; Jos. 10. 26; 22. 8; Jg. 1. 6, 28; 5. 30; 7. 25; 8. 7, 20; 9. 45; 1 Sam. 11. 2; 17. 51; 31. 9; 2 Kgs. 3. 25; 8. 12; 14. 14; 15. 16; Is. 13. 16; Hos. 10. 14; 13. 16; Amos 1. 6, 13. [30] Ex. 15. 1, 20; Jg. 5; 1 Sam. 18. 6; 30. 16; Ps. 21; 60. 6 . . . [31] 1 Sam. 7. 12. [32] 1 Sam. 21. 9; 31. 10; 2 Sam. 8. 10 . . . [33] Jos. 15. 16; 1 Sam. 17. 25; 2 Sam. 18. 11. [34] 1 Sam. 30. 21–25; (Num. 31. 27.) [35] 2 Sam. 1. 17 . . .; 3. 31 . . .; 1 Kgs. 11. 15. [36] Dt. 20. 5–8. [37] Dt. 20. 19–20 [38] 1 Kgs. 20. 31. [39] Num. 31. 19.

WASP

Of the wasp family the Bible mentions only the largest species: the hornet*.

Watch-tower.

WATCH-TOWER

The Israelites erected in their fields, but especially in vineyards,[1] dry-stone towers from the height of which a watchman kept an eye on the fruits and crops, to protect them against marauders and against jackals and foxes. Built in the form of a truncated cone, some 10 ft. from the ground, they terminated with a terrace, shaded with branches from the sun. Projecting stones served as an external staircase; and the inside could be used as a storehouse [2] for food. Structures of the same kind are still to be seen in Palestine, where they are one of the characteristic features of the countryside in the vine-growing areas.

[1] Is. 5. 2; Matt. 21. 33; Mk. 12. 1; cf. 2 Kgs. 17. 9; 18. 8. [2] 1 Chr. 27. 25.

WATER

As is well known, water is of very great value in the East, for it is not usually abundant. It is even sold, still today as formerly, in the streets of Damascus and Jerusalem.[1] The right to use certain water-holes was often paid for with silver,[2] and the watering of flocks at the wells sometimes gave rise to disputes.[3] But to refuse water to the traveller or to the thirsty would have been villainous.[4]

At all times Palestinians have devoted the greatest care to hydraulic works († canal, cistern, reservoir, well) and practised irrigation, the efficacy of which they knew well.[5] They particularly appreciated water from springs—living or running water.[6]

Water quite naturally inspired the poets and prophets of the Bible with numerous images. They praise its freshness,[7] its fertilizing virtues,[8] the beauty of trees planted near rivers and streams.[9] It is, moreover, the essential element of the world in ancient cosmogonies.[10]—God himself is compared with a spring of living water;[11] "He that believeth on me," says Jesus, "out of his belly shall flow rivers of living water",[12] and the Apocalypse sings of the springs of living water of the new world.[13]

In the Jewish religion water was used for sacred ablutions; water thus became the symbol of the purification of the soul: the part it played in John's baptism is well known, as also the place it occupies in Christian baptism.

[1] Is. 55. 1. [2] Num. 20. 19; 2 Kgs. 19. 24; Prov. 5. 15; 9. 17; Lam. 5. 4. [3] Gen. 26. 20; Ex. 2. 16, 17. [4] Gen. 24. 17; Job 22. 7; Is. 32. 6; Matt. 10. 42; 25. 42; Jn. 4. 7. [5] Ps. 65. 9; 104. 10; Eccl. 2. 6; Ez. 17. 7, 8; 31. 4. [6] Gen. 26. 19; Lev. 14. 5; 15. 13. [7] Ps. 23. 2; 42. 2; Prov. 25. 25. [8] Job 8. 11; 14. 9; Is. 44. 14. [9] Ps. 1. 3; Jer. 17. 8, 13. [10] Gen. 1. [11] Jer. 2. 13; 17. 13. [12] Jn. 7. 38 (cf. Jn. 4). [13] Rev. 7. 17; 21. 6.

WAX

Beeswax is mentioned only in certain beautiful and vigorous figures of speech in the O.T. When Yahweh comes forth out of his place "the valleys shall be cleft, as wax before the fire," says Micah.[1] "As wax melteth before the fire, so let the wicked perish at the presence of God," the Psalmist declares,[2] while in his grief he also exclaims: "My heart is like wax; it is melted in the midst within my breast."[3]—We know that the ancient world, from the Hellenistic period onwards, sometimes used wax-coated wooden tablets for writing on.[4]

[1] Mic. 1. 4; cf. Ps. 97. 5. [2] Ps. 68. 2. [3] Ps. 22. 14. [4] Cf. Lk. 1. 63.

WEASEL

There are two species in Palestine. The name occurs only in the Leviticus list[1] of unclean animals; some prefer to translate this word by "mole" or "marten".

[1] Lev. 11. 29.

WEAVING

Primitive conditions in the life of the Israelites reserved for women the tasks of spinning* and weaving;[1] but they succeeded only in preparing coarse materials used for tent cloth or to make the ancient loin-cloth, the sack*, worn into a later age as a sign of mourning. Still today, among the Bedouin, it is the women who busy themselves with this work, and the weaving loom they use could easily be very similar to the one used by the Israelites in former times, even though they may have had still more primitive contrivances.

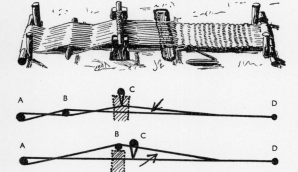

Loom, with sections showing its two positions.

The warp threads, which constituted two superimposed sheets, were stretched between two large wooden uprights (A and D) (acting as rollers), wedged behind stakes firmly fixed into the ground; even threads were attached to a cross-piece (C), while the odd ones were raised at the desired moment by a second bar placed at the back (B). In this way the shuttle could perform a back-and-forth movement now above, now below one of these series of threads.

Finally, a removable flat lath allowed the fabric to be tightened.

It was doubtless in this way that relatively narrow bands of material were woven, barely a few yards long; mats of reeds were also made in this way. At Lachish the workshop of a weaver called Hilkija ben Moas has recently been discovered. This man lived in the last years of the Judaean monarchy; his seal has been discovered among the remains of a vertical loom of which a half-calcined upright was still in place.

In order to obtain more solid materials several threads were twisted together.[2] The High Priest's robe had to be woven with a gold thread,[3] and the historian Josephus says that Herod's contained a silver thread.[4] It is known that in the days of the kings the weaver's profession had so greatly developed that there was a guild of weavers.[5] But that was far from excluding foreign imports,[6] whether from Egypt, Phoenicia,[7] or Babylonia.[8]

The staff of Goliath's[9] spear was so big that it was likened to a weaver's beam.

One single passage in the Bible mentions the shuttle; it was Job who saw in its unvarying, swift motion an image of the monotonous rapidity of the passing of the days, so painful to the weary eyes of an invalid.[10]

[1] 1 Sam. 2. 19; Prov. 31. 19, 24. [2] Ex. 26. 1, 36; 28. 6, 15, etc. [3] Ex. 39. 3. [4] Acts 12. 21. [5] 1 Chr. 4. 21. [6] Ez. 27. 7. [7] Ez. 27. 16. [8] Jos. 7. 21. [9] 1 Sam. 17. 7; 1 Chr. 20. 5. [10] Job 7. 6.

WEEK

Among the ancient Israelites, the lunar month, of twenty-nine days and a fraction, doubtless provided four weeks of seven days each.[1] The cycle commenced afresh with each new moon, the difference between 4×7 days = 28 days and the length of the month being accounted for by some method or other —perhaps by making the new moon a day apart ($28 + 1$ days, or even sometimes $28 + 2$ days). Later, at a period difficult to fix, the week was detached from the moon's course and repeated itself every seven days without interruption through the whole year.

The origins of the seven-day week are obscure († Sabbath); it has been connected with the phases of the moon, and this seems more obvious than to relate it to the planets or the sacred character of the number seven. It is doubtful whether traces of a ten-day week exist in the O.T., as some have claimed.[2] Apart from the Sabbath day, the different days of the Israelite week bear no name, but a mere ordinal number: they spoke of the 1st, the 2nd . . . day of the week;[3] however, the 6th day was called later the eve of, or the preparation* for, the Sabbath.

[1] Cf. Gen. 29. 27. [2] Cf. Gen. 24. 55; Ex. 12. 3; Lev. 16. 29; 23. 27; 25. 9. [3] Ex. 16. 5; Matt. 28. 1.

WEEKS, FEAST OF

From ancient times the Israelites who had established themselves in Palestine celebrated a feast to mark the end of the harvest, called the Feast of the Harvest, the Day of First Fruits, or Feast of Weeks [1] because it took place, according to Deuteronomy, seven weeks after the sickle was put into the corn.[2] It was an agrarian feast, doubtless inherited from the Canaanites, and was eminently joyful [3] and dominated by the idea of the gratitude due to Yahweh. Only the Priestly Code [4] gives a few details about it: it states that it lasts one day only, that is to say, the 50th after the offering of the sheaf of corn presented during the Feast of the Passover* (whence the name "Pentecost"—i.e., Greek for "the 50th" [day]— which it bears in the N.T.); it also states that the Feast is characterized by the putting into the sanctuary of two loaves made, of course, with the new flour and baked with leaven*; according to the text, it might seem that every Israelite had to make this gift, but it is rather a matter of two loaves offered in the name of the whole community as a mark of gratitude. A whole series of important blood sacrifices [5] enhanced this Feast, which was also marked by a sacred convocation of the people and by the cessation of all work.[6]

In the later period of Judaism the Feast of Weeks was related to the promulgation of the Law on Sinai,[7] and thus assumed an historical significance. In the time of Christ and the apostles the Feast seems to have acquired more importance than in the past: it attracted large numbers of pilgrims to Jerusalem.[8] It is known that Christianity commemorates the foundation of the church on the day of Pentecost.

[1] Ex. 23. 16; 34. 22; Num. 28. 26; 2 Chr. 8. 13. [2] Dt. 16. 9, 10. [3] Dt. 16. 11; cf. Is. 9. 3. [4] Lev. 23. 15 . . . [5] Lev. 23. 18 . . .; Num. 28. 27. [6] Lev. 23. 21; Num. 28. 26. [7] Cf. Ex. 19. 1 . . . [8] Acts 2; 20. 16.

WEIGHTS AND MEASURES

While in Mesopotamia a degree of unity was created from the 3rd millennium between the measures of length, capacity, and weight, great variety seems to have long persisted in Israelite usage. The Bible period covers so long a stretch of time that it is not really surprising that the same words can cover quantities which differ; but the divergences of a given epoch are noticeably parallel. Moreover, archaeological excavations have not produced a single intact measures of capacity. This is why the estimates that can be made are only approximate.

1. *Measures of length.* Very naturally, parts of the body were used for this purpose. The smallest unit was the fingerbreadth; four fingerbreadths evidently gave a handbreadth or palm; the span followed, which is the measure of the open hand from thumb to little finger, and then the cubit—measured from the elbow to the tip of the middle finger. Their relationship may be tabulated thus:

1 handbreadth* = 4 fingers*
1 span* = 12 fingers = 3 palms
1 cubit* = 24 fingers = 6 palms = 2 spans

To measure distances the Bible first uses approximate indications, such as a bow-shot [1] or a day's journey.[2] But in the N.T. the influence of other civilizations gave precision to the measurements; there we find, in fact, the furlong* (about 623 ft.) and the mile* (about 4,922 ft.); though again we have there "a Sabbath* day's journey", that is the length of journey permitted by the Law for a Sabbath day (about 3,850 ft.). In addition, Acts uses the Roman fathom* (about 6 ft.).

2. *Measure of surfaces.* Surfaces are invariably indicated by the length of their sides, measured by line* or measuring-reed*. The solitary measure of area is the yoke*, still actually in use in Syria.

3. *Measures of capacity for solids.* A duodecimal system of measurement here seems to have been combined with a decimal system; the following relationships can be established:

1 log* = 0·89 pints
1 kab* = 4 logs = 1·78 quarts
1 seah* = 6 kabs = 24 logs = 2·67 gallons
1 ephah* = 3 seahs = 18 kabs = 72 logs = 1 bushel
1 homer* = 10 ephahs = 30 seahs = 180 kabs = 720 logs = 10 bushels

The Talmud also speaks of $\frac{1}{2}$, $\frac{1}{4}$, and $\frac{1}{8}$ kab.

4. *Measures of capacity for liquids.* These are often identical with those used for solids; the table of their relationship is as follows:

1 log* = 0·89 pints
1 kab* = 4 logs = 1·78 quarts.
1 hin* = 3 kabs = 12 logs = 1·34 gallons
1 bath* = 6 hins = 18 kabs = 72 logs = 1 bushel (1·29 cu. ft.)
1 cor* = 10 baths = 60 hins = 180 kabs = 720 logs = 10 bushels (12·87 cu. ft.)

5. *Weights.* The word weight in Hebrew (viz., šekel, shekel) comes from a verb common to the Semitic languages which denotes the action of weighing money, and which, by extension, means "to pay". So originally, when there was no coined money, payments were made by a quantity of gold or silver which evidently had to be weighed out.[3]

The Israelite system of weights was inspired by the Babylonian, in which each weight was sixty times greater than the preceding one; in Bible texts we find:

1 talent* = 60 minas = 360 shekels
1 mina* = 60 shekels*

But the shekel, which was the unit of weight, was subdivided into $\frac{1}{2}$, $\frac{1}{4}$, and $\frac{1}{20}$ shekel.

It is practically impossible to fix an exact equivalence, particularly because the relation of one weight to another varied (at one time the mina was worth only 50 instead of 60 shekels), and also because royal weights were heavier than ordinary ones. A certain number of weights in the form of living

Assyrian and Persian weights.

creatures—lion, duck, frog, insects, etc.—have been recovered in excavations; but many others have no particular form. They are made of various materials: basalt, porphyry, marble, limestone, lead, bronze, glass, etc. Unfortunately only a very few are provided with inscriptions, and the deciphering of these does not afford satisfactorily precise determination of their value. The smallest weights were kept in a bag [4] or purse.[5]

The Roman pound is the only weight mentioned in the N.T.; [6] it weighed 0·72 lb.

[1] Gen. 21. 16. [2] Gen. 30. 36. [3] Gen. 23. 16; Jer. 32. 9.
[4] Dt. 25. 13. [5] Prov. 16. 11. [6] Jn. 12. 3; 19. 39.

WELL

While the cistern* gathers rain-water, the well is an artificial pit intended to reach "the living water" of an underground spring or water-level. In a country such as Palestine, often poor in springs, a well was a real source of wealth, and its possession the object of disputes and conflicts.[1] To fill in a well, to fill it purposely with earth was a true act of war.[2] Situated near certain localities which sometimes owed their prosperity and their name to them,[3] or along caravan routes for which they constituted quite obvious stopping-places in the waste-lands, the wells were carefully constructed and walled up; their opening was closed by slabs, leaving in the centre only a hole over which was rolled a large stone,[4] sometimes covered over with earth to make the use of the well impossible for those who might not know its exact position. The water was drawn by means of devices ranging from the simple bucket provided with a rope

to the more ingenious systems of the later periods. Watering-places and drinking-troughs were at the disposal of flocks, which naturally gathered there, led by their shepherds.[5] One of the most ancient texts of the O.T. is a song intended either to mark the rhythm of the sinking of a well or to obtain or celebrate the gushing forth of the water.[6] There exist still today in Palestine wells which go back more or less to remote antiquity, such as the one called Jacob's Well (or the well of the woman of Samaria),[7] which was supposed to be 8 ft. in diameter and over 100 ft. deep, and the one discovered at Tell ed Duweir (Lachish), which reaches 120 ft. in depth.

[1] Gen. 26. 19 . . . [2] Gen. 26. 15; 2 Kgs. 3. 19. [3] Gen. 26. 33. [4] Gen. 29. 3. [5] Gen. 24. 11, 20; Ex. 2. 16; Jg. 5. 11. [6] Num. 21. 17, 18. [7] Jn. 4. 12.

WHALE

There is little probability that the Israelites knew of whales; the word sometimes thus translated— even in the Book of Jonah (and Matt. 12. 40)— simply means a large fish or sea-monster.[1]

[1] Gen. 1. 21; Job 7. 12; Ps. 148. 7; Is. 27. 1; Jonah 2. 1.

WHEAT

The cultivation of wheat, one of the chief kinds of corn, began in Palestine as early as the Bronze Age. The Bible very often mentions it and, indeed, describes the promised land as a land of wheat and barley, of vines and fig trees, etc.[1] In the days of the monarchy agriculture was so prosperous, particularly in the Plain of Jezreel, that the Israelites were able to export considerable quantities of wheat to Phoenicia.[2]

(† Agriculture, corn.)

[1] Dt. 8. 8. [2] 1 Kgs. 5. 11.

WHIP

A whip was used for driving certain domesticated animals, especially the horse: "A whip for the horse . . . and a rod for the back of fools," says the Book of Proverbs [1] and, in his prophecy against Nineveh, Nahum hears, with the gallop of horses, the crack of the whip and the din of wheels.[2]

But the whip also played its part in educating children: "The whip and correction are wisdom at every season," Ben-Sira declares, and "he that loveth his son will apply the whip to him generously".[3]

On the eve of the schism, Rehoboam openly told the assembly of the people at Shechem: "My father chastised you with whips, but I will chastise you with scorpions",[4] meaning by that either whips provided with points, or perhaps prickly plants.[5]

We know that Jesus made himself a whip of cords († rope) to drive the merchants and money-changers out of the Temple.[6] As for the whip with which he was beaten by the Romans before his death, although the Gospel texts [7] use the verbs "to scourge" and "to whip", the instrument of torture is not stated, and we may hesitate between the *flagrum* made of very heavy cords, sometimes armed with knuckle-bones and metal balls, and the *flagellum*, perhaps still more terrible, because it was made of thin, sharp thongs that easily lacerated the flesh.—On the other hand, the tribune in Jerusalem threatened St Paul [8] with a "whip", such as is mentioned again in the Epistle to the Hebrews.[9]—To punish some guilty people the Jews doubtless most often used, in the synagogues, whips made of three leather thongs that could be lengthened at will.

The word "whip" is used metaphorically in the O.T. and N.T.[10] in the sense of punishment, suffering, infirmity, or scourge. Thus the prophet [11] announces that Yahweh of hosts will brandish the whip against Assyria, while the poem of Job speaks of the "whip of the tongue".[12]

(† Scourging.)

[1] Prov. 26. 3. [2] Nahum 3. 2. [3] Ecclus. 22. 6; 23. 2; 30. 1. [4] 1 Kgs. 12. 11, 14. [5] Jg. 8. 16. [6] Jn. 2. 15. [7] Matt. 20. 19; 27. 26; Mk. 10. 34; 15. 15; Lk. 18. 33; Jn. 19. 1. [8] Acts 22. 24. [9] Heb. 11. 36. [10] Jos. 23. 13; Mk. 3. 10; 5. 29, 34 (Gk. and R.V. mg); Lk. 7. 21. [11] Is. 10. 26. [12] Job 5. 21.

WIDOW

The lot of the widow—who wore special clothing [1]—seems to have been generally rather precarious in Israel. She did not inherit from her husband († inheritance § 4) and possessed only what she had provided at the time of her marriage. On the death of her husband, the eldest son took over the management of the house; there was even a time when the widow was part of the inheritance left by her husband and when a son could become the spouse of his father's wife (step-mother). The position of the widow could be particularly serious if she had children in infancy or no relative ready to keep her. The childless widow usually returned to her father's family.[2] Every widow could re-marry,[3] but a priest was not allowed to marry a widow,[4] unless she had been the wife of a priest.[5]

Deprived of their protector and husband, widows were exposed to all sorts of mean actions and extortions, for so the Bible texts imply on many occasions.[6] And so the law kept them under its protection,[7] and the prophets upheld their cause,[8] which Yahweh himself,[9] moreover, and those who feared him, took in hand.[10]

Widows had to be invited to the meals celebrated at the time of the great public feasts; [11] they shared in the tithe,[12] and they were allowed to glean in the fields and vineyards.[13]—The Christian communities dealt from the beginning with the widows' lot; [14] it seems, moreover, that certain of them, who answered to some definite qualifications, formed a definite group [15] in the church, distinct from deaconesses*.

[1] Gen. 38. 14, 19. [2] Gen. 38. 11; Lev. 22. 13; Ruth 1. 8. [3] 1 Cor. 7. 8. [4] Lev. 21. 14. [5] Ez. 44. 22. [6] 2 Sam. 14. 4 . . .; 2 Kgs. 4. 1; Job 22. 9; 24. 3, 21; Ps. 94. 6; Is. 1. 23; 10. 2; Ez. 22. 7; Lk. 18. 3. [7] Ex. 22. 22; Dt. 24. 17; 27. 19. [8] Is. 1. 17; Jer. 7. 6; 22. 3; Zech. 7. 10; Mal. 3. 5; Mk. 12. 40; Lk. 20. 47. [9] Dt. 10. 18; Ps. 68. 5; 146. 9; Prov. 15. 25; 1 Ti. 5. 5. [10] Job 29. 13; 31. 16. [11] Dt. 16. 11, 14. [12] Dt. 14. 28, 29; 26. 12. [13] Dt. 24. 19–21. [14] Acts 6. 1; 9. 39; Jas. 1. 27. [15] 1 Ti. 5. 9–16.

WILD ASS

This is a general way of referring to several species of untamed asses. Our versions usually translate in this way two Hebrew terms regarded as synonymous, and some scholars have even questioned whether these words do not designate a particular species, viz., the hybrid ass, which is intermediate in stature between the horse and the ass, and the hunting of which may be depicted on certain Assyrian bas-reliefs. For linguistic reasons other commentators believe that only the word *'arôd* [1] means "wild ass", while the other, more frequently used term (*pere'*) in fact means the zebra.[2]

The O.T. alludes particularly to the lonely places favoured by these animals, while the poem of Job alone gives a brief account of them.[3] Genesis finely compares Ishmael (i.e., the Bedouin of the desert) with a wild ass (or a zebra); his hand will be against everyone, and everyone's hand against him.[4]

[1] Job 39. 5; Dan. 5. 21. [2] Gen. 16. 12; Job 6. 5; 11. 12; 24. 5; 39. 5–8; Ps. 104. 11; Is. 32. 14; Jer. 14. 6; Hos. 8. 9. [3] Job 39. 5–8. [4] Gen. 16. 12.

WILD GOAT

Its Hebrew name could mean "climber". The species to be met with in Palestine, in Arabia, and especially Sinai, differs from the ibex of the Alps by

Wild goat.

its lighter coat and by the curvature of its knarled horns, at times more than a yard long. This extraordinarily savage animal, which inhabits high, precipitous places, is mentioned in some O.T. texts:

298

Saul pursued David right up to the rocks of the wild goats;[1] the high mountains are the haunt of the wild goats, says Ps. 104,[2] and God asks Job if he knows the time when the wild goats bring forth their young.[3] The Book of Proverbs compares a young woman with the graceful female wild goat[4] (often translated by gazelle, doe!).

[1] 1 Sam. 24. 2. [2] Ps. 104. 18. [3] Job 39. 1. [4] Prov. 5. 19.

WILD-GOURD

2 Kgs. 4. 39 tells how the disciples of Elisha thought one day that they were being poisoned by fruits, which one of them had gathered in the fields and which he had cut up and put in the pot to stew. Usually the Hebrew word for these fruits is taken to mean "colocynth". The colocynth belongs to the genus of the cucumbers; its globular fruit, about the

Colocynth (*Citrullus colocynthis*).

size of an orange and yellow when ripe, has a very bitter taste and contains a powerful medicinal principle.

Moreover, the colocynth was a very decorative plant, and there is good reason for thinking that it provided the motif for the cedarwood carvings which ornamented the interior of Solomon's Temple.[1] The Bronze Sea*, one of the marvels of the Temple, also bore under its rim two rows of colocynths, cast with it in a single piece.[2]

[1] 1 Kgs. 6. 18. [2] 1 Kgs. 7. 24.

WILL

Some men in the O.T. (e.g., Jacob, Joseph, David[1]) gave expression to their last wishes on the eve of death; but the use of wills as such, to which the Epistles to the Galatians and the Hebrews allude,[2] was relatively late among the Jews.

[1] Gen. 49. 29 . . .; 50. 25; 1 Kgs. 2. 2 . . .; cf. 2 Kgs. 20. 1.
[2] Gal. 3. 15; Heb. 9. 16, 17.

WILLOW

Several species of willow are to be met with in Palestine. The O.T. mentions five or six times[1] a

tree which grows at the water's edge and whose name might be used for various willows, though some translators think that it refers rather to the poplar*, e.g., Ps. 137. 2 is given as: "Upon the poplars of the country we hanged up our *kinnôrim*." It is difficult to decide. The translation "willow" is that of the ancient versions (LXX, Vulgate, etc.). Moreover, willows and poplars form a natural family (the Salicaceae). (The text of Ez. 17. 5 is uncertain.)

[1] Lev. 23. 40; Job 40. 17; Ps. 137. 2; Is. 44. 4; 15. 7 (Amos 6. 14).

WINDOW

The usual Palestinian dwellings, like those of the fellaheen of today, had only very few windows; while permitting ventilation and the escape of smoke,[1] these generally narrow openings left the house in a half-darkness which was favourable to coolness. Their narrowness and their rarity naturally made the work of the architect and builder easier; in some cases, even, the door acted as the sole window! However, the window was sometimes big enough to let a man through, as is proved by more than one Bible text[2] and by the statement that thieves used them.[3] It is true that in some of these texts—and in that relating the death of Jezebel in particular—the references are to windows belonging to palaces.[4]

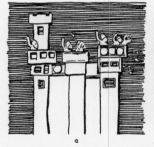

Windows: fragment of Assyrian bas-relief and ivory plaque.

Houses of well-to-do people were provided with windows often of a fine size, and more or less numerous. An idea of them can be gained from various bas-reliefs (a), for hardly more than the foundations of ancient buildings themselves remain. It has even been supposed that some houses possessed a kind of balcony or loggia. The prophet Jeremiah regarded stone houses with spacious rooms and wide windows as an insolent luxury, and condemned them.[5]

The theme of the woman at the window has often been engraved on ivory (b); from this it is possible to picture the usually small dimensions of these openings; frequently, too, they were divided into two by a cross-bar or even half blocked by a little balustrade.

WINNOW

As glass for panes did not exist, the window was closed by means of mats, curtains, or panels of wood which were held back "to open the window".[6] It could also be provided with a grill of wood or worked stone, usually fixed, like those used in Arab windows;[7] these gratings enabled people to see what was happening outside without being seen: it was thus that the mother of Sisera watched for the return of her son[8] and that Michal followed David's dance before the Ark.[9]

The First Book of Kings[10] speaks, in obscure terms, of the three rows of windows in the house of the Forest of Lebanon, which doubtless belonged to a Syrian type of palace called a "house with windows". It is difficult to form a precise idea of the windows, closed by a wooden lattice, which were apparently in the upper part of Solomon's Temple,[11] as also the numerous barred windows listed in the description of Ezekiel's Temple.[12]

[1] Hos. 13. 3. [2] Jos. 2. 15; Acts 9. 25; 20. 9; 2 Cor. 11. 33. [3] Joel 2. 9. [4] 1 Sam. 19. 12; 2 Kgs. 1. 2; 9. 30 ff. [5] Jer. 22. 14. [6] Gen. 26. 8; 2 Kgs. 13. 17; Eccl. 12. 3; Dan. 6. 10. [7] Prov. 7. 6; Cant. 2. 9; 5. 4 (?). [8] Jg. 5. 28. [9] 2 Sam. 6. 16. [10] 1 Kgs. 7. 4, 5. [11] 1 Kgs. 6. 4. [12] Ez. 40. 16; etc.

WINNOW

Winnowing in the literal sense comes only into the Book of Ruth[1] († agriculture). Everywhere else the Bible texts speak only figuratively of this operation

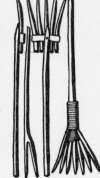

Left: winnowing; *right:* wooden winnowing forks.

and the implements employed[2] in it (forks and shovels rather than osier winnowing-fans).

[1] Ruth 3. 2. [2] Is. 30. 24, 28; 41. 16; Jer. 4. 11; 15. 7; 51. 2; Ez. 5. 2; Matt. 3. 12; Lk. 3. 17.

WITNESS

In law at least two witnesses were required to bring about a death sentence[1] and even for other penalties.[2] In the case of stoning* it was the witnesses who started to carry out the sentence: their responsibility for it was expressed in this way.[3] The following

had no power to act as witnesses: women, slaves, minors, close relatives, the deaf, blind or dumb, or any who had been convicted of falsehood.—False witnesses who were detected suffered the same punishment they had wished to bring upon the accused[4] (the Babylonian Code of Hammurabi made similar provisions). Judging from the Decalogue,[5] from the complaints and assertions of the Psalms and Proverbs[6]—not to mention the trials of Naboth, Christ, and Stephen[7]—false witness seems to have been very frequent. On the other hand, a witness who evaded giving evidence was also culpable.[8]

Important contracts and solemn engagements or affirmations required the presence of witnesses, and sometimes also their signatures.[9]

[1] Num. 35. 30; Dt. 17. 6; Heb. 10. 28. [2] Dt. 19. 15; Jn. 8. 17; 2 Cor. 13. 1; 1 Ti. 5. 19. [3] Dt. 17. 7. [4] Dt. 19. 19. [5] Ex. 20. 16. [6] Ps. 27. 12; 35. 11; Prov. 6. 19; 12. 17; 14. 5, 25; 19. 5, 28; 25. 18. [7] 1 Kgs. 21. 10, 13; Matt. 26. 59 . . .; Mk. 14. 55 . . .; Acts 6. 13. [8] Lev. 5. 1. [9] Ruth 4. 9; Is. 8. 2; 43. 9; Jer. 32. 10, 12, 25, 44; Matt. 18. 16; 1 Ti. 6. 12; 2 Ti. 2. 2.

WOLF

The wolf is still met with today in Palestine, though less frequently in Cisjordania than in Transjordania. It has always been a terror to shepherds in the countryside, because it is more ferocious than the jackal. Naturally the Bible in its figurative language does not fail to allude to this carnivore, which it treats, along with the lion and leopard, as a symbol of destruction.[1] "Benjamin is a ravenous wolf," says the Blessing of Jacob,[2] "in the morning he devours the prey and in the evening he divides the spoil." Still more striking is Isaiah's promise that the day will come when the wolf and the lamb will feed and dwell together.[3]

Jesus sent his disciples out as sheep (or lambs) in the midst of wolves;[4] he condemned the bad shepherd who abandons his flock when he sees the wolf coming;[5] and issued a warning against false prophets disguised as sheep who are in reality ravenous wolves.[6] St Paul warned the Ephesian elders that one day after his departure cruel wolves might unexpectedly appear among them who would not spare the flock.[7] All these figures of speech have become classic.

[1] Jer. 5. 6. [2] Gen. 49. 27; cf. Ez. 22. 27; Hab. 1. 8; Zeph. 3. 3. [3] Is. 11. 6; 65. 25. [4] Matt. 10. 16; Lk. 10. 3. [5] Jn. 10. 12. [6] Matt. 7. 15. [7] Acts 20. 29.

WOMAN

In Israel, although the husband had no formal rights over the person of his wife, he was nevertheless her lord and master, and a wife was, to some extent, her husband's property.[1] She owed him absolute fidelity, without being able to demand it in return;

similarly, he could easily send his wife away, while she had no right of divorce*. However, a husband could not sell his wife. From all points of view, a woman occupied an inferior position: there was less rejoicing over the birth of a daughter than a son, her education was less elaborate than that of the boys; generally the woman had to stand aside, men would not take meals with her; [2] the disciples were less surprised that Jesus spoke to a Samaritan woman than that their Master spoke to a woman at all; [3] "you shall not speak to women in the market-place," says the Talmud, "least of all to your wife." Even in the religious field, men and women did not have equal rights; women were relegated to the background in the Temple at Jerusalem, and even today they have a place apart in the synagogue. They were exempted from certain religious duties without being actually forbidden to perform them. A woman could not inherit from her husband, nor, as a rule, a daughter from her father († inheritance). A husband or father had the right to disclaim or to annul any undertakings entered into by a wife or daughter [4] and, from Josephus and the Talmud, we know that women could not normally give evidence in court.

However, the position of the married woman was not so serious as it might at first appear. Certainly she was her husband's property, but, as a daughter, she was in her father's power, and he could even sell her as a slave*. Children owed full and complete obedience to their mother,[5] and even Leviticus says,[6] "Let each of you honour mother [mentioned first] and father." Of course, the wife had to be housed, fed, and kept by her husband; and she could always appeal for protection to the family or clan to which she had belonged before her marriage. It is not unusual in the O.T. to find women playing a part in the rejoicing over a victory [7] or taking part in sacrifices or religious festivals.[8] Any intelligent and respectable woman could easily create an honourable position for herself in the family group: the Bible has preserved the memory of women whose good sense, skill, and dignity [9] it loved to stress. A few were ranked as prophetesses,[10] and without mentioning queens, it is enough to recall Deborah to show how much influence certain women could exert outside the domestic scene.

Furthermore, Israelite law sought to protect the woman's weakness, to safeguard her rights; [11] and her position improved in the course of time. It is certain that, in a general way, the Israelite woman enjoyed greater consideration than does the Muslim or Arab woman of today, and greater freedom, too.

Israel's spiritual leaders always advocated respect for women—bone of Adam's bone and flesh of his flesh [12]—and were quick to praise their diligence, piety, and qualities, which they valued more highly than beauty. "He who finds a wife," says the Book of Proverbs, "finds a good thing and obtains favour from the Lord." [13] "House and wealth are inherited from fathers, but a prudent wife is from the Lord." [14] At greater length, Ecclesiasticus (Apocrypha) states:

"Happy is the husband of a virtuous wife,
The number of his days is doubled.
A worthy wife is the joy of her husband,
And he passes his years in peace.
The virtuous wife is a good gift;
She shall be given to those who fear the Lord.
Rich or poor, her husband has a joyful heart,
And gaiety shines from his face at all times." [15]

Or again:

"The grace of a wife delighteth her husband,
And her understanding fatteneth his bones.
A silent woman is a gift from the Lord
And a well instructed woman is above worth.
Grace upon grace is a modest wife
And there is no price worthy of a chaste woman." [16]

These texts are the more significant because it is only after such statements that the writer praises feminine beauty:

"As the sun arising in the highest places of the heavens,
So the beauty of a good wife shines in her well-ordered home;
As the lamp shining on the holy candlestick,
So is the beauty of a face on a stately figure.
Like golden pillars upon silver bases,
So are elegant feet upon firm heels." [17]

The eulogy in Proverbs [18] of the virtuous and courageous woman is classical, and the Mishnah strikes the same note when it says, for example: "A man owes great respect to his wife, for it is only through his wife that prosperity comes to a man." "The death of a good wife is for him who loves her a misfortune as great as the ruin of Jerusalem." "A man should love his wife as himself and honour her more than himself."

It follows that judgment against unworthy women is all the more severe: Amos [19] vigorously attacks the dissolute women of Samaria, Isaiah [20] mocks and threatens the coquettes of Jerusalem, and Ecclesiasticus has no words strong enough for the wicked woman:

"There is no poison worse than the poison of a snake,
And there is no wrath greater than the wrath of a woman.
I would rather dwell with a lion and a dragon,
Than keep house with a wicked woman . . .
Grief of heart and sorrow is a jealous wife,
And the whip of a tongue that tells its griefs to all the world.
An evil wife is like a yoke of oxen in disaccord;
He that takes hold of her has seized a scorpion." [21]

The wife's task was often onerous. In addition to the duties of motherhood, all the household cares devolved on her. Rising before dawn, she would grind flour and cook the day's bread, fetch water and wood, keep the house tidy, supervise the children, prepare meals, help in the fields, or go to the town to sell the garden produce, and when she stayed at home she would still find time to sew, spin, weave cloth, or plait straw.

We know the place held by the women of the N.T., the fine women who appear in the background of the life of Jesus,[22] the zeal and diligence of the first Christian women,[23] the part played by widows in the early church.[24] The teaching of Christ and the apostles has given full dignity to the woman and to marriage;[25] it has been claimed that certain N.T. recommendations concerning a wife's subjection, or her conduct in assemblies,[26] bear the mark of the time and its circumstances, just as it is claimed that the foundations of the equality of men and women were laid down there;[27] in any case St Paul could not have paid greater homage to woman than he did when making her the symbol of the church beloved and sanctified by Jesus Christ.[28]

(† Marriage, divorce, widow, family, dress, head-dress.)

[1] Gen. 12. 18; Ex. 20. 17; 21. 3. [2] Gen. 18. 9; cf. Ruth 2. 14. [3] Jn. 4. 27. [4] Num. 30. 4 ff. [5] Ex. 20. 12; Dt. 5. 16; 21. 18. [6] Lev. 19. 3. [7] Ex. 15. 20; Jg. 11. 34; 1 Sam. 18. 6; Ps. 68. 25. [8] Jg. 13. 20, 23; 1 Sam. 1. 1–4; 2. 19; Neh. 8. 3; 12. 43. [9] Ruth; 1 Sam. 19. 11 ff.; 25. 14 ff.; 2 Sam. 21. 7 ff.; 2 Kgs. 4. 8 ff. [10] Ex. 15. 20; Num. 12. 2; Jg. 4. 4; 2 Kgs. 22. 14; cf. Lk. 2. 36; Acts 21. 8; 1 Cor. 11. 5. [11] Dt. 21. 10 ff.; 22. 13 ff.; 22. 28 ff. [12] Gen. 2. 23. [13] Prov. 18. 22. [14] Prov. 19. 14. [15] Ecclus. 26. 1–4.* [16] Ecclus. 26. 13–15.* [17] Ecclus. 26. 16–18.* [18] Prov. 31. 10 ff. [19] Amos 4. 1 ff. [20] Is. 3. 16 ff. [21] Ecclus. 25. 15–16; 26. 6–7.* [22] Mk. 15. 40–41; 16. 1–10; Lk. 1. 26 ff.; 2. 5 ff.; 8. 2, 3; 10. 38; 23. 49, 55–56; 24. 1–10; Jn. 11. 2, 5; 12. 1–3; 20. 1 ff. [23] Acts 9. 36; 12. 12; 16. 14; 17. 34; 18. 2, 26; 21. 9; Rom. 16. 1; 2 Ti. 1. 5. [24] 1 Ti. 5. 3 ff. [25] Matt. 5. 31, 32; 19. 3–9; Mk. 10. 11, 12; Lk. 16. 18; 1 Cor. 7. 10 ff.; Eph. 5. 31. [26] 1 Cor. 11. 2 ff.; 14. 34–35; 1 Ti. 2. 11 ff. [27] 1 Cor. 11. 11; Gal. 3. 28. [28] Eph. 5. 23, 25.

[* The quoted passages present many textual difficulties, and in places the French has been followed more closely than any English version.—A. H.]

WOOD

Palestine has no doubt never been very rich in wood, but in former times it was less rare than it is today: some regions possessed forests*,[1] but the country is now almost totally denuded of them. Then again, the O.T. shows that wood was often used for making domestic or agricultural objects,[2] carts,[3] idols,[4] and in the construction of houses (roofs, doors, window lattices, locks), but only great buildings, such as palaces, afforded the luxury of boarded floors, wainscoting, colonnades of wood, or carved panels.[5] (Solomon's Temple*, house* of the Forest of Lebanon.) Generally speaking, stone was less precious than wood, because it was widely available.

While dead wood gathered carefully [6] was used for cooking and heating, the sacrifices required considerable quantities of wood fuel;[7] one of the small courts within Herod's Temple was called "the timber room": there the priests closely examined the official offerings of the faithful,[8] which had to be of good quality and, in particular, undamaged by worms. One of the thirteen collecting boxes in Herod's Temple took gifts intended for the purchase of wood for the altar.

The people of Palestine made use of the services of woodcutters, carpenter-joiners, cabinet makers, and wood-carvers, whose tools we know about from texts and from excavation—axes, saws, drills, hammers, chisels, knives, nails of wood or bronze, compass, measure, pencil, and plumb-line—but these craftsmen were probably not very numerous, at least in early days, when each person made for himself what he needed.

The chief woods used came from the sycomore*, cypress*, oak*, wild olive* (or pine), acacia*, sandalwood*, but the best of all was the greatly famed cedarwood*, which Solomon used extensively for his buildings;[9] he imported it from Lebanon, through the Phoenicians.[10]

[1] Jos. 17. 15 . . .; 1 Sam. 23. 15; 2 Sam. 18. 6; Ez. 20. 46; etc. [2] Lev. 11. 32. [3] 1 Sam. 6. 14. [4] Dt. 29. 17; Is. 40. 20; 44. 13 . . .; Hos. 4. 12. [5] Jer. 22. 14; Hagg. 1. 8; etc. [6] Num. 15. 32; Jos. 9. 21, 27; 1 Kgs. 17. 10. [7] Gen. 22; Lev. 1; etc. [8] Neh. 10. 34; 13. 31. [9] 1 Kgs. 6. 9 . . . [10] 1 Kgs. 5. 6 . . .

WOODCUTTER

Although the Israelites naturally knew how to cut down the trees they needed for their own use,[1] it seems that the profession of woodcutting was little practised. The Book of Joshua records that they imposed upon the Gibeonites the task of being "hewers of wood and drawers of water for the community and for the altar",[2] while Solomon, on the eve of building the Temple and asking the king of Tyre for help, said: "There is no one among us who knows how to fell trees like the Sidonians." [3]—In a vigorous metaphor the prophet Jeremiah compares Egypt's enemy to woodcutters who come, armed with axes, to cut down a forest.[4]

[1] Dt. 19. 5; 2 Kgs. 6. 4; Ez. 39. 10. [2] Jos. 9. 21, 27. [3] 1 Kgs. 5. 6; 2 Chr. 2. 10. [4] Jer. 46. 22.

WOOL

At all times this textile material has been of first importance for the Israelites, and for Easterners in general, because their most used garments were of wool. Hence the raising of sheep* was one of the main resources of Palestine, and wool was the object of a trade the echo of which we often hear in the Bible.[1] Does not the Second Book of Kings claim that the king of Moab, a leading sheep-breeder, paid 100,000 lambs and the wool of 100,000 rams as tribute to the king of Israel?[2]

In spring each year sheep-shearing took place, with much popular rejoicing, and the great sheep owners, such as Nabal or Absalom, made a feast for their shepherds and shearers, and for the relations and friends they invited for the occasion.[3]

The whiteness of wool, which had undergone various cleaning operations, provided the poets of the O.T. with some beautiful comparisons:[4] "Though your sins are red as crimson, they shall be [white] as wool,"[5] said Isaiah. The wool could be tinted with various colours, and it was important to protect it from mites and larvae of all kinds.[6] (For the working of wool see † spinning, weaving, fuller.)

We may note that the law forbade the wearing of a garment woven of two kinds of threads, wool and linen,[7] and that priests serving in the Temple had to dress in linen and not in wool, which might cause perspiration.[8]

[1] Prov. 31. 13; Ez. 27. 18; Hos. 2. 5, 9. [2] 2 Kgs. 3. 4. [3] Gen. 38. 12; 1 Sam. 25. 4 . . .; 2 Sam. 13. 23, 27. [4] Ps. 147. 16; Cant. 4. 2; 6. 6; Dan. 7. 9; (Rev. 1. 14.) [5] Is. 1. 18. [6] Is. 51. 8; Matt. 6. 19–20. [7] Lev. 19. 19; Dt. 22. 11. [8] Ez. 44. 17–19.

WORK

From our point of view here we need only stress that, contrary to current opinion, the Bible regards work as the destiny normally prescribed for man by the Creator.

God instituted work *before* the Fall, when he placed man in the garden "to till it and keep it".[1] The curse that followed the Fall is a reminder that it is sin which makes work difficult and laborious.

At Sinai God enjoined through Moses the fourth Commandment: "Six days shalt thou labour."[2] After that the Bible contains numerous texts urging men to work: the O.T. moralists,[3] Jesus himself,[4] the apostle Paul, insist in turn on the value of work. In face of Graeco-Roman society, which so often regarded leisure as the ideal life, the Israelites and the Christians contributed to the rehabilitation of work.[5]

Work is used figuratively for the action of Jesus himself,[6] and for the missionary activity which the disciples have to undertake.[7]

(† Agriculture, hireling, Nethinim, slave, vine.)

[1] Gen. 2. 15. [2] Ex. 20. 9. [3] Prov. 13. 4; 20. 4, 13; 21. 25; 24. 30; 26. 13; Eccl. 9. 10. [4] Jn. 5. 17. [5] 1 Cor. 4. 12; 9. 6; Eph. 4. 28; 2 Th. 3. 8, 10–12. [6] Jn. 9. 4; Matt. 9. 36–38. [7] 1 Cor. 15. 58; Phil. 2. 16; 1 Th. 2. 9; 5. 12; etc.

WORM

Bible texts sometimes speak of worms, both literally and figuratively, but usually what is meant are the larvae of certain insects that attack foodstuffs,[1] plants,[2] sick bodies,[3] and corpses.[4]

[1] Ex. 16. 20. [2] Dt. 28. 39; Jonah 4. 7. [3] Job 7. 5; Acts 12. 23. [4] Job 17. 14; 21. 26; 24. 20; Is. 14. 11; (cf. Is. 66. 24; Mk. 9. 48).

WORMWOOD

There are several species of wormwood (*Artemisia*) in Palestine. The Hebrew name signifies "accursed plant", not because the Israelites used it to make a harmful liquor, but because of its taste; it symbolized bitterness, and it was linked with gall*, poison, iniquity, and the curse.[1]

[1] Amos 6. 12; Lam. 3. 19; Rev. 8. 11; etc.

WRITING

1. The *invention* of alphabetic writing is a capital discovery in the history of mankind. In particular, it introduced an important transformation into social life by placing within the reach of all a means of transmitting thought, which up till then had been the prerogative of a privileged class of clerks and scribes. This discovery, whose origin and derivation are not yet established definitely, was made in the second half of the 2nd millennium, and spread throughout the world from the east coast of the Mediterranean Sea. The Israelites lived in this region, and there is every reason to think, first of all, that if they did not play a creative part in this discovery, they were at any rate among the first to benefit from it, and then that the social evolution to which it gave rise was probably not unconnected with the advent of the monarchy which dates precisely from the end of the 2nd millennium.

As a matter of fact, the O.T. hardly mentions the degree of instruction († school) attained by the subjects of the kings of Israel and Judah. For ancient times, it is basically only a matter of letters written by eminent people. However, a scribe is mentioned among David's officials;[1] noticing that he bears an Aramaic name, it can be wondered whether he were not at the court in order to teach a new method of writing. It seems likely that David himself wrote the letter which caused the downfall of Uriah,[2] as later Jezebel herself wrote the message(s) which provoked the death of Naboth.[3] Jehu wrote letters to the leaders of Samaria,[4] and the kings of Syria, Assyria, and Babylon address themselves in writing to their colleagues in Palestine.[5] It seems likely that in the 8th century, generally speaking, cultured people could write fluently, and that gradually reading and writing spread to the rank and file to a great extent;

this is shown by the ostraca* and graffiti discovered in Palestine. Mention of written texts, official or otherwise, increase also in the O.T.: royal writings, annals, legislative and prophetic texts, juridical sentences, contracts of purchase, letters of divorce, complaints, etc.; [6] finally, everyone knows how important the Epistles of the N.T. are.

2. *What script did the Israelites use?* The problem is very complex because the Israelites came under the influence of various civilizations, on the one hand, and on the other, because economic and political conditions propagated at certain periods a particular language, and consequently a particular form of writing.

(*a*) It is very likely that Abraham, of whom no passage in the Bible implies that he could read or write, had nevertheless a knowledge from his home-country of cuneiform writing (i.e., in the shape of wedges or triangular impressions). In the first place,

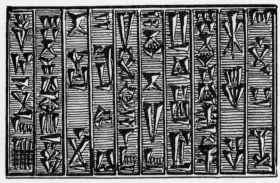

Syllabic cuneiform writing (Code of Hammurabi).

this script was ideographic (i.e., the ideas to be expressed were drawn), but it was transformed and became almost exclusively syllabic; this was a new method, which had as its principle the drawing of the words themselves and no longer of the things they represented; and in order to reduce the number of signs to be used at the same time as to fix them, each word was divided into syllables which could be found in other words. However, it was necessary to create a very great number of signs to be able to write all that one said.

(*b*) Moses, who, according to tradition, "was instructed in all the wisdom of the Egyptians",[7] might well have learnt to read and write Egyptian. Now, Egyptian writing presents a development analogous to the preceding writing, but much less rigorous. The scribes often placed side by side the sign which represented the sound of a word and the one which drew its idea; and the fine designs of writing engraved in the stone of monuments were simplified and often modified by those who had to write fluently; finally, the language itself was lacking

enough in precision, especially in its vocalic elements, to give rise to a simplification in writing in which some signs became syllabic and even one-lettered. But because of a rather curious conservatism, these various writing signs subsisted alongside one another, which is enough to explain the complicated nature of this system of writing.

(*c*) But Moses and his people spoke Hebrew, a Semitic language very like that of the Phoenicians.

Alphabetic cuneiform writing (from Ras Shamra).

The latter had been seeking a simplified way of writing and had found the system which we call alphabetic; the principle of this new notation consisted of representing by a very few signs, no longer words or syllables, but the essential elements of these syllables, i.e., consonants only; in fact, the use made of vowels by Semitic languages permits them if need be to be dispensed with altogether. We know that at the time when the Israelites entered Canaan several sorts of

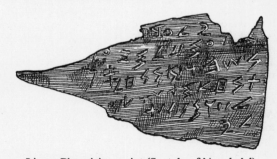

Linear Phoenician script (Spatula of 'Azarba'al).

alphabet had come into being; they can be divided into two types:

(i) That of Ugarit (former name of the *tell* of Ras Shamra), which is a script with cuneiform characters, impressed on clay tablets by means of a bevelled engraving-needle; a large number of little clay tablets covered with this script have been dug up.

(ii) That of Byblos, a linear form of script which could evidently be engraved on stone, but which

304

could also, and above all, be painted on a smooth surface much more easily than cuneiform script, even when it was simplified.

It was this second type of script which passed to the Canaanites (taking the place of a primitive script in which very few documents exist), then to the Israelites, Moabites, and Aramaeans, to impose itself next—while undergoing, it is true, certain transformations—first on the Greek world, and then, through it, on the Etruscans and Romans, who transmitted it to the Celts and Teutons, on the one hand, and on the other, to the Arabs and through them to the peoples of Africa and Asia.

The Israelites' writing, therefore, was of the linear type. It was with characters of this nature that people wrote not only the letters and documents mentioned above but also the texts of the O.T. themselves, at least until the return from Exile. We can have a clear idea of it from an examination of the monuments of the time dug up in the area: tablets from Gezer (10th century), the Moabite Stone (9th), ostraca* from Samaria (9th), the Siloam inscription († reservoir) (7th), seals*, coins († money), etc.

Phoenician script on the Moabite Stone (the enclosed letters form the word: Israel).

However, about the 6th century B.C. Aramaic was taking the dominant place in the Semitic world which Accadian had occupied until then. In a parallel way, Aramaic writing, too, infiltrated everywhere, due to the activity of the traders of Damascus; although it stemmed from Phoenician, it was more cursive, and was fairly rapidly adopted by the Israelites, except, however, for official and religious texts. The Talmud claims that it was in Exile (586–538) that they learnt this script, but it is known that there were serious

discussions among the priests in the course of the 5th and 4th centuries, to find out if it were permissible to transcribe the Bible into a new script: some thought so, realizing that hardly anyone knew the ancient writing any longer, whereas others felt they were

Hebrew and Greek alphabets.

Opening lines of the Epistle to the Colossians, according to a papyrus of about A.D. 230. The original writing may have looked like this.

being more faithful to God by keeping the texts in ancient Hebrew. These priests were in the minority and joined the Samaritans, who kept their Bible, through the centuries until today, in the ancient script, though in a more decorative form.

The Aramaic script had rapidly assumed a particular, angular shape which won for it the name of square Hebrew script, replacing the one which, by comparison, could be called triangular Hebrew. The first engraved inscriptions in square Hebrew date only from the 2nd and 1st centuries B.C., but in the time of Jesus Christ it was the script the Law was written in—since it is in square Hebrew and not in the old style that the letter i (yod, iota) is the smallest letter.[8]

Finally, it should be said that the Hebrew alphabet (ancient or square) comprises twenty-two consonantal letters; the vowels were represented by points and little marks placed above or beneath the consonants only after the 6th century A.D.; Hebrew is written from right to left and from top to bottom of the page. The order of letters in the Hebrew alphabet is given by the Bible itself in fairly numerous poetical pieces which represent it in acrostic.[9]

אַשְׁרֵי הָאִישׁ אֲשֶׁר לֹא הָלַךְ
בַּעֲצַת רְשָׁעִים וּבְדֶרֶךְ חַטָּאִים
לֹא עָמָד וּבְמוֹשַׁב לֵצִים לֹא יָשָׁב:

Hebrew writing.

(d) When the authors of the N.T. wrote in Greek it was naturally Greek script which they used. It was a script derived, as we have said, from triangular Hebrew.

3. *Material.* The first writings were probably done on *stone*,[10] a process which continued for monumental inscriptions and seals. White-washed stones were also used. On these the characters were painted.[11] Metal and especially lead plaques[12] were also used, or objects of gold, silver, or bronze—*metals* in which the writing was engraved. There have recently been found in a cave near the Dead Sea two scrolls comprising three sheets of copper (each sheet about 31 in. long, 11·8 in. high, 0·3 in. thick) covered with a deeply incised text. The tablets of clay in general use in Babylon and Nineveh, so well made for cuneiform writing, were much less suitable for the ancient Hebrew alphabet; they hardly appear to have been used by the Israelites (the deed of purchase mentioned by Jer. 32. 10 may have been written on papyrus like the Aramaic Jewish contracts of Elephantine at this period). For correspondence and short texts, potsherds* were used on

which writing was usually done in ink with a reed pen* cut with a little knife. *Tablets of wood* were useful to the scribes, for example, for writing rapid reports. The most common form was the dyptich, made of two tablets joined by a thong, and which opened and closed like a book; from the Hellenistic period, these little boards were often coated with wax, the surface of the wax being protected by a raised frame. But only the use of *parchment* and papyrus enabled the Israelites to preserve long texts; this material, which was so suited to cursive writing, remarkably encouraged its wider use. Writing was done by means of a stylus*. The preparation of sheep and goat skin for this purpose was perfected at Pergamum at the end of the 2nd century; thence its name parchment (Latin, *pergamena*).[13] It gradually

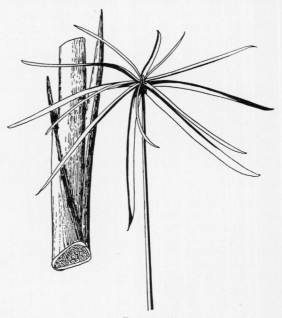

Papyrus.

supplanted *papyrus*, which had been used in Egypt since the 3rd millennium and in Syria from at least the end of the 2nd. The O.T. mentions it only at the end of the monarchy. Papyrus belongs to the family of Cyperaceae, and the genus Cyperus, which is the characteristic type of this family. This species of reed has branches which can attain more than 10 ft. in length; they are triangular at the top and terminate in an elegant bunch of sword-like leaves. Boats were made of papyrus (as they are, indeed, still today) either by crushing the biggest stems to weave them afterwards into the shape of a basket († ark) or by assembling them in bundles, afterwards attached together side by side († boat). In order to make the kind of paper for which the papyrus is chiefly famous,

306

the central part of strong branches stripped of their bark was used; these fibres were separated into thin strips placed and stuck side by side in two super-imposed layers, the first in one direction and the second cross-wise. The sheets thus obtained were beaten with a hammer (to make them thinner) and polished with pumice-stone; they could measure 3 to 8 in., by 6 to 18 in. Sometimes a certain number of them were stuck consecutively to make a wide strip which was wound round one or two cylindrical rollers. The same process was adopted for parchment leaves. These rolls [14] constituted the "books" of antiquity; their text was separated into columns, and the "pages" appeared by simple rotation of the rollers. The "codices", or books made of leaves placed on top of one another and then bound, date only from the 2nd century A.D. A label indicated the contents of the rolls, which were generally kept in a little chest or an earthenware jar. In order to write on papyrus or parchment, ink* and a reed were used.[15]

[1] 2 Sam. 8. 17. [2] 2 Sam. 11. 14. [3] 1 Kgs. 21. 8. [4] 2 Kgs. 10. 1. [5] 2 Kgs. 5. 5. [6] Dt. 6. 9; 24. 1; Jos. 10. 13; 1 Sam. 10. 25; 1 Kgs. 14. 19; Ezr. 1. 1; 4; 7. 11; Job 31. 35; Is. 8. 1; 10. 1; 30. 8; 34. 16; Jer. 29; 32. 11; Hos. 8. 12. [7] Acts 7. 22. [8] Matt. 5. 18. [9] Ps. 25; 34; 37; 111; 119; etc. [10] Ex. 32. 16; 34. 1, 28; Jos. 8. 32; Job 19. 24; 2 Cor. 3. 3. [11] Dt. 27. 2. [12] Ex. 28. 36; Job 19. 24; Jer. 17. 1. [13] 2 Ti. 4. 13. [14] Ps. 40. 7; Is. 34. 4; Jer. 36. 2; Ez. 2. 9; Zech. 5. 1; Lk. 4. 17; Acts 8. 28; Rev. 6. 14. [15] 3 Jn. 13.

XYSTUS

The historian Josephus several times mentions the existence in Jerusalem of an area surrounded by porticoes designed for gymnastic exercises, between the Temple and the Hasmonaean palace, in the Tyropoeon Valley. Called Xystus (= planed), the name of Hellenistic gymnasia, this enclosure had been fitted out by Herod the Great and constituted also a kind of "agora" or "forum", well suited for public assemblies. Some scholars have thought that Pilate held his tribunal there at the time of the trial of Jesus.

(† Praetorium.)

YEAR

It is likely that in ancient times the Hebrew year had been a lunar year of 12 months of 29 or 30 days, i.e., 354 days, about 11 less than a solar year. Such a system would quickly show a shifting of the seasons in relation to the months (compare the Moham-medan calendar). To avoid the inconvenience of this, an attempt was soon made to synchronize the lunar year with the earth's rotation round the sun (the solar year); various ways were used, until finally, every two or three years a 13th month was added to the 12 lunar months.—Very naturally, the autumnal

equinox marked the start of the new year; it was, in-deed, the end of the cycle of agricultural work [1]—the harvests were gathered in and the earth yearned for the rain which would make all things new. But after the Exile (and perhaps even before it) the Israelites must have adopted for their civil calendar that of Babylonia, in which the year commenced with the spring equinox. However, they retained (and have retained up to the present) the ancient system for their religious calendar; so that the 1st month of the religious year is the 7th of the civil year, and New Year* is celebrated on 1st Tishri, in the autumn.[2]

[1] Ex. 23. 16; 34. 22. [2] Lev. 23. 24; Num. 29. 1.

YOKE

The wooden yoke used by the Israelites hardly differed from the present Palestinian yoke. Formed of a transverse bar, with long pins fixed vertically for enclosing the neck of the ox, mule, or horse which bore it, and also for fixing it over the shaft, it was also kept in place by thongs passed under the animal's throat.[1]

It should be noted that it was forbidden to put two animals of different species under one yoke,[2] either to spare the more feeble or from opposition to all cross-breeding. Only animals which had never borne the yoke could be offered in sacrifice.[3]

Oxen under a primitive yoke.

The same name was also given to a land measure equivalent to the area a pair of oxen could plough in one day [4] († acre).—The iron yoke [5] with which the prophets threaten the people is only a figure of speech for violent oppression; yokes were not made of metal. Finally, the word "yoke" is most often used metaphorically in the Bible; among many texts which might be quoted we limit ourselves to the famous say-ing of Jesus: "My yoke is easy (it does not chafe) and my burden is light." [6]

(† Agriculture, plough.)

[1] Jer. 27. 2; Ez. 34. 27; Nahum 1. 13. [2] Dt. 22. 10; Lev. 19. 19. [3] Num. 19. 2; Dt. 21. 3; 1 Sam. 6. 7. [4] 1 Sam. 14. 14 (?); Is. 5. 10. [5] Dt. 28. 48; Jer. 28. 13. [6] Matt. 11. 29, 30.

ZEALOT

Two disciples of Jesus were named Simon—one was Simon Peter, and the other was Simon "the Zealot" (according to Luke's Gospel [1]), or "the

Cananaean" (according to Mark and Matthew [2]). These two terms designate one and the same group of extreme Israelite nationalists who formed themselves into a party a few years before the birth of Jesus. Under the inspiration of Judas of Gamala and a Pharisee named Zadok, they revolted against the Romans, but these made short work of them. The zealots who survived only attracted more sympathy from the populace, which had a ready ear for extremists. In the end it was this hot-headed group which, some years before A.D. 70, provoked a fresh revolt against the Romans and thus the arrival of Vespasian's army which destroyed Jerusalem, its Temple, and the Jewish State.

[1] Lk. 6. 15. [2] Mk. 3. 18; Matt. 10. 4.

ZODIAC

Some O.T. passages probably allude to the signs of the zodiac, in particular the text in the Second Book of Kings which, among the cults Josiah suppressed, speaks of one celebrated in honour of the *mazzalôt* ("stations").[1] The same word, with a slight emendation, may also be read in the poem of Job.[2] But some translations prefer to take it as the name of a particular star of some constellation, or as meaning the constellations in general. The same could hold in the case of the "chambers of the south" mentioned in Job 9. 9, which are hardly to be equated with the signs of the zodiac. Josephus and Philo connect the twelve precious stones on the breastplate of the High Priest* with these signs, while some modern authors think to find them in the Blessing of the twelve sons of Jacob,[3] and elsewhere besides. These associations are extremely questionable; but, on the other hand, the correspondences between some of the signs of the zodiac and certain symbols in the Book of Revelation [4] have more in their favour.

[1] 2 Kgs. 23. 5. [2] Job 38. 32. [3] Gen. 49. [4] Rev. 4. 4, 6 . . .; 9. 3, 5; 12. 1; 21. 19 . . .

SOURCES OF ILLUSTRATIONS

The illustrations in this Dictionary have either been executed from the originals, or from privately owned photographs, or drawn from the following sources:

Encyclopédie photographique de l'Art, Paris 1935–1938.

Revue biblique, 1933, 1934, 1950, 1951, 1952, 1954.

BABELON, J. *Le portrait dans l'antiquité d'après les monnaies*, 1942.

BARROIS, A.-G. *Manuel d'archéologie biblique*, 1939, 1953.

BEAULIEU, M. *Le costume antique*, 1951.

BERG and SCHMIDT. *Officinellen Pflanzen.*

BERTIN, L. *La vie des animaux*, 1950.

BIDAULT, J. *Pirogues et pagaies.*

BONNET, H. *Die Waffen der Völker des Alten Orients*, 1926.

CONTENAU, G. *La civilisation phénicienne*, 1926.

— *La civilisation des Hittites et des Metanniens*, 1934.

DALMAN, G. *Arbeit und Sitte in Palästina*, 1928–1939.

DAREMBERG and SAGLIO. *Dictionnaire d'archéologie grecque et romaine.*

DUFOURCQ, N. *La musique, des origines à nos jours*, 1946.

ERMAN, A. *La religion des Egyptiens*, 1937.

GALLING, K. *Biblisches Reallexikon.*

GORCÉ, M. and MORTIER, R. *Histoire générale des religions*, 1948.

GRESSMANN, H. *Altorientalische Bilder zum Alten Testament*, 1927.

GROHMEYER and BENZINGER (Tr. Breitenstein, J.). *Vues et documents bibliques.*

GROLLENBERG, L. H. *Atlas de la Bible*, 1955.

HALL, H. R. *La sculpture assyrienne et babylonienne au British Museum*, 1928.

JÉQUIER, G. *Histoire de la civilisation égyptienne*, 1930.

LAHY-HOLLENBECQUE, M. *L'évolution humaine*, 1951.

LALLEMAND, F. *Journal de M. Sestios.*

LODS, AD. *Israël*, 1930.

LOND, G. *The Megiddo Ivories.*

MONNIER, M. *Pompéï.*

PARROT, A. *Les fouilles de Mari*, Rapport préliminaire, 1935.

— *Archéologie mésopotamienne.*

ROTH, C. *Histoire du peuple juif*, 1948.

SÉBILLE, A. *Histoire de la marine.*

SKIRA, A. *Les grands siècles de la peinture: La peinture étrusque*, 1952; *la peinture romaine*, 1953; *la peinture égyptienne*, 1954.

THÉZARD, J. *Autour du lac de Tibériade.*

UCELLI. *Navi di Nemi.*

VINCENT, H. *Canaan*, 1914.

VOLZ, P. *Die biblishen Altertümer.*

WATZINGER, C. *Denkmähler Palästinas*, 1933.

WESTPHAL, A. *Dictionnaire encyclopédique de la Bible*, 1935.

WOOLLEY, L. *Ur en Chaldée*, 1938.